The Color of Justice

Race, Ethnicity, and Crime in America

FOURTH EDITION

SAMUEL WALKER
University of Nebraska at Omaha

CASSIA SPOHN
Arizona State University

MIRIAM DELONE
University of Nebraska at Omaha

THOMSON
™
WADSWORTH

Australia • Brazil • Canada • Mexico • Singapore • Spain
United Kingdom • United States

THOMSON

™

WADSWORTH

The Color of Justice:
Race, Ethnicity, and Crime in America,
Fourth Edition
Samuel Walker, Cassia Spohn, Miriam DeLone

Senior Acquisitions Editor, Criminal Justice: Carolyn Henderson Meier

Assistant Editor: Rebecca Johnson

Technology Project Manager: Amanda Kaufmann

Marketing Manager: Terra Schultz

Marketing Assistant: Jaren Boland

Marketing Communications Manager: Linda Yip

Project Manager, Editorial Production: Jennie Redwitz

Creative Director: Rob Hugel

Art Director: Vernon Boes

Print Buyer: Linda Hsu

Permissions Editor: Joohee Lee

Production Service: Graphic World Inc.

Copy Editor: Graphic World Inc.

Illustrator: Graphic World Illustration Studio

Cover Designer: Yvo

Cover Image: © Terry W. Eggers/Corbis

Compositor: Integra Software Services

Text and Cover Printer: West Group

© 2007, 2004 Thomson Wadsworth, a part of the Thomson Corporation. Thomson, the Star logo, and Wadsworth are trademarks used herein under license.

Printed in the United States of America
1 2 3 4 5 6 7 10 09 08 07 06

Library of Congress Control Number: 2006904963

ISBN 0-534-62446-4

Thomson Higher Education
10 Davis Drive
Belmont, CA 94002-3098
USA

For more information about our products, contact us at:
Thomson Learning Academic Resource Center
1-800-423-0563

For permission to use material from this text or product, submit a request online at
http://www.thomsonrights.com.
Any additional questions about permissions can be submitted by e-mail to
thomsonrights@thomson.com.

Brief Contents

Contents

Foreword

Today, there are more African American men in prison and jail than in college. This statistic, reported by The Sentencing Project, a Washington, DC–based policy research group, is alarming for what it says about national priorities and the collateral consequences of criminal justice policy. We know, for example, that going to college improves one's life chances in several respects, including lifelong earnings and other measures of well-being. We also know that being incarcerated affects most of those same prospects negatively. Putting these facts together, we can say that as a result of today's incarceration policies, more African American men will experience the lifelong debilitating effects of incarceration than the lifelong beneficial effects of college.

College is not the only racial contrast with criminal justice. The odds of an African American male born today going to prison are nearly one in three, and this rate is several times higher than the odds for white males and more than 10 times higher than the odds for white females. The concentration of prison and jail activity among people of color living in impoverished urban neighborhoods is at least 10 and sometimes as much as 50 times higher than that in other neighborhoods.

When it comes to the understanding the color of justice, however, studies of African Americans are not the only story. Justice for "brown" Americans—people with Hispanic and Latino cultural roots—is rapidly becoming as important an issue in some parts of America as has historically been true for "black" Americans, who are the offspring of former slaves. Increasing concern about illegal immigration has fueled an interest in racial and ethnic profiling that goes well beyond young African American men. As our nation's attention becomes focused on the prospect of terrorism, today's interest in profiling extends past the traditional enforcement on roads and highways to include national security at points of entry. Immigration enforcement has raised the possibility of a new application for racial profiling.

There can be no denying that criminal justice policy and practice operate under the cloud of a racial dynamic. People may dispute what causes that dynamic, and they may disagree about its consequences, but there is no disputing the fact that criminal justice means something different for people of color than it does for others in the United States. This difference in personal experience of justice translates into significant impediments to a larger sense of justice and fairness among those of minority racial and ethnic backgrounds.

As editor of *The Wadsworth Contemporary Issues in Crime and Justice Series*, I am pleased to introduce the fourth edition of *The Color of Justice: Race, Ethnicity, and Crime in America*. The series is devoted to providing in-depth investigation of current issues in crime and justice that cannot receive adequate treatment in standard introductory textbooks. Surely there can be no topic of more burning importance than that of racial and ethnic fairness in the criminal justice system.

This edition of *The Color of Justice* provides the best, most comprehensive exploration available today of the problem of race and ethnic variability in criminal justice practices. Professors Walker, Spohn, and DeLone have assembled the most up-to-date statistics, and they have supplied the most insightful and incisive analysis of any book on this topic now available. The new edition covers the topics that made previous editions bestsellers in this series, and the authors have updated their review of research to incorporate new and provocative studies of race, strengthened the treatment of Hispanic and Latino issues, and added material on immigration and homeland security that arise from a new and pressing concern about terrorism.

This book has become a standard text in its area, and the reasons are several. First, the presentation of data and interpretation of studies are comprehensive, covering a wide range of material within a broad understanding of criminal justice, from the passage of laws to their enforcement and the consequential sanctions imposed. Second, the analysis is fair-minded and dispassionate. When dealing with a topic in which emotions often run stronger than reason, this book offers a careful analysis and an impartial interpretation of what is known about the subject. People whose views run to divergent conclusions can all find value in this book because it provides the data people need to be informed about a topic deserving of more thoughtful attention.

Third, the book goes beyond the usual division of black and white. America today is multiracial and multiethnic, and one cannot study these topics without recognizing the substantial diversity that is the U.S. population. This book makes a conscious effort to go beyond the usual distinctions and to investigate racial and ethnic questions of a much wider variety. Fourth, this book does not hawk a particular point of view. The evidence is provided to the reader as a guidepost to an informed perspective, but the perspective itself is left to the reader to develop as the evidence is pondered and digested.

To these four strengths must be added an observation: No aspect of criminal justice is left out. The book addresses the broad questions of social structure and social values, just as it confronts the much more narrow questions of law enforcement decisions and criminal justice system classification. In this sense, the book will address a topic that will be of direct importance to almost any reader who picks it up.

What this book represents, then, is a rare gem of a contribution. Comprehensive, critical, and authoritative, but not at all pedantic, the authors provide a book that will inform the reader, stimulate class discussion, and take the intellectual understanding of those who read it to a higher level. I recommend it to you with enthusiasm.

Todd R. Clear
Series Editor

Preface

Since the third edition of *The Color of Justice* was published, issues of race and ethnicity with respect to crime have become even more prominent in American political life. The issue of immigration, in particular, has become a major controversy. Unlike most books on criminal justice, this edition of *The Color of Justice* provides a wealth of information on the fastest-growing minority segment of the American population, the Hispanic and Latino community. The question of racial profiling—for example, police making traffic stops solely on the basis of the driver's race or ethnicity—continues to be a national controversy. Questions of profiling are not confined to traffic stops, however; they have been raised with regard to national security and immigration enforcement as well. The debate over the death penalty has also entered a new phase in just the last few years, with new and disturbing evidence of miscarriages of justice, including innocent people being sentenced to death. Many of the convicted offenders who have been exonerated through DNA evidence have been African Americans. In short, controversies involving race and ethnicity continue to pervade the criminal justice system, with new issues continually arising.

ORGANIZATION

This book is divided into 11 chapters. The organization is designed to guide students through a logical exploration of the subject, beginning with a discussion of the broader social context for race and ethnicity in American society and then moving to the different components of the criminal justice system: police, courts, corrections, the death penalty, and juvenile justice.

NEW TO THIS EDITION

In the Fourth Edition, we have significantly updated research and included the most current statistics available, particularly with regard to Hispanic groups. Also included is material on some of the most important recent developments in the field—racial profiling in the context of homeland security, for instance, as well as hate crime legislation, challenges to affirmative action, the disproportionate attention given to crime victims according to race, minority youth victimization rates, the intersection of race and domestic violence, and much more.

■ Chapter 1, "Race, Ethnicity, and Crime," has been revised to reflect changes in the state of racial and ethnic relations in the United States and how those changes relate to the criminal justice system.

■ Chapter 2, "Victims and Offenders," includes a reexamination of media depictions of crime victims, especially the race of victims, and also includes expanded discussions of the victimization of college students, gangs, domestic terrorism, and the different theoretical perspectives on victimization.

■ In Chapter 3, "Race, Ethnicity, Social Structure, and Crime," the data on the social and economic status of African Americans, Hispanics, and white Americans has been completely updated.

■ Chapter 4, "Justice on the Street?" contains greatly expanded coverage of racial profiling, incorporating new data from studies of traffic enforcement and new perspectives on the nature of the problem and how it can be controlled.

■ Chapter 5, "The Courts," includes new material reflecting recent research on bail and charging decisions and a discussion of African American law students and affirmative action.

■ In Chapter 6, "Justice on the Bench?" there is a discussion of the case of Walter Rideau, who was exonerated of his alleged crime; and as a result of the continuing controversy over race discrimination in jury selection, there is an expanded discussion of efforts to achieve a more diverse jury pool. This chapter also includes a new section on rape, race, and mistaken eyewitness identification.

■ Chapter 7, "Race and Sentencing," includes a summary of important new reports from The Sentencing Project; also included is new material on the drug-free school zone, racial differences in perceptions of the severity of criminal sanctions, and the constitutionality of hate crime sentencing enhancements.

■ Chapter 8, "The Color of Death," features a detailed discussion of the important events in Illinois that emptied the state's death row; also included are discussions of recent research on racial patterns in death sentences, research exploring the question of whether those who kill white women get the death penalty at a higher rate, and updated material on wrongful convictions.

■ Chapter 9, "Corrections in America: A Colorful Portrait," contains much more data on Hispanic Americans and Native Americans, new material on Native

American Drug Courts, and new material on the controversy involving the attempt by California correctional officials to segregate prisoners by race.

■ Chapter 10, "Minority Youth and Crime," includes a more extensive discussion of explanations for the higher violent victimization rate among racial and ethnic minority youth and new material on racial and ethnic disparities in arrests of juveniles. Also featured are the use of official gang databases and data on racial and ethnic patterns in the waiver of juveniles to adult court and placement of juveniles in residential treatment facilities.

■ Chapter 11, "The Color of Justice," provides a final overview of race, ethnicity and crime in America. Our conclusions from the first three editions of this book still stand. Criminal justice in America is pervaded with problems related to race and ethnicity. Disentangling the many factors associated with these problems is extremely difficult, however. Patterns of discrimination are often deeply embedded in the administration of justice and difficult to specify precisely. Nonetheless, discrimination is a serious problem in the American criminal justice system.

SUPPLEMENTS

An extensive package of supplemental aids accompanies this edition. It is available to qualified adopters; please consult your local sales representative for details.

For the Instructor

■ *Instructor's Resource Manual with Test Bank* by Gordon Armstrong, Oakland Community College: For the first time, an *Instructor's Resource Manual with Test Bank* has been developed for *The Color of Justice*. The manual includes learning objectives, chapter outlines, key terms, class discussion exercises/lecture suggestions, and a test bank containing approximately 50 questions per chapter in multiple choice, true–false, fill-in-the-blank, and essay formats, with a full answer key.

■ *Microsoft® PowerPoint® Presentations* by David Montague, University of Arkansas, Little Rock: Also for the first time, Microsoft PowerPoint presentations have been developed to accompany this text. This valuable resource will enhance your classroom lectures and save you time in preparing for your course. Choose from the ready-made dynamic slides offered or customize them to create a unique set.

■ *The Wadsworth Criminal Justice Video Library:* So many exciting, new videos— so many great ways to enrich your lectures and spark discussion of the material in this text. View our full video offerings and download clip lists with running times at www.thomsonedu.com/criminaljustice/media_center/index.html. Your Thomson Wadsworth representative will be happy to provide details on our video policy by adoption size. The library includes these selections and many others:

ABC Videos: The ABC video series includes Introduction to Criminal Justice, Volume I; Corrections, Volume I; and Terrorism, Volume I. Launch your lectures with exciting video clips from the award-winning news coverage of ABC. Addressing topics covered in a typical course, these videos are divided into short segments—perfect for introducing key concepts in contexts relevant to students' lives. Contact your local Thomson representative to learn more.

The Wadsworth Custom Videos for Criminal Justice, Volumes 2 and 3: Produced by Wadsworth and Films for the Humanities, these videos include short 5- to 10-minute segments that encourage classroom discussion. Topics include cocaine wars, prison gangs and racism behind bars, the life of an African American cop, three strikes laws, and more. Both volumes are available on either VHS or DVD.

Court TV Videos: These 1-hour videos present seminal and high-profile cases, such as *Florida v. Pitts and Lee* (death penalty), *Michigan v. Budzyn* (police force), and *Florida v. Campbell* ("driving while black"). Each case is followed from initial investigation to the penalty phase, with commentary by offenders, victims, witnesses, counsel, and experts in the field.

A&E American Justice Series: There are 40 videos to choose from, on topics such as deadly force, gang activity, juvenile justice, and death row.

Films for the Humanities: There are nearly 200 videos to choose from on a variety of topics such as understanding prejudice, hate crimes, hate groups, racism online, and more.

For the Student

■ *Six Steps to Effective Writing in Criminal Justice:* This compact resource helps students develop strong writing skills while preparing them for their academic and professional pursuits. The text includes sample writing topics, examples, formats, and papers that reflect the criminal justice discipline. When packaged with this text it is available at no cost to students.

■ *Writing for Criminal Justice:* This handy guide pulls together various articles and excerpts on writing skills to give students an introduction to academic, professional, and research writing, along with a basic grammar review and a survey of verbal communication on the job. The voices of practitioners and people who use these techniques every day will help students see the relevance of these skills to their future careers.

■ *The Wadsworth Criminal Justice Resource Center* (www.thomsonedu.com/criminaljustice): This website now includes a direct link to "Terrorism: An Interdisciplinary Perspective," an intriguing site that provides thorough coverage of terrorism in general and the issues surrounding the events of September 11. This website also provides a variety of tools and resources such as critical-thinking exercises from Jonathan White's *Terrorism: An Introduction,* InfoTrac® College Edition exercises, and links to online journals for updated information.

- *Internet Guide for Criminal Justice,* Second Edition: Internet beginners will appreciate this helpful booklet. With explanations and the vocabulary necessary for navigating the Web, it features customized information on criminal justice–related websites and presents Internet project ideas.

- *Internet Activities for Criminal Justice,* Second Edition: This completely revised 96-page booklet shows how to best use the Internet for research through searches and activities.

- *Criminal Justice Internet Explorer,* Third Edition: This colorful brochure lists the most popular Internet addresses for criminal justice–related websites. It includes URLs for corrections, victimization, crime prevention, high-tech crime, policing, courts, investigations, juvenile justice, research, and fun sites.

ACKNOWLEDGMENTS

We would like to thank the reviewers of this and all previous editions: Mary Atwell, Radford University; George S. Bridges, University of Washington; Orie A. Brown, California State University, Fresno; Stephanie Bush-Baskette, Florida State University; Christina Caifano, California State University, San Bernardino; Charles Crawford, Western Michigan University; James G. Fox, Buffalo State College; Jeannine Gailey, Texas Christian University; Tara Gray, New Mexico State University, Las Cruces; Marty Gruher, Rogue Community College; Robert G. Huckabee, Indiana State University; Peter Kratcoski, Sr., Kent State University; Martha A. Myers, University of Georgia; Marianne O. Nielson, Northern Arizona University; Elaine Premo, Chemeketa Community College; Elise Rego, University of Massachusetts; Gregory D. Russell, California State University, Chico; Katheryn Russell, University of Maryland; Susan Sharp, University of Oklahoma; Jill Shelley, Northern Kentucky University; Jed Stone, Lake Forest College; Becky L. Tatum, Georgia State University; Mary Ann Zager, Northeastern University; and Marjorie Zatz, Arizona State University.

1

🌱

Race, Ethnicity, and Crime
The Present Crisis

More than 100 years ago, the great African American scholar W. E. B. Du Bois declared, "The problem of the twentieth century is the problem of the color line."[1] Racism and racial discrimination, he argued, were the central problems facing modern society.

Much the same can be said about crime and justice in American society today. Nearly every problem related to criminal justice issues involves matters of race and ethnicity:

- In 2003 the incarceration rate for African American males in state and federal prisons was 7.3 times the rate for whites (3,405 vs. 465, respectively, per 100,000). The incarceration rate for Hispanic Americans was 2.6 times greater than for whites (1,231 per 100,000). There were also disparities in the incarceration of white and African American females, but not as great as for males.[2]

- Demographic changes are posing new challenges for criminal justice agencies. Hispanics and Latinos are the fastest-growing group in the U.S. population, increasing from 9 percent of the population in 1990 to 14 percent in 2005—and projected to be 18 percent by the year 2020. Language barriers involving recent immigrants with limited English proficiency raise a number of problems for the criminal justice system—the inability of people to communicate with police officers, the lack of translators for court proceedings, and so on. Asian Americans and Pacific Islanders now constitute 4 percent of the population.[3]

- Some immigrant groups practice traditional holistic medical practices that are often misunderstood in this country. A report by the Charlotte-Mecklenburg (North Carolina) Police Department points out that the practices of coining and cupping "leave temporary marks on the body that may be misconstrued as abuse." There have been cases where police arrested parents for child abuse because they did not understand the nature of these practices. The report adds that many recent immigrants are not aware of public health laws that require immunization of children.[4]

- In a 2005 survey the Pew Hispanic Center found that 82 percent of Hispanics believe that discrimination is preventing them from succeeding in the United States (and 44 percent see discrimination as a "major problem").[5]

- Conflict between the police and the African American community continues to trouble many cities. In Cincinnati, the fatal shooting of a young African American man in April 2001, the 15th such shooting in 6 years, sparked a riot with significant property destruction and the imposition of a citywide curfew. This riot was only the latest in a long series of urban disorders that have punctuated the last 100 years in the United States.[6]

- Native American reservations experience very high crime rates and inadequate law enforcement protection, according to a Justice Department report.[7]

- The national controversy over "racial profiling"—the allegation that police officers stop African American drivers because of the color of their skin and not because of actual violations of traffic laws—represents a new chapter in the long history of discrimination based on race.[8]

Since the mid-1960s, crime has been a central issue in American politics. For many white Americans, the crime issue is an expression of racial fears: fear of victimization by African American offenders and fear of racial integration of neighborhoods. For its annual report on *The State of Black America*, The National Urban League surveyed 800 African Americans. One question asked, "In general, do you think the criminal justice system in the United States is biased in favor of blacks, is it biased against blacks, or does it generally give blacks fair treatment?" Seventy-four percent of the respondents thought that it is biased against African Americans, whereas only 15 percent thought that the system is fair.[9]

In short, on both sides of the color line, there are suspicion and fear: a sense of injustice on the part of racial minorities and fear of black crime on the part of whites. American society is deeply polarized over the issues of crime, justice, and race. This polarization of attitudes toward crime is especially strong with respect to the death penalty. In 2003, 54 percent of African Americans opposed the death penalty for persons convicted of murder, compared with 29 percent of whites. (In previous polls, Latino Americans fell somewhere in between whites and African Americans).[10]

Although African Americans are more likely to be the victims of crime, whites express very high levels of fear of crime. For many whites, *crime* is a code word for fears of social change, and fears of racial change in particular. A study of community crime control efforts in Chicago, for example, found that neighborhood organizations usually were formed in response to perceived changes in the racial composition of their neighborhoods.[11]

THE SCOPE OF THIS BOOK

This book offers a comprehensive, critical, and balanced examination of the issues of crime and justice with respect to race and ethnicity. We believe that none of the existing books on the subject is completely adequate.[12]

First, other books do not offer a comprehensive treatment of all the issues on crime and the administration of criminal justice. There are many excellent articles and books on particular topics, such as the death penalty or police use of deadly force, but none covers the full range of topics in a complete and critical fashion. As a result, there are often no discussions of whether relatively more discrimination exists at one point in the justice system than at others. For example, is there more discrimination by the police in making arrest decisions than, say, by prosecutors in charging? Christopher Stone, former director of the Vera Institute of Justice, points out that our knowledge about most criminal justice issues is "uneven."[13] There are many important questions about which we just do not have good information.

Second, the treatment of race and ethnicity in introductory criminal justice textbooks is very weak. The textbooks do not identify race and ethnicity as a major issue and fail to incorporate important literature on police misconduct, felony sentencing, the employment of racial minorities, and other important topics.[14]

Third, few books or articles discuss all racial and ethnic groups. Most focus entirely on African Americans. Coramae Richey Mann points out that "the available studies focus primarily on African Americans and neglect other racial minorities."[15] There is relatively little research on Hispanic Americans and even less on Native Americans or Asian Americans. *The Color of Justice* includes material on these groups, along with material on Americans of Middle Eastern origin, who, in the wake of the terrorist attacks on September 11, 2001, allege that they have been the victims of racial profiling and other forms of discrimination.

The evidence we do have clearly indicates important differences between the experiences of various racial and ethnic groups with respect to crime and justice. African Americans and Latinos, for example, have different experiences with the police and different attitudes toward their local police departments. The experience of Native Americans is completely different from those two groups.

The Color of Justice takes a *contextual approach* and emphasizes the unique historical, political, and economic circumstances of each group. Alfredo Mirandé, author of *Gringo Justice*, argues that historically "a double standard of justice" has existed, one for Anglo Americans and one for Chicanos.[16] Marianne O. Nielsen, meanwhile, argues that the subject of Native Americans and criminal justice "cannot be understood without recognizing that it is just one of many interrelated issues that face native peoples today," including "political power, land, economic development, [and] individual despair."[17]

Because there has been little comparative research, it is difficult to make useful comparisons of the experiences of different groups. We do not know, for example, whether Hispanic Americans are treated worse, better, or about the same as African Americans. We have chosen to title this book *The Color of Justice* because it covers *all* people of color.

Fourth, few books on this subject offer a critical perspective on the available evidence. The handling of the data on arrests or sentencing is often superficial, ignoring many important complexities. Traffic stop data, for example, have proved to be extremely complex, and as we will see in Chapter 4 it is often difficult to make easy judgments about whether existing disparities indicate a pattern of illegal discrimination exists. Too often authors rely only on evidence that supports their preconceptions.

We strongly disagree with William Wilbanks's argument that racism in the criminal justice system is a "myth."[18] This book presents abundant evidence on racial and ethnic disparities in the administration of justice that can only be explained in terms of biased attitudes and practices. We also reject Christopher Stone's conclusion, in his report to the President's Initiative on Race, that there is "strong reason for optimism" in the data on race and criminal justice.[19] The authors of this book are not quite so optimistic. There are indeed some areas of progress in the direction of greater equality and fairness in the criminal justice system. The employment of African Americans and Latinos in the justice system has made some real progress. At the same time, however, persistent patterns of racial and ethnic disparities remain. Discrimination appears to be deeply rooted in the application of the death penalty, for example.

Finally, as Hawkins points out, American sociologists and criminologists have done a very poor job of studying the relationship of race, ethnicity, and crime. In particular, there is an absence of solid theoretical work that would provide a comprehensive explanation for this extremely important phenomenon. The main reason for this, Hawkins argues, is that "public discourse about both crime and race in the United States has always been an ideological and political mine field."[20] On the one side racist theories of biological determinism attribute high rates of crime among racial and ethnic minorities to genetic inferiority. On the other side, the mainstream of American criminology has downplayed racial differences in criminal behavior and emphasized the inadequacy of official crime data. The extreme sensitivity of the subject has tended to discourage rather than stimulate the development of theoretical studies of race, ethnicity, and crime.

OBJECTIVES OF THE BOOK

The Color of Justice has several objectives. First, it seeks to synthesize the best and most recent research on the relevant topics: the patterns of criminal behavior and victimization, police practices, court processing and sentencing, the death penalty, and prisons and other correctional programs.

Second, it offers an interpretation of what the existing research means. Is there systematic discrimination in the criminal justice system? Can patterns of discrimination be explained better in terms of contextual discrimination? What does that term mean? If this pattern exists, where do we find it? How serious is it? What are the causes? Have any reforms succeeded in reducing it?

Third, *The Color of Justice* offers a multiracial and multiethnic view of crime and justice issues. The United States is a multicultural society, with many different races, ethnic groups, and cultural lifestyles. Unfortunately, most of the research has ignored the rich diversity of contemporary society. There is a great deal of research on African Americans and criminal justice but relatively little on Hispanics, Native Americans, and Asian Americans. In addition, much of the criminal justice research confuses race and ethnicity.

Finally, *The Color of Justice* does not attempt to offer a comprehensive theory of the relationship of race, ethnicity, and crime. Although Hawkins makes a persuasive case for the need for such a theory, this book has a more limited objective. It seeks to lay the groundwork for a comprehensive theory by emphasizing the general patterns in the administration of justice with respect to race and ethnicity. We feel that the available evidence permits us to draw some conclusions about that subject. The development of a comprehensive theory will have to be the subject of a future book.

GOALS OF THE CHAPTER

As an introduction to the book, Chapter 1 provides a foundation for a discussion of race, ethnicity, and crime involving several basic issues. The first issue involves *race* and *ethnicity*. When we speak of race and ethnicity, what are we talking about? What is the difference between race and ethnicity? Which groups belong in which category? The second issue is the question of *disparities* and *discrimination*. What exactly is the difference between disparity and discrimination? What kind of evidence is necessary to establish that discrimination exists?

The first section of this chapter describes the racial and ethnic categories used in the United States. It also discusses the quality of data on race and ethnicity reported by the different criminal justice agencies.

The second section examines the distribution of racial and ethnic groups in the United States. The uneven distribution of racial and ethnic groups across the country means that race and ethnicity have a very different impact on the criminal justice systems in different cities and states.

The third section addresses the distinction between disparity and discrimination. One of the central controversies in criminal justice is whether the over-representation of racial minorities in the justice system is the result of discrimination or whether it represents disparities that can be explained by other factors.

THE COLORS OF AMERICA:
RACIAL AND ETHNIC CATEGORIES

The 2000 census revealed that the United States is increasingly a multiracial, multiethnic society. The population was 69.4 percent non-Hispanic white, 12.7 percent Black or African American, 0.9 percent Native American, and 3.8 percent Asian/Pacific Islander. Within these four racial categories, 12.6 percent reported Hispanic ethnicity. These figures represent significant changes from

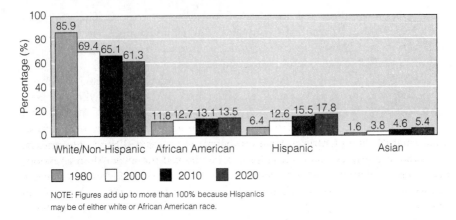

FIGURE 1.1 U.S. Population, 1980–2020 (projected)

SOURCE: U.S. Bureau of the Census. *Interim Projections by Age, Sex, Race, and Hispanic Origin* (Washington, DC: Bureau of the Census, March 2004).

20 years ago, and demographers are predicting steady changes in the immediate future. As Figure 1.1 indicates, Hispanics are the fastest-growing racial or ethnic group in the United States, increasing from 6.4 percent of the population in 1980 to an estimated 17.8 percent by the year 2020. In the summer of 2005 the Census Bureau announced that Texas had become the fourth state where Latinos and African Americans constituted a majority of the population (50.2 percent). The other states are Hawaii (77 percent), New Mexico (57 percent), and California (56 percent), along with the District of Columbia (70 percent).[21]

Racial and Ethnic Categories

Race and ethnicity are extremely complex and controversial subjects. The categories the Census Bureau and other government agencies use, and that most people use in everyday conversation, are problematic and do not accurately reflect the reality of American life.

Race Traditionally, race has referred to the "major biological divisions of mankind," which are distinguished by color of skin, color and texture of hair, bodily proportions, and other physical features.[22] The traditional approach identifies three major racial groups: Caucasian, Negroid, and Mongoloid.

Anthropologists and sociologists do not accept the strict biological definition of race. Because of intermarriage and evolution over time, it is virtually impossible to identify exclusive racial categories. Scientists have not been able to determine meaningful differences between people who are referred to as white, black, and Asian. Yinger maintains that "we cannot accept the widespread belief that there are a few clearly distinct and nearly immutable races. Change and intermixture are continuous."[23]

Experts regard the concept of race as "primarily a social construct."[24] That is to say, groups define themselves and have labels applied to them by other groups.

Usually, the politically and culturally dominant group in any society defines the labels that are applied to other groups. At times, however, subordinate groups assert themselves by developing their own labels. Racial designations have changed over the centuries as a result of changes in both political power and racial attitudes. Yinger argues that the critical categories for social analysis are the "socially visible 'racial' lines, based on beliefs about race and on administrative and political classifications, rather than genetic differences."[25]

A good example of the politics of racial categories is the history of the classification and labeling of African American people in the United States. Historically, the attitudes of whites—and official policy—embodied the racist "drop of blood" theory: anyone with the slightest African ancestry was defined as "black," even when a majority of that person's ancestors were white or Caucasian.[26] Following this approach, many datasets in the past used the categories of "white" and "nonwhite." The federal government today prohibits the use of the "nonwhite" label.[27]

The problem with traditional racial categories is obvious when we look at American society. Many people have mixed ancestry. What, for example, is the "race" of the child whose father is African American and mother is of Irish American heritage? Or the child whose mother is Japanese American and whose father is of European background? Or the child whose mother is Native American and whose father is Hispanic? Many "white" Americans have some ancestors who were African American or Native American. Few African Americans have ancestries that are purely African.

Issues related to classifying multiracial and multiethnic people are not abstract ideas; they have very real, and often cruel, human meaning. An article in the *New Yorker* magazine highlighted the case of Susan Graham of Roswell, Georgia, who complained, "When I received my 1990 census form, I realized that there was no race category for my children." She is white, and her husband is African American. She called the Census Bureau and was finally told that children should take the race of their mother. No rational reason was given about why the race of her husband, the children's father, should be arbitrarily ignored. Then, when she enrolled the children in kindergarten, the school classified them as "black." Thus, she pointed out, "My child has been white on the United States census, black at school, and multiracial at home—all at the same time."[28]

The bureaucratic problems related to classification of people have important human implications. Classification systems label people and inevitably tend to imply that some groups are inferior to others. The Association of Multi-Ethnic Americans and related groups are particularly concerned about the impact of classifications and labels on children.[29]

The problem of classifying multiethnic and multiracial people has important implications for criminal justice data. What if the National Crime Victimization Survey (NCVS) calls the Graham household? Would their household be classified as "white" or "black"? What if one of their children were the victim of a robbery? Would the victimization survey record that as a "white" or "black" victimization?

Members of the major racial and ethnic groups are divided among themselves about which term they prefer. The National Urban League surveyed 800 African American adults, asking them which term they preferred. About half (51 percent)

Focus on an Issue
The Bell Curve *Controversy: Race and IQ*

A national storm of controversy erupted in the fall of 1994 over a book titled *The Bell Curve* (Herrnstein & Murray, 1994). The authors argue that success in life is determined largely by IQ: the smarter people succeed, whereas those with lower intelligence, as measured by standard IQ tests, fail and end up at the bottom of the social scale. The authors contend that those at the low end of the IQ scale do poorly in school and are more likely to be unemployed, receive welfare, and commit crime.

The most provocative and controversial parts of their thesis are the points that intelligence is inherited and that there are significant differences in intelligence between races. The authors cite data indicating that Asian Americans consistently score higher on IQ tests than white European Americans, who, in turn, score higher than African Americans. Herrnstein and Murray are very clear about the policy implications of their argument: Because intelligence is mainly inherited, social programs designed to improve the performance of poor children, such as Head Start, are doomed to failure and should be abandoned.

The Bell Curve was attacked by psychologists, anthropologists, and sociologists, among others (Fraser, 1995). Critics disputed the authors' assumptions that there is some entity called "intelligence" that is inherited and that IQ tests are a valid measure of intellectual capacity.

Critics also disputed their handling of the evidence regarding intelligence tests, the impact of environmental factors as opposed to inherited factors, and the effect of programs such as Head Start. There is evidence, for example, that Head Start does improve IQ test scores in addition to children's later success in life.

One point is relevant to the discussion in this chapter. Herrnstein and Murray argue that there are basic, inherited differences in intelligence between races. We reject that argument on the grounds that the vast majority of anthropologists and sociologists do not accept the idea of separate races as distinct biological entities. If there are no scientifically valid racial differences, the basic argument of *The Bell Curve* falls apart.

In response to the long controversy, the American Anthropological Association (AAA) in 1994 issued an official "Statement on 'Race' and Intelligence." (Note in this statement and the one cited in Box 1.1 that the AAA places the word *race* in quotation marks as a way of indicating that the concept does not have any scientific validity.) The AAA makes the following statement:

> The American Anthropological Association (AAA) is deeply concerned by recent public discussions which imply that intelligence is biologically determined by race. Repeatedly challenged by scientists, nevertheless these ideas continue to be advanced. Such discussions distract public and scholarly attention from and diminish support for the collective challenge to ensure equal opportunities for all people, regardless of ethnicity or phenotypic variation.

Earlier AAA resolutions against racism (1961, 1969, 1971, 1972) have spoken to this concern. The AAA further resolves:

WHEREAS all human beings are members of one species, *Homo sapiens*, and

WHEREAS, differentiating species into biologically defined "races" has proven meaningless and unscientific as a way of explaining variation (whether in intelligence or other traits),

THEREFORE, the American Anthropological Association urges the academy, our political leaders and our communities to affirm, without distraction by mistaken claims of

racially determined intelligence, the common stake in assuring equal opportunity, in respecting diversity and in securing a harmonious quality of life for all people.

The full AAA statement is available on the organization's website (www.aaanet.org).

> **B O X 1.1** **American Anthropological Association, Statement on "Race," 1998 (excerpt)**
>
> In the United States both scholars and the general public have been conditioned to viewing human races as natural and separate divisions within the human species based on visible physical differences. With the vast expansion of scientific knowledge in this century, however, it has become clear that human populations are not unambiguous, clearly demarcated, biologically distinct groups. Evidence from the analysis of genetics (e.g., DNA) indicates that most physical variation, about 94%, lies *within* so called racial groups. Conventional geographic "racial" groupings differ from one another only in about 6% of their genes. This means that there is greater variation within "racial" groups than between them. In neighboring populations there is much overlapping of genes and their phenotypic (physical) expressions.
>
> Throughout history whenever different groups have come into contact, they have interbred. The continued sharing of genetic materials has maintained all of humankind as a single species.
>
> ———
>
> SOURCE: The full statement, along with other materials, can be found on the website of the American Anthropological Association (www.aaanet.org).

---

preferred *black*, and 43 percent preferred *African American*.[30] Reports by the Pew Hispanic Center find complex patterns of self-identification among Hispanics. When asked what is the first term they use to identify themselves, slightly more than half use their country of origin (i.e., Mexico, Nicaragua). About one third (34%) prefer "Hispanic" and 13% prefer Latino.

As these examples suggest, the complex multicultural reality of American society means that the categories used by government agencies such as the Census Bureau are, as one person put it, "illogical."[31]

The U.S. Census Bureau classifies people on the basis of self-identification—that is, your racial or ethnic identity is what *you* say it is. Many people have protested the requirement of having to choose one or another racial category. The Association of MultiEthnic Americans (AMEA) was established to fight for the right of people with mixed heritage to acknowledge their full identity. AMEA proclaimed "victory" in October 1997 when the Office of Management and Budget (OMB) adopted new federal guidelines allowing people to identify themselves in terms of more than just one race.[32] Most of the data in this book use the racial categories established by the OMB, which are required for use by all federal agencies, including the Census Bureau.

The OMB also revised the names used for many of the racial groups.[33] The new categories are (1) American Indian or Alaska Native; (2) Asian; (3) Black or African American; (4) Hispanic or Latino; (5) Native Hawaiian or Other Pacific Islander; and (6) white. Previously, OMB used only the term *black*; the new category is *Black or African American*. Persons may also identify themselves as Haitian or Negro. Previously, only the term *Hispanic* was used. The new guidelines use *Hispanic or Latino*. The OMB considered, but rejected, a proposal to use *Native American* and retained the old term *American Indian*.

The OMB defines a black or African American person as anyone "having origins in any of the black racial groups of Africa." It defines a white person as anyone "having origins in any of the original peoples of Europe, the Middle East, or North Africa." Accordingly, a person who is from Morocco or Iran is classified as "white," and someone from Nigeria or Tanzania is classified as "black." The category of American Indians includes Alaska Natives and "original peoples of North and South America (including Central America)." Asian includes people from the Far East, Southeast Asia, or the Indian subcontinent. Pacific Islanders are no longer in the same category with Asians and are now included with Native Hawaiians in a separate category.

The OMB concedes that the racial and ethnic categories it created "are not anthropologically or scientifically based." Instead, they represent "a socialpolitical construct." Most important, OMB warns that the categories "should not be interpreted as being primarily biological or genetic in reference."[34]

Ethnicity Ethnicity is not the same thing as race. *Ethnicity* refers to differences between groups of people based on cultural customs, such as language, religion, foodways, family patterns, and other characteristics. Among white Americans, for example, there are distinct ethnic groups based primarily on country of origin: Irish Americans, Italian Americans, Polish Americans, and so on.[35] Yinger uses a three-part definition of ethnicity: (1) The group is perceived by others to be different with respect to such factors as language, religion, race, ancestral homeland, and other cultural elements; (2) the group perceives itself to be different with respect to these factors; and (3) members of the group "participate in shared activities built around their (real or mythical) common origin and culture."[36]

The Hispanic or Latino category is extremely complex. First, Hispanic is an ethnic designation, and individuals may belong to any racial category. Thus, some Hispanics identify themselves as white, others consider themselves African American, and some identify as Native Americans. In the past, criminal justice agencies, following the federal guidelines, have classified Hispanics as white but have not also collected data on ethnic identity. As a result, most criminal justice data sets do not provide good longitudinal data on Hispanics.

Second, the Hispanic American population is extremely diverse with respect to place of origin, which includes Mexico, Puerto Rico, Cuba, Central America,

South America, and others. Although widely used, these categories are not consistent or logical. Mexico and Cuba are countries, whereas Central America and South America are regions consisting of several nations. Mexican Americans are the largest single group within the Hispanic community, making up 58.4 percent of the total in the 2000 census. Puerto Ricans are the second largest (9.6 percent), and Cubans are third (3.2 percent).[37]

Arab Americans   Arab Americans represent a special case because the community is extremely diverse and does not fit into any of the categories used by the U.S. Census. The Census records most Arab Americans as "caucasian," but that label does not adequately describe the diverse community. With respect to the physical indicators that are popularly used to define "race," such as skin color or hair texture, Arab Americans are as diverse as are "white" and "black" Americans. The term Arab Americans is, in fact, a social construct that includes people of many different national origins, religions, and ethnicities.[38]

Many people assume that Arab Americans are all Muslim, but this is not true. Arab Americans are Muslim, Christian, Druze, and other religions. Even the Christians are divided among Protestant, Catholic, and Greek Orthodox. In terms of national origins, Arab Americans trace their heritage to Lebanon, Syria, Iraq, Kuwait, Morocco, Algeria, and many other countries. (Many people assume that Turkish people are Arabs, but they are not.) Finally, with regard to ethnicity, Arab Americans may be Kurds, Berbers, Armenian, Bedu, or members of other groups.

The Immigration Controversy   Immigration erupted as a major political controversy in the spring of 2006. Hundreds of thousands of demonstrators marched in cities across the country to protest an immigration bill that had been passed by the U.S. House of Representatives. If it became law, it would make it a felony to be in the United States without proper immigration status. Under present law, violation of federal immigration laws is a civil offense. A person may be detained and deported, but it is not a crime and definitely not a felony.

Obviously, the law would have a major impact on American criminal justice. There are an estimated 12 million undocumented immigrants in the United States as of the spring of 2006. The law would instantly create 12 million new "criminals." Critics of the law point out that attempting to arrest, detain, and prosecute that many people is not possible. The law contains other provisions that critics oppose. One provision makes it a crime to knowingly assist an undocumented immigrant. This would appear to make it a crime to operate a soup kitchen or shelter that serves even one undocumented immigrant. For this reason, many religious leaders opposed the law. As this book is being written, the future of federal immigration law, and its impact on American criminal justice, is very uncertain.

"Minority Groups" as a Label   The term *minorities* is widely used as a label for people of color. The United Nations defines minority groups as "those nondominant groups in a population which possess and wish to preserve stable ethnic, religious or linguistic traditions or characteristics markedly different from those of the rest of the population."[39] The noted sociologist Louis Wirth adds the element of discrimination to this definition: Minorities are those who "are singled out from the others in the society in which they live for differential and unequal treatment, and who therefore regard themselves as objects of collective discrimination."[40]

Use of the term *minority* is increasingly criticized. Among other things, it has a pejorative connotation, suggesting "less than" something else, which in this context means less than some other groups. The new OMB guidelines for the Census Bureau and other federal agencies specifically "do *not* identify or designate certain population groups as 'minority groups.'"[41] Many people today prefer to use the term *people of color*.

Diversity within Racial and Ethnic Groups　Another important complicating factor is the diversity that exists within racial and ethnic groups. As our previous discussion indicates, both the Latino and the Arab American communities include people of very different national origins. The African American community, meanwhile, consists of people whose families have been in the United States for hundreds of years and recent immigrants from Africa. Some recent immigrants from Africa, for example, do not wish to be labeled African Americans because they consider themselves strictly African. The Native American community is divided among 562 tribal governments recognized by the Bureau of Indian Affairs (which does not necessarily include all tribes), some of which have very different languages, cultural traditions, and tribal political institutions. Each racial and ethnic group, meanwhile, is divided by social class, with both wealthy and poor members. Social class has a major impact on peoples' experiences with the criminal justice system.

A Vera Institute study of police relations with immigrant communities in New York City concluded that "immigrant groups are not monolithic, [but] are made up of ethnically, culturally, socio-economically, and often linguistically diverse subgroups . . . ." This has important implications for criminal justice agencies. The Vera Institute report advised that police departments must "reach out to a variety of community representatives," even within one racial or ethnic group.[42]

One reason criminal justice agencies need to reach out to immigrant groups is that recent arrivals to the United States do not necessarily understand our legal system. A number of scholars have noted that they do not share the "legal consciousness" that long-time American residents have.[43] This legal consciousness includes a sense of "inherent rights" and entitlements regarding the legal system. In practice, this includes a sense of your right to call the police if you have a problem, a right to be treated respectfully by the police and other officials, and a right to file a complaint if you are not treated properly.

The Politics of Racial and Ethnic Labels

There has always been great controversy over what term should be used to designate different racial and ethnic groups. The term *African American*, for example, is relatively new and became widely used only in the 1980s. It has begun to replace *black* as the preferred designation, which replaced *Negro* in the 1960s. *Negro*, in turn, replaced *colored* about 25 years earlier. The leading African American civil rights organization is the National Association for the Advancement of Colored People

(NAACP), founded in 1909. Ironically, *colored* replaced *African* much earlier. In some respects, then, we have come full circle in the past 150 years. As John Hope Franklin, the distinguished African American historian and former chair of President Clinton's Initiative on Race, points out in his classic history of African Americans, *From Slavery to Freedom*, the subjects of his book have been referred to by "three distinct names . . . even during the lifetime of this book."[44]

Preferred labels can change quickly in a short time. The term *African American*, for example, replaced *black* as the preferred label among African Americans in just 5 years (although a majority say that it does not matter).[45]

The controversy over the proper label is *political* in the sense that it often involves a power struggle between different racial and ethnic groups. It is not just a matter of which label but who chooses that label. Wolf argues that "the function of racial categories within industrial capitalism is exclusionary."[46] The power to control one's own label represents an important element of police power and autonomy. Having to accept a label placed on you by another group is an indication of powerlessness.

The term *black* emerged as the preferred designation in the late 1960s as part of an assertion of pride in blackness and quest for power by African Americans themselves. The African American community was making a political statement to the majority white community: "This is how we choose to describe ourselves." In a similar fashion, the term *African American* emerged in the 1980s through a process of self-designation on the part of the African American community. In this book, we use the term *African American*. It emerged as the preferred term by spokespersons for the African American community and has been adopted by the OMB for the 2000 census (and can be used along with *black, Negro,* and *Haitian*). It is also consistent with terms commonly used for other groups. We routinely refer to Irish Americans, Polish Americans, and Chinese Americans, for instance, using the country of origin as the primary descriptor.

It makes sense, therefore, to designate people whose country of origin is Africa as African Americans. The term *black* refers to a color, which is an imprecise descriptor for a group of people whose members range in skin color from a very light yellow to a very dark black.

A similar controversy exists over the proper term for Hispanic Americans (see Box 1.2). Not everyone, including some leaders of the community itself, prefers this term. Some prefer *Latino*, and others use *Chicano*. As we previously noted, a majority of Hispanics refer to themselves by their country of origin, while about one third use the term *Hispanic* and the remainder prefer *Latino*.[47] The 2005 Pew Hispanic Center survey found that among third-generation Hispanic Americans (that is, the third generation to live in the United States), 21 percent identify themselves by their country of origin, 20 percent identify as Latino or Hispanic, and 57 percent identify themselves as American.[48] Some white Americans incorrectly refer to Hispanics as Mexican Americans, ignoring the many people who have a different country of origin. The OMB has accepted the term *Latino*, and the 2000 census uses the category of Hispanic or Latino. In this book we use the term *Hispanic*. It is more comprehensive than other terms and includes all of the different countries of origin.

B O X 1.2 Donde está la justicia?

The term *Hispanic* has been used to refer to people of Spanish descent. The term refers, in part, to people with ties to nations where Spanish is the official language. The U.S. government and legal system historically have insisted on categorizing all Spanish-speaking people as Hispanic and treating them as a monolithic group, regardless of cultural differences.

The term *Latino*, however, generally refers to people with ties to the nations of Latin America and the Caribbean, including some nations where Spanish is not spoken such as Brazil. It also encompasses people born in the United States whose families immigrated to this country from Latin America in the recent past and those whose ancestors immigrated generations ago. Like the term *Hispanic*, the categorization *Latino* is a general one that does not recognize the diversity of ethnic subgroups (for example, Puerto Rican, Dominican, Guatemalan, Peruvian, and Mexican).

SOURCE: Adapted from Francisco A. Villarruel and Nancy E. Walker, *Donde está la justicia? A Call to Action on Behalf of Latino and Latina Youth in the U.S. Justice System* (East Lansing, MI: Institute for Youth, Children, and Families, 2002).

We use the term *Native Americans* to designate those people who have historically been referred to as American Indians. The term *Indians*, after all, originated through a misunderstanding, as the first European explorers of the Americas mistakenly thought they had landed in Asia.

The term *Anglo* is widely used as a term for white Americans, but it is not an accurate descriptor. Only a minority of white Americans trace their ancestry back to the British Isles, to which the term Anglo refers. The often-used pejorative term *WASP* (white, Anglo-Saxon, Protestant) is also inaccurate because many white Americans are Catholic, Jewish, or members of some other religious group, and are not Anglo-Saxon.

In short, the term *white* is as inaccurate as *black*. People who are commonly referred to as white include a wide range of skin colors, from very pale white to a dark olive or brown. The term *Caucasian* may actually be more accurate.

The Quality of Criminal Justice Data on Race and Ethnicity

Serious analysis of the racial and ethnic dimensions of crime and justice requires good data. Unfortunately, the data reported by criminal justice agencies are not always reliable. The first problem is that on many important subjects there are no data at all on race or ethnicity. The majority of the published research to date involves African Americans. Although there are important gaps and much remains to be done, we do have a reasonably good sense of how African Americans fare at the hands of the police, prosecutors, judges, and correctional officials. Hispanic Americans, however, have until very recently been neglected. Even less research is available on Native Americans and Asian Americans. Consequently, we will not be able to discuss many important subjects in detail in this book (for example, the patterns of police arrest of Hispanics compared with those of whites and African Americans).

A second problem involves the quality of the data. Criminal justice agencies do not always use the same racial and ethnic categories. The problem is particularly acute with respect to Hispanic Americans. Many criminal justice agencies collect data only on race and use the census categories of white and black, counting Hispanics as whites. This approach, however, masks potentially significant differences between Hispanics and non-Hispanic whites. This has important implications for analyzing the nature and extent of disparities in the criminal justice system. If we assume that Hispanics are arrested at a higher rate than non-Hispanic whites (a report finds that Hispanic drivers are arrested by the police at a much higher rate than whites),[49] the available data not only eliminate Hispanics as a separate group but also raise the overall non-Hispanic arrest rate. This result would narrow the gap in arrest rates between whites and African Americans and understate the real extent of racial disparities in arrest.

Some data systems use the categories of "white" and "nonwhite." This approach incorrectly treats all people of color as members of the same race. As noted earlier, the OMB prohibits government agencies from using the term *nonwhite*.

Classifying Hispanics and non-Hispanic whites as "white" has a major impact on official data and the picture that is presented of the criminal justice system. Holman analyzed how using a "white/black" classification system results in an overcount of non-Hispanic whites in prison and an undercount of Hispanics. Data from 1997 indicated that 58 percent of all federal prisoners were white. In fact, however, only 31.3 were non-Hispanic whites and 26.7 were Hispanic. In New Mexico, the misrepresentation was even worse. Official data indicated that 83 percent of prisoners were white, when in fact only 28.9 percent were non-Hispanic white and 54.1 percent were Hispanic.[50]

The Uniform Crime Reports (UCR) data from the Federal Bureau of Investigation (FBI) are useless with respect to many important issues related to race, ethnicity, and crime. First, the data used to create the Crime Index, "crimes known to police," do not include data on race and therefore do not tell us anything about victimization by race. Second, the FBI data on arrests use the categories of white, black, American Indian or Alaska Native, and Asian or Pacific Islander. There is still no separate category for Hispanics. Fortunately, the National Crime Victimization Survey (NCVS) does collect data on Hispanics and non-Hispanics, and it is a rich source of data on this issue. The BJS National Prisoner Statistics program also reports data on white, black, and Hispanic prisoners.

With respect to Native Americans, LaFree points out that they "fall under the jurisdiction of a complex combination of native and nonnative legal entities" that render the arrest data "problematic."[51] Snyder-Joy characterizes the Native American justice system as "a jurisdictional maze" in which jurisdiction over various criminal acts is divided among federal, state, and tribal governments.[52] It is not clear, for example, that all tribal police agencies report arrest data to the FBI's UCR system. Thus, Native American arrests are probably significantly undercounted.

A third problem is that the FBI has changed the categories for Asian Americans over the years, making longitudinal analysis impossible.

B O X   1.3   Who is "Juanita"?

The report *Donde esta la justicia?* illustrated the problem with reference to "Juanita," whose father is Puerto Rican and mother is African American. How would she be classified if she were arrested? In Arizona she would define her own race or ethnicity. In California she would be counted as African American. In Michigan she would be classified as Hispanic and then be assigned to a racial group. In Ohio she would be recorded as biracial.

SOURCE: Adapted from Building Blocks for Youth, *Donde esta la justicia?* (East Lansing: Michigan State University, 2002).

The appendices in the *Sourcebook of Criminal Justice Statistics* reveal a serious lack of consistency in the use of the Hispanic designation among criminal justice agencies.[53] In the National Corrections Reporting Program, for example, Colorado, Illinois, Minnesota, New York, Oklahoma, and Texas record Hispanic prison inmates as "unknown" race. Ohio records Native Americans and Asian Americans as "unknown" race. California, Michigan, and Oklahoma classify only Mexican Americans as Hispanic, apparently classifying people from Puerto Rico, Cuba, and South America as non-Hispanic.

In addition, the criminal justice officials responsible for classifying persons may be poorly trained and may rely on their own stereotypes about race and ethnicity. The race of a person arrested is determined by what the arresting officer puts on the original arrest report. In the Justice Department's Juvenile Court Statistics, race is "determined by the youth or by court personnel."[54] We are not entirely sure that all of these personnel designate people accurately.

In short, the official data reported by criminal justice agencies are very problematic, which creates tremendous difficulties when we try to assess the fate of different groups at the hands of the criminal justice system. The disparities that we know to exist today could be greater or smaller, depending on how people have been classified. We will need to be sensitive to these data problems as we discuss the various aspects of the criminal justice system in the chapters ahead.

THE GEOGRAPHY OF RACIAL AND ETHNIC JUSTICE

Because of two factors, the "geography of justice" in the United States varies across the country. First, the primary responsibility for criminal justice lies with city, county, and state governments. The federal government plays a very small role in the total picture of criminal justice. Second, the major racial and ethnic groups are not evenly distributed across the country. California and Texas alone have a disproportionate share of the Hispanic population, for example. As a result, the salience of race and ethnicity varies widely from jurisdiction to jurisdiction.

Although the United States as a whole is becoming more diverse, most of this diversity is concentrated in a few regions and metropolitan areas. One study concluded that "most communities lack true racial and ethnic diversity."[55] In 1996 only 745 of the 3,142 counties had a white population that was below the national average. Only 21 metropolitan areas qualified as true "melting pots" (with the percentage of the white population below the national average and at least two minority groups with a greater percentage than their national average).[56]

More than half of all racial and ethnic minorities live in just five states (California, Texas, New York, Florida, and Illinois), with 20 percent in California alone. More than half (52.3 percent) of the African American population is located in the 17 states in the Southeast. The other major concentration is in the big cities of the North and the Midwest. For example, African Americans represent 82 percent of the population in Detroit, 67 percent in Atlanta, and 46 percent in Cleveland.[57]

The distribution of the Hispanic population is even more complex. More than half (51 percent) live in just two states, Texas and California. About 83 percent of these people are Mexican Americans. Puerto Rican Americans are concentrated on the East Coast, with almost 41 percent living in New York and New Jersey. In New York City, Puerto Ricans are the largest Hispanic national origins group (789,172 people in 2000, out of a total of 8 million Hispanics), and Dominicans are second, with 406,806 people. People from Mexico are a relative small part of the New York City population, with only 186,872 people. About 67 percent of all Cuban Americans live in Florida.[58] Native Americans are also heavily concentrated. Just less than half (45 percent) live in four states: Oklahoma, Arizona, New Mexico, and California.[59]

The uneven distribution of the major racial and ethnic groups is extremely important for criminal justice. Crime is primarily the responsibility of state and local governments. Thus, racial and ethnic issues are especially salient in those cities where racial minorities are heavily concentrated. For example, the context of policing is very different in Detroit, which is 82 percent African American, than in Minneapolis, where African Americans are only 18 percent of the population. Similarly, Hispanic issues are far more significant in San Antonio, which is 59 percent Hispanic, than in many other cities where few Hispanics live.[60]

The concentration of racial and ethnic minority groups in certain cities and counties has important implications for criminal justice agencies. Population concentration translates into political power and the ability to control agencies. Mayors, for example, appoint police chiefs. If a country is a majority African American or Hispanic, those groups are able to control the election of the sheriff. African Americans have served as mayors of most of the major cities: New York; Los Angeles; Chicago; Philadelphia; Detroit; Atlanta; Washington, DC, and others. There have also been African American police chiefs or commissioners in each of these cities.

The concentration of African Americans in the Southeast has at least two important effects. This concentration gives this group a certain degree of political power that translates into elected African American sheriffs and mayors. These officials, in turn, may appoint African American police chiefs. For instance, by 2001 the State of Mississippi had 892 elected African American officials, more than any other state, including several elected sheriffs.[61] In 2004, Texas led the nation with 2,013 elected Hispanic officials.

DISPARITY VERSUS DISCRIMINATION

Perhaps the most important question with respect to race and ethnicity is whether there is discrimination in the criminal justice system. Many people argue that it is pervasive, whereas others believe that intentional discrimination does not exist. Mann presents "a minority perspective" on the administration of justice, emphasizing discrimination against people of color.[62] Wilbanks, however, argues that the idea of systematic racism in the criminal justice system is a "myth."[63]

Debates over the existence of racial discrimination in the criminal justice system are often muddled and unproductive because of confusion over the meaning of "discrimination." It is, therefore, important to make two important distinctions. First, there is a significant difference between disparity and discrimination. Second, discrimination can take different forms and involve different degrees of seriousness. Box 1.4 offers a schematic diagram of the various forms of discrimination, ranging from total, systematic discrimination to pure justice.

Disparity refers to a difference but one that does not necessarily involve discrimination. Look around your classroom. If you are in a conventional college program, almost all of the students will be relatively young (between the ages of 18 and 25). This represents a disparity in age compared with the general population. There are no children, few middle-aged people, and probably no elderly students. This is not a result of discrimination, however. These older groups are not enrolled in the class mainly because the typical life course is to attend college immediately after high school. The age disparity, therefore, is the result of factors other than discrimination.

The example of education illustrates the point that a disparity is a difference that can be explained by legitimate factors. In criminal justice, the crucial distinction is between legal and extralegal factors. *Legal factors* include the seriousness of the offense, aggravating or mitigating circumstances, or an offender's prior criminal record. These are considered legitimate bases for decisions by most criminal justice officials because they relate to an individual's criminal behavior. *Extralegal factors* include race, ethnicity, gender, social class, and lifestyle. They are not legitimate bases for decisions by criminal justice officials because they involve group membership and are unrelated to a person's criminal behavior. It would be illegitimate, for example, for a judge to sentence all male burglars to prison but place all female burglars on probation, despite the fact that women had committed the same kind of burglary and had prior records similar to those of many of the men. Similarly, it would be illegitimate for a judge to sentence all unemployed persons to prison but grant probation to all employed persons.

Discrimination, however, is a difference based on *differential treatment* of groups without reference to an individual's behavior or qualifications. A few examples of employment discrimination will illustrate the point. Until the 1960s, most Southern police departments did not hire African American officers. The few that did,

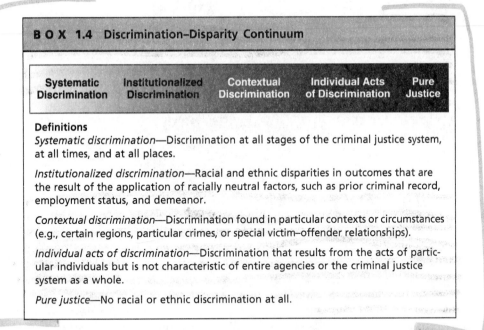

B O X 1.4 Discrimination–Disparity Continuum

Systematic Discrimination	Institutionalized Discrimination	Contextual Discrimination	Individual Acts of Discrimination	Pure Justice

Definitions

Systematic discrimination—Discrimination at all stages of the criminal justice system, at all times, and at all places.

Institutionalized discrimination—Racial and ethnic disparities in outcomes that are the result of the application of racially neutral factors, such as prior criminal record, employment status, and demeanor.

Contextual discrimination—Discrimination found in particular contexts or circumstances (e.g., certain regions, particular crimes, or special victim–offender relationships).

Individual acts of discrimination—Discrimination that results from the acts of particular individuals but is not characteristic of entire agencies or the criminal justice system as a whole.

Pure justice—No racial or ethnic discrimination at all.

moreover, did not allow them to arrest whites. Many Northern police departments, meanwhile, did not assign African American officers to white neighborhoods.[64] These practices represented differential treatment based on race—in short, discrimination. Also during that time period, airlines hired only young women as flight attendants. This approach represented a difference in treatment based on gender rather than individual qualifications. The flight attendants were also automatically terminated if they married; because no male employees were fired for being married, this practice represented a form of sexual discrimination.

African Americans were excluded from serving on juries because they were illegally disenfranchised as voters and, therefore, were not on jury lists. This practice represented racial discrimination in jury selection. Let's imagine a rural county in the northwestern United States, however, where there are no African American residents. The absence of African Americans from juries would represent a racial disparity but not discrimination. Consider another hypothetical case. Imagine that a police department arrested only African Americans for suspected felonies and never arrested a white person. That situation would represent racial discrimination in arrest.

The questions we deal with in the real world, of course, are not quite so simple. There are, in fact, racial disparities in jury selection and arrest: African Americans are less likely to serve on juries, and more African Americans are arrested than whites. The question is whether these disparities reflect discrimination. The evidence on these two difficult issues is discussed in Chapter 4 (arrests) and Chapter 6 (jury selection).

It is also important to remember that the word *discrimination* has at least two different meanings. One has a positive connotation. It is a compliment to say that someone has "discriminating taste" in music, food, or clothes. The person discriminates against bad food and bad music. The other meaning of *discrimination* has a negative connotation. When we say that someone "discriminates against African Americans or Hispanics," we mean that he or she makes invidious distinctions based on negative judgments about an entire group of people—that is, the person discriminates against all African Americans without reference to a particular person's qualities (e.g., ability, education, or experience). Acts that involve racial or ethnic discrimination in employment, housing, or the administration of justice are illegal.

The Law of Discrimination

Discrimination occurs whenever people are treated differently. An act of discrimination is illegal when it is prohibited by law. Several different parts of the American legal system make discrimination illegal. The Fourteenth Amendment to the Constitution declares that "nor shall any state ... deny to any person within its jurisdiction the equal protection of the law." This provision applies to the states and not the federal government. If a state barred African Americans or women from serving on juries (as some states once did) it would be a violation of the Fourteenth Amendment.

A number of federal laws also forbid discrimination. Title VII of the 1964 Civil Rights Act holds that "It shall be an unlawful employment practice for an employer to fail or refuse to hire or to discharge any individual, or otherwise to discriminate against any individual with respect to his compensation, terms, conditions, or, privileges of employment, because of such individual's race, color, religion, sex, or national origin ..." This law covers employment discrimination by private employers and government agencies, which would include police, court, and correctional agencies. Other federal laws prohibit other forms of discrimination, such as in housing or on the basis of age.

State constitutions and laws also prohibit discrimination. The constitution of each of the 50 states has a provision similar to the Fourteenth Amendment. All states also have laws prohibiting discrimination in employment, housing, and other areas. Finally, cities have municipal ordinances that also make discrimination illegal.

Although the Fourteenth Amendment and federal, state, and local laws prohibit discrimination, in court a plaintiff has to prove that his or her experience involved discrimination. An African American who is stopped while driving and given a traffic ticket has to prove that the stop and the ticket were based on race. A Hispanic defendant sentenced to prison has to prove that the sentence was based on national origin. A Native American who is not hired as a parole officer has to prove that it was based on race. Proving discrimination in court is often very difficult. In most cases, other factors entered into the decision, and the decision was not clearly based on race or ethnicity. In Chapter 4 we will discuss the difficulty of proving racial profiling based on official data on traffic enforcement.

The Discrimination–Disparity Continuum

To help clarify the debate over this issue, let's review Box 1.4. *Systematic discrimination* means that discrimination occurs at all stages of the criminal justice system, in all places, and at all times. That is to say, there is discrimination in arrest, prosecution, and sentencing (stages); in all parts of the country (places); and without any significant variation over time.

Institutionalized discrimination involves disparities in outcomes (for example, more African Americans than whites are sentenced to prison) that result from established (institutionalized) policies. Such policies do not directly involve race. As Georges-Abeyie explains, "The key issue is result, not intent. Institutionalized racism is often the legacy of overt racism, of de facto practices that often get codified, and thus sanctioned by de jure mechanisms."[65]

Some criminal courts, for example, have bail policies granting pretrial release to defendants who are currently employed. This policy is based on the reasonable assumption that an employed person has a greater stake in the community and is less likely to flee than an unemployed person. The policy discriminates against the unemployed, and, because racial minorities are disproportionately represented among the unemployed, they are more likely to be denied bail. Thus, the bail policy has a race effect: a racial disparity in the outcomes that is the result of a criterion other than race. The racial disparity exists not because any judge is racially prejudiced, but because judges apply the rules consistently.

Employment discrimination law recognizes the phenomenon of institutionalized discrimination with reference to "disparate impact." A particular hiring policy may be illegal if it has an especially heavy impact on a certain group and is not demonstrably job related. In policing, for example, police departments formerly did not hire people who were shorter than 5'6". This standard had a disparate impact on women, Hispanics, and Asian Americans and is now no longer used.

Contextual discrimination involves discrimination in certain situations or contexts. There are a number of examples in the criminal justice system. Racial profiling involves discrimination in the context of traffic enforcement. (In the same department there may not be a similar pattern in routine felony arrests.) Some unprofessional court systems may have patterns of extreme racial or ethnic disparities that are not found in more professionalized court systems where court officials are better trained and guided by formal policies. One important example is discrimination based on victim–offender relationship. As we will see in Chapter 8, the odds that the death penalty will be given are greatest when an African American murders a white person, whereas there is almost no chance of a death sentence when a white person murders an African American.[66] This factor has been found in the context of other felony sentencing as well. It also appears that drug enforcement has a much heavier impact on African Americans and Hispanics than routine police work does.[67]

Organizational factors represent another contextual variable. Some police departments encourage aggressive patrol activities (e.g., frequent stops and frisks). The Kerner Commission found that "aggressive preventive patrol" aggravated tensions between the police and racial minority communities.[68]

Thus, departments with different patrol policies may have less conflict with minority communities. Some police departments have very bad records in terms of use of physical force, but others have taken steps to curb misconduct.

Individual acts of discrimination involve those carried out by particular justice officials. For instance one police officer is biased in making arrests, whereas others in the department are not; one judge sentences minorities very harshly, whereas other judges in the same court do not. These are discriminatory acts, but they do not represent general patterns of how the criminal justice system operates.

Finally, at the far end of the spectrum in Box 1.4 is the condition we label *pure justice*. This means that there is no discrimination at any time or place in the criminal justice system.

In a controversial analysis of the administration of justice, Wilbanks argues that the idea of a racist criminal justice system is a "myth." He claims that "there is racial prejudice and discrimination within the criminal justice system" but denies that "*the system* is characterized by racial prejudice and discrimination."[69]

Using our discrimination–disparity continuum, Wilbanks falls somewhere in the area of contextual discrimination and individual discrimination. Mann, however, argues that there is systematic discrimination: "The law and the legal system [have] perpetuated and [continue] to maintain an ingrained system of injustice for people of color."[70]

Throughout the chapters that follow, we will grapple with the question of whether disparities represent discrimination. For example, there are racial and ethnic disparities in arrests by the police. In Chapter 4, we examine the evidence on whether these data indicate a clear pattern of discrimination—and if so, what kind of discrimination (contextual, individual, or systematic). Chapter 4 also examines the difficulties in interpreting traffic stop data to determine whether there is a pattern of illegal racial profiling. There is also evidence of disparities in plea bargaining and sentencing. Chapters 5, 6, and 7 wrestle with the problem of interpreting the data to determine whether there are patterns of discrimination. Chapter 8 examines the data on the death penalty and the race of persons executed.

A THEORETICAL PERSPECTIVE ON RACE, ETHNICITY, AND CRIME

There are many different theories of crime and criminal justice. We believe that the available evidence on race, ethnicity, and crime is best explained by a theoretical perspective known as *conflict theory*.

The basic premise of conflict theory is that the law is used to maintain the power of the dominant group in society and to control the behavior of individuals who threaten that power.[71] A classic illustration of conflict theory involves the law of vagrancy. Vagrancy involves merely being out in public with little or no money and no clear "purpose" for being there. Vagrancy is something engaged in only by the poor. To make vagrancy a criminal act and to enforce vagrancy laws are means by which the powerful attempt to control the poor.

Conflict theory explains racial disparities in the administration of justice as products of broader patterns of social, economic, and political inequality in U.S. society. These inequalities are the result of prejudicial attitudes on the part of the white majority and discrimination against minorities in employment, education, housing, and other aspects of society. Chapter 3 explores these inequalities in detail. Conflict theory explains the overrepresentation of racial and ethnic minorities in arrest, prosecution, imprisonment, and capital punishment as both the product of these inequalities and an expression of prejudice against minorities.

Conflict theory has often been oversimplified by both advocates and opponents. Criminal justice research has found certain "anomalies" in which racial minorities are not always treated more harshly than whites. For example, there are certain situations in which African American suspects are less likely to be arrested than white suspects. Hawkins argues that these anomalies can be explained through a revised and more sophisticated conflict theory that takes into account relevant contingencies.[72]

One contingency is crime type. Hawkins claims that African Americans may be treated more leniently for some crimes because officials believe that these crimes are "more normal or appropriate for some racial and social class groups than for others."[73] In the South during the segregation era, for example, African Americans often were not arrested for certain crimes, particularly crimes against other African Americans. The dominant white power structure viewed this behavior as "appropriate" for African Americans. The fact that minority offenders were being treated leniently in these situations is consistent with conflict theory because the outcomes represent a racist view of racial minorities as essentially "childlike" people who cannot control their behavior.

A second contingency identified by Hawkins involves the race or ethnicity of the offender relative to the race of the victim. Much research has found that the criminal justice system responds more harshly when the offender is a person of color and the victim is white, particularly in rape and potential death penalty murder cases. According to conflict theory, such crimes are viewed as challenges to the pattern of racial dominance in society. The same crime is not perceived as a threat when it is intraracial (for example, white offender/white victim, African American offender/African American victim). A relatively lenient response to crimes by minorities against minorities or crimes in which a racial or ethnic minority is the victim is explained by conflict theory in terms of a devaluing of the lives of minority victims.

There may also be important contingencies based on population variables. It may be that crimes by racial minorities are treated more harshly when minorities represent a relatively large percentage of the population and therefore are perceived as a social and political threat. A substantial body of research has explored the "minority threat" thesis, which holds that racial or ethnic disparities will be greater where the white majority feels threatened by a large or growing racial or ethnic minority population in that jurisdiction.[74] At the same time, some research on imprisonment has found that the disparity between white and African American incarceration rates is greatest in states with small minority populations.[75] In this context, minorities have little political power.

Alternative Theories

Conflict theory is a sociological explanation of criminal behavior and the administration of justice in that it holds that social factors explain which kinds of behavior are defined as criminal; which people commit crime; and how crimes are investigated, prosecuted, and punished. Sociological explanations of crime are alternatives to biological, psychological, and economic explanations. These other factors may contribute in some way to explaining crime but, according to the sociological perspective, do not provide an adequate general theory of crime.[76]

Conflict theory also differs from other sociological theories of crime. Consensus theory holds that all groups in society share the same values and that criminal behavior can be explained by individual acts of deviance. Conflict theory does not see consensus in society regarding the goals or operation of the criminal justice system. Conflict theory also differs from Marxist theory, although there are some areas of agreement. Conflict theory and Marxist theory both emphasize differences in power between groups. Marxist theory, however, holds that there is a rigid class structure with a ruling class. Conflict theory, meanwhile, maintains a pluralistic view of society in which there are different centers of power—business and labor, farmers and consumers, government officials and the news media, religious organizations, public interest groups, and so forth—although they are not necessarily equal. The pluralistic view also allows for changes in the relative power of different groups.

CONCLUSION

The question of race and ethnicity is a central issue in American criminal justice—perhaps the central issue. The starting point for this book is the over-representation of racial and ethnic minorities in the criminal justice system. This chapter sets the framework for a critical analysis of this fact about contemporary American society. We have learned that the subject is extremely complex. First, the categories of race and ethnicity are extremely problematic. Much of the data we use are not as refined as we would like. Second, we have learned that there is much controversy over the issue of discrimination. An important distinction exists between disparity and discrimination. Also, there are different kinds of discrimination. Finally, we have indicated the theoretical perspective about crime and criminal justice that guides the chapters that follow.

DISCUSSION QUESTIONS

1. What are the differences between *race* and *ethnicity*? Give some examples that illustrate the differences.
2. When social scientists say that the concept of race is a "social construct," what exactly do they mean?
3. Do you think the U.S. census should have a category of "multicultural" for race and ethnicity? Explain why or why not. Would it make a difference in the accuracy of the census? Would it make a difference to you?
4. Explain the difference between *discrimination* and *disparity*. Give one example from some other area of life.

NOTES

1. W. E. B. Du Bois, *The Souls of Black Folk* (Chicago: McClurg, 1903), p. 13.

2. Bureau of Justice Statistics, *Prisoners in 2003*, NCJ 205335 (Washington, DC: U.S. Government Printing Office, 2004). Available at www.ncjrs.org, NCJ 205335.

3. U.S. Census Bureau, *Statistical Abstract of the United States, 2006* (Washington, DC: U.S. Government Printing Office, 2006), Tables 2, 3. Available at www.census.gov/statab/www/.

4. Charlotte-Mecklenburg Police Department, International Relations Unit, *Law Enforcement Services to a Growing International Community* (Charlotte: Charlotte-Mecklenburg Police Department, 2004, p. 18.). www.charmeck.org/departments/police/.

5. Pew Hispanic Center, *Hispanics: A People in Motion* (Washington, DC: Pew Hispanic Center, 2005), p. 18. www. pewhispanic.org.

6. The Cincinnati consent decree is discussed in Samuel Walker, *The New World of Police Accountability* (Thousand Oaks, CA: Sage, 2005). The consent decree is available at the website of the Special Litigation Section of the U.S. Department of Justice and also at the website of the City of Cincinnati. Available at www.usdoj.gov/crt/split/.

7. Stewart Wakeling, Miriam Jorgensen, Susan Michaelson, and Manley Begay, *Policing on American Indian Reservations: A Report to the National Institute of Justice*, NCJ 188095 (Washington, DC: U.S. Government Printing Office, 2001). Available at www.ncjrs.org.

8. David Harris, *Profiles in Injustice: Why Racial Profiling Doesn't Work* (New York: New Press, 2002); ACLU, *Driving While Black* (New York: ACLU, 1999). See www.profilesininjustice.com.

9. National Urban League, *State of Black America, 2001* (New York: National Urban League, 2001). Available at www.nul.org/soba.

10. Bureau of Justice Statistics, *Sourcebook of Criminal Justice Statistics, 2003*, online edition, Table 2.52, p. 146. Available at www.albany.edu/sourcebook.

11. Dennis Rosenbaum, D. A. Lewis, and J. Grant, "Neighborhood-Based Crime Prevention: Assessing the Efficacy of Community Organizing in Chicago," in *Community Crime Prevention: Does It Work?* Dennis Rosenbaum, ed. (Newbury Park, CA: Sage, 1986), pp. 109–136.

12. See, for example, Shaun L. Gabbidon and Helen Taylor Greene, *Race and Crime* (Thousand Oaks: Sage Publications, 2005); David Cole, *No Equal Justice: Race and Class in the American Criminal Justice System* (New York: The New Press, 1999); Katheryn K. Russell, *The Color of Crime* (New York: New York University Press, 1998); Gregg Barak, Jeanne M. Flavin, and Paul S. Leighton, *Class, Race, Gender, and Crime* (Los Angeles: Roxbury, 2001); Michael Tonry, *Malign Neglect* (New York: Oxford University Press, 1996); Coramae Richey Mann, *Unequal Justice* (Bloomington: Indiana University Press, 1988); Ronald Barri Flowers, *Minorities and Criminality* (Westport, CT: Greenwood, 1988); William Wilbanks, *The Myth of a Racist Criminal Justice System* (Monterey, CA: Brooks/Cole, 1987); Joan Petersilia, *Racial Disparities in the Criminal Justice System* (Santa Monica, CA: Rand, 1983).

13. Christopher Stone, "Race, Crime, and the Administration of Justice: A Summary of the Available Facts," paper presented to the Advisory Board of the President's Initiative on Race, May 19, 1998.

14. Samuel Walker and Molly Brown, "A Pale Reflection of Reality: The Neglect of Racial and Ethnic Minorities in Introductory Criminal Justice Textbooks,"

Journal of Criminal Justice Education 6 (spring 1995), pp. 61–83.

15. Mann, *Unequal Justice*, p. viii.

16. Alfredo Mirandé, *Gringo Justice* (Notre Dame, IN: University of Notre Dame Press, 1987), p. ix.

17. Marianne O. Nielsen, "Contextualization for Native American Crime and Criminal Justice Involvement," in *Native Americans, Crime, and Justice*, Marianne O. Nielsen and Robert A. Silverman, eds. (Boulder, CO: Westview, 1996), p. 10.

18. Wilbanks, *The Myth of a Racist Criminal Justice System*.

19. Stone, "Race, Crime, and the Administration of Justice," p. 1.

20. Darnell F. Hawkins, "Ethnicity, Race, and Crime: A Review of Selected Studies," in *Ethnicity, Race, and Crime*, D. F. Hawkins, ed. (Albany: State University of New York, 1995), p. 40.

21. Bureau of the Census, "Texas Becomes the Newest 'Majority-Minority' State," Bulletin, August 11, 2005.

22. The concept of race is both problematic and controversial. For a starting point, see Ashley Montagu, *Statement on Race*, 3rd ed. (New York: Oxford University Press, 1972), which includes the text of and commentary on four United Nations statements on race.

23. J. Milton Yinger, *Ethnicity: Source of Strength? Source of Conflict?* (Albany: State University of New York Press, 1994), p. 19.

24. Paul R. Spickard, "The Illogic of American Racial Categories," in *Racially Mixed People in America*, Marla P. Root, ed. (Newbury Park, CA: Sage, 1992), p. 18.

25. Yinger, *Ethnicity*, p. 19.

26. Christine B. Hickman, "The Devil and the One Drop Rule: Racial Categories, African Americans, and the U.S. Census," *Michigan Law Review* 95 (March 1997), pp. 1161–1265.

27. U.S. Office of Management and Budget, Directive 15, *Race and Ethnic Standards for Federal Statistics and Adminis-trative Reporting*, OMB Circular No. A-46 (1974), rev. 1977 (Washington, DC: U.S. Government Printing Office, 1977).

28. Lawrence Wright, "One Drop of Blood," *The New Yorker* (July 25, 1994), p. 47.

29. See the Association of MultiEthnic Americans website at www.ameasite.org.

30. National Urban League, *State of Black America, 2001*. Available at www.nul.org/soba.

31. Pew Hispanic Center, *2002 National Survey of Latinos* (Los Angeles: Pew Hispanic Center, 2002). See also Pew Hispanic Center, *Hispanic Trends: A People in Motion* (Los Angeles: Pew Hispanic Center, 2005). Available at www.pewhispanic.org.

32. AMEA website: www.ameasite.org.

33. Office of Management and Budget, "Revisions to the Standards for the Classification of Federal Data on Race and Ethnicity" (October 30, 1997). Available at www.whitehouse.gov/omb/fedreg/ombdir15.html.

34. Ibid.

35. James Paul Allen and Eugene James Turner, *We the People: An Atlas of America's Ethnic Diversity* (New York: Macmillan, 1988).

36. Yinger, *Ethnicity*, pp. 3–4.

37. U.S. Bureau of the Census, *U.S. Hispanic Latino Population, Census 2000* (Washington, DC: Census Bureau, 2004). Available at www.census.gov. See also reports by the Pew Hispanic Center at www.pewhispanic.org.

38. Nadine Naber, "Ambiguous Insiders: An Investigation of Arab American Invisibility," *Ethnic and Racial Studies*, 23 (January 2000), pp. 37–61.

39. Quoted in Yinger, *Ethnicity*, p. 21.

40. Louis Wirth, "The Problem of Minority Groups," in *The Science of Man in the World Crisis*, Ralph Linton, ed. (New York: Columbia University Press, 1945), p. 123.

41. Office of Management and Budget, "Revisions to the Standards."

42. Anita Khashu, Robin Busch, Zainab Latif, and Francesca Levy. *Building Strong Police-Immigrant Community Relations: Lessons from a New York City Project* (New York: Vera Institute, 2005). Available at www.vera.org.

43. Cecilia Menjivar and Cynthia L. Beharano, "Latino Immigrants' Perceptions of Crime and Police Authorities: A Case Study from the Phoenix Metropolitan Area, *Ethnic and Racial Studies*, 27 (January 2004), pp. 120–148.

44. John Hope Franklin and Alfred A. Moss Jr., *From Slavery to Freedom: A History of African Americans*, 7th ed. (New York: Knopf, 1994), p. xix.

45. George Gallup Jr., *The Gallup Poll Monthly* (August 1994), p. 30.

46. Eric R. Wolf, *Europe and the People without History* (Berkeley: University of California Press, 1982), pp. 380–381.

47. Pew Hispanic Center, *2002 National Survey of Latinos,* and Pew Hispanic Center, *Hispanic Trends: A People in Motion.* Available at www.pewhispanic.org.

48. Pew Hispanic Center, *Hispanics: A People in Motion* (2005), p. 19.

49. Bureau of Justice Statistics, *Contacts Between the Police and the Public: Findings from the 2002 National Survey* (Washington, DC: U.S. Department of Justice, 2005). NCJ 207845.

50. Barry Holman, *Masking the Divide: How Officially Reported Prison Statistics Distort the Racial and Ethnic Realities of Prison Growth* (Alexandria: National Center on Institutions and Alternatives, 2001).

51. Gary LaFree, "Race and Crime Trends in the United States, 1946–1990," in *Ethnicity, Race, and Crime,* pp. 173–174.

52. Zoann K. Snyder-Joy, "Self-Determination and American Indian Justice: Tribal versus Federal Jurisdiction on Indian Lands," in *Ethnicity, Race, and Crime,* p. 310.

53. Bureau of Justice Statistics, *Sourcebook of Criminal Justice Statistics, 2003, Online edition* (Washington, DC: U.S. Government Printing Office, 2005), app. 4.

54. Ibid., app. 13.

55. William H. Frey, "The Diversity Myth," *American Demographics* 20 (June 1998), p. 41.

56. Ibid.

57. U.S. Census Bureau, *Statistical Abstract, 2006*, Table 23.

58. Ibid., Table 23.

59. Ibid., Table 24, p. 27.

60. U.S. Census Bureau, Statistical Abstract of the United States, 2003, Tables 27, 29.

61. U.S. Census Bureau, Statistical Abstract, 2006, Tables 403, 404.

62. Mann, *Unequal Justice*, pp. vii–xiv.

63. Wilbanks, *The Myth of a Racist Criminal Justice System.*

64. W. Marvin Dulaney, *Black Police in America* (Bloomington: Indiana University Press, 1996).

65. D. E. Georges-Abeyie, "Criminal Justice Processing of Non-White Minorities," in *Racism, Empiricism, and Criminal Justice,* B. D. MacLean and D. Milovanovic, eds. (Vancouver: Collective, 1990), p. 28.

66. David C. Baldus, George G. Woodworth, and Charles A. Pulaski, *Equal Justice and the Death Penalty: A Legal and Empirical Analysis* (Boston: Northeastern University Press, 1990).

67. Jerome G. Miller, *Search and Destroy* (New York: Cambridge University Press, 1996).

68. National Advisory Commission on Civil Disorders [Kerner Commission], *Report* (New York: Bantam Books, 1968), p. 304.

69. Wilbanks, *The Myth of a Racist Criminal Justice System*, p. 5.

70. Mann, *Unequal Justice*, p. 160.

71. Richard Quinney, *The Social Reality of Crime* (Boston: Little, Brown, 1970).

72. Darnell Hawkins, "Beyond Anomalies: Rethinking the Conflict Perspective on Race and Criminal Punishment," *Social Forces* 65 (March 1987), pp. 719–745.

73. Ibid.

74. Malcolm D. Holmes, "Minority Threat and Police Brutality: Determinants of Civil Rights Criminal Complaints in U.S. Municipalities," *Criminology* 38 (May 2000), p. 343.

75. Alfred Blumstein, "Prison Populations: A System out of Control," in *Crime and Justice: A Review of Research*, Michael Tonry and Norval Morris, eds., vol. 10 (Chicago: University of Chicago Press, 1988), p. 253.

76. Freda Adler, Gerhard O. W. Mueller, and William S. Laufer, *Criminology*, 2nd ed. (New York: McGraw-Hill, 1995).

Victims and Offenders

Myths and Realities About Crime

Some crime stories capture the attention of the public more than others, arguably because of the nature of the offense, the type of victim, and the type of offender. Recently, media outlets have been charged with favoring the presentation of some crime stories over others. The media consistently portray violent crime as more common than property crime, when the opposite is true. Additionally, the media often present crime stories that suggest crime is increasing at astronomical rates, when crime rates are at historical lows.

Some critics also charge that the media show bias in the coverage of missing persons, arguing that print and television coverage of stories focuses on missing white women and tends to ignore missing women of color. *Essence* magazine contends, for example, that "when black women disappear, the media silence is deafening."[1] Specifically, some media critics charge that attention the media give to such cases as Laci Peterson, Natalee Holloway, and Chandra Levy far out-weighs the emphasis placed on such cases as Evelyn Hernandez, LaToyia Figueroa, and Ardena Carter.

Perhaps the typical American recognizes the details of one of the following pairs of missing person victims but not the other.

The first pair of victims is connected by time and location/geography:

In 2004 Laci Peterson, a missing white female who was 8 months pregnant, was found dead in the San Francisco Bay area. Most Americans know not just the details of her disappearance from her home, the search for her whereabouts, and the subsequent recovery of her body, but also that her husband, Scott Peterson, was charged and convicted of this offense.

Few Americans are aware that a few months before Laci Peterson's body was discovered, the decapitated body of a young, pregnant Hispanic woman, Evelyn Hernandez, was found. Details of her missing person/murder case were not extensively covered by the national media.

The second pair of victims is connected by time, but not geography:

> In May 2005, Natalee Holloway, a white American teenager, was reported missing in Aruba. Her story made headlines almost from the moment that she was reported missing. Print and news media covered the incident extensively for weeks following her disappearance.

> In July 2005, 24-year-old LaToyia Figueroa, who was pregnant, was reported missing. Her body was later recovered, and her boyfriend was charged with murder. However, her story was initially ignored by the national media, some suggest because she wasn't white.

The third pair of victims is connected by time and occupation:

> In 2003 Chandra Levy, a white female intern in Washington, DC, disappeared on a morning jog. Considerable attention was paid to her search and recovery in nationwide news stories.[2]

> In 2003 Ardena Carter, a young African American graduate student in Georgia, went missing on her way to the library. Her disappearance and the subsequent recovery of her body garnered no more than regional news coverage.[3]

Critics of the media coverage of these types of missing person cases argue that the public is being misled about who is really missing.[4] Figures from the U.S. Department of Justice, for example, indicate that in California, nearly twice as many Latina women (7,453) are missing than white women (4,032).[5] The National Center for Missing Adults reports that of the more than 47,000 people missing in 2005, 29,553 were white or Hispanic, 13,859 were African American, 1,199 were Asian American, and 685 were Native American.[6] Of these missing persons, 53 percent were men.

This pattern of more media emphasis on white, female missing persons is not necessarily intentional; nonetheless it does seem to signal a devaluation of the lives of nonwhite victims of crime. Professor Todd Boyd notes that the media's decision to focus on white women and not minority women may be "an unconscious decision about who matters and who doesn't."[7] He asserts, "In general, there is an assumption that crime is such a part of black and Latino culture that these things happen all the time. In many people's minds it's regarded as being commonplace and not a big deal."

GOALS OF THE CHAPTER

In this chapter we describe the context of crime in the United States. We use several different sources of data to paint a picture of the crime victim and the offender. We compare victimization rates for racial and ethnic minorities to the rates for whites, focusing on both household victimization and personal victimization. We also compare offending patterns for racial minorities and whites. We then present statistics to document the fact that crime is predominantly an intra-racial, rather than an interracial, event. We also focus on the most noted exception to the intraracial crime pattern: hate crime. We end the chapter with a discussion of ethnic youth gangs and their role in American society.

A BROADER PICTURE OF THE CRIME VICTIM

Our perceptions of crime are shaped to a large extent by the highly publicized crimes featured on the nightly news and sensationalized in newspapers. We read about young African American or Hispanic males who sexually assault, rob, and murder whites, and we assume that these crimes are typical. We assume that the typical crime is a violent crime, that the typical victim is white, and that the typical offender is African American or Hispanic. As Silberman observes, this topic is difficult to address:

> In the end, there is no escaping the question of race and crime. To say this is to risk, almost guarantee, giving offense; it is impossible to talk honestly about the role of race in American life without offending and angering both whites and blacks—and Hispanic browns and Native American reds as well. The truth is terrible, on all sides; and we are all too accustomed to the soothing euphemisms and inflammatory rhetoric with which the subject is cloaked.[8]

In short, compelling evidence suggests that the arguably prominent picture of crime, criminal, and victim just described is at best incomplete and at worst inaccurate, particularly as it concerns race and ethnicity of crime victims. Victimization data, in fact, reveal that racial minorities are more likely than whites in most circumstances to be victimized by crime.

In the sections that follow, we use victimization data to paint a broad picture of the crime victim, allowing for a view of which racial and ethnic groups are disproportionately the victims of crime. We begin by discussing the National Crime Victimization Survey, the source of most data on criminal victimization in the United States. We then compare the household victimization rates of African Americans and whites, as well as Hispanics and non–Hispanics. Personal victimization rates (property and violent offense) are then compared for African Americans, Hispanics, and whites. We conclude the discussion with a discussion of homicide victimization events.

The National Crime Victimization Survey

The most systematic source of victimization information is the National Crime Victimization Survey (NCVS).[14] The survey, which began in 1973, is conducted by the Bureau of Census for the Bureau of Justice Statistics (BJS).[15] Survey data are used to produce annual estimates of the number and rate of personal and household victimizations for the nation as a whole and for various subgroups of the population.

Focus on an Issue
Central Park Jogger

In 1989 a group of minority male teen-agers were convicted of attacking and raping a woman who was jogging in New York's Central Park. The Central Park Jogger Case has long been used to illustrate the media emphasis on certain types of crimes (violent crime), with certain types of crime victims (white females), and with certain types of offenders (a "gang" of young, minority males). Does this incident reflect a "typical" criminal event? Many people believe that it does: a white victim falling prey to the violence of minority gang activity. But the evidence suggests that it is *not* the typical criminal event. First, more than 80 percent of crimes reported to the police are property crimes.[9] Second, a disproportionate number of crime victims are minorities. Third, interracial (between-race) crimes are the exception, not the rule. Finally, not all group activity is gang activity, not all gang actions are criminal, and not all gang members are racial or ethnic minorities.

Additionally, an article in the *New York Times* several weeks after the well-publicized event described here helps put this victimization in perspective. A total of 29 rapes were reported in the city that week (April 16–22, 1989), with 17 African American female victims, 7 Hispanics, 3 whites, and 2 Asians.[10] Thus, the typical rape victim was in fact a *minority* female. Although the 29 reports from the New York Police Department did not indicate the race of the offender, other sources, including the national victimization data discussed later in this chapter, demonstrate that rape is predominantly an intrarracial (within-race) crime.[11]

Subsequent to the investigation of this event, five young minority males were eventually convicted and incarcerated for perpetrating this attack, serving up to 8 years in prison. In 2002, with the assistance of DNA analysis, it was revealed that the five convicted youth were not the actual offenders.[12] Now, the actual offender has been identified and has confessed to the offense.[13] Note, these details became known only after the young offenders had served their sentences. Thus, this infamous case of minority youth crime has become an example of wrongful prosecution based on faulty police work that involved questionable interrogation techniques.

Interviews are conducted at 6-month intervals to ask whether household members have been the victims of selected major crimes during the last 6 months.[16] Information is collected from persons age 12 and older who are members of the household selected in the sample. The sample is chosen on the basis of the most recent census data to be representative of the nation as a whole. The NCVS data presented here are estimates based on the interviews of 834,360 households and 149,000 people aged 12 years and older.[17] The response rates for the 2004 survey were very high: 91.3 percent of eligible households and 85.5 percent of eligible individuals responded.[18]

Members of selected households are contacted either in person or by phone every 6 months for 3 years. Household questionnaires are completed to describe the demographic characteristics of the household (income, number of members, etc.). The race and ethnicity of the adult completing the household questionnaire is recorded from self-report information as the race and ethnicity of the household. Starting in 2003, respondents can self-report more than one race. Incident questionnaires are completed for both household offenses and personal victimizations. The designated head of the household is questioned about the incidence of household burglary, household larceny, and motor-vehicle theft. Personal victimization incident questionnaires are administered to household members age 12 and older, probing them to relay any victimizations of rape, robbery, assault, and personal larceny. Those who report victimizations to interviewers are asked a series of follow-up questions about the nature of the crime and the response to the crime. Those who report personal victimizations are also asked to describe the offender and their relationship (if any) with the offender. Some sample personal victimization questions are as follows:

During the last six months:

Did anyone beat you up, attack you, or hit you with something such as a rock or a bottle?

Did anyone take something directly from you by using force, such as by a stickup, mugging, or threat?

Was anything stolen from you while you were away from home—for instance, at work, in a theater or restaurant, or while traveling?

In many ways, the NCVS produces a more complete picture of crime and the characteristics of those who are victimized by crime than official police records. For one thing, respondents are asked about victimizations not reported to the police. In addition, the survey includes questions designed to elicit detailed information concerning the victim, the characteristics of the offender(s), and the context of the victimization. This information is used to calculate age-, sex-, and race-specific estimates of victimization. In addition, estimates of inter-racial and intraracial crime can be calculated.

The NCVS also has several limitations. For example, it does not cover commercial crime, kidnapping, or homicide; the estimates produced are for the nation as a whole, central city compared to suburban areas, but not for states or local jurisdictions; homeless people are not interviewed; and responses are susceptible to memory loss and interviewer bias. In addition, the information on race is often limited to white, African American, and "other," and ethnicity is generally limited to Hispanic and non-Hispanic only, with the latter being available for selected issues only. It is important to remember that Hispanics may be of any race (see Chapter 1). NCVS designations are determined by census categories, so the Hispanic category includes all individuals of Spanish origin (Mexican American, Chicano, Mexican, Puerto Rican, Cuban, Central or South American) regardless of racial identity.

Household Victimization

As noted, the NCVS questions the designated head of household about crimes against the household—burglary, household larceny, and motor vehicle theft. It is clear that household victimization rates vary by race and ethnicity, indicating that

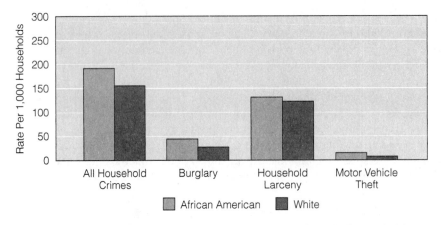

FIGURE 2.1 Household Victimization Rates, by Race of Head of Household, 2003
SOURCE: *Criminal Victimization Data, 2003*. Available at www.ojp.usdoj.gov/bjs/cvict_v.htm.

African American households are more vulnerable than white households and Hispanic households are more vulnerable than non-Hispanic ones.[19]

In 2003 households headed by African Americans had a higher victimization rate than white households (Figure 2.1) for all designated household offenses (190 per 1,000 households compared to 159 per 1,000 households). This general pattern also characterized each of the three household crimes—that is, the rate for African American households exceeded the rate for white households by burglary (39 compared to 28) and household larceny (136 compared to 122). The greatest disparity was present in motor vehicle theft rates, with African American households at a rate nearly twice that of white households (15 compared to 8).

The BJS also estimates that victimization rates for Hispanics households are markedly higher than the victimization rates for non-Hispanic households.[20] Figure 2.2 shows higher rates for Hispanics for all household crimes combined (207 per 1,000 households compared to 158 per 1,000 households). Burglary and household larceny rates indicate that Hispanic-headed households have higher victimization rates than non-Hispanic ones (34 compared to 29; 160 compared to 121), with motor vehicle theft reflecting the greatest disparity, with rates nearly twice as high for Hispanic households (14 compared to 8).

The newest data available from the NCVS reveals that the victimization rates of persons reporting two or more races (recall this is a recent change based on U.S. Census racial classification rules) is substantially higher than any other racial groups. For example, while overall victimization rates for whites and African Americans are below 200 per 1,000 population, the mixed race group reports a 50 percent higher victimization rate (299 per 1,000).[20a]

The Effect of Urbanization   The racial differences in household victimization rates discussed thus far are differences for the United States as a whole. These patterns vary, however, depending on the degree of urbanization (Table 2.1).[21]

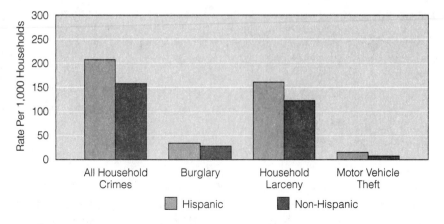

FIGURE 2.2 Household Victimization Rates, by Ethnicity of Head of Household, 2004

SOURCE: *Criminal Victimization Data, 2004.* Available at www.ojp.usdoj.gov/bjs/cvict_v.htm.

TABLE 2.1 Racial and Ethnicity Property Crime Victimization Rate by Urban, Suburban, and Rural Setting, 1993–1998

	Crime Rate Per 1,000 Households		
	Urban	Suburban	Rural
Race			
African American	348.6	295.5	200.0
White	341.7	252.4	210.6
Other	295.4	253.9	342.8
Ethnicity			
Hispanic	386.4	337.8	271.6
Non-Hispanic	335.2	249.9	209.6

SOURCE: Detis T. Duhart, *Urban, Suburban, and Rural Victimization, 1993–1998* (Washington, DC: Bureau of Justice Statistics, 2000). Available at www.ojp. usdoj.gov/bjs/.

Household victimization rates are highest for African Americans in urban areas, for white households in suburban areas, and for the combined "other" racial group (Native American/Alaska Native and Asian Pacific Islander) in the rural areas. The pattern stated in Figure 2.1 of African American households having higher victimization rates than white households does reverse under some circumstances.[22] Specifically, rural area data reflect slightly higher victimization rates for white households than for African American households.

Although the analysis presented in Table 2.1 offers no information by crime type, analysis of earlier years of victimization data indicate even more variations in

T A B L E 2.2 Personal Victimization Rates by Type of Crime and by Race and Ethnicity of Victims, 2004

| | Victimization Rates[a] | | | | | |
| | Race | | | | Ethnicity | |
	White	African American	Other	Multi-Race	Hispanic	Non-Hispanic
Crimes of Violence						
Rape	0.8	1.7	0.1	2.4	0.6	0.9
Robbery	1.8	3.7	2.6	3.8	2.8	2.0
Assault	18.4	20.7	10.1	45.3	14.9	19.1
Aggravated	4.0	6.7	1.8	5.5	3.2	4.4
Simple	14.4	13.9	8.3	39.8	11.7	14.6
Crimes of Theft	0.8	1.5	1.0	3.2	0.7	0.7
All Offenses	21.0	26.0	12.7	51.6	18.2	21.6

[a]Victimization rates per 1,000 persons age 12 and older.

SOURCE: Shannan M. Catalano, *Criminal Victimization 2004*. Bureau of Justice Statistics, 2001. Available at www.ojp.usdoj.gov/bjs.

the typical victimization pattern. Specifically, crime-specific data from suburban areas reflected higher burglary and household larceny figures for white households compared to the higher combined victimization rate for suburban African American households.[23] In rural areas, crime-specific data indicated that African American households had higher motor vehicle theft rates than white rural households, which had the highest combined victimization rates.[24]

Personal Victimization

In addition to questioning the head of the household about crimes against the household, the NCVS interviewers ask all household members age 12 or older whether they themselves have been the victim of an act of rape (worded as sexual assault), robbery, assault, or personal theft within the past 6 months. This information is then used to estimate victimization rates for the nation as a whole and for the various subgroups in the population.

Consistent with the pattern of racial disparity found in household victimizations, these estimates reveal that African Americans are more likely than either whites or members of "other" racial groups to be the victims of personal crimes. Additionally, respondents selecting two or more racial categories to describe themselves have the highest victimization rates. As shown in Table 2.2, the overall victimization rate (which combines crimes of violence and personal theft) for African Americans is 26.0 per 1,000 persons in the population age 12 or older, 21.0 per 1,000 for whites, 12.7 per 1,000 for other races (combined group of Native American/Alaska Native and Asian/Pacific Islanders), and 51.6 per 1,000 for the multi-race respondents.

The racial differences are much larger for crimes of violence than for crimes of theft. In particular, African Americans are more than two times as likely as whites to be the victims of robbery and are slightly more likely to be the victims of aggravated assault than whites or other races. Notably, the victimization rates for the multi-race category is similar to the robbery victimization rate for African Americans; this group has a substantially higher risk than for all other groups for assault. Analysis of multiple years of the NCVS dataset also indicate that from 1992 to 1996, African American's were three times as likely to be victims of carjackings than whites.[25] The information in rape victimization again shows African Americans and the multi-race category as having the highest victimization rates, at two and three times higher than the rates reported for whites and "other" race.

The victimization rates for African Americans and whites are far more similar for simple assaults, with notable exception of the multi-race category, which reports a rate of three times higher than the other groups. Finally, the personal theft rates are highest for African Americans and the multi-race category compared to whites and "other races," with the multi-racial group reporting a rate two times higher than African Americans.

Table 2.2 also displays personal victimization rates by ethnicity. Overall, in 2004 non-Hispanics had slightly higher victimization rates than Hispanics. This comparison does not hold for all years of the NCVS reports—for example, in 2000 Hispanic respondents reported higher victimization rates (30.8 per 1,000 persons age 12 or older compared to 28.8 per 1,000).[26] Victimization rates for 2004 also vary by type of crime. Hispanics have the highest victimization rates for robbery, whereas non-Hispanics have higher victimization rates for rape, assaults, and personal theft. Box 2.1 offers insight into the rates of violent crime victimization for college students by race and ethnicity.

The Effects of Urbanization   An analysis of victimization trends by the BJS using NCVS data from 1993 to 1998 indicates that urbanization is a key aspect of understanding violent victimization. As the data in Table 2.3 (see p. 40) reveal, victimization rates for all groups are highest in urban areas and lowest in rural areas. This pattern also characterizes the victimization rates for African Americans and whites and for Hispanics and non-Hispanics. In contrast, the violent victimization rate for "other races" (e.g., Native Americans and Asian Americans) is substantially higher in rural areas than in urban areas. Victimization rates for African Americans and whites are very similar in suburban and rural areas, with whites having a higher rate (34 per 1,000 population) than African Americans (31 per 1,000 population) in rural areas. In urban areas, the rate for African Americans (68 per 1,000 population) is higher than the rate for whites (59 per 1,000 population).

The BJS report also indicated that urban residents, who accounted for 29 percent of the U.S. population, reported 38 percent of all violent and property crime victimizations.[27] Suburban residents comprise 50 percent of the population and experience 47 percent of the victimizations.[28] Rural residents are least likely to experience criminal victimization; they comprise 20 percent of the population and experience 20 percent of all criminal victimizations.[29]

The most recent victimization data indicate that although the overall property victimization rate is highest for African Americans and highest in urban areas, there are some interesting differences when we look more closely.[30] Personal theft victimization rates are always higher for whites, particularly in urban areas.

(continued on p. 40)

B O X 2.1   College Students and Violent Victimization

The Bureau of Justice Statistics has pooled several years of National Crime Victimization Survey (NCVS) data (1995–2002) to offer a picture of violent victimization of college students. About 7.9 million people per year from ages 18 to 24 years were enrolled in college during this time. The consistent pattern of age, race, and victimization from the NCVS dataset is that young minorities have routinely higher violent victimization rates than whites. However, white college students have higher rates of violent victimization than African American students and students of "other" races (65 per 1,000 students compared to 52 and 37 per 1,000 students, respectively). Nonstudent victimization rates (ages 18–24) are substantially higher, with African American and whites having the highest rates (83 and 65 per 1,000 population compared to the numbers outlined previously). African American students have the highest victimization rates for robbery and aggravated assault, but white students have higher rates of victimization for simple assault and rape victimization.

A unique aspect of this dataset is that Hispanics are coded to be of any race, so their victimization rates can be compared to whites and African Americans, rather than simply non-Hispanics. A review of these data indicates that Hispanics have an overall violent victimization rate that is higher than the rate for African Americans but lower than the rate for whites. The exception to this pattern is the Hispanic victimization rate for rape—it is higher than any other racial/ethnic group in the study.

SOURCE: Katrina Baum and Patsy Klaus, "Violent Victimization of College Students, 1995-2000," *Bureau of Justice Statistics Report* (Washington, DC: Government Printing Office, January 2005).

Focus on an Issue
Violent Victimization and Women of Color

Research on the characteristics of victims of violent crime generally focuses on the race of the victim, the ethnicity of the victim, or the sex of the victim. There are relatively few studies that examine the interrelationships among race, ethnicity, sex, and violent victimization or that attempt to determine if the risk factors for violent victimization are different for white women and women of color.

Two studies of nonlethal violent victimization addressed these issues. Lauritsen and White (Janet L. Lauritsen and Norman A. White, "Putting Violence in Its Place: The Influence of Race, Ethnicity, Gender, and Place on the Risk for Violence," *Crime and Public Policy* 1 (2001): 37–59) used data from the National Crime Victimization Survey

(NCVS) to identify the risk of violence for African American, white, and Hispanic females. Because they were interested in the potential relationship between neighborhood characteristics and risk for violence, they classified violent incidents according to whether they occurred within respondents' neighborhoods (i.e., within 1 mile of their homes). They also differentiated between incidents involving strangers and those involving nonstrangers.

Lauritsen and White found that the overall risk of nonlethal violence was lowest for white females and highest for African American females, with Hispanic females in the middle. They also found that (1) women, regardless of race/ ethnicity, faced a lower risk of violence in their own neighborhoods; (2) African

American women faced a substantially higher risk of violence at the hands of nonstrangers than either white or Hispanic women; and (3) both African American and Hispanic women faced higher risks of violence at the hands of strangers than did white women. These racial/ethnic differences, which persisted when the authors controlled for other characteristics of the respondent that might be associated with risk of victimization, diminished or disappeared when they included a measure of neighborhood disadvantage in their models. When neighborhood disadvantage was taken into consideration, they found that Hispanic females, but not African American females, had a higher risk of nonstranger violence than white females and that neither Hispanic females nor black females faced a higher risk of stranger violence than white females. Further analysis revealed that African American, white, and Hispanic women who lived in disadvantaged neighborhoods had higher risks for stranger and nonstranger violence than African American, white, and Hispanic women who lived in more advantaged communities. According to the authors, this means that "the reduction of violence is unlikely to require group-specific solutions, but will require attention to both community and individual factors that foster safety and harm reduction" (p. 51).

Dugan and Apel (Laura Dugan and Robert Apel, "An Exploratory Study of the Violent Victimization of Women: Race/Ethnicity and Situational Context," *Criminology* 41 (2003): 959–977) took a somewhat different approach to studying violent victimization of women of color. They combined 8 years of NCVS data, which generated enough cases to explore risk factors for white, African American, Hispanic, Asian/Pacific Islander, and Native American females. In predicting violent victimization, the authors controlled for the respondent's age; home environment (i.e., type of residence, marital status,

number of children younger than age 12, and whether the respondent went out every night); and such things as the respondent's income, education, and job situation. They found that Native American women faced the greatest risk of violent victimization, followed by black women, Hispanic women, white women, and Asian/Pacific Islander women. The rate for Native American women, in fact, was almost twice the rate for black women (p. 967).

The authors of this study discovered that the factors that predicted violent victimization were not the same for each group of women. Although being married was a protective factor for all women and going out every night and moving often were risk factors across the board, the other factors had more variable effects. Living in an urban area, for example, increased the risk of violent victimization only for African American and Native American women, and living in public housing was a risk factor only for Hispanic women. Living alone with at least one child, having a job, and working while in college all had particularly strong effects on victimization of Asian/Pacific Islander woman.

The authors also found interesting racial/ethnic differences in the characteristics of the violent victimization incidents that women experienced. White women were the least likely to be victimized by someone using a weapon but were the most likely to be victimized by a spouse. African American women, however, were the group most likely to be victimized by a boyfriend or at home; they also were the most likely to be victimized using a weapon and to be seriously injured. Asian/Pacific Islander women were the most likely to be victims of impersonal crimes (for example, robbery), to be victimized by strangers, and to be victimized by more than one offender. African American women were the most likely to call the police to report the victimization; Asian women were the

(continued)

(*continued*)
least likely to do so. Hispanic females were the least likely to be victimized in the home, and Native American females were the most likely to be victimized by someone who was using drugs or alcohol at the time of the incident.

The results of these two studies suggest that explanations for the violent victimization of women are complicated and that it is "naive to assume that all women are uniformly put at risk or protected regardless of their cultural background" (p. 972).

T A B L E 2.3   **Violent Crime Victimization Rates by Race and Ethnicity for Urban, Suburban, and Rural Areas, 1993–1998**

| | Rate per 1,000 persons age 12 or older | | |
	Urban	Suburban	Rural
Overall Rate	48	37	28
By Race			
African American	68	48	31
White	59	44	34
Other Races	36	35	68
By Ethnicity			
Hispanic	52	50	46
Non-Hispanic	61	43	34

SOURCE: Detis T. Duhart, *Urban, Suburban, and Rural Victimization, 1993–1998* (Washington, DC: Bureau of Justice Statistics, 2000). Available at www.ojp.usdoj.gov/bjs/.

The household burglary and motor vehicle theft rates for African Americans and whites nearly converge in rural areas.

Trends in Household and Personal Victimization

A review of NCVS data from 1973 to 2004[31] indicates that most of the general pattens of victimization noted in the preceding section have not changed over time. The household victimization data for these years illustrate that property victimization rates for African American households consistently exceed the rates for white households and Hispanic victimization rates exceed those of non–Hispanic households; however, some variations occur when considering urbanization and crime type. Moreover, rates of robbery and aggravated assault victimization for African Americans are repeatedly higher, whereas simple assault rates remain similar to white victimization rates. Violent victimization rates are higher for Hispanics than non-Hispanics, driven mostly by higher robbery rates. Personal theft rates are characterized by a convergence of rates for these two groups over time; however, African American rates remain somewhat higher than the rate for whites and Hispanic rates remain somewhat higher than the non-Hispanics rate.

The addition of urbanization to the discussion of race, ethnicity, and victimization offers an interesting, although divergent, pattern for different race and ethnicity groups. Urban areas consistently have the highest household and personal victimization rates. African Americans consistently have the most disproportionately high violent and household victimization rates but only in urban areas. Suburban victimization rates are more similar across racial groups. However, rural victimization rates often reflect African Americans with the lowest victimization rates, whereas the other combined racial groups have disproportionately high victimization rates in rural areas. Similarly, the highest victimization rates for African Americans are in urban areas, whereas the victimization rates for the other racial group are highest in the rural areas.

Hispanic victimization rates reflected a combination of these patterns: Hispanic household victimization rates are similar to African American victimization rates in that the highest victimization rates are in urban areas, however; Hispanics retain the disproportionately higher victimization rate than non-Hispanics in urban, suburban, and rural areas. Personal victimization rates for Hispanics are similar to the other combined racial group, with disproportionately high rates for Hispanics only in suburban and rural areas.

Perhaps the pattern of higher victimization for African Americans in urban areas and higher victimization for other minority groups in rural areas has to do with issues of racial composition. Urban populations are disproportionately African American, whereas rural areas are disproportionately white.[32] For example, the movement of Hispanic populations to fill labor needs in rural areas that have traditionally been predominantly (90 percent or more) white has left such groups open to higher risks of victimization.

The NCVS has also been used to explore trends in violence by gang members. Although fewer than 10 percent of violent victimizations are reported as being perpetrated by perceived gang members, the BJS has pooled 10 years of NCVS data for respondents who were able to identify there attackers as gang members.[33] These data are used to calculate violent victimization rates per 1,000 persons in each group. Similar to the trends discussed earlier, racial groups have different violent victimization rates by perceived gang members. The highest rate of violent victimization is for African American respondents, at 4.1 per 1,000 population; the "other" (both Asian American and Native American) category has a rate of 3.0 per 1,000 population, and the white respondents have the lowest rate of 2.6 per 1,000 population. The trend that emerges from these data is that Hispanic respondents are more likely than non-Hispanic respondents to report being victimized by gang members (5.7 acts of violence per 1,000 compared to 2.4 acts of violence per 1,000). See Boxes 2.2 and 2.3 for information on Native Americans and Asian Americans, respectively, as victims of violent crimes.

Lifetime Likelihood of Victimization

Although annual victimization rates are important indicators of the likelihood of victimization, they "do not convey the full impact of crime as it affects people."[36] To gauge the impact of crime, we must consider not just the odds of

---

B O X 2.2 **Native Americans and Violent Crimes**

Information on the victimization rates of Native Americans is difficult to compile. This group represents less than 1 percent (0.5 percent) of the sample population of non-Hispanic respondents in the National Crime Victimization Survey (NCVS). Given that the incidence of victimization in the general population is rare, documenting a rare event in a small population is challenging. The Bureau of Justice Statistics has pooled a number of years (1992–2001) to reveal a picture of Native American (nonfatal) violent victimization: 101 violent victimizations occurred per 1,000 population of Native Americans age 12 and older. The average violent victimization rate for Native Americans was 2.5 times the rate for whites (41 per 1,000), twice the rate for African Americans (51 per 1,000), and 4.5 times that rate for Asians (22 per 1,000).[34]

When the victimization rates are disaggregated by crime type, Native Americans have higher victimization rates in almost all categories. Their robbery and assault victimization rates are twice that of whites and African Americans. However, the rape victimization rate for Native Americans is higher than for whites but lower than for African Americans.

In contrast to the general intraracial victimization patterns of white and African American crime, Native Americans report that 6 of 10 violent offenses were committed by someone they perceived to be white.[35]

B O X 2.3 **Asian Americans and Violent Crime**

Asian Americans make up less than 4 percent of the population. To estimate their victimization rates, the BJS pooled several years of NCVS (1993–1998) data. These rates indicate that Asian Americans have the lowest overall victimization rates (25.5 per 1,000 population age 12 and older) compared to whites (45.5 per 1,000), African Americans (56.5 per 1,000), and Native Americans (188.8 per 1,000).[38] Rates for individual violent victimizations indicated that only for robbery are Asian victimization rates higher than the next lowest group (whites).[39] The persistent pattern of intraracial crime events does not hold true for Asian American victimizations. When Asian American respondents were asked to report the perceived race of the offender, less than 30 percent of offenders were identified as Asian Americans, whereas 35 percent were identified as white and 26 percent as African American.[40]

---

being victimized within the next few weeks or months but the possibility of being robbed, raped, assaulted, or burglarized at some time in our lives. Although the odds of being victimized during any 12-month period are low, the odds of ever being victimized may be high. Whereas only 16 out of 10,000 women are rape victims annually, for example, the lifetime likelihood of being raped is much greater: nearly 1 out of every 12 females (and 1 out of every 9 black females) will be the victim of a rape at some time during her life.[37]

The BJS used annual victimization rates for a 10-year period to calculate lifetime victimization rates. These rates, which are presented in Table 2.4, indicate that about five out of six people will be victims of a violent crime at least once during their lives

TABLE 2.4 Lifetime Likelihood of Victimization

	Percentage Who Will Be Victimized [a]	
	African Americans	Whites
Violent crimes	87	82
Robbery	51	27
Assault	73	74
Rape (females only)	11	8
Personal theft	99	99

[a]Percentage of persons who will experience one or more victimizations starting at 12 years of age.

SOURCE: Bureau of Justice Statistics, U.S. Department of Justice, *Lifetime Likelihood of Victimization* (Washington, DC: U.S. Government Printing Office, 1987).

and that nearly everyone will be the victim of a personal theft at least once. There is no difference in the African American and white rates for personal theft, and only a slight difference in the rates for violent crimes.

For the individual crimes of violence, the lifetime likelihood of being assaulted is nearly identical for African Americans and whites; about three of every four people, regardless of race, will be assaulted at some time during their lives. There are, however, large racial differences for robbery, with African Americans almost twice as likely as whites to be robbed. The lifetime likelihood of rape is also somewhat higher for African American females than for white females. Thus, for the two most serious (nonmurder) violent crimes, the likelihood of victimization is much higher for African Americans than for whites.

Homicide Victimization

The largest and most striking racial differences in victimization are for the crime of homicide. In fact, all of the data on homicide point to the same conclusion: African Americans, and particularly African American males, face a much greater risk of death by homicide than do whites.

Although the NCVS does not produce estimates of homicide victimization rates, there are a number of other sources of data. A partial picture is available from the Supplemental Homicide Reports (SHR) submitted by law enforcement agencies to the U.S. Federal Bureau of Investigation (FBI) as part of the Uniform Crime Reports (UCR) Program. This information is collected when available for single victim–single offender homicides. These data reveal that a disproportionate number of homicide victims are African American. From 1976 to 2002, African Americans constituted no more than 15 percent of the population but comprised more than 46 percent of all homicide victims. Whites are underrepresented in homicide figures, compared to the population, but they did make up the majority of victims from 1976 to 2002, with whites comprising 51 percent of homicide victims.[41]

Focus on an Issue
Victim Assistance: Should Race Matter?

Although most observers agree that the American criminal justice system should treat suspects and offenders in a colorblind fashion, how should we treat victims? Barak, Flavin, and Leighton[44] argue that victim assistance should take the race, ethnicity, gender, and even class of the victim into consideration. They state, "Victim counseling needs to be sensitive to cultural values through which the victimization experience is interpreted. Rehabilitation and intervention programs likewise need to build on cultural values for maximum effectiveness."[45] For example, a victim of domestic violence may need different services depending on their social realities: a Hispanic woman with children, no employment history, and a limited working knowledge of English will require different services than a white woman with children, a professional employment history, and a command of English.

Do you agree? Should the criminal justice system be entirely color blind? Or, does justice actually require the system to be color conscious in some situations?

The SHR data reveal that homicide is a more significant risk factor for African Americans than for whites. Whereas homicide rates have decreased among all groups since the early 1990s, the homicide rate in 2002 indicated that African Americans were 6 times more likely to be murdered than whites (20.8 per 100,000 population compared to 3.3 per 100,000 population).[42] Even more striking, the rate for African American males was nearly 8 times the rate for white males and was 24 times the rate for white females. The rate for African American females exceeded the rate for white females, appearing closer to that of white males.

The BJS analysis of homicide trends from 1976 to 2002 reveals that the circumstance of homicides often varies by race.[43] For example, although white and African American victims are equally likely to be gun homicides, whites constitute more than half of the victims in arson and poison cases. Additionally, African American are the majority of victims in homicides involving drugs, and whites are the majority victim in sex-related homicides and in gang-related homicides.

Summary: A More Comprehensive Picture of the Crime Victim

The victimization data presented in the preceding sections offer a more comprehensive picture of the crime victim than is found in common perceptions and media presentations. These data reveal that African Americans, Asian/Pacific Islanders, Native Americans, and Hispanics are often more likely than whites and non-Hispanics to be victims of household and personal crimes. These racial and ethnic differences are particularly striking for violent crimes, especially robbery. African Americans—especially African American males—also face a much greater risk of death by homicide than whites. It thus seems fair to conclude that in the United States, the groups at greatest risk of becoming crime victims are those that belong to racial and ethnic minority groups.

Focus on an Issue
The Creation of Victims and Offenders of Color

Silberman makes the following observation on the common misconceptions of race and crime:[46]

> For most of their history in this country ... blacks were victims, not initiators, of violence. In the Old South, violence against blacks was omnipresent—sanctioned both by customs and by law. Whites were free to use any methods, up to and including murder, to control 'their Negros.' ... There was little blacks could do to protect themselves. To strike back at whites, or merely to display anger or insufficient deference, was not just to risk one's own neck, but to place the whole community in danger. It was equally dangerous, or at best pointless, to appeal to the law.

Indeed, the purpose of the 14th amendment to the U.S. Constitution following the Civil War was to create a situation of full citizenship for former slaves. One of the implications of this newfound status of citizenship was that African Americans were formally conferred the status of victim and offender in the eyes of the law. Prior to this time, actions of assault, rape, and theft against slaves and by slaves were handled informally or even as civil matters. Even African American offenders were not necessarily viewed as subject to formal criminal trial and adjudication, especially if the "victims" were slaves, too.

One frequently told example of a slave's lack of status as a citizen is the case of Margaret Garner. This female slave escaped with her children to Ohio from a Kentucky plantation in 1855. Once discovered by her master, who was given the right of retrieval under federal law, she responded to the threat of capture by murdering one of her children and attempting to murder her other children. Outrage at her actions lead to the rather unprecedented call for the intervention of the formal justice of the American judicial system. This situation was complicated by the legal issue of citizenship. In short, the slave could not be tried as a citizen and the victim of the murder was not a citizen either. The issues were merely of a civil nature. Although most would agree the child was a victim, she was not so in the eyes of the law. Garner was in fact tried for her destructive actions to the master's property. This case became the foundation for the story *Beloved,* first in a novel by Toni Morrison (1988) and later adapted to a movie (1998) of the same title.[47]

PICTURE OF THE TYPICAL OFFENDER

For many people the term "crime" evokes an image of a young African American male who is armed with a handgun and who commits a robbery, a rape, or a murder. In the minds of many Americans, "crime" is synonymous with "black crime."

It is easy to see why the average American believes that the typical offender is African American. The crimes that receive the most attention—from the media, from politicians, and from criminal justice policymakers—are "street crimes" such as murder, robbery, and rape. These are precisely the crimes for which African Americans are arrested at a disproportionately high rate. In 2003, for example, 48.5 percent of those arrested for murder, 54.5 percent of those arrested for robbery, and 33.3 percent of those arrested for rape were African American.[48]

Arrest rates for serious violent crimes, of course, do not tell the whole story. Although violent crimes may be the crimes we fear most, they are not the crimes that occur most frequently. Moreover, arrest rates do not necessarily present an accurate picture of offending. Many crimes are not reported to the police, and many of those reported do not result in an arrest.

In this section we use a number of criminal justice data sources to paint a picture of the typical criminal offender. We summarize the offender data presented in official police records, victimization reports, and self-report surveys. Because each of these data sources varies both in terms of the offender information captured and the "point of contact" with the offender, the picture of the typical offender that each produces also differs somewhat. We note these discrepancies and summarize the results of research designed to reconcile them.

Official Arrest Statistics

Annual data on arrests are produced by the UCR system, which has been administered by the FBI since 1930. Today, the program compiles reports from more than 17,000 law enforcement agencies across the country, representing 95 percent of the total U.S. population. The annual report, *Crime in the United States,* offers detailed information from local, state, and federal law enforcement agencies on crime counts and rates as well as arrest information.

Problems with UCR Data   The information on offenders gleaned from the Uniform Crime Reports is incomplete and potentially misleading because it includes only offenders whose crimes result in arrest. The UCR data exclude offenders whose crimes are not reported to the police and offenders whose crimes do not lead to arrest. A second limitation is that the UCR reports include arrest statistics for four racial groups (white, African American, Native American, and Asian), but they do not present any information by ethnicity (Hispanic versus non-Hispanic). See "Focus on an Issue: A Proposal to Eliminate Race from the Uniform Crime Report" for further discussion of the controversy surrounding the reporting of race in UCR figures.

A substantial proportion of crimes are not reported to the police. In fact, the NCVS reveals that fewer than half of all violent victimizations and only one-third of all property victimizations are reported to the police.[49] Factors that influence the decision to report a crime include the seriousness of the crime and the relationship between the victim and the offender; violent crimes are more likely than property crimes to be reported, as are crimes committed by friends or relatives rather than strangers.[50]

Victimization surveys reveal that victims often fail to report crimes to the police because of a belief that nothing could be done, the event was not important enough, the police would not want to be bothered, or it was a private matter.[51]

Focus on an Issue
A Proposal to Eliminate Race from the Uniform Crime Report

In October 1993, a group of mayors, led by Minneapolis Mayor Donald Fraser, sent a letter to the U.S. Attorney General's office asking that the design of the Uniform Crime Report (UCR) be changed to eliminate race from the reporting of arrest data. The mayors were concerned about the misuse of racial data from crime statistics. They charged that the current reporting policies "perpetuate racism in American society" and contribute to the general perception "that there is a causal relationship between race and criminality." Critics of the proposal argued that race data are essential to battling street crime because they reveal who the perpetrators are.

Although the federal policy of reporting race in arrest statistics has not changed, Fraser was instrumental in pushing a similar request through the Minnesota Bureau of Investigation. The final result in Minnesota was the following disclaimer in state crime publications:

"Racial and ethnic data must be treated with caution ... [E]xisting research on crime has generally shown that racial or ethnic identity is not predictive of criminal behavior within data which has been controlled for social and economic factors." This statement warns that descriptive data are not sufficient for causal analysis and should not be used as the sole indication of the role of race and criminality for the formation of public policy.

Using inductive reasoning, the overrepresentation of minority race groups in arrest data can be suggestive of at least two causal inferences: (1) certain racial groups characterized by differential offending rates, or (2) arrest data reflective of differential arrest patterns targeted at minorities. What steps must a researcher take to move beyond descriptions of racial disparity in arrest data to an exploration of causal explanations for racial patterns evident in arrest data?

Failure to report also might be based on the victim's fear of self-incrimination or embarrassment resulting from criminal justice proceedings that result in publicity or cross-examination.[52]

The NCVS indicates that the likelihood of reporting a crime to the police also varies by race. African Americans are slightly more likely than whites to report crimes of theft and violence to the police, whereas Hispanics are substantially less likely than non-Hispanics to report victimizations to the police.[53] Hindelang found that victims of rape and robbery were more likely to report the victimization to the police if there was an African American offender.[54]

Even if the victim does decide to report the crime to the police, there is no guarantee that the report will result in an arrest. The police may decide that the report is "unfounded"—in this case, an official report is not filed and the incident is not counted as an "offense known to the police." Furthermore, even if the police do file an official report, they may be unwilling or unable to make an arrest. In 2003 only about 20 percent of all index crimes were cleared by the police; the clearance rate for serious crimes ranged from 13.1 percent for burglary to 62.4 percent for murder.[55]

Police officer and offender interactions also may influence the inclination to make an arrest, and cultural traditions may influence police–citizen interactions. For instance, Asian communities often handle delinquent acts informally, when other communities would report them to the police.[56] Hispanic cultural traditions may increase the likelihood of arrest if the Hispanic's tradition of showing respect for an officer by avoiding direct eye contact is interpreted as insincerity.[57] African Americans who appear "hostile" or "aggressive" also may face a greater likelihood of arrest.[58]

The fact that many reported crimes do not lead to an arrest, coupled with the fact that police decisionmaking is highly discretionary, suggests that we should exercise caution in drawing conclusions about the characteristics of those who commit crime based on the characteristics of those who are arrested. To the extent that police decisionmaking reflects stereotypes about crime or racially prejudiced attitudes, the picture of the typical offender that emerges from official arrest statistics may be racially distorted. If police target enforcement efforts in minority communities or concentrate on crimes committed by racial minorities, then obviously racial minorities will be overrepresented in arrest statistics.

A final limitation of UCR offender information centers around the information not included in these arrest reports. The UCR arrest information fails to offer a full picture of the white offender entering the criminal justice system. Specifically, additional sources of criminal justice data present the white offender as typical in the case of many economic, political, and organized crime offenses. Russell, in detailing the results of her "search for white crime" in media and academic sources, supports the view that the occupational (white-collar) crimes for which whites are consistently overrepresented may not illicit the same level of fear as the street crimes highlighted in the UCR but nonetheless have a high monetary and moral cost.[59] (See Box 2.4 for information on the "operationalization," or measurement, of race in crime data.)

Arrest Data The arrest data presented in Table 2.5 reveal that the public perception of the "typical criminal offender" as an African American is generally inaccurate. Examination of the arrest statistics for all offenses, for instance, reveals that the typical offender is white; more than two-thirds (70.6 percent) of those arrested in 2003 were white, less than one-third (27.0 percent) were African American, and less than 3 percent were Native American or Asian. Similarly, more than half of those arrested for violent crimes and nearly two-thirds of those arrested for property crimes were white. In fact, the only crimes for which the typical offender was African American were robbery and gambling.[62]

Examining the percentage of all arrests involving members of each racial group must be done in the context of the distribution of each group in the population. In 2003 whites comprised approximately 83 percent of the U.S. population, African Americans comprised 13 percent, Native Americans comprised less than 1 percent, and Asians comprised 3 percent. A more appropriate comparison, then, is the percentage in each racial group arrested *in relation to* that group's representation in

B O X 2.4 The Operationalization of Race in Criminal Justice Data

The concept of race is measured—operationalized—in a number of ways, depending on the discipline and depending on the research question. Most biologists and anthropologists recognize the difficulties with using traditional race categories (white, black, red, yellow) as an effective means of classifying populations, and most social scientists rely on administrative definitions for recordkeeping, empirical analysis, and theory testing. Given these conditions, however, the term "race" still carries the connotation of an objective measurement with a biological/genetic basis.

As Knepper[60] notes, the recording of race in the UCR can be traced to a practice that has no formal theoretical or policy relevance. From available accounts, this information was recorded because it was "available" and may be a side effect of efforts to legitimize fingerprint identification. Currently, the UCR manual gives detailed information on the definitions for index offenses and Part 2 offenses and provides specific instructions about the founding of crimes and the counting rules for multiple offenses. What is lacking, however, are specific instructions on the recording of race information. Administrative/census definitions provided by local law enforcement agencies on agency arrest forms are calculated and reported, but no criteria for the source of the information are given. Thus, some records will reflect self-reporting by the offender, whereas others will reflect observations of police personnel. Some police arrest reports have "black," "white," "Native American," and "Asian," whereas many use the category of "other." Still others use "Hispanic" in the race category, rather than a separate ethnicity. Given that the FBI does not currently request or report ethnicity in the UCR, much information is lost.

The FBI's National Incident-Based Reporting System does log additional information based on race and ethnicity for victims and offenders, but the information available in that dataset for 2004 reflects on only 20 percent of the U.S. population in 26 states.[61]

the general population, rather than simply stating the "typical offender" by the largest proportion of offenders by racial group.

Thus, although whites are the people most often arrested in crime categories reported in the UCR, it appears that African Americans are arrested at a disproportionately high rate for *nearly* all offenses. The total combined rate for all offenses (see Table 2.5) indicates that the arrest rate for African Americans is two times higher than would be predicted by their representation in the population. The disproportion is even larger for the most serious Part 1/index offenses reported in the UCR; the arrest rate is two and a half times higher for African Americans than predicted by their representation in the population.

Among the individual offenses, however, the degree of African American overrepresentation varies. The largest disparities are found for robbery and murder. The arrest rate for African Americans is nearly four times what we would expect for murder and robbery. The differences also are pronounced for rape, motor vehicle theft, gambling, vagrancy, stolen property offenses, and weapons offenses.

TABLE 2.5 Percent Distribution of Arrests by Race, 2003

	White (%)	African American (%)	Native American (%)	Asian American (%)
Total	70.6	27.0	1.3	1.2
Part 1 Crimes				
Murder and nonnegligent manslaughter	49.1	48.5	1.1	1.2
Forcible rape	64.1	33.3	1.3	1.3
Robbery	43.9	54.4	0.6	1.1
Aggravated assault	63.5	34.0	1.1	1.3
Burglary	70.5	27.5	1.0	1.0
Larceny-theft	68.5	28.8	1.3	1.5
Motor-vehicle theft	61.3	35.9	1.0	1.8
Arson	77.5	20.9	0.9	0.7
Violent Crime	60.5	37.2	1.0	1.2
Property Crime	68.2	29.1	1.2	1.4
Part 2 Crimes				
Other assaults	65.7	31.8	1.3	1.2
Forgery and counterfeiting	69.3	28.9	0.6	1.2
Fraud	68.8	29.9	0.6	0.7
Embezzlement	68.3	29.8	0.5	1.4
Stolen property: buying, receiving, possessing	60.6	37.6	0.7	1.0
Vandalism	76.2	21.2	1.4	1.2
Weapons: carrying, possessing, etc.	62.1	36.1	0.7	1.1
Prostitution and commercialized vice	58.0	39.3	.5	2.2
Sex offenses (except forcible rape and prostitution)	73.7	23.9	1.0	1.4
Drug abuse violations	66.0	32.6	0.6	0.8
Gambling	26.6	69.7	0.2	3.5
Offenses against family and children	67.2	30.4	1.3	1.2
Driving under the influence (DUI)	88.2	9.6	1.4	1.0
Liquor law violations	87.3	8.9	2.8	1.0
Drunkenness	84.1	12.8	2.6	0.6
Disorderly conduct	67.5	30.2	1.5	0.8
Vagrancy	55.9	41.6	1.8	0.7

	White (%)	African American (%)	Native American (%)	Asian American (%)
All other offenses (except traffic)	66.9	30.4	1.4	1.3
Suspicion	64.5	34.0	0.6	0.8
Curfew and loitering law violations	67.9	30.0	0.8	1.3

SOURCE: *Crime in the United States, 2003*. (Washington, DC: U.S. Department of Justice, 2003). Available at www.fbi.gov/ucr/ucr.htm.

Table 2.5 also presents arrest statistics for whites, Native Americans, and Asians. Whites are overrepresented for some UCR offenses. Specifically, whites are overrepresented for driving under the influence (DUIs) and liquor law violations compared to their representation in the general population whites are found in numbers consistent with their representation in the population for drunkenness arrests.

The overall pattern for Native American arrest figures is a slight overrepresentation compared to their representation in the population (1.3 percent of those arrested versus 0.8 percent in the population); however, the pattern across crimes is more erratic. For Part 1/index crimes, Native Americans are slightly more likely to be arrested for property crimes (particularly larceny-theft) than their representation in the population suggests. Native Americans are overrepresented in several Part 2 offenses, including other assaults, vandalism, liquor law violations, drunkenness, disorderly conduct, and vagrancy. The proportion of Native American offenders arrested for a number of offenses—robbery, fraud, embezzlement, receiving stolen property, prostitution/commercialized vice, and gambling—is lower than what is expected given their proportion in the population. Additionally, the arrest figures for a number of other offenses—murder, robbery, aggravated assault, burglary, and drug abuse violations—are consistent with their proportion in the general population.

Caution is required when interpreting Native American arrest figures because arrests made by tribal police and federal agencies are not recorded in UCR data. Using information from the Bureau of Indian Affairs, Peak and Spencer[63] found that, although UCR statistics revealed lower-than-expected homicide arrest rates for Native Americans, homicide rates were nine times higher than expected across the 207 reservations reporting.

For overall figures and each index offense, Asian Americans are underrepresented in UCR arrest data (1.2 percent of arresters in 2003 compared to 3 percent of the population). The notable exception to the pattern of underrepresentation is the Part 2 offense of gambling. Although 2003 data reveal 3.5 percent of arrests for gambling are of Asians, UCR arrest figures have been as high as 6.7 percent. The arrest rate for this offense can reach twice what is expected given the representation of Asians in the population. Notably, Asian Americans are underrepresented in arrest figures for arson, fraud, drug abuse violations, disorderly conduct, and vagrancy.

Focus on an Issue
Racial and Ethnic Identification of Terrorists

Identifying a profile of terrorists through the traditional format of the Uniform Crime Report (UCR) system will be difficult. First, terrorist acts, even those resulting in deaths, are not always reported in the UCR. For example, the deaths that occurred as a result of the domestic terrorist bombing in Oklahoma City on April 19, 1995 were recorded in the Oklahoma UCR figures; however, the deaths that occurred in various locations on September 11, 2001, as a result of international terrorist actions are not recorded in the UCR. Second, if there is no recorded event, there will be no recorded arrest and no subsequent offender information by race, age, or gender. For example, Timothy McVeigh's arrest for the Oklahoma City bombing appeared in the arrest figures in Oklahoma, including his race, gender, and age; however, the suspected terrorists from September 11—even if they were alive—would not be included in arrest figures.

An argument can be made that terrorist acts are also hate crimes; however, additional concerns arise with the recording of hate-crime incidents because it is a challenge to identify victims and offenders. The FBI reports ask for victim and offender to be identified by racial categories used in the U.S. census: white, African American, Native American/Alaska Native, and Asian/Pacific Islanders. These categories are very broad—for example, victims from Saudi Arabia and Iraq are identified as white, whereas victims from Pakistan and India are identified as Asian. Moreover, ethnicity is only recorded for victims, not offenders; and is defined as Hispanic or non-Hispanic.

Perceptions of Offenders by Victims

Clearly African Americans are arrested at a disproportionately high rate. The problem, of course, is that we do not know the degree to which arrest statistics accurately reflect offending. As noted previously, not all crimes are reported to the police and not all of those that are reported lead to an arrest.

One way to check the accuracy of arrest statistics is to examine data on offenders produced by the NCVS. Respondents who report a "face-to-face" encounter with an offender are asked to indicate the race of the offender. If the percentage of victims who report being robbed by an African American matches the percentage of African Americans who are arrested for robbery, we can have greater confidence in the validity of the arrest statistics. We can be more confident that differences in the likelihood of arrest reflect differences in offending.

If, however, the percentage of victims who report being robbed by an African American is substantially smaller than the percentage of African Americans who are arrested for robbery, we can conclude that at least some of the disproportion in the arrest rate reflects what Hindelang refers to as "selection bias" in the criminal justice system. As Hindelang notes, "If there are substantial biases in the UCR data for *any* reason, we would expect, to the extent that victimization survey reports are unbiased, to find large discrepancies between UCR arrest data and victimization survey reports on racial characteristics of offenders."[64]

Problems with NCVS Offender Data   There are obvious problems in relying on victims' "perceptions" of the race of the offender. Respondents who report a victimization are asked if the offender was white, African American, or some other race. These perceptions are of questionable validity because victimizations often occur quickly and involve the element of shock. In addition, victim memory is subject to decay over time and to "retroactive reconstruction" to fit the popular conception of a criminal offender. If a victim believes that the "typical criminal" is African American, this may influence his or her perception of the race of the offender.

There is another problem in relying on victims' perceptions of offender race. To the extent that these perceptions are based on skin color, they may be unreliable indicators of the race of offenders whose self-identification reflects their lineage or heritage rather than the color of their skin. Thus, individuals may appear in different racial groupings in victimization reports than they do on a police arrest report. A light-skinned offender who identifies himself as Hispanic and whose race is thus recorded as "other" in arrest data might show up in victimization data as "white." If this occurs with any frequency, it obviously will affect the picture of the offender that emerges from victimization data.

Perceptions of Offenders   With these caveats in mind, we present the NCVS data on the perceived race of the offender for single-offender violent victimizations. As Table 2.6 shows, although the typical offender for all of the crimes except robbery is white (or is perceived to be white), African Americans are overrepresented as offenders for all of the offenses listed. The most notable disproportion revealed by Table 2.6 is for robbery, with just less than 40 percent of the offenders in single-offender robberies identified as African American. Also, African Americans are overrepresented as offenders for rape/sexual assault, aggravated assault, and simple assault, but not as severely as with robbery.

We argued earlier that one way to check the accuracy of arrest statistics is to *compare* the race of offenders arrested for various crimes with victims' perceptions of the race of the offender. These comparisons are found in Table 2.7. There is a relatively close match in the figures for white offenders for robbery and for simple assault. However, noticeable gaps in the rape and aggravated assault comparisons suggest whites may be underrepresented in arrest data compared to the victim-perception data. Moreover, whites appear to be overrepresented in arrest data compared to victim perceptions for only one offense: robbery. For African Americans, however, the pattern is more consistent—that is, African Americans are represented in arrest figures in much higher proportions than the perception of offenders from victim interviews for all offenses examined, with more than one-third higher representation in arrest figures than in victim-perception percentages.[65] These comparisons indicate that the racial disproportion found in arrest rates for these four offenses cannot be used to resolve the dilemma of differential arrest rates by race versus a higher rate of offending among African Americans. It may be reasonably argued that such evidence actually suggests the

T A B L E 2.6   Perceived Race of Offender for Single-Offender Crimes of Violence

Type of Crime	Perceived Race of the Offender		
	White	African American	Other
All Crimes of Violence	63.0%	21.3%	12.6%
Rape/Sexual Assault	47.9	24.4	22.4
Robbery	40.8	39.5	15.2
Assault	65.4	19.7	12.0
Aggravated	58.0	22.6	15.3
Simple	67.4	18.9	11.1

SOURCE: Bureau of Justice Statistics, *Criminal Victimization in the United States, 2003* (Washington, DC: U.S. Department of Justice, 2004).

T A B L E 2.7   A Comparison of UCR and NCVS Data on Offender Race, 2003

	Whites		African Americans		Other	
	Arrested	Perceived	Arrested	Perceived	Arrested	Perceived
Rape	64.1	47.9	33.3	24.4	2.6	22.4
Robbery	43.9	40.8	54.4	39.5	1.7	5.2
Aggravated Assault	63.5	58.0	34.0	22.6	2.4	15.3
Simple Assault	65.7	67.4	31.8	18.9	2.5	11.1

SOURCE: Federal Bureau of Investigation, *Crime in the United States, 2003* (Washington, DC: U.S. Government Printing Office, 2004); Bureau of Justice Statistics, *Criminal Victimization in the United States, 2003* (Washington, DC: U.S. Government Printing Office, 2004).

presence of both differentially high offending rates by African Americans for serious violent offenses *and* the presence of differentially high arrest rates for African Americans, particularly for rape offenses.

The comparison of other race figures offers a consistent pattern of under-representation of "other" race in arrest figures compared to the victim-perception figures. This observation could mean that Asian/Pacific Islander and Native American/Alaska Native are committing crimes at a higher rate than they are arrested for. However, these figures also suggest that NCVS respondents may be classifying offenders they perceive as Hispanic/Latino/Mexican in appearance to be of "other" race. Citizens commonly assume that Hispanic is a racial category, not an ethnic category. It may be argued, then, that dark-skinned offenders who do not appear African American may be classified as other because Hispanic is not an option to the race–identification question. Additionally, NCVS respondents are not asked to identify the perceived ethnicity of the offender.

Hindelang used early victimization data to determine which of these explanations (differential offending vs. differential enforcement) was more likely. His initial comparison of 1974 arrest statistics with victimization data for rape, robbery, aggravated assault, and simple assault revealed some evidence of "differential selection for criminal justice processing"[66] for two of the offenses examined. For rape and aggravated assault, the percentage of African American offenders in the victimization data was smaller (9 percentage points for rape, 11 percentage points for aggravated assault) than the proportion found in UCR arrest statistics.

However, once Hindelang controlled for victimizations that were reported to the police, the discrepancies disappeared and the proportions of offenders identified as African American and white were strikingly similar. Hindelang concluded that "it is difficult to argue (from these data) that blacks are no more likely than whites to be involved in the common law crimes of robbery, forcible rape, assault."[67]

Hindelang's analysis of victimizations reported to the police also revealed a pattern of differential reporting by victims. Specifically, Hindelang found that for rape and robbery, those victimized by African Americans were more likely than those victimized by whites to report the crime to the police. Hindelang suggested that this is a form of selection bias—victim-based selection bias.

Hindelang concluded his comparison of UCR arrest rates and victimization survey data by separating the elements of criminal justice–system selection bias, victim-based selection bias, and differential offending rates. He argued that both forms of selection bias were present but that each was outweighed by the overwhelming evidence of differential involvement of African Americans in offending. These findings are supported by a more recent analysis using NIBRS arrest data (17 states) by D'Alessio and Stolzenberg. They report that the odds of arrest were actually higher for whites in three of the four crime types examined. They conclude that their findings suggest that "the disproportionately high arrest rate for black citizens is most likely attributable to differential involvement in reported crime rather than to racially biased law enforcement practices.[67a]

Self-Report Surveys

Self-report surveys are another way to paint a picture of the criminal offender. These surveys question respondents about their participation in criminal or delinquent behavior. Emerging in the 1950s, the self-report format remains a popular source of data for those searching for descriptions and causes of criminal behavior. One of the advantages of asking people about their behavior is that it gives a less distorted picture of the offender than an official record because it is free of the alleged biases of the criminal justice system. However, it is not at all clear that self-report survey results provide a more *accurate* description of the criminal offender.[68]

Problems with Self-Report Surveys   One of the major weaknesses of the self-report format is that there is no single design used. Moreover, different surveys focus on different aspects of criminal behavior. Not all self-report surveys ask the same questions or use the same or similar populations, and very few follow the same group over time. Usually, the sample population is youth from school settings or institutionalized groups.

In addition to the problems of inconsistent format and noncomparable samples, self-report surveys suffer from a variety of other limitations. The accuracy of self-report data is influenced by the respondents' honesty and memory and by interviewer bias.

One of the most confounding limitations in criminal justice datasets is present with self-report surveys: the comparisons are overwhelmingly comparisons of African Americans and whites. Little can be said about Native Americans, Asian Americans, or Hispanic Americans. Some studies suffer from the additional limitation of homogenous samples, with insufficient racial representation. These limitations make it difficult to draw conclusions about how many members of a racial group commit delinquent activity (prevalence) and how frequently racial minorities commit crime (incidence).

Although self-report surveys generally are assumed to be reliable and valid, this assumption has been shown to be less tenable for certain subgroups of offenders.[69] Specifically, it has been shown that there is differential validity for white and African American respondents. Validity is the idea that, as a researcher, you are measuring what you think you are measuring. Reverse record checks (matching self-report answers with police records) have shown that there is greater concurrence between respondent answers and official police arrest records for white respondents than for African American respondents.[70] This indicates that African American respondents tend to underreport some offending behavior.

Elliot and colleagues caution against a simplistic interpretation of these findings.[71] They find that African American respondents are more likely to underreport index-type offenses than less serious offenses. Therefore, they suggest that this finding may indicate the differential validity of official police records rather than differential validity of the self-report measures by race. An example of differential validity of police records would occur if police report the clearly serious offenses for whites and African Americans but report the less serious offenses for African Americans only. In short, most self-report researchers conclude that racial comparisons must be made with caution.

Characteristics of Offenders   Usually juvenile self-report surveys record demographic data and ask questions about the frequency of certain delinquent activities in the last year. The delinquent activities included range in seriousness from skipping class, drinking liquor, stealing something worth more than $50, stealing a car, or assaulting someone.[72]

Early self-report studies, those conducted before 1980, found little difference in delinquency rates across race (African American and white only). Later, more refined self-report designs have produced results that challenge the initial assumption of similar patterns of delinquency.[73] Some research findings indicate that African American males are more likely than white males to report serious criminal behavior (prevalence). Moreover, a larger portion of African Americans than whites report a high frequency of serious delinquency (incidence).[74]

B O X 2.5 Monitoring the Future

The only student-based self-report survey done on a yearly basis with a nationwide sample is Monitoring the Future.[76] Responses to their delinquency questions reveal few differences in self-report delinquent behavior by white compared to African American youth. White youth were slightly more likely to report having been in a serious fight in the last year, having used a weapon to get something from a person, taken something from a store, and taking a car that didn't belong to someone in the family. African American youth were slightly more likely to report having taken something from a store without paying for it, taking something not belonging to you worth less than $50, and going into some house or building without permission.

Huizinga and Elliot explored whether African American youth have a higher prevalence of offending than whites and whether a higher incidence of offending by African Americans can explain differential arrest rates. Their analysis revealed few consistent racial differences across the years studied, either in the proportion of African American and white youth engaging in delinquent behavior or the frequency with which African American and white offenders commit delinquent acts. Contrary to Hindelang, they suggest that the differential selection bias hypothesis cannot be readily dismissed because the differential presence of youth in the criminal justice system cannot be explained entirely by differential offending rates.

Perhaps the most recent and comprehensive analysis of the race and prevalence and race and incidence issues was done by Huizinga and Elliot[75] with six waves of the National Youth Survey (NYS) data. This self-report survey is a longitudinal study that began in 1976 and uses a national panel design. This study offers the only national assessment of individual offending rates based on self-report studies for a 6-year period. See Box 2.5, "Monitoring the Future," for additional information on self-report drug use.

Drug Offenders A prevalent image in the news and entertainment media is the image of the drug user as a person of color. In particular, arrest data for non-alcoholic drug abuse violations reflect an overrepresentation of African Americans and an overrepresentation of Native Americans for alcohol-related offenses. A more comprehensive picture of drug users emerges from self-report data that asks respondents to indicate their use of and prevalence of use behavior for particular drugs. In a recent report on the use of drugs among people of color, the National Institutes of Health (NIH) summarizes the current body of research as indicating:[77]

- African American youth report less alcohol use than white youth and report similar prevalence levels for use of illicit drugs compared to other racial and ethnic groups. (NIH does note research suggesting that African Americans experience higher rates of drug-related health problems than users from other race/ethnicity groups).

- Asian/Pacific Islander youth responding to sporadic state level surveys and several years of pooled national data consistently report less drug use than other non-Asian populations.

- Native American youth begin using a variety of drugs (not limited to alcohol) at an earlier age than white youth. Inhalant use is twice as high among Native American youth.

- Hispanics are found to have a higher reported use of illicit drug use than non-Hispanic whites.

In short, there is no clear picture of the typical drug user/abuser. Additional race differences are evident in results from a school-based survey by the Centers for Disease Control and Prevention, which indicate that self-reported lifetime crack use is highest among Hispanic students, followed by lower percentages for whites and even lower percentages for African Americans. However, the National Household Survey on Drug Abuse data reveal the disturbing observation that a far greater number of African American and Hispanic youth (approximately one-third) reported seeing people sell drugs in the neighborhood occasionally or more often than whites did (less than 10 percent).

Summary: A Picture of the Typical Criminal Offender

The image of the typical offender that emerges from the data examined here conflicts somewhat with the image in the minds of most Americans. If by the phrase "typical offender" we mean the offender who shows up most frequently in arrest statistics, then for all crimes except murder and robbery the typical offender is white, not African American.

As we have shown, focusing on the *number* of persons arrested is somewhat misleading. It is clear from the data discussed thus far that African Americans are arrested at a disproportionately high *rate*. This conclusion applies to property crime and violent crime. Moreover, victimization data suggest that African Americans may have higher offending rates for serious violent crime, but examinations of victim perception of offender with official arrest data reveal that some of the overrepresentation of African American offenders may be selection bias on the part of criminal justice officials, but this dilemma remains unsettled.

If part of the view of the typical criminal offender is that the typical drug offender is a minority, we have shown that self-report data from youth populations in the United States reveal that people of color do not have consistently higher drug-use rates than whites. This picture varies slightly by type of drug, with Hispanic youth showing higher rates of use with some drugs and Native American youth with other drugs but little evidence of differential patterns of higher use rates by African Americans than other racial groups.

CRIME AS AN INTRARACIAL EVENT

In the minds of many Americans, the term "crime" conjures up an image of an act of violence against a white victim by an African American offender.[78] In the preceding sections we demonstrated the inaccuracy of these perceptions of victims and offenders; we illustrated that the typical victim is a racial minority and that the typical offender, for all but a few crimes, is white. We now turn to a discussion of crime as an *intraracial* event.

National Crime Victimization Survey

Few criminal justice data sources, including the NCVS, offer comprehensive information on the racial makeup of the victim–offender dyad. Recall that the NCVS asks victims about their perceptions of the offender's race in crimes of violence and data presented distinguish among only African Americans, whites, and "others"(victims perceptions of the offender as Hispanic are not available).

With these limitations in mind, NCVS data on the race of the victim and the perceived race of the offender in single-offender violent victimizations can be examined.[79] These data indicate that almost all violent crimes by white offenders were committed against white victims (73 percent). This pattern also characterized the individual crimes of robbery, sexual assault, aggravated assault, and simple assault. The typical white offender, in other words, commits a crime against another white person.

This intraracial pattern of violent crime is also reported by African American victims. In short, crimes of robbery, sexual assault, aggravated assault, and simple assault of African Americans is predominantly intraracial. The only NCVS crime type that does not follow this pattern is a white robbery victim with injury. These victims are nearly as likely to be victimized by perceived offenders who are white *or* African American.

Uniform Crime Report Homicide Reports

A final source of data on the victim–offender pair is the Supplemental Homicide Report. Contrary to popular belief, a 26-year review of UCR SHRs reveals that homicide is essentially an intraracial event.[80] Specifically, 94 percent of African American murder victims were slain by other African Americans and 86 percent of whites were victimized by whites.[81] Of the small percentage of interracial homicides they are more likely to be occur with young victims and young offenders and are slightly more likely to be black-on-white offenses than white-on-black offenses.[82] This analysis also reveals that when crimes are interracial they are more likely to be stranger homicides (3 in 10 are interracial) than homicides by victim or acquaintance (1 in 10 are interracial).[83]

Summary

The general pattern revealed by the data discussed previously is one in which white offenders consistently victimize whites, whereas African American offenders, and particularly African American males, more frequently victimize both African Americans and whites. As noted, the politicizing of black criminality continues,

Focus on an Issue
Politicizing Black-on-Black Crime

"Much attention has been devoted to 'black-on-black' crime . . . It is not unusual to see in the written press or to hear in the electronic media stories depicting the evils of living in the black community.[This] has occurred with such frequency that some individuals now associate black people with criminality. Simply put, it has become fashionable to discern between crime and black-on-black crime. Rarely does one read or hear about white crime or 'white-on-white' crime. This is troubling when one considers that most crimes, including serious violent crimes, are committed by and against whites as well as blacks."[84]

and the emergence of and subsequent focus on racial hoaxes persists.[85] See "Focus on an Issue" sections for a discussion of the politicizing of black criminality and the persistence of racial hoaxes.

Some researchers have challenged the assertion that crime is predominantly intraracial.[86] These critics point to the fact that a white person has a greater likelihood of being victimized by an African American offender than an African American has of being victimized by a white offender. Although this is true, it does not logically challenge the assertion that crime is predominantly an intraracial event. Remember that the NCVS reveals that the typical offender is white, not African American.

The exception to the predominant intraracial pattern of crime occurred with the examination of Native American and Asian victimization patterns. Native Americans report most victimizations occurring by whites, and Asians report victimizations occurring almost equally by whites, African Americans, and other racial groups (with no group committing the majority of offenses).

CRIME AS AN INTERRACIAL (HATE) EVENT

Not all interracial criminal events are considered hate crimes. The term "hate crime" (or bias crime) is most often defined as a common law offense that contains an element of prejudice based on the race, ethnicity, national origin, religion, sexual orientation, or disability status of the victim (some statutes add gender). Generally, hate-crime legislation is enacted in the form of enhancement penalties for common law offenses (ranging from assault to vandalism) that have an element of prejudice. Justifications for the creation of such legislation include the symbolic message that certain actions are exceptionally damaging to an individual when they are "provoked" by the status of race and ethnicity and that such actions are damaging to the general community and should be condemned.

The FBI has been mandated by Congress to collect and disseminate information on hate crime in the United States.[87] In 2003 the FBI Hate Crime Data Collection Program received reports from nearly 12,000 law enforcement

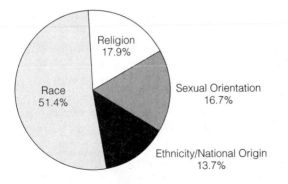

FIGURE 2.3 Hate-Crime Offenses, by Bias Type, 2003

SOURCE: *FBI Hate Crime Report*, 2003.
NOTE: Disability status (antiphysical and antimental) constitutes 0.4 percent of offenses in 2003 and is not included in this figure.

agencies (representing 49 states and the District of Columbia), representing nearly 85 percent of the U.S. population.[88] The FBI offers this caution in its annual report: "The reports from these agencies are insufficient to allow a valid national or regional measure of the volume and types of crimes motivated by hate; they offer perspectives on the general nature of hate crime occurrence."[89]

The FBI received reports of 7,489 bias-motivated criminal incidents in 2003, consisting of 8,706 offenses.[90] Most offenses reported (63.3 percent) involved crimes against a person, with 36.0 percent of the offenses designated as property offenses.[91] A small number of offenses (0.7 percent) were designated as crimes against society.[92] The most common offense was the crime of intimidation (31.5 percent), followed by destruction/vandalism of property (30.0 percent), simple assault (20.8 percent), and aggravated assault (10.6 percent).[93]

More than half of the reported hate-crime offenses involved race bias (51.4 percent), with another 17.9 percent reflecting bias based on religion, and 13.7 percent reflecting a bias based on ethnicity/national origin (Figure 2.3). The victims of race bias crimes were reflective of all race categories, including a multiracial group category. The ethnicity/national origin information is available for Hispanic and other ethnicity/national origin. African Americans and Hispanics are the most common hate-crime victims in their respective categories, with Asian and mixed-race victims being overrepresented as well. White victims are not overrepresented in relation to their presence in the population but are the second largest group of hate-crime victims.

Offender information is also available in the FBI Hate Crime Reporting Program reports. This information is provided by victims reporting their perceptions, rather than arrest information, to the police. In 56.9 percent of the hate-crime offenses reported, the offender was known and the perception of race was reported by the victim.[94] In these cases suspected offenders were most often identified as white (73.8 percent), but suspected offenders represented all four race categories and were occasionally identified as multi-racial.[95] In short, all race groups have individuals who have been victimized by bias crimes and all race groups have individuals who are suspected offenders of bias crimes.

Information on the trends of victimization and offending in bias-crime events is limited, but patterns for both whites and African Americans have emerged. Whites are most often victimized by African Americans, and African Americans are most often victimized by whites.[96] In 2003 Native Americans were most likely to identify whites as the typical offender in bias-crime incidents. Additionally, although Native Americans are rarely identified as offenders, they were as likely to have white victims as African American victims.[97] Asian Americans most often identify their offenders as white, whereas the offender identified as Asian American is found to victimize African Americans more than the other racial groups.[98]

In 2005 the Bureau of Justice Statistics released a Special Report comparing the picture of hate crime incidents and offenders that appear in victim self-report survey in formation (the NCVS) with the picture found in police based data (UCR).[98a] The NCVS requires corroborating evidence of hate-based motivation before it records an event as a hate crime. Specifically, the offender must use derogatory language, display a hate symbol, or have a confirmed hate crime report by local law enforcement. Pooling several years of NCVS data (2000–2003), results in an average of 191,000 hate incidents, of which 92,000 were reported to police (44 percent).[98b] These data reveal approximately 3 percent of all violent crimes reported in the NCVS were perceived by the victim as hate crimes. Nearly one-third of the offenses were violent crimes such as rape and serious assault, and nearly 25 percent of the offenses were household vandalism that was perceived to be motivated by hate. The most common motivation identified by victims was based on race (55 percent), association with someone of a different race (such as a multi-racial couple; 31 percent), or ethnicity (29 percent).

Key information describing the offender and the incident is also available from the NCVS data.[98c] Offenders are predominately male and most likely to be white and a stranger to the victim. The event is most likely to be a violent crime and occur in a public place. When comparing hate offenders to non-hate offenders, NCVS data reveals that perceived gang membership and use of weapons does not vary from hate to non-hate related events. However, a larger percentage of females are identified as offenders in hate events compared to non-hate events. Similarly, the perceived racial make-up of offenders is different with hate and non-hate related events. Forty-four percent of offenders are white in hate events, while 62 percent of offenders are identified as white in non-hate events. Conversely, a larger percentage of hate offenders are perceived as African American, compared to the percent of non-hate offenders (39 percent compared to 24 percent).

When the racial composition of victims and offenders is examined, interesting differences appear. First, white victims report that nearly half of their offenders were white offenders and nearly half of the offenders were African American.[98d] However, African American victims perceive their offenders to be white in more than 85 percent of offenses, with African American offenders identified in only 15 percent of cases.[98e]

The official UCR recording of hate crime incidence from this time period (2000–2003) gives an annual averaged of 8,227 incidents.[98f] What accounts for the disparity? First, the motivation of association is not recognized by the UCR classification system (identified above as the second most common motivation

Focus on an Issue
Racial Hoaxes

Katherine Russell asserts that a racial hoax occurs "when someone fabricates a crime and blames it on another person because of his race OR when an actual crime has been committed and the perpetrator falsely blames someone because of his race."[102] One infamous racial hoax was the case of Susan Smith's assertion that an African American man stole her car and kidnapped her children.[103] She was a white women, who it was later revealed drove her car, with her children trapped in their car seats, into a nearby lake. Russell argues that such hoaxes have social and psychological consequences for individuals and the community and significant legal costs.[104] In this 1994 case in South Carolina, state and federal officials spent 9 days looking for the alleged offender before she confessed to driving the car into the lake and killing her children. Smith's attempt to blame someone else for the crime was successful (even if temporarily) because it tapped in to widely held societal fears about the typical criminal.

Russell documents known racial hoaxes in the United States from 1987 to 1996. Although she found that racial hoaxes "are perpetrated by people of all races, classes, geographic regions and ages,"[105] the majority of racial hoax cases were perpetrated by a white person

charging an African American person (70 percent of the cases), with a smaller number of African Americans charging whites in racial hoaxes.[106] Hoax perpetrators have been charged with filing false police reports, but this occurs in less than half of the documented cases.[107]

In her book, *The Color of Crime,* Russell makes a compelling argument for a strong legal response to the perpetration of racial hoaxes. She argues that legislation should be passed, similar to hate-crime legislation, that allows for a sentence enhancement to such charges as filing a false police report in the case of racial hoaxes. Such a law would be similar to one proposed in New Jersey in 1995, which would punish citizens who falsely incriminate another as the perpetrator of a crime or submit a fictitious report based on race, color, or ethnicity (as well as religion and sexual orientation).[108] In addition, to a sentence enhancement (fine, fee, additional supervision/incarceration), the person convicted would have to reimburse the law enforcement agencies whose search actions resulted from the racial hoax.

What do you think? Should states have racial hoax sentence enhancement statutes? What should the content of such legislation be?

in the NCVS). Second is the lack of victimization reporting to the police. The NCVS respondents reveal the hate incidents they report to the police are confirmed by police investigation in fewer than 10 percent of incidents. This study also reveals that victims are less likely to report hate related events to the police than similar non-hate related events. Additionally, the NCVS data may reflect an overreporting by respondents, perhaps due to telescoping events forward in time.

Jacobs[99] argued that hate-crime statutes create a law unlikely to deter and its implementation will widen social division. He also argued that hate-crime legislation represents an ill-advised insertion of the civil rights paradigm into the criminal law. Specifically, he reasons that civil rights legislation is an attempt to extend "positive rights and opportunities to minorities and women . . . directed at the conduct of government officials and private persons who govern, regulate, or sell goods and services. By contrast, hate crime law deals with conduct that is already criminal and with wrongdoers who are already criminals."[100] He concluded that the "possibility that criminals can be threatened into not discriminating in their choice of crime victims is slight."[101]

ETHNIC YOUTH GANGS

In the minds of most Americans, the words *gang, race,* and *crime* are inextricably linked. Recall the incident described at the beginning of this chapter in "Focus on an Issue" (p. 32)—a woman raped and attacked by a group of minority teenagers in Central Park. The media labeled these youth a "gang." This designation, however, was challenged by those who argued that the teenagers allegedly involved in the incident were not organized, had no gang identity, and behaved more like a mob than a gang.[109]

A comprehensive review of recent research on ethnic youth gangs is beyond the scope of this chapter. Instead, we discuss some of the prevailing myths about gangs and gang membership and summarize research on ethnic gang activities. Although there is no universally accepted definition of a gang, the term is generally used to refer to a group of young people who recognize some sort of organized membership and leadership and who, in addition, are involved in criminal activity.[110]

Gang Myths and Realities

We have shown that popular perceptions of crime, crime victims, and criminal offenders often are inaccurate. Many of the prevailing beliefs about gangs are similarly mistaken. In the sections that follow we discuss some of the myths surrounding gangs and gang activity. We show that, although there is an element of truth in each of these myths, there also are a number of inaccuracies.

Myth 1: All gang members are African American and belong either to the Bloods or Crips. The Bloods and the Crips *are* predominantly African American and are very widely known. These two gangs are heavily involved in illegal drug activities and are characterized by a confederation of local gangs that stretch across the country.[111] They are not, however, exclusively African American. Mydans[112] provided examples of well-to-do white youth joining California Crips and Bloods.

Although members of the racial minority groups we focus on in this book are overrepresented in gangs, they do not comprise the entire gang problem. (It is somewhat misleading to categorize gangs as Hispanic or Asian. The terms "Hispanic" and "Asian" are very broad and mask the variety within each group. In reality, gangs are ethnically specific by nationality; there are Puerto Rican, Cuban, Mexican American, Vietnamese, Cambodian, Korean, Chinese, and Japanese gangs.)

The earliest gangs in the United States were predominantly white. The first documentation of youth gangs is just after the Revolutionary War.[113] Moreover, the seminal studies of youth gangs conducted in the early 1900s documented predominantly white ethnic gangs composed of youth from Eastern European countries.[114] Currently, white ethnic gangs are not as prevalent. Covey and colleagues[115] argue that "the relative absence of white ethnic gangs in official studies may be a product of a number of factors including the difficulty of identifying them[116] and biases in reporting and public perception."[117] Many of the white ethnic groups that do exist are characterized by white supremacist activities or satanism.

Myth 2: Gangs are only found in large cities. It is important to understand that the gang phenomenon is not a homogeneous one. Although many gangs *are* located in urban areas, gangs are increasingly found in suburban and rural communities and on Indian reservations.[118] The 2002–2003 National Youth Gang Survey, collected by the National Youth Gang Center from law enforcement agencies, reported gangs were present in 95 percent of cities with a population of 250,000 and 91 percent of cities with a population of 100,000 to 249,999. Cities of smaller sizes also reported the presence of gangs, with 70 percent of cities with 50,000 to 99,999 residents and 32 percent in cities with 2,500 to 49,999 residents reporting a gang presence in their jurisdictions. Additionally, this survey revealed that suburban and rural counties each reported the presence of gangs (41 percent and 14 percent).[119]

Myth 3: All gangs are involved in selling drugs and drug trafficking. Many, but not all, gangs are involved in illegal drug activities. Moreover, at least some of these gangs existed before they began selling drugs. It is possible that gangs have been exploited because of their structure and organization to sell drugs and that this lucrative activity serves as a reason for recruitment and expansion.

Drug use is common in most gangs, but the emphasis placed on drug sales varies by the character and social organization of the gang.[120] Many researchers challenge the idea that selling drugs is usually an organized gang activity involving all gang members.[121] In their study of Denver youth, Esbensen and Huizinga distinguished between a gang involved in drug activity and individual gang members selling drugs. They found that 80 percent of youth respondents said that their gangs were involved in drug sales, but only 28 percent admitted to selling drugs themselves.[122] In short, although gang members were found to be more active in drug-related crimes (use and sales) than nongang youth, not all gang members sold drugs.

In the 1999 National Youth Gang Survey, law enforcement agencies reported that 51 percent of all gangs in rural counties were believed to be organized specifically for the purpose of drug trafficking, whereas 41 percent of those in large cities were identified as organized for drug trafficking.[123] Drug trafficking by gangs is perceived as being less common in suburban areas (39 percent of all gangs) and small cities (26 percent of all gangs).[124]

Related to the myth that all gang members sell drugs is the notion that drugs and violence are inextricably linked. In fact, there is a complex relationship between drugs and violence in gangs. Fagan found that, regardless of the level of drug dealing within a gang, violent behaviors still occurred, with the majority of incidents unrelated to drug sales.[125] He concluded that "for gang members, violence is not an inevitable consequence of involvement in drug use and dealing."[126] Curry and Decker also noted the prevalence of violence in gang activity, pointing out that much of this violence is intraracial.[127]

Moreover, an assessment of gang activity across the country documents the emerging trend toward the use of technology in the commission of crime. These new criminal endeavors are identified as identity theft, pirating of videos and movies, and email fraud schemes.[128]

Myth 4: Gangs are the result of poverty and a growing underclass. It is overly simplistic to attribute the existence of gangs solely to poverty. The National Youth Gang Survey indicated that, although the majority of gang members are identified as underclass, 35 percent were identified as working class, 12 percent as middle class, and 3 percent as upper middle class.[129] Gangs exist for a variety of reasons: the growth of the underclass,[130] the disintegration of the African American and Hispanic family,[131] poverty,[132] difficulty assimilating into American culture,[133] marginality,[134] political and religious reasons,[135] and general rebellion against adult and conventional society.[136] However, Curry and Decker did argue that gang formation and gang delinquency are more likely to be explained at a community level rather than at an individual level.[137]

Myth 5: All gang members are males. Although it is true that males are over-represented in gang membership, there are female gang members and female gangs. The early sociological literature on gangs only discussed males; females who accompanied male gang members were often described in terms of an "auxiliary"—present, but not a formal part of the criminal activity.

More recent studies have found both fully active female gang members and a few solely female gangs. Researchers estimate that females represent between 10 percent[138] and 25 percent[139] of all gang members, with nearly 40 percent of all youth gangs having female members.[140] Campbell identified several all-female gangs in New York City. "The Sandman Ladies," for example, were Puerto Rican females with a biker image. "The Sex Girls" were African American and Hispanic females who were involved in drug dealing. Currently, female gang members are known to assist with the "movement of drugs and weapons for male gang members and gather intelligence from rival gangs."[141]

The presence of female gang members differs by ethnicity as well. Females are found in Hispanic gangs, African American gangs, and white ethnic gangs, but they appear to be conspicuously absent in both journalistic and scholarly accounts of Asian American gangs.[142]

Myth 6: Youth gangs involve only young people and have few ties to organized crime. For a number of years gang researchers have documented generational patterns of gang membership in a number of Hispanic and African American gangs. More than 25 percent of all law enforcement agencies in one survey indicated that gangs in their jurisdiction were associated with organized crime.[143] Law enforcement agencies report that street gangs are associated with Mexican drug organizations, Asian organized crime groups, Russian organized crime, and outlaw motorcycle gangs.[144]

Varieties of Ethnic Gangs

We already noted that, contrary to popular wisdom, all gang members are not African Americans. There are also Hispanic, Native American, Asian, and white gangs. The National Youth Gang Survey indicated that 47 percent of gang members are identified as Hispanic, 31 percent as African American, 13 percent as white, 7 percent as Asian, and 2 percent as other.[145]

Covey and colleagues stated, "[Ethnicity] is not the only way to understand gangs, but gangs are organized along ethnic lines, and it would be a mistake to ignore ethnicity as a variable that may affect the nature of juvenile gangs."[146] Most ethnic gangs reflect a mixture of their members' culture of origin and the American "host" culture; indeed, many gangs form as the result of a clash between the two cultures.

African American The most widely known African American gangs are the Bloods and the Crips. Each gang has unique "colors" and sign language to reinforce gang identity. It is believed that these gangs are really "national con-federations of local gangs" in American cities.[147] They are characteristically very territorial and often are linked to drug distribution.

Other African American gangs exist across the United States. Researchers have identified many big-city African American gangs that are oriented toward property crime rather than drug sales.[148] In addition, African American gangs have formed around the tenets of Islam, with corresponding political agendas.[149]

Native American The circumstances among which Native American youth are becoming part of the gang culture in the United States include the emerging presence of gangs in the semi-sovereign tribal lands throughout the country and as members of gangs located in urban and rural nonreservation areas. Specifically, the Navajo nations have documented the presence of youth gangs consisting of tribal members. They have reported the presence of more than 50 gangs with nearly 1,000 members on the tribal lands.[150] Some Native American gangs identify themselves with the native culture of their unique areas (such as the Native Outlawz and Native Mob), whereas other gang names indicate alliances with more nationally recognized groups like the Bloods and Gangster Disciplines (with names like the Indian Bloods and Native Gangster Disciples).[151] Actual evidence of structural alliances with these other urban gangs seems to be in doubt. Some gang researchers speculate that such affiliation is "utilized for the purposes of notoriety and intimidation."[152] Most gang crimes on tribal lands seem to be property-based, but there is increasing concern about violence and drug distribution (especially methamphetamine and marijuana).[153]

Asian American As previously stated, there are a variety of Asian ethnic gangs. Most Asian gang researchers attribute the formation of these gangs, at least in part, to feeling alienated because of difficulty assimilating into American culture.[154] Similarities between Asian gangs include an emphasis on economic activity and a pattern of intraracial victimization. The tendency to victimize others in the Asian community may contribute to lower reporting rates of gang victimization to local law enforcement. Asian gangs are found in coastal cities in Western states, such as California and Oregon, but also in east coast cities in the states of New York, Massachusetts, and Connecticut.[155]

The origins of Chinese American gangs can be traced to the early 1890s and the secret "Tong" societies.[156] Chinese American gang activity has increased with the relaxation of immigration laws in the mid 1960s.[157] The research on Chinese

American gangs shows a commitment to violence for its own sake (gang warfare) and as a means for attaining income (robbery, burglary, extortion, protection).[158] Gang researchers report that it is not unusual for Asian organized crime groups to work with street gangs in such activities as "drug trafficking, credit card fraud, illegal gambling and money laundering."[159] Chin[160] noted that, generally, the structure of Chinese American gangs is very hierarchical; he also explains that gang members may participate in legitimate business, establish drug distribution and sale networks, and form national and international networks.

Vietnamese American gang activity is not as structured as that of Chinese American gangs. The increase in gang activity for this ethnic group can also be tied to an influx in immigration. Overall, Vietnamese American gang activity is less violent, usually economically oriented, and most likely to target other Vietnamese Americans.[161]

Hispanic Hispanic gangs have identifiable core concerns: brotherhood/sister-hood, machismo, and loyalty to the barrio (neighborhood).[162] Many Hispanic gangs have adult and juvenile members,[163] and gang members may be involved in the use and sale of drugs. The importance of machismo may explain the emphasis of many Hispanic gangs on violence, even intragang violence.

Hispanic gangs make up the largest ethnic population of gang membership in the country. Prominent Hispanic gangs vary by region. In the western part of the country, Sur 13 and The Latin Kings are most evident. The former is strongly associated with the prison gang Mexican Mafia (discussed in Chapter 9).[164] Law enforcement agencies have identified Hispanic gangs in Northern California in alliance with outlaw motorcycle gangs to transport drugs (primarily methamphet-amine).[165] International connections emerge with such gangs as the MS-13 (Mara Salvatrucha), which has El Salvadoran roots.[166] Other gangs are reported to have connections to crime groups in Honduras, Guatemala, and other Central American countries.[167]

The National Alliance of Gang Investigators reports that some Central American gang members, from El Salvador and Honduras, have gained Temporary Protective Status (granted by the Bureau of Immigration and Custom's Enforcement) in the United States as a result of the gang prosecution efforts in their own countries.[168] The Department of Homeland Security requires migrants to be deported if they have been convicted of a felony or two or more misdemeanors, but some gang members are able to remain for a period of time if they are looking for work.[169]

White The white ethnic gangs—composed of Irish, Polish, and Italian youth—identified by researchers earlier in this century are less evident in today's cities. Contemporary white ethnic gangs are most often associated with rebellion against adult society; with suburban settings; and with a focus on white supremacist, domestic terrorist, or satanist ideals.

"Skinheads" may be the most well-known example of a white ethnic gang. Covey and colleagues describe them in this way: "Skinhead gangs usually consist of European American youths who are non-Hispanic, non-Jewish, Protestant, working class, low income, clean shaven and militantly racist and white supremacist."[170] Skinheads have been located in cities in every region of the country and have been linked to adult domestic terrorist organizations such as the White Aryan Resistance (WAR) and other Neo-Nazi movements. Skinheads are unique in the sense that they use violence not to protect turf, protect a drug market, or commit robberies, but rather "for the explicit purpose of promoting political change by instilling fear in innocent people."[171]

Youth gangs with connections to domestic terrorist groups comprise less than 10 percent of known gang activity.[172] These groups include the Ku Klux Klan, Aryan Resistance, National Socialist Movement, and various militia groups.[173] Little evidence exists of youth gang connections with international terrorist groups because most evidence suggests recruitment is more common in adult prisons (see Chapter 9).[174]

"Stoner" gangs, another form of white ethnic gangs, are characterized by an emphasis on satanic rituals. This doctrine is supplemented by territoriality and the heavy use of drugs.[175]

In recognizing the racial nature of gangs it is important to clarify the role of racism in the formation of gangs. Most gangs are racially and ethnically homogenous. Some researchers argue that this situation is merely reflective of the racial and ethnic composition of neighborhoods and primary friendships—that is, "where schools and neighborhoods are racially and ethnically mixed, gangs tend to be racially and ethnically mixed."[176]

Although violent conflicts do occur between and within ethnic gangs, violence is seldom the reason for gang formation. Racism as a societal phenomenon that creates oppressive conditions can contribute to gang formation. However, individual racism explains very little in terms of the formation of gangs or the decision to join gangs. Skinhead membership is a notable exception, being almost exclusively a function of individual racism.[177]

CONCLUSION

We began this chapter with a discussion of the presentation of crime stories in the media in comparison to their actual occurrence. We argued that incidents like missing person reports and racial hoaxes shape perceptions of crime in the United States. In the minds of many Americans, the typical crime is an act of violence involving a white victim and a minority offender. We have used a variety of data sources to illustrate the inaccuracy of these perceptions and offer a more comprehensive view of victimization and offending.

We have shown that people of color are overrepresented as victims of both household and personal crime and have demonstrated that this pattern is particularly striking for crimes of violence. We have demonstrated that the typical offender for all crimes except robbery and gambling is white; however, African Americans are arrested at a disproportionately high rate. We also have shown that most crimes involve an offender and victim of the same race, which means that crime is predominantly an intraracial event.

The information provided in this chapter may raise as many questions as it answers. Although we have attempted to paint an accurate picture of crime and victimization in the United States, we are hampered by limitations inherent in existing data sources. Some victimization events are not defined as crimes by the victims, many of those that are defined as crimes are not reported to the police, and many of those reported to the police do not lead to an arrest. There is no dataset that provides information on all crimes that occur.

We have attempted to address this problem by using several different sources of data. We believe that we can have greater confidence in the conclusions we reach if two or more distinct types of data point in the same direction. The fact that both NCVS data and data from the SHRs consistently reveal that racial and ethnic minorities are more likely than whites to fall victim to crime, for example, lends credence to the need for a more comprehensive picture of victims and offenders. Similarly, the fact that a variety of data sources suggest that crime is predominantly an intraracial event enhances our confidence in this conclusion as well.

We have less confidence in our conclusions concerning the racial makeup of the offender population. Although it is obvious that African Americans are arrested at a disproportionately high rate, particularly for murder and robbery, it is not clear that this reflects differential offending rather than selective enforcement of the law. Arrest statistics and victimization data both indicate that African Americans have higher rates of offending than whites, but some self-report studies suggest that there are few, if any, racial differences in offending. We suggest that this discrepancy limits our ability to draw definitive conclusions about the meaning of the disproportionately high arrest rates for African Americans.

One final caveat seems appropriate. The conclusions we reach about victims and offenders are based primarily on descriptive data; they are based primarily on percentages, rates, and trends over time. These data are appropriate for describing a disproportionate representation of people of color as the victims of crime and as the criminal offender, but these data are not sufficient for drawing conclusions concerning causality. The data we have examined in this chapter can tell us that the African American arrest rate is higher than the white arrest rate for a particular crime, but they cannot tell us why this is so. We address issues of causation in subsequent chapters.

DISCUSSION QUESTIONS

1. Does the media systematically discriminate against crime victims, favoring white victims? Or, is the discrimination contextual (see Chapter 1)? How does the media cover racial hoaxes? Does this coverage perpetuate the view of young African American males as the typical criminal offenders?

2. What are some of the possible explanations for the overrepresentation of minorities as crime victims? Are minority communities particularly vulnerable to crime? Why?

3. The descriptive information in UCR arrest data depicts an overrepresentation of African American offenders for most violent and property crimes. What are the possible explanations for such disparity? Is this picture of the offender the result of differential offending rates or differential enforcement practices? What must a researcher include in a study of "why people commit crime" to advance beyond a description of disparity to test for a causal explanation?

4. "Should hate be a crime?" What arguments can be made to support the use of sentencing enhancement penalties for hate crimes? What arguments can be made to oppose such statutes? Are hate-crime laws likely to deter offenders and reduce crime?

5. What are the social and psychological costs of racial hoaxes? Should perpetuating a racial hoax be a crime? What should the penalty for such an offense be?

6. If most youth gangs are racially and ethnically homogenous, should law enforcement use race- and ethnic-specific strategies to fight gang formation and to control gang crime? Or, should law enforcement strategies be racially and ethnically neutral? What dilemmas are created for police departments who pursue each of these strategies? Is the likely result institutional or contextual discrimination?

NOTES

1. Quoted in Anne-Marie O'Connor, "Media Coverage of Missing Women Draws Ire." Monday, August 8, 2005, *Lincoln Journal Star*, p. 8A.

2. Erin Bruno, quoted in Alim, Fahizah, "Missing White Women Get Lion's Share of Media Coverage." June 28, 2005, *Sacramento Bee*.

3. Ibid.

4. Erin Bruno, quoted in Alim, Fahizah, "Missing White Women Get Lion's Share of Media Coverage." June 28, 2005, *Sacramento Bee*.

5. Ibid.

6. Erin Bruno quoted in Anne-Marie O'Connor, "Media Coverage of Missing Women Draws Ire." Monday, August 8, 2005, *Lincoln Journal Star*, p. 8A.

7. Quoted in Anne-Marie O'Connor, "Media Coverage of Missing Women Draws Ire." Monday, August 8, 2005, *Lincoln Journal Star*, p. 8A.

8. Charles Silberman, *Criminal Violence, Criminal Justice* (New York: Random House, 1978), pp. 177–118.

9. According to Uniform Crime Report index crime totals for 2000, roughly 90 percent of crimes were property crimes. It is believed that rapes are severely underreported, but similar arguments can be made for property crimes, especially fraud. Even if the rape numbers are low, the numbers of violent criminal events do not overshadow property crime.

10. *New York Times* (May 29, 1989), p. 25.

11. Robert M. O'Brien, "The Interracial Nature of Violent Crimes: A Reexamination," *American Journal of Sociology* 92 (1987): 817–835.

12. Joe Mahony, "Five Cleared in Central Park Jogger Assault," January 7, 2005, *Daily News* (New York).

13. Ibid.

14. The National Crime Survey (NCS) was recently renamed the National Crime Victimization Survey (NCVS) to clearly emphasize the focus of measuring victimizations.

15. The Bureau of Justice Statistics was formerly the National Criminal Justice and Information Service of the Law Enforcement Assistance Administration.

16. Bureau of Justice Statistics, *Criminal Victimizations in the United States: 1973-92 Trends* (Washington, DC: Government Printing Office, 1994).

17. Shannan M. Catalano, *Criminal Victimization 2004* (Washington, DC: Government Printing Office, 2005). Available at www.ojp.usdoj.gov/bjs/.

18. Ibid.

19. Sourcebook of Criminal Justice Statistics Online (Tables 3.22.2003 and 3.23.2003). Available at www.albany.edu/sourcebook.

20. Ibid.

20a. Ibid.

21. Detis T. Duhart, *Urban, Suburban and Rural Victimization, 1993–1998* (Washington, DC: U.S. Department of Justice, 2000). Available at www.ojp.usdoj/bjs/.

22. Ibid.

23. Bureau of Justice Statistics, *Criminal Victimization in the United States, 1994* (Washington, DC: U.S. Government Printing Office, 1996).

24. Ibid.

25. *Criminal Victimization, 2004.* Available at www.ojp.usdoj.gov/bjs/cvict_v.htm.

26. Rennison, *Criminal Victimization, 2000.*

27. Duhart, *Urban, Suburban and Rural Victimization, 1993–1998.*

28. Ibid.

29. Ibid.

30. *Criminal Victimization in the U.S., 2002.* Available at www.ojp.usdoj.gov/bjs.

31. Lawrence Greenfeld and Steven K. Smith, *American Indians and Crime* (Washington, DC: Bureau of Justice Statistics, 1999); Rennison, *Criminal Victimization 2000*; Catalano, *Criminal Victimization 2004.*

32. Duhart, *Urban, Suburban and Rural Victimization, 1993–1998.*

33. Erika Harrell, *Violence by Gang Members, 1993–2003* (Washington, DC: Bureau of Justice Statistics, 2005). NCJ 208875.

34. Callie Rennison, *Violent Victimization and Race, 1993–1998.* Available at www.ojp.usdoj.gov/bjs/pub/pdf/vvr98.pdf. See also: Lawrence A. Greenfeld and Steven K. Smith, *American Indians and Crime* (Washington, DC: Bureau of Justice Statistics, 1999).

35. Ibid.

36. Bureau of Justice Statistics, *Lifetime Likelihood of Victimization* (Washington, DC: U.S. Department of Justice, 1987), p. 1.

37. Ibid., p. 3.

38. Renisson, *Violent Victimization and Race.*

39. Ibid.

40. Ibid.

41. *Homicide Trends in the US, 1976–2002.* Available at www.ojp.usdoj.bjs/homicide/race.htm.

42. Ibid.

43. Ibid.

44. Gregg Barak, Jeanne M. Flavin, and Paul S. Leighton, *Class, Race, Gender and Crime: Social Realities of Justice in America* (Los Angeles: Roxbury, 2001).

45. Ibid., p. 102.

46. Silberman, *Criminal Violence, Criminal Justice.*

47. Steven Weisenburger, *Modern Medea* (New York: Hill and Wang, 1998); Toni Morrison, *Beloved: A Novel* (New York: Plume, 1988).

48. U.S. Department of Justice, *Crime in the United States, 2000*. Available at www.fbi.gov/ucr/ucr.htm.

49. Rennison, *Criminal Victimization, 2000*.

50. Ibid.

51. Ibid.

52. D. L. Decker, D. Shichor, and R. M. O'Brien, *Urban Structure and Victimization* (Lexington, MA: D.C. Heath, 1982), p. 27.

53. Rennison, *Criminal Victimization, 2000*.

54. Michael J. Hindelang, "Race and Involvement in Common Law Personal Crimes," *American Sociological Review* 43 (1978): 93–109.

55. U.S. Department of Justice, *Crime in the United States, 2003*.

56. John Huey-Long Song, "Attitudes of Chinese Immigrants and Vietnamese Refugees Toward Law Enforcement in the United States," *Justice Quarterly* 9 (1992): 703–719.

57. Margorie Zatz, "Pleas, Priors and Prison: Racial/Ethnic Differences in Sentencing," *Social Science Research* 14 (1985): 169–193.

58. Donald Black, "The Social Organization of Arrest," in *The Manners and Customs of the Police*, Donald Black, ed. (New York: Academic Press, 1980), pp. 85–108.

59. Katheryn K. Russell, *The Color of Crime* (New York: New York University Press, 1998).

60. Paul Knepper, "Race, Racism and Crime Statistics." *Southern Law Review*, 24 (1996): 71–112.

61. Available at www.fbi.gov/ucr/faqs.htm.

62. In some years, UCR arrest data indicate that African Americans make up half of the murder arrestees, but this pattern is not constant.

63. K. Peak and J. Spencer, "Crime in Indian Country: Another Trail of Tears,"

Journal of Criminal Justice 15 (1987): 485–494.

64. Hindelang, "Race and Involvement in Common Law Personal Crimes," p. 93.

65. Granted, the robbery arrest figures do include commercial offenses, but we are not looking at the volume of offenses; we are looking at the demographics of who is arrested.

66. Hindelang, "Race and Involvement in Common Law Personal Crimes," p. 99.

67. Ibid., pp. 100–101.

67a. Stewart J. D'Alessio and Lisa Stolzenberg, "Race and the Probability of Arrest." *Social Forces* 80 (2003): 1381–1397.

68. Gwynn Nettler, *Explaining Crime*, 3rd ed. (New York: McGraw-Hill, 1984).

69. Patrick G. Jackson, "Sources of Data" in *Measurement Issues in Criminology*, Kimberly Kempf, ed. (New York: Springer-Verlag, 1990).

70. Michael Hindelang, Travis Hirschi, and Joseph G. Weis, *Measuring Delinquency* (Beverly Hills, CA: Sage, 1981); Delbert Elliot, David Huizinga, Brian Knowles, and Rachel Canter, *The Prevalence and Incidence of Delinquent Behavior: 1976–1980: National Estimates of Delinquent Behavior by Sex, Race, Social Class and Other Selected Variables* (Boulder, CO: Behavioral Research Institute, 1983); Robert M. O'Brien, *Crime and Victimization Data* (Beverly Hills, CA: Sage, 1985).

71. Elliot et al. *The Prevalence and Incidence of Delinquent Behavior: 1976–1980: National Estimates of Delinquent Behavior by Sex, Race, Social Class and Other Selected Variables*.

72. National Youth Survey questionnaire in O'Brien, *Crime and Victimization Data*.

73. O'Brien, *Crime and Victimization Data*.

74. Delbert S. Elliot and S. S. Ageton, "Reconciling Race and Class Differences in Self-Reported and Official Measures of Delinquency," *American Sociological Review*

45 (1980): 95–110. Hindelang et al., *Measuring Delinquency*.

75. David Huizinga and Delbert S. Elliot, "Juvenile Offenders: Prevalence, Offender Incidence, and Arrest Rates by Race," *Crime and Delinquency* 33 (1987): 206–223.

76. Principal Investigators of the Monitoring the Future Project are Lloyd D. Johnston, Jerald G. Bachman and Patrick M. O'Malley. Data available in the *Sourcebook of Criminal Justice Statistics 2000*. Available at www.albany.edu/sourcebook/.

77. National Institute of Health, *Drug Use Among Racial/Ethnic Minorities*, Report No. 95–3888. (Washington, DC: U.S. Government Printing Office, 1995).

78. Lori Dorfman and Vincent Scharaldi, "Off Balance: Youth, Race and Crime in the News," Berkeley Media Studies Group, 2001. Available at www.buildingblocks foryouth.org/media.html.

79. NCVS, 2003.

80. *Homicide Trends in the United States, 1976–2002*. Available at www.ojp.us-doj.gov/bjs/homicide/race.htm.

81. Ibid.

82. Ibid.

83. Ibid.

84. Robert Bing, "*Politicizing Black-on-Black Crime: A Critique of Terminological Preference*," in *Black-on-Black Crime,* P. Ray Kedia, ed. (Bristol, TN: Wyndham Hall Press, 1994).

85. Bing, "*Politicizing Black-on-Black Crime*"; Katheryn K. Russell, *The Color of Crime* (New York: New York University Press, 1998).

86. William Wilbanks, "Is Violent Crime Intraracial?" *Crime and Delinquency* 31 (1985): 117–128.

87. Hate Crimes Act of 1990; Violent Crime and Law Enforcement Act of 1994; Church Arson Prevention Act.

88. Federal Bureau of Investigation, Hate Crime Statistics, 2003. Available at www.fbi.gov/ucr/hatecm.htm.

89. Ibid., p. 5.

90. Ibid.

91. Ibid.

92. Ibid.

93. Ibid., p. 6.

94. Ibid., p. 11.

95. Ibid., p. 11.

96. Ibid., p. 14.

97. Ibid., p. 14.

98. Ibid., p. 14.

98a. Caroline Wolf Harlow, *Hate Crime Reported by Victims and Police* (Washington, DC: BJS, 2005).

98b. Ibid.

98c. Ibid.

98d. Ibid.

98e. Ibid.

98f. Hate Crime, 2000–2003. Available at www.fbi.gov/ucr.

99. James Jacobs, "Should Hate be a Crime?" *Public Interest* (1993): 3–14.

100. Jacobs, "Should Hate be a Crime?" p. 11.

101. Ibid., pp. 11–12.

102. Katheryn K. Russell, *The Color of Crime* (New York: New York University Press, 1998), p. 70.

103. Ibid.

104. Ibid.

105. Ibid., p. 76.

106. Ibid., p. 76.

107. Ibid., p. 75.

108. Ibid., p. 88.

109. A. K. Cohen, "Foreword and overview," in *Gangs in America*, C. Ronald Huff, ed. (Newbury Park, CA: Sage, 1990).

110. Herbert C. Covey, Scott Menard and Robert J. Franzese, *Juvenile Gangs* (Springfield, IL: Charles C. Thomas, 1992).

111. Covey, et al. *Juvenile Gangs*.

112. S. Mydans, "Not Just the Inner City: Well To Do Join Gangs," *New York Times* National (April 10, 1991): A–7.

113. James Howell, *Youth Gangs: An Overview* (Washington, DC: Office of Juvenile Justice and Delinquency Prevention, 1998).

114. Frank Thrasher, *The Gang* (Chicago: University of Chicago Press, 1927).

115. Covey, et al., *Juvenile Gangs*, p. 64.

116. C. J. Friedman, F. Mann, and H. Aldeman, "Juvenile Street Gangs the Victimization of Youth," *Adolescence* 11 (1976): 527–533.

117. William J. Chambliss, "The Saints and The Roughnecks," *Society* 11 (1973): 341–355.

118. National Alliance of Gang Investigators Association. 2005 National Gang Threat Assessment. Available at ojp.usdoj.gov/BJA/what/2005_threat_assesment.pdf.

119. Highlights of the 2002–2003 National Youth Gang Surveys. Office of Juvenile Justice and Delinquency Prevention, 2005. Available at www.ncjrs.gov/pdffiles1/ojjdp/fs200501.pdf.

120. C. Ronald Huff ("Youth Gangs and Public Policy," *Crime and Delinquency* 35[1989]: 528–537) identifies three gang types: hedonistic, instrumental, or predatory. Jeffrey Fagan ("The Social Organization of Drug Use and Drug Dealing Among Urban Gangs," *Criminology* [1989]: 633–666) identified four gang types: social gangs, party gangs, serious delinquents, and organized gangs.

121. Malcomb W. Klein, Cheryl Maxson, and Lea C. Cunningham "'Crack,' Street Gangs and Violence," *Criminology* 29 (1991): 623–650; Scott H. Decker and Barrick Van Winkle, "Slinging Dope: The Role of Gangs and Gang Members in Drug Sales," *Justice Quarterly* 11 (1994): 583–604.

122. Finn-Aage Esbensen and David Huizinga "Gangs, Drugs and Delinquency," *Criminology* 31 (1993): 565–590.

123. Highlights of the 1999 National Youth Gang Survey.

124. Ibid.

125. Fagan, "The Social Organization of Drug Use and Drug Dealing Among Urban Gangs."

126. Ibid.

127. David G. Curry and Scott H. Decker, *Confronting Gangs: Crime and Community* (Los Angeles: Roxbury, 1998).

128. NAGIA. 2005 Threat Assessment, p. 3–5.

129. Highlights of the 1999 National Youth Gang Survey.

130. J. M. Hagedorn, *People and Folks* (Chicago: Lake View Press: 1989); D. Ronald Huff, *Gangs in America*.

131. W. K. Brown, "Graffiti, identity, and the delinquent gang," *International Journal of Offender Therapy and Comparative Criminology* 22 (1978): 39–45.

132. J. W.C. Johnstone, "Youth Gangs and Black Suburbs," *Pacific Sociological Review* 24 (1981):355–375.

133. Thrasher, *The Gang*; J.D. Moore and Vigil R. Garcia, "Residence and Territoriality in Chicano Gangs," *Social Problems* 31 (1983): 182–194; Ko-Lin Chin, Jeffrey Fagan, and Robert J. Kelly, "Patterns of Chinese Gang Extortion," *Justice Quarterly* 9 (1992): 625–646; Calvin Toy, "A Short History of Asian Gangs in San Francisco," *Justice Quarterly* 9 (1992): 645–665.

134. M.G. Harris, *Cholas: Latino Girls in Gangs* (New York: AMS Press, 1988); J.D. Vigil, *Bario Gangs* (Austin, TX: University of Texas Press, 1988).

135. Anne Campbell, "Girls in the Gang: A Report from New York City" (Oxford: Basil Blackwell, 1984); E. G. Dolan and S. Finney, *Youth Gangs*.

136. James F. Short, Jr., and Fred L. Strodbeck, *Group Process and Gang Delinquency* (Chicago: University of Chicago Press, 1965).

137. Curry and Decker, *Confronting Gangs.*

138. Mydans, "Not Just the Inner City."

139. Esbensen and Huizinga, "Gangs, Drugs and Delinquency"; Jeffrey Fagan, "Social Process of Delinquency and Drug Use Among Urban Gangs," in *Gangs in America*, C. Ronald Huff, ed. (Newbury Park, CA: Sage, 1990); Anne Campbell, *The Girls in the Gang*, 2nd ed. (Cambridge, MA: Basil Blackwell, 1991).

140. National Alliance of Gang Investigators Association. p. 10.

141. Ibid., p. 11.

142. Covey et al. *Juvenile Gangs.*

143. NAGIA. p. 2.

144. Ibid., pp. 2–3.

145. Highlights of the 1999 National Youth Gang Survey, Office of Juvenile Justice and Delinquency Prevention, 2000. Available at www.iir.com/nygc/.

146. Ibid., p. 49.

147. Ibid., p. 52.

148. C. Ronald Huff, "Youth Gangs and Public Policy," *Crime and Delinquency* 35 (1989): 524–537; Campbell, *Girls in the Gang.*

149. Campbell, *Girls in the Gang.*

150. *Omaha World Herald* (September 18, 1997).

151. National Alliance of Gang Investigators Association, 2005 Threat Assessment, pp. 11–12.

152. Ibid., p. 12.

153. Ibid., p. 12.

154. James D. Vigil and S.C. Yun "Vietnamese Youth Gangs in Southern California," in *Gangs in America*; Chin et al. "Patterns in Chinese Gang Extortion"; Toy, "A Short History."

155. Covey et al., *Juvenile Gangs*, p. 67; NAGIA, 2005 Threat Assessment, p. 18.

156. Ibid.

157. Chin et al. "Patterns of Chinese Gang Extortion"; Toy, "A Short History."

158. Chin et al. "Patterns of Chinese Gang Extortion."

159. FIND fn24 from NAGIA, p. 3.

160. K. Chin, "Chinese gangs and extortion," in *Gangs in America*, C. Ronald Huff, ed. (Newbury Park, CA: Sage, 1990).

161. Vigil and Yun, "Vietnamese Youth Gangs in Southern California."

162. Covey et al. *Juvenile Gangs.*

163. Ibid.

164. NAGIA, 2005 Threat Assessment, pp. 7–8.

165. Ibid.

166. Ibid.

167. Ibid.

168. Ibid.

169. Ibid., p. 9.

170. Covey et al., *Juvenile Gangs*, p. 65.

171. Mark S. Hamm, *American Skinheads* (Westport, CT: Praeger; 1994), p. 62.

172. NAGIA, 2005 Threat Assessment, p. 5.

173. Ibid.

174. Ibid.

175. I. A. Spergel, "Youth Gangs: Continuity and Change," in *Crime and Delinquency: An Annual Review of Research*, vol 12, Michael Tonry and Norval Morris, eds. (Chicago: University of Chicago Press; 1990).

176. Covey et al., *Juvenile Gangs.*

177. Hamm, *American Skinheads.*

⁂

Race, Ethnicity, Social Structure, and Crime

THE IMAGES FROM HURRICANE KATRINA

The images from New Orleans following Hurricane Katrina exposed the deep cleavages in American society. It was impossible not to notice that the overwhelming majority of people stranded in the city and seeking shelter in the Superdome or the Convention Center were African American and poor. Whites and middle-class residents of New Orleans left the city before the hurricane struck, but an estimated 100,000 people were left behind. True, some chose to stay, but most had no way to leave: no car or truck. And being left behind meant that they not only lost their homes, as did those who got out of town, but they were stuck in the degrading conditions of the Superdome and the Convention Center: little food or water, no medical care, no functioning toilets, and no safety from criminals.

Some critics accused the federal government of not caring about the African American victims of the hurricane. But was the problem race or social class? Many African Americans did flee the city beforehand. The vast majority of those who could not were people of color.

The Hurricane Katrina crisis exposed the interplay of race and class in America and the impact of social class on well-being. The majority of those at the bottom are people of color and suffer the most when disaster strikes. The simple fact of not having a car because you are poor compounds your problems. You can't flee a hurricane when you need to. Later in this chapter we will explore how not having a car makes it very difficult to find and hold a job in this country—which places a huge obstacle on your chances of escaping poverty.

Two Societies?

In 1968 the Kerner Commission warned that "our Nation is moving toward two societies, one black, one white—separate and unequal."[1] Twenty-four years later, political scientist Andrew Hacker published a book on American race relations titled *Two Nations: Black and White, Separate, Hostile, Unequal.*[2] Hacker's subtitle indicates that the Kerner Commission's dire warning has come true: instead of moving toward greater equality and opportunity, since the 1960s we have moved backward. The images from Hurricane Katrina provided vivid support for this argument.

GOALS OF THE CHAPTER

Race discrimination and social and economic inequality have a direct impact on crime and criminal justice. They account for many of the racial disparities in the criminal justice system. The goals of this chapter are to examine the broader structure of American society with respect to race and ethnicity and to analyze the relationship between social structure and crime. As we learned in Chapter 2, racial and ethnic minorities are disproportionately involved in the criminal justice system, both as crime victims and as offenders. In very general terms, there are two possible explanations for this overrepresentation. The first is discrimination in the criminal justice system. We explore the data related to this issue in Chapters 4 through 10. The second explanation involves structural inequalities in American society. This chapter examines the relationships among race and ethnicity, the social structure, and crime.

We should first define what we mean by social structure. *Social structure* is "a general term for any collective social circumstance that is unalterable and given for the individual."[3] The analysis of social structure reveals *patterned relationships between groups of people* that form the basic contours of society. The patterned relationships are related to employment, income, residence, education, religion, gender, and race and ethnicity. In combination, these factors explain a person's circumstances in life, relationships with other groups, attitudes and behavior on most issues, and prospects for the future.

This chapter explores three distinct issues related to the relationships among inequality, race and ethnicity, and crime:

1. *The extent of racial and ethnic inequality.* The first issue we examine is the nature and extent of inequality in American society with respect to the economic status of racial and ethnic minorities. What is the economic status of people of color compared with that of whites? Is the gap between whites and people of color narrowing or growing?

2. *Inequality and crime.* The second issue is the relationship between inequality and crime. In what ways is inequality associated with crime? To what extent do the leading theories of crime help explain the relationship between inequality and crime?

3. *The impact of the civil rights movement.* The third issue is the impact of efforts designed to reduce inequality. Have civil rights laws effectively eliminated discrimination in employment, housing, and other areas of American life? If Hacker is right that the United States is "two nations: separate, hostile, [and]

unequal," how do we explain the failure of the national effort to eliminate discrimination? At the same time, have various economic programs designed to increase economic opportunity—from the liberal War on Poverty in the 1960s to conservative Reaganomics in the 1980s to the neoliberal policies of President Bill Clinton in the 1990s—achieved their goals and reduced poverty? If not, how do we explain the persistence of economic inequality?

ECONOMIC INEQUALITY

The first important issue is the nature and extent of inequality in the United States. The data indicate three important patterns: (1) a large gap between rich and poor, without regard to race or ethnicity; (2) a large economic gap between white Americans and racial minorities; and (3) the growth of the very poor—a group some analysts call an underclass—in the past 30 years. The standard measures of economic inequality are income, wealth, unemployment, and poverty status. All of these measures indicate deep and persistent inequality in society generally and with respect to race and ethnicity.

Income

Median family income is a standard measure of economic status. U.S. Census Bureau data reveal wide gaps between racial and ethnic groups. In 2004, the median household income in the United States was $44,389. But it was $30,134 for African American families and $34,241 for Hispanic families (Figure 3.1). (Keep in mind that the Census reports income data in different ways, including by families and by households, resulting in different and often confusing figures).[4] African Americans made significant progress relative to whites in the 1950s and 1960s but then stagnated in the 1970s. The National Research Council concluded, "Since the early 1970s, the economic status of blacks relative to whites has, on average, stagnated or deteriorated."[5]

The median household income figures mask significant differences *within* racial and ethnic groups. One of the most significant developments over the past 40 years has been the growth of an African American middle class.[6] A similar class difference exists within the Hispanic community. These cleavages are the result of two factors. First, the civil rights movement opened the door to employment for racial and ethnic minorities in many job categories where they previously had been excluded: white-collar, service, and professional-level jobs. At the same time, the changing structure of the American economy has been characterized by tremendous growth in the white-collar sector. An increasing number of African Americans and Hispanics have been able to take advantage of these new opportunities; however, the percentage of African Americans among the very poor has also increased. Thus, among racial and ethnic minorities there is a greater gap between the middle class and the poorest than at any other time in our history.

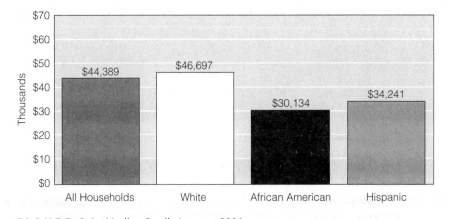

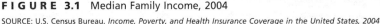

FIGURE 3.1   Median Family Income, 2004

SOURCE: U.S. Census Bureau, *Income, Poverty, and Health Insurance Coverage in the United States, 2004* (Washington, DC: Department of Commerce, 2005), Table 1.

Wealth

The data on household wealth reveal an even larger gap between whites and minorities. The distinction between income and wealth is important. *Income* measures how much a person or family earns in any given period. *Wealth,* however, includes all accumulated assets: home, cars, savings, stocks, and so forth. The family that owns a house, for example, has far more wealth than the family that rents. The 2000 median net worth of White households was $79,400, compared with only $7,500 for African Americans and $9,750 for Hispanic households (Figure 3.2).[7] In short, whites have 10 times the net worth of African Americans and 8 times the net worth of Hispanics. These huge gaps have major implications, both direct and indirect, for crime and criminal justice.

The reasons for the huge gap in net worth are easy to understand. Middle-class people are able to save each month; the poor are not. These savings are used to buy a house, stocks, or other investments. The family's net wealth increases as the value of their home increases. Affluent whites, moreover, usually buy houses in neighborhoods where property values are rising rapidly. Lower-middle-class families, regardless of race, are often able to buy homes only in neighborhoods where property values are stagnant. As a result, their wealth does not increase very much. The poor, of course, are not able to save or invest anything, and they continually fall behind everyone else in terms of wealth.

Wealth plays an important role in perpetuating inequality. It cushions a family against temporary hard times, such as loss of a job. The lower-middle-class person who is laid off, even temporarily, may lose his or her home; as a result, the family slides down the economic scale. Wealth is also transferred to the next generation. Families with savings can afford to send their children to private colleges and graduate or professional schools. They can also help their children buy their first home by giving or loaning them all or part of the down payment.

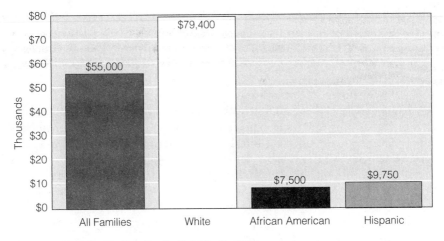

FIGURE 3.2 Median Family Net Worth, 2000

SOURCE: U.S. Census Bureau, *Net Worth and Asset Ownership of Households: 1998 and 2000* (Washington, DC: Department of Commerce, 2003), Figure 6.

Finally, when they die, their children inherit their estate in the form of cash, stock, or property. Poor and even many lower-middle-class families are not able to help their children in any of these ways. Wealth, in these respects, forms an important part of the social capital (see discussion later in the chapter) that shapes a person's advantages, or lack of advantages, in life.

Unemployment

In mid-2005 the official unemployment rate for the United States was 5.0 percent, higher than the 4.0 rate in mid-2000 but still lower than the rates in the mid-1990s and much better than 1985 when it reached a high point of 7.2 percent.[8] It is worth noting that the crime rate in the late 1990s was the lowest it had been since the 1960s. There have always been significant differences in the unemployment rates for different racial and ethnic groups. The unemployment rate for whites in mid-2005 was 4.2 percent, compared with 9.6 percent for African Americans, 5.8 percent for Hispanics, and 3.6 percent for Asians. The African American unemployment rate has been consistently twice as high as or higher than the white rate. In 1985, for example, the African American unemployment rate was 15.1 percent, compared with 6.2 percent for whites and 10.5 percent for Hispanics.[9] Thus, although African Americans benefit from economic good times, they have not been able to overcome their relative disadvantage with respect to the unemployment rate.

The official data on unemployment tell only part of the story, however. First, there are serious problems with the official unemployment rate, just as there are problems with the official crime rate. The official unemployment rate counts only those people who are actively seeking employment. It does not count three important groups: (1) discouraged workers who have given up and are not looking for work; (2) part-time employees who want full-time jobs but cannot find them; and (3) workers in the "underground economy," who are paid in cash to avoid paying taxes and Social Security withholding. Many economists believe that racial minorities are disproportionately represented among those not counted by the official unemployment rate.[10]

Equally important, the official unemployment rate is much higher for teenagers than for adults. The unemployment rate for African Americans between the ages of 16 and 19 was 31.7 percent in 2004, compared with 15.0 percent for white teenagers and 20.4 percent for Hispanic teenagers. The African American teenage unemployment rate had fallen dramatically since 1985, when it was a staggering 40.2 percent, but in 2004 it was still twice the white rate.[11] The unemployment rates for all three groups increased between 2000 and 2004, but the relative gaps between the three groups remained the same.

The unemployment rate data reveal important differences within the Hispanic community related to national origins. The unemployment rate for Hispanics of Mexican and Puerto Rican origin is consistently higher than for those of Cuban origin.[12]

Later in this chapter we discuss the major theories of crime as they relate to race and ethnicity. For virtually every theory, the teenage unemployment rate is particularly important in terms of the likelihood of participation in crime. The peak years of criminal activity for Index crimes are for people between the ages of 14 and 24. Official arrest data indicate that involvement in crime peaks at age 18 for violent crimes and at age 16 for property crimes. The lack of meaningful job opportunities for teenagers is an important factor in the high rates of crime. The persistently higher rates of unemployment for African American and Hispanic teenagers help explain their higher rates of criminal activity compared with those of whites.

Poverty Status

Yet another measure of economic status is the percentage of families in poverty. The federal government first developed an official definition of poverty in 1964, designed to reflect the minimum amount of income needed for an adequate standard of living. In 2005 the official poverty line was $19,350 for a family of four.[12] In 2003, 12.5 percent of all Americans were below the poverty line. The percentage has fluctuated over time, from 22.2 percent in 1960 to 11.4 percent in 1978. In 2003, 10.5 percent of all non–Hispanic whites were below the poverty line, compared with 24.4 percent of African Americans and 22.5 percent of Hispanics. Even worse, economists have estimated that the official government poverty line is actually only half of what people really need to live adequately. Thus, a family of four really needs an income of $38,700 a year.[13]

The most disturbing aspect of the poverty figures is the percentage of children living below the poverty line. About 38 percent of all children in the United States—27 million total—live in families in poverty. The impact of poverty is especially strong on racial and ethnic minority groups. An estimated 60 percent of African American and 62 percent of Hispanic children live in low-income families.[14] Because childhood low-income status is associated with so many other social problems—inadequate nutrition, single-parent households, low educational achievement, high risk of crime victimization, and high rate of involvement in crime—the data suggest a grim future for a very large percentage of racial and ethnic minority children.

Insurance Coverage

Another important measure of well-being is insurance coverage. An estimated 45 million Americans had no health insurance in 2003. That included 14.6 percent of whites, 19.6 percent of African Americans, and 32.7 percent of Hispanics.[15]

Lack of health insurance makes a big difference. It means you cannot take care of routine health problems, which in turn lead to major health problems that limit your ability to hold a job. Prenatal health care is possibly even more important. Lack of adequate care can result in developmental problems that affect how a child performs in school and, as a result, his or her life chances. Perhaps even more important, lack of health care creates insecurity and a more general alienation from society. People who think society does not care about them are less likely to care about society and the community they live in. Later in this chapter we will examine how these factors relate to different criminological theories.

Social Capital and Cultural Capital

The perpetuation of poverty and inequality from one generation to another is heavily determined by access to capital on the part of an individual or group. The theorist Pierre Bourdieu identifies three different types of capital. Economic capital, obviously, refers to financial resources. Social capital refers to a person's network of friends, relationships, and other contacts. Cultural capital includes education, knowledge, or skills that give a person an advantage.[16] Social and cultural capital have huge implications for individuals and their likelihood of becoming criminals. A family member who owns a business and can offer you a job is a form of social capital. Having a job and a chance to move up in the business means you are much more likely to establish a law-abiding lifestyle. Knowing how to repair cars or air conditioning units is a skill—a form of cultural capital—that is also likely to lead to employment. People often learn these skills from their father or uncle and so a stable family often contributes directly to the development of cultural capital. These examples illustrate how inequality is perpetuated as social and cultural capital are transmitted from one generation to the next.[17]

Sociologists and psychologists generally agree that the family is the primary unit for transmitting values to children. These values include, for example, self-respect, self-reliance, hard work, and respect for other people. If a family is dysfunctional, these values are not effectively transmitted to the children. The condition of poverty is generally associated with single-parent families, which are less able to transmit positive values.

Social capital is defined by the World Bank as "the institutions, relationships, and norms that shape the quality or quantity of a society's social interactions."[18]

The sources of social capital include families, communities, and organizations. With respect to employment, one important form of social capital is having family, friends, or neighbors who are able to offer jobs (for example, in a small family business) or personal referral to someone who is able to offer a job. This process is often referred to as *networking* and is generally recognized as extremely important in terms of finding jobs and advancing careers. In extremely poor neighborhoods, however, there are few people with jobs to offer or with family or friends who can make good job references. Criminologist Elliot Currie illustrated the point by citing a comparative study of juvenile delinquents who graduated from the Lyman School in Massachusetts and the Wiltwyck School in New York in the 1950s. The predominantly white Lyman graduates often had personal connections who helped them find good employment. One graduate explained: "I fooled around a lot when I was a kid.... But then I got an uncle on the [police] force. When I was twenty he got me my first job as a traffic man."[19] The predominantly African American and Hispanic graduates of Wiltwyck did not have similar kinds of personal resources. As a result, they recidivated into criminal activity at a much higher rate. In short, the conditions of extreme poverty diminish the human and social capital that young people possess and, as a consequence, contribute to higher rates of criminal activity.

The noted sociologist Alejandro Portes points out, however, that social capital can have a downside. Different communities in a large metropolitan area may each be well organized but still be in conflict and working at cross-purposes. For example, several may be demanding improvements in the streets and parks in *their* neighborhoods. All may be demanding more police protection at the same time, when police resources are already stretched thin. Finally, effective networks of groups in neighborhoods may direct their activity to criminal enterprises: drug trafficking, gambling, and so on. All of these aspects of social capital can hinder positive social and economic development.[20]

The World Bank argues that government institutions, "the public sector," are an important part of the network of social capital. Assume for the moment that a neighborhood has stable families and a strong sense of community. Responsive government institutions can help translate their aspirations and efforts into effective services: good schools, attractive parks for recreation, a public transportation system that allows people to find and hold jobs, and so on. Obviously, the police and the criminal justice system are an important element of this process. If the police effectively control crime and disorder, community members will feel better about their neighborhood and feel empowered to work for its improvement. The community policing movement of the past 20 years has been built on the idea that policing can be made more effective through partnerships with community organizations.

If, however, neighborhood residents do not trust the police, they are less likely to cooperate with them in solving crime and other problems. Residents will also feel worse about their neighborhood. For this reason, the quality of police–community relations is extremely important. Chapter 4 discusses in detail the state of police–community relations and the effectiveness of programs to improve them.

Progress, Stagnation, or Regression? The Debate over the Status of African Americans

In a comprehensive survey of American race relations, the National Research Council concluded, "The status of black Americans today can be characterized as a glass that is half full." Despite considerable progress in race relations since the 1960s, there remain "persisting disparities between black and white Americans." Although civil rights laws and economic change have allowed "a substantial fraction of blacks to enter the mainstream of American life," the majority of African Americans have not achieved social or economic equality with whites.[21] Hispanics, Native Americans, and other racial and ethnic minorities experience similar inequalities in social and economic status.

Not everyone agrees with this pessimistic assessment, however. In *America in Black and White: One Nation, Indivisible*, Stephan and Abigail Thernstrom argue that African Americans have made remarkable progress since the 1940s, economically, socially, and politically. "The signs of progress are all around us," they observe, "although we now take that progress for granted."[22] Using Gunnar Myrdal's classic study of American race relations, *An American Dilemma* (1944), as their baseline, they find that the percentage of African American families in poverty fell from 87 percent in 1940 to 21.9 percent in 2000. The number of African Americans enrolled in college increased 30-fold in the same period, increasing from 45,000 students in 1940 to 1.4 million in the late 1990s.

Whereas 60 percent of employed African American women worked as domestics in 1940, today more than half are in white-collar jobs. The number of African American elected officials rose from a national total of only 103 in 1960 to 8,896 by 1999. African Americans serve as mayors and police chiefs in major cities all across the country. Contrary to Andrew Hacker's pessimistic assessment that we are "two nations," the Thernstroms argue that we are today less separate; less unequal; and, in their view, less hostile than was the case in 1940.[23]

Where does the truth lie? Is the United States progressing, stagnating, or regressing in terms of social and economic inequality? The answer is that there is a degree of truth in all three interpretations. It depends on which segment of the population we are talking about. We can make sense of this complex subject by taking the approach we suggested in Chapter 1: disaggregating it into distinct components and contexts.

First, different time frames lead to different interpretations. The Thernstroms' optimistic interpretation uses 1940 as a baseline. Few can question their data on racial progress since that time. After all, 1940 was still a time of institutionalized racial segregation in the South and blatant discrimination in other parts of the country. But even the Thernstroms concede that progress has stagnated in the past 30 years. Using 1973 as a baseline leads to a far more pessimistic interpretation.

Second, the aggregate status of African Americans encompasses two divergent trends: the generally rising status of a new middle class and the deteriorating status of the very poor.[24] The same is true for other people of color. Some Hispanics are also doing very well and are integrating into the mainstream of American life. Others are trapped at the bottom of society, and in many respects

TABLE 3.1 Percentage of Aggregate Wealth Held by the Richest and the Poorest Households

	Poorest 20%	Richest 20%	Richest 5%
1998	3.6	49.2	21.4
1988	3.8	46.3	18.3
1978	4.3	43.7	16.2
1968	4.2	42.8	16.6

SOURCE: U.S. Census Bureau, *Current Population Survey, March 1968–1999* (Washington, DC: U.S. Government Printing Office, 2000), Table 2.

they are doing much worse than before. Asian Americans are also divided into those who are doing well and those who are not.

The 2000 census figures reveal that the gap between the richest and poorest Americans actually grew during the prosperous 1990s (the Clinton years), just as it did during the 1980s (the Reagan years). Table 3.1 indicates the share of all national income earned by the richest 5 percent of the population, the richest 20 percent, and the poorest 20 percent. The gap was narrowest in the 1970s but has steadily increased ever since. A disproportionate percentage of the very poor are African American and Hispanic. Their economic status has been getting worse over the last 25 years.[25]

This book is concerned with crime and criminal justice. From that perspective, the persistence of a very poor group at the bottom of society assumes special importance. Predatory crime has always been concentrated among the very poor. In 2000 the violent crime rate was more than twice as high for the poorest Americans as for the wealthiest: 60.3 per 1,000 for people with incomes of $7,500 or less and 22.3 per 1,000 for those with incomes of $75,000 or more.[26] The reasons for this are explained later in this chapter in the discussion of the different theories of crime.

The real point of disagreement between those who take an optimistic view, such as the Thernstroms, and those who take a more pessimistic view is the *cause* of the stagnation over the past 30 years. Many observers blame the changes in the economy, including the disappearance of industrial-level jobs, particularly from the inner city. The Thernstroms blame affirmative action and racial preferences in particular. They argue that the greatest gains in racial equality were made during the years when the civil rights movement emphasized color-blind policies and that stagnation set in during the 1970s when civil rights leaders emphasized racial preferences.

We would reply by arguing that the civil rights movement eliminated the most blatant forms of discrimination (for example, disenfranchisement of African Americans in the South and law schools not admitting African Americans). It is not surprising that the elimination of these barriers would lead to some rapid progress, primarily by those who were equipped to take advantage of the new opportunities. The growth of political and civil rights, however, did not necessarily address *economic* inequality, particularly for those not yet equipped to take advantage of expanding opportunities. The Thernstroms have a point that affirmative action programs have not really helped those at the very bottom. But they are also wrong in arguing that affirmative action is the *cause* of the plight of the very poor.

The Debate over the Underclass

Those observers who take the most pessimistic view often use the term *underclass* to describe the very poor who are concentrated in the inner cities.[27] The question of the existence of an underclass is more than a matter of semantics. It makes a great deal of difference whether the term is merely another euphemism for poor people (that is, "the poor," "the deprived," "the impoverished," "the disadvantaged," "the at-risk," and so on), which implies that the economic status of people at the bottom has not changed in any fundamental way, or whether it describes the emergence of a new kind of poverty in America.[28]

From our perspective, the crucial point about the development of an underclass is that the conditions affecting the very poor have three important effects. First, they tend to perpetuate poverty. Second, they create conditions, such as family breakdown, that lead to higher involvement in crime. Third, members of the underclass lack and are unable to develop the social capital—education, skills, and networks—that are likely to help individuals rise out of severe poverty (see the discussion of social capital later).

Evidence suggests that the nature of urban poverty has changed in significant ways. First, the industrial sector of the economy has eroded, eliminating the entry-level jobs that were historically available to the poor. Second, conditions in the underclass generate circumstances and behavior that perpetuate poverty.[29] Gary Orfield and Carole Ashkinaze's study of economic conditions in Atlanta during the 1980s found growing inequality amid overall growth and prosperity. The authors found that although most people in the Atlanta metropolitan area fared better economically, "the dream of equal opportunity is fading fast for many young blacks in metropolitan Atlanta." For the African American poor in the inner city, "many of the basic elements of the American dream—a good job, a decent income, a house, college education for the kids—are less accessible … than was the case in the 1970s."[30] Most of the economic growth occurred in the largely white suburbs, whereas opportunities declined in the predominantly African American inner city. At the same time, most of the expanding opportunities occurred in the service sector of the economy: either in white-collar professional-level jobs or in minimum-wage service jobs (for example, fast food). The poor cannot realistically compete for the professional-level jobs, and many of the service-sector jobs do not pay enough to support a family. A minimum-wage job paying \$5.15 per hour (the federally mandated level in 2005) yields an annual income of \$10,300 (\$5.15 × 40 hours/week × 50 weeks). This is substantially less than the official poverty line of \$19,350 for a family of four.

Patterns of residential segregation contribute to the development of the urban underclass. Job growth over the past 20 years has been strongest in suburban areas outside the central cities. Inner-city residents, regardless of color, find it extremely difficult both to learn about job opportunities and to travel to and from work. Public transportation systems are either weak or nonexistent in most cities, particularly with respect to traveling to suburban areas. A private car is almost a necessity for traveling to work. Yet one of the basic facts of poverty is the lack of sufficient money to buy a reliable car. Concentration of the very poor and their isolation from the rest of society erode the social networks that are extremely important for finding employment.

Studies of the job-seeking process have found that whites are more likely to be referred to jobs by friends or family who have some information about a job or connection with an employer. Racial and ethnic minorities are less likely to have these kinds of contacts, which are an important element of social capital. The problem is especially acute for members of the underclass, who are likely to have very few personal contacts that lead to good jobs.[31]

The pessimistic analysis of the changes in Atlanta in *The Closing Door* is still compatible with the more optimistic aspects of the Thernstroms' analysis. Atlanta has a large and growing African American professional and middle class. These individuals and families live in the suburbs, as do their white counterparts. Their very real progress, however, coexists in the Atlanta metropolitan area with the lack of progress by very poor African Americans trapped in the inner city. Crutchfield explains the economic situation in the inner city in terms of a *dual labor market*. What economists call the *primary* market consists of good, well-paying jobs with fringe benefits (especially health care coverage) and good prospects for the future. The *secondary* market consists of low-paying jobs with limited fringe benefits and uncertain prospects for the future. He argues that the secondary market "has an effect on individual propensity to engage in crime." Individuals are less "bonded" to their work (and, by extension, to society as a whole) and to the idea that hard work will lead to a brighter future. Additionally, the inner city involves concentrations of people in the secondary market, who then "spend time with each other, socialize with one another, and at times even victimize each other."[32]

The pattern of economic change that affected Atlanta, a growing city, had even more negative effects on declining industrial cities such as New York and Chicago. Economic expansion there was concentrated in the suburban areas, and the inner cities declined significantly. Such older industrial cities did not experience the same rate of growth in the suburbs, and the decline in industrial jobs was even more severe. The relationship of the underclass to crime becomes clearer when we look at it from the standpoint of neighborhood community social structure.

COMMUNITY SOCIAL STRUCTURE

The social structure of communities has an important impact on crime. *Community* in this respect refers to both large metropolitan communities and local neighborhoods. The social structure of a community involves the spacial distribution of the population, the composition of local neighborhoods, and patterns of interaction between and within neighborhoods.

Residential Segregation

American metropolitan communities are characterized by strong patterns of residential segregation. As already indicated, this has an impact on patterns of criminal activity.

Residential segregation itself is nothing new. Historically, American cities have always been segregated by race, ethnicity, and income. New arrivals to the city—either immigrants from other countries or migrants from rural areas—settled in the central city, with older immigrant groups and the middle class moving to neighborhoods farther out or to suburban communities. Racial and ethnic segregation in housing has been the result of several factors: the historic practice of de jure segregation, covert discrimination, and group choice. In the South and some Northern communities, local ordinances prohibited African Americans from living in white neighborhoods.

Particularly in the North, many property owners adopted restrictive covenants that prohibited the sale of property to African Americans or Jews. Real estate agents maintained segregation by steering minority buyers away from white neighborhoods. Banks and savings and loan companies refused to offer mortgages in poor and minority neighborhoods—a practice known as "redlining." Finally, segregation has been maintained by personal choice. People often prefer to live among members of their own group. Thus, European immigrants tended to form distinct ethnic neighborhoods, many of which still exist (for example, Little Italy and Chinatown).

Despite federal and state laws outlawing housing discrimination, residential segregation persists today. Social scientists have devised an index of residential segregation that measures the proportion of neighborhoods in any city that are racially homogeneous. The data indicate that in the 1980s, from 70 to 90 percent of the people in the major cities lived in racially homogeneous neighborhoods.

The residential segregation indices for both Detroit and Chicago in 1980 were 88, meaning that 88 percent of all people lived in either all-white or all–African American neighborhoods. In practical terms, this means that for a white person living in Detroit, an estimated 93 percent of the "potential" contacts with other people would involve other whites. For African Americans, 80 percent of the "potential" contacts would involve other African Americans. In New York City and Los Angeles, the residential segregation indices were 78 and 79, respectively.[33]

Residential Segregation and Crime   Residential segregation has a direct impact on crime. Most important, it concentrates high-rate offenders in one area, which has two significant consequences. First, the law-abiding residents of those areas suffer high rates of robbery, burglary, and other predatory crimes. The National Crime Victimization Survey consistently finds that racial and ethnic minorities and poor people are victimized more than white and middle-class people. The violent crime rate for the very poor (60.3 per 1,000) is more than twice that of the richest Americans (22.3 per 1,000).[34]

Second, the concentration of high-rate offenders in one area has an important effect on the propensity of individuals to engage in criminal activity. Several of the theories of crime discussed later place this phenomenon in a broader framework. Teenagers in those areas are subject to disproportionate contact with people who are already involved in criminal activity. These teenagers have comparatively less contact with law-abiding peers. As Crutchfield points out, unemployed or marginally employed people in the secondary labor market "spend more time with each other," and as a result, they are more likely to influence each other in the direction of a greater propensity to commit crime.[35]

Even in stable families, the sheer weight of this peer influence overwhelms positive parental influence. In the worst of situations, teenagers are coerced into joining crime-involved gangs. Thus, many individuals are socialized into crime when this would not be the case if they lived in a more diverse neighborhood with lower crime. In one of the great ironies of recent history, some of the great gains of the civil rights movement have hurt the poorest racial minority communities. Since the 1960s, the civil rights movement has opened up employment opportunities in business and the professions, creating a greatly expanded African American middle class. At the same time, the end of blatant residential segregation has created housing opportunities for families in the new African American middle class. Following the example of their white counterparts, these families move out of low-income, inner-city neighborhoods and into the suburbs.

The result is that the old neighborhoods abandoned by the African American middle class are stripped of important stabilizing elements—what Wilson refers to as a "social buffer."[36] The neighborhood loses its middle-class role models, who help socialize other children into middle-class values, and an important part of its natural leadership, the people who are active in neighborhood associations and local school issues. Skogan reports that educated, middle-class, home-owning residents are more likely to be involved in neighborhood organizations than are less educated, poorer, renting residents.[37] And, as we have already noted, the middle class is composed of the people who can provide the social networks that lead to good jobs.

All of these factors contribute directly to neighborhood deterioration and indirectly to crime. As more of the people with better incomes move out, the overall economic level of the neighborhood declines. Houses often go from owner-occupied to rental property. As the area loses purchasing power, neighborhood stores lose business and close. Wilson and Kelling, two of the early theorists of community policing, argue that the physical deterioration of a neighborhood (abandoned buildings and cars, unrepaired houses, and so forth) is a sign that people do not care and, consequently, is an "invitation" to criminal behavior.[38] As the composition of the neighborhood changes, meanwhile, an increasing number of crime-involved people move in, changing the context of peer pressure in the neighborhood.

Skogan describes the impact of fear of crime on neighborhood deterioration as a six-stage process. It begins with withdrawal. People choose to have less contact with other neighborhood residents; the ultimate form of withdrawal is to move away. This leads to a reduction in informal control over behavior by residents: people no longer monitor and report on the behavior of, say, their neighbors' children. Then, organizational life declines: fewer residents are active in community groups. These factors lead to an increase in delinquency and disorder. As the neighborhood becomes poorer, commercial decline sets in. Local shops close and buildings are abandoned. The final stage of the process is collapse. At this point, according to Skogan, "there is virtually no 'community' remaining."[39] Community policing, it should be noted, is designed to stop this process of deterioration. First, many community policing efforts address small signs of disorder that cause people to withdraw. Second, police-initiated partnerships and block meetings are designed to strengthen networks among residents and help to give them a feeling of empowerment or collective efficacy in dealing with neighborhood problems.[40]

The Impact of Crime and Drugs   Crime has a devastating impact on neighborhoods—an impact that is intensified in very poor neighborhoods. First, it results in direct economic loss and physical harm to the crime victims. Second, the resulting high fear of crime damages the quality of life for everyone in the area. Third, persistent high rates of crime cause employed and law-abiding people to move out of the neighborhood, thereby intensifying the concentration of the unemployed and high-rate offenders. Fourth, crime damages local businesses, in the form of both direct losses and inability to obtain insurance. Eventually, many of these businesses move or close, with the result that the immediate neighborhood loses jobs. Those that stay frequently charge higher prices to make up for their losses.

The drug problem has hit poor neighborhoods with devastating effect, particularly with the advent of crack cocaine in the mid-1980s. Drug trafficking fostered the growth of gangs and led to an increase in gang-related violence, including drive-by shootings that sometimes kill innocent people. Moreover, crack cocaine appears to be more damaging to family life than other drugs are. Mothers addicted to crack seem more likely to lose their sense of parental responsibility. The phenomenon of pregnant women becoming addicted to crack has resulted in a serious problem of crack-addicted babies.[41]

In some drug-ridden neighborhoods, the drug trade is the central feature of neighborhood life. Entire blocks have become "drug bazaars" with open drug sales. The drug trade is often a highly organized and complex activity, with people watching for the police, negotiating the sale, obtaining the drugs, and holding the main supply. The buyers are frequently outsiders, and the drug market represents what economists call *economic specialization*, with one part of society providing services to the rest of society.[42] Police departments have experimented with drug enforcement crackdowns (short-term periods of intensive arrest activity), but there is no evidence that this strategy has any long-term effect on reducing the drug trade.[43]

When drug and gang activity begins to dominate a neighborhood, it becomes virtually impossible for law-abiding residents to shield themselves and their children from illegal activity. The peer pressure on juveniles to join gangs becomes extremely intense. Often, kids join gangs for their own protection.

Because of drive-by shootings and other gang-related violence, the streets are even less safe than before. This is the stage that Skogan describes as neighborhood "collapse."[44]

THEORETICAL PERSPECTIVES ON INEQUALITY
AND CRIME

The second important issue addressed in this chapter is the relationship between inequality and crime. We have established that significant economic inequality prevails between the white majority and racial and ethnic minorities. To what extent does this inequality contribute to the racial and ethnic disparities in crime and criminal justice? To help answer this question, we turn to the major theories of criminal behavior. In different ways, each one posits a relationship between inequality and crime that helps explain the disparities within crime and criminal justice.

Social Strain Theory

Robert Merton's social strain theory holds that each society has a dominant set of values and goals along with acceptable means of achieving them. Not everyone is able to realize these goals, however. The gap between approved goals and the means people have to achieve them creates what Merton terms *social strain.*[45]

As Steven F. Messner and Richard Rosenfeld argue in *Crime and the American Dream,* the dominant goals and values in American society emphasize success through individual achievement.[46] Success is primarily measured in terms of material goods, social status, and recognition for personal expression (for example, through art or athletics). The indicators of material success include a person's job, income, place of residence, clothing, cars, and other consumer goods.

The accepted means of achieving these goals are also highly individualistic, emphasizing hard work, self-control, persistence, and education. The American work ethic holds that anyone can succeed if only he or she will work hard enough and keep trying long enough. Failure is regarded as a personal, not a social, failure. Yet, as we have seen, many people in America do not enjoy success in these terms: unemployment rates remain high, and millions of people are living in poverty. Minorities are the victims of racial and ethnic discrimination.

Merton's theory of social strain holds that people respond to the gap between society's values and their own circumstances in several different ways: rebellion, retreatism, and innovation. Some of these involve criminal activity.

Rebellion involves a rejection of society's goals and the established means of achieving them, along with an attempt to create a new society based on different values and goals. This stage includes revolutionary political activity, which in some instances might be politically related criminal activity such as terrorism.

Retreatism entails a rejection of both the goals and the accepted means of achieving them. A person may retreat, for example, into drug abuse, alcoholism, vagrancy, or a countercultural lifestyle. Retreatism helps explain the high rates of drug and alcohol abuse in America. Many forms of drug abuse involve criminal behavior: the buying and selling of drugs, robbery or burglary as a means of obtaining money to purchase drugs, or involvement in a drug trafficking network that includes violent crime directed against rival drug dealers.

There is considerable debate among criminologists over the relationship between drugs and crime.[47] There is no clear evidence that drug abuse is a direct cause of crime. Studies of crime and drugs have found mixed patterns: some individuals began their criminal activity before they started using drugs, whereas for others, drug use preceded involvement in crime. Moreover, some individuals "specialize" and either use (and/or sell) drugs but engage in no other criminal activity, or they commit crimes but do not use illegal drugs.[48]

Innovation involves an acceptance of society's goals but a rejection of the accepted means of attaining them—that is, some forms of innovation can be negative rather than positive. Crime is one mode of innovation. The person who embezzles money seeks material success but chooses an illegitimate (criminal) means of achieving it. Gang formation and drug trafficking are manifestations of entrepreneurship and neighborhood networking. Unfortunately, they lead to lawbreaking and often have destructive side effects (for example, gang-related shootings) rather than law obedience. These are examples of what Portes and Landolt refer to as the "downside" of social capital.[49] The person who steals to obtain money or things is seeking the external evidence of material success through illegal means.

Applying the Theory Social strain theory helps explain the high rates of delinquency and criminal behavior among racial and ethnic minorities in the United States. Criminal activity will be higher among those groups that are denied the opportunity to fulfill the American dream of individual achievement. The theory also explains far higher rates of retreatist (for example, drug abuse) and innovative (for example, criminal activity) responses. The high levels of economic inequality experienced by minorities, together with continuing discrimination based on race and ethnicity, mean that minorities are far less likely to be able to achieve approved social goals through conventional means.

Differential Association Theory

Edwin Sutherland's theory of differential association holds that criminal behavior is learned behavior. The more contact a person has with people who are already involved in crime, the more likely that person is to engage in criminal activity.[50]

Applying the Theory Given the structure of American communities, differential association theory has direct relevance to the disproportionate involvement of racial and ethnic minorities in the criminal justice system. Because of residential segregation based on income and race, a person who is poor, a racial or ethnic minority, or both is more likely to have personal contact with people who are already involved in crime. The concentration of people involved in crime in underclass neighborhoods produces enormous peer pressure to become involved in crime. In neighborhoods where gangs are prevalent, young people often experience tremendous pressure to join a gang simply as a means of personal protection. In schools where drug use is prevalent, juveniles will have more contact with drug users and are more likely to be socialized into drug use themselves. As noted earlier, Crutchfield argues that the secondary labor market brings together high concentrations of people with a weak attachment to their work and the future, who then socialize with each other and influence each other's propensity to commit crime.[51] Most parents have a basic understanding of differential association theory: they warn their children to avoid the "bad" kids in the neighborhood and encourage them to associate with the "good" kids.

Social Disorganization Theory

Followers of the Chicago school of urban sociology developed the social disorganization theory of crime.[52] Focusing on poor inner-city neighborhoods, this theory holds that the conditions of poverty undermine the institutions that socialize people into conventional, law-abiding ways of life. As a result, the values and behavior leading to delinquency and crime are passed on from one generation to another. The Chicago sociologists found that recent immigrants tended to have lower rates of criminality than the first American-born generation.

They argued that immigrants were able to preserve old-world family structures that promoted stability and conventional behavior. These older values broke down in the new urban environment, however, which led to higher rates of criminality among the next generation. The Chicago sociologists noted the spatial organization of the larger metropolitan areas, with higher rates of criminal behavior in the poorer inner-city neighborhoods and lower rates in areas farther out.

The conditions of poverty contribute to social disorganization and criminality in several ways. Poverty and unemployment undermine the family, the primary unit of socialization, which leads to high rates of single-parent families. Lack of parental supervision and positive role models contributes to crime and delinquency. The concentration of the poor in certain neighborhoods means that individuals are subject to strong peer group influence tending toward nonconforming behavior. Poverty is also associated with inadequate prenatal care and malnutrition, which contribute to developmental and health problems that, in turn, lead to poor performance in schools.

Applying the Theory   Social disorganization theory helps explain the high rates of crime and delinquency among racial and ethnic minorities. As our discussion of inequality suggests, minorities experience high rates of poverty and are geographically concentrated in areas with high rates of social disorganization.

Social disorganization theory is consistent with other theories of crime. It is consistent with social strain theory, in that persons who are subject to conditions of social disorganization are far less likely to be able to achieve the dominant goals of society through conventional means and, therefore, are more likely to turn to crime. It is consistent with differential association theory, in that neighborhoods with high levels of social disorganization will subject individuals, particularly young men, to strong influences tending toward delinquency and crime.

Culture Conflict Theory

Culture conflict theory holds that crime will be more likely to flourish in heterogeneous societies where there is a lack of consensus over society's values.[53] Human behavior is shaped by norms that are instilled through socialization and embodied in the criminal law. In any society, the majority not only defines social norms but controls the making and the administration of the criminal law. In some instances, certain groups do not accept the dominant social values. They may reject them on religious or cultural grounds or feel alienated from the majority because of discrimination or economic inequality. Conflict over social norms and the role of the criminal law leads to certain types of lawbreaking.

One example of religiously based culture conflict involves peyote, a cactus that has mild hallucinogenic effects when smoked and that some Native American religions use as part of their traditional religious exercises.[54] Today, many observers see national politics revolving around a "culture war" involving such issues as abortion, homosexuality, and religion in the public schools.[55] Some groups believe that abortion is murder and should be criminalized; others argue that it is a medical procedure that should be governed by the individual's private choice.

Applying the Theory   Culture conflict theory helps explain some of the differential rates of involvement in crime in society, which is extremely heterogeneous, characterized by many different races, ethnic groups, religions, and cultural lifestyles. The theory encompasses the history of racial conflict—from the time of slavery, through the Civil War, to the modern civil rights movement—as one of the major themes in U.S. history. There is also a long history of ethnic and religious conflict. Americans of white, Protestant, and English background, for instance, exhibited strong prejudice against immigrants from Ireland and southern and eastern Europe, particularly Catholics and Jews.[56]

An excellent example of cultural conflict in American history is the long struggle over the consumption of alcohol that culminated in national Prohibition (1920–1933). The fight over alcohol was a bitter issue for nearly 100 years before Prohibition. To a great extent, the struggle was rooted in ethnic and religious differences. Protestant Americans tended to take a very moralistic attitude toward alcohol, viewing abstinence as a sign of self-control and a means of rising to middle-class status. For many Catholic immigrant groups, particularly Irish and German, alcohol consumption was an accepted part of their cultural lifestyle. The long crusade to control alcohol use represented an attempt by middle-class Protestants to impose their lifestyle on working-class Catholics.[57]

Conflict Theory

Conflict theory holds that the administration of criminal justice reflects the unequal distribution of power in society.[58] The more powerful groups use the criminal justice system to maintain their dominant position and to repress groups or social movements that threaten it.[59] As Hawkins argues, conflict theory was developed primarily with reference to social class, with relatively little attention to race and ethnicity.[60]

The most obvious example of conflict theory in action was the segregation era in the South (1890s–1960s), when white supremacists instituted de jure segregation in public schools and other public accommodations.[61] The criminal justice system was used to maintain the subordinate status of African Americans.

Because African Americans were disenfranchised as voters, they had no control or influence over the justice system. As a result, crimes by whites against African Americans went unpunished, and crimes by African Americans against whites were treated very harshly—including alleged or even completely fabricated offenses.[62] Meanwhile, outside of the South, discrimination also limited the influence of minorities over the justice system. The civil rights movement has eliminated de jure segregation and other blatant forms of discrimination. Nonetheless, pervasive discrimination in society and the criminal justice system continues.

Applying the Theory   Conflict theory explains the overrepresentation of racial and ethnic minorities in the criminal justice system in several ways. The criminal law singles out certain behavior engaged in primarily by the poor. Vagrancy laws are the classic example of the use of the criminal law to control the poor and other perceived "threats" to the social order. The criminal law has also been used against political movements challenging the established order: from sedition laws against unpopular ideas to disorderly conduct arrests of demonstrators.

Finally, "street crimes" that are predominantly committed by the poor and disproportionately by racial and ethnic minorities are the target of more vigorous enforcement efforts than are those crimes committed by the rich. The term *crime* refers more to robbery and burglary than to white-collar crime. In these ways, conflict theory explains the overrepresentation of racial and ethnic minorities among people arrested, convicted, and imprisoned.

Routine Activity Theory

Routine activity theory shifts the focus of attention from offenders to criminal incidents. Felson explains that the theory examines "how these incidents originate in the routine activities of everyday life."[63] Particularly important, the theory emphasizes the extent to which the daily routine creates informal social control that helps prevent crime or undermines those informal controls and leads to higher involvement in crime. (Informal social control includes, for example, the watchfulness of family, friends, and neighbors. Formal social control is exercised by the police and the rest of the criminal justice system.) Felson offers the example of parental supervision of teenagers. He cites data indicating that between 1940 and the 1970s, American juveniles spent an increasing amount of time away from the home with no direct parental supervision.[64]

These changes are rooted in the changing nature of work and family life in contemporary society (as opposed to some kind of moral failing). These circumstances increase the probability that young people will engage in crime. To cite an earlier example, in the 1920s many people were alarmed that the advent of the automobile created the opportunity for young men and women to be alone together without direct parental supervision, with a resulting increase in premarital sexual behavior.

Applying the Theory   Routine activity theory is particularly useful in explaining crime when it is integrated with other theories. If parental supervision represents an important informal social control, then family breakdown and single-parent households will involve less supervision and increase the probability of more involvement in crime. High rates of teenage unemployment will mean that more young people will have free time on their hands, and if unemployment is high in the neighborhood, they will have more association with other unemployed young people, including some who are already involved in crime.

The Limits of Current Theories

All of the theories discussed here attempt to explain the relationships among race, ethnicity, and crime in terms of social conditions. Hawkins argues that this approach represents the liberal political orientation that has dominated American sociology and criminology through most of this century.[65] He also believes that there are important limitations to this orientation. The liberal emphasis on social conditions arose out of a reaction to racist theories of biological determinism, which sought to explain high rates of crime among recent European immigrants and African Americans in terms of genetic inferiority. Herrnstein and Murray's controversial book, *The Bell Curve*, represents a recent version of this approach. The liberal emphasis on social conditions, however, tends to become a form of social determinism, as criminologists focus on the social pathologies of both minority communities and lower-class communities. Although consciously avoiding biologically based stereotypes, much of the research on social conditions has the unintended effect of perpetuating a different set of stereotypes about racial and ethnic minorities.

Hawkins suggests that if we seek a comprehensive explanation of the relationships among race, ethnicity, and crime, the most promising approach will be to combine the best insights from liberal criminology regarding social conditions and conflict perspectives regarding both the administration of justice and intergroup relations.[66]

INEQUALITY AND SOCIAL REFORM

The most disturbing aspect of social inequality in America has been its persistence over 30 years despite a national effort to reduce or eliminate it. Peterson refers to this as the "poverty paradox": not just the persistence of poverty in the richest country in the world but its persistence in the face of a major attack on it.[67] The civil rights movement fought to eliminate racial discrimination, and several different government policies sought to create economic opportunity and eliminate poverty. In the 1960s, liberals adopted the War on Poverty and other Great Society programs; in the 1980s, conservative economic programs of reducing both taxes and government spending sought to stimulate economic growth and create job opportunities.

Not only has inequality persisted, but as Hacker, Orfield, and Ashkinaze argue, the gap between rich and poor and between whites and minorities has gotten worse in many respects. What happened? Did all the social and economic policies of the past generation completely fail?

There are four major explanations for the persistence of inequality, poverty, and the growth of the underclass.[68] Many liberals argue that it is the result of an inadequate welfare system. Social welfare programs in the United States are not nearly as comprehensive as those in other industrialized countries, lacking guaranteed health care, paid family leave, and comprehensive unemployment insurance. Other liberals argue that it is the result of the transformation of the national (and international) economy that has eliminated economic opportunities in the inner city and reduced earnings of many blue-collar jobs. Many conservatives argue that the persistence of poverty is the result of a "culture of poverty" that encourages attitudes and behavior patterns that keep people from rising out of poverty. Closely related to this view is the conservative argument that many government social and economic programs provide disincentives to work. These conservatives believe, for example, that the welfare system encourages people not to work and that the minimum wage causes employers to eliminate rather than create jobs.

The prominent African American social critic Cornell West argues that the traditional liberal–conservative debate on the relative importance of social structure versus individual character is unproductive. He points out that "structures and behavior are inseparable, that institutions and values go hand in hand."[69] In short, the problem of the persistence of inequality is extremely complex. The next section examines some of the major forces that have reshaped American life in the past generation and their impact on inequality.

The Impact of the Civil Rights Movement

The civil rights movement of the post–World War II years has been one of the most important events in U.S. history. The years between 1954 and 1965 witnessed nothing less than a revolution in American law, establishing equality as national policy. The legal assault on segregation, led by the NAACP, reached its apex in the landmark 1954 case of *Brown v. Board of Education*. The U.S. Supreme Court declared segregated public schools unconstitutional under the Fourteenth Amendment and invalidated the underlying doctrine of "separate but equal." Other cases invalidated other forms of race discrimination.[70] In 1967, for example, the Court declared unconstitutional a Virginia law barring interracial marriage.[71]

Legislation also attacked discrimination. The 1964 Civil Rights Act outlawed racial discrimination in employment, housing, public accommodations, and other areas of American life. In 1965 Congress passed the Voting Rights Act to eliminate racial discrimination in voting. President Lyndon Johnson issued Executive Order 11246 directing federal agencies to adopt affirmative action policies. Many states and municipalities, meanwhile, enacted their own civil rights statutes. The following federal civil rights laws are particularly important:

1964 Civil Rights Act

1965 Voting Rights Act

1972 Equal Opportunity Act

1990 Americans with Disabilities Act

Impact on American Society   The civil rights revolution had a profound impact on the American social structure. By outlawing overt or *de jure* racial discrimination it "opened" society to a degree unprecedented in U.S. history. It also had a profound effect on the operations of every social institution, including the criminal justice system. The most important changes occurred in the states of the South. The integration of the public schools between 1966 and 1973 was dramatic. In 1966, 80 percent of all minority students attended a school in which 90 percent or more of the students were also minorities. By 1973 the figure was only 25 percent. Public schools in the South went from being the most segregated to the most integrated in the entire country. At the same time, however, schools in the Northeast became more segregated between the 1960s and 1980s.[72]

The impact of the civil rights movement is also evident in electoral politics. African American voter registration, African American voter participation, and election of African American officials have dramatically increased. The change has been most profound in the South, where systematic disenfranchisement existed until the 1960s. In 1940 only 3.1 percent of voting-age African Americans were registered to vote; registration increased to 28.7 percent in 1960 and 66.9 percent in 1970.[73] The increase between 1960 and 1970 was clearly the result of the 1965 Voting Rights Act.

As a result of greater voter participation, the number of African American elected officials increased dramatically, from 33 nationwide in 1941 to 280 in 1965 and 9,061 in 2001. The number of African American members of the House of Representatives increased from 1 in 1940 to 4 in 1965, 20 in 1985, and 41 in 2006. The total number of Hispanic elected officials increased from 3,174 in 1985 to 4,561 in 2004. The number of Hispanic members of the House increased from 2 in 1941 to 25 in 2006.[74]

In 2001 there were 802 African American elected officials in Mississippi, including 8 elected sheriffs and 25 mayors. Throughout the Deep South, the Voting Rights Act has helped elect minorities as county commissioners, school board members, sheriffs, and officials in other important positions.[75] In Northern cities, African American mayors are common. In Cleveland in 1967, Carl Stokes was the first African American to be elected mayor of a major U.S. city. African Americans are serving or have recently served as mayors of New York, Chicago, Los Angeles, Philadelphia, Atlanta, New Orleans, Seattle, and many other cities.

The Civil Rights Movement and the Criminal Justice System   The civil rights movement also transformed the criminal justice system. Again, the greatest changes occurred in the South. Under the old system of institutionalized segregation, the entire criminal justice system was an instrument for maintaining the subordination of African Americans. Disenfranchised as voters, African Americans did not serve on juries and had no voice in the election and appointment of officials who ran the criminal justice system.[76] As a result, there were no African American police officers in the Deep South, and in the border states the few African American officers who were hired were confined to policing the African American community and not allowed to arrest whites, no matter what their offense. There also were no African American sheriffs, prosecutors, judges, or correctional officials.

By the late 1970s, the South had become "integrated" into the national social structure. The distinctive racial caste system was abolished, and the problems facing Southern criminal justice agencies were essentially the same as those facing agencies in the North and West. Problems certainly persist with respect to police–community relations, but the situation in Atlanta or New Orleans is not fundamentally different from the situation in Boston or Seattle.[77] There is evidence of racial discrimination in criminal sentencing, but this problem has been found in states from all regions of the country.

The civil rights movement also had a profound effect on the criminal justice system outside the South. Racial discrimination was identified as a major problem in the justice system, and various reforms were undertaken to eliminate it. Police departments adopted police–community relations programs to improve relations with minority communities. The Supreme Court declared unconstitutional the practice of prosecutors or defense attorneys using peremptory challenges to exclude jurors because of race.[78] Racially segregated prisons were declared unconstitutional.[79]

African Americans and Hispanics, meanwhile, experienced increased employment in justice agencies and in a number of instances assumed positions of leadership. The percentage of all sworn police officers in city police departments who are African American increased from 3.6 percent in 1960 to 11.7 percent in 2003. Hispanics represented 4.1 percent of all municipal sworn officers in 1988 and 9.1 percent in 2003.[80]

The Attack on Economic Inequality

The economic policies of both liberal Democratic and conservative Republican presidents since the 1960s have attempted to stimulate the economy, create jobs, and eliminate poverty. The major liberal Democratic effort was the War on Poverty, begun in 1965 with the Economic Opportunity Act. The federal attack on poverty and inequality also included major programs related to health care, education, Social Security, food stamps, and other forms of government assistance. The major conservative Republican effort in the 1980s involved "Reaganomics" or "supply-side economics," which sought to stimulate the economy by lowering taxes and government spending. Conservatives also sought to reduce or eliminate many government assistance programs, arguing that they create disincentives to work.

The impact of these different measures is a matter of great controversy. Conservatives argue that the War on Poverty and other liberal policies of the 1960s not only failed to eliminate poverty but actually made things worse by impeding economic growth and removing the incentives for poor people to seek employment.[81] Liberals, meanwhile, argue that Reaganomics increased the gap between rich and poor, benefiting the wealthy and eliminating programs for the poor. The data suggest that neither the economic policies of the liberals nor those of the conservatives have eliminated the structural inequalities in American society. As we have already suggested, the long-term trends have had contradictory effects. Some people have been able to take advantage of the new economic opportunities, whereas others have become even more deeply trapped in poverty—with the creation of a new underclass.

These trends have affected racial and ethnic minorities as well as whites. As Thernstrom and Thernstrom argue, many African Americans have been able to move into the middle class as a result of the elimination of job discrimination and the expansion of white-collar job opportunities.[82] These individuals are much better off than their parents were. For example, 75 percent of employed African American men in 1940 were either farm laborers or factory machine operators; 68 percent of the employed African American women were either domestic servants or farm laborers. By 1982, 20 percent of all employed African American men were in professional or managerial occupations, compared with only 6 percent in 1950.[83] Many Hispanic Americans have experienced similar social and economic progress.

Other members of minority communities, however, have been hit hard by the shrinking opportunities and are worse off than their parents were or even worse off than they themselves were 15 or 20 years earlier. These are the people who are trapped in the underclass. The National Research Council found a noticeable "contrast between blacks who have achieved middle-class status and those who have not."[84] As we discussed earlier, the conditions of poverty inhibit the transmission of human and social capital from one generation to another, thereby perpetuating poverty across generations.

The complex changes in the economy over the past three decades have directly affected the racial and ethnic dimensions of crime and criminal justice. The persistence of severe inequality and the growth of the underclass have created conditions conducive to high rates of crime. The different theories of crime we discussed earlier—social strain theory, differential association theory, social disorganization theory, culture conflict theory, conflict theory, and routine activity theory—all would predict high rates of crime, given the changes in the economy that have occurred. Because racial and ethnic minorities have been disadvantaged by these economic trends, these theories of crime help explain the persistently high rates of crime among minorities.

It is important to note that the economic trends have coincided with the increased opportunities for minorities over the same time period—at least for those able to take advantage of them. As we have already stated, some minorities have been able to move into the middle class. At the same time, the civil rights movement has resulted in greater political empowerment among minorities, as measured by voter participation, election of public officials, and employment in the criminal justice system.

Political empowerment by itself, however, is not sufficient to reduce criminal behavior. African Americans were elected as mayors in Cleveland, Detroit, Newark, Atlanta, Washington, D.C., and other cities at exactly the time when these cities faced the financial crisis resulting from the transformation of the economy. The financial crisis consisted of two parts: the tax base eroded as factories closed and middle-class people moved to the suburbs, and, at the same time, there were increased demands for public services in terms of welfare, police protection, and so forth.

In short, the civil rights movement has had a mixed effect on the inequalities in American social structure. It has opened the doors of opportunity for some racial and ethnic minorities. Often forgotten, these accomplishments are very substantial. The achievements of the civil rights movement, however, have not addressed the worsening economic conditions of the urban underclass.

CONCLUSION

The American social structure plays a major role in shaping the relationships among race, ethnicity, and crime. American society is characterized by deep inequalities related to race, ethnicity, and economics. There is persistent poverty, and minorities are disproportionately represented among the poor. In addition, economic changes have created a new phenomenon known as the urban underclass.

The major theories of crime explain the relationship between inequality and criminal behavior. In different ways, social strain, differential association, social disorganization, culture conflict, conflict, and routine activity theories all predict higher rates of criminal behavior among the poor and racial and ethnic minorities.

DISCUSSION QUESTIONS

1. Do you agree with the Kerner Commission's conclusion that we are "moving toward two societies, one black [and] one white"? Explain your answer.

2. Explain how residential discrimination contributes to crime.

3. What is meant by the concepts of human capital and social capital? How do they affect criminal behavior?

4. What has been the impact of the civil rights movement on crime and criminal justice?

5. Which theory of crime do you think best explains the prevalence of crime in the United States?

NOTES

1. Kerner Commission, *Report of the National Advisory Commission on Civil Disorders* (New York: Bantam Books, 1968), p. 1.

2. Andrew Hacker, *Two Nations: Black and White, Separate, Hostile, Unequal* (New York: Scribner's, 1992).

3. E. F. Borgatta and M. L. Borgatta, *Encyclopedia of Sociology*, vol. 4 (New York: Macmillan, 1992), p. 1970.

4. Bureau of the Census, *Census of the Population, 2000.* Current estimates available at www.census.gov.

5. Gerald David Jaynes and Robin Williams Jr., eds., *A Common Destiny: Blacks and American Society* (Washington, DC: National Academy Press, 1989), p. 6.

6. Stephan Thernstrom and Abigail Thernstrom, *America in Black and White: One Nation, Indivisible* (New York: Simon & Schuster, 1997).

7. Bureau of the Census, *Net Worth and Asset Ownership of Household: 1998 and 2000* (Washington, DC: Bureau of the Census, May 2005). Available at www.census.gov.

8. U.S. Bureau of Labor Statistics, *The Unemployment Situation: August 2005* (Washington, DC: Department of Labor, 2005). Available at www.dol.gov.

9. Bureau of the Census, *Statistical Abstract of the United States, 2006* (Washington, DC: U.S. Bureau of the Census, 2006), Table 610. Available at www.census.gov.

10. Hacker, *Two Nations*, p. 105.

11. Bureau of the Census, *Statistical Abstract, 2006*, Table 610.

12. Ibid., Table 41.

13. National Center for Children in Poverty, *Basic Facts About Low-Income Children: Birth to Age 18* (New York: Columbia University, July 2005).

14. Ibid. See also Bureau of the Census, *Poverty in the United States: 2002* (Washington, DC: Bureau of the Census, 2003).

15. U.S. Bureau of the Census, *Income, Poverty, and Health Insurance Coverage in the United States: 2003* (Washington, DC: Bureau of the Census, 2004).

16. Pierre Bourdieu and Jean-Claude Passeron, *Reproduction in Education, Society and Culture* (Newbury Park, CA: Sage, 1990).

17. Toby L. Parcel and Elizabeth G. Menaghan, *Parents' Jobs and Children's Lives* (New York: Aldine deGruyter, 1994), p. 1.

18. "What Is Social Capital?" World Bank Group, PovertyNet. Available at www.worldbank.org/poverty.

19. Elliot Currie, *Confronting Crime* (New York: Pantheon Books, 1985), p. 243. The original study is by William McCord and Jose Sanchez, "The Treatment of Deviant Children: A Twenty-Five Year Follow-Up Study," *Crime and Delinquency* 29 (March 1983): 239–251.

20. Alejandro Portes and Patricia Landolt, "The Downside of Social Capital," *The American Prospect* 26 (May–June 1996): 18–21, 94.

21. Jaynes and Williams, *A Common Destiny*, p. 4.

22. Thernstrom and Thernstrom, *America in Black and White*, p. 17.

23. Ibid., p. 534.

24. Ibid., Chapter 7, "The Rise of the Black Middle Class," pp. 183–202.

25. U.S. Census Bureau, *Current Population Survey, March 1968–1999* (Washington, DC: U.S. Government Printing Office, 2000), Table 2.

26. Bureau of Justice Statistics, *Criminal Victimization in the United States, 2000: Changes 1999–2000 with Trends 1993–2000* (Washington, DC: U.S. Government Printing Office, 2001).

27. William Julius Wilson, *The Truly Disadvantaged* (Chicago: University of Chicago Press, 1987); Christopher Jencks and Paul E. Peterson, eds., *The Urban Underclass* (Washington, DC: Brookings Institution, 1991); William Julius Wilson, ed., *The Ghetto Underclass* (Newbury Park, CA: Sage, 1993).

28. Hacker, *Two Nations*, p. 52.

29. Hacker, *Two Nations*; Andrew J. Winnick, *Toward Two Societies: The Changing Distributions of Income and Wealth in the U.S. Since 1960* (New York: Praeger, 1989); Gary Orfield and Carole Ashkinaze, *The Closing Door: Conservative Policy and Black Opportunity* (Chicago: University of Chicago Press, 1991).

30. Orfield and Ashkinaze, *The Closing Door*, p. xiii.

31. Jaynes and Williams, *A Common Destiny*, p. 321.

32. Robert D. Crutchfield, "Ethnicity, Labor Markets, and Crime," in *Ethnicity, Race, and Crime*, D. F. Hawkins, ed. (Albany: State University Press of New York, 1995), p. 196.

33. Jaynes and Williams, *A Common Destiny*, pp. 78–79.

34. Bureau of Justice Statistics, *Criminal Victimization, 2000* (Washington, DC: Department of Justice, 2004). Available at www.ncjrs.org, NCJ 205455.

35. Crutchfield, "Ethnicity, Labor Markets, and Crime," p. 196.

36. Wilson, *The Truly Disadvantaged*, pp. 137, 144; see also Bill E. Lawson, "Uplifting the Race: Middle-Class Blacks and the Truly Disadvantaged," in *The Underclass Question*, Bill E. Lawson, ed. (Philadelphia: Temple University Press, 1992), pp. 90–113.

37. Wesley G. Skogan, *Disorder and Decline* (New York: Free Press, 1990), pp. 132–133.

38. James Q. Wilson and George Kelling, "Broken Windows: The Police and Neighborhood Safety," *Atlantic Monthly* 249 (March 1982) 29–38.

39. Wesley Skogan, "Fear of Crime and Neighborhood Change," in *Communities and Crime*, A. Reiss and M. Tonry, eds. (Chicago: University of Chicago Press, 1986), pp. 215–220.

40. Wesley G. Skogan and Susan M. Hartnett, *Community Policing, Chicago Style* (New York: Oxford University Press, 1997).

41. The problem has been exaggerated in much of the news media coverage but is a serious problem nonetheless. See Dale Gieringer, "How Many Crack Babies?" in *Drug Prohibition and the Conscience of Nations*, Arnold Trebach and Kevin B. Zeese, eds. (Washington, DC: Drug Policy Foundation, 1990), pp. 71–75.

42. Peter Reuter, Robert MacCoun, and Patrick Murphy, *Money from Crime: A Study of the Economics of Drug Dealing in Washington, D.C.* (Santa Monica, CA: Rand Corporation, 1990).

43. Lawrence W. Sherman, "Police Crackdowns", in *Crime and Justice: An Annual Review of Research*, vol. 12, Michael Tonry and Norval Morris, eds. (Chicago: University of Chicago Press, 1990).

44. Skogan, "Fear of Crime and Neighborhood Crime," p. 220.

45. Robert K. Merton, *Social Theory and Social Structure* (New York: Free Press, 1957).

46. Steven F. Messner and Richard Rosenfeld, *Crime and the American Dream*, 3rd ed. (Belmont, CA: Wadsworth, 2001).

47. Michael Tonry and James Q. Wilson, eds., *Drugs and Crime, Crime and Justice: A Review of Research*, vol. 13 (Chicago: University of Chicago Press, 1990).

48. David N. Nurco, Timothy W. Kinlock, and Thomas E. Hanlon, "The Drugs–Crime Connection," in *Handbook of Drug Control in the United States*, James A. Inciardi, ed. (New York: Greenwood, 1990), pp. 71–90.

49. Alejandro Portes and Patricia Landolt, "Unsolved Mysteries: The Tocqueville Files II," *The American Prospect* 7, 26 (May–June 1996): 10.

50. Edwin H. Sutherland, *Principles of Criminology*, 3rd ed. (Philadelphia: Lippincott, 1939).

51. Crutchfield, "Ethnicity, Labor Markets, and Crime," p. 196.

52. W. I. Thomas and Florian Znaniecki, *The Polish Peasant in Europe and America* (Boston: Gorham, 1920); Clifford R. Shaw, Frederick M. Forbaugh, and Henry D. McKay, *Delinquency Areas* (Chicago: University of Chicago Press, 1929).

53. Thorsten Sellin, *Culture Conflict and Crime*, bulletin 41 (New York: Social Science Research Council, 1938).

54. Christopher Vecsey, ed., *Handbook of American Indian Religious Freedom* (New York: Crossroad, 1991).

55. James Davison Hunter, *Culture Wars: The Struggle to Define America* (New York: Basic Books, 1991).

56. Gustavus Myers, *History of Bigotry in the United States* (New York: Random House, 1943).

57. Joseph R. Gusfield, *Symbolic Crusade* (Urbana: University of Illinois Press, 1966).

58. Austin T. Turk, *Criminality and Legal Order* (Chicago: Rand McNally, 1969); Richard Quinney, *The Social Reality of Crime* (Boston: Little, Brown, 1970).

59. Allen E. Liska, ed., *Social Threat and Social Control* (Albany: State University Press of New York, 1992).

60. Darnell F. Hawkins, "Beyond Anomalies: Rethinking the Conflict Perspective on Race and Criminal Punishment," *Social Forces* 65 (March 1987): 719–745; Darnell F. Hawkins, "Ethnicity: The Forgotten Dimension of American Social Control," in *Inequality, Crime, and Social Control*, George S. Bridges and Martha A. Myers, eds. (Boulder, CO: Westview, 1994), pp. 99–116.

61. C. Vann Woodward, *The Strange Career of Jim Crow*, 3rd ed., rev. (New York: Oxford University Press, 1974).

62. Gunnar Myrdal, *An American Dilemma* (New York: Harper & Brothers, 1944).

63. Marcus Felson, *Crime and Everyday Life* (Thousand Oaks, CA: Pine Forge Press, 1994), p. xi.

64. Ibid., p. 104.

65. Darnell F. Hawkins, "Ethnicity, Race, and Crime: A Review of Selected Studies," in *Ethnicity, Race, and Crime*, pp. 31, 39–41.

66. Ibid.

67. Paul E. Peterson, "The Urban Underclass and the Poverty Paradox," in *The Urban Underclass*, pp. 3–27.

68. Summarized in Peterson, "The Urban Underclass and the Poverty Paradox," in *The Urban Underclass*, pp. 9–16.

69. Cornell West, *Race Matters* (Boston: Beacon, 1993), p. 12.

70. Richard Kluger, *Simple Justice* (New York: Vintage Books, 1977).

71. *Loving v. Virginia*, 388 U.S. 1 (1967).

72. Jaynes and Williams, *A Common Destiny*, pp. 76–77.

73. Ibid., p. 233.

74. Bureau of the Census, *Statistical Abstract of the United States, 2006*, Tables 503, 404. Congressional Hispanic Caucus Institute, website: www.chci.org.

75. Bureau of the Census, *Statistical Abstract of the United States, 2006*, Table 403.

76. Myrdal, *American Dilemma*, especially Chapter 28, "The Police and Other Public Contacts."

77. Samuel Walker, "A Strange Atmosphere of Consistent Illegality: Myrdal on 'The Police and Other Public Contacts,'" in *An American Dilemma Revisited: Race Relations in a Changing World*, Obie Clayton Jr., ed. (New York: Russell Sage Foundation, 1996), pp. 226–246.

78. *Batson v. Kentucky*, 476 U.S. 79 (1986).

79. *Washington v. Lee*, 390 U.S. 266 (1968).

80. Bureau of Justice Statistics, *Local Police Departments, 2003* (Washington, DC: U.S. Department of Justice, 2006); Samuel Walker and Charles M. Katz, *The Police in America: An Introduction*, 5th ed. (New York: McGraw-Hill, 2005).

81. Charles Murray, *Losing Ground: American Social Policy, 1950–1980* (New York: Basic Books, 1984).

82. Thernstrom and Thernstrom, *America in Black and White*.

83. Jaynes and Williams, *A Common Destiny*, p. 312.

84. Ibid., p. 4.

4

⊥

Justice on the Street?
The Police and Racial and Ethnic Minorities

UNEQUAL JUSTICE?

Cincinnati is a city torn by conflict between the police and the African American community: 15 African Americans were shot and killed by the police between 1996 and 2001. The fifteenth shooting in April 2001 provoked a riot that resulted in significant property damage and a citywide curfew. At the same time, the police department was the subject of a lawsuit alleging racial profiling and was also being investigated by the Civil Rights Division of the U.S. Justice Department. One year after the riot the city entered into a consent decree with the Justice Department, the American Civil Liberties Union (ACLU), and the local Black United Front that required sweeping reforms in the police department, including a new use of force policy, limits on the use of the canine unit, a new citizen complaint procedure, and other changes.[1]

A survey of Cincinnati residents had found that nearly half (46.6 percent) of all African Americans said they had been personally "hassled" by the police, compared with only 9.6 percent of all whites. *Hassled* was defined as being "stopped or watched closely by a police officer, even when you had done nothing wrong."[2]

The events in Cincinnati, which resembled those in the turbulent 1960s, represent perhaps the worst single case of police–community relations problems. Similar tensions over shootings and excessive use of force by police are found in other cities as well. The most controversial recent issue is racial profiling. Civil rights groups allege that police target African American drivers for traffic stops on the basis of their race rather than for actual violations of the law. Robert Wilkins,

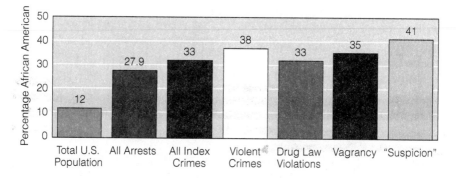

FIGURE 4.1   Racial Disparities in Arrests, 2002

SOURCE: Federal Bureau of Investigation, *Crime in the United States, 2002* (Washington, DC: Department of Justice, 2003).

an African American attorney, was stopped by the Maryland state police on Interstate 95 and subjected to a prolonged detention and illegal search. To support Wilkins's case, his lawyers sponsored observational research on traffic and enforcement patterns on I-95. The research found that African Americans did not speed on I-95 at a higher rate than that of white drivers but constituted 73 percent of all drivers stopped for possible violations. Even worse, they represented 81 percent of all drivers whose cars were searched after being stopped.[3]

The issue of racial profiling in traffic stops is only part of a larger pattern of racial disparities in the criminal justice system. Racial and ethnic minorities are arrested, stopped and questioned, and shot and killed by the police out of proportion to their representation in the population. African Americans represent only 12 percent of the population but in 2003 were 28 percent of all people arrested, 33 percent of all Index crime arrests, 38 percent of all violent crime arrests, and 35 percent of all arrests for vagrancy (Figure 4.1). They are shot and killed by police 4 times as often as whites, down from a ratio of 8:1 in the early 1970s.[4]

Hispanic communities, meanwhile, are often underserved by the police. Many Latinos are reluctant to call the police for routine problems, in part because of fear they will be subject to immigration law enforcement.[5] The federal government has authorized local police to enforce federal immigration laws—a power they did not previously have. Some Hispanic people do not call the police because they either do not speak English or have limited English proficiency.

Native American reservations have seriously inadequate law enforcement agencies, according to a Justice Department survey, despite crime rates that are much higher than in the rest of American society.[6]

A report by the Police Executive Research Forum (PERF) places the issue of racial profiling in a broader context. Racial bias does not occur just in traffic enforcement but can occur in any and all phases of law enforcement—traffic stops, arrests, failure to provide service, and so forth. This chapter examines the full range of police activities to identify possible patterns of bias.[7]

Complex and Ambiguous Evidence

Relations between the police and racial and ethnic minority communities is extremely complex—and not as simple as many people believe. A good indicator of this complexity is the public opinion poll data about attitudes toward the police. African Americans consistently rate the police less favorably than white Americans. In a 2004 poll, only 41 percent of African Americans expressed a "great deal of confidence" in the police, compared with 70 percent of whites. Latino Americans also have less favorable attitudes than whites, but they are not as negative as are African Americans.[8]

Nonetheless, a majority of African Americans have generally favorable attitudes toward the police (combining the 41 percent expressing "a great deal of confidence" with 46 percent expressing "some"). The combined total of 87 percent is a higher rating than for most other institutions in society. When asked about specific aspects of policing, such as use of force, however, the gap between the attitudes of African Americans and whites widens even further. People are very sensitive to how police officers do their jobs. We will discuss this issue and its implications for policy later in this chapter.

GOALS OF THE CHAPTER

This chapter explores the complex issues in the relationship between the police and racial and ethnic minority communities and helps sort through the sometimes conflicting evidence on race, ethnicity, and criminal justice.[9] The first section outlines a contextual approach that helps resolve the apparent contradictions in the available evidence. The second section examines public opinion about the police, comparing the attitudes of whites, African Americans, and Hispanics (unfortunately, there is little evidence on other racial and ethnic groups). The third section reviews the evidence on police behavior, beginning with the most serious action, use of deadly force, and proceeding through the less serious police activities. The fourth section deals with citizen complaints against the police, reviewing the evidence on the extent of misconduct and the ways police departments handle citizen complaints. The final section examines police employment practices. Particular attention is given to the law of employment discrimination and the historic problem of discrimination against racial and ethnic minorities.

A CONTEXTUAL APPROACH

This chapter adopts a contextual approach to help understand the complex and at times contradictory evidence related to police and racial and ethnic minorities. This approach disaggregates the general subject of policing into four specific contexts that affect relations between the police and minorities (Table 4.1).[10]

T A B L E 4.1 Contexts of Policing

Variations by racial and ethnic group

African American, Hispanic, Native American, Vietnamese, etc.

Variations by police department

More professional vs. less professional

High rates of use of deadly force vs. low rates

Variations within each racial and ethnic group

By social class and by nationality group

Recent immigrants vs. long-time residents

Middle class vs. poor

Variations by department units and tactics and policing philosophy

Patrol unit vs. gang unit vs. traffic enforcement unit

First, different racial and ethnic groups have very different experiences with the police. As noted in Chapter 1, we cannot talk about "minorities," or even "racial and ethnic minorities," as a homogeneous category. African Americans, Hispanics, Native Americans, and Asian Americans all have somewhat different experiences with the police. Hispanics are less likely to be stopped by the police than either African Americans or non-Hispanic whites. African Americans, meanwhile, have the least favorable attitudes toward the police. We will look at these variations throughout this chapter.[11]

A survey of six racial and ethnic groups in New York City found "major differences" in how they respond to being a crime victim. If there were an incident of "family violence," 80 percent of Dominicans and Colombians said they would be "very likely" to report it to the police, compared with 66 percent of African Americans and 65 percent of Asian Indians. Similar differences were found for break-ins and drug sales.[12] The most important factor, however, was a sense of ethnic group community empowerment. People were more likely to report crimes to the police if they believe their own racial or ethnic community "was likely to work together to solve local problems" and if they believe their community had some political power. A sense of community powerlessness reduced the likelihood of reporting crimes. In short, the experience of a racial or ethnic community itself—its cohesion and political power—plays a major role in its relationship with the police, and these experiences vary considerably from group to group.

Nielsen, meanwhile, argues that the Native American experience with the criminal justice system "cannot be understood without recognizing that it is just one of many interrelated issues that face Native peoples today," including "political power, land, economic development, [and] individual despair."[13]

Second, police departments have very different records with regard to racial and ethnic minority community relations. Some departments do a much better job of controlling officer use of deadly force. A 2001 survey by the *Washington Post* found that the rate of fatal shootings by police is seven or eight times higher in some cities than in others.[14] As noted earlier, Cincinnati has had serious conflict between its police department and its African American community. The Boston Police Department, however, has been credited with developing improved relations with racial and ethnic minority communities, in particular by working through the Boston Ten Point Coalition, a group of community religious institutions.[15]

Third, social class makes a difference, with the result that there are important differences within racial and ethnic minority communities. Ronald Weitzer's research in Washington, DC, found significant differences in perceptions of the police by low-income and middle-class African Americans in the city. Low-income and middle-class African Americans believe that race makes a difference in how police treat individuals, whereas middle-class whites had a much more favorable view of police–community relations in their own neighborhood.[16] Not all African Americans and Hispanics are poor. All the public opinion surveys indicate that young men have a very different—and far more negative—experience with the police than do adults or young women (discussed later).

Fourth, variations by police units and tactics and policing philosophy have very different impacts on communities. Aggressive patrol tactics with frequent stops of citizens, for example, create resentment among young men. Drug enforcement efforts are disproportionately directed at minority communities. Community policing, meanwhile, has been found to have a positive effect on confidence and trust in the police. Later in this chapter we will explain how racial profiling in traffic stops occurs in three different contexts: the war on drugs, people being "out of place," or crackdowns on crime. In short, profiling does not necessarily occur in all places and times in one jurisdiction.

In short, we have to be careful about generalizing about racial or ethnic groups, including whites, and the police. We have to focus on particular kinds of police actions and their effects on particular groups of people in society.

A LONG HISTORY OF CONFLICT

Conflict between the police and racial and ethnic minorities is nothing new. There have been three major eras of riots related to police abuse: 1917–1919, 1943, and 1964–1968. The Cincinnati riots of 2001 were only the latest chapter in a long history of conflict and violence.[17] The pattern of civil disorders in this country is depressingly similar. Noted African American psychologist Kenneth Clark told the Kerner Commission in 1967 that reading the reports of the earlier riots was like watching the same movie "re-shown over and over again, the same analysis, the same recommendations, and the same inaction."[18]

Alfredo Mirandé, meanwhile, defines the long history of conflict between Hispanics and the police in terms of "gringo justice." Taking a broad historical and political perspective, he sees a fundamental "clash between conflicting and competing cultures, world views, and economic, political and judicial systems."[19] Conflict with the police is a product of the political and economic subordination of Hispanics, their concentration in distinct neighborhoods or barrios, and stereotyping of them as criminals. The so-called Zoot Suit Riot in Los Angeles in 1943 involved attacks on Hispanic men by police and by white Navy personnel on shore leave.[20] Major conflicts between the police and the Los Angeles Hispanic community also erupted in 1970 and 1971.

THE POLICE AND A CHANGING AMERICA

The changing demographic face of the United States because of immigration presents a special challenge for the police. Between 1980 and 2000, the Hispanic population increased from 6.4 percent of the U.S. population to 11.8 percent. By 2005 the Hispanic population had grown to 14 percent of the total population and is now the largest people of color community in the country.[21] These changes create potential conflict related to race, ethnicity, cultural values, lifestyles, and political power. Many new American residents do not speak English and are not familiar with U.S. laws and police practices. Historically, the police have often aggravated conflicts with new arrivals and powerless people. The police have represented the established power structure, resisted change, and reflected the prejudices of the majority community.

A report by PERF argues that, contrary to past practice, the police can "help prevent open conflict, mitigate intergroup tensions within a community and build meaningful partnerships among the diverse populace of modern cities."[22]

The Charlotte-Mecklenburg, North Carolina, Police Department created a special International Unit to help the department respond more effectively to all of the new immigrant groups in the community, which include Hispanic, Hmong, Vietnamese, and Asian Indians.[23]

One starting point is for the police to develop language skills that enable them to communicate effectively with all segments of the community. One private firm (Network Omni Translation [www.networkomni.com]) provides translation services in a number of languages under contract with law enforcement agencies and other organizations. The Minneapolis Civilian Police Review Authority published brochures explaining how to file a citizen complaint in seven languages (English, Spanish, Lakota, Ojibway, Vietnamese, Cambodian, and Hmong).[24]

PUBLIC ATTITUDES ABOUT THE POLICE

Public attitudes about the police provide a good starting point for understanding relations between the police and racial and ethnic minority communities in context. Race and ethnicity are consistently the most important factor in shaping attitudes about the police. Yet, public attitudes are complex and surprising. The vast majority of all Americans express confidence in the police. Among white Americans in 2004, 92 percent express either a "great deal" or "some" confidence, and only 8 percent express "very little" confidence. By comparison,

T A B L E 4.2   Attitudes Toward the Police

| | "Have You Ever Been Unfairly Stopped by Police?" | | |
	Yes	No	Don't Know
African American	37%	61%	2%
Hispanic	20	79	1
Asian	11	85	3
White	4	96	-

National Survey, 1,709 Adults, 2001

SOURCE: *The Washington Post*, "Discrimination in America," June 21, 2001.

17 percent of "nonwhites" express "very little" confidence (unfortunately, this poll did not distinguish between Hispanics and non-Hispanic whites).

At the same time, African Americans consistently report that they believe that the police treat African Americans unfairly or have experienced unfair treatment themselves. In a 2001 survey, 37 percent said they had been "unfairly stopped by police," compared with only 4 percent of whites (Table 4.2).[25] In another poll, more than half of African Americans (58 percent) felt that the police in their community did not treat all races fairly, compared with only 20 percent of whites and 27 percent of Hispanics.[26]

The public opinion data contradict the popular image of total hostility between the police and minorities. The vast majority of African Americans and Hispanics are similar to most whites in their experience and attitudes: they are law-abiding people who rarely have contact with the police. Their major complaint is a lack of adequate police protection. A recent Police Foundation survey in Washington, DC, found that 54.8 percent of African American residents feel there are "too few" police officers, compared with only 25.7 percent of whites.[27]

Attitudes toward the police are also heavily shaped by residents' perceptions of the quality of life in their neighborhood. People who live in high crime areas generally rate the police less favorably. Because African American and Hispanic neighborhoods tend to have higher crime rates than white neighborhoods, this results in less favorable attitudes toward the police. Weitzer found that middle-class African Americans in Washington, DC, had a much more favorable view of relations with the police in their neighborhood than did poor African Americans. Their attitudes on this point, in fact, were much closer to those of white, middle-class Washington residents than of poor African Americans.[28]

Surveys over the past 30 years have found that public attitudes toward the police have been remarkably stable. In 1967 the President's Crime Commission reported that only 16 percent of nonwhites rated the police as "poor," and a 1977 survey found that only 19 percent of African Americans rated their police as "poor," compared with 9 percent of whites. A survey of 500 Hispanic residents of Texas found that only 15 percent rated their local police as "poor."[29]

Highly publicized controversial incidents have a short-term effect on public attitudes. In the immediate aftermath of the 1991 Rodney King beating, the percentage of white Los Angeles residents who said they "approve" of the Los

Angeles police fell from more than 70 percent to 41 percent. The approval ratings by African Americans and Hispanics in the city, which were low to begin with, also fell. The approval ratings of all groups eventually returned to their previous levels, but white attitudes did so much more quickly than those of minority groups.[30]

Age is the second most important factor in shaping attitudes toward the police. Young people, regardless of race, consistently have a more negative view of the police than do middle-aged and elderly people. This is not surprising. Young men are more likely to be out on the street, have contact with the police, and engage in illegal activity. At the same time, lower-income people have more negative attitudes toward the police than do upper-income people.

Hostile relations between the police and young, low-income men are partly a result of conflict over lifestyles. Werthman and Piliavin found that juvenile gang members in the early 1960s regarded their street corner hangouts as "a sort of 'home' or 'private place.'" They sought to maintain control over their space, particularly by keeping out rival gang members. Their standards of behavior for their space were different from what adults, especially middle-class adults, and the police considered appropriate for a public area.[31]

Our contextual approach, in short, indicates that the heart of the conflict between police and racial and ethnic minorities involves young people, particularly young men, and especially those in low-income neighborhoods. The experiences of these individuals are not the same as those of older, middle-class members of minority neighborhoods.

The Impact of Police Officer Conduct

A growing body of research indicates that citizen attitudes are heavily influenced by how they feel officers treat them in an encounter. It is not necessarily what the police do, but how they do it. This research is based on the concept of procedural justice, which holds that in any situation levels of satisfaction are mainly determined not by the outcome but by the process.[32] For example, it is not whether someone is stopped by the police and given a traffic ticket, but whether the officer is courteous and respectful. Another example would be a student's grade. A student is less likely to be upset by a low grade (e.g., a D) if the teacher takes the time to explain the basis for the grade (failure to mention important points covered in class, incomplete sentences, etc.).

In his survey of citizen satisfaction with the police, Skogan found that people who had been stopped by the police had more favorable attitudes if they felt they were *treated fairly*, if the officer(s) *explained the situation* to them, were *polite*, and *paid attention* to what they had to say on their own behalf. The procedural justice research consistently finds that people are more satisfied if they feel they had a chance to tell their side of the story. Skogan found important racial and ethnic differences in citizen perceptions, however. African Americans and Spanish-speaking Latinos, for example, were "far less likely to report that police had explained why they had been stopped." Less than half of the African Americans and Latinos thought the police treated them politely, and both groups thought they were treated unfairly.[33]

These findings have important policy implications. They clearly indicate that it is possible for the police to improve public attitudes and improve relations with racial and ethnic minority communities. Policies that increase officer courtesy and willingness to listen to people they deal with are very likely to improve police–community relations. Possible policies are discussed later in this chapter.

POLICING RACIAL AND ETHNIC MINORITY COMMUNITIES

As already noted, it is not appropriate to talk about "racial and ethnic minorities" as a homogeneous group. These individuals have different types of experiences with the police.

The African American Community

Historically, the primary focus of police–community relations problems has involved the African American community. Thirty years ago, Bayley and Mendelsohn observed, "[T]he police seem to play a role in the life of minority people out of all proportion to the role they play in the lives of the dominant white majority."[34] This is still true today and is the result of differences in income level, reported crime, and calls for police service.

African Americans are more likely than other Americans to be the victims of crime. The National Crime Victimization Survey (NCVS) reports that in 2003, the robbery rate for African Americans was three times that of whites (5.9 per 1,000 versus 1.9 per 1,000). And as we have already noted, the quality of neighborhood life has a major impact on attitudes toward the police. It is interesting to note, however, that despite less favorable opinions about the police, African Americans report crimes to the police at a slightly higher rate than whites do. African American women, for example, reported 60.2 percent of all violent victimizations to the police, compared with 47.1 for white women. The racial gap is much narrower for males and for property crimes, however.[35]

African Americans are shot and killed by the police at a much higher rate than the rate for whites and are more likely to be arrested than whites. Because of these factors, African American neighborhoods generally receive higher levels of police patrol than do white neighborhoods. Some African American parents are so fearful of the police that they make special efforts to teach their children to be very respectful when confronted by a police officer. They are afraid that their children (and particularly their sons) might be beaten or shot if they displayed any disrespect.[36]

The Hispanic Community

A report to the U.S. Justice Department concluded, "Latinos may have unique experiences with police which shape attitudes toward law enforcement officials."[37] The Hispanic community also experiences higher rates of crime than does the non-Hispanic white community. The robbery rate is about 43 percent higher for Hispanics than for non-Hispanics. Hispanics, however, are slightly less likely to report crimes than non-Hispanics. Hispanic men report 40 percent of violent crimes, versus 45.6 percent for non-Hispanic men. It is interesting to note, however, that Hispanic women are much more likely to report violent crimes (54.8%) compared with non-Hispanic women (49.3).[38]

Hispanics initiate contact with the police *less* frequently (167 per 1,000 people) than either whites (221 per 1,000) or African Americans (189 per 1,000) and are also *less* likely to be stopped by the police for a traffic violation.[39] One study found that the police did not stop many Hispanic drivers because officers decided that they probably would not be able to communicate with Spanish-speaking drivers, and, therefore, nothing would result from the stop.[40]

Several factors help explain the patterns of interactions between Hispanics and the police. Hispanics who do not speak English have difficulty communicating with the police and may not call. Some Hispanics fear that calling the police will expose members of their community to investigation regarding immigration status. Carter found that the Hispanic community's sense of family often regards intervention by an "outsider" (such as a police officer) as a threat to the family's integrity and, in the case of an arrest, as an attack on the father's authority.[41] (Other studies of Hispanic families, however, have found considerable variations that suggest that Carter employed inappropriate stereotypes.)

A series of focus groups in a Midwestern city found significant differences between how Hispanic, African American, and white residents would respond to an incident of police misconduct. Members of the predominantly Spanish-speaking group were far more fearful of the police, far less knowledgeable about the U.S. legal system, and less likely to file a complaint than either whites or African Americans. Much of the fear of the police was related to concern about possible immigration problems.[42]

Skogan's survey of Chicago residents is the first to explore the differences between English-speaking and non–English-speaking Hispanics. The study found significant differences in virtually all aspects of relations with the police. Non–English-speaking Hispanics were much less likely to report crimes: only 9 percent of respondents, compared with 35 percent of English-speaking Hispanics and 27 percent of African Americans. They were also less likely to report a neighborhood problem to the police (8 percent, compared with 19 percent of English-speaking Hispanics and 14 percent of African Americans).[43]

The Native American Community

Native Americans occupy a unique legal status in the United States, which has an important effect on their relations with the police. Native American tribes are recognized as semi-sovereign nations with broad (although not complete) powers of self-government within the boundaries of the United States. There are more than 500 federally recognized Native American tribes and about 330 federally recognized reservations, and approximately 200 have separate law enforcement agencies.[44]

This results in extremely complex problems related to the jurisdiction of tribal police agencies, county sheriff or city police departments, and federal authorities for particular crimes. In any specific case, jurisdiction depends on where the crime was committed, who committed the crime, and what crime was committed. Tribal police have jurisdiction only over crimes committed on Indian lands by Native Americans. A crime committed by any other person on a reservation is the responsibility of the county sheriff. In addition, tribal authorities have jurisdiction only over less serious crimes. Murder and robbery, for example, are the responsibility of federal authorities.[45]

Native American policing is also complex because there are five different types of tribal law enforcement agencies: (1) Those operated and funded by the federal Bureau of Indian Affairs (BIA); (2) those federally funded but operated by the tribe under an agreement with the BIA (called PL 96–638 agencies); (3) those operated and funded by the tribes themselves; (4) those operated by tribes under the 1994 Indian Self-Determination Act; and (5) those operated by state and local governments under Public Law 280.[46]

A 2001 report to the National Institute of Justice (NIJ) found serious problems with policing on Native American lands. Not only has there been increasing crime on reservations, but tribal police departments suffer from inadequate budgets and equipment, poor management, high levels of personnel turnover, and considerable political influence.[47] The Bureau of Justice Statistics (BJS) reports that the victimization rate for violent crimes among Native Americans is twice that of other Americans;[48] reservations have problems with youth gangs and domestic violence. Most tribal agencies are very small (10 or fewer sworn officers), and only half have a 911 emergency telephone service. About half (42.6 percent) cross-deputize their officers with the local county sheriff's department, meaning that their officers have law enforcement powers off the reservation. About two-thirds of all sworn officers employed by tribal departments are Native Americans, and about 56 percent are members of the tribe they serve. The NIJ report concludes that most of these problems are the legacy of federal Native American policy that has historically served the interests of the federal government rather than the goal of tribal autonomy and self-governance.[49]

The Middle Eastern Community

The terrorist attack on the United States on September 11, 2001 raised fears of discrimination against Arab Americans on the basis of national origin, religion, or immigration status. There are an estimated 4 million Arab Americans in the United States, representing about 2 percent of the U.S. population. The American-Arab Anti Discrimination Committee (ADC; www.adc.org) reports increased incidents of discrimination following 9/11, including 80 incidents where Arab Americans were removed from airplanes solely because of their appearance and not any illegal conduct.[50]

Several policing issues concern the Arab American community. The first is racial profiling, whereby the police, particularly federal authorities, identify individuals as suspects solely on the basis of their national origin. In the wake

Focus on an Issue
Enforcing Federal Immigration Laws

The enforcement of immigration laws represents a special problem for the Hispanic community—and for Asian, Middle Eastern, and African communities. Traditionally, local police have not enforced immigration laws because the laws are federal. The Immigration and Customs Enforcement (ICE) is responsible for enforcement.

In the aftermath of 9/11, the federal government has proposed authorizing local law enforcement to enforce federal immigration laws. The terrorists who destroyed the World Trade Center and damaged the Pentagon were foreign nationals, some of whom were in the United States illegally. The Justice Department argues that local police involvement in immigration law enforcement would greatly increase the possibility of catching potential terrorists. The Mexican American Legal Defense Fund (MALDEF) and other civil rights groups oppose the Clear Law Enforcement for Criminal Alien Removal

(CLEAR) Act introduced in Congress that would require state and local authorities to enforce federal immigration laws during the courts of their normal duties.[52]

Many local police officials have objected to this new role. In the fall of 2001, the Portland, Oregon, police department and a few others refused to cooperate with the Federal Bureau of Investigation in its effort to interview 5,000 men of Middle Eastern origin. The California Police Chiefs Association sent a letter to Attorney General John Ashcroft, opposing local police enforcement of immigration laws.[53] The Association and other local police officials fear that enforcing immigration laws will create conflict with immigrant communities with whom they want to develop good relations. As we have seen, Hispanics call the police at a lower rate than do other groups, in part because of fears of potential problems with immigration laws.

of 9/11, there were a number of incidents involving discrimination against Arab Americans attempting to fly on airlines. In some instances, the acts of discrimination were committed by private individuals or companies. In the summer of 2005 the ADC protested a statement by a New York City Council member who called for profiling of men of Arab descent.[51]

A second issue involves hate crimes, specifically attacks on Arab Americans because of their national origin or religion. The ADC reported more than 700 violent attacks on Arab Americans in the first 9 weeks following the 9/11 terrorist attack.

There are also issues related to the federal war on terrorism. Soon after 9/11, the FBI set out to interview 5,000 Arab American men in the United States, not as criminal suspects but simply as potential sources of information about possible terrorists. Many Arab Americans regarded this as intimidating and a form of racial profiling. The special issue of enforcing federal immigration laws—which affects Hispanics as well as Arab Americans—is discussed in the "Focus on an Issue: Enforcing Federal Immigration Laws" box.

POLICE USE OF DEADLY FORCE

The fatal shooting of an African American man by the Cincinnati police sparked the riots in that city in April 2001. Historically, police shootings have been the most explosive issue in police–community relations. In the 1970s, the police fatally shot eight African Americans for every one white person. By 1998 the ratio had been reduced to 4:1.[54] James Fyfe, one of the leading experts on the subject, asked whether the police have "two trigger fingers," one for whites and one for African Americans and Hispanics.[55]

On October 3, 1974, two Memphis police officers shot and killed Edward Garner, a 15-year-old African American. Garner was 5'4" tall, weighed 110 pounds, and was shot in the back of the head while fleeing with a stolen purse containing $10. The Memphis officers acted under the old *fleeing felon rule*, which allowed a police officer to shoot to kill, for the purpose of arrest, any fleeing suspected felon. The rule gave police officers very broad discretion, allowing them to shoot, for example, a juvenile suspected of stealing a bicycle worth only $50. Edward Garner's parents sued, and in 1985 the Supreme Court declared the fleeing felon rule unconstitutional in *Tennessee v. Garner*. The Court ruled that the fleeing felon rule violated the Fourth Amendment protection against unreasonable searches and seizures, holding that shooting a person was a seizure.[56]

Police officers, of course, do not shoot every suspected fleeing felon. The data, however, suggest that they were much more likely to shoot African Americans than whites. Between 1969 and 1974, for example, police officers in Memphis shot and killed 13 African Americans in the "unarmed and not assaultive" category but only one white person (Table 4.3). In fact, half of all the African Americans shot were in that category.[57] The permissive fleeing felon rule allowed officers to act on the basis of prejudices and stereotypes. White officers were more likely to feel threatened by African American suspects than by white suspects in similar situations. Because the typical shooting incident occurs at night, in circumstances in which the officer has to make a split-second decision, it is often not clear whether the suspect has a weapon.

There is little data on the shootings of Hispanics and none of Native Americans or Asian Americans. The BJS report on deadly force trends from 1976 to 1998 uses the categories of "white" and "black," however. Presumably, Hispanics shot and killed by the police were classified as "white." The result is that the gap between African Americans and non-Hispanic whites is probably even greater than the report indicates. In an earlier study, Geller and Karales found that between 1974 and 1978 Hispanics were about twice as likely to be shot and killed by the Chicago police as whites, but only half as likely to be shot as African Americans.[58] One of the problems with studying this issue—as discussed in Chapter 1—is that criminal justice agencies have traditionally classified Hispanics as "white," not distinguishing between Hispanic and non-Hispanic whites.

There are substantial differences among police departments regarding the number and rate of citizens shot and killed. Controlling for violent crime (an extremely relevant variable on this issue), Washington, DC, police shot and killed

TABLE 4.3 Citizens Shot and Killed by Police Officers, Memphis

	1969–1974		1985–1989	
	White	African American	White	African American
Armed & assaultive	5	7	6	7
Unarmed & assaultive	2	6	1	5
Unarmed & not assaultive	1	13	0	0
Totals, by race	8	26	7	12
Total	34		19	

SOURCE: Adapted from Jerry R. Sparger and David J. Glacopassi, "Memphis Revisited: A Reexamination of Police Shootings after the Garner Decision," *Justice Quarterly* 9 (June 1992): 211–225.

almost 7 times as many citizens as did Boston police officers between 1990 and 2000 (6.35 per 10,000 violent crimes versus 0.91 per 10,000).[59] These variations highlight the importance of the contextual approach to police–community relations and the importance of differences in departmental policies and the enforcement of those policies and discipline of officers.

Disparity versus Discrimination in Police Shootings

The data on people shot and killed by the police raise the question that pervades all studies of race, ethnicity, and criminal justice: When does evidence of a disparity indicate discrimination? The data clearly indicate a racial disparity in people shot and killed by the police. Over the last 20 years, the ratio has been narrowed from 8:1 to 4:1.[60] Does the 4:1 ratio represent discrimination, or does it reflect a disparity that can be explained by factors other than race?

Geller and Karales addressed this question by controlling for the "at-risk" status of persons shot and killed by the Chicago police in the 1970s. People are not equally at risk of being shot by the police. Virtually all shooting victims are men rather than women; young men are also disproportionately represented compared with older men. Young men are more likely to engage in the behavior that places them at risk—namely, use of a weapon in street crime. Geller and Karales found when they controlled for at-risk status, defined in terms of arrest for "forcible felonies" (murder, rape, armed and strong-arm robbery, aggravated battery, aggravated assault, and burglary), the racial disparity disappeared. In fact, whites were shot and killed at a slightly higher rate.[61]

Controlling Police Shootings

One clear point emerges from the long-term data on police shootings: department policies can reduce the number of people shot and killed by the police and in the process narrow the racial disparity. In the 1970s, in response to protests by civil rights groups, police departments began to replace the old fleeing felon rule in favor of the *defense of life* rule, limiting shootings to situations that pose a threat to the life of the officer or some other person. Many departments also prohibit warning shots, shots to wound, and shots at or from moving vehicles. Officers are now required to fill out a report any time they discharge their weapon. These reports are then subject to an automatic review by supervisors.

Fyfe found that the defense of life rule reduced firearms discharges in New York City by almost 30 percent in just a few years.[62] Across the country, the number of people shot and killed by police declined from a peak of 559 in 1975 to 300 in 1987. Follow-up data on Memphis illustrate that the defense of life rule reduced the racial disparity in shootings. As Table 4.3 indicates, between 1985 and 1989 no people of either race were shot and killed in the fleeing felon category. The overall number of people shot and killed decreased significantly, and the racial disparity was cut in half.[63] The defense of life rule may not have changed police officer attitudes, but it did alter their behavior, curbing the influence of racial prejudice. Similar policies in departments across the country had the same effect. Nationally, the racial disparity between African Americans and whites declined from 8:1 in the 1970s to 4:1 by 1998.[64]

"POLICE BRUTALITY": POLICE USE OF PHYSICAL FORCE

Q: Did you beat people up who you arrested?

A: No. We'd just beat people in general. If they're on the street, hanging around drug locations . . .

Q: Why?

A: To show who was in charge.[65]

This exchange between the Mollen Commission and a corrupt New York City police officer in the mid-1990s dramatized the unrestrained character of police brutality in poor, high-crime neighborhoods in New York City. Police brutality has been a historic problem with U.S. police. As far back as 1931 the Wickersham Commission reported that the "third degree," the "inflicting of pain, physical or mental, to extract confessions or statements is extensively practiced."[66] The 1991 Rodney King beating is probably the most notorious recent example of police use of excessive physical force. A 1998 report by Human Rights Watch concluded, "Race continues to play a central role in police brutality in the United States."[67]

The Mollen Commission defined brutality as the "threat of physical harm or the actual infliction of physical injury or pain."[68] Many people use an even broader definition. The President's Crime Commission found that 70.3 percent of African Americans included rudeness as police brutality, compared with 54.6 percent of whites.[69] The New York City Civilian Complaint Review Board classifies 16 specific police officer actions in the "force" category, including firing a gun, pointing a gun, using pepper spray, and using a police radio or flashlight as a club.[70]

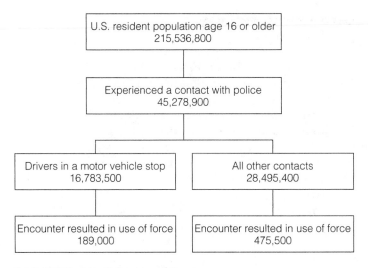

U.S. resident population age 16 or older
215,536,800

Experienced a contact with police
45,278,900

Drivers in a motor vehicle stop
16,783,500

All other contacts
28,495,400

Encounter resulted in use of force
189,000

Encounter resulted in use of force
475,500

FIGURE 4.2 Police Use of Force

SOURCE: Bureau of Justice Statistics, *Contacts Between Police and the Public: Findings from the 1999 National Survey* (Washington, DC: Government Printing Office, 2001), p. 1.

The term *police brutality* is a political slogan with no precise meaning. We use the term *excessive force*, defined as any physical force that is more than reasonably necessary to accomplish a lawful police purpose. It is important to distinguish between *force* and *excessive force*. A police officer is legally justified in using force to protect himself or herself from physical attack or to subdue a suspect who is resisting arrest. Any amount of force more than the minimal amount needed is excessive.

There is much disagreement over the prevalence of police use of excessive force.[71] Critics of the police argue that it is a routine, nightly occurrence, whereas others believe that it is a rare event. The most systematic national study of police use of force is the BJS police–citizen contact survey. The 2002 report found police officers used force or threatened to use force (an important factor that is not included in most studies) in about 1.5 percent of all encounters with citizens.[72] This represents an estimated total of 664,500 people who experienced force or threatened use for force (Figure 4.2). The BJS survey then asked people if they felt the force used was excessive. An astounding 75.4 percent felt that it was excessive, and whites (71.6 percent) were almost as likely as African Americans (77.7 percent) to report feeling it was excessive. These responses, of course, represent the perception of the citizen. Observational studies of police work have found that in the judgment of the independent observer, about one-third of all uses of force are excessive or unjustified.[73]

There are substantial racial and ethnic disparities in police use of force. The BJS report found that African Americans were more than 3 times as likely to experience force or threatened force (3.5 percent of all encounters) than whites (1.1 percent). Hispanics were more likely than whites but less likely than African

Americans to experience police use of force (2.5 percent). The BJS findings are roughly consistent with previous studies of use of force.[74]

Some critics of the police have trouble believing the estimate that police use or threaten to use force only 1.5 percent of the time. Our contextual approach puts a different perspective on the data. Most encounters between citizens and the police involve routine, trouble-free order maintenance and service situations. Certain situations, however, tend to be problematic. Studies consistently find that police use force 4 or 5 times more often against people being arrested, people who challenge their authority, and people who are drunk or on drugs. The issue of challenges to police authority raises some questions. Some people believe that the police overreact to even legitimate questions from citizens. They refer to this police practice as "contempt of cop."[75] Reiss found that almost half of the victims of excessive force had either defied the officer's authority (39 percent of all cases) or resisted arrest (9 percent of all cases). Black's data revealed another important pattern, however—African Americans were far more likely to be disrespectful to the police than were whites after controlling for all other variables.[76] It seems obvious that African American males are more likely to be disrespectful because of the long history of police–community relations problems. The impact of this pattern on arrests is discussed later in this chapter.

Reiss concluded that race *per se* is not a determining factor in the use of excessive force: "Class rather than race determines police misconduct."[77] The typical victim of excessive force is a lower-class male, regardless of race. Other observers, however, disagree with this interpretation and see a systematic pattern of police use of force against young minority men.

The race or ethnicity of the officer has little apparent influence on the use of physical force. The majority of excessive force incidents are intraracial—that is, citizens are mistreated by a police officer of the same racial or ethnic group. The data on citizen complaints against police are revealing. In New York City, whites represented 62 percent of all officers in 2003 and 65 percent of all officers receiving citizen complaints; African Americans represented 15 percent of all officers and 13 percent of those receiving complaints; Hispanics represented 21 percent of all officers and 20 percent of those receiving complaints. A similar pattern exists in San Jose, California.[78] Worden found a very complex pattern of use of force, with African American officers somewhat more likely than white officers to use reasonable levels of force but less likely to use improper force.[79]

At the same time, however, police officers of different races have very different perceptions of how the police in general use force and treat people of color and the poor. A Police Foundation survey of officers nationwide found that 57 percent of African American officers agreed or strongly agreed with the statement "Police officers are more likely to use physical force against blacks and other minorities than against whites in similar situations," compared with only 5 percent of white officers. The responses to this statement reflected not what officers said they personally do, but what they perceived officers in general do (which probably means other officers in their own department).[80]

The data on officer involvement in excessive use of force parallel the data on the use of deadly force. In neither case is it a simple matter of white officers shooting or beating minority citizens. In both cases, officer behavior is heavily determined by the contextual or situational variables: location (high-crime versus low-crime precinct); the perceived criminal involvement of the citizen; the demeanor of the citizen; and in the case of physical force, the social status of the citizen.

Our contextual approach suggests that the use of physical force has special significance for racial minority communities. Even if the overall rate of use of force is only 1.5 percent of all encounters, incidents are concentrated among lower-class men and criminal suspects, which means they are disproportionately concentrated among racial and ethnic minorities. Reiss pointed out that incidents accumulate over time, creating a perception of systematic harassment.[81] Weitzer and Tuch asked Washington, DC, residents if they felt police used excessive force in their neighborhood. Among African Americans, 30 percent felt it happened "very often" or "fairly often," compared with only 8 percent of whites and 23 percent of Hispanics.[82]

Finally, police use of force has special political significance for minorities. Because the police are the symbolic representatives of the established order, incidents of excessive force are perceived as part of the broader patterns of inequality and discrimination in society.

DISCRIMINATION IN ARRESTS?

Racial minorities are arrested far more often than whites. African Americans are about 12 percent of the population, but in 2003 they represented 27 percent of all arrests, 32.9 percent of arrests for Index crimes, and 37.2 percent of arrests for violent crimes (see Figure 4.1). Tillman found that in California, 66 percent of all African American men were likely to be arrested before the age of 30 years, compared with only 34 percent of white men.[83] The FBI does not report data on ethnicity, so there are no national data on arrest rates for Hispanics. Native Americans represent 0.8 percent of the U.S. population but 1.1 percent of all persons arrested.[84]

The arrest data again raise the question of whether the racial disparities indicate a pattern of systematic racial discrimination or a disparity that is related to other factors such as involvement in crime (see Chapter 1, Box 1.3). In his study of arrest discretion, Donald Black found that police officers consistently underenforce the law, arresting only about half of the people they could have arrested (58 percent of felony suspects and only 44 percent of misdemeanor suspects). The decision to arrest is discretionary and primarily influenced by situational factors. Officers are more likely to arrest when (1) the evidence is strong; (2) the crime is of a more serious nature; (3) the complainant or victim requests an arrest; (4) the relationship between the victim and offender is distant (that is, strangers rather than acquaintances or spouses); and (5) the suspect is disrespectful toward the officer. In Black's study, the race of the suspect was not a major determinant of arrest decisions.[85]

Black did, however, find that African Americans were arrested more often than whites, mainly because they were more often disrespectful to police officers. This phenomenon represents a vicious circle in racial discrimination. Because of the broader patterns of racial inequality in U.S. society, young African American men have more negative attitudes toward the police (see discussion earlier in this chapter). Expressing their hostility toward police officers results in higher arrest rates, which only heightens their feelings of alienation and hostility.

Klinger, however, questioned Black's interpretation of the impact of demeanor. He argued that the study did not specify when the hostile demeanor occurred. If it occurred after the actual arrest was made—and it is understandable that a person might express anger at that point—it did not cause the arrest.[86]

Another factor contributing to the racial disparity in arrests is the greater involvement of African Americans in the more serious crimes. The NCVS reports that victims perceived the offender to be African American in 46.5 percent of all single-offender robberies but only 22 percent of all assaults.[87] Because robbery is generally regarded as a more serious crime than assault, and because greater seriousness increases the probability of arrest, it follows that more African Americans will be arrested than whites.

Smith, Visher, and Davidson concluded that race does have an effect on arrest discretion. Analyzing 5,688 police–citizen encounters in 24 police departments in three major metropolitan areas, they found that police officers were more likely to arrest when the victim was white and the suspect was African American, and more likely to comply with a white victim's request that the suspect be arrested. After controlling for all relevant variables, they concluded that "race does matter" and that African American suspects were more likely to be arrested than whites.[88]

Other studies have suggested that African Americans are more likely to be arrested on less stringent evidentiary criteria than whites.[89] Petersilia's study of racial disparities in California found that African American and Hispanic arrestees were more likely to be released by the police without the case going to the prosecutor and more likely to have the prosecutor reject the case. At first glance, it might appear that African Americans and Hispanics are being treated more leniently in these two postarrest decisions. Petersilia, however, suggested that racial and ethnic minorities are arrested more often on weaker evidence than whites, particularly in "on-view" situations rather than with a warrant. The weak evidence in on-view arrests is then more likely to result in a release or rejection later in the criminal process.[90] Nonetheless, an arrest, even one that does not lead to prosecution, represents a significant form of punishment and is often perceived as harassment.

The race of the officer does not appear to influence arrest decisions. African American, Hispanic, and white officers arrest people at similar rates and for generally the same reasons. Black found some evidence that African American officers were slightly more likely to arrest African American suspects, in part because these officers appeared to be more willing to comply with requests for arrests made by African American citizens. He admitted, however, that the subject has not been researched as thoroughly as it needs to be.[91]

Zero-Tolerance Policing

One of the important new developments in law enforcement is zero-tolerance or "quality of life" policing. Under this approach, the police concentrate on relatively minor crimes, such as public urination or loitering. In New York City, there was particular emphasis on "fare-beaters," individuals who try to cheat the subway system by jumping over the turnstile. People arrested for a minor crime often turn out to have an illegal gun in their possession or are wanted on outstanding warrants.[92] City officials, including the police, claim that the great reduction in crime in New York City in the 1990s was a result of quality of life policing. Critics, however, argue that this aggressive style of policing results in harassment of citizens, particularly young men of color.[93] In fact, New York City experienced severe police–community relations problems in the 1990s as a result of several controversial shootings and the savage beating of Abner Louima in 1997. Most American cities experienced dramatic reductions in serious crime in the 1990s. Boston and San Diego, in particular, experienced dramatically lower crime rates without zero-tolerance policing and the controversies it generates.[94]

One of the important differences in policing styles is the extent to which an anticrime program is focused on suspected lawbreakers. The highly praised Boston Gun Project targets a specific list of known gang leaders and relies heavily on enforcement of probation and parole restrictions. This is a focused approach to law enforcement, concentrating on known individuals. It is very different from traditional police "crackdowns" or "sweeps" that involve massive and indiscriminate stops and frisks and arrests of young men in African American or Hispanic neighborhoods without any suspicion of actual gang membership or criminal activity. Crackdowns and sweeps involve a form of racial profiling because people are stopped and arrested solely on the basis of race, gender, and age.[95]

In sum, patterns of arrest by race are extremely complex. Racial minorities, especially African Americans, are arrested far more frequently than are whites. Much of this disparity, however, can be attributed to the greater involvement of minorities in serious crime. Greater disrespect for the police also contributes to arrest disparity. Even after all the relevant variables are controlled, however, some evidence of arrest discrimination against African Americans persists.

TRAFFIC STOPS: RACIAL PROFILING

Racial profiling in traffic stops has been the major controversy surrounding police practices in recent years. *Racial profiling* is defined as the use of race as an indicator in a profile of criminal suspects, with the result that drivers are stopped either entirely or in part because of their race or ethnicity and not because of any illegal activity. Civil rights leaders coined the term "driving while black" to describe this practice. A 2004 Gallup Poll found that 53 percent of all Americans believe that

Focus on an Issue
The Chicago Gang Ordinance

Gangs are a serious problem in many cities. Gangs have controlled drug trafficking, been responsible for gun violence, and intimidated law-abiding citizens, creating a climate of fear in neighborhoods. In an effort to control gangs, Chicago enacted a Gang Congregation Ordinance in 1992. The story of the law is an excellent case study in the use of police discretion to fight crime.

The Chicago gang ordinance made it a crime for a known "gang member" to "loiter" on the street with one or more people with "no apparent purpose." In enforcing the law, Chicago police officers had to "reasonably believe" the person was a gang member, order the person to disperse, and make an arrest if the person did not disperse. Violations could be punished by a fine of $500 and/or 6 months in jail and/or 120 days of community service.

In three years, the Chicago police issued 80,000 dispersal orders and arrested 42,000 people. Enforcement of the law fell heavily on the African American and Hispanic communities in Chicago. The Police Department enforced it only in areas where it believed gangs were a problem, but it did not inform the public about which areas they were. The basic question became, "Did the law give the police too much discretion in enforcing the law?"

The Supreme Court ruled the Chicago Gang Ordinance unconstitutional in the case of *Chicago v. Morales* (1999). The Court found the law unconstitutionally vague. The definition of loitering was vague and did not distinguish between standing on the street for a good purpose (waiting for a friend) or a bad purpose (planning a crime). There was no *mens re* requirement—that is, the police did not have to show that a person had criminal intent. Almost comically, the law did not apply to people who were moving and excluded specific acts that are the most intimidating kinds of conduct (e.g., approaching someone in a possibly threatening manner). Finally, the law violated the First Amendment right of freedom of association, which includes the right to freely travel in public places.

The law also raised the issue of lists of gang members compiled by police departments. The Chicago law authorized officers to enforce the law against people it "reasonably believed" to be gang members. But how does an officer know that? Is there an official list, or is the officer making a subjective judgment on the spot? If the department does have a list, how was it compiled? Who provided the information? Was the information verified? If a young man dropped out of a gang he belonged to was he still listed as a "gang member"? How do you ever get off the list? In many cities there have been controversies over the arbitrary and discriminatory uses of police department gang lists.

Further Reading

Chicago v. Morales, 527 U.S. 41 (1999).

Malcolm Klein, *The American Street Gang* (New York: Oxford, 1995).

Charles M. Katz, "The Establishment of a Police Gang Unit: An Examination of Organizational and Environmental Factors," *Criminology* 39 (2001): 37–75.

racial profiling is "widespread." It is surprising that 50 percent of white Americans believe it, compared with 67 percent of African Americans and 63 percent of Hispanics. The issue is not confined to traffic enforcement either. All racial and ethnic groups also believe that racial profiling is widespread in shopping malls and stores.[96]

The racial profiling controversy involves several related issues: Does racial profiling in fact exist? How can we measure police activity to determine whether it exists? What is the best method of controlling officer behavior in traffic enforcement and eliminating any racial or ethnic bias?[97]

The Use of Race in Law Enforcement

It is important to clarify when race or ethnicity can and cannot be used in law enforcement. This includes traffic enforcement, pedestrian stops, frisks, and arrests. Several basic points need to be clarified. Most important, stopping someone *solely* because of race or ethnicity is clearly an illegal form of discrimination. In practice, however, traffic stops and arrests usually involve a complex mix of factors—gender, location, height, weight, clothing, behavior, and so on—and it is often difficult to determine if race was the real reason. This leads to the important but difficult question, "Can the police use race as one of several factors in making a traffic stop" (for example, along with make of the vehicle, the location of the stop, and so on)? If race is one element in a general profile (for example, young black male driving a BMW), a stop or arrest is probably illegal. A stop or arrest is legal, however, in a situation where race or ethnicity is one of several descriptors of a particular individual suspect (for example, male, young, tall, wearing baseball jacket and cap, and white).[98]

Profiling Contexts

Racial profiling occurs in at least three different contexts. One is the *War on Drugs*, where officers are targeting African Americans or Hispanics in the belief that they are very likely to be engaged in drug trafficking. This approach represents a profile of criminal suspects based on racial and ethnic stereotypes. The ACLU and others argue that the Drug Enforcement Administration (DEA) has encouraged racial profiling by state and local departments through its "Operation Pipeline." DEA training materials, they claim, stereotype African Americans and Hispanics as drug traffickers.[99]

A second context involves stopping citizens who appear to be *out of place*, such as an African American in a predominantly white neighborhood or a white in a predominantly African American neighborhood. This approach is also based on racial stereotypes, specifically the assumption that this person does not "belong" in this area and therefore must be engaged in some criminal activity. It ignores the fact that the African American in a white neighborhood may in fact live there, may have friends who live there, or may be visiting someone for business or professional purposes (for example, an insurance salesperson calling on a potential customer). Similarly, the white person in a predominantly African

T A B L E 4.4 Experiences with Traffic Stops, 2002

	Drivers of Vehicles		
	Ticketed	Arrested	Force Used
White	56.5%	2.0%	0.8%
African American	58.4	5.8	2.7
Hispanic	71.5	5.2	2.4

SOURCE: Bureau of Justice Statistics, *Contacts Between Police and the Public: Findings from the 2002 National Survey* (Washington, DC: Department of Justice, 2005), Table 9.

T A B L E 4.5 Outcomes of Traffic Stops, by Race and Ethnicity, 2002

Race/ Ethnicity	Issued a Warning	Driver Ticketed	Driver Searched	Driver Arrested	Force Used	Excessive Force Used
White	27.4%	56.5%	2.5%	2.0%	0.8%	0.7%
African American	18.3	58.4	8.1	5.8	2.7	2.5
Hispanic	18.2	71.5	8.3	5.2	2.4	2.0

SOURCE: Bureau of Justice Statistics, *Contacts Between Police and the Public: Findings from the 2002 National Survey* (Washington, DC: Department of Justice, 2005), Table 9.

American neighborhood might have some legitimate personal or business–related reason for being there (for example, real estate sales). In a study of traffic stops in a predominantly white community bordering a largely African American city, Meehan and Ponder confirmed this interpretation. They found that the "proactive surveillance" of African American drivers "significantly increases as African Americans travel farther from 'black' communities and into white communities."[100]

A third context involves a *crackdown on crime*. In this case, the police department has decided to get tough on street crime through an aggressive stop, question, and frisk policy. It is likely to focus on a high-crime neighborhood, which, in turn, is likely to be an African American or Hispanic community. As a result, virtually all of the people stopped will be racial or ethnic minorities.[101]

The Data on Traffic Stops

The BJS national survey of police–citizen contacts provides the best data on police traffic stop practices (Table 4.4). Several important patterns emerge from this study. First, traffic stops are the most common form of encounter between police officers and citizens, accounting for 40 percent of all contacts in 2002.[102]

Second, African American drivers are more likely to be stopped (9.1 percent) than white drivers (8.7 percent) or Hispanic drivers (8.6 percent). The racial differences are even more pronounced with regard to more specific traffic stop practices. Twice as many African American drivers as white drivers reported being stopped five or more times (3.4 percent compared with 1.6 percent). This clearly suggests that some African American drivers are being targeted by police. Whites were more likely to be stopped for speeding and drunk driving, whereas African Americans and Hispanics were more likely to be stopped for vehicle defects and record checks.

Third, the greatest racial disparities exist with respect to what happens *after* the initial stop. In the 2002 survey whites and African Americans were issued tickets almost equally, whereas Hispanic drivers were more likely to be ticketed. Both African Americans (5.8 percent) and Hispanics (5.2 percent) were more than twice as likely as whites (2 percent) to be arrested in a traffic stop.

Finally, African Americans (2.7 percent) and Hispanics (2.4 percent) were three times as likely to have force used against them as whites (0.8 percent). Similar findings regarding what happens after the initial stop have been reported in almost all other studies of traffic enforcement.[103]

Interpreting Traffic Stop Data

As is the case with the deadly force and physical force data, the traffic stop data raise difficult questions related to interpretation. There is a question of whether racial and ethnic disparities in traffic stops represent a pattern of discrimination. The basic problem, which criminologists have been wrestling with, is, what *benchmark* or *baseline* should be used to interpret the traffic stop data? How would we know whether a certain percentage stops of African Americans is too high? When does a disparity become a pattern of discrimination? Lorie Fridell's comprehensive discussion of this issue, *By the Numbers*, makes it very clear that there are no simple answers and that great care must be taken when interpreting a set of traffic stop data.[104]

Most traffic stop data collection efforts have used the resident population data as a benchmark. The report by the San Jose Police Department, for example, found that Hispanics represented 43 percent of all drivers stopped but only 31 percent of the San Jose population. These data clearly indicate a disparity in the percentage of Hispanics stopped by the police. But do they represent a pattern of illegal discrimination? Other studies have found similar disparities.[105]

Resident population data are not good benchmarks or baselines for traffic stop data, however. They do not represent who is at *risk of being stopped* for a possible traffic violation. An at-risk estimate would take into account the percentage of a racial or ethnic group who are licensed drivers and who actually drive and, most important, the percentage of actual traffic law violators who are members of various racial and ethnic groups.[106] The BJS study found significant racial and ethnic differences in driving patterns. Among whites, 93.3 percent drive "a few times a year or more," compared with only 78.9 percent of African Americans and 77.7 percent of Hispanics.[107] In short, whites are far more at risk for being stopped than either of the other two groups for the simple reason that they drive more. Low-income status and the consequent lack of a car probably account for the lower driving rates among African Americans and Hispanics.

In the racial profiling lawsuits in Maryland and New Jersey, the plaintiffs avoided the problems with population data by conducting direct observation of traffic on the interstate highways in question. Observers drove on the highways and estimated the percentage of all drivers who were African American and the percentage of traffic law violators by race and ethnicity, and then they measured these data against the racial breakdown of drivers actually stopped. In both Maryland and New Jersey, African Americans were not observed violating the law at a higher rate than white drivers were. These data provided convincing evidence that African American drivers were being stopped not because of their driving behavior or the condition of their cars but for some other reason—their race.[108]

The research strategy used in the lawsuits in Maryland and New Jersey was facilitated by the fact that it occurred on interstate highways, which are confined spaces with limited access and where the police have only one task: traffic enforcement. This research strategy, however, is very difficult to apply in normal city traffic situations. Cities are large geographic areas where citizens are moving about in many different ways and where the police are performing many different tasks: law enforcement, order maintenance, and service. In this constantly changing environment, it is difficult to estimate the number of traffic violators.[109]

Although direct observation is the best method for studying traffic enforcement, it is also very expensive. It requires a number of trained observers surveying traffic over an extended period. Consequently, it has been used only on special occasions, either through a research grant or as part of a lawsuit.

An alternative approach is to use peer officer comparisons. Walker argues that this approach adapts the basic principles behind police Early Intervention Systems (EIS). EIS are data-based management tools that collect and analyze police officer performance data (citizen complaints, officer use of force reports, and so on) for the purpose of identifying those officers who have an unusually high number of indicators of problematic behavior.[110] Many EIS operate by comparing officers' performance records against those of their peers who are working similar assignments. The system identifies officers whose performance is out of line with the average for their peers (e.g., more uses of force or complaints).

Applying the EIS approach to traffic stop data, officers are compared with other officers having the same assignment (for example, same shift or same precinct or neighborhood). The system is capable of identifying officers who stop more African American or Hispanic drivers than their peers. Because the work environment is the same, activity levels should be roughly comparable. And because the racial and ethnic composition of the area is the same for all officers, any disparities in traffic stops or arrests suggest that bias might be a factor. EIS result in a formal intervention for officers identified by the system. This can involve counseling, training over issues related to traffic stops or cultural diversity, or reassignment.

Eliminating Bias in Traffic Enforcement

Several strategies have been developed to combat racial and ethnic bias in traffic stops. The traditional strategy of law enforcement organizations involves a combination of *exhortation and training*. The chief executive issues a statement that race discrimination is prohibited and then officers are offered training on nondiscrimination. Many critics, however, argue that these actions do not necessarily control officer actions on the street.

The second strategy, favored by civil rights groups, has been to demand that law enforcement agencies *collect data on all traffic stops*. Several states have passed laws requiring data collection, and a large number of departments have begun data collection voluntarily. A federal data collection law has been pending in Congress for several years.[111] As our previous discussion of interpreting traffic stop data suggested, however, official data do not necessarily reveal patterns of discrimination.

A third strategy involves law enforcement agencies adopting *policies and procedures* governing how officers conduct traffic stops. The consent decree in the Justice Department suit against the New Jersey State Police, for example, requires officers to notify their dispatcher when they are about to make a stop and to report the vehicle license number and the reason for the stop. Officers must also complete detailed reports on each stop, and supervisors are required to review each report carefully.[112] Many other departments have adopted similar policies. These requirements are designed to ensure that officers are accountable for each stop by documenting it. Many departments have also installed video cameras in patrol cars. The cameras provide a visual record of the stop and also document any inappropriate behavior by the officer or challenge false claims of officer misconduct raised by citizens.

The PERF Policy on Traffic Enforcement

The most comprehensive set of recommendations for handling traffic stops is contained in a PERF report, *Racially Biased Policing: A Principled Response*.[113] The policy includes specific guidelines on when race (or ethnicity) may and may *not* be used in stopping citizens (Box 4.1). It clearly states that race cannot be the sole or even the primary factor in determining whether to stop a citizen. Officers may, however, take race or ethnicity into account when it is information related to a "specific suspect or suspects" that links the suspect or suspects to a particular crime. (See our earlier discussion of the use of race in law enforcement.) Moreover, this information must come from a "trustworthy" source. In short, the police can use race as an indicator when they have a report of a robbery committed by a young male, white/African American/Hispanic, wearing a baseball cap and a red coat, and driving a white, late-model sedan. They cannot, however, begin stopping all white/African American/Hispanic males simply because police have reports of robberies committed by a male in one of those ethnic or racial categories. If they see an individual fitting the racial or ethnic category who also exhibits suspicious behavior, a stop would be justified.

The PERF policy also recommends specific steps that police officers should take to help reduce the perception of bias. Officers should "be courteous and professional" when stopping a citizen, they should "state the reason for the stop as soon as practical," they should "answer any questions the citizen may have" and "provide his or her name and badge number when requested," and "apologize

B O X 4.1   Police Executive Research Forum (PERF) Recommended Policy on Traffic Stops

Title: Addressing Racially Biased Policing and the Perceptions Thereof

Purpose: This policy is intended to reaffirm this department's commitment to unbiased policing, to clarify the circumstances in which officers can consider race/ethnicity when making law enforcement decisions, and to reinforce procedures that serve to assure the public that we are providing service and enforcing laws in an equitable way.

Policy:

A. Policing Impartially
    1. Investigative detentions, traffic stops, arrests, searches, and property seizures by officers will be based on a standard of reasonable suspicion or probable cause in accordance with the Fourth Amendment of the U.S. Constitution. Officers must be able to articulate specific facts and circumstances that support reasonable suspicion or probable cause for investigative detentions, traffic stops, arrests, nonconsensual searches, and property seizures.

    Except as provided below, officers shall not consider race/ethnicity in establishing either reasonable suspicion or probable cause. Similarly, except as provided below, officers shall not consider race/ethnicity in deciding to initiate even those nonconsensual encounters that do not amount to legal detentions or to request consent to search.

    Officers may take into account the reported race or ethnicity of a specific suspect or suspects based on trustworthy, locally relevant information that links a person or persons of a specific race/ethnicity to a particular unlawful incident(s). Race/ethnicity can never be used as the sole basis for probable cause or reasonable suspicion.
    2. Except as provided above, race/ethnicity shall not be motivating factors in making law enforcement decisions.

B. Preventing Perceptions of Biased Policing
    In an effort to prevent inappropriate perceptions of biased law enforcement, each officer shall do the following when conducting pedestrian and vehicle stops:

    Be courteous and professional.

    Introduce himself or herself to the citizen (providing name and agency affiliation), and state the reason for the stop as soon as practical, unless providing this information will compromise officer or public safety. In vehicle stops, the officer shall provide this information before asking the driver for his or her license and registration.

    Ensure that the detention is no longer than necessary to take appropriate action for the known or suspected offense, and that the citizen understands the purpose of reasonable delays.

    Answer any questions the citizen may have, including explaining options for traffic citation disposition, if relevant.

    Provide his or her name and badge number when requested, in writing or on a business card.

    Apologize and/or explain if he or she determines that the reasonable suspicion was unfounded (e.g., after an investigatory stop).

Compliance: Violations of this policy shall result in disciplinary action as set forth in the department's rules and regulations.

Supervision and Accountability: Supervisors shall ensure that all personnel in their command are familiar with the content of this policy and are operating in compliance with it.

SOURCE: Police Executive Research Forum, *Racially Biased Policing: A Principled Response* (Washington, DC: Author, 2001), pp. 51–53.

and/or explain if he or she determines that the reasonable suspicion was unfounded."[114]

Adoption of all the PERF recommendations by police departments could reduce a major source of public dissatisfaction with the police among people of all racial and ethnic groups. As we mentioned earlier, a growing body of research finds that citizens are very concerned about how police treat them during an encounter. This includes behavior that expresses respect or disrespect. One study, for example, found that many citizens accept the fact that the police have to engage in intrusive behavior (e.g., stop and question citizens on the street), but they resent being treated in a disrespectful manner.[115]

A Success Story: The Customs Bureau

The U.S. Customs Bureau represents a case study in how racial bias can be effectively controlled. A 2000 report on the Customs Bureau found significant disparities in searches of passengers entering the United States. African American women were more likely to be searched than either white women or African American males. Despite a high rate of intrusive searches, African American women were less likely to be found possessing contraband. A major problem was that Customs agents had almost unlimited discretion to choose who to search. Additionally, the guidelines for identifying suspicious people were extremely vague.[116]

In a series of reforms, the Customs Bureau developed a much shorter, more specific list of indicators that could justify a search and clear guidelines on agents' exercise of discretion, including requirements that they obtain supervisors' approval for particular kinds of searches. These reforms drastically reduced the number of searches, but the "hit rate," the percentage of times they found contraband, increased equally dramatically. At the same time, there were far fewer unnecessary searches of innocent people, the vast majority of whom are people of color. In short, the Customs Bureau was "working smarter": instead of indiscriminate searches that are unproductive and offend many innocent people, searches are better targeted toward possible suspects.[117] The lesson of the Customs Bureau experience is that racial bias in searches can be effectively reduced without harming effective law enforcement.

STREET STOPS AND FRISKS

Closely related to traffic stops is the police practice of stopping pedestrians on the street and questioning or frisking them, or both. This practice has long been a source of police–community tensions and is often referred to as a field interrogation (FI). The police have traditionally used FIs as a crime-fighting policy designed to "emphasize to potential offenders that the police are aware of" them and to "reassure the general public that the patrol officers are actively engaged in protecting law-abiding citizens." Patrol officers have full discretion to conduct FIs. As we have seen with respect to deadly force, uncontrolled discretion opens the door for discriminatory practices. Some police departments use an "aggressive preventive patrol" strategy to encourage FIs. More than 30 years ago, the Kerner Commission found that such a strategy aggravated tensions with minority communities.[118]

Young African American and Hispanic men believe they are singled out for frequent and unjustified harassment in such actions. In Chicago, 71 percent of high school students surveyed reported that they had been stopped by the police, and 86 percent felt the police had been disrespectful.[119]

Studies of FIs have produced conflicting findings. In the San Diego Field Interrogation study from the 1970s, nearly half of all people stopped and questioned were African Americans, although they represented only 17.5 percent and 4.8 percent of the population of the two precincts in the study. All of the people stopped and questioned were male, and about 60 percent were juveniles.[120] The San Diego study also found, however, that 75 percent of all the people stopped and questioned thought the officer had a right to stop them. In some respects, this seems to be a highly positive response; however, if 25 percent of all people stopped and questioned did not feel that it was legitimate, there would be a significant number of unhappy or even angry people over the course of a year.[121]

A report by the Massachusetts attorney general found that "Boston police officers engaged in improper, and unconstitutional, conduct in the 1989–1990 period with respect to stops and searches of minority individuals."[122] Interviews with more than 50 individuals revealed a pattern of African American men and women being stopped and questioned without any basis for suspicion, threatened by the officers if they asked why they were being stopped, and subjected to highly intrusive and embarrassing strip searches in public.

The most sophisticated study of street stops was commissioned by the New York state attorney general. The study found that even after investigators had controlled for crime rates and the racial composition of particular neighborhoods, African Americans and Hispanics were stopped at rates that could not be explained by factors other than race and ethnicity. The data indicated that police actions were not explained by an effort to control disorder or to improve the quality of life in neighborhoods, but in terms of "policing poor people in poor places."[123]

An ethnographic study of a low-income, high-crime neighborhood in St. Louis found that police officers had deeply divided opinions about how to police the area. They wanted to establish close relations with residents and help them deal with their problems. At the same time, however, many officers wanted to "kick ass," meaning they wanted to be free to use their own judgment to deal with crime in the neighborhood. They did not engage in these tactics because of their fear of being disciplined by the department (being "written up").[124]

Special Issue: Stereotyping and Routine Police Work

An underlying problem in the traffic stop and stop-and-frisk issues is the tendency of police officers to stereotype certain kinds of people and to act on those stereotypes. Jerome Skolnick argued many years ago that stereotyping is built into police work. Officers are trained to be suspicious and look for criminal activity.

As a result, they develop "a perceptual shorthand to identify certain kinds of people" as suspects, relying on visual "cues": dress, demeanor, context, gender, and age. Thus, a young, low-income man in a wealthy neighborhood presents several cues that trigger an officer's suspicion in a way that a middle-aged woman or even a young woman in the same context does not.[125] Race is also often a "cue." A young, racial minority man in a white neighborhood is likely to trigger an officer's suspicion because he "looks out of place"—although he could be an honors student who attends church regularly and has never committed a crime. By the same token, the presence of two middle-class, white men in a minority neighborhood known to have a high level of drug trafficking is likely to trigger the suspicion that they are seeking to purchase drugs. Because racial minority men are disproportionately arrested for robbery and burglary, police officers can fall into the habit of stereotyping all young, racial minority men as offenders. With traffic stops, certain types of vehicles also serve as "cues": officers believe that certain kinds of persons drive certain kinds of cars, with the result that vehicles are a proxy for race and class. In their study of how police officers form suspicions about citizens, Dunham and Alpert found that "behavior" was the most important, followed by specific information about a suspect, the time and place of the event, and the citizens' appearance.[126]

Harvard law professor Randall Kennedy asks the question, "Is it proper to use a person's race as a proxy for an increased likelihood of criminal conduct?"[127] Can the police stop an African American man simply because the suspect in a crime is in that category or because of statistical evidence that young, African American men are disproportionately involved in crime, drug, or gang activity? He points out that the courts have frequently upheld this practice as long as race is one of several factors involved in a stop or an arrest and the stop is not done for purposes of harassment.

Kennedy then makes a strong argument that race should never be used as the basis for a police action "except in the most extraordinary of circumstances." First, if the practice is strictly forbidden, it will reduce the opportunity for the police to engage in harassment under the cloak of "reasonable" law enforcement measures. Second, the current practice of using race "nourishes powerful feelings of racial grievance against law enforcement authorities." Third, the resulting hostility to the police creates barriers to police–citizen cooperation in those communities "most in need of police protection." Fourth, permitting the practice contributes to racial segregation because African Americans will be reluctant to venture into white neighborhoods for fear of being stopped by the police.[128]

VERBAL ABUSE

Verbal abuse by police officers is one of the more common criticisms by citizens about the police. Some words, such as racial, ethnic, or gender epithets, are clearly wrong. Whether certain words are offensive depends on the specific context and how those words are perceived by the citizen. The mildest form of abuse is simple rudeness or discourtesy. An officer may speak in a sharp tone of voice or refuse to answer a citizen's question. Even if discourteous words do not have an explicit racial or ethnic component, they may be perceived as offensive in a certain context. Calling a citizen a name such as "asshole" or "scumbag" may not appear racially or ethnically motivated, but these words may be perceived as such in an encounter on the street between a white officer and a minority citizen.

Even simple rudeness, such as calling a citizen "stupid," can have a major impact on police–community relations. As we have already discussed, citizens are very sensitive to how they are treated, and the lack of politeness by an officer has a major impact on public attitudes. Racial or ethnic slurs represent a serious form of verbal abuse. They demean citizens, deny them equal treatment on the basis of their race or ethnicity, and aggravate police–community tensions.

For police officers, derogatory language is a control technique. White, Cox, and Basehart argue that profanity directed at citizens serves several functions: to get their attention; keep them at a distance; and label, degrade, dominate, and control them.[129] It is also often a moral judgment. As middle-class professionals, police officers often look down on people who do not live by their standards, including criminals, chronic alcoholics, and the homeless.

Verbal abuse is especially hard to control. The typical incident occurs on the street, often without any witnesses except other police officers or friends of the citizen, and leaves no tangible evidence (unlike a physical attack). Consequently, most complaints about verbal abuse become "swearing contests" in which the citizen says one thing and the officer says just the opposite. Few people bother to file formal complaints about this kind of behavior, however. In 2001, only 4 of the nearly 2,000 allegations investigated by the San Francisco Office of Citizen Complaints involved racial slurs. Other agencies have reported similarly low rates of racial slur allegations.[130]

POLICE OFFICER ATTITUDES AND BEHAVIOR

Are police officers prejudiced? What is the relationship between police officer attitudes and the behavior of police on the street? The evidence on these questions is extremely complex. As Smith, Graham, and Adams explain, "Attitudes are one thing and behavior is another."[131]

Bayley and Mendelsohn compared the attitudes of Denver police officers with those of the general public and found that police officers were prejudiced "but only slightly more so than the community as a whole." Eight percent of the officers indicated that they disliked Spanish-surnamed people, compared with 6 percent of the general public. When asked about specific social situations (for example, "Would you mind eating together at the same table?" or "Would you mind having someone in your family marry a member of a minority group?"), the officers were less prejudiced against Spanish-surnamed people than the general public was but were more prejudiced against African Americans.[132]

Bayley and Mendelsohn's findings are consistent with other research indicating that police officers are not significantly different from the general population in terms of psychological makeup and attitudes, including attitudes about race and ethnicity. Police departments, in other words, do not recruit a distinct group of prejudiced or psychologically unfit individuals. Bayley and Mendelsohn found that on all personality scales, Denver police officers were "absolutely average people."[133]

The attitudes of officers are often contradictory, however. Smith and colleagues found that the overwhelming majority of police officers (79.4 percent) agreed or strongly agreed with the statement "Most people in this community respect police officers."[134] At the same time, however, most (44.2 percent) believed that the chances of being abused by a citizen were very high. The characteristics of an officer's assignment affect perception of the community. Officers assigned to racial or ethnic minority communities, high-crime areas, and poor neighborhoods thought they received less respect from the public than did officers working in other areas. Reiss noted a significant contradiction between the attitudes and behavior of the officers observed in his study. About 75 percent of the officers were observed making racially derogatory remarks, yet they did not engage in systematic discrimination in arrest or use of physical force.[135]

In short, attitudes do not translate directly into behavior. One of the main reasons involves the bureaucratic nature of police work. An arrest is reviewed first by a supervising officer and then by other criminal justice officials (prosecutor, defense attorney, and judge). News media coverage is also possible. The potentially unfavorable judgments of these people serve to control the officer's behavior. Verbal abuse, however, is much harder to control for the simple reason that it rarely comes to the attention of anyone else.

Much of the research on police officer attitudes was conducted in the 1960s or early 1970s. Since then, police employment practices have changed substantially. Far more African American, Hispanic, female, and college-educated officers are employed today (as discussed later). The earlier research, which assumed a disproportionately white, male police force, may no longer be valid.[136] In fact, the Police Foundation study of police abuse of authority found striking differences in the attitudes of white and African American officers. African American officers, by a huge margin, are more likely to believe that police officers use excessive force and use excessive force more often against racial and ethnic minorities and the poor.[137]

Most police departments offer sensitivity or cultural diversity training programs for their officers. These programs usually cover the history of race relations, traditional racial and ethnic stereotypes, and explanations of different racial and ethnic cultural patterns. Questions have been raised about the effectiveness of these programs, however. Some critics fear that they may be counterproductive, serving only to reinforce negative attitudes and focusing on attitudes rather than behavior. Most important, classroom training does not necessarily address on-the-street behavior of officers. Policies that directly address behavior—such as the PERF policy on traffic enforcement—are more likely to produce positive changes.[138] Alpert, Smith, and Watters argue that, "Mere classroom lectures . . . are insufficient" and emphasis needs to be placed on actual on-the-street behavior.[139]

POLICE CORRUPTION AND PEOPLE OF COLOR

Police corruption has a special impact on minority communities. Most police corruption involves vice activities—drugs, gambling, prostitution, after-hours night clubs—that historically have been segregated in low-income and racial minority neighborhoods.

In the 1970s, the Knapp Commission found that payoffs to New York City police officers were about $300 per month in midtown Manhattan, the central business district, and $1,500 in Harlem, the center of the African American community.[140] In the 1990s, the Mollen Commission exposed a pattern of corruption and violence in the poorest African American and Hispanic neighborhoods. Officers took bribes for protecting the drug trade, beat up drug dealers, broke into apartments, and stole drugs and money.[141] Historically, police corruption has been concentrated in poor and racial minority neighborhoods because that is where illegal vice crimes have been concentrated. This pattern reflects a more general pattern of unequal law enforcement. The poor and minorities have not had the political power to demand the kind of law enforcement available to white and middle-class people. The result has been that vice and the resulting corruption are concentrated in poor and minority neighborhoods. The non-enforcement of the law is as much a form of discrimination as overenforcement.

Police corruption harms racial and ethnic minorities in several ways. First, allowing vice activities to flourish in low-income and minority communities represents an unequal and discriminatory pattern of law enforcement. Second, the existence of open drug dealing or prostitution degrades the quality of neighborhood life. Third, vice activities encourage secondary crime—the patrons of prostitutes are robbed; afterhours clubs are the scenes of robbery and assault; and competing drug gangs have shoot-outs with rival gangs. Fourth, community awareness of police corruption damages the reputation of the police. In 1993, 26 percent of African Americans thought the ethical standards of the police were "low" or "very low," compared with only 8 percent of whites.[142] In Washington, DC, a study by the Police Foundation found that 19.4 percent of Hispanic residents and 14 percent of African Americans, compared with only 7.2 percent of whites, feel that police officers in the city are "dishonest."[143]

POLICE–COMMUNITY RELATIONS PROGRAMS

Police departments have tried different strategies for improving police–community relations. Some have proved to be more effective than others.

Special Units

In response to the riots of the 1960s, most big-city police departments established special police–community relations (PCR) programs to resolve racial and ethnic tensions. Most involved a separate PCR unit within the department. PCR unit officers spent most of their time speaking in schools or to community groups.[144] Some PCR units also staffed neighborhood storefront offices to make the department more accessible to community residents who either were intimidated by police headquarters or found it difficult to travel downtown. Another popular program was the "ride-along," which allowed citizens to ride in a patrol car and view policing from an officer's perspective.

The PCR programs of the 1960s were not effective. A Justice Department report concluded that they "tended to be marginal to the operations of the police department," with little direct impact on patrol and other key operations.[145] Public education and ride-along programs mainly reached people who already had favorable attitudes toward the police. In the 1970s, most departments reduced or abolished their PCR programs.

Community Policing

Community policing represents an entirely new approach to policing, and as a result some community policing programs have had positive effects on police–community relations. The ambitious Chicago Alternative Police Services (CAPS) program includes a series of regular meetings between patrol beat officers and community residents.[146] The major difference is that under community policing, these meetings are designed to develop two-way communication, with citizens providing input into police policies. The old PCR programs mainly involved one-way communication from the police to the community—in short, a standard public relations effort where the organization attempts to sell itself to the public.

Although it was not labeled community policing *per se*, the Boston Gun Project involved activities that were consistent with the philosophy of community policing. In its effort to fight gun crimes, the Boston Police Department developed a close working relationship with religious leaders in Boston, developing what was called the Ten Point Coalition. This effort had a positive effect on relations between the African American community and the police department.[147]

In a national survey of public attitudes about the police, Weitzer and Tuch found that people who believe that community policing is practiced in their neighborhood are less likely to believe that the police frequently use excessive force. The study did not verify whether the police were actually practicing community policing in particular neighborhoods or whether it had a real effect on police conduct. Nonetheless, the belief that it exists has a positive effect on attitudes.[148] Skogan and Hartnett found that community policing had a positive effect on citizens' attitudes toward the police in Chicago. Both African Americans and whites who lived in community policing districts were less likely to believe that police use of excessive force was a problem; similarly they were less likely to believe that the police stopped too many people.[149]

Community policing works only if residents are aware of and involved in the program. Skogan found that in Chicago Latinos who spoke Spanish were significantly less aware of the CAPS (Chicago Alternative Policing Strategy) than were other groups. They were also the group least likely to have attended a neighborhood beat meeting to discuss neighborhood problems with community policing officers. African Americans, by contrast, were the most likely to have attended a beat meeting. Latinos now represent more than 26 percent of the Chicago population, and an estimated 60 percent of them indicate that they prefer to speak Spanish. Spanish-speaking Latinos were least likely to have learned about CAPS from another person (as opposed to television or a printed brochure). In short, special efforts are needed to involve this component of Chicago residents in the community policing program.[150]

Responding to Specific Community Concerns

Some departments have made special efforts to respond to specific community concerns. In one of the best examples, the San Diego Police Department voluntarily decided to collect traffic stop data to determine if there was a pattern of racial profiling. San Diego was the first police department in the country to conduct voluntary data collection. San Jose, California, quickly did the same, and many other departments have followed their example.

In his introduction to the first traffic stop data report, San Jose police chief William Landsdowne explained that his department "prides itself upon being responsive to the needs and concerns of everyone who lives, works, learns, plays, and travels within San Jose."[151] Undertaking data collection—a difficult, time-consuming effort that is not popular with all the officers—indicates that the chief was willing to give real meaning to those words.

The Boston Police Department is widely credited with both reducing crime and improving relations with minority communities in the 1990s. The main program for reducing crime was the Boston Gun Project, a series of specific actions designed to reduce handgun violence among young people and gang members in particular. One of the main programs to improve police–community relations was the Ten Point Coalition, a partnership between the police department and the religious community. The Ten Point Coalition represents a combination of the principles underlying both community policing and problem-oriented policing. These principles include a recognition that the police cannot fight crime alone, that citizens are important "coproducers" of law enforcement services, and that police departments need to build working partnerships with established community groups. In African American communities, churches have historically been one of the most important institutions.[152]

The Ten Point Coalition established a number of specific efforts: "Adopt-a-Gang" programs where churches provide drop-in centers for young people, neighborhood crime-watch programs, partnerships with community health centers to provide counseling for families with problems, and rape crisis centers for battered women.[153]

A major concern among racial and ethnic minority communities is that police departments do not care about them and are unwilling to acknowledge mistakes that affect their communities. In 2005 the Los Angeles Sheriff's Department took a dramatic step in the direction of expressing concern about a controversial incident. Sheriff's deputies fired 120 shots at an African American man in a vehicle who they believed was an armed suspect. He was wounded and arrested but found to be not the suspect. In a remarkable gesture, the deputies involved publicly apologized to the community for the impact of the incident on the community. There is no record of officers in any department ever apologizing for their actions in this manner. At the same time, the Sheriff personally expressed his concern, speedily revised the department's shooting policy, and disciplined the officers. All of these steps represented an effort to repair the damage done by an excessive use of force by officers.[154]

A report by the Vera Institute on police and immigrant communities found that community leaders want to see results. It concluded that "if community participants do not see immediate changes in police policy and procedures," they may perceive a department's outreach efforts "as little more than public relations."[155] In the 120 shots incident in Los Angeles, the Sheriff's Department demonstrated its responsiveness by revising its shooting policy within a month.

Reduce Officer Misconduct

The National Academy of Sciences report concluded that one way to improve police–community relations is to improve officer conduct and to reduce specific incidents of misconduct.[156] As mentioned earlier, citizens are sensitive to how officers treat them. In Skogan's study of Chicago, citizen attitudes were heavily influenced by whether they felt they were treated fairly, whether the officer explained the situation to them, whether the officer was polite, and whether the officer listened to what they had to say about the situation.[157]

Concern about how officers treat people arises from the field of procedural justice. Research by Tom Tyler and other experts in this field has found that people's attitudes are affected by how they are treated and not necessarily by the outcome of the interaction.[158]

Police departments can take positive steps to improve officer conduct. The PERF policy on traffic stops, for example, recommends that officers explain the reason for the stop. If there is no violation of the law or the stop was based on a mistaken identity, PERF recommends that officer apologize for the inconvenience. More courteous officer performance in traffic stops could have a major impact on citizen attitudes. The BJS study of police citizen encounters found that traffic stops are the most frequent reason for police–citizen contacts.[159]

Controlling police use of deadly force is also extremely important. The 2001 riot in Cincinnati was sparked by the fifteenth fatal shooting of an African American in 5 years by the police department. The failure to control officer use of deadly force obviously had a negative effect on how African Americans perceive the police. Similarly, controlling officer use of less lethal force, particularly the use of the police baton or Taser stun guns, is also likely to improve community relations.

Police departments can also take steps to ensure the *cultural competency* of their officers. The New York Police Department (NYPD), for example, prepared a Fact Sheet on Arab communities. It includes a section on "What Codes of Conduct Should I Know When Entering an Arab's Home?" It explains that in "many Arab Muslim households [people] remove their shoes at the door because carpeting is used for prayers."[160]

Ensuring Cultural Competence

Because American society is becoming so much more diverse, experts argue that the police and other criminal justice agencies need to ensure that their employees possess cultural competence. Cultural competence is defined as being aware of the dynamics of interactions between people of different cultures and developing both agency policies and skills among agency personnel to address these dynamics. Issues related to cultural competence arise not just in criminal justice, but in health care, education, and other social services. Georgetown University sponsors a National Center for Cultural Competence devoted to research and training on this issue.[161]

The Charlotte-Mecklenburg, North Carolina Police Department created a special International Unit to respond to all of the new cultural groups in the community. The country had experienced high rates of immigration of Hispanics, Hmong, Vietnamese, and Indians. The unit produced a manual for all officers in the department that, for example, explained traditional medical practices of coining and cupping that leave marks on the body and are often misinterpreted as physical abuse.[162]

CITIZEN COMPLAINTS AGAINST THE POLICE

One of the greatest sources of tension between the police and minorities is the perceived failure of police departments to respond adequately to citizen complaints about police misconduct. The development of external citizen oversight agencies, which now exist in virtually all big cities, is a response to this problem.[163]

African Americans file a disproportionate number of all complaints against the police. In New York City, for example, African Americans made 52.2 percent of all complaints filed with the Civilian Complaint Review Board, even though they represent only 24.5 percent of the city's population.[164] Hispanics, however, are less likely to file complaints. Language barriers are a problem for Hispanics who do not speak English, and many police departments do not provide information or complaint forms in Spanish (or Asian languages). Many recent immigrants do not understand the nature of the citizen complaint process and assume that they need an attorney. A study based on interviews with Hispanic immigrants found that many immigrants do not have the "legal consciousness" of long-time resident Americans and do not understand that they have a right to file a complaint against a government official.[165] Also, many recent immigrants from Mexico or other Latin American countries are extremely fearful of the police because complaining about an officer in those countries can result in serious retaliation, even death.

T A B L E 4.6 **Race and Ethnicity of Officers Receiving Complaints, Compared to Composition of the Department, New York City, 2004**

Percentage of Officers	Receiving Complaints	Percentage of Officers in the Department
White	60.1	61.1
African American	15.3	14.9
Hispanic	21.7	21.4
Asian	2.8	2.2

SOURCE: New York City Civilian Complaint Review Board, *Status Report, January–December 2004* (New York: Civilian Complaint Review Board, 2005), Table 9.

Racial and ethnic minorities accuse police departments of failing to adequately investigate complaints and do not discipline officers who are guilty of misconduct. There is a widespread belief that the complaint review process is just a "cover-up."[166] A survey in Washington, DC, found that 75.3 percent of African Americans believe that police department investigations of alleged officer misconduct are biased. Meanwhile, 65.6 percent of Hispanic residents and 81.8 percent of Asians also feel the process is biased. It is surprising that more than half of whites (56.1 percent) also think that complaint investigations are biased.[167] Most people who feel they are victims of police abuse do not even file a formal complaint. One study found that only 30 percent of those people who felt they had a reason to complain about a police officer took any kind of action, and only some of them contacted the police department. Most people called someone else (a friend or some other government official).[168]

Historically, some departments have actively discouraged citizen complaints. The Kerner Commission found evidence of this in the 1960s.[169] In the 1990s the Christopher Commission found that officers at Los Angeles police stations discouraged people from filing complaints and sometimes even threatened them with arrest. Additionally, officers frequently did not complete Form 1.81, which records an official complaint.[170] In response to criticisms about how it handled complaints, the Los Angeles Police Department established a special toll-free number as a complaint hotline. A study by the American Civil Liberties Union in Los Angeles, however, found that only 13 percent of the people calling local police stations were given the toll-free number. Other callers (71.9 percent) were told that there was no such number or that the officer could not give it out or they were put on hold indefinitely.[171]

Police department internal affairs (IA) or professional standards units traditionally have handled citizen complaints. The police subculture is very strong, however, and IA officers tend to protect their colleagues and the department against external criticism. Westley found that the police subculture emphasizes "silence, secrecy, and solidarity." Under the informal "code of silence," officers often are willing to lie to cover up misconduct by fellow officers.[172] The Christopher Commission concluded that in Los Angeles, "the greatest single barrier to the effective investigation and adjudication of complaints is the officers' unwritten 'code of silence.'" The code "consists of one simple rule: an officer does not provide adverse information against a fellow officer."[173] The Mollen Commission investigating police corruption in New York City found the "pervasiveness" of the code of silence "alarming." The Commission asked one officer, "Were you ever afraid that one of your fellow officers might turn you in?" He answered, "Never," because "cops don't tell on cops."[174]

As a result, most citizen complaints become "swearing contests": the citizen alleges one thing, and the officer denies it. Few citizen complaints are sustained by police investigators. Police departments sustain only 10.4 percent of all complaints.[175]

One alternative to traditional complaint investigation is to mediate complaints. Mediation is a voluntary process in which the complainant and the officer meet face-to-face (usually for about an hour) with a professional mediator supervising the session. The point of mediation is not to establish guilt but to foster a dialogue that leads to better understanding on both sides of the issue. The end result is often simply an agreement that each side has listened to and understands the other person's point of view. Vivian Berger, an experienced mediator in New York City, argues that mediation is particularly appropriate for complaints when the officer and the complainant are of different races or ethnic groups. She explains that many complaints are not formally about race (for example, the allegation is discourtesy) but that "they are really about race"—that is, the complaint is the result of misunderstandings that are rooted in racial or cultural differences. Mediation provides a structured process in which both sides have to listen to each other. In many cases, this can help bridge the racial divide.[176]

CITIZEN OVERSIGHT OF THE POLICE

To ensure better handling of complaints against the police, civil rights groups have demanded external or citizen oversight of complaints. Citizen oversight is based on the idea that people who are not police officers will be more independent and objective in investigating complaints. Despite strong opposition from police unions, citizen review has spread rapidly in recent years. By 2001 there were more than 100 oversight agencies in the United States, covering almost all of the big cities and many smaller cities.[177]

Some citizen oversight procedures investigate complaints themselves (for example, the San Francisco Office of Citizen Complaints). Others provide some citizen input into investigations conducted by IA officers (for example, the Kansas City Office of Citizen Complaints). Some procedures systematically audit the performance of the IA unit (for example, the Portland Independent Police Review Office, which is located in the office of the city auditor).[178]

There is some evidence that citizen review enhances public confidence in the complaint process. In 1991, for example, San Francisco had five times as many complaints per officer as Los Angeles. Some observers argue that San

Francisco generates more complaints because its civilian review procedure enhances citizens feelings that their complaints will receive a fair hearing, whereas the Los Angeles Police Department (before recent reforms) was actively discouraging complaints.[179]

To better serve citizens who want to file a complaint, an increasing number of departments and citizen oversight agencies are taking a number of steps: (1) accepting complaints at locations other than police headquarters; (2) accepting complaints over the phone or by email; (3) accepting anonymous complaints; (4) providing a toll-free telephone number for complaints; (5) providing detailed information about the complaint process on their websites; and (6) providing information and complaint forms in all of the languages appropriate for the community.

POLICE EMPLOYMENT PRACTICES

Discrimination in the employment of racial and ethnic minorities as police officers has been a long-standing problem. During the segregation era (1890s–1960s), Southern cities did not hire any African American officers and police departments in Northern states engaged in systematic employment discrimination.[180] In 1967, for example, African Americans made up 23 percent of the population in Oakland but only 2.3 percent of the police officers.[181] Employment discrimination occurs in three different areas of policing: recruitment, promotion to supervisory ranks, and assignment to shifts and specialized units.

The former Boston police commissioner Paul Evans recognized the need for a diverse workforce in terms of practical law enforcement. He stated, "I know that having African American and Hispanic and Vietnamese officers, people of different backgrounds and cultures who can conduct comfortable interviews with crime victims and can infiltrate crime rings that aren't white—I know the need for that is just common sense."[182]

Trends in African American and Hispanic Employment

Since the 1960s, some progress has been made in the employment of racial and ethnic minority police officers (Figure 4.3). In 1960 an estimated 3.6 percent of all sworn officers in the United States were African Americans. By 2003 the figure had increased to 11.7 percent. Hispanics represented about 9.1 percent of all sworn officers that year. (Little data exist on Hispanic officers for earlier years.)[183]

The aggregate figures on employment are misleading because, as noted in Chapter 1, the racial and ethnic minority groups are not evenly distributed across the country. It is more useful to look at particular police departments to see whether they represent the communities they serve. The accreditation standards for law enforcement agencies require that "the agency has minority group and female employees in the sworn law enforcement ranks in approximate proportion

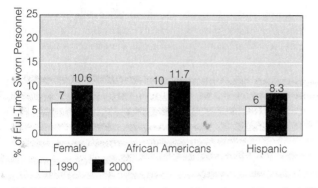

FIGURE 4.3   African American, Hispanic, and Female Officers, 1990–2000

SOURCE: Bureau of Justice Statistics, *Law Enforcement Management and Administrative Statistics, 1990,* (Washington, DC: Department of Justice, 1992); Bureau of Justice Statistics, *Law Enforcement Management and Administrative Statistics, 2000,* (Washington, DC: Department of Justice, 2003).
NOTE: Survey methodologies are not exactly comparable.

to the makeup of the available work force in the law enforcement agency's service community."[184]

The Equal Employment Opportunity (EEO) Index provides a good measure of whether a department represents the community it serves. The EEO Index compares the percentage of minority group officers with the percentage of that group in the local population. If, for example, a community is 40 percent African American and 30 percent of the officers are African American, the EEO Index is 0.75.[185] The EEO Index puts an interesting perspective on individual departments. In 2000 New York City Police Department's EEO Index for African Americans was only 48.8. The city population was 26.6 percent African American but only 13 percent of the officers were. The NYPD EEO Index for Hispanic officers was 66.6 (27 percent Hispanic population and 18 percent Hispanic officers). In short, the NYPD was less than halfway toward meeting the goal of matching the African American population.[186]

The Boston Police Department provides an example of how an employer can take active steps to increase racial and ethnic minority employment. Former Police Commissioner Paul Evans found that the local civil service rules made exceptions for job candidates with special skills. Because Boston has a significant Haitian population, Evans was able to use these rules to hire officers who could speak French Creole and thus could communicate better with Haitian residents. Evans then extended this practice to include job applicants who could speak Spanish, Vietnamese, or Chinese.[187]

Los Angeles offers another interesting perspective on minority employment. In 1992 the police department had a perfect EEO Index (1.00) for African Americans (14 percent of both the population and the sworn officers). Yet the Rodney King incident revealed that the department had a serious race relations problem. The Christopher Commission found a racist climate within the department, with officers making racist comments over the department's computerized message system.[188] In short, merely employing racial minority officers does not automatically eliminate police–community relations problems. The quality of policing is largely determined by the organizational culture of the department, which is the combined product of leadership by the chief, formal policies on critical issues such as the use of force, and rank-and-file officer peer culture.

In some police departments, non–Hispanic white officers are now the minority. The City of Miami Police Department in 2000 was 54 percent Hispanic, 27 percent African American, and only 19 percent non-Hispanic white. Non-Hispanic whites were only 34 percent of the Detroit Police Department officers in 2000.[189]

Recent immigration trends have heightened the importance of having bilingual officers who can communicate in Spanish or Asian languages. The Christopher Commission found that in 1991 in the heavily Hispanic communities of Los Angeles, often no Spanish-speaking officers were available to take citizen complaints.[190] Similar problems arise in communities with significant Asian American populations, representing different nationalities and languages.

A study of police and Hispanic citizen interactions in a Midwestern city found that, although language barriers did not create any major crises (even violent incidents arising from an inability to communicate), they did create delays in the delivery of services and some frustration on the part of officers. When handling a situation in which the citizens did not speak English, officers either found a family member or bystander who could translate or simply "muddled through" with "street Spanish."[191]

Relatively few Native Americans and Asian Americans are employed as sworn police officers in departments other than tribal law enforcement agencies (where Native Americans are about 56 percent of all officers). The Justice Department's report *Law Enforcement Management and Administrative Statistics* provides the most systematic set of data. A few police departments do have a significant number of Asian American officers. They represent 13 percent of the officers in San Francisco in 2000. Native Americans, however, are substantially underrepresented, even in states with the largest Native American populations. They are only 1 percent of the sworn officers in Albuquerque, New Mexico, for example.[192]

The Law of Employment Discrimination

Employment discrimination based on race or ethnicity is illegal. The Fourteenth Amendment to the U.S. Constitution provides that "No state shall ... deny to any person ... the equal protection of the laws." Title VII of the 1964 Civil Rights Act prohibits employment discrimination based on race, color, national origin, religion, or sex. The 1972 Equal Employment Opportunity Act extended the coverage of Title VII to state and local governments. In addition, state civil rights laws prohibit employment discrimination on the basis of race or ethnicity. According to Section 703, "It shall be an unlawful employment practice for an employer ... to fail or refuse to hire or to discharge any individual, or otherwise to discriminate against any individual with respect to his compensation, terms, conditions, or privileges of employment, because of such individual's race, color, religion, sex, or national origin."[193]

The most controversial aspect of employment discrimination is the policy of affirmative action. The Office of Federal Contract Compliance defines affirmative action as "results-oriented actions [taken] to ensure equal employment opportunity [which may include] goals to correct under-utilization...[and] backpay, retroactive seniority, makeup goals and timetables." Affirmative action originated in 1966 when President Lyndon Johnson issued Executive Order 11246 directing all federal contractors to have affirmative action programs. Some affirmative action programs are voluntary, whereas others are court ordered; some have general goals, whereas others have specific quotas.

An affirmative action program consists of several steps. The first is a census of employees to determine the number and percentage of racial minorities and women in different job categories. The data are then used to identify under-utilization. *Underutilization* exists where the percentage of employees in a particular job category is less than the percentage of potentially qualified members of that group in the labor force. If underutilization exists, the employer is required to develop a plan to eliminate it. Recruitment programs usually include active outreach to potential minority applicants, mainly through meetings with community groups and leaders. The New Haven, Connecticut, police department successfully increased the representation of racial minority officers from 22 percent in 1991 to 40 percent by 2000. The department recognized that its traditional methods of recruiting, such as placing ads in the newspaper, were not working effectively for groups other than whites. To overcome this problem, the department worked closely with community groups, holding focus groups to discuss the issue, for example. These sessions generated ideas about which messages were most effective with different racial and ethnic groups, and focus group members later helped with the recruitment effort. Also, police officer recruiters were carefully selected on the basis of their enthusiasm, communication skills, and ability to relate to different groups.[194]

An employer may voluntarily adopt an affirmative action plan with quotas. In 1974 the Detroit Police Department adopted a voluntary quota of promoting one African American officer for each white officer promoted. As a result, by 1992 half of all the officers at the rank of sergeant or higher were African American. Most affirmative action plans have been court ordered, as a result of discrimination suits under Title VII of the 1964 Civil Rights Act. A 1980 consent decree settling the suit against the Omaha, Nebraska, police department, for example, established a long-term goal of having 9.5 percent African American officers in the department within 7 years. At the time of the suit, African Americans were only 4 percent of the sworn officers, and the figure had been declining. To achieve the 9.5 percent goal, the court ordered a 3-stage recruitment plan: African Americans would be 40 percent of all new recruits until they were 6 percent of the department, 33 percent of recruits until they were 8 percent, and then 25 percent of recruits until the final 9.5 percent goal was reached. The city reached the goals of the court order ahead of schedule, and by 1992 African American officers were 11.5 percent of the police department.

Discrimination in Assignment

Discrimination also occurs in the assignment of police officers. In the South during the segregation era, African American officers were not assigned to white neighborhoods and were not permitted to arrest whites.[195] Many Northern cities also confined minority officers to minority neighborhoods. Reiss found that some police departments assigned their incompetent white officers to racial minority neighborhoods.[196] Seniority rules that govern the assignment in most departments today make blatant discrimination difficult. Officers with the most seniority, regardless of race, ethnicity, or gender, have first choice for the most desirable assignments. Seniority rules can have an indirect race effect, however. In a department that has only recently hired a significant number of racial or ethnic minorities, these officers will be disproportionately assigned to high-crime areas because of their lack of seniority. Fyfe found that this seniority-based assignment pattern explained why African American officers in New York City fired their weapons more often than white officers did (although the rates were virtually the same for all officers assigned to the high crime areas, regardless of race).[197]

There is also discrimination in assignment to special and desirable units. The special counsel to the Los Angeles County Sheriff Department identified two categories of desirable positions. "Coveted" positions were those that officers sought because they are interesting, high paying, or convenient (in terms of work schedule). In the Los Angeles Sheriff Department, these included the Special Enforcement Bureau, the Narcotics Bureau, and precinct station detective assignments. "High-profile" positions, however, are those likely to lead to promotion and career advancement. These include operations deputy, the Recruitment Training Bureau, and field training officer positions.[198]

An investigative study by the *New York Times* found that African American male officers were seriously underrepresented in the elite units of the NYPD. The 124-officer mounted patrol unit had only 3 African Americans, and there were only 2 in the 159-officer harbor patrol unit. It is well understood in the NYPD that selection for an elite unit depends on having a friend who will sponsor you—a "hook" or a "rabbi" in the slang of the NYPD. With few people in high command and in elite units, African American officers often find their career paths blocked in those areas.[199]

The assignment of African American officers to plainclothes detective work has created a new problem. In 1992 an African American transit police officer in New York City wearing plain clothes was shot and seriously wounded by a white officer who mistook him for a robber. Similar incidents have occurred in other cities. The *New York Times* report found that in New York City, virtually all of the many of African American officers interviewed had at some time been stopped and questioned—sometimes at gunpoint—by white officers.[200]

The Impact of Diversity

Civil rights leaders and police reformers have fought for increased employment of racial and ethnic minorities with three different goals in mind. First, employment discrimination is illegal and must be eliminated for that reason alone. Second,

Focus on an Issue

Would It Make a Difference? Assigning African American Officers to African American Neighborhoods

Some civil rights activists argue that police departments should assign African American officers exclusively to African American neighborhoods. They believe that these officers would be more sensitive to community needs, more polite and respectful to neighborhood residents, and less likely to act in a discriminatory manner.

Is this a good idea? Would it, in fact, improve the quality of policing in minority neighborhoods? The evidence does not support this proposal.

First, as we have already seen, no evidence suggests that African American, Hispanic, and white officers behave in significantly different ways. Fyfe's (1981) research on deadly force found that officers assigned to high-crime precincts fired their weapons at similar rates, regardless of race. Reiss (1968) found that white and African American officers used excessive physical force at about the same rate. Black (1980) found no significant differences in the arrest patterns of white and African American officers. It is worth noting that male and female officers have also been found to behave in roughly similar ways. Thus, most experts on the police argue that situational and departmental factors, not race or gender, influence police officer behavior (Sherman, 1980).

Second, assigning only African American officers to African American neighborhoods, or Hispanic officers to Hispanic neighborhoods, would discriminate against the officers themselves.

It would "ghettoize" them and deny them the variety of assignments and experience that helps lead to promotion. The policy would also perpetuate racial stereotypes by promoting the idea that only African American officers could handle the African American community.

Third, the proposal is based on a faulty assumption about the nature of American urban communities. Although there are all-white, all–African American, and all-Hispanic neighborhoods, there are also many mixed neighborhoods. It is impossible to draw a clear line between the "white" and the "black" communities. Under the proposed policy, which officers would be assigned to mixed neighborhoods? Moreover, the racial and ethnic composition of neighborhoods is constantly changing (Reiss, 1971). Today's all-white neighborhood is tomorrow's multiracial and multiethnic neighborhood. Any attempt to draw precinct boundaries based on race or ethnicity would be quickly outdated.

some reformers believe that minority officers will behave in different ways than white officers on the street and be less likely to discriminate in making arrests or using physical force.[201] Third, many experts argue that police departments should reflect the communities they serve to create a positive public image.

With respect to the first objective, increased minority employment means that the agency is complying with the law of equal employment opportunity. Obeying the law is an important consideration, regardless of any other effects of minority employment. Along these lines, failure to hire an adequate number of racial or ethnic minorities frequently results in an employment discrimination suit, which is expensive and tends to create organizational turmoil.

With respect to the second goal, there is no clear evidence that white, African American, or Hispanic police officers behave in different ways on the job (see "Focus on an Issue: Would It Make a Difference? Assigning African American Officers to African American Neighborhoods," p. 150). They arrest and use physical and deadly force in similar fashions. For the most part, they are influenced by situational factors: the seriousness of the offense, the demeanor of the suspect, and so forth.

There is increased recognition of the importance of having officers with skills in languages other than English. Common sense suggests that officers who can communicate effectively in Spanish or Cambodian will be better able to serve people who speak those languages.[202] At present, however, there are no studies that would confirm this hypothesis. Diversifying a police department does have an impact on the police subculture, bringing in people with different attitudes. African American and Hispanic officers have formed their own organizations at both the local and national levels.

The National Black Police Officers Association and the Guardians, for example, represent African American officers. Hispanic officers have formed the National Latino Peace Officers Association and the Hispanic American Command Officers Association. These organizations offer a different perspective on police issues from the one presented by white police officers. After the Rodney King incident, for example, members of the African American Peace Officers Association in Los Angeles stated, "Racism is widespread in the department."[203] This was a very different point of view than that expressed by white Los Angeles officers. In this respect, minority employment breaks down the solidarity of the police subculture.

The National Black Police Officers Association published a brochure titled "Police Brutality: A Strategy to Stop the Violence," urging officers to report brutality by other officers. This brochure represents a sharp break with the traditional norms of the police subculture, which emphasize protecting other officers from outside investigations.[204] The Police Foundation's national survey of police officers found that African American officers are far more likely to believe that officers in their department use excessive force than are white officers.[205] Finally, an evaluation of community policing in Chicago found that African American officers were more receptive to change—including community policing—than were white officers.[206]

In short, minority officers do have a different perspective on policing and police problems than white officers. The extent to which these attitudes are translated into different behavior on the street is not clear, however. At the same time, differences in attitudes among officers of different race and ethnicity can cause conflict within the department. In a number of departments, race relations have been strained when African American officers file employment discrimination suits and white officers file countersuits challenging affirmative action programs. In a study of a Midwestern police department, Robin Haarr found little daily interaction between white and African American officers. In particular, she asked officers who they would seek out if they had a problem or question that needed answering.[207] In short, the racial divisions that exist in society at large are reproduced within police departments.

With respect to the third goal, improved police–community relations, there is some limited evidence that increased minority employment improves public opinion about the police. A survey of Chicago residents found a small but significant number of people who felt that the Chicago Police Department has improved because of increased numbers of minority officers in supervisory positions. Significantly, no respondents felt that the department had gotten worse because of increased minority employment.[208] A study in Detroit found that, unlike in all other surveys, African American residents rated the police department more favorably than did white residents, suggesting that this more favorable rating was the result of the significant African American representation in city government, including the police department.[209] As already mentioned, having bilingual officers on the force may improve the ability of the police to serve communities of recent immigrants and in that respect improve police–community relations with those groups.

People of Color as Supervisors and Chief Executives

African American and Hispanic officers are also seriously underrepresented in supervisory ranks. In 1992 African Americans were 11.5 percent of all sworn officers in New York City but only 6.6 percent of the officers at the rank of sergeant and higher. In Los Angeles, Hispanics were 22.3 percent of all sworn officers but only 13.4 percent of those at the rank of sergeant and higher.[210]

Female African American and Hispanic officers encounter both race and gender discrimination. Women, regardless of race or ethnicity, are significantly underrepresented among all sworn officers and even more underrepresented in the supervisory ranks. A 1992 survey found that white female officers were being promoted at a faster rate than either African American or Hispanic female officers. In Chicago, for example, there were 73 white females, 37 African American females, and 2 Hispanic females above the rank of sergeant in a department of 12,291 sworn officers. The data contradict the popular belief that minority women enjoy a special advantage because employers count them in two affirmative action categories. Hispanic women, in fact, were almost completely unrepresented at the rank of sergeant and higher.

Racial and ethnic minorities have been far more successful in achieving the rank of police chief executive. In recent years, African Americans have served as chief executive in many of the largest police departments in the country: New York City, Los Angeles, Chicago, Philadelphia, Atlanta, and New Orleans, among others. Several African American individuals have established distinguished careers as law enforcement chief executives. Lee P. Brown served as sheriff of Multnomah County, Oregon, and then police chief in Atlanta, Houston, and New York City. In 1993 he became President Clinton's director of the Office of Drug Control Policy and later was elected mayor of Houston. Hubert Williams served as police commissioner in Newark, New Jersey, and then became president of the Police Foundation, a private police research organization. Charles Ramsey was appointed superintendent of the Washington, DC, police department in 1998 after directing the Chicago Police Department's community policing program.

CONCLUSION

Significant problems persist in the relations between police and racial and ethnic communities in the United States. African Americans and Hispanics rate the police lower than do white Americans. There is persuasive evidence that minorities are more likely than white Americans to be shot and killed, arrested, and victimized by excessive physical force. Although some progress has been made in recent years in controlling police behavior, particularly with respect to the use of deadly force, significant racial and ethnic disparities remain. In addition, there is evidence of misconduct directed against racial and ethnic minorities and of police departments failing to discipline officers who are guilty of misconduct. Finally, police department employment discrimination continues.

With reference to the discrimination–disparity continuum we discussed in Chapter 1, the evidence about the police suggests a combination of three of the different patterns. Some disparities are institutionalized discrimination resulting from the application of neutral criteria (as in the greater likelihood of arrest for the more serious crimes). Some represent contextual discrimination (as in the greater likelihood of arrest of minorities suspected of crimes against whites). And some are individual acts of discrimination by prejudiced individuals. There is no basis for saying that a situation of pure justice exists or that racism is a "myth," as William Wilbanks argued.

The evidence supports the conflict perspective regarding the police and racial and ethnic minorities. The data suggest that police actions such as arrest, use of deadly force, and verbal abuse reflect the broader patterns of social and economic inequality in U.S. society that we discussed in detail in Chapter 3.

Those inequalities are both racial and economic. Thus, the injustices suffered by racial and ethnic minorities at the hands of the police are a result of both discrimination against ethnic and racial minorities and the disproportionate representation of minorities among the poor.

The evidence also supports Hawkins's call for a modified conflict perspective that takes into account evident complexities and contingencies. Some of the evidence we have reviewed, for example, indicates that in certain situations, African Americans receive less law enforcement protection than do whites.

Discrimination can result from too little policing as well as excessive policing. Other evidence suggests that the race of the suspect must be considered in conjunction with the race of the complainant. Finally, the evidence indicates significant changes in some important areas of policing with respect to racial and ethnic minorities. On the positive side, the number of people shot and killed by the police has declined. On the negative side, the War on Drugs has been waged most heavily against racial and ethnic minorities. In terms of employment, some slow but steady progress has been made in the employment of African Americans and Hispanics as police officers.

DISCUSSION QUESTIONS

1. What is meant by a contextual approach to examining policing, race, and ethnicity?

2. How is policing in Native American communities different from policing in the rest of the United States?

3. When does police use of force become "excessive" or "unjustified"? Give a definition of *excessive force*.

4. Are there any significant differences between how Hispanics and African Americans interact with the police? Explain.

5. Is there racial or ethnic discrimination in arrests? What is the evidence on this question?

6. Define the concept of *affirmative action*. Do you support or oppose affirmative action in the employment of police officers? Do you think affirmative action is more important in policing than in other areas of life? Explain.

NOTES

1. The Cincinnati consent decree and other consent decrees can be found at the U.S. Civil Rights Division website (http://www.usdoj.gov/crt/split/).

2. Sandra Lee Browning, Francis T. Cullen, Liqun Cao, Renee Kopache, and Thomas J. Stevenson, "Race and Getting Hassled by the Police: A Research Note," *Police Studies* 17, no. 1 (1994): 1–11.

3. David Harris, *Profiles in Injustice: Why Racial Profiling Won't Work* (New York: New Press, 2001); for the latest news, reports, and legislation on racial profiling, see Harris's website: www. profilesininjustice.com; ACLU, *Driving While Black* (New York: ACLU, 1999).

4. Bureau of Justice Statistics, *Policing and Homicide, 1976–98: Justifiable Homicide by Police, Police Officers Murdered by Felons*, NCJ 180987 (Washington, DC: U.S. Government Printing Office, 2001). Available at www.ncjrs.org.

5. Cecilia Menjivar and Cynthia L. Bejarano, "Latino Immigrants' Perceptions of Crime and Police Authorities in the United States: A Case Study from the Phoenix Metropolitan Area," *Ethnic and Racial Studies*, 27 (January 2004): 120–148.

6. Stewart Wakeling, Miriam Jorgensen, Susan Michaelson, and Manley Begay, *Policing on American Indian Reservations: A Report to the National Institute of Justice*, NCJ 188095 (Washington, DC: U.S. Government Printing Office, 2001). Available at www.ncjrs.org.

7. Police Executive Research Forum, *Racially Biased Policing: A Principled Response* (Washington, DC: PERF, 2001).

8. Gallup Poll data cited in Bureau of Justice Statistics, *Sourcebook of Criminal Justice Statistics, 2003*, p. 109. Online edition available at www.albany.edu.

9. It is drawn heavily from Samuel Walker and Charles M. Katz, *The Police in America: An Introduction*, 5th ed. (New York: McGraw-Hill, 2005), chap. 12.

10. Samuel Walker, *Police Interactions with Racial and Ethnic Minorities: Assessing the*

Evidence and Allegations (Washington, DC: Police Executive Research Forum, 2000).

11. Bureau of Justice Statistics, *Contacts Between Police and the Public: Findings from the 2002 National Survey*, NCJ 207845 (Washington, DC: U.S. Government Printing Office, 2005). Available at www.ncjrs.org.

12. Robert C. Davis and Nicole J. Henderson, "Willingness to Report Crimes: the Role of Ethic Group Membership and Community Efficacy," *Crime and Delinquency*, 49 (October 2003): 564–580.

13. Marianne O. Nielsen, "Contextualization for Native American Crime and Criminal Justice Involvement," in *Native Americans, Crime, and Justice*, Marianne O. Nielsen and Robert A. Silverman, eds. (Boulder, CO: Westview, 1996), p. 10.

14. "Officers Killed with Impunity," *Washington Post* (July 1, 2001), p. 1.

15. U.S. Department of Justice, *Youth Violence: A Community-Based Response: One City's Success Story* (Washington, DC: U.S. Department of Justice, 1996).

16. Ronald Weitzer, "Racialized Policing: Residents' Perceptions in Three Neighborhoods," *Law and Society Review* 34, no. 1 (2000): 129–156.

17. Walker and Katz, *Police in America*, chap. 2.

18. National Advisory Commission on Civil Disorders [Kerner Commission], *Report* (New York: Bantam Books, 1968).

19. Alfredo Mirandé, *Gringo Justice* (Notre Dame, IN: University of Notre Dame Press, 1987).

20. A video documentary, *Zoot Suit Riots*, along with supporting educational material, can be found on the Public Broadcasting System website at www.pbs.org.

21. Pew Hispanic Center, *Hispanics: A People in Motion* (Washington, DC: Pew Hispanic Center, 2005).

22. Henry I. DeGeneste and John P. Sullivan, *Policing a Multicultural Community* (Washington, DC: Police Executive Research Forum, 1997), p. 15.

23. Charlotte-Mecklenburg Police Department, International Unit, *Law Enforcement Services to a Growing International Community* (Charlotte, NC: Charlotte Mecklenburg Police Department, 2004).

24. Minneapolis Civilian Review Authority, *How to File a Complaint* (Minneapolis MN: CRA, n.d.).

25. Gallup Poll data cited in Bureau of Justice Statistics, *Sourcebook of Criminal Justice Statistics, 2003*, p. 109.

26. "Discrimination in America," *Washington Post* (June 21, 2001).

27. The Police Foundation, Metropolitan Police Department, *Biased Policing Project, Final Report* (Washington, DC: The Police Foundation, 2004), p. 67.

28. Ronald Weitzer, "Racialized Policing: Residents' Perceptions in Three Neighborhoods," *Law and Society Review*, 34, no. 1 (2000): 129–155.

29. A comprehensive overview of public opinion trends is in Steven A. Tuch and Ronald Weitzer, "Racial Differences in Attitudes toward the Police," *Public Opinion Quarterly* 61 (1997): 643–663.

30. Ronald Weitzer, "Incidents of Police Misconduct and Public Opinion, *Journal of Criminal Justice*, 30 (2002): 397–408.

31. Carl Werthman and Irving Piliavin, "Gang Members and the Police," in *The Police: Six Sociological Essays*, David J. Bordua, ed. (New York: Wiley, 1967), p. 58.

32. A. Allen Lind and Tom R. Tyler, *The Social Psychology of Procedural Justice* (New York: Plenum, 1988).

33. Wesley G. Skogan, "Citizen Satisfaction with Police Encounters," *Police Quarterly*, 8 (September 2005): 298–321.

34. David H. Bayley and Harold Mendelsohn, *Minorities and the Police: Confrontation in America* (New York: Free Press, 1969), p. 109.

35. Bureau of Justice Statistics, *Criminal Victimization 2000: Changes 1999–2000 with Trends 1993–2000*, NCJ 187007 (Washington, DC: U.S. Government Printing Office, 2001). Available at www.ncjrs.org.

36. "From Some Parents, Warnings about Police," *New York Times* (October 23, 1997), p. A18.

37. Cynthia Perez McCluskey, *Policing the Latino Community* (East Lansing, MI: Julian Samora Research Institute, 1998), p. 3.

38. Bureau of Justice Statistics, *Criminal Victimization 2003* (Washington, DC: Department of Justice, 2004). Available at www.ncjrs.org, NCJ 205445.

39. Bureau of Justice Statistics, *Contacts Between Police and the Public: Findings from the 1999 National Survey* (Washington, DC: Department of Justice, 2001). These data are not reported in the report on the more recent 2002 survey.

40. Leigh Herbst and Samuel Walker, "Language Barriers in the Delivery of Police Services: A Study of Police and Hispanic Interactions in a Midwestern City," *Journal of Criminal Justice* 29, no. 4 (2001): 329–340.

41. David L. Carter, "Hispanic Perceptions of Police Performance: An Empirical Assessment," *Journal of Criminal Justice* 13 (1985): 487–500.

42. Samuel Walker, "Complaints against the Police: A Focus Group Study of Citizen Perceptions, Goals, and Expectations," *Criminal Justice Review* 22, no. 2 (1997): 207–225.

43. Wesley G. Skogan, "Citizen Satisfaction with Police Encounters," *Police Quarterly*, 8 (September 2005): 298–321.

44. Stewart Wakeling, Miriam Jorgensen, Susan Michaelson, and Manley Begay, *Policing on American Indian Reservations: A Report to the National Institute of Justice*, NCJ 188095 (Washington, DC: U.S. Government Printing Office, 2001). Available at www.ncjrs.org.

45. Ibid., p. 9. William C. Canby, *American Indian Law* (St. Paul: West, 1998).

46. Eileen M. Luna, "The Growth and Development of Tribal Police," *Journal of Contemporary Criminal Justice*, 14, no. 1 (1998): 75–86; Wakeling et al., *Policing on American Indian Reservations*, p. 7.

47. Stewart Wakeling, Miriam Jorgensen, Susan Michaelson, and Manley Begay, *Policing on American Indian Reservations: A Report to the National Institute of Justice*, NCJ 188095 (Washington, DC: U.S. Government Printing Office, 2001). Available at www.ncjrs.org

48. Bureau of Justice Statistics, *American Indians and Crime* (Washington, DC: Department of Justice, 1999); NCJ 173386. OJJDP, *Youth Gangs in Indian Country* (Washington, DC: Department of Justice, 2004); Eileen Luna-Firebaugh, "Violence Against Indian Women and the STOP VAIW Program," *Violence Against Women*, 12 (2006): 125–136.

49. Wakeling et al., *Policing on American Indian Reservations*; Clarice Fineman, "Police Problems on the Navajo Reservation," *Police Studies*, 9 (Winter 1986): 194–198.

50. Arab American Anti-Discrimination Committee, *Report on Hate Crimes and Discrimination Against Arab Americans* (Washington, DC: ADC, 2003).

51. Arab American Anti-Discrimination Committee, *ADC-NY Calls for Racial Profiling in New York Must be Addressed*. Available at http://www.adc.org.

52. Mexican American Legal Defense Fund (MALDEF), *Annual Report 2003* (Washington, DC, 2004), p. 6.

53. California Police Chiefs Association, letter to Attorney General John Ashcroft (April 10, 2002).

54. Bureau of Justice Statistics, *Policing and Homicide, 1976–98.*

55. James J. Fyfe, "Reducing the Use of Deadly Force: The New York Experience," in *Police Use of Deadly Force*, U.S. Department of Justice (Washington, DC: U.S. Government Printing Office, 1978), p. 29.

56. *Tennessee v. Garner*, 471 U.S. 1 (1985).

57. Jerry R. Sparger and David J. Giacopassi, "Memphis Revisited: A Reexamination of Police Shootings after the Garner Decision," *Justice Quarterly* 9 (June 1992): 211–225. See also James J. Fyfe, "Blind Justice: Police Shootings in Memphis," *Journal of Criminal Law and Criminology* 73, no. 2 (1982): 707–722.

58. William A. Geller and Kevin J. Karales, *Split-Second Decisions* (Chicago: Chicago Law Enforcement Study Group, 1981), p. 119.

59. "Officers Killed with Impunity," p. 1.

60. Bureau of Justice Statistics, *Policing and Homicide, 1976–98*.

61. Geller and Karales, *Split-Second Decisions*.

62. James J. Fyfe, "Administrative Interventions on Police Shooting Discretion," *Journal of Criminal Justice* 7 (winter 1979): 309–323.

63. Jerry R. Sparger and David J. Giacopassi, "Memphis Revisited: A Reexamination of Police Shootings after the Garner Decision," *Justice Quarterly* 9 (June 1992): 211–225.

64. Bureau of Justice Statistics, *Policing and Homicide, 1976–98*.

65. City of New York, Commission to Investigate Allegations of Police Corruption [Mollen Commission], *Commission Report* (New York: Author, 1994), p. 48.

66. National Commission on Law Observance and Enforcement, *Lawlessness in Law Enforcement* (Washington, DC: U.S. Government Printing Office, 1931), p. 4.

67. Human Rights Watch, *Shielded from Justice: Police Brutality and Accountability in the United States* (New York: Author, 1998), p. 39.

68. City of New York, *Commission Report*, p. 44, n. 4.

69. President's Commission on Law Enforcement and Administration of Justice, *Field Surveys*, vol. 5: *A National Survey of Police and Community Relations* (Washington, DC: U.S. Government Printing Office, 1967), p. 151.

70. New York City Civilian Complaint Review Board, *Status Report, January–December 2001* (New York: Author, 2002), p. 38.

71. The best review of the available studies is in Kenneth Adams, "Measuring the Prevalence of Police Abuse of Force," in *And Justice for All*, William A. Geller and Hans Toch, eds. (Washington, DC: Police Executive Research Forum, 1995), pp. 61–98; see also Anthony M. Pate and Lorie Fridell, *Police Use of Force*, 2 vols. (Washington, DC: Police Foundation, 1993).

72. Bureau of Justice Statistics, *Contacts Between Police and the Public*.

73. Ibid.

74. Ibid.

75. Robert E. Worden, "The 'Causes' of Police Brutality: Theory and Evidence on Police Use of Force," in Geller and Toch, eds. *And Justice for All*.

76. Albert Reiss, *The Police and the Public* (New Haven, CT: Yale University Press, 1971); Donald Black, "The Social Organization of Arrest," in *The Manners and Customs of the Police*, Donald Black, ed. (New York: Academic Press, 1980), pp. 85–108.

77. Reiss, *The Police and the Public*, pp. 149, 155.

78. New York City Civilian Complaint Review Board, Status Report Jan–Dec 2003 (2004). Available at www.nyc.gov/html/ccrb/. San Jose Independent Police Auditor, *2004 Year End Report* (San Jose: Independent Police Auditor, 2005). Available at www.sanjoseca.gov/ipa.

79. Worden, "The 'Causes' of Police Brutality," pp. 52–53.

80. David Weisburd, Rosann Greenspan, Edwin E. Hamilton, Kellie A. Bryant, and Hubert Williams, *The Abuse of Police Authority: A National Study of Police Officers' Attitudes* (Washington, DC: Police Foundation, 2001).

81. Reiss, *The Police and the Public*, p. 151.

82. Ronald Weitzer and Steven A. Tuch, "Race and Perceptions of Police Misconduct," *Social Problems*, 51, no. 4 (2004): 305–325.

83. Robert Tillman, "The Size of the Criminal Population: The Prevalence and Incidence of Adult Arrest," *Criminology* 25 (August 1987): 561–579.

84. Federal Bureau of Investigation, *Crime in the United States* (Washington, DC: Department of Justice, annual).

85. Black, "The Social Organization of Arrest," pp. 85–108.

86. David A. Klinger, "Demeanor or Crime? Why 'Hostile' Citizens Are More Likely to Be Arrested," *Criminology* 32, no. 3 (1994): 475–493.

87. Bureau of Justice Statistics, *Criminal Victimization in the United States, 2003* (Washington, DC: U.S. Government Printing Office, 2004).

88. Douglas A. Smith, Christy Visher, and Laura A. Davidson, "Equity and Discretionary Justice: The Influence of Race on Police Arrest Decisions," *Journal of Criminal Law and Criminology* 75 (spring 1984): 234–249; Douglas A. Smith and Christy A. Visher, "Street-Level Justice: Situational Determinants of Police Arrest Decisions," *Social Problems* 29 (December 1981): 167–177.

89. John R. Hepburn, "Race and the Decision to Arrest: An Analysis of Warrants Issued," *Journal of Research in Crime and Delinquency* 15 (1978): 54–73.

90. Joan Petersilia, *Racial Disparities in the Criminal Justice System* (Santa Monica, CA: Rand Corporation, 1983), pp. 21–26.

91. Black, *The Manners and Customs of the Police*, p. 108.

92. George L. Kelling and Catherine M. Coles, *Fixing Broken Windows* (New York: Free Press, 1996).

93. New York Civil Liberties Union, *Deflecting Blame* (New York: Author, 1998), p. 48.

94. John E. Eck and Edward R. Maguire, "Have Changes in Policing Reduced Violent Crime? An Assessment of the Evidence," in *The Crime Drop in America*, Alfred Blumstein and Joel Wallman, eds. (New York: Cambridge University Press, 2000), pp. 224–228.

95. Bureau of Justice Statistics, *Reducing Gun Violence: The Boston Gun Project's Operation Ceasefire* (Washington, DC: Department of Justice, 2001). Available at www.ncjrs.org, NCJ 188741.

96. Bureau of Justice Statistics, *Sourcebook of Criminal Justice Statistics 2003*, Table 2.26, p. 126.

97. Harris, *Profiles in Injustice;* ACLU, *Driving While Black.*

98. Police Executive Research Forum, *Racially Biased Policing.*

99. ACLU, *Driving While Black;* Harris, *Profiles in Injustice.*

100. Albert J. Meehan and Michael J. Ponder, "Race and Place: The Ecology of Racial Profiling African American Motorists," *Justice Quarterly*, 19 (September 2002): 399–430.

101. Michael W. Smith, "Police-led Crackdowns and Cleanups: An Evaluation of a Crime Control Initiative in Richmond," *Crime and Delinquency* (2001): 60–83.

102. Bureau of Justice Statistics, *Contacts between Police and the Public;* Bureau of Justice Statistics, *Characteristics of Drivers Stopped by Police, 1999*, NCJ 191548 (Washington, DC: U.S. Government Printing Office, 2002).

103. Ibid.

104. Samuel Walker, *The New World of Police Accountability*. (Thousand Oaks, CA: Sage, 2005); Lorie A. Fridell, *By the Numbers: A Guide for Analyzing Race Data from Traffic Stops* (Washington, DC: Police Executive Research Forum, 2004).

105. San Jose Police Department, *Vehicle Stop Demographic Study: First Report* (San Jose: Author, 1999).

106. Samuel Walker, "Searching for the Denominator: Problems with Police Traffic Stop Data and an Early Warning System Solution," *Justice Research and Policy* 3 (spring 2001): 63–95.

107. Bureau of Justice Statistics, *Contact Between Police and the Public: Findings from the 2002 National Survey*, Table 7.

108. Harris, *Profiles in Injustice*.

109. Walker, "Searching for the Denominator."

110. Internal benchmarking is explained in Walker, *The New World of Police Accountability* (Sage, 2005); Fridell, *By the Numbers*, pp. 143–160.

111. Current information about data collection laws and data reports is available at http://www.profilesininjustice.com.

112. Walker, *The New World of Police Accountability*. The New Jersey consent decree and others are available on the U.S. Department of Justice website (http://www.usdoj.gov/crt/split).

113. Police Executive Research Forum, *Racially Biased Policing*.

114. Ibid., pp. 51–53.

115. Sara E. Stoudtland, "The Multiple Dimensions of Trust in Resident/Police Relations in Boston," *Journal of Research in Crime and Delinquency*, 38 (August 2001): 226–256.

116. General Accounting Office, *U.S. Customs Service: Better Targeting of Airline Passengers for Personal Searches Could Produce Better Results*, GAO/GGD-00-38 (March 2000).

117. Harris, *Profiles in Injustice*.

118. National Advisory Commission, *Report*, pp. 301, 304–305.

119. Warren Friedman and Marsha Hott, *Young People and the Police* (Chicago: Chicago Alliance for Neighborhood Safety, 1995), p. 111.

120. John E. Boydston, *San Diego Field Interrogation: Final Report* (Washington, DC: Police Foundation, 1975), pp. 16, 62.

121. Boydston, *San Diego Field Interrogation*, p. 62.

122. Massachusetts Attorney General, *Report of the Attorney General's Civil Rights Division on Boston Police Department Practices* (Boston: Attorney General's Office, 1990).

123. Jeffrey Fagan and Garth Davies, "Street Stops and Broken Windows: Terry, Race, and Disorder in New York City," *Fordham Urban Law Journal*, 28 (2001): 457–504.

124. Carolyn M. Ward, "Policing in the Hyde Park Neighborhood, St. Louis: Racial Bias, Political Pressure, and Community Policing," *Crime, Law and Social Change* 26 (1997): 171–172.

125. Jerome Skolnick, *Justice without Trial: Law Enforcement in a Democratic Society*, 3rd ed. (New York: Macmillan, 1994), pp. 44–47.

126. Roger G. Dunham, Geoffrey P. Alpert, Megan S. Stroshine, and Katherine Bennett, "Transforming Citizens into Suspects: Factors that Influence the Formation of Police Suspicion," *Police Quarterly*, 8 (September 2005): 366–393.

127. Randall Kennedy, *Race, Crime, and the Law* (New York: Vintage Books, 1998), p. 137.

128. Ibid., pp. 151, 153.

129. Mervin F. White, Terry C. Cox, and Jack Basehart, "Theoretical Considerations of Officer Profanity and Obscenity in Formal Contacts with Citizens," in *Police Deviance*, 2nd ed., Thomas Barker and David L. Carter, eds. (Cincinnati: Anderson, 1991), pp. 275–297; John Van Maanen, "The Asshole," in *Policing: A View from the Street*,

John Van Maanen and Peter Manning, eds. (Santa Monica, CA: Goodyear, 1978), pp. 221–238.

130. San Francisco, Office of Citizen Complaints, *Annual Report* (San Francisco: Office of Citizen Complaints, 2001). Available at www.sfgov.org/occ.

131. Douglas A. Smith, Nanette Graham, and Bonney Adams, "Minorities and the Police: Attitudinal and Behavioral Questions," in *Race and Criminal Justice*, Michael J. Lynch and E. Britt Patterson, (New York: Harrow & Heston, 1991), p. 31.

132. Bayley and Mendelsohn, *Minorities and the Police*, p. 144.

133. Ibid., pp. 15–18.

134. Smith et al., "Minorities and the Police," p. 28.

135. Reiss, *The Police and the Public*, p. 147.

136. Samuel Walker, "Racial-Minority and Female Employment in Policing: The Implications of 'Glacial' Change," *Crime and Delinquency* 31 (October 1985): 555–572.

137. Weisburd et al., *The Abuse of Police Authority*.

138. Jerome L. Blakemore, David Barlow, and Deborah L. Padgett, "From the Classroom to the Community: Introducing Process in Police Diversity Training," *Police Studies* 18, no. 1 (1995): 71–83.

139. Geoffrey P. Alpert, William C. Smith, and Daniel Watters, "Law Enforcement: Implications of the Rodney King Beating," *Criminal Law Bulletin* 28 (September–October 1992): 477.

140. New York City, *The Knapp Commission Report on Police Corruption* (New York: Braziller, 1972), p. 1.

141. City of New York, *Commission Report*.

142. Bureau of Justice Statistics, *Sourcebook of Criminal Justice Statistics, 1993*, p. 165.

143. Police Foundation, Metropolitan Police Department, *Biased Policing, Final Report*, p. 81.

144. Fred A. Klyman and Joanna Kruckenberg, "A National Survey of Police–Community Relations Units," *Journal of Police Science and Administration* 7 (March 1979): 74.

145. U.S. Department of Justice, *Improving Police/Community Relations* (Washington, DC: Department of Justice, 1973).

146. Wesley G. Skogan and Susan M. Hartnett, *Community Policing: Chicago Style* (New York: Oxford University Press, 1997).

147. Bureau of Justice Statistics, *Reducing Gun Violence*.

148. Weitzer and Tuch, "Race and Perceptions of Police Misconduct."

149. Skogan and Hartnett, *Community Policing: Chicago Style*, p. 217.

150. Wesley Skogan, et al., *Community Policing and The New Immigrants: Latinos in Chicago* (Washington, DC: Department of Justice, 2002. NCJ 189908.

151. San Jose Police Department, *Vehicle Stop Demographic Study*.

152. PolicyLink, *Community-Centered Policing: A Force for Change* (Oakland, CA: Department of Justice, Author, 2001), pp. 16–20.

153. U.S. Department of Justice, *Youth Violence*.

154. Samuel Walker, *120 Shots: What Real Police Accountability Looks Like* (Omaha, NE: Police Professionalism Initiative, 2005). Available at www.policeaccountability.org.

155. Anita Khashu, et al., *Building Strong Police-Immigrant Community Relations: Lessons from a New York City Project* (New York: Vera Institute, 2005), Executive Summary.

156. National Academy of Sciences, *Fairness and Effectiveness in Policing: The Evidence* (Washington, DC: National Academy Press, 2004), p. 298.

157. Skogan and Hartnett, *Community Policing, Chicago Style*.

158. Lind and Tyler, *The Social Psychology of Procedural Justice*.

159. Bureau of Justice Statistics, *Contacts Between Police and the Public: Findings from the 2002 National Survey*.

160. New York City Police Department, *Fact Sheet, New York City's Arab Communities*. Available at http://www.vera.com.

161. Georgetown University website (http://www.georgetown.edu).

162. Charlotte-Mecklenburg Police Department, International Unit, *Law Enforcement Services to a Growing International Community* (Charlotte, NC: Charlotte Mecklenburg Police Department, 2004).

163. Samuel Walker, *Police Accountability: The Role of Citizen Oversight* (Belmont, CA: Wadsworth, 2001).

164. New York City Civilian Complaint Review Board, *Status Report, 2001*, p. 1.

165. Cecilia Menjivar and Cynthia L. Bejarano, "Latino Immigrants' Perceptions of Crime and Police Authorities in the United States: A Case Study from the Phoenix Metropolitan Area," *Ethnic and Racial Studies*, 27 (January 2004): 120–148.

166. Human Rights Watch, *Shielded from Justice*, pp. 63–65.

167. Police Foundation, Metropolitan Police Department, *Biased Policing Project, Final Report* (Washington, DC: Police Foundation, 2004).

168. Samuel Walker and Nanette Graham, "Citizen Complaints in Response to Police Misconduct: The Results of a Victimization Survey," *Police Quarterly* 1 (1998): 65–89.

169. National Advisory Commission, *Report*.

170. Christopher Commission, *Report of the Independent Commission*, Los Angeles: Christopher Commission, 1991, pp. 153–161.

171. ACLU of Southern California, *The Call for Change Goes Unanswered* (Los Angeles: Author, 1992), p. 23.

172. William A. Westley, *Violence and the Police* (Cambridge, MA: MIT Press, 1970).

173. Christopher Commission, *Report of the Independent Commission*, p. 168.

174. City of New York, *Commission Report*, p. 53.

175. Pate and Fridell, *Police Use of Force*, vol. 1, p. 118. A discussion of the reasons why so few complaints are sustained is in Walker, *Police Accountability*, pp. 121–137.

176. Samuel Walker, Carol Archbold, and Leigh Herbst, *Mediating Citizen Complaints* (Washington, DC: Department of Justice, 2002).

177. Walker, *Police Accountability*, p. 6.

178. Information about different citizen oversight agencies is available at www.policeaccountability.org.

179. Walker, *Police Accountability*, p. 122.

180. W. Marvin Dulaney, *Black Police in America* (Bloomington, IN: Indiana University Press, 1996).

181. President's Commission on Law Enforcement and Administration of Justice, *Task Force Report: The Police* (Washington, DC: U.S. Government Printing Office, 1967), p. 168.

182. "From Court Order to Reality: A Diverse Boston Police Force," *New York Times* (April 4, 2001), p. 1.

183. Bureau of Justice Statistics, *Local Police, 2003*.

184. Commission on Accreditation for Law Enforcement Agencies, *Standards for Law Enforcement Agencies*, 3rd ed., Standard 31–2 (Fairfax, VA: Author, 1994).

185. Samuel Walker and K. B. Turner, *A Decade of Modest Progress* (Omaha, NE: University of Nebraska at Omaha, 1992).

186. Bureau of Justice Statistics, *Law Enforcement Management and Administrative Statistics, 2000* (Washington, DC: Department of Justice, 2004).

187. "From Court Order to Reality," p. 1.

188. Christopher Commission, *Report of the Independent Commission.*

189. Bureau of Justice Statistics, *Law Enforcement Management and Administrative Statistics, 2000,* Table 3a.

190. Christopher Commission, *Report of the Independent Commission.*

191. Herbst and Walker, "Language Barriers in the Delivery of Police Services."

192. Bureau of Justice Statistics, *Law Enforcement Management and Administrative Statistics, 2000.*

193. U.S. Department of Labor, Office of Federal Contract Compliance, *Employment Standards Administration* (n.d.).

194. PolicyLink, *Community-Centered Policing,* p. 33.

195. Gunnar Myrdal, "Police and Other Public Contacts," in *An American Dilemma* (New York: Harper & Brothers, 1944); W. Marvin Dulaney, *Black Police in America* (Bloomington, IN: Indiana University Press, 1996).

196. Reiss, *The Police and the Public,* p. 167.

197. James J. Fyfe, "Who Shoots? A Look at Officer Race and Police Shooting," *Journal of Police Science and Administration* 9, no. 4 (1981): 367–382.

198. Merrick J. Bobb, Special Counsel, *9th Semiannual Report* (Los Angeles: Los Angeles County, 1998), pp. 59–61.

199. "For Black Officers, Diversity Has Its Limits," *New York Times* (April 2, 2001), p. 1; "Alone, Undercover, and Black: Hazards of Mistaken Identity," *New York Times* (November 22, 1992), p. A1.

200. "Alienation Is a Partner for Black Officers," *New York Times* (April 3, 2001) p. 1.

201. The Kerner Commission, for example, argued that "Negro officers can also be particularly effective in controlling disorders"; National Advisory Commission, *Report,* p. 315.

202. PolicyLink, *Community-Centered Policing,* pp. 36–37.

203. "Los Angeles Force Accused from Within," *New York Times* (March 29, 1991), p. A18.

204. National Black Police Officers Association, *Police Brutality: A Strategy to Stop the Violence* (Washington, DC: Author, n.d.).

205. Weisburd et al., *The Abuse of Police Authority.*

206. Skogan and Hartnett, *Community Policing, Chicago Style.*

207. Robin N. Haarr, "Patterns of Interaction in a Police Patrol Bureau: Race and Gender Barriers to Integration," *Justice Quarterly* 14 (March 1997): 53–85.

208. Samuel E. Walker and Vincent J. Webb, "Public Perceptions of Racial and Minority Employment and Its Perceived Impact on Police Service." Paper presented at the American Society of Criminology Annual Meeting, 1997.

209. Frank et al., "Reassessing the Impact of Race on Citizens' Attitudes toward the Police."

210. Samuel Walker, Susan E. Martin, and K. B. Turner, "Through the Glass Ceiling? Promotion Rates for Minority and Female Police Officers." Paper presented at the American Society of Criminology, November 1994.

5

The Courts

A Quest for Justice
During the Pretrial Process

> [I]t is clear to me that if America ever is to eradicate racism, lawyers will
> have to lead. We must cleanse the justice system, because until the
> justice system is truly colorblind, we cannot have any genuine hope for
> the elimination of bias in the other segments of American life.
> —PHILIP S. ANDERSON, PRESIDENT, AMERICAN BAR ASSOCIATION[1]

In March 1931, nine African American teenage boys were accused of raping two white girls on a slow-moving freight train traveling through Alabama. They were arrested and taken to Scottsboro, Alabama, where they were indicted for rape, a capital offense. One week later, the first case was called for trial. When the defendant appeared without counsel, the judge hearing the case simply appointed all members of the local bar to represent him and his co-defendants. An out-of-state lawyer also volunteered to assist in the defendants' defense, but the judge appointed no counsel of record.

The nine defendants were tried and convicted, and eight were sentenced to death. They appealed their convictions, arguing that their right to counsel had been denied. In 1932, the United States Supreme Court issued its ruling in the case of *Powell v. Alabama*,[2] one of the most famous Supreme Court cases in U.S. history. The Court reversed the defendants' convictions and ruled that due process of law required the appointment of counsel for young, inexperienced, illiterate, and indigent defendants in capital cases.

The Supreme Court's ruling in *Powell* provided the so-called Scottsboro Boys with only a short reprieve. They were quickly retried, reconvicted, and resentenced to death, despite the fact that one of the alleged victims had recanted and questions were raised about the credibility of the other victim's testimony. Once again, the defendants appealed their convictions, this time contending that their right to a fair trial by an impartial jury had been denied. All of the defendants had been tried by all-white juries. They argued that the jury selection procedures used in Alabama were racially biased. Although African Americans who were registered to vote were eligible for jury service, they were excluded in practice because state officials refused to place their names on the lists from which jurors were chosen. In 1935, the Supreme Court, noting that the exclusion of all African Americans from jury service deprived African American defendants of their right to the equal protection of the laws guaranteed by the Fourteenth Amendment, again reversed the convictions.[3]

The Supreme Court's decision was harshly criticized in the South. The Charleston *News and Courier*, for example, stated that racially mixed juries were "out of the question" and asserted that the Court's decision "can and will be evaded."[4] Southern sentiment also strongly favored yet another round of trials. Thomas Knight, Jr., the attorney who prosecuted the Scottsboro cases the second time, noted that "Approximately ninety jurors have been found saying the defendants were guilty of the offense with which they are charged and for which the penalty is death." Knight reported that he had been "retained by the State to prosecute the cases and [would] prosecute the same to their conclusion."[5]

Less than 8 months after the Supreme Court's decision, a grand jury composed of 13 whites and 1 African American returned new indictments against the 9 defendants. Haywood Patterson, the first defendant to be retried, again faced an all-white jury. Although there were 12 African Americans among the 100 potential jurors, 7 of the 12 asked to be excused and the prosecutor used his peremptory challenges to remove the remaining 5 African Americans. In his closing argument, the prosecutor also implied that an acquittal would force the women of Alabama "to buckle six-shooters about their middles" in order to protect their "sacred secret parts." He pleaded with the jurors to "Get it done quick and protect the fair womanhood of this great State."[6]

Patterson was convicted and sentenced to 75 years in prison. The sentence, although harsh, represented "a victory of sorts."[7] As the Birmingham *Age-Herald* noted, the decision "represents probably the first time in the history of the South that a Negro has been convicted of a charge of rape upon a white woman and has been given less than a death sentence."[8]

Three of the remaining eight defendants were tried and convicted in July 1937. One of the three, Clarence Norris, was sentenced to death; the other two received prison sentences of 75 and 99 years. Shortly thereafter, Ozie Powell pled guilty to assaulting an officer after the State agreed to dismiss the rape charge. That same day, in an unexpected and controversial move, the State dropped all charges against the remaining four defendants. In a prepared statement, Attorney General Thomas Lawson asserted that the State was "convinced beyond any question of doubt . . . that the defendants that have been tried are guilty." However, "after careful consideration of all the testimony, every lawyer connected with the prosecution is convinced that the defendants Willie Roberson and Olen Montgomery are not guilty." Regarding the remaining two defendants, who were 12 and 13 years old when the crime occurred, Dawson stated that "the ends of justice would be met at this time by releasing these two juveniles on condition that they leave the State, never to return."[9]

The State's decision to drop charges against four of the nine defendants led editorial writers for newspapers throughout the United States to call for the immediate release of the defendants who previously had been convicted. The Richmond *Times-Dispatch* stated that the State's action "serves as a virtual clincher to the argument that all nine of the Negroes are innocent," and the *New York Times* called on the state to "do more complete justice later on."[10]

Charles Norris's death sentence was commuted to life imprisonment in 1938, but the Alabama Pardon and Parole Board repeatedly denied the five defendants' requests for parole. One of the defendants finally was granted parole in 1943, and by 1950 all of them had gained their freedom. Collectively, the nine Scottsboro Boys served 104 years in prison for a crime that many believe was "almost certainly, a hoax."[11]

THE SITUATION TODAY

The infamous Scottsboro Case illustrates overt discrimination directed against African American criminal defendants. However, those events took place in the 1930s and 1940s, and much has changed since then. Legislative reforms and Supreme Court decisions protecting the rights of criminal defendants, coupled with changes in attitudes, have made it less likely that criminal justice officials will treat defendants of different races differently. Racial minorities are no longer routinely denied bail and then tried by all-white juries without attorneys to assist them in their defense. They are no longer brought into court in chains and shackles. They no longer receive "justice" at the hands of white lynch mobs.

Despite these reforms, inequities persist. Racial minorities, and particularly those suspected of crimes against whites, remain the victims of unequal justice. In 1983, for example, Lenell Geter, an African American man, was charged with the armed robbery of a Kentucky Fried Chicken restaurant in Balch Springs, Texas. Despite the absence of any physical evidence to connect him to the crime and despite the prosecution's failure to establish his motive for the crime, Geter was convicted by an all-white jury and sentenced to life in prison.

Geter's conviction was particularly surprising given the fact that he had an ironclad alibi. Nine of his co-workers, all of whom were white, testified that Geter was at work on the day of the crime. His supervisor testified that there was no way Geter could have made the 50-mile trip from work to the site of the crime by 3:20 P.M., the time the robbery occurred. According to one co-worker, "Unless old Captain Kirk dematerialized him and beamed him over there, he couldn't have made it back by then. He was here at work. There's no question in my mind—none at all."[12]

Prosecutors in the county where Geter was tried denied that race played a role in Geter's conviction. As one of them put it, "To say this is a conviction based on race is as far out in left field as you can get."[13] Geter's co-workers disagreed; they argued that Geter and his codefendant (who also was African American) wouldn't have been charged or convicted if they had been white.

Events that occurred following the trial suggest that Geter's co-workers were right. Another man arrested for a series of armed robberies eventually was linked to the robbery of the Kentucky Fried Chicken restaurant. Geter's conviction and sentence were overturned after the employees who originally identified Geter picked this suspect out of a lineup. Geter served more than a year in prison for a crime he did not commit.

Like Lenell Geter, James Newsome, an African American sentenced to life in prison for the armed robbery and murder of a white man, also had an alibi. At his trial for the 1979 murder of Mickey Cohen, the owner of Mickey's Grocery Store in Chicago, Newsome's girlfriend and her two sisters testified that he was with them at the time of the murder. The prosecutor trying the case argued that Newsome's girlfriend, who was a convicted burglar, was not a credible witness. He also introduced the testimony of three eyewitnesses who identified Newsome as Cohen's killer.[14]

Despite the fact that there was no physical evidence linking Newsome to the crime, and despite the fact that Newsome's fingerprints were not found on the items in the store handled by the killer, the jury hearing the case found Newsome guilty. Although Cook County prosecutors had sought the death penalty, the jury recommended life in prison.

Newsome, who steadfastly maintained his innocence, spent the next 15 years appealing his conviction. With the help of Norval Morris, a University of Chicago Law School Professor, and two noted Chicago defense attorneys, Newsome was able to convince the Cook County Circuit Court to order that the fingerprints obtained from the crime scene be run through the Police Department's computerized fingerprint database to see if they matched any of those on file. The tests revealed that the fingerprints matched those of Dennis Emerson, a 45-year-old Illinois death row inmate who, at the time of Cohen's murder, was out on parole after serving 3 years for armed robbery.

Two weeks later, Newsome was released from prison. Shortly thereafter, Illinois governor Jim Edgar pardoned Newsome and ordered his criminal record expunged. Following his release, James Newsome, who spent 15 years in prison for a crime he didn't commit, said, "I finally felt vindicated. I had defeated a criminal-justice giant. Fifteen years ago, they told me that I would never walk the streets again in my life. What did I do? I slayed a giant—a criminal justice giant."[15]

Like Geter, Newsome contended that race played a role in his arrest and conviction. "In the most [racially] polarized city in the world," Newsome stated, "racism was a factor. I was a suspect and I was convenient."[16]

Race also played a role in the case of Clarence Brandley, an African American who was sentenced to death for the rape and murder of Cheryl Dee Fergeson, a white student at a high school north of Houston where Brandley worked as a janitor. Brandley and a co-worker found the body and were the initial suspects in the case. Brandley's co-worker, who was white, reported that during their interrogation one of the police officers stated, "One of you two is going to hang for this." Then he turned to Brandley and said, "Since you're the nigger, you're elected."[17] The police investigating the case claimed that three hairs found on the victim implicated Brandley. Although the hairs were never forensically tested, the police claimed that they were identical "in all observable characteristics" to Brandley's.

Brandley was indicted by an all-white grand jury and tried before an all-white jury, which hung 11-1 in favor of conviction. He was retried by a second all-white jury after the district attorney trying the case used his peremptory challenges to strike all of the prospective African American jurors. During his closing argument, the district attorney referred to Brandley as a "necrophiliac" and a "depraved sex maniac." This time, the jurors found Brandley guilty and recommended a death sentence, which the judge imposed.

Brandley spent 6 years on death row before a Texas district court, citing misconduct on the part of police and prosecutors, threw out his conviction. The judge, who noted that there was strong evidence that the crime was committed by two white men, stated that "the color of Clarence Brandley's skin was a substantial factor which pervaded all aspects of the State's capital prosecution against him, and was an impermissible factor which significantly influenced the investigation, trial and post-trial proceedings of [Brandley's] case."[18]

These three recent cases, of course, do not prove that there is a pattern of *systematic* discrimination directed against racial minorities in courts throughout the United States. One might argue, in fact, that these three cases are simply exceptions to the general rule of impartiality. As we explained in Chapter 1, the validity of the discrimination thesis rests not on anecdotal evidence but on the results of empirical studies of criminal justice decisionmaking.

GOALS OF THE CHAPTER

In this chapter and in Chapter 6, we discuss the treatment of racial minorities in court. The focus in this chapter is on pretrial decisionmaking. Our goal is to determine whether people of color are more likely than whites to be tried without adequate counsel to represent them or to be denied bail or detained in jail prior to trial. In addition, we review research on prosecutors' charging and plea bargaining decisions for evidence of differential treatment of racial minorities and whites. We argue that recent reforms adopted voluntarily by the states or mandated by court decisions have reduced, but not eliminated, racial discrimination in the pretrial process.

DECISIONS REGARDING COUNSEL AND BAIL

As we explained in Chapter 3, racial minorities are at a disadvantage in court both because of their race and because they are more likely than whites to be poor. This "double jeopardy" makes it more difficult for minority defendants to obtain competent attorneys or secure release from jail prior to trial. This, in turn, hinders their defense and may increase the odds that they will be convicted and sentenced harshly. Given these consequences, decisions regarding provision of counsel and bail obviously are important.

Racial Minorities and the Right to Counsel

The Sixth Amendment to the U.S. Constitution states, "In all criminal prosecutions, the accused shall enjoy the right to have the assistance of counsel for his defense." Historically, this meant simply that if someone had an attorney, he could bring him along to defend him. The problem, of course, was that this was of no help to the majority of defendants, and particularly minority defendants, who were too poor to hire their own attorneys.

The U.S. Supreme Court, recognizing that defendants could not obtain fair trials without the assistance of counsel, began to interpret the Sixth Amendment to require the appointment of counsel for indigent defendants. The process began in 1932, when the Court ruled in *Powell v. Alabama*[19] that states must provide attorneys for indigent defendants charged with capital crimes (see the earlier discussion of the Scottsboro case). The Court's decision in a 1938 case, *Johnson v. Zerbst*,[20] required the appointment of counsel for all indigent defendants in federal criminal cases, but the requirement was not extended to the states until *Gideon v. Wainwright*[21] was decided in 1963. In that 1963 decision, Justice Black's majority opinion stated:

> [R]eason and reflection require us to recognize that in our adversary system of criminal justice, any person haled into court, who is too poor to hire a lawyer, cannot be assured a fair trial unless counsel is provided for him . . . The right of one charged with crime to counsel may not be deemed fundamental and essential to fair trials in some countries, but it is in ours.

In subsequent decisions, the Court ruled that "no person may be imprisoned for any offense, whether classified as petty, misdemeanor, or felony, unless he was represented by counsel"[22] and that the right to counsel is not limited to trial, but applies to all "critical stages" in the criminal justice process.[23] As a result of these rulings, most defendants must be provided with counsel from arrest and interrogation through sentencing and the appellate process. As illustrated in Box 5.1, the Supreme Court also has ruled that defendants are entitled to *effective* assistance of counsel.[24]

At the time the *Gideon* decision was handed down, 13 states had no statewide requirement for appointment of counsel except in capital cases.[25] Other states relied on members of local bar associations to defend indigents, often on a *pro bono* basis. Following *Gideon*, it became obvious that other procedures would be required if all felony defendants were to be provided attorneys.

States moved quickly to implement the constitutional requirement articulated in *Gideon*, either by establishing public defender systems or by appropriating money for court-appointed attorneys. The number of public defender systems

---

B O X 5.1 The Supreme Court and "Effective" Assistance of Counsel

In 1984 the Supreme Court articulated constitutional standards for determining whether a defendant had ineffective assistance of counsel. The Court ruled, in the case of *Strickland v. Washington* (466 U.S. 668 [1984], at 687), that to establish ineffectiveness, a defendant must prove:

- First, "that counsel's performance was deficient. This requires showing that counsel made errors so serious that counsel was not functioning as the 'counsel' guaranteed the defendant by the Sixth Amendment."

- Second, "that the deficient performance prejudiced the defense. This requires showing that counsel's errors were so serious as to deprive the defendant of a fair trial, a trial whose result is reliance."

The Court also stated that to establish ineffectiveness, a "defendant must show that counsel's representation fell below an objective standard of reasonableness." To establish prejudice, he "must show that there is a reasonable probability that, but for counsel's unprofessional errors, the result of the proceeding would have been different."

The Court revisited this issue in 2000, ruling that Terry Williams had been denied effective assistance of counsel (*Williams v. Taylor* 529 U.S. 420 [2000]). Williams was convicted of robbery and murder and sentenced to death after a Virginia jury concluded that he had a high probability of future dangerousness.

At the sentencing hearing, Williams' lawyer failed to introduce evidence that Williams was borderline mentally retarded and did not advance beyond sixth grade. He also failed to introduce the testimony of prison officials, who described Williams as among the inmates "least likely to act in a violent, dangerous, or provocative way." Instead, Williams' lawyer spent most of his time explaining that he realized it would be difficult for the jury to find a reason to spare Williams' life. His comments included the following: "I will admit too that it is very difficult to ask you to show mercy to a man who maybe has not shown much mercy himself.... Admittedly, it is very difficult to ... ask that you give this man mercy when he has shown so little of it himself. But I would ask that you would."

The Supreme Court ruled that Williams' right to effective assistance of counsel had been violated. According to the Court, "there was a reasonable probability that the result of the sentencing proceeding would have been different if competent counsel had presented and explained the significance of all the available evidence."

---

grew rapidly. In 1951 there were only seven public defender organizations in the United States; in 1964 there were 136; by 1973 the total had increased to 573.[26] A recent national survey of indigent defense services among all U.S. prosecutorial districts found that 21 percent used a public defender program, 19 percent used an assigned counsel system, and 7 percent used a contract attorney system; the remaining districts (43 percent) reported that a combination of methods was used.[27] A survey of inmates incarcerated in state and federal prisons in 1997 revealed that about 73 percent of the state inmates and 60 percent of the federal inmates were represented by a public defender or assigned counsel. This survey also revealed that African Americans and Hispanics were more likely than whites to be represented by a public defender or assigned counsel. Among state prison inmates, for example, 77 percent of the African Americans, 73 percent of the Hispanics, and 69 percent of the whites reported that they were represented by a publicly funded attorney.[28]

Quality of Legal Representation   As a result of Supreme Court decisions expanding the right to counsel and the development of federal and state policies implementing these decisions, African Americans and other racial minorities are no longer routinely denied legal representation at trial or at any of the other critical stages in the process. Questions have been raised, however, about the quality of legal representation provided to indigent defendants by public defenders. A recent article in the *Harvard Law Review*, for example, claimed:

> Nearly four decades after *Gideon*, the states have largely, and often outrageously, failed to meet the Court's constitutional command. The widespread, lingering deficiencies in the quality of indigent counsel have led some to wonder whether this right, so fundamental to a fair and accurate adversarial criminal process, is unenforceable.[29]

According to this author, the fact that most criminal defendants are indigent, coupled with the "low quality of indigent defense," raises fundamental questions about the "overall fairness of the criminal justice system."[30]

There is evidence suggesting that defendants share this view. In fact, one of the most oft-quoted statements about public defenders is the answer given by an unidentified prisoner in a Connecticut jail to the question of whether he had a lawyer when he went to court. "No," he replied, "I had a public defender."[31] Neubauer similarly notes that in prison " 'PD' stands not for 'public defender' but for 'prison deliverer.' "[32] Some social scientists echo this negative assessment, charging that public defenders, as part of the courtroom workgroup, are more concerned with securing guilty pleas as efficiently and as expeditiously as possible than with aggressively defending their clients.[33] As Weitzer[34] notes (and as the examples in Box 5.2 confirm), "In many jurisdictions, public defenders and state-appointed attorneys are grossly underpaid, poorly trained, or simply lack the resources and time to prepare for a case—a pattern documented in cases ranging from the most minor to the most consequential, capital crimes."

Other social scientists disagree. Citing studies showing that criminal defendants represented by public defenders do not fare worse than those represented by private attorneys,[35] these researchers suggest that critics "have tended to underestimate the quality of defense provided by the public defender."[36] Wice, in fact, concluded that the public defender is able to establish a working relationship with prosecutors and judges "in which the exchange of favors, so necessary to greasing the squeaky wheel of justice, can directly benefit the indigent defendant."[37] As part of the courtroom workgroup, in other words, public defenders are in a better position than private attorneys to negotiate favorable plea bargains and thus to mitigate punishment.

A recent report by the Bureau of Justice Statistics (BJS) revealed that case outcomes for state and federal defendants represented by public attorneys do not differ dramatically from those represented by private counsel.[38] There were only very slight differences in the conviction rates of defendants represented by public

---

B O X 5.2   **Are Indigent Capital Defendants Represented by Incompetent Attorneys?**

In "Judges and the Politics of Death," Stephen Bright and Patrick Keenan (1995, p. 800) claimed, "Judges often fail to enforce the most fundamental protection of an accused, the Sixth Amendment right to counsel, by assigning an inexperienced or incompetent lawyer to represent the accused." In support of their assertion, they offered the following examples:

- A capital defendant who was represented by a lawyer who had passed the bar exam only 6 months earlier, had not taken any classes in criminal law or criminal procedure, and had never tried a jury or a felony trial.

- An attorney who described his client as "a little old nigger boy" during the penalty phase of the trial.

- A judge in Harris County, Texas, who responded to a capital defendant's complaints about his attorney sleeping during the trial with the assertion that, "The Constitution doesn't say the lawyer has to be awake."

- A Florida attorney who stated during the penalty phase of a capital case, "Judge, I'm at a loss. I really don't know what to do in this type of proceeding. If I'd been through one, I would, but I've never handled one except this time."

- A study of capital cases in Philadelphia that found that "even officials in charge of the system say they wouldn't want to be represented in Traffic Court by some of the people appointed to defend poor people accused of murder."

---

and private attorneys but somewhat larger differences in the incarceration rates. At the federal level, 87.6 percent of the defendants represented by public attorneys were sentenced to prison, compared to 76.5 percent of the defendants with private attorneys. The authors of the report attributed this to the fact that public counsel represented a higher percentage of violent, drug, and public-order offenders, whereas private attorneys represented a higher percentage of white-collar defendants. Felony defendants in state courts also faced lower odds of incarceration if they were represented by private attorneys (53.9 percent) rather than public defenders (71.3 percent). In both state and federal court, on the other hand, defendants represented by private attorneys got longer sentences than those represented by public defenders. At the federal level, the mean sentences were 58 months (public attorneys) and 62 months (private attorneys); at the state level, they were 31.2 months (public attorneys) and 38.3 months (private attorneys).[39]

Race, Type of Counsel, and Case Outcome   The data presented thus far do not address the question of racial discrimination in the provision of counsel. Although it is true that African American and Hispanic defendants are more likely than white defendants to be represented by public defenders, it does not necessarily follow from this that racial minorities will be treated more harshly than whites as their cases move through the criminal justice system. As we have noted, studies have not consistently shown that defendants represented by public defenders fare worse than defendants represented by private attorneys.

Most studies have not directly compared the treatment of African American, Hispanic, and white defendants represented by public defenders and private attorneys. It is possible that racial minorities represented by public defenders receive more punitive sentences than whites represented by public defenders, or that whites who hire their own attorneys receive more lenient sentences than racial minorities who hire their own attorneys. To put it another way, it is possible that hiring an attorney provides more benefits to whites than to racial minorities, and representation by a public defender has more negative consequences for racial minorities than for whites.

Holmes, Hosch, Daudistel, Perez, and Graves found evidence supporting these possibilities in one of the two Texas counties where they explored the interrelationships among race/ethnicity, legal resources, and case outcomes.[40] The authors of this study found that in Bexar County (San Antonio) both African American and Hispanic defendants were significantly less likely than white defendants to be represented by a private attorney, even after such things as the seriousness of the crime, the defendant's prior criminal record, and the defendant's gender, age, and employment status were taken into account. The authors also found that defendants who retained a private attorney were more likely to be released prior to trial and received more lenient sentences than those represented by a public defender.[41] In this particular jurisdiction, then, African American and Hispanic defendants were less likely than whites to be represented by a private attorney and, as a result, they received more punitive treatment than whites.

An examination of the sentences imposed on defendants convicted of felonies in three large urban jurisdictions in 1993 and 1994 produced somewhat different results. Spohn and DeLone[42] compared the proportions of white, African American, and Hispanic defendants who were represented by a private attorney in Chicago, Miami, and Kansas City. As shown in Table 5.1, in all three jurisdictions whites were substantially more likely than African Americans to have private attorneys. In Chicago, 22.5 percent of white defendants, but only 6.9 percent of African American defendants, had a private attorney. In Miami, Hispanics also were less likely than whites to be represented by a private attorney.

Although the data presented in Table 5.1 reveal that smaller proportions of racial minorities than whites had access to the services of a private attorney, they do not provide evidence of differential treatment based on either type of attorney or race/ethnicity. In fact, when Spohn and DeLone examined the sentences imposed on racial minorities and whites in each jurisdiction, they found an interesting pattern of results. As shown in Figure 5.1, in Chicago and Kansas City only whites benefitted from having a private attorney. Among African Americans, the incarceration rates for defendants represented by private attorneys were only slightly lower than the rates for defendants represented by public defenders; among Hispanics in Chicago, the rate for defendants with private attorneys was actually somewhat *higher* than the rate for those with public defenders. In Miami, both whites and African Americans benefited from representation by private counsel but Hispanics with private attorneys were sentenced to prison at a slightly *higher* rate than Hispanics represented by the public defender.

TABLE 5.1 Race/Ethnicity and Type of Attorney in Chicago, Miami, and Kansas City

Race of Defendant	Percentage Represented by a Private Attorney		
	Chicago	Miami	Kansas City
White	22.5	34.5	37.8
African American	6.9	23.4	24.8
Hispanic	21.2	27.3	NA[a]

[a]There were only 47 Hispanic defendants in Kansas City.

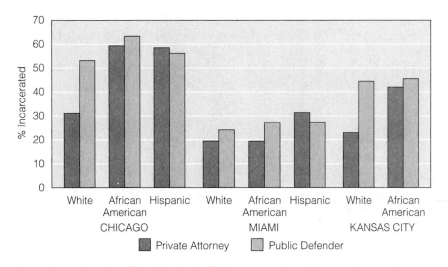

FIGURE 5.1 Race/Ethnicity, Type of Attorney, and Incarceration Rates in Chicago, Miami, and Kansas City

The incarceration rates displayed in Figure 5.1 do not take into account differences in the types of cases handled by private attorneys and public defenders. It is certainly possible that the incarceration rates for defendants represented by private attorneys generally are lower than the rates for defendants represented by public defenders, not because private attorneys are more experienced, more competent, and more zealous, but because the types of cases they handle are less serious or because the defendants they represent have less serious prior criminal records. If private attorneys, in other words, usually represent first offenders charged with relatively minor crimes and public defenders represent recidivists as well as first offenders and violent offenders as well as nonviolent offenders, we would expect the sentences imposed on defendants with private attorneys to be less severe than those imposed on defendants with public defenders, irrespective of the quality of representation provided by the attorney.

To test this possibility, Spohn and DeLone analyzed the relationship between race/ethnicity, type of attorney, and the likelihood of incarceration, controlling for several indicators of the seriousness of the crime and for the offender's prior criminal record, age, gender, and employment status. They found that, with one exception, the type of attorney had no effect on the odds of incarceration for any racial/ethnic group in any jurisdiction. The only exception was in Miami, where African Americans represented by private attorneys faced significantly lower odds of incarceration than African Americans represented by public defenders.

These results cast doubt on assertions that racial minorities are disadvantaged by their lack of access to private counsel. At least in these three jurisdictions, public defenders do not appear to "provide a lower caliber defense than what private attorneys offer."[43]

In summary, although it would be premature to conclude on the basis of research conducted to date either that decisions concerning the provision of counsel are racially neutral or that the consequences of these decisions for racial minorities are unimportant, significant changes have occurred since the 1930s. (See the "Focus on an Issue: Racial Minorities and the Legal Profession" box for a discussion of racial minorities and the legal profession.) It is clear that scenes from the infamous Scottsboro Case will not be replayed in the 21st century. The Supreme Court has consistently affirmed the importance of the right to counsel and has insisted that states provide attorneys to indigent criminal defendants at all critical stages in the criminal justice process. Although some critics have questioned the quality of legal services afforded indigent defendants, particularly in capital cases where the stakes are obviously very high, the findings of a number of methodologically sophisticated studies suggest that "indigent defenders get the job done and done well."[44] In short, it is no longer true that racial minorities "are without a voice"[45] in courts throughout the United States.

Racial Minorities and Bail Decisionmaking

Critics of the traditional money bail system, in which defendants either pay the amount set by the judge or pay a bail bondsman to post bond for them, argue that the system discriminates against poor defendants. They also charge that the system discriminates, either directly or indirectly, against racial minorities. Critics contend that historically African American and Hispanic defendants were more likely than white defendants to be detained prior to trial, either because the judge refused to set bail or because the judge set bail at an unaffordable level.[64] "As a result," according to one commentator, "the country's jails are packed to overflowing with the nation's poor—with red, brown, black, and yellow men and women showing up in disproportionate numbers."[65]

Bail Reform Concerns about the rights of poor defendants and about the consequences of detention prior to trial led to the first bail reform movement, which emerged in the 1960s and emphasized reducing pretrial detention. Those who lobbied for reform argued that the purpose of bail was to ensure the defendant's appearance in court and that bail therefore should not exceed the

(continued on p. 178)

Focus on an Issue
Racial Minorities and the Legal Profession

In the early 1930s, one of the defendants in the Scottsboro case described the courtroom where he was convicted and sentenced to death as "one big smiling white face" (Carter, 1969, p. 302). With the exception of the defendants themselves, no racial minorities were present in the courtroom.

Although the situation obviously has changed since then, racial minorities still represent a very small proportion of the lawyers and judges in the United States. Among those enrolled in law schools in 2003, only 20.6 percent were African American, Hispanic, Asian, or Native American.[46] In 2000, 88.8 percent of all licensed lawyers were white, 4.2 percent were African American, 3.4 percent were Hispanic, and 2.2 percent were Asian.[47]

Racial minorities also comprise a very small proportion of the judiciary. A 2004 report by the American Bar Association revealed that only 10.1 percent of all state court judges were racial minorities. Of these judges, 5.9 percent were African American, 2.8 percent were Hispanic, 1.1 percent were Asian, and only 13 (0.1 percent) were Native American.[48] The situation is somewhat more positive in the federal level, where 11.3 of all district court judges and 6.9 percent of all court of appeals judges on the bench in 2000 were African American. Hispanics comprised 5.0 percent of the district court bench and 6.2 percent of the appellate court bench. There were, however, very few Asian Americans or Native Americans on the federal bench.[49] Most of the racial minorities on the federal bench were men. Among district court judges, there were 54 African American men but only 16 African American women; there were 26 Hispanic men and 5 Hispanic women.[50]

The American Bar Association's 2000 report on the progress of minorities in the legal profession concluded that minority entry into the profession had stalled and that the obstacles to minority entry into the profession had grown more formidable. The report noted that the campaign to end affirmative action in law school admissions, which had spread rapidly throughout the United States, threatened "to stifle minority entry and advancement in the profession for years to come."[51] According to the American Bar Association, "the legal profession—already one of the least integrated professions in the country—threatens to become even less representative of the citizens and society it serves."[52]

ARE BLACK LAW STUDENTS HURT OR HELPED BY AFFIRMATIVE ACTION?

In 1997 Barbara Grutter, a white resident of Michigan with a 3.8 undergraduate GPA and a 161 LSAT score, was denied admission to the University of Michigan Law School. (See "In the Courts: *Grutter v. Bollinger*" for a more detailed discussion of this case.) She sued, claiming that she was rejected because the law school used race as a "predominant factor" and gave preference to applicants from certain minority groups. She argued that doing so violated the equal protection clause of the 14th Amendment and Title VI of the Civil Rights Act of 1964. In 2003 the United States Supreme Court ruled that "the law school's narrowly tailored use of race in admissions decisions to further a compelling interest in obtaining the educational benefits that flow from a diverse student body is not prohibited by the Equal Protection Clause or Title VI" (*Grutter v. Bollinger*, 288 F.3d 732 [2003]).

One year later, Richard Sander, a law professor at the University of California Los Angeles, argued in the

(*continued*)

(continued)

Stanford Law Review that affirmative action policies hurt, not help, African American law students.[53] Sander contended that the African American students who get preferential treatment as a result of affirmative action enter law school with weaker grades and lower LSAT scores—the two best predictors of law school success—than white students. Noting that 43% of the African American students who entered law school in the fall of 1991 either did not graduate or did not pass the bar exam, Sander asserted that affirmative action sets African American students up for failure by placing them in schools where they cannot compete academically. He also predicted that "the number of black lawyers produced by American law schools each year and subsequently passing the bar would probably increase if those schools collectively stopped using racial preferences."[54]

Sander's methods and conclusions were called into question by social scientists and legal scholars. The harshest criticism came from Chambers, Clydesdale, Kidder, and Lempert, who argued in the *Stanford Law Review* that Sander's conclusions were "simple, neat, and wrong."[55] They asserted that ending affirmative action would lead, not to an increase in the number of African American lawyers, as Sander had predicted, but to a 30 percent to 40 percent decline in the number of African Americans entering the legal profession.[56] Other critics stated that even if Sander's findings were correct, his study failed to take into consideration the academic benefits of diversity, for which "there is universal celebration" on college campuses.[57]

THE PERCEPTIONS OF AFRICAN AMERICAN AND WHITE LAWYERS: DIVIDED JUSTICE?

A 1998 survey of African American and white lawyers commissioned by the *ABA Journal* and the *National Bar Association*

Magazine revealed stark racial differences in perceptions of the justice system.[58] When asked about the amount of racial bias that currently exists in the justice system, more than half of the African American lawyers, but only 6.5 percent of the white lawyers, answered "very much." In fact, 29.6 percent of the white lawyers stated that they believed there was "very little" racial bias in the justice system.

Responses to other questions also varied by race:

■ How does the amount of racial bias in the justice system compare with other segments of society?

	African Americans	Whites
More	22.7%	5.7%
Same	69.6	40.5
Less	5.9	45.8

■ Have you witnessed an example of racial bias in the justice system in the past three years?

	African Americans	Whites
Yes	66.9%	15.1%
No	31.1	82.4

■ What is your assessment of the ability of the justice system to eliminate racial bias in the future?

	African Americans	Whites
Hopeful	59.1%	80.7%
Pessimistic	38.2	15.1

■ Should police be allowed to create profiles of likely drug dealers or other criminals as a way to combat crime?

	African Americans	Whites
Yes	17.8%	48.6%
No	74.6	36.9

■   Should race be a factor in creating the profiles?

	African Americans	Whites
Race OK	5.5%	19.5%
Race Not OK	91.2	67.9

■   Have you seen an attempt to skew a jury racially because of the race of the defendant?

	African Americans	Whites
Yes	51.7%	22.4%
No	45.8	73.6

■   Are minority women lawyers treated less fairly than white women lawyers in hiring and promotion?

	African Americans	Whites
Yes	66.5%	10.9%
No	14.3	60.4

As these results clearly suggest, African American lawyers are substantially more likely than white lawyers to believe that the justice system is racially biased. As the author of the study noted, "Though they have made the justice system their life's work, many black lawyers believe the word 'justice' has a white spin that says 'just us.'"[59]

In the Courts: *Grutter v. Bollinger*

In 1997 Barbara Grutter, a white resident of Michigan with a 3.8 undergraduate GPA and a 161 LSAT score, was denied admission to the University of Michigan Law School. She filed suit, arguing the law school's admissions policies discriminated against her on the basis of race in violation of the 14th Amendment and Title VI of the Civil Rights Acts of 1974.

The law school's admission policy, which was designed to achieve a diverse study body, required officials to evaluate the candidate's undergraduate GPA and LSAT score along with the quality of the undergraduate institution; the difficulty of the courses taken as an undergraduate; and the candidate's personal statement, letters of recommendation, and essay describing how he or she "would contribute to law school life and diversity." Although the policy did not define diversity solely in terms of race and ethnicity or restrict the types of diversity that would be given substantial weight in admissions decisions, it did state that the goal was to accept "a mix of students with varying backgrounds and

experiences who will respect and learn from each other."[60] The policy stated explicitly that the law school was committed to "racial and ethnic diversity with special reference to the inclusion of students from groups which have been historically discriminated against, like African Americans, Hispanics, and Native Americans, who without this commitment might not be represented in our student body in meaningful numbers."[61]

Barbara Grutter claimed that she was not admitted to the University of Michigan Law School in large part because the school took the race/ethnicity of the applicant into account and, in doing so, gave African American and Hispanic applicants a significantly greater chance of admission than white students with similar credentials. She argued that the school did not have a "compelling interest" to justify the use of race as an admissions factor.

The United States Supreme Court did not agree with Grutter's arguments. The court

(continued)

(continued)

ruled that "The Law School's narrowly tailored use of race in admissions decisions to further a compelling interest in obtaining the educational benefits that flow from a diverse student body is not prohibited by the Equal Protection Clause" or Title VI of the Civil Rights Act of 1964.[62] The Supreme Court stated that student body diversity was, in fact, a compelling state interest "that can justify using race in university admissions." The court acknowledged that it would be "patently unconstitutional" to enroll a certain number of minority students "simply to assure some specified percentage of a particular group," but stated that this was not the case with respect to the law school's admission policy. Rather, "the Law School defines its critical mass concept by reference to the substantial, important, and laudable educational benefits that diversity is designed to produce, including cross-racial understanding and the breaking down of racial stereotypes."[63]

The Supreme Court also noted that the admissions plan was "narrowly tailored," in that it considered each applicant's race/ethnicity as only one factor among many. The court reiterated that, although "universities cannot establish quotas for members of certain racial or ethnic groups or put them on separate admission track," they can structure their admission policies to give serious consideration to all of the ways an applicant might contribute to a diverse educational environment.

amount necessary to guarantee that the defendant would show up for all court proceedings. Proponents of this view asserted that whether a defendant was released or detained prior to trial should not depend on his or her economic status or race. They also cited research demonstrating that the type and amount of bail imposed on the defendant and the time spent by the defendant in pretrial detention affected the likelihood of a guilty plea, the likelihood of conviction at trial, and the severity of the sentence.[66]

Arguments such as these prompted state and federal reforms designed to reduce pretrial detention. Encouraged by the results of the Manhattan Bail Project, which found that the majority of defendants released on their own recognizance did appear for trial,[67] local jurisdictions moved quickly to reduce reliance on money bail and to institute programs modeled after the Manhattan Bail Project. Many states revised their bail laws, and in 1966 Congress passed the Bail Reform Act, which proclaimed release on recognizance the presumptive bail decision in federal cases.

Then, as Walker noted, "the political winds shifted."[68] The rising crime rate of the 1970s generated a concern for crime control and led to a reassessment of bail policies. Critics challenged the traditional view that the only function of bail was to assure the defendant's appearance in court. They argued that guaranteeing public safety was also a valid function of bail and that pretrial detention should be used to protect the community from "dangerous" offenders.

These arguments fueled the second bail reform movement, which emerged in the 1970s and emphasized preventive detention. Conservative legislators and policymakers lobbied for reforms allowing judges to consider "public safety" when making decisions concerning the type and amount of bail.[69] By 1984, 34 states had enacted legislation giving judges the right to deny bail to defendants deemed dangerous.[70] Also in 1984, Congress passed a law authorizing preventive detention of dangerous defendants in federal criminal cases.[71]

TABLE 5.2 Race/Ethnicity and Bail Outcomes in King County, Washington

	Whites	All Racial Minorities	African Americans	Hispanics	Native Americans	Asian Americans
Released on personal recognizance	25%	14%	14%	10%	8%	18%
Monetary bail set	34%	56%	46%	60%	60%	50%
Median bail amount	$10,000	$10,000	$10,000	$10,000	$10,000	$15,000
In custody prior to trial	28%	39%	36%	54%	55%	35%

SOURCE: George S. Bridges, *A Study on Racial and Ethnic Disparities in Superior Court Bail and Pre-Trial Detention Practices in Washington* (Olympia: Washington State Minority and Justice Commission, 1997), Table 1.

The Effect of Race on Bail Decisionmaking Proponents of bail reform argued that whether a defendant was released or detained prior to trial should not depend on his or her economic status or race. They argued that bail decisions should rest either on assessments of the likelihood that the defendant would appear in court or on predictions of the defendant's dangerousness.

The problem, of course, is that there is no way to guarantee that judges will not take race into account in making these assessments and predictions. As Mann asserted, even the seemingly objective criteria used in making these decisions "may still be discriminatory on the basis of economic status or skin color."[72] If judges stereotype African Americans and Hispanics as less reliable and more prone to violence than whites, they will be more inclined to detain people of color and release whites, irrespective of their more objective assessments of risk of flight or dangerousness.

Studies examining the effect of race on bail decisions have yielded contradictory findings. Some researchers conclude that judges' bail decisions are based primarily on the seriousness of the offense and the defendant's prior criminal record and ties to the community; race has no effect once these factors are taken into consideration.[73] Other researchers contend that the defendant's economic status, not race, determines the likelihood of pretrial release.[74] If this is the case, one could argue that bail decisionmaking reflects *indirect* racial discrimination because African American and Hispanic defendants are more likely than white defendants to be poor.

A number of studies document *direct* racial discrimination in bail decisions. A study by Bridges of bail decisionmaking in King County, Washington, for example, examined the effect of race/ethnicity on four bail outcomes: whether the defendant was released on his or her own recognizance; whether the court set monetary bail; the amount of bail required; and whether the defendant was held in custody pending trial.[75] As shown in Table 5.2, he found that racial minorities were less likely than whites to be released on their own recognizance and were more likely than whites to have bail set. Racial minorities also were held in pretrial detention at higher rates than whites. The detention rate was 55 percent for Native Americans, 54 percent for Hispanics, 36 percent for African American, and 28 percent for whites. There were, however, no differences in the median amount of bail required.

Bridges noted that, although "at face value these differences may seem alarming,"[76] they might be the result of legitimate factors that criminal justice officials take into consideration when establishing the conditions of pretrial release: the defendant's ties to the community, the perceived dangerousness of the defendant, and any previous history of the defendant's failure to appear at court proceedings. When he controlled for these legally relevant variables and for the defendant's age and gender, however, he found that the race effects did not disappear. Racial minorities and men were less likely than whites and women to be released on their own recognizance and more likely than whites and women to be required to pay bail as a condition of release. For both of these decisions, the prosecutor's recommendation regarding the type and amount of bail was the strongest predictor of outcome. In contrast, race had no effect on the likelihood of pretrial detention once the bail conditions and the amount of bail set by the judge were taken into account.

Interviews with King County criminal justice officials revealed that most of them believed the racial differences in bail outcomes could be attributed to three factors: racial minorities' lack of resources and consequent inability to retain a private attorney; the tendency of judges to follow the recommendations of prosecutors; and cultural differences and language barriers that made it difficult to contact the defendant's references or verify information provided by the defendant. Because racial minorities were more likely than whites to be poor, they were more likely to be represented by public defenders with large caseloads and limited time to prepare for bail hearings. Resource constraints similarly limited the amount of time that judges and pretrial investigators were able to devote to bail decisions, which led to reliance on the recommendations proffered by the prosecutor. Although Bridges stressed that his study produced no evidence "that disparities are the product of overt, prejudicial acts by court officials," he nonetheless concluded that "race and ethnicity matter in the disposition of criminal cases."[77] He added that this "is a serious concern for the courts in Washington" because it "implies that, despite the efforts of judges and others dedicated to fairness in the administration of justice, justice is not administered fairly."[78]

Other evidence of direct racial discrimination is found in an analysis of pretrial release outcomes for felony defendants in the nation's 75 largest counties during the 1990s.[79] As shown in Figure 5.2, Demuth and Steffensmeier found that African Americans and Hispanics were more likely than whites to be detained in jail prior to trial. Among female defendants, the detention rates were 23.5 percent (whites), 28.4 percent (African Americans), and 34.7 percent (Hispanics). Among males, the rates were 33.1 percent (whites), 44.8 percent (African Americans), and 50.5 percent (Hispanics). The pretrial detention rate for Hispanic males, in other words, was more than twice the rate for white females.

As was the case with the Washington State study, these differences did not disappear when the authors controlled for the seriousness of the charges against the defendant, the number of charges the defendant was facing, whether the defendant previously had failed to appear for a court proceeding, and the defendant's prior record and age. Demuth and Steffensmeier found that males were more likely than females and that African Americans and Hispanics were more likely than whites to be detained in jail prior to trial. They also found that white

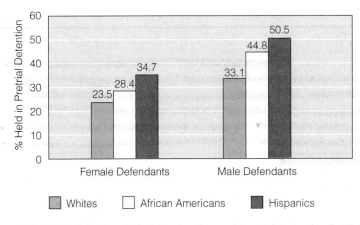

FIGURE 5.2 Race/Ethnicity, Gender, and Pretrial Detention in 75 U.S. Counties

SOURCE: Stephen Demuth and Darrell Steffensmeier, "The Impact of Gender and Race-Ethnicity in the Pretrial Release Process," *Social Problems* 51 (2004): 222–242.

females faced a significantly smaller likelihood of pretrial detention than any of the other groups, particularly Hispanic males and African American males.[80]

Findings from this study also provided some clues as to the reasons why defendants were held in jail prior to trial. For African Americans, the increased likelihood of detention was because they were almost two times more likely than whites to be held on bail; African Americans, in other words, were less likely than whites to be able to pay bail and secure their release. For Hispanics, however, the increased likelihood of detention reflected not only their inability to pay bail, but also the fact that they were more likely than whites to have to pay bail for release and the amount they were required to pay was higher than the amount that similarly situated whites were required to pay.[81] The authors also found that both female and male white defendants were more likely than their racial/ethnic counterparts to be released prior to trial and that this was largely because of their greater ability to make bail. As they noted, "white defendants of both sexes apparently have greater financial capital or resources either in terms of their personal bankroll/resources, their access to family or social networks willing to post bail, or their greater access to bail bondsmen for purposes of making bail."[82]

There also is evidence that defendant race interacts with other variables related to bail severity. Farnworth and Horan,[83] for example, found that the amount of bail imposed on white defendants who retained private attorneys was less than the amount imposed on African American defendants who retained private attorneys. Chiricos and Bales similarly found that the likelihood of pretrial detention was greatest for African American defendants who were unemployed.[84]

A study of bail decisionmaking in 10 federal district courts also found evidence of an indirect relationship between race/ethnicity and bail decisions. This study revealed that race did not have a direct effect on bail outcomes, but it did interact with a number of other variables to produce harsher bail outcomes for some types of African American defendants.[85] More specifically, the authors found that having a prior felony conviction had a greater negative effect on bail severity for African American defendants than for white defendants, and having more education or a higher income had a greater positive effect for whites than for African Americans.

Bail and Case Outcomes   Concerns about discrimination in bail decisionmaking focus on two facts: African American and Hispanic defendants who are presumed to be innocent are jailed prior to trial *and* those who are detained prior to trial are more likely to be convicted and receive harsher sentences than those who are released pending trial. These concerns focus, in other words, on the possibility that discrimination in bail decisionmaking has "spillover" effects on other case processing decisions.

An analysis of pretrial release of felony defendants by the BJS attests to the validity of these concerns.[86] Using data from 2000, BJS compared the conviction rates for released and detained defendants in the 75 largest counties in the United States. They found that 77 percent of those who were detained prior to trial, but only 55 percent of those who were released, were convicted. There were similar disparities for each of the four types of offenses analyzed. Among offenders charged with violent crimes, for example, the conviction rates were 69 percent for those who were detained and 45 percent for those who were released; the figures for drug offenders were 80 percent (detained offenders) and 55 percent (released offenders). A BJS study using data from 1992 revealed that pretrial status also affected the likelihood of incarceration: 50 percent of the detained defendants were sentenced to prison, compared to only 19 percent of those who were released prior to trial.[87]

Although these data suggest that pretrial release does have important spillover effects on case outcomes, the higher conviction and imprisonment rates for defendants who were detained pending trial could result from the fact that defendants who are held in jail prior to trial tend to be charged with more serious crimes, have more serious prior criminal histories, and have a past history of nonappearance at court proceedings. The BJS study discussed previously, for example, found that defendants charged with murder had the lowest release rate and that defendants with more serious prior records or a history of nonappearance were more likely to be detained prior to trial.[88] Given these findings, it is possible that the relationship between pretrial status and case outcomes would disappear once controls for case seriousness and prior criminal record were taken into consideration.

Data collected for a study of sentencing outcomes in Chicago, Miami, and Kansas City during 1993 and 1994 were used to explore this possibility.[89] Spohn and DeLone found that the offender's pretrial status was a strong predictor of the likelihood of imprisonment, even after other relevant legal and extralegal variables were taken into account. In all three cities, offenders who were released prior to trial faced substantially lower odds of a prison sentence than did offenders who were detained pending trial. Further analysis of sentences imposed by judges in Chicago and Kansas City revealed that pretrial detention had a similar effect on incarceration for each racial/ethnic group and for males and females.[90] As shown in Table 5.3, among both males and females, African American, Hispanic, and white defendants who were detained prior to trial faced substantially greater odds

T A B L E 5.3 The Effect of Pretrial Detention on Incarceration Rates for Typical Felony Offenders in Chicago and Kansas City

	% Sentenced to Prison	
	Detained Prior to Trial	Released Prior to Trial
Chicago		
African American male	73	23
Hispanic male	72	22
White male	63	16
African American female	53	11
Hispanic female	55	11
White female	42	7
Kansas City		
African American male	29	16
White male	24	13
African American female	13	6
White female	10	5

NOTE: These probabilities were calculated for defendants who were 30 years old, were charged with one count of possession of narcotics with intent, had one prior felony conviction, were not on probation at the time of the current offenses, were represented by a public defender, and pled guilty.

of incarceration than African American, Hispanic, and white defendants who were released pending trial. In Chicago, the highest incarceration rates were found for African American (73 percent), Hispanic (72 percent), and white (63 percent) males who were detained prior to trial; the lowest rates for were found for white (7 percent), African American (11 percent), and Hispanic (11 percent) females who were released pending trial.

The results of this study suggest that defendants who were detained prior to trial received more punitive sentences than those who were released and that the highest incarceration rates were for African Americans and Hispanics who were detained prior to trial. In Chicago, this "detention penalty" is compounded by the fact that African Americans were significantly more likely than whites to be detained prior to trial. Because they were detained more often than whites in the first place, African American defendants were more likely than whites to suffer both the pains of imprisonment prior to trial and the consequences of pretrial detention at sentencing.

Although the findings are somewhat contradictory, it thus appears that the reforms instituted since the 1960s have not produced racial equality in bail decisionmaking. It is certainly true that racial minorities are no longer routinely jailed prior to trial because of judicial stereotypes of dangerousness or because they are too poor to obtain their release. Nevertheless, there is evidence that judges in some jurisdictions continue to take race into account in deciding on the type and amount of bail. There also is evidence that race interacts with factors such as prior record or employment status to produce higher pretrial detention rates for African American defendants than for white defendants. Given the consequences of pretrial detention, these findings are an obvious cause for concern.

CHARGING AND PLEA BARGAINING DECISIONS

> Regrettably, the evidence is clear that prosecutorial discretion is systematically exercised to the disadvantage of black and Hispanic Americans. Prosecutors are not, by and large, bigoted. But as with police activity, prosecutorial judgment is shaped by a set of self-perpetuating racial assumptions.[91]

Thus far we have examined criminal justice decisions concerning appointment of counsel and bail for evidence of racial discrimination. We have shown that, despite reforms mandated by the Supreme Court or adopted voluntarily by the states, inequities persist. African Americans and Hispanics who find themselves in the arms of the law continue to suffer discrimination in these important court processing decisions.

In this section, we examine prosecutors' charging and plea bargaining decisions for evidence of differential treatment of minority and white defendants. We argue that there is compelling evidence of racial *disparity* in charging and plea bargaining. We further contend that this disparity frequently reflects racial *discrimination*.

Prosecutors' Charging Decisions

Prosecutors exercise broad discretion in deciding whether to file formal charges against individuals suspected of crimes and in determining the number and seriousness of the charges to be filed. According to the Supreme Court, "So long as the prosecutor has probable cause to believe that the accused committed an offense defined by statute, the decision whether or not to prosecute, and what charge to file or bring before a grand jury, generally rests entirely in his discretion."[92] As Justice Jackson noted in 1940, "the prosecutor has more control over life, liberty, and reputation than any other person in America."[93]

The power of the prosecutor is reflected in the fact that in most states, from one-third to one-half of all felony cases are dismissed by the prosecutor prior to a determination of guilt or innocence.[94] Prosecutors can reject charges at the initial screening, either because they believe the suspect is innocent or, more typically, because they believe the suspect is guilty but a conviction would be unlikely. Prosecutors also can reject charges if they feel it would not be in the "interest of justice" to continue the case—because the crime is too trivial; because of a perception that the suspect has been punished enough; or because the suspect has agreed to provide information about other, more serious, cases.[95] Finally, prosecutors can reject charges as felonies but prosecute them as misdemeanors.

If a formal charge is filed by the prosecutor, it still can be reduced to a less serious felony or to a misdemeanor during plea bargaining. It also can be dismissed by the court on a recommendation by the prosecutor. This usually happens when the case "falls apart" prior to trial. A witness may refuse to cooperate or may fail to appear at trial, or the judge may rule that the confession or other essential evidence is inadmissible. Unlike the prosecutor's initial decision to reject the charge, the decision to dismiss a charge already filed requires official court action.

The Effect of Race on Charging Decisions   Although the prosecutor's discretion is broad, it is not unlimited. The Supreme Court, in fact, has ruled that the decision to prosecute may not be "deliberately based upon an unjustifiable standard such as race, religion, or other arbitrary classification."[96] The prosecutor, in other words, cannot legitimately take the race of the suspect into account in deciding whether to file charges or in deciding on the seriousness of the charge to be filed.

Gunnar Myrdal, a Swedish social scientist and the author of a book examining the "Negro Problem" in the Unites States in the late 1930s and early 1940s, found substantial discrimination against African Americans in the decision of whether to charge. As Myrdal noted:

> State courts receive indictments for physical violence against Negroes
> in an infinitesimally small proportion of the cases. It is notorious that
> practically never have white lynching mobs been brought to court in the
> south, even when the killers are known to all in the community and are
> mentioned by name in the local press. When the offender is a Negro,
> indictment is easily obtained, and no such difficulty at the start will meet
> the prosecution of the case.[97]

Only a few studies have examined the effect of race on prosecutorial charging decisions, reaching contradictory conclusions. Some researchers found either that race did not affect charging decisions at all,[98] or that race played a very minor role in the decision of whether to prosecute.[99] The authors of these studies concluded that the decision to prosecute was based primarily on the strength of evidence in the case.

Several studies concluded that prosecutors' charging decisions *are* affected by race. An analysis of the decision to reject or dismiss charges against felony defendants in Los Angeles County, for example, revealed a pattern of discrimination in favor of female defendants and against African American and Hispanic defendants.[100] The authors controlled for the defendant's age and prior criminal record, the seriousness of the charge against the defendant, and whether the defendant used a weapon in committing the crime. As shown in Table 5.4, they found that Hispanic males were most likely to be prosecuted fully, followed by African American males, white males, and females of all ethnic groups.

The authors of this study speculated that prosecutors took both race and gender into account in deciding whether to file charges in "marginal cases." They reasoned that strong cases would be prosecuted and weak cases would be dropped, regardless of the race or gender of the suspect. In marginal cases, however,

**T A B L E 5.4   The Effect of Race and Gender on Prosecutors'
Charging Decisions**

Group	Adjusted Means[a]		
	Rejected at Screening	**Dismissed by Court**	**Fully Prosecuted**
African American male	46%	34%	39%
African American female	57	42	30
Hispanic male	46	33	42
Hispanic female	54	43	31
White male	54	33	26
White female	59	42	19

[a] Means have been adjusted for the effect of four independent variables: age of the
defendant, prior record of the defendant, seriousness of the charge, and whether the
defendant used a weapon.

SOURCE: Table adapted from Cassia Spohn, John Gruhl, and Susan Welch, "The Impact of the
Ethnicity and Gender of Defendants on the Decision to Reject or Dismiss Felony Charges,"
Criminology 25 (1987): 175–191.

prosecutors may simply feel less comfortable prosecuting the dominant
rather than the subordinate ethnic groups. They might feel the dominant
groups are less threatening. Or they might believe they can win convictions more often against blacks and Hispanics than against Anglos.[101]

Similar results surfaced in a study of prosecutors' charging decisions in King
County, Washington.[102] When the authors of this study examined the prosecutor's decision to file felony charges (rather than file misdemeanor charges or
decline to prosecute the case), they found that prosecutors were substantially
more likely to file felony charges against racial minorities than against whites.
These differences were especially pronounced for violent crimes and drug
offenses. Moreover, the racial disparities did not disappear when the authors
controlled for the seriousness of the crime, the defendant's prior criminal record,
and the defendant's age and gender. Even taking these factors into account,
Native Americans were 1.7 times more likely than whites to be charged with a
felony and African Americans were 1.15 times more likely than whites to face
felony charges.[103]

Crutchfield and his co-authors stressed that these racial differences were not
"necessarily the result of individuals making biased decisions."[104] Rather, the
differences probably reflected race-linked legal, economic, and social factors that
prosecutors take into account in deciding whether to charge, as well as officials'
focus on drug offenses involving crack cocaine. As we have repeatedly emphasized, however, this type of subtle or indirect discrimination is problematic. It is
difficult to disentangle the effects of race/ethnicity, social class, employment
history, and family situation. Even if criminal justice officials are justified in
taking these social and economic factors into account, doing so will necessarily
produce unintended race effects.

The Effect of Offender Race and Victim Race on Charging Decisions The research discussed thus far suggests that the race/ethnicity of the offender affects prosecutors' charging decisions. There also is evidence that charging decisions vary depending on the race of the offender and the race of the victim. LaFree,[105] for example, found that African Americans arrested for raping white women were more likely to be charged with felonies than were either African Americans arrested for raping African American women or whites arrested for raping white women. One study found that defendants arrested for murdering whites in Florida were more likely to be indicted for first-degree murder than those arrested for murdering African Americans.[106] Another study of prosecutors' charging decisions in death penalty cases found that homicide cases involving African American defendants and white victims were more likely than similar cases involving other offender–victim racial combinations to result in first-degree murder charges.[107] The prosecutor in the Midwestern jurisdiction where this study was conducted was also more likely to file a notice of aggravating circumstances and to proceed to a capital trial if the defendant was an African American who was accused of killing a white.

Research on sexual assault case processing decisions in Detroit reached a different conclusion. Spohn and Spears[108] used data on sexual assaults bound over for trial in Detroit Recorder's Court to examine the effect of offender race, victim race, and other case characteristics on the decision to dismiss the charges against the defendant (versus the decision to fully prosecute the case). Building on previous research demonstrating that African Americans who murder or rape whites receive more punitive treatment than other victim–offender racial combinations, they hypothesized that black-on-white sexual assaults would be more likely than either black-on-black or white-on-white sexual assaults to result in the dismissal of all charges. They found just the opposite: the likelihood of charge dismissal was significantly *greater* for cases involving African American offenders and white victims than for the other two groups of offenders. They also found that African Americans prosecuted for assaulting whites were *less* likely to be convicted than whites charged with sexually assaulting whites.[109]

Spohn and Spears concluded that their "unexpected findings" suggest that African American-on-white sexual assaults with weaker evidence are less likely to be screened out during the preliminary stages of the process.[110] Police and prosecutors, in other words, may regard sexual assaults involving African American men and white women as inherently more serious than intraracial sexual assaults; consequently, they may be more willing to take a chance with a reluctant victim or a victim whose behavior at the time of the incident was questionable. According to the authors of this study:

> The police may be willing to make an arrest and the prosecutor may be willing to charge, despite questions about the procedures used to obtain physical evidence or about the validity of the defendant's confession. If this is true, then cases involving black offenders and white victims will be more likely than other types of cases to 'fall apart' before or during trial.[111]

A study of charging decisions in California reached a similar conclusion. Petersilia found that white suspects were *more* likely than African American or

Hispanic suspects to be formally charged.[112] Her analysis of the reasons given for charge rejection led her to conclude that the higher dismissal rates for nonwhite suspects reflected the fact that "blacks and Hispanics in California are more likely than whites to be arrested under circumstances that provide insufficient evidence to support criminal charges."[113] Prosecutors were more reluctant to file charges against racial minorities than against whites, in other words, because they viewed the evidence against racial minorities as weaker and the odds of convicting them as lower.

Race, Drugs, and Selective Prosecution   The results of Petersilia's study in Los Angeles and Spohn and Spears' study in Detroit provide evidence suggestive of a pattern of *selective prosecution*—that is, cases involving racial minorities, or certain types of racial minorities, are singled out for prosecution, whereas similar cases involving whites are either screened out very early in the process or never enter the system in the first place.

This argument has been made most forcefully with respect to drug offenses. In *Malign Neglect*, for example, Michael Tonry[114] argues, "Urban black Americans have borne the brunt of the War on Drugs." More specifically, he charges that "the recent blackening of America's prison population is the product of malign neglect of the war's effects on black Americans."[115] Miller[116] similarly asserts that "from the first shot fired in the drug war African-Americans were targeted, arrested, and imprisoned in wildly disproportionate numbers."

There is ample evidence that the War on Drugs is being fought primarily in African American and Hispanic communities. In 1997, for example, racial minorities comprised nearly three-fourths of all offenders prosecuted in federal district courts for drug trafficking: 25 percent of these offenders were white, 33 percent were African American, and 41 percent were Hispanic.[117] These figures are inconsistent with national data on use of drugs, which reveal that whites are more likely than either African Americans or Hispanics to report having "ever" used a variety of drugs, including cocaine, PCP, LSD, and marijuana.[118]

Some commentators cite evidence of a different type of selective prosecution in drug cases (see Box 5.3 for the U.S. Attorney General's memorandum regarding racial neutrality in federal prosecution). Noting that the penalties for use of crack cocaine mandated by the federal sentencing guidelines are substantially harsher than the penalties provided under many state statutes, these critics suggest that state prosecutors are more likely to refer crack cases involving racial minorities to the federal system for prosecution.[120] Berk and Campbell, for example, compared the racial makeup of defendants arrested for sale of crack cocaine in Los Angeles to the racial makeup of defendants charged with sale of crack cocaine in state and federal courts. They found that the racial makeup of arrestees was similar to the racial makeup of those charged with violating state statutes. However, African Americans were overrepresented in federal cases; in fact, over a 4-year period, no whites were prosecuted for the sale of crack cocaine in federal court.

This issue was addressed by the Supreme Court in 1996. The five defendants in the case of *U.S. v. Armstrong et al.*[121] alleged that they were selected for prosecution in federal court (i.e., the U.S. District Court for the Central District of California) rather than in state court because they were African American. They further alleged that this decision had serious potential consequences.

**B O X 5.3   The U.S. Attorney General and Racial Neutrality
in Prosecution**

In January 1999, Janet Reno, then Attorney General for the United States, issued a memorandum on "Ensuring Racial Neutrality in Prosecution Practices" to all United States Attorneys.[119] Excerpts from the memo included the following:

- "Each United States Attorney should examine his or her office's practices and procedures and take all necessary measures to ensure the use of race-neutral policies in the exercise of prosecutorial discretion within a district. Absent compelling, specific law enforcement imperatives there is ordinarily no justification for differing policies and practices within a district with respect to similarly situated defendants. Moreover, any race-neutral policy that has a disparate racial impact should be carefully reviewed to determine whether the disparity is justified by law enforcement necessity and not the product of conscious or unconscious racial bias."

- "Care must be taken to ensure that race plays no part in the Government's decision whether to file a substantial assistance motion or the amount of any recommended reduction."

- "As the chief federal law enforcement officer in the district, the United States Attorney should take a leadership role in ensuring that all agencies within the district are aware of issues of racial disparity ... [O]ur constant vigilance will ensure that there is no perception of racial disparity in the discharge of our duties. The public recognition that our policies are administered in a race-neutral fashion is as important as the reality that we do so administer them."

Christopher Armstrong, for example, faced a prison term of 55 years to life under federal statutes, compared to 3 to 9 years under California law. Another defendant, Aaron Hampton, faced a maximum term of 14 years under California law but a mandatory life term under federal law.

Following their indictment for conspiring to possess with intent to distribute more than 50 grams of crack cocaine, the defendants filed a motion for discovery of information held by the U.S. Attorney's office regarding the race of people prosecuted by that office. In support of their motion, they offered a study showing that all of the defendants in the crack cocaine cases closed by the Federal Public Defender's Office in 1991 were African American.

The U.S. District Court ordered the U.S. Attorney's office to provide the data requested by the defendants. When federal prosecutors refused to do so, noting that there was no evidence that they had refused to prosecute white or Hispanic crack defendants, U.S. District Judge Consuelo Marshall dismissed the indictments. The 9th Circuit U.S. Court of Appeals affirmed Judge Marshall's dismissal of the indictments. The appellate court judges stated that they began with "the presumption that people of all races commit all types of crimes—not with the premise that any type of crime is the exclusive province of any particular racial or ethnic group."[122] They stated that the defendant's evidence showing that all 24 crack defendants were African American required some response from federal prosecutors.

The U.S. Supreme Court disagreed. In an 8-to-1 decision that did not settle the issue of whether the U.S. Attorney's Office engaged in selective prosecution,

BOX 5.4   Are African American Pregnant Women Who Abuse Drugs Singled Out for Prosecution Under Child Abuse/Neglect Statutes?

Prosecution of Pregnant Women Who Abuse Drugs

In 1989 Jennifer Clarise Johnson, a 23-year-old African American crack addict, became the first woman in the United States to be convicted for exposing a baby to illegal drugs during pregnancy. The Florida court gave Johnson 15 to 20 years probation and required her to enter drug treatment and report subsequent pregnancies to her probation officer. According to the prosecutor who filed charges against Johnson, "We needed to make sure this woman does not give birth to another cocaine baby."[126]

Other prosecutions and convictions in other state courts followed; by 1992 more than 100 women in 24 states had been charged with abusing an unborn child through illegal drug use during pregnancy.

Many of these cases were appealed and, until 1997, all of the appeals resulted in the dismissal of charges. Then in October 1997, the South Carolina Supreme Court became the first court in the United States to rule that a viable fetus could be considered a person under child abuse laws and that a pregnant woman who abused drugs during the third trimester of pregnancy therefore could be charged with child abuse or other, more serious, crimes.[127] Two months later, Talitha Renee Garrick, a 27-year-old African American woman who admitted that she smoked crack cocaine an hour before she gave birth to a stillborn child, pled guilty to involuntary manslaughter in a South Carolina courtroom.

Do Prosecutors "Target" Pregnant Black Women?

A number of commentators contend that prosecutors' charging decisions in these types of cases reflect racial discrimination. Humphries and colleagues, for example, asserted, "The overwhelming majority of prosecutions involve poor women of color."[128] Roberts[129] similarly argued that "Poor Black women are the primary targets of prosecutors, not because they are more likely to be guilty of fetal abuse, but because they are Black and poor."[130]

To support her allegations, Roberts cited evidence documenting that most of the women who have been prosecuted have been African American; she notes that the 52 women prosecuted through 1990 included 35 African Americans, 14 whites, 2 Hispanics, and 1 Native American. Ten out of 11 cases in Florida, and 17 out of 18 cases in South Carolina, were brought against African American women.[131] According to Roberts, these glaring disparities create a presumption of racially selective prosecution.

the Court ruled that federal rules of criminal procedure regarding discovery do not require the government to provide the information requested by the defendants. Although prosecutors *are* obligated to turn over documents that are "material to the preparation of the . . . defense," this applies *only* to documents needed to mount a defense against the government's "case-in-chief" (i.e., the crack cocaine charges) and not to documents needed to make a selective prosecution claim. Further, the Court ruled that "For a defendant to be entitled to discovery on a claim that he was singled out for prosecution on the basis of his race, he must make a threshold showing that the Government declined to prosecute similarly situated suspects of other races."[123]

Justice Stevens, the lone dissenter in the case, argued that the evidence of selective prosecution presented by the defendants "was sufficiently disturbing to require some response from the United States Attorney's Office." According to Stevens:

Randall Kennedy, an African American professor of law at Harvard University and the author of *Race, Crime, and the Law*, acknowledged that Roberts' charges of selective prosecution and racial misconduct "are surely plausible." As he noted, "Given the long and sad history of documented, irrefutable racial discrimination in the administration of criminal law...no informed observer should be shocked by the suggestion that some prosecutors treat black pregnant women more harshly than identically situated white pregnant women."[132]

Kennedy claimed, however, that Roberts' contention that prosecutors target women "*because* they are black and poor,"[133] although plausible, is not persuasive. He noted that Roberts relied heavily on evidence from a study designed to estimate the prevalence of alcohol and drug abuse among pregnant women in Pinellas County, Florida. This study revealed that there were similar rates of substance abuse among African American and white women but that African American women were 10 times more likely than white women to be reported to public health authorities (as Florida law required).

Kennedy argued that the Florida study does not provide conclusive evidence of racial bias. He noted, in fact, that the authors of the study themselves suggested that the disparity in reporting rates might reflect either the fact that newborns who have been exposed to cocaine exhibit more severe symptoms at birth or the fact that black pregnant women are more likely than white pregnant women to be addicted to cocaine (rather than to alcohol, marijuana, or some other drug). Kennedy asserted that Roberts failed to address these alternative hypotheses and simply insisted "'racial prejudice and stereotyping must be a factor' in the racially disparate pattern of reporting ..."[134]

Kennedy also contended that Roberts' analysis failed to consider the problem of underprotection of the law. Imagine, he asked, what the reaction would be if the situation were reversed and prosecutors brought child abuse charges solely against drug-abusing white women. "Would that not rightly prompt suspicion of racially selective devaluation of black babies on the grounds that withholding prosecution deprives black babies of the equal *protection* of the laws?"[135]

What do you think? Do prosecutors "target" pregnant women who are poor and African American? What would the reaction be (among whites? among African Americans?) if only white women were prosecuted?

If a District Judge has reason to suspect that [the United States Attorney for the Central District of California], or a member of her staff, has singled out particular defendants for prosecution on the basis of their race, it is surely appropriate for the Judge to determine whether there is a factual basis for such a concern.[124] (See Box 5.4 for a discussion of whether African American pregnant women who abuse drugs are singled out for prosecution under child abuse/neglect laws.)

Stevens added that the severity of federal penalties imposed for offenses involving crack cocaine, coupled with documented racial patterns of enforcement, "give rise to a special concern about the fairness of charging practices for crack offenses." His concerns are echoed by U.S. District Court Judge Consuelo B. Marshall, who observed, "We do see a lot of these [crack] cases and one does ask why some are in state court and some are being prosecuted in federal court . . . and if it's not based on race, what's it based on?"[125]

Race and Plea Bargaining Decisions

There has been relatively little research focusing explicitly on the effect of race on prosecutors' plea bargaining decisions. Few studies have asked if prosecutors take the race of the defendant into consideration in deciding whether to reduce or drop charges in exchange for a guilty plea. Moreover, the studies that have been conducted have reached contradictory conclusions.

Research reveals that prosecutors' plea bargaining decisions are strongly determined by the strength of evidence against the defendant, by the defendant's prior criminal record, and by the seriousness of the offense.[136] Prosecutors are more willing to offer concessions to defendants who commit less serious crimes and have less serious prior records. They also are more willing to alter charges when the evidence against the defendant is weak or inconsistent.

A number of studies conclude that white defendants are offered plea bargains more frequently and get better deals than racial minorities. A study of the charging process in New York, for example, found that race did not affect charge reductions if the case was disposed of at the first presentation. Among defendants who did not plead guilty at the first opportunity, however, African Americans received less substantial reductions than whites.[137] An analysis of 683,513 criminal cases in California concluded that "Whites were more successful in getting charged reduced or dropped, in avoiding 'enhancements' or extra charges, and in getting diversion, probation, or fines instead of incarceration."[138]

An analysis of plea bargaining under the federal sentencing guidelines also concluded that whites receive better deals than racial minorities.[139] This study, which was conducted by the United States Sentencing Commission, examined sentence reductions for offenders who provided "substantial assistance" to the government. According to §5K1.1 of the *Guidelines Manual*, if an offender assists in the investigation and prosecution of another person who has committed a crime, the prosecutor can ask the court to reduce the offender's sentence. Because the guidelines do not specify either the types of cooperation that "count" as substantial assistance or the magnitude of the sentence reduction that is to be given, this is a highly discretionary decision.

The Sentencing Commission estimated the effect of race/ethnicity on both the probability of receiving a substantial assistance departure and the magnitude of the sentence reduction. They controlled for other variables such as the seriousness of the offense, use of a weapon, the offender's prior criminal record, and other factors deemed relevant under the sentencing guidelines. They found that African Americans and Hispanics were less likely than whites to receive a substantial assistance departure; among offenders who did receive a departure, whites received a larger sentence reduction than either African Americans or Hispanics.[140] According to the Commission's report, "the evidence consistently indicated that factors that were associated with either the making of a §5K1.1

motion and/or the magnitude of the departure were not consistent with princi-ples of equity."[141]

Similar results were reported by Albonetti,[142] who examined the effect of guideline departures on sentence outcomes for drug offenders. She found that guideline departures (most of which reflected prosecutors' motions to reduce the sentence in return for the offenders' "substantial assistance") resulted in larger sentence reductions for white drug offenders than for African American or Hispanic drug offenders. A guideline departure produced a 23 percent reduction in the probability of incarceration for white offenders, compared to a 14 percent reduction for Hispanic offenders and a 13 percent reduction for African Amer-ican offenders.[143] Albonetti concluded that her findings "strongly suggest that the mechanism by which the federal guidelines permit the exercise of discretion operates to the disadvantage of minority defendants."[144]

Two studies found that race did not affect plea bargaining decisions in the predicted way. An examination of the guilty plea process in nine counties in Illinois, Michigan, and Pennsylvania revealed that defendant race had no effect on four measures of charge reduction.[145] The authors of this study concluded that "the allocation of charge concessions did not seem to be dictated by blatantly discriminatory criteria or punitive motives."[146] A study of charge reductions in two jurisdictions found that racial minorities received more *favorable* treatment than whites. In one county, African Americans received more favorable charge reductions than whites; in the other county, Hispanics were treated more favorably than whites.[147] The authors of this study speculated that these results might reflect devaluation of minority victims. As they noted, "if minority victims are devalued because of racist beliefs, such sentiments could, paradoxically, produce more favorable legal outcomes for minority defendants." The authors also suggested that the results might reflect overcharging of minority defendants by the police; prosecutors may have been forced "to accept pleas to lesser charges from black defendants because of the initial overcharging."[148]

In sum, although the evidence concerning the effect of race on prosecutors' charging and plea bargaining decisions is both scanty and inconsistent, a number of studies have found that African American and Hispanic suspects are more likely than white suspects to be charged with a crime and prosecuted fully. There also is evidence supporting charges of selective prosecution of racial minorities, especially for drug offenses. The limited evidence concerning the effect of race on plea bargaining is even more contradictory. Given the importance of these initial charging decisions, these findings "call for the kind of scrutiny in the pretrial stages that has been so rightly given to the convicting and sentencing stages."[149]

CONCLUSION

The court system that tried and sentenced the Scottsboro Boys in 1931 no longer exists, in the South or elsewhere. Reforms mandated by the U.S. Supreme Court or adopted voluntarily by the states have eliminated much of the blatant racism directed against racial minorities in court. African American and Hispanic criminal defendants are no longer routinely denied bail and then tried by all-white juries without attorneys to assist them in their defense. They are not consistently prosecuted and convicted with less-than-convincing evidence of guilt.

Implementation of these reforms, however, has not produced equality of justice. As shown in the preceding sections of this chapter, there is evidence that defendant race/ethnicity continues to affect decisions regarding bail, charging, and plea bargaining. Some evidence suggests that race has a direct and obvious effect on these pretrial decisions; other evidence suggests that the effect of race is indirect and subtle. It is important to note, however, that discriminatory treatment during the pretrial stage of the criminal justice process can have profound consequences for racial minorities at trial and sentencing. If racial minorities are more likely than whites to be represented by incompetent attorneys or detained in jail prior to trial, they may, as a result of these differences, face greater odds of conviction and harsher sentences. Racially discriminatory charging decisions have similar "spillover" effects at trial.

DISCUSSION QUESTIONS

1. Some commentators have raised questions about the quality of legal representation provided to the poor. They also have suggested that racial minorities, who are more likely than whites to be poor, are particularly disadvantaged. Is this necessarily the case? Are racial minorities represented by public defenders or assigned counsel treated more harshly than those represented by private attorneys? If you were an African American, Hispanic, or Native American defendant and could choose whether to be represented by a public defender or a private attorney, which would you choose? Why?

2. Racial minorities comprise a very small proportion of the lawyers and judges in the United States. What accounts for this? What difference, if any, would it make if more of the lawyers representing criminal defendants were racial minorities?

3. Do you agree or disagree with the Supreme Court's decision (*Grutter v. Bollinger*) in the case in which the University of Michigan Law School's admission procedures were challenged? What is the basis for your agreement or disagreement?

4. Assume that racial minorities *are* more likely than whites to be detained prior to trial. Why is this a matter for concern? What are the consequences of pretrial detention? How could the bail system be reformed to reduce this disparity?

5. Randall Kennedy, the author of *Race, Crime and the Law*, argues (p. 10) that it is sometimes difficult to determine "whether, or for whom, a given disparity is harmful." Regarding the prosecution of pregnant women who abuse drugs, he states that "Some critics attack as racist prosecutions of pregnant drug addicts on the grounds that such prosecutions disproportionately burden blacks." But,

he asks, "on balance, are black communities *hurt* by prosecutions of pregnant women for using illicit drugs harmful to their unborn babies or *helped* by intervention which may at least plausibly deter conduct that will put black unborn children at risk?" How would you answer this question?

6. Assume that there is evidence that prosecutors in a particular jurisdiction offer more favorable plea bargains to racial minorities than to whites–that is, they are more willing to reduce the charges or to recommend a sentence substantially below the maximum permitted by law if the defendant is a racial minority. What would explain this seemingly "anomalous" finding?

7. What evidence would the defendants in *U.S. v. Armstrong et al.*, the Supreme Court case in which five black defendants challenged their prosecution for drug offenses in federal rather than state court, need to prove that they had been the victims of unconstitutional selective prosecution? How would they obtain this evidence? Has the Supreme Court placed an unreasonable burden on defendants alleging selection prosecution?

NOTES

1. Philip S. Anderson, "Striving for a Just Society," *ABA Journal* (February 1999), p. 66.

2. *Powell v. Alabama*, 287 U.S. 45 (1932).

3. *Norris v. Alabama*, 294 U.S. 587 (1935).

4. Dan T. Carter, *Scottsboro: A Tragedy of the American South* (Baton Rouge: Louisiana State University Press, 1969), p. 326.

5. Ibid., p. 328.

6. Ibid., pp. 344–345.

7. Ibid., p. 347.

8. Birmingham *Age-Herald*, January 24, 1936 (quoted in Carter, *Scottsboro*, p. 347).

9. Carter, *Scottsboro*, pp. 376–377.

10. Ibid., p. 377.

11. Randall Kennedy, *Race, Crime, and the Law* (New York: Vintage Books, 1997), p. 104.

12. Peter Applebome, "Facts Perplexing in Texas Robbery," *The New York Times* (December 19, 1983), p. 17.

13. Ibid., p. 17.

14. *Chicago Tribune*, August 9, 1995, Section 5, pp. 1–2.

15. Ibid., p. 2.

16. Ibid.

17. Available at The Justice Project website at http://www.justice.policy.net/cjreform/profiles.

18. Kennedy, *Race, Crime, and the Law*, p. 127.

19. *Powell v. Alabama*, 287 U.S. 45 (1932).

20. *Johnson v. Zerbst*, 304 U.S. 458 (1938).

21. *Gideon v. Wainwright*, 372 U.S. 335 (1963).

22. *Argersinger v. Hamlin*, 407 U.S. 25 (1972).

23. A defendant is entitled to counsel at every stage "where substantial rights of the accused may be affected" that require the "guiding hand of counsel" (*Mempa v. Rhay*, 389 U.S. 128, 1967). These critical stages include arraignment, preliminary hearing, entry of a plea, trial, sentencing, and the first appeal.

24. *Strickland v. Washington*, 466 U.S. 668 (1984).

25. Anthony Lewis, *Gideon's Trumpet* (New York: Vintage Books, 1964).

26. Lisa J. McIntyre, *The Public Defender: The Practice of Law in the Shadows of Repute* (Chicago: University of Chicago Press, 1987).

27. Bureau of Justice Statistics, *Defense Counsel in Criminal Cases* (Washington, DC: U.S. Department of Justice, 2000), Table 5.

28. Ibid., Tables 16 and 19.

29. "Notes: Gideon's Promise Unfulfilled: The Need for Litigated Reform of Indigent Defense," *Harvard Law Review* 113 (2000): 2062–2079.

30. Ibid., p. 2065.

31. Jonathan D. Casper, "Did You Have a Lawyer When You Went to Court? No, I Had a Public Defender," *Yale Review of Law & Social Action* 1 (1971): 4–9.

32. David W. Neubauer, *America's Courts and the Criminal Justice System*, 7th ed. (Belmont, CA: Wadsworth, 2002), p. 186.

33. See, for example, Abraham S. Blumberg, "The Practice of Law as a Confidence Game: Organizational Cooptation of a Profession," *Law & Society Review* 1 (1967): 15–39; David Sudnow, "Normal Crimes: Sociological Features of the Penal Code in the Public Defender's Office," *Social Problems* 12 (1965): 255–277.

34. Ronald Weitzer, "Racial Discrimination in the Criminal Justice System: Findings and Problems in the Literature," *Journal of Criminal Justice* 24 (1996): 313.

35. Jonathan D. Casper, *Criminal Courts: The Defendant's Perspective* (Englewood Cliffs, NJ: Prentice-Hall, 1978); Richard D. Hartley, "Type of Counsel and Its Effects on Criminal Court Outcomes in a Large Midwestern Jurisdiction: Do You Get What You Pay For?" Diss. University of Nebraska at Omaha, 2005; Martin A. Levin, *Urban Politics and the Criminal Courts* (Chicago: University of Chicago Press, 1977); Lisa J. McIntyre, *The Public Defender: The Practice of Law in the Shadow of Repute* (Chicago: University of Chicago Press,

1987); Dallin H. Oaks and Warren Lehman, "Lawyers for the Poor," in *The Scales of Justice*, Abraham S. Blumberg, ed. (Chicago: Aldine, 1970); Lee Silverstein, *Defense of the Poor* (Chicago: American Bar Foundation, 1965); Gerald R. Wheeler and Carol L. Wheeler, "Reflections on Legal Representation of the Economically Disadvantaged: Beyond Assembly Line Justice," *Crime and Delinquency* 26 (1980): 319–332.

36. Jerome Skolnick, "Social Control in the Adversary System," *Journal of Conflict Resolution* 11 (1967): 67.

37. Paul B. Wice, *Chaos in the Courthouse: The Inner Workings of the Urban Municipal Courts* (New York: Praeger, 1985).

38. Bureau of Justice Statistics, *Defense Counsel in Criminal Cases*. (Washington, DC: U.S. Department of Justice, 2000).

39. Ibid.

40. Malcolm D. Holmes, Harmon M. Hosch, Howard C. Daudistel, Dolores A. Perez, and Joseph B. Graves, "Ethnicity, Legal Resources, and Felony Dispositions in Two Southwestern Jurisdictions," *Justice Quarterly* 13 (1996): 11–30.

41. Ibid., p. 24.

42. The findings reported in this chapter are unpublished. For a discussion of the overall conclusions of this study, see Cassia Spohn and Miriam DeLone, "When Does Race Matter? An Examination of the Conditions Under Which Race Affects Sentence Severity" *Sociology of Crime, Law, and Deviance*, 2 (2000): 3–37.

43. Weitzer, "Racial Discrimination in the Criminal Justice System," p. 313.

44. Roger A. Hanson and Brian J. Ostrom, "Indigent Defenders Get the Job Done and Done Well," in *Criminal Justice: Law and Politics*, 6th ed., George Cole, ed. (Belmont, CA: Wadsworth, 1993).

45. Gunnar Myrdal, *An American Dilemma: The Negro Problem and Modern Democracy* (New York: Harper and Brothers, 1944), p. 547.

46. American Bar Association, "Lawyer Demographics." Available at http://www.abanet.org/legaled/statistics.html.

47. Ibid.

48. American Bar Association, National Database on Judicial Diversity in State Courts. Available at http://www.abanet.org/judind/diversity/national.html

49. American Bar Association Commission on Racial and Ethnic Diversity in the Profession. *Miles to Go 2000: Progress of Minorities in the Legal Profession* (Chicago: American Bar Association, 2000), Table 42 and Table 46.

50. Ibid., Table 44.

51. Ibid., p. 28.

52. Ibid., p. x.

53. Richard H. Sander, "A Systematic Analysis of Affirmative Action in American Law Schools," *Stanford Law Review* 57 (2004): 367–585.

54. Ibid., p. 474.

55. David L. Chambers, Timothy T. Clydesdale, William C. Kidder, and Richard O. Lempert, "The Real Impact of Eliminating Affirmative Action in American Law Schools: An Empirical Critique of Richard Sander's Study," *Stanford Law Review* 57 (2005): 1855–1898.

56. Ibid., p. 1857.

57. John Hechinger, "Critics Assail Study of Race, Law Students." *Wall Street Journal* November 5, 2004. Available at http://www.wsj.com.

58. American Bar Association, "Race and the Law: Special Report," February (1999): 42–70.

59. Terry Carter, "Divided Justice," *ABA Journal* February (1999): 42–45.

60. The University of Michigan Law School, *Report and Recommendations of the Admissions Committee*. Available at http://www.law.umich.edu/admissionspolicy.pdf.

61. Ibid.

62. *Grutter v. Bollinger*, 288 F.3d 732 (2003).

63. Ibid.

64. Myrdal, *An American Dilemma*, p. 548.

65. Haywood Burns, "Black People and the Tyranny of American Law," *The Annals of the American Academy of Political and Social Sciences* 407 (1973): 156–166.

66. Celesta A. Albonetti, "An Integration of Theories to Explain Judicial Discretion," *Social Problems* 38 (1991): 247–266; Ronald A. Farrell and Victoria L. Swigert, "Prior Offense Record as a Self-Fulfilling Prophecy," *Law & Society Review* 12 (1978): 437–453; Caleb Foote, "Compelling Appearance in Court: Administration of Bail in Philadelphia," *University of Pennsylvania Law Review* 102 (1954): 1031–1079; Joan Petersilia, *Racial Disparities in the Criminal Justice System* (Santa Monica, CA: Rand Corporation, 1978); Gerald R. Wheeler and Carol L. Wheeler, "Reflections on Legal Representation of the Economically Disadvantaged."

67. Wayne Thomas, *Bail Reform in America* (Berkeley, CA: University of California Press, 1976).

68. Samuel Walker, *Taming the System: The Control of Discretion in Criminal Justice, 1950–1990* (New York: Oxford University Press, 1993).

69. J. Austin, B. Krisberg and P. Litsky, "The Effectiveness of Supervised Pretrial Release," *Crime and Delinquency* 31 (1985): 519–537; John S. Goldkamp, "Danger and Detention: A Second Generation of Bail Reform," *The Journal of Criminal Law and Criminology* 76 (1985): 1–74; Walker, *Taming the System*.

70. Goldkamp, "Danger and Detention."

71. This law was upheld by the U.S. Supreme Court in *United States v. Salerno*, 481 U.S. 739 (1987).

72. Coramae Richey Mann, *Unequal Justice: A Question of Color* (Bloomington, IN: Indiana University Press, 1993), p. 168.

73. R. Stryker, Ilene Nagel, and John Hagan, "Methodology Issues in Court

Research: Pretrial Release Decisions for Federal Defendants," *Sociological Methods and Research* 11 (1983): 460–500; Charles M. Katz and Cassia Spohn, "The Effect of Race and Gender on Bail Outcomes: A Test of an Interactive Model," *American Journal of Criminal Justice* 19 (1995): 161–184.

74. S. H. Clarke and G. G. Koch, "The Influence of Income and Other Factors on Whether Criminal Defendants Go To Prison," *Law & Society Review* 11 (1976): 57–92.

75. George S. Bridges, *A Study on Racial and Ethnic Disparities in Superior Court Bail and Pre-Trial Detention Practices in Washington* (Olympia, WA: Washington State Minority and Justice Commission, 1997).

76. Ibid., p. 54.

77. Ibid., p. 98.

78. Ibid.

79. Stephen Demuth and Darrell Steffensmeier, "The Impact of Gender and Race-Ethnicity in the Pretrial Release Process," *Social Problems* 51 (2004): 222–242.

80. Ibid., Tables 2 and 4.

81. Ibid., p. 233.

82. Ibid., p. 238.

83. Margaret Farnworth and Patrick Horan, "Separate Justice: An Analysis of Race Differences in Court Processes," *Social Science Research* 9 (1980): 381–399.

84. Theordore G. Chiricos and William D. Bales, "Unemployment and Punishment: An Empirical Assessment," *Criminology* 29 (1991): 701–724.

85. Celesta A. Albonetti, Robert M. Hauser, John Hagan, and Ilene H. Nagel, "Criminal Justice Decision Making as a Stratification Process: The Role of Race and Stratification Resources in Pretrial Release," *Journal of Quantitative Criminology* 5 (1989): 57–82.

86. Bureau of Justice Statistics, *Felony Defendants in Large Urban Counties, 2000* (Washington, DC: U.S. Department of Justice, 2003), Table 24.

87. Bureau of Justice Statistics, *Pretrial Release of Felony Defendants, 1992* (Washington, DC: U.S. Department of Justice, 1994), pp. 13–14.

88. Bureau of Justice Statistics, *Felony Defendants in Large Urban Counties, 2000* (Washington, DC: U.S. Department of Justice, 2003), Tables 13 and 18.

89. Spohn and DeLone, "When Does Race Matter?" Table 2.

90. Spohn and DeLone, unpublished data.

91. Leadership Conference on Civil Rights, *Justice on Trial: Racial Disparities in the American Criminal Justice System* (Washington, DC: Leadership Conference on Civil Rights, 2000).

92. *Bordenkircher v. Hayes*, 434 U.S. 357, 364.

93. Kenneth Culp Davis, *Discretionary Justice* (Baton Rouge: Louisiana State University Press, 1969), p. 190.

94. Barbara Boland (INSLAW Inc.), *The Prosecution of Felony Arrests* (Washington, DC: Bureau of Justice Statistics, 1983); Kathleen B. Brosi, *A Cross-City Comparison of Felony Case Processing* (Washington, DC: Institute for Law and Social Research, 1979); Vera Institute of Justice, *Felony Arrests: Their Prosecution and Disposition in New York City's Courts* (New York: Longman, 1981).

95. Charles E. Silberman, *Criminal Violence, Criminal Justice* (New York: Random House, 1978), p. 271.

96. *Bordenkircher v. Hayes*, supra, 434 U.S. 357, at 364.

97. Myrdal, *An American Dilemma*, pp. 552–553.

98. Ilene Nagel Bernstein, William R. Kelly, and Patricia A. Doyle, "Societal Reaction to Deviants: The Case of Criminal Defendants," *American Sociological Review* 42 (1977): 743–755; Malcolm M. Feeley, *The Process Is the Punishment: Handling Cases in a Lower Criminal Court* (New York: Russell Sage Foundation, 1979); John Hagan, "Parameters of

Criminal Prosecution: An Application of Path Analysis to a Problem of Criminal Justice," *Journal of Criminal Law and Criminology* 65 (1975): 536–544.

99. Celesta A. Albonetti, "Criminality, Prosecutorial Screening, and Uncertainty: Toward a Theory of Discretionary Decision Making in Felony Case Processing," *Criminology* 24 (1986): 623–644; Martha A. Myers, *The Effects of Victim Characteristics in the Prosecution, Conviction, and Sentencing of Criminal Defendants*, unpublished Ph.D. dissertation (Bloomington, IN: Indiana University, 1977).

100. Cassia Spohn, John Gruhl, and Susan Welch, "The Impact of the Ethnicity and Gender of Defendants on the Decision To Reject or Dismiss Felony Charges," *Criminology* 25 (1987): 175–191.

101. Ibid., p. 186.

102. Robert D. Crutchfield, Joseph G. Weis, Rodney L. Engen, and Randy R. Gainey, *Racial and Ethnic Disparities in the Prosecution of Felony Cases in King County* (Olympia, WA: Washington State Minority and Justice Commission, 1995).

103. Ibid., p. 32.

104. Ibid., p. 58.

105. Gary D. LaFree, "The Effect of Sexual Stratification by Race on Official Reactions to Rape," *American Sociological Review* 45 (1980): 842–854.

106. Michael L. Radelet, "Racial Characteristics and the Imposition of the Death Penalty," *American Sociological Review* 46 (1981): 918–927.

107. Jon Sorensen and Donald H. Wallace, "Prosecutorial Discretion in Seeking Death: An Analysis of Racial Disparity in the Pretrial Stages of Case Processing in a Midwestern County," *Justice Quarterly* 16 (1999): 559–578.

108. Cassia Spohn and Jeffrey Spears, "The Effect of Offender and Victim Characteristics on Sexual Assault Case Processing Decisions," *Justice Quarterly* 13 (1996): 649–679.

109. Ibid., pp. 661–662.

110. Ibid., p. 673.

111. Ibid., p. 674.

112. Joan Petersilia, *Racial Disparities in the Criminal Justice System* (Santa Monica, CA: Rand, 1983).

113. Ibid., p. 26.

114. Michael Tonry, *Malign Neglect: Race, Crime, and Punishment in America* (New York: Oxford University Press, 1995), p. 105.

115. Ibid., p. 115.

116. Jerome Miller, *Search and Destroy: African-American Males in the Criminal Justice System* (Cambridge: Cambridge University Press, 1996), p. 80.

117. United States Sentencing Commission, *1997 Sourcebook of Federal Sentencing Statistics* (Washington, DC: United States Sentencing Commission, 1998), Table 4.

118. U.S. Department of Health and Human Services, Substance Abuse and Mental Health Services Administration, *National Household Survey on Drug Abuse: Population Estimates 1994* (Rockville, MD: U.S. Department of Health and Human Services, 1995).

119. Available at http://www.usdoj. gov/ag/readingroom/.

120. Richard Berk and Alec Campbell, "Preliminary Data on Race and Crack Charging Practices in Los Angeles," *Federal Sentencing Reporter* 6 (1993): 36–38.

121. *U.S. v. Armstrong et al.*, 517 U.S. 456 (1996).

122. 48 F. 3d 1508 (9th Cir.1995).

123. *U.S. v. Armstrong et al.*, 517 U.S. 456 (1996).

124. Ibid., (Stevens, J., dissenting).

125. Leadership Conference on Civil Rights, *Justice on Trial*, p. 14.

126. Drew Humphries, John Dawson, Valerie Cronin, Phyllis Keating, Chris Wisniewski, and Jennine Eichfeld, "Mothers and Children, Drugs and Crack: Reactions to Maternal Drug

Dependency," in *The Criminal Justice System and Women*, 2nd ed., Barbara Raffel Price and Natalie J. Sokoloff, eds. (New York: McGraw-Hill, 1995), p. 169.

127. *Whitner v. State of South Carolina* (1996).

128. Ibid., p. 173.

129. Dorothy Roberts, "Punishing Drug Addicts Who Have Babies: Women of Color, Equality, and the Right of Privacy," *Harvard Law Review* 104 (1991): 1419–1454.

130. Ibid., p. 1432.

131. Ibid., p. 1421, n. 6.

132. Kennedy, *Race, Crime, and the Law*, p. 354.

133. Ibid., p. 359.

134. Ibid., p. 360.

135. Ibid., p. 363.

136. Lynn M. Mather, *Plea Bargaining or Trial?* (Lexington, MA: Heath, 1979).

137. Ilene Nagel Bernstein, Edward Kick, Jan T. Leung, and Barbara Schultz, "Charge Reduction: An Intermediary State in the Process of Labelling Criminal Defendants," *Social Forces* 56 (1977): 362–384.

138. Weitzer, "Racial Discrimination in the Criminal Justice System," p. 313.

139. Linda Drazga Maxfield and John H. Kramer, *Substantial Assistance: An Empirical Yardstick Gauging Equity in Current Federal Policy and Practice* (Washington, DC: United States Sentencing Commission, 1998).

140. Ibid., pp. 14–19.

141. Ibid., p. 21.

142. Celesta A. Albonetti, "Sentencing Under the Federal Sentencing Guidelines: Effects of Defendant Characteristics, Guilty Pleas, and Departures on Sentence Outcomes for Drug Offenses, 1991–92," *Law & Society Review* 31 (1997): 789–822.

143. Ibid., p. 813.

144. Ibid., p. 818.

145. Peter F. Nardulli, James Eisenstein, and Roy B. Flemming, *The Tenor of Justice: Criminal Courts and the Guilty Plea Process* (Chicago: University of Chicago Press, 1988).

146. Ibid., p. 238.

147. Malcolm D. Holmes, Howard C. Daudistel, and Ronald A. Farrell, "Determinants of Charge Reductions and Final Dispositions in Cases of Burglary and Robbery," *Journal of Research in Crime and Delinquency* 24 (1987): 233–254.

148. Ibid., pp. 248–249.

149. Spohn, Gruhl, and Welch, "The Impact of the Ethnicity and Gender of Defendants on the Decision To Reject or Dismiss Felony Charges," p. 189.

6

⟵⊥⟶

Justice on the Bench?
Trial and Adjudication in Criminal Court

> In our courts, when it's a white man's word against a black man's, the
> white man always wins. They're ugly but those are the facts of life. The
> one place were a man ought to get a square deal is a courtroom, be he
> any color of the rainbow, but people have a way of carrying their
> resentments right into a jury box.
> —HARPER LEE, *TO KILL A MOCKINGBIRD*[1]

We began the previous chapter with a discussion of the Scottsboro case, a
case involving nine young African American males who were convicted
of raping two white girls in the early 1930s. We noted that the defendants were
tried by all-white juries and that the Supreme Court overturned their convictions
because of the systematic exclusion of African Americans from the jury pool.

However, the Scottsboro Boys were tried in the 1930s, and much has changed
since then. Race relations have improved and decisions handed down by the
Supreme Court have made it increasingly difficult for court systems to exclude
African Americans from jury service. Nevertheless, "racial prejudice still sometimes
seems to sit as a 'thirteenth juror.'"[2] All-white juries continue to convict African
American defendants on less-than-convincing evidence. All-white juries continue
to acquit whites who victimize African Americans despite persuasive evidence of
guilt. And police and law enforcement officials sometimes bend the law in their
zeal to obtain a conviction. Consider the following recent cases:

1987: A jury of 10 whites and two African Americans acquitted Bernie
Goetz, the so-called "subway vigilante," of all but one relatively minor
charge in the shooting of four young men on a New York City subway.
Goetz, a white man, was accused of shooting and seriously wounding four
African American youths who Goetz said had threatened him. A man outside

the courtroom held up a sign reading, "Congratulations! Bernie Goetz wins one for the good guys."

1991: Four white Los Angeles police officers were charged in the beating of Rodney King, an African American man stopped for a traffic violation. A videotape of the incident, which showed the officers hitting King with their batons and kicking him in the head as he lay on the ground, was introduced as evidence at the trial. Los Angeles exploded in riots after a jury composed of 10 whites, one Asian American, and one Hispanic American acquitted the officers on all charges.

1997: Orange County (California) Superior Court Judge Everett Dickey reversed Geronimo Pratt's 1972 conviction for first-degree murder, assault with intent to commit murder, and robbery.[3] Pratt, a decorated Vietnam War veteran and a leader in the Black Panther Party, was accused of killing Caroline Olsen and shooting her ex-husband Kenneth Olsen on the Lincoln Park tennis court in Santa Monica. Pratt, who claimed he had been in Oakland on Panther business at the time of the crime, was convicted based in large part on the testimony of another member of the Black Panther Party, Julius Butler. It was later revealed that Butler had been a paid police informant and that police and prosecutors in Los Angeles conspired to keep this information from the jury hearing Pratt's case. Over the next 25 years, Pratt's lawyers filed a series of appeals, arguing that Pratt's conviction "was based on false testimony knowingly presented by the prosecution."[4] Their requests for a rehearing were repeatedly denied by California courts, and the Los Angeles District Attorney's Office refused to reopen the case. Then, in May 1997, Judge Dickey granted Pratt's petition for a writ of habeas corpus and reversed his conviction. Citing errors by the district attorney who tried the case, Judge Dickey stated, "The evidence which was withheld about Julius Butler and his activities could have put the whole case in a different light, and failure to timely disclose it undermines confidence in the verdict."[5] Geronimo Pratt, who spent 25 years in prison—including 8 years in solitary confinement—was released on June 10, 1997. In April 2000, Pratt's lawsuit for false imprisonment and violation of his civil rights was settled out of court: The City of Los Angeles agreed to pay Pratt $2.75 million, and the federal government agreed to pay him $1.75 million. Pratt's attorney, Johnnie Cochran Jr., described the settlement as "unprecedented" and praised Pratt for "the relentless pursuit of justice." Cochran also stated that the settlement puts "to rest a matter that has dragged on for more than three decades."[6]

2005: Walter Rideau, a 62-year-old African American whom *Life Magazine* once called "the most rehabilitated prisoner in America," walked out of a Calcasieu (Louisiana) Parish jail a free man after a jury that included four African Americans found him guilty of manslaughter rather than murder. Rideau, who had previously been sentenced to death three times by all-white, all-male juries, spent 44 years in prison for the 1961 murder of a white female bank teller, a crime he did not deny. Each of his convictions and death sentences were overturned by federal courts. His first conviction was overturned by the U.S.

Supreme Court, which referred to his trial as "kangaroo court proceedings." A federal appellate court overturned his second conviction and death sentence because the prosecutor removed potential jurors who said they would be hesitant, but not completely unwilling, to sentence Rideau to death. In 2000, a federal appellate court overturned his third conviction because of racial discrimination in the selection of the grand jury. Following this decision, the State of Louisiana decided to retry Rideau a fourth time, despite the fact that many of the prosecution witnesses were dead or otherwise unable to testify. The Calcasieu Parish District Attorney (with the approval of the judge in the case) had the testimony of the state's witnesses in the earlier trial read to the new jury. The jury found him guilty of manslaughter, which under Louisiana law carried a maximum penalty of 21 years in prison. Theodore M. Shaw, president of the NAACP Legal Defense and Educational Fund, which represented Rideau in the most recent case, stated, "This was not a case about innocence. It was about fairness and redemption—fairness, because even the guilty are entitled to a trial untainted by racial discrimination and misconduct, and redemption, because in a real sense the teenager who committed the tragic crime died while incarcerated for 44 years and was reborn as the man who paid the price and struggled for redemption."[7]

GOALS OF THE CHAPTER

In this chapter we focus on trial and adjudication in criminal court. We begin with an examination of race and the jury selection process. We focus on both the procedures used to select the jury pool and the process of selecting the jurors for a particular case. We also discuss the issue of "playing the race card" in a criminal trial. We end the chapter by summarizing the scholarly debate surrounding the issue of racially based jury nullification.

SELECTION OF THE JURY POOL

Three facts about jury discrimination are largely undisputed. First, the all-white jury has been a staple of the American criminal justice system for most of our history. Second, the Supreme Court has long condemned discrimination in jury selection. And third, race discrimination in jury selection remains a pervasive feature of our justice system to this day. The interesting question is how all of these facts can be true at the same time.
—DAVID COLE, *NO EQUAL JUSTICE*[8]

The jury plays a critically important role in the criminal justice system. Indeed, "the jury is the heart of the criminal justice system."[9] Although it is true that most cases are settled by plea and not by trial, many of the cases that do go to trial involve serious crimes in which defendants are facing long prison terms, or even the death penalty. In these serious—and highly publicized—cases, the jury serves as the conscience of the community and, in the words of the United States Supreme Court, as "an inestimable safeguard against the corrupt or overzealous prosecutor and against the compliant, biased, or eccentric judge."[10] As the Court has repeatedly emphasized, the jury also serves as "the criminal defendant's fundamental 'protection of life and liberty against race or color prejudice.'"[11]

The Supreme Court first addressed the issue of racial discrimination in jury selection in its 1880 decision of *Strauder v. West Virginia*.[12] The Court ruled that a West Virginia statute limiting jury service to white males violated the equal protection clause of the Fourteenth Amendment and therefore was unconstitutional. The Court concluded that the statute inflicted two distinct harms. The first was a harm that affected the entire African American population. According to the Court,

> The very fact that colored people are singled out and expressly denied by a statute all right to participate in the administration of the law, as jurors, because of their color ... is practically a brand upon them affixed by the law, an assertion of their inferiority, and a stimulant to that race prejudice which is an impediment to securing to individuals of the race that equal justice which the law aims to secure to all others.[13]

The Court stated that the West Virginia statute inflicted a second harm that primarily hurt African American defendants, who were denied even the *chance* to have people of their own race on their juries. "How can it be maintained," the Justices asked, "that compelling a man to submit to trial for his life by a jury drawn from a panel from which the State has expressly excluded every man of his race, because of his color alone, however well qualified in other respects, is not a denial to him of equal legal protection?"[14] The Court added that this was precisely the type of discrimination the equal protection clause was designed to prevent.

After *Strauder v. West Virginia*, it was clear that states could not pass laws excluding African Americans from jury service. This ruling, however, did not prevent states, and particularly Southern states, from developing techniques designed to preserve the all-white jury. In Delaware, for example, local jurisdictions used lists of taxpayers to select "sober and judicious" persons for jury service. Under this system, African American taxpayers were eligible for jury service but were seldom, if ever, selected for the jury pool. The state explained this result by noting that few of the African Americans in Delaware were intelligent, experienced, or moral enough to serve as jurors. As the Chief Justice of the Delaware Supreme Court concluded: "That none but white men were selected is in nowise remarkable in view of the fact—too notorious to be ignored—that the great body of black men residing in this State are utterly unqualified by want of intelligence, experience, or moral integrity to sit on juries."[15]

The U.S. Supreme Court refused to accept this explanation. In *Neal v. Delaware*, decided 2 years after *Strauder*, the court ruled that the practice had systematically excluded African Americans from jury service and was therefore a case of purposeful—and unconstitutional—racial discrimination.[16] Justice Harlan, writing for the Court, stated that it was implausible "that such uniform exclusion of [Negroes] from juries, during a period of many years, was solely because ... the black race in Delaware were utterly disqualified, by want of intelligence, experience, or moral integrity."[17]

These early court decisions did not eliminate racial discrimination in jury selection, particularly in the South. Gunnar Myrdal's analysis of the "Negro problem" in the United States in the late 1930s and early 1940s concluded that the typical jury in the South was composed entirely of whites.[18] He noted that some courts had taken steps "to have Negroes on the jury list and call them in occasionally for service."[19] He added, however, that many Southern courts, and particularly those in rural areas, had either ignored the constitutional requirement or had developed techniques "to fulfill legal requirements without using Negro jurors."[20] As a result, as Wishman noted, "For our first hundred years, blacks were explicitly denied the right to be jurors, which meant that if a black defendant was not lynched on the spot, an all-white jury would later decide what to do with him."[21]

Since the mid-1930s, the Supreme Court has made it increasingly difficult for court systems to exclude African Americans or Hispanics from the jury pool. It consistently has struck down the techniques used to circumvent the requirement of racial neutrality in the selection of the jury pool. The Court, for example, ruled that it was unconstitutional for a Georgia county to put the names of white potential jurors on white cards, the names of African American potential jurors on yellow cards, and then "randomly" draw cards to determine who would be summoned.[22] Similarly, the Court struck down the "random" selection of jurors from tax books in which the names of white taxpayers were in one section and the names of African American taxpayers were in another.[23] As the Justices stated in *Avery v. Georgia*, "the State may not draw up its jury lists pursuant to neutral procedures but then resort to discrimination at other stages in the selection process."[24]

The states' response to the Supreme Court's increasingly vigilant oversight of the jury selection process was not always positive.[25] The response in some southern jurisdictions "was a new round of tokenism aimed at maintaining as much of the white supremacist status quo as possible while avoiding judicial intervention."[26] These jurisdictions, in other words, included a token number of racial minorities in the jury pool in an attempt to head off charges of racial discrimination. The Supreme Court addressed this issue as late as 1988.[27] The Court reversed the conviction of Tony Amadeo, who was sentenced to death for murder in Putnam County, Georgia, after it was revealed that the Putnam County district attorney asked the jury commissioner to limit the number of African Americans and women on the master lists from which potential jurors were chosen.

Although these Supreme Court decisions have made it more difficult for states to discriminate overtly on the basis on race, the procedures used to select the jury pool are not racially neutral. Many states obtain the names of potential jurors from lists of registered voters, automobile registrations, or property tax rolls. The problem with this seemingly objective method is that in some jurisdictions racial minorities are less likely than whites to register to vote or to own automobiles or taxable property. As a result, racial minorities are less likely than

---

B O X 6.1   Excerpts from Massachusetts Jury Selection Statute

Juror Service

Juror service in the participating counties shall be a duty which every person who qualifies under this chapter shall perform when selected. All persons selected for juror service on grand and trial juries shall be selected at random from the population of the judicial district in which they reside. All persons shall have equal opportunity to be considered for juror service. All persons shall serve as jurors when selected and summoned for that purpose except as hereinafter provided. No person shall be exempted or excluded from serving as a grand or trial juror because of race, color, religion, sex, national origin, economic status, or occupation. Physically handicapped persons shall serve except where the court finds such service is not feasible. This court shall strictly enforce the provisions of this section.

Disqualification from Juror Service

As of the date of receipt of the juror summons, any citizen of the United States, who is a resident of the judicial district or who lives within the judicial district more than fifty per cent of the time, whether or not he is registered to vote in any state or federal election, shall be qualified to serve as a grand or trial juror in such judicial district unless one of the following grounds for disqualification applies:

1. Such person is under the age of eighteen years.
2. Such person is seventy years of age or older and indicates on the juror confirmation form an election not to perform juror service.
3. Such person is not able to speak and understand the English language.
4. Such person is incapable by reason of a physical or mental disability of rendering satisfactory juror service.
5. Such person is solely responsible for the daily care of a permanently disabled person living in the same household and the performance of juror service would cause a substantial risk of injury to the health of the disabled person.
6. Such person is outside the judicial district and does not intend to return to the judicial district and does not intend to return to the judicial district at any time during the following year.
7. Such person has been convicted of a felony within the past seven years or is defendant in pending felony cases or is in the custody of a correctional institution.
8. Such person has served as a grand or trial juror in any state or federal court within the previous three calendar years or the person is currently scheduled to perform such service.

SOURCE: 234A M.6.L.A. § et seq.

---

whites to receive a jury summons. Further compounding the problem is the fact that "for a number of reasons, from skepticism and alienation to the inability to take time off from their jobs, minorities and the poor are also less likely to respond to those summonses they receive."[28] The result is a jury pool that overrepresents white middle- and upper-class persons and underrepresents racial minorities and those who are poor (see Box 6.1).

Techniques for Increasing Racial Diversity

State and federal jurisdictions have experimented with a number of techniques for increasing the racial diversity of the jury pool. When officials in Hennepin County (St. Paul), Minnesota, which is 9 percent nonwhite, discovered that most grand juries were all white, they instituted a number of reforms designed to make jury service less burdensome. They doubled the pay for serving, provided funding to pay jurors' day-care expenses, and included a round-trip bus pass with each jury summons.[29] As a result of these measures, the number of racial minorities selected for grand juries increased.

A more controversial approach involves "race-conscious jury selection."[30] Some jurisdictions, for example, send a disproportionate number of summonses to geographic areas with large populations of racial minorities. Others attempt to select a more representative jury pool by subtracting the names of white prospective jurors until the proportion of racial minorities in the pool matches the proportion in the population. A more direct effort to ensure racial diversity involves setting aside a certain number of seats for racial minorities. Although no jurisdiction has applied this approach to the selection of trial jurors, judges in Hennepin County are required to select two minority grand jurors for every grand jury.[31]

A somewhat different approach was tried in a U.S. District Court. In 2005, a federal district court judge in Boston ordered court administrators to send a new summons to another person in the same zip code if a summons was returned as undeliverable.[32] Judge Nancy Gertner took this step in an attempt to increase the pool of African American jurors available for a federal death penalty case involving two African American men. Massachusetts pioneered the use of resident lists rather than lists of registered voters in an attempt to increase the racial diversity of the jury pool. However, defense attorneys in the case argued that resident lists are more likely to be inaccurate in areas with the highest percentage of blacks, resulting in a large number of summonses returned as undeliverable. According to Patricia Garin, one of the defense attorneys, Gertner's remedy, although unlikely to make juries truly representative of the community, was "a step in the right direction" and would increase the chances that people of color would serve on juries.[33]

Opinions regarding these techniques are divided. Randall Kennedy argued that "officials should reject proposals for race-dependent jury reforms."[34] Although he acknowledged that these proposals are well-intentioned, Kennedy maintained that they would have unintended consequences (for example, jurors selected because of their race might believe they are expected to act as representatives of their race during deliberations) and would be difficult to administer (for example, officials would be required to determine the race of potential jurors and defendants, which would inevitably result in controversies over racial identification). Kennedy also suggested that the more direct techniques may be unconstitutional. As he noted, "Over the past decade, the U.S. Supreme Court has become increasingly hostile to race-dependent public policies, even when they have been defended as efforts to include historically oppressed racial minorities in networks of economic opportunity and self-government."[35] Although the

Supreme Court has not yet addressed this issue, in 1998 the U.S. Court of Appeals for the Sixth Circuit ruled that subtracting nonwhites from jury panels so that all panels matched the racial makeup of the community violated the equal protection rights of white jurors.[36]

Those on the other side contend that race-conscious plans that create representative jury pools should be allowed because they reduce the likelihood that people of color will be tried by all-white juries. Albert Alschuler, an outspoken advocate of racial quotas for juries, asserted that "few statements are more likely to evoke disturbing images of American criminal justice than this one: 'the defendant was tried by an all-white jury.'"[37] He and other critics of jury selection procedures contend that lack of participation by racial minorities on juries that convict the African Americans and Hispanics who fill court dockets in many jurisdictions leads to questions regarding the legitimacy of their verdicts. Advocates of race-conscious plans also argue that the inclusion of greater numbers of racial minorities will counteract the cynicism and distrust that minorities feel toward their government. As David Cole, a professor at Georgetown University Law Center, wrote, "If the criminal justice system is to be accepted by the black community, the black community must be represented on juries. The long history of excluding blacks from juries is one important reason why blacks as a class are more skeptical than whites about the fairness of the criminal justice system."[38]

THE PEREMPTORY CHALLENGE: RACIAL PROFILING IN THE COURTROOM?

The Supreme Court consistently has ruled that the jury should be drawn from a representative cross-section of the community and that race is not a valid qualification for jury service. These requirements, however, apply only to the selection of the jury pool. They do not apply to the selection of individual jurors for a particular case. In fact, the Court has repeatedly stated that a defendant is *not* entitled to a jury "composed in whole or in part of persons of his own race."[39] Thus, prosecutors and defense attorneys can use their peremptory challenges— "challenges without cause, without explanation, and without judicial scrutiny"[40]— as they see fit (for evidence of this, see Box 6.2) They can use their peremptory challenges in a racially discriminatory manner.

It is clear that lawyers do take the race of the juror into consideration during the jury selection process. Prosecutors assume that racial minorities will side with minority defendants, and defense attorneys assume that racial minorities will be more inclined than whites to convict white defendants. As a result of these assumptions, both prosecutors and defense attorneys have used their peremptory challenges to strike racial minorities from the jury pool. Kennedy, in fact, characterized the peremptory challenge as "a creature of unbridled discretion that, in the hands of white prosecutors and white defendants, has often been used to sustain racial subordination in the courthouse."[41]

B O X 6.2 Selecting a Jury: Stereotypes and Prejudice

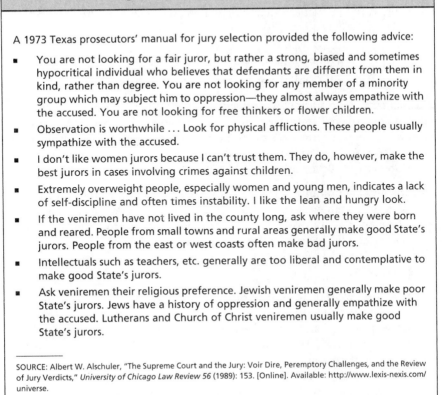

A 1973 Texas prosecutors' manual for jury selection provided the following advice:

- You are not looking for a fair juror, but rather a strong, biased and sometimes hypocritical individual who believes that defendants are different from them in kind, rather than degree. You are not looking for any member of a minority group which may subject him to oppression—they almost always empathize with the accused. You are not looking for free thinkers or flower children.

- Observation is worthwhile … Look for physical afflictions. These people usually sympathize with the accused.

- I don't like women jurors because I can't trust them. They do, however, make the best jurors in cases involving crimes against children.

- Extremely overweight people, especially women and young men, indicates a lack of self-discipline and often times instability. I like the lean and hungry look.

- If the veniremen have not lived in the county long, ask where they were born and reared. People from small towns and rural areas generally make good State's jurors. People from the east or west coasts often make bad jurors.

- Intellectuals such as teachers, etc. generally are too liberal and contemplative to make good State's jurors.

- Ask veniremen their religious preference. Jewish veniremen generally make poor State's jurors. Jews have a history of oppression and generally empathize with the accused. Lutherans and Church of Christ veniremen usually make good State's jurors.

SOURCE: Albert W. Alschuler, "The Supreme Court and the Jury: Voir Dire, Peremptory Challenges, and the Review of Jury Verdicts," *University of Chicago Law Review 56* (1989): 153. [Online]. Available: http://www.lexis-nexis.com/universe.

Dramatic evidence of this surfaced recently in Philadelphia. In April 1997, Lynne Abraham, Philadelphia's District Attorney, released a 1986 videotape made by Jack McMahon, a former assistant district attorney and her electoral opponent. In the hour-long training video, McMahon advised fellow prosecutors that "young black women are very bad for juries" and that "blacks from the low-income areas are less likely to convict." He also stated, "There's a resentment for law enforcement. There's a resentment for authority. And as a result, you don't want *those people* on your jury"[42] (emphasis added). A Philadelphia defense attorney characterized the videotape as "an abuse of the office," noting, "It was unconstitutional then, and it's unconstitutional now. You don't teach young attorneys to exclude poor people, or black people or Hispanic people."[43]

These comments notwithstanding, there is compelling evidence that prosecutors do use their peremptory challenges to strike racial minorities from the jury pool. As a result, African American and Hispanic defendants are frequently tried by all-white juries. In 1964, for example, Robert Swain, a 19-year-old African American, was sentenced to death by an all-white jury for raping a white woman in Alabama. The prosecutor had used his peremptory challenges to strike all six

African Americans on the jury panel. In 1990, the State used all of its peremptory challenges to eliminate African Americans from the jury that would try Marion Barry, the African American mayor of Washington, D.C., on drug charges.

The Supreme Court and the Peremptory Challenge: From *Swain* to *Batson*

The Supreme Court initially was reluctant to restrict the prosecutor's right to use peremptory challenges to excuse jurors on the basis of race. In 1965, the Court ruled in *Swain v. Alabama* that the prosecutor's use of peremptory challenges to strike all six African Americans in the jury pool did not violate the equal protection clause of the Constitution.[44] The Court reasoned,

> The presumption in any particular case must be that the prosecutor is using the State's challenges to obtain a fair and impartial jury ... The presumption is not overcome and the prosecutor therefore subjected to examination by allegations that in the case at hand all Negroes were removed from the jury or that they were removed because they were Negroes.[45]

The Court went on to observe that the Constitution did place some limits on the use of the peremptory challenge. The Justices stated that a defendant could establish a *prima facie* case of purposeful racial discrimination by showing that the elimination of African Americans from a particular jury was part of a pattern of discrimination in that jurisdiction.

The problem, of course, was that the defendants in *Swain*, and in the cases that followed, could not meet this stringent test. As Wishman observed, "A defense lawyer almost never has the statistics to prove a pattern of discrimination, and the state under the *Swain* decision is not required to keep them."[46] The ruling, therefore, provided no protection to the individual African American or Hispanic defendant deprived of a jury of his peers by the prosecutor's use of racially discriminatory strikes. As Supreme Court Justice William Brennan later wrote:

> With the hindsight that two decades affords, it is apparent to me that *Swain's* reasoning was misconceived ... *Swain* holds that the state may presume in exercising peremptory challenges that only white jurors will be sufficiently impartial to try a Negro defendant fairly .... Implicit in such a presumption is profound disrespect for the ability of individual Negro jurors to judge impartially. It is the race of the juror, and nothing more, that gives rise to the doubt in the mind of the prosecutor.[47]

Despite harsh criticism from legal scholars and civil libertarians,[48] who argued that *Swain* imposed a "crushing burden ... on defendants alleging racially discriminatory jury selection,"[49] the decision stood for 21 years. It was not until 1986 that the Court, in *Batson v. Kentucky*,[50] rejected *Swain's* systematic exclusion requirement and ruled "that a defendant may establish a *prima facie* case of purposeful discrimination in selection of the petit jury solely on evidence concerning the prosecutor's

B O X 6.3 White Defendants and the Exclusion of Black Jurors

The Equal Protection Clause of the Fourteenth Amendment declares that "No State shall...deny to any person within its jurisdiction the equal protection of the law." Enacted in the wake of the Civil War, the Fourteenth Amendment was designed to protect the rights of the newly freed slaves. As Congressman Stevens, one of the amendment's sponsors stated, "Whatever law punishes a white man for a crime shall punish the black man precisely in the same way and to the same degree. Whatever law protects the white man shall afford 'equal' protection to the black man" (Mason & Beancy, 1972, p. 379).

The Supreme Court has interpreted the equal protection clause to prohibit prosecutors from using their peremptory challenges in a racially discriminatory manner—that is, to forbid prosecutors from striking African Americans or Hispanics from the pool of potential jurors in cases involving African American and Hispanic defendants. But what about cases involving white defendants? Are prosecutors prohibited from using their challenges to strike racial minorities when the defendant is white?

The Supreme Court has ruled that white defendants *can* challenge the exclusion of racial minorities from the jury. In 1991, for example, the Court ruled that "a criminal defendant may object to the race-based exclusion of jurors effected through peremptory challenges regardless of whether the defendant and the excluded juror share the same race" (*Powers v. Ohio*, 499 U.S. 400 [1991]). This case involved a white criminal defendant on trial for homicide who objected to the prosecutor's use of peremptory challenges to remove African Americans from the jury. In 1998, the Court handed down a similar decision regarding the grand jury, ruling that whites who are indicted by grand juries from which African Americans have been excluded can challenge the constitutionality of the indictment (*Campbell v. Louisiana*, 523 U.S. 392 [1998]).

In both of these cases, the Court stated that a white defendant has the right to assert a violation of equal protection on behalf of excluded African American jurors. According to the Court, the discriminatory use of peremptory challenges by the prosecution, "casts doubt upon the integrity of the judicial process and places the fairness of the criminal proceeding in doubt." And, although an individual juror does not have the right to sit on any particular jury, "he or she does possess the right not to be excluded from one on account of race." As the Court stated, "Both the excluded juror and the criminal defendant have a common interest in eliminating racial discrimination from the courtroom." Because it is unlikely that the excluded juror will challenge the discriminatory use of the peremptory challenge, the defendant can assert this right on his or her behalf (*Powers v. Ohio*, 499 U.S. 400 [1991]).

What do you think? Should a white defendant be allowed to challenge the prosecutor's use of peremptory challenges to exclude African Americans and other racial minorities from his or her jury?

exercise of peremptory challenges at the defendant's trial."[51] The justices added that once the defendant makes a *prima facie* case of racial discrimination, the burden shifts to the state to provide a racially neutral explanation for excluding African American jurors. (See Box 6.3 for a discussion of the use of the peremptory challenge to exclude African American jurors in cases involving white defendants.)

Interpreting and Applying the *Batson* Standard   Although *Batson* seemed to offer hope that the goal of a representative jury was attainable, an examination of cases decided since 1986 suggests otherwise. State and federal appellate courts have ruled, for example, that leaving one or two African Americans on the jury precludes any inference of purposeful racial discrimination on the part of the prosecutor,[52] and that striking only one or two jurors of the defendant's race does not constitute a "pattern" of strikes.[53]

Trial and appellate courts have also been willing to accept virtually any explanation offered by the prosecutor to rebut the defendant's inference of purposeful discrimination.[54] As Kennedy[55] noted, "judges tend to give the benefit of the doubt to the prosecutor." Kennedy cited as an example *State v. Jackson*, a case in which the prosecutor used her peremptory challenges to strike four African Americans in the jury pool. According to Kennedy,

> The prosecutor said that she struck one black prospective juror because she was unemployed and had previously served as a student counselor at a university, a position that bothered the prosecution because it was 'too liberal a background.' The prosecution said that it struck another black prospective juror because she, too, was unemployed, and, through her demeanor, had displayed hostility or indifference. By contrast, two whites who were unemployed were seated without objection by the prosecution.[56]

Although Kennedy acknowledged that "one should give due deference to the trial judge who was in a position to see directly the indescribable subtleties," he stated that he "still has difficulty believing that, had these prospective jurors been white, the prosecutor would have struck them just the same." Echoing these concerns, Serr and Maney conclude, "The cost of forfeiting truly peremptory challenges has yielded little corresponding benefit, as a myriad of 'acceptable' explanations and excuses cloud any hope of detecting racially based motivations."[57] For a more detailed discussion of the peremptory challenge, see "Focus on an Issue: Should We Eliminate the Peremptory Challenge?"

The validity of their concerns is illustrated by a 1995 Supreme Court case, *Purkett v. Elem*.[58] Jimmy Elem, an African American on trial for robbery in Missouri, objected to the prosecutor's use of peremptory challenges to strike two African American men from the jury panel. The prosecutor provided the following racially neutral explanation for these strikes:

> I struck [juror] number twenty-two because of his long hair. He had long curly hair. He had the longest hair of anybody on the panel by far. He appeared to me to not be a good juror for that fact, the fact that he had long hair hanging down shoulder length, curly, unkempt hair. Also, he had a mustache and a goatee type beard. And juror number twenty-four also has a mustache and goatee type beard. Those are the only two people on the jury ... with the mustache and goatee type beard ... And I don't like the way they looked, with the way the hair is cut, both of them. And the mustaches and the beards look suspicious to me.[59]

Focus on an Issue
Should We Eliminate the Peremptory Challenge?

In theory, the peremptory challenge is used to achieve a fair and impartial jury. The assumption is that each side will "size up" potential jurors and use its challenges "to eliminate real or imagined partiality or bias that may be based only on a hunch, an impression, a look, or a gesture" (Way, 1980, p. 344). Thus, a prosecutor may routinely strike "liberal" college professors, whereas a defense attorney may excuse "prosecution-oriented" business executives. The result of this process, at least in principle, is a jury that will decide the case based on the evidence alone.

The reality is that both sides use their peremptory challenges to "stack the deck" (Levine, 1992, p. 51). The prosecutor attempts to pick a jury that will be predisposed to convict, whereas the defense attorney attempts to select jurors who will be inclined to acquit. In other words, rather than choosing open-minded jurors who will withhold judgment until they have heard all of the evidence, each attorney attempts to pack the jury with sympathizers. According to one attorney, "Most successful lawyers develop their own criteria for their choices of jurors. Law professors, experienced lawyers, and a number of technical books suggest general rules to help select *favorable jurors*" [emphasis added] (Wishman, 1986, p. 105).

DO PROSECUTORS USE PEREMPTORY CHALLENGES IN A RACIALLY DISCRIMINATORY MANNER?

The controversy over the use of the peremptory challenge has centered on the prosecution's use of its challenges to eliminate African Americans from juries trying African American defendants. It centers on what Justice Marshall called "the shameful practice of racial discrimination in the selection of juries" (*Batson v. Kentucky*, 479 U.S. 79 [1986]). Critics charge that the process reduces minority participation in the criminal justice system and makes it difficult, if not impossible, for racial minorities to obtain a "jury of their peers." They assert that peremptory challenges "can transform even a representative venire into a white, middle-class jury," thereby rendering "meaningless the protections provided to the venire selection process by *Strauder* and its progeny" (Serr & Maney, 1988, pp. 7–8).

There is substantial evidence that prosecutors exercise peremptory challenges in a racially discriminatory manner. A study of challenges issued in Calcasieu Parish, Louisiana, from 1976 to 1981, for example, found that prosecutors excused African American jurors at a disproportionately high rate (Turner, Lovell, Young, & Denny, 1986, pp. 61–69). Although the authors also found that defense attorneys tended to use their challenges to excuse whites, they concluded that "Because black prospective jurors are a minority in many jurisdictions, the exclusion of most black prospective jurors by prosecution can be accomplished more easily than the similar exclusion of Caucasian prospective jurors by defense" (Turner et al., 1986, p. 68; Hayden, Senna, & Seigel, 1978).

African American defendants challenging their convictions by all-white juries also have produced evidence of racial bias. One defendant, for example, showed that Missouri prosecutors challenged 81 percent of the African American jurors available for trial in 15 cases with African American defendants (*United States v. Carter*, 528 F. 2d 844, 848 [CA 8 1975]). Another defendant presented evidence indicating that in 53 Louisiana cases involving African

(continued)

(*continued*)
American defendants, federal prosecutors used more than two-thirds of their challenges against African Americans, who comprised less than one-fourth of the jury pool (*United States v. McDaniels*, 379 F. Supp. 1243 [ED La. 1974]). A third defendant showed that South Carolina prosecutors challenged 82 percent of the African American jurors available for 13 trials involving African American defendants (*McKinney v. Walker*, 394 F. Supp. 1015, 1017–1018 [SC 1974]). Evidence such as this supports Justice Marshall's contention (in a concurring opinion in *Batson v. Kentucky*) that "Misuse of the peremptory challenge to exclude black jurors has become both common and flagrant" (*Batson v. Kentucky*, 106 Sct. 1712, 1726 [1986] [Marshall, J., concurring]).

ARE ALL-WHITE JURIES INCLINED TO CONVICT AFRICAN AMERICAN DEFENDANTS?

Those who question the prosecutor's use of peremptory challenges to eliminate African Americans from the jury pool argue that African American defendants tried by all-white juries are disproportionately convicted. They assert that white jurors take the race of the defendant and the race of the victim into account in deciding whether to convict the defendant.

Researchers have examined jury verdicts in actual trials and in mock jury studies for evidence of racial bias. Kalven and Zeisel (1966), for example, asked the presiding judge in more than 1,000 cases if he or she agreed with the jury's verdict. Judges who disagreed with the verdict were asked to explain the jury's behavior. Judges disagreed with the jury's decision to convict the defendant in 22 cases; in four of these cases they attributed the jury's conviction to prejudice against African American defendants involved in interracial sex. Kalven and Zeisel also found that juries were more likely than judges to acquit African American defendants who victimized other African Americans.

Johnson (1985) argued, "Mock jury studies provide the strongest evidence that racial bias frequently affects the determination of guilt." She reviewed nine mock jury studies in which the race of the defendant was varied while other factors were held constant. According to Johnson, white "jurors" in all of the studies were more likely to convict minority-race defendants than they were to convict white defendants (p. 1626).

One mock jury study found evidence of racial bias directed at both the defendant and the victim (Klein & Creech, 1982, p. 21). In this study, white college students read two transcripts of four crimes in which the race of the male defendant and the race of the female victim were varied; they then were asked to indicate which defendant was more likely to be guilty. For the crime of rape, the probability that the defendant was guilty ranged from 70 percent for crimes with black offenders and white victims, to 68 percent for crimes with white offenders and white victims, 52 percent for crimes with black offenders and black victims, and 33 percent for crimes with white offenders and black victims (Klein & Creech, 1982, p. 24).

SHOULD THE PEREMPTORY CHALLENGE BE ELIMINATED?

Defenders of the peremptory challenge, although admitting that there is inherent tension between peremptory challenges and the quest for a representative jury, argue that the availability of peremptories ensures an *impartial* jury. Defenders of the process further argue that restricting the number of peremptory challenges or requiring attorneys to provide reasons for exercising them would make selection of an impartial jury more difficult. Those who advocate elimination of the peremptory challenge assert that prosecutors and defense attorneys can use the challenge for cause to eliminate biased or prejudiced jurors. They argue that because prosecutors exercise their peremptory challenges in a racially discriminatory manner, African American defendants are often tried by all-white juries predisposed toward conviction.

In a concurring opinion in the *Batson* case, Justice Marshall called on the Court to ban the use of peremptory challenges by the prosecutor and to allow states to ban their use by the defense (*Batson v. Kentucky*, 106 Sct. 1712, 1726 [1986] [Marshall, J., concurring]). Marshall argued that the remedy fashioned by the Court in *Batson* was inadequate to eliminate racial discrimination in the use of the peremptory challenge. He noted that a black defendant could not attack the prosecutor's discriminatory use of peremptory challenges at all unless the abuse was "so flagrant as to establish a *prima facie* case," and that prosecutors, when challenged, "can easily assert facially neutral reasons for striking a juror" (*Batson v. Kentucky*, at 1727).

Other commentators, who acknowledge that the solution proposed in *Batson* is far from ideal and that reform is needed, propose more modest reforms. Arguing that the chances for abolition of the peremptory challenge are slim, they suggest that a more feasible alternative would be to limit the number of challenges available to each side. As one legal scholar noted, "Giving each side fewer challenges will make it more difficult to eliminate whole groups of people from juries" (Note, *Batson v. Kentucky*, 1988, p. 298). Another argued that courts must "enforce the prohibition against racially discriminatory peremptory strikes more consistently and forcefully than they have done thus far" (Kennedy, 1997, p. 230). Another, more radical, suggestion is to allow each side to designate one or two prospective jurors who cannot be challenged peremptorily (see, for example, Ramirez, 1998, p. 161).

Those who lobby for reform of the peremptory challenge maintain that the system would be fairer without them. As Morris B. Hoffman (2000) put it, "Imagine a jury selection process that sends the message to all 50 prospective jurors in the courtroom that this is a rational process. That we have rules for deciding who is fair and not fair, just as we have rules for deciding who prevails in the end and who does not."

The U.S. Court of Appeals for the Eighth Circuit ruled that the prosecutor's reasons for striking the jurors were not legitimate race-neutral reasons because they were not plausibly related to "the person's ability to perform his or her duties as a juror." Thus, the trial court had erred in finding no intentional discrimination.

The Supreme Court reversed the Circuit Court's decision, ruling that *Batson v. Kentucky* required only "that the prosecution provide a race-neutral justification for the exclusion, not that the prosecution show that the justification is plausible." Noting that neither beards nor long, unkempt hair are characteristics peculiar to any race, the Court stated that the explanation offered by the prosecutor, although it may have been "silly or superstitious," was race-neutral. The trial court, in other words, was required to evaluate the *genuineness* of the prosecutor's explanation, not its *reasonableness*. As the Court noted, "At this step of the inquiry, the issue is the facial validity of the prosecutor's explanation.

In the Courts: *Miller-El v. Dretke*

In 1986 Thomas Miller-El was convicted and sentenced to death by a Dallas County (Texas) jury composed of 11 whites and one African American. The jury found Miller-El, an African American, guilty of killing a hotel employee and severely wounding another during the course of a robbery. During jury selection, Miller-El challenged the prosecutor's use of peremptory strikes against 10 of the 11 African Americans eligible to serve on the jury. He claimed that the strikes were based on race, citing as proof both the prosecutor's questioning of potential jurors in his trial and the fact that the Dallas County District Attorney had a history of excluding African Americans from criminal juries. The Texas courts that heard his appeal ruled against him, stating that there was no evidence that the jurors were struck because of their race and that the race-neutral reasons given by the prosecutor were "completely credible and sufficient" (*Miller-El v. State*, 748 S. W. 2d 459 [1988]).

Following a round of appeals in the federal courts, all of which agreed with the state courts' conclusions, Miller-El's case reached the United States Supreme Court. In June 2005, the Supreme Court reversed Miller-El's conviction, ruling 6-3 that there was strong evidence of racial prejudice during jury selection and that the state court's conclusions were therefore "unreasonable as well as erroneous" (*Miller-El v. Dretke*, 537 US 322, 336 [2005]). Justice David H. Souter, writing for the majority, said, "The prosecutors' chosen race-neutral reasons for the strikes do not hold up and are so far at odds with the evidence that pretext is the fair conclusion, indicating the very discrimination the explanations were meant to deny." To support their conclusion, the justices cited the following evidence:

- Out of 20 African American members of the 108-person jury panel for Miller-El's trial, only one served. Nine of the 20 were excused for cause; of the remaining 11 African Americans, 10 were peremptorily struck by the prosecution. As the court noted, "Happenstance is unlikely to produce this disparity."

- The "racially-neutral" reasons given by the prosecution to explain the strikes of African Americans applied just as well to whites who were not struck and, in some cases, mischaracterized the testimony of African Americans regarding such things as their willingness to impose the death penalty. In fact, the court stated that one of the African Americans who was struck expressed strong support of the death penalty and, therefore, should have been "an ideal juror in the eyes of a prosecutor seeking a death sentence." The fact that he was struck, and that whites who expressed less support for the death penalty were not, "supports a

Unless a discriminatory intent is inherent in the prosecutor's explanation, the reason offered will be deemed race neutral."

The two dissenting judges—Justice Stevens and Justice Breyer—were outraged. They argued that the Court in this case actually overruled a portion of the opinion in *Batson v. Kentucky*. They stated that, the majority's conclusions notwithstanding, *Batson* clearly required that the explanation offered by the prosecutor must be "related to the particular case to be tried." According to Justice Stevens,

> In my opinion, it is disrespectful to the conscientious judges on the Court of Appeals who faithfully applied an unambiguous standard articulated in one of our opinions to say that they appear "to have seized on our admonition in *Batson* . . . that the reason must be 'related to the particular

conclusion that race was significant in determining who was challenged and who was not." According to Justice Souter, "it blinks reality" to deny that some of the African America jurors were struck because of their race.

- Prosecutors repeatedly used their right to reshuffle the cards bearing potential jurors' names to reseat the African Americans at the back of the panel, where they were less likely to be questioned during the *voir dire* (and more likely to be dismissed without being questioned). The prosecution did not offer a racially neutral reason for shuffling the jury. Justice Souter wrote, "At least two of the jury shuffles conducted by the state make no sense except as efforts to delay consideration of black jury panelists."

- The questions posed to African American and white jurors during *voir dire* were different. Before asking potential jurors about their feelings regarding the death penalty, for example, prosecutors gave them a description of the death penalty. Ninety-four percent of the white jurors heard a bland description ("We anticipate that we will be able to present to a jury the quantity and type of evidence necessary to convict him of capital murder"), whereas more than half of the African American jurors heard a graphic description that described the method of execution in detail ("at some point Mr. Thomas Joe Miller-El—the man sitting right down there—will be taken ... to the death house and placed on a gurney and injected with a lethal substance until he is dead). The Court concluded that the graphic script was used "to make a case for excluding black panel members opposed to or ambivalent about the death penalty." Race, according to the court, "was the major consideration when the prosecution chose to follow the graphic script."

The Supreme Court concluded that the evidence proffered by Miller-El, which clearly documented that prosecutors were selecting and rejecting potential jurors because of race, "is too powerful to conclude anything but discrimination."

Less than 1 month after the Supreme Court handed down its decision, Dallas District Attorney Bill Hill announced that the State would retry Miller-El and would seek the death penalty. Hill, who noted that Miller-El's "guilt of this heinous crime is not in question," stated that his office was committed to fairness. Hill added that "we as a community and we as a district attorney's office have come far in making unlawful bias and discrimination a thing of the past."[62]

case to be tried.' Of course, they 'seized on' that point because *we told them to*. The Court of Appeals was following *Batson*'s clear mandate. To criticize those judges for doing their jobs is singularly inappropriate.[60]

Justice Stevens went on to say, "Today, without argument, the Court replaces the *Batson* standard with the surprising announcement that any neutral explanation, no matter how 'implausible or fantastic,' even if it is 'silly or superstitious,' is sufficient to rebut a prima facie case of discrimination."

Critics of *Batson* and its progeny maintain that until the courts articulate and apply a more meaningful standard or eliminate peremptory challenges altogether (see In the Courts: *Miller-El v. Dretke*), "peremptory strikes will be color-blind in theory only."[61]

B O X 6.4   Exonerations in the United States: Rape, Race, and Mistaken Eyewitness Identification

In 1989 a Cook County (Chicago) Circuit Judge vacated Gary Dotson's conviction for rape and dismissed the charges against him. Dotson thus became the first prisoner in the United States to be exonerated by DNA identification technology. As the technology improved and became more widely available, the number of DNA exonerations increased, from one or two a year in the early 1990s, to about six per year in the mid-1990s, to an average of 20 per year from 2000 to 2003.[65]

A recent analysis of 340 exonerations in the United States from 1989 to 1990 revealed that DNA exonerations were especially prevalent in rape cases.[66] These cases also were characterized by eyewitness misidentification. In fact, in 107 of the 121 exonerations for rape, the defendant was the victim of eyewitness misidentification and in 105 of these cases the defendant was eventually cleared by DNA evidence. About half (102/205) of the exonerations in murder cases also involved eyewitness misidentification, but only 39 of the 205 defendants were cleared as a result of DNA evidence.[67]

Rape, Race, and Misidentification

Although the percentages of African Americans, Hispanics, and whites who were exonerated for all crimes were similar to the percentages of each group incarcerated in state prisons, this was not the case for rape. In 2002, 58 percent of all people incarcerated for rape were white, 29 percent were African American, and 13 percent were Hispanic. Among defendants who were convicted of rape but later exonerated, the percentages were reversed: 64 percent were African American, 28 percent were white, and 7 percent were Hispanic. African Americans, in other words, comprised only 29 percent of all persons incarcerated for rape but 64 percent of all defendants exonerated for rape.[68]

The authors of this study suggested that the key to the explanation for the over-representation of African Americans among defendants falsely convicted for rape "is probably the race of the victim."[69] As they pointed out, the race of the victim was known in 52 of the 69 exonerations of African Americans for rape. In 78 percent of these cases, the victim was white. As they noted, "Inter-racial rape is uncommon, and rapes of white women by black men in particular account for well under 10 percent of all rapes. But among rape exonerations for which we know the race of both parties, almost exactly half (39/80) involve a black man who was falsely convicted of raping a white woman."[70]

The authors, who admitted that there were many possible explanations for this finding, stated that the "most obvious explanation for this racial disparity is probably also the most powerful: the perils of cross-racial identification."[71] Almost all of the exonerations in the interracial rape cases included in their study were based at least in part on eyewitness misidentification.

There is substantial evidence that cross-racial eyewitness identifications, and particularly eyewitness identifications of African Americans by whites, are unreliable.[72] What seems to happen, then, is that a white victim of a rape case mistakenly identifies an African American as the perpetrator of the crime, the defendant is found guilty at trial based at least in part on the eyewitness identification, and the defendant is exonerated when DNA evidence reveals that he was not the man who committed the crime.

There is incontrovertible evidence that the reforms implemented since the Scottsboro boys were tried, convicted, and sentenced to death by all-white juries have reduced racial discrimination in the jury selection process. Decisions handed down by the Supreme Court have made it difficult, if not impossible, for courts to make "no pretense of putting Negroes on jury lists, much less calling or using them in trials."[63] However, the jury selection process remains racially biased. Prosecutors continue to use the peremptory challenge to exclude African American and Hispanic jurors from cases with African American and Hispanic defendants[64] and appellate courts continue to rule that their "racially neutral" explanations adequately meet the standards articulated in *Batson*. Supreme Court decisions notwithstanding, the peremptory challenge remains an obstacle to impartiality. For a discussion of other issues concerning trials of racial minorities, see Box 6.4, "Exonerations in the United States: Rape, Race, and Mistaken Eyewitness Identification."

PLAYING THE "RACE CARD"
IN A CRIMINAL TRIAL

In 1994 O. J. Simpson, an African American actor and former All-American football star, was accused of murdering his ex-wife, Nicole Brown Simpson, and Ronald Goldman, a friend of hers. On October 4, 1995, a jury composed of nine African American women, two white women, one Hispanic man, and one African American man acquitted Simpson of all charges. Many commentators attributed Simpson's acquittal at least in part to the fact that his attorney, Johnnie L. Cochran, Jr., had "played the race card" during the trial. In fact, another of Simpson's attorneys, Robert Shapiro, charged that Cochran not only played the race card, he "dealt it from the bottom of the deck."[73]

Cochran was criticized for attempting to show that Mark Fuhrman, a Los Angeles police officer who found the bloody glove that linked Simpson to the crime, was a racist who planted the evidence in an attempt to frame Simpson. He also was harshly criticized for suggesting during his closing argument that the jurors would be justified in nullifying the law by acquitting Simpson. Cochran encouraged the jurors to take Fuhrman's racist beliefs into account during their deliberations. He urged them to "send a message" to society that "we are not going to take that anymore."[74]

Although appeals to racial sentiment—that is, "playing the race card"—are not unusual in U.S. courts, they are rarely used by defense attorneys representing African Americans accused of victimizing whites. Much more typical are *prosecutorial* appeals to bias. Consider the following examples:

- An Alabama prosecutor, who declared, "Unless you hang this Negro, our white people living out in the country won't be safe."[75]

- A prosecutor in North Carolina, who dismissed as implausible the claim of three African American men that the white woman they were accused of raping had consented to sex with them. The prosecutor stated that "the average white woman abhors anything of this type in nature that had to do with a black man."[76]

- A prosecutor in a rape case involving an African American man and a white woman who asked the jurors, "Gentlemen, do you believe that she would have had intercourse with this black brute?"[77]

- A prosecutor in a case involving the alleged kidnapping of a white man by two African American men, who said in his closing argument that "not one *white* witness has been produced" to rebut the victim's testimony [emphasis added].[78]

- A prosecutor who stated, during the penalty phase of a capital case involving Walter J. Blair, an African American man charged with murdering a white woman, "Can you imagine [the victim's] state of mind when she woke up at 6 o'clock that morning, staring into the muzzle of a gun held by this black man?"[79]

All of these appeals to racial sentiment, with the exception of the last, resulted in reversal of the defendants' convictions. A federal court of appeals, for example, ruled in 1978 that the North Carolina prosecutor's contention that a white woman would never consent to sex with a black man was a "blatant appeal to racial prejudice." The court added that when such an appeal involves an issue as "sensitive as consent to sexual intercourse in a prosecution for rape...the prejudice engendered is so great that automatic reversal is required."[80]

A federal court of appeals, however, refused to reverse Walter Blair's conviction and death sentence. Its refusal was based on the fact that Blair's attorney failed to object at trial to the prosecutor's statement. The sole dissenter in the case suggested that the court should have considered whether the defense attorney's failure to object meant that Blair had been denied effective assistance of counsel. He also vehemently condemned the prosecutor's statement, which he asserted "played upon white fear of crime and the tendency of white people to associate crime with blacks."[81]

According to Harvard law professor Randall Kennedy, playing the race card in a criminal trial is "virtually always morally and legally wrong." He asserted that doing so encourages juries to base their verdicts on irrelevant considerations and loosens the requirement that the state prove the case beyond a reasonable doubt. As he noted, "Racial appeals are not only a distraction but a menace that can distort interpretations of evidence or even seduce jurors into believing that they should vote in a certain way irrespective of the evidence."[82] As the case discussed in the "Focus on an Issue: The Lynching of an Innocent Man and Defiance of the U.S. Supreme Court" makes clear, appeals to racial bias also can seduce individuals into believing that they have a right to take matters into their own hands.[83]

Race-Conscious Jury Nullification:
Black Power in the Courtroom?

In a provocative essay published in the *Yale Law Journal* shortly after O.J. Simpson's acquittal, Paul Butler, an African American professor of law at George Washington University Law School, argued for "racially based jury nullification"[85]—that is, he

Focus on an Issue
The Lynching of an Innocent Man and Defiance of the U.S. Supreme Court

On January 23, 1906, Nevada Taylor, a 21-year-old white woman who worked as a bookkeeper for a shop in Chattanooga, Tennessee, was sexually assaulted after she got off the trolley near the home she shared with her father and her brothers and sisters (Curriden & Phillips, 1999). Miss Taylor did not see her attacker and initially could describe him only as about her height and dressed in a black outfit and a hat. When asked by Hamilton County Sheriff Joseph Shipp if her attacker was "a white man or a Negro," she first said that she didn't know, that she hadn't gotten a good look at him. She then changed her mind, stating that she believed the man was black (Curriden & Phillips, 1999, p. 31).

The next day, the *Chattanooga News* reported the attack in a story with the headline "Brutal Crime of Negro Fiend." According to the *News*, "The fiendish and unspeakable crime committed in St. Elmo last night by a Negro brute, the victim being a modest, pretty, industrious and popular girl, is a sample of the crimes which heat southern blood to the boiling point and prompt law abiding men to take the law into their own hands and mete out swift and horrible punishment" (Curriden & Phillips, 1999, p. 33).

There were no clues as to the identity of the suspect, other than a leather strap found at the scene of the crime. A reward of $375—more money than many people in Chattanooga earned in a year—was offered for information leading to the arrest of Miss Taylor's attacker. Two days later, a man by the name of Will Hixson called Sheriff Shipp, asked if the reward was still available, and stated that he had seen a black man near the trolley station on the evening in question. He told Sheriff Shipp that he thought he could identify the man, and later that afternoon he fingered Ed Johnson.

Ed Johnson denied the allegations, stating that he had been at work at the Last Chance Saloon that afternoon and evening. He gave the sheriff the names of witnesses, most of whom were black, who could vouch for him. Despite the fact that there was no evidence, other than Hixson's identification, linking him to the crime and that he had an alibi, Johnson was arrested and charged with the rape of Nevada Taylor.

As news of Johnson's arrest spread, a mob began to gather at the jail. Within hours, more than 1,500 people had congregated, and many of them were urging the jailers to turn Johnson over to them. When informed by Hamilton County Criminal Court Judge Sam D. McReynolds that Johnson was no longer in Chattanooga, that he had been transported to Knoxville for safekeeping until trial, the crowd dispersed. As Curriden & Phillips (1999, p. 50) noted, the leaders of the mob "had put Sheriff Shipp and Judge McReynolds on notice: convict and punish this Negro quickly or they would be back."

Seventeen days after the attack on Nevada Taylor, a jury of 12 white men found Ed Johnson, who had steadfastly insisted that he was innocent, guilty of rape. The trial was replete with references to the fact that Johnson was black and his victim was white. The prosecutor, for example, asked Miss Taylor to point out "the Negro brute" who assaulted her. Miss Taylor pointed to Ed Johnson, who was the only black person in the courtroom. The prosecutor trying the case concluded his final argument by stating that the jurors should "Send that black brute to the gallows and prove to the world that in Chattanooga and Hamilton

(continued)

(continued)
County the law of the country does not countenance such terrible crimes, has not ceased to mete out the proper punishment for such horrible outrages" (Curriden & Phillips, 1999, p. 118).

The judge in the case also allowed the people in the audience—and the jurors—to express their opinions about the case and about Ed Johnson. When Johnson testified, the pro-prosecution spectators booed and heckled him. The audience cheered when prosecutors made a point and hissed and jeered when the defense objected. At one point in the trial, one of the jurors leaped to his feet, pointed at Johnson, and yelled, "If I could get at him, I'd tear his heart out right now" (Curriden & Phillips, 1999, Chapter 5).

Judge McReynolds sentenced Ed Johnson to die and scheduled his execution for March 13, 1906. When Johnson's attorneys announced that they did not intend to appeal his conviction, two prominent local African American attorneys stepped in and filed a motion for a new trial. Noah Parden and Styles Hutchins believed that the evidence did not support a conviction and that there had been numerous violations of Johnson's constitutional rights. After their motion for a new trial was denied, they appealed to the Tennessee Supreme Court, which ruled that there had been "no serious errors" in the case.

Parden and Hutchins then appealed to the U.S. District Court, arguing that Johnson had not received a fair trial. District Court Judge C.D. Clark ruled that although "there was great haste in this trial" and "counsel were to an extent terrorized on account of the fear of a mob," the district court had no authority to intervene. The problem, according to Judge Clark, was that the right to a fair trial guaranteed by the Sixth Amendment did not apply to state-court cases. Nonetheless, Judge Clark did issue a stay of execution to allow Johnson's lawyers to

appeal to the U.S. Supreme Court (Curriden and Phillips, 1999, p. 168).

In a precedent-setting decision, the Supreme Court decided to intervene in the case. On March 18, 1906, Supreme Court Justice John M. Harlan sent a telegram to Judge Clark announcing that the court would hear Johnson's appeal. The Court also sent a telegram to Sheriff Shipp and Judge McReynolds informing them that Johnson's execution was to be stayed pending the outcome of his appeal.

The citizens of Chattanooga were outraged that "people in Washington, D.C." were interfering in the case and telling them how to run their court system. The *Chattanooga News* issued what amounted to a call to arms, predicting that mob violence would result if "by legal technicality the case is prolonged and the culprit finally escapes" (Curriden & Phillips, 1999, p. 197).

On March 19, the newspaper's prediction of violence came true. A mob gathered at the jail and, led by 25 determined men, bashed in the doors of the jail, grabbed Johnson from his cell, and dragged him through town to the bridge that spanned the Tennessee River. The leaders of the mob urged Johnson to confess. Instead, he repeated his claim of innocence, stating, "I am going to tell the truth. I am not guilty." His words enraged the crowd, and as they prepared to hang him from the bridge, Ed Johnson uttered his last words, "God bless you all. I am innocent" (Curriden & Phillips, 1999, pp. 210–214).

Although the citizens of Chattanooga blamed the lynching of Ed Johnson on the interference of the federal courts, the justices of the Supreme Court, and especially Justices Harlan and Holmes, were outraged that their order staying the execution had been ignored. President Theodore Roosevelt also condemned the lynching, which he called "contemptuous of the court" and "an affront to the highest tribunal in the land that cannot go by without proper action being taken." As Justice Harlan told the *Washington Post*, "the mandate of the Supreme Court has for the first time in the history of the country been openly defied by a community" (Curriden & Phillips, 1999, p. 222).

The events that transpired next shocked the citizens of Chattanooga. In May 1906, the U.S. Department of Justice charged Sheriff Shipp, his deputies, and the ringleaders of the lynch mob with contempt of court. In December of that year, the Supreme Court announced that it had jurisdiction in the case and that the justices, sitting as a trial court, would determine the fate of the defendants. According to Curriden & Phillips (1999, p. 284), the Supreme Court was sending a message "that its authority was supreme" and that defiance of its orders "would not and could not be tolerated."

Although charges were eventually dropped against 17 of the 26 defendants and three of the remaining nine were found not guilty, the Supreme Court found Sheriff Shipp, one of his deputies, and four members of the lynch mob guilty of contempt of court. Shipp and two members of the mob were sentenced to 90 days in prison; the others received sentences of 60 days. Noah Parden, the lawyer who filed the appeal with the Supreme Court, told the *Atlanta Independent* that the court's actions sent an important message. "We are at a time," he said, "when many of our people have abandoned the respect for the rule of law due to the racial hatred deep in their hearts and souls, and nothing less than our civilized society is at stake" (Curriden & Phillips, 1999, p. 336).

Ninety-four years later, Hamilton County Criminal Court Judge Doug Meyer, overturned Johnson's conviction. "It really is hard for us in the White community to imagine how badly Blacks were treated at that time," said Judge Meyer. "Something I don't believe the White community really understands is that, especially at that time, the object was to bring in a Black body, not necessarily the person who had committed the crime. And I think that's what happened in this case. There was a rush to find somebody to convict and blame."[84] The attorney who filed the petition to overturn Johnson's conviction was Leroy Phillips, one of the co-authors of *Contempt of Court*.

---

urged African American jurors to refuse to convict African American defendants accused of nonviolent crimes, regardless of the strength of the evidence mounted against them. According to Butler, "it is the moral responsibility of black jurors to emancipate some guilty black outlaws."[86]

Jury nullification, which has its roots in English common law, occurs when a juror believes that the evidence presented at trial establishes the defendant's guilt but nonetheless votes to acquit. The juror's decision may be motivated either by a belief that the law under which the defendant is being prosecuted is unfair or by an objection to the application of the law to a particular defendant. In the first instance, a juror might refuse to convict a defendant tried in federal court for possession of more than 50 grams of crack cocaine, based on her belief that the draconian penalties mandated by the law are unfair. In the second instance, a juror might vote to acquit a father charged with child endangerment after his 2-year-old daughter, who was not restrained in a child safety seat, was thrown from the car and killed when he lost control of his car on an icy road. In this case, the juror does not believe that the law itself is unfair, but, rather, that the defendant has suffered enough and that nothing will be gained by additional punishment.

Jurors clearly have the power to nullify the law and to vote their conscience. If a jury votes unanimously to acquit, the double jeopardy clause of the Fifth Amendment prohibits reversal of the jury's decision. The jury's decision to acquit, even in the face of overwhelming evidence of guilt, is final and cannot be reversed by the trial judge or by an appellate court. In most jurisdictions, however, jurors do not have to be told that they have the right to nullify the law.[87]

Butler's position on jury nullification is that the "black community is better off when some nonviolent lawbreakers remain in the community rather than go to prison."[88] Arguing that there are far too many African American men in prison, Butler suggested that there should be "a presumption in favor of nullification"[89] in cases involving African American defendants charged with *nonviolent, victimless,* crimes like possession of drugs. Butler claimed that enforcement of these laws has a disparate effect on the African American community and does not "advance the interest of black people."[90] He also suggested that white racism, which "creates and sustains the criminal breeding ground which produces the black criminal,"[91] is the underlying cause of much of the crime committed by African Americans. He thus urged African American jurors to "nullify without hesitation in these cases."[92]

Butler did not argue for nullification in all types of cases. In fact, he asserted that defendants charged with violent crimes such as murder, rape, and armed robbery should be convicted if there is proof beyond a reasonable doubt of guilt. He contended that nullification is not morally justifiable in these types of cases because "people who are violent should be separated from the community, for the sake of the nonviolent."[93] Violent African American offenders, in other words, should be convicted and incarcerated to protect potential innocent victims. Butler was willing to "write off" these offenders based on his belief that the "black community cannot afford the risks of leaving this person in its midst."[94]

The more difficult cases, according to Butler, involve defendants charged with nonviolent property offenses or with more serious drug-trafficking offenses. He discussed two hypothetical cases, one involving a ghetto drug dealer and the other involving a thief who burglarizes the home of a rich family. His answer to the question "Is nullification morally justifiable here?" is "It depends."[95] Although he admitted that "encouraging people to engage in self-destructive behavior is evil" and that therefore most drug dealers should be convicted, he argued that a juror's decision in this type of case might rest on the particular facts in the case. Similarly, although he is troubled by the case of the burglar who steals from a rich family because the behavior is "so clearly wrong," he argued that the facts in the case—for example, a person who steals to support a drug habit—might justify a vote to acquit. Nullification, in other words, may be a morally justifiable option in both types of cases.

Randall Kennedy's Critique   Randall Kennedy[96] raised a number of objections to Butler's proposal, which he characterized as "profoundly misleading as a guide to action."[97] Although he acknowledged that Butler's assertion that there is racial injustice in the administration of the criminal law is correct, Kennedy nonetheless objected to Butler's portrayal of the criminal justice system as a "one-dimensional system that is totally at odds with what black Americans need and want, a system that unequivocally represents and unrelentingly imposes 'the white man's law'."[98] Kennedy faulted Butler for his failure to acknowledge either the legal reforms implemented as a result of struggles *against* racism or the significant presence of African American officials in policymaking positions and the criminal justice system. The problems inherent in the criminal justice system, according to Kennedy, "require judicious attention, not a campaign of defiant sabotage."[99]

Kennedy objected to the fact that Butler expressed more sympathy for nonviolent African American offenders than for "the law-abiding people compelled by circumstances to live in close proximity to the criminals for whom he is willing to urge subversion of the legal system."[100] He asserted that law-abiding African Americans "desire *more* rather than *less* prosecution and punishment for *all* types of criminals,"[101] and suggested that, in any case, jury nullification "is an exceedingly poor means for advancing the goal of a racially fair administration of criminal law."[102] He claimed that a highly publicized campaign of jury nullification carried on by African Americans will not produce the social reforms that Butler demands. Moreover, such a campaign might backfire. Kennedy suggested that it might lead to increased support for proposals to eliminate the requirement that the jury be unanimous in order to convict, restrictions on the right of African Americans to serve on juries, or widespread use of jury nullification by white jurors in cases involving white-on-black crime.

According to Kennedy, the most compelling reason to oppose Butler's call for racially based jury nullification is that it is based on "an ultimately destructive sentiment of racial kinship that prompts individuals of a given race to care more about "their own" than people of another race."[103] He objected to the implication that it is proper for African American jurors to be more concerned about the fate of African American defendants than white defendants, more disturbed about the plight of African American communities than white communities, and more interested in protecting the lives and property of African American than white citizens. "Along that road," according to Kennedy, "lies moral and political disaster." Implementation of Butler's proposal, Kennedy insisted, would not only increase but legitimize "the tendency of people to privilege in racial terms 'their own'."[104]

CONCLUSION

In Chapter 5, we concluded that the reforms implemented during the past few decades have substantially reduced racial discrimination during the pretrial stages of the criminal justice process. Our examination of the jury selection process suggests that a similar conclusion is warranted. Reforms adopted voluntarily by the states or mandated by appellate courts have made it increasingly unlikely that African American and Hispanic defendants will be tried by all-white juries. An important caveat, however, concerns the use of racially motivated peremptory challenges. Supreme Court decisions notwithstanding, prosecutors still manage to use the peremptory challenge to eliminate African Americans and Hispanics from juries trying African American and Hispanic defendants. More troubling, prosecutors' "racially neutral" explanations for strikes alleged to be racially motivated, with few exceptions, continue to be accepted at face value. Coupled with anecdotal evidence that prosecutors are not reluctant to "play the race card" in a criminal trial, these findings regarding jury selection suggest that the process of adjudication, like the pretrial process, is not free of racial bias.

Based on the research reviewed in this chapter and the previous one, we conclude that contemporary court processing decisions are not characterized by *systematic* discrimination against racial minorities. This may have been true at the time that the Scottsboro Boys and Ed Johnson were tried, but it is no longer true. As we have shown, the U.S. Supreme Court has consistently affirmed the importance of protecting the rights of criminal defendants and has insisted that the race of the defendant not be taken into consideration in making case processing decisions. Coupled with reforms adopted voluntarily by the states, these decisions make systematic racial discrimination unlikely.

We are not suggesting, however, that these reforms have produced an equitable, or color-blind, system of justice. We are not suggesting that contemporary court processing decisions reflect *pure justice*. Researchers have demonstrated that court processing decisions in some jurisdictions reflect racial discrimination, whereas decisions in other jurisdictions are racially neutral. Researchers also have shown that African American and Hispanics who commit certain types of crimes are treated more harshly than whites and that being unemployed, having a prior criminal record, or being detained prior to trial may have a more negative effect on court outcomes for people of color than for whites.

These findings lead us to conclude that discrimination against African Americans and other racial minorities is not universal but is confined to certain types of cases, certain types of settings, and certain types of defendants. We conclude that the court system of today is characterized by *contextual discrimination*.

DISCUSSION QUESTIONS

1. The Supreme Court has repeatedly asserted that a defendant is not entitled to a jury "composed in whole or in part of persons of his own race." Although these rulings establish that states are not *obligated* to use racially mixed juries, they do not *prohibit* states from doing so. In fact, a number of policymakers and legal scholars have proposed reforms that use racial criteria to promote racial diversity on American juries. Some have suggested that the names of majority race jurors be removed from the jury list (thus ensuring a larger proportion of racial minorities); others have suggested that a certain number of seats on each jury be set aside for racial minorities. How would you justify these reforms to a state legislature? How would an opponent of these reforms respond? Overall, are these good ideas or bad ideas?

2. Evidence suggesting the prosecutors use their peremptory challenges to preserve all-white juries in cases involving African American or Hispanic

defendants has led some commentators to call for the elimination of the peremptory challenge. What do you think is the strongest argument in favor of eliminating the peremptory challenge? In favor of retaining it?

3. Given that the Supreme Court is unlikely to rule that the peremptory challenge violates the right to a fair trial and is therefore unconstitutional, are there any remedies or reforms that could be implemented?

4. Should a white defendant be allowed to challenge the prosecutor's use of peremptory challenges to exclude African Americans and other racial minorities from his or her jury? Why or why not?

5. Why do you think the U.S. Supreme Court decided to intervene in the Ed Johnson case (see the "Focus on an Issue: The Lynching of an Innocent Man")?

6. In this chapter, we present a number of examples of lawyers who "played the race card" in a criminal trial. Almost all of them involved prosecutors who appealed to the potential racist sentiments of white jurors. But what about defense attorneys representing African American defendants who attempt to appeal to the potential racist sentiments of African American jurors? Does this represent misconduct? How should the judge respond?

7. Why does Paul Butler advocate "racially based jury nullification"? Why does Randall Kennedy disagree with him?

NOTES

1. Harper Lee, *To Kill a Mockingbird* (New York: Warner Books, 1960), p. 220.

2. James P. Levine, *Juries and Politics* (Pacific Grove, CA: Brooks/Cole Publishing, 1992).

3. For an excellent discussion of this case, see Jack Olsen, *Last Man Standing: The Tragedy and Triumph of Geronimo Pratt* (New York: Doubleday, 2000).

4. Ibid., p. 367.

5. Ibid., p. 465.

6. Jeremy Engel, "Federal Judge Approves $4.5 Million Settlement in Pratt Case," *Metropolitan News-Enterprise, Capitol News Service,* May 1, 2000.

7. NAACP Legal Defense and Educational Fund, "Justice Prevails in Louisiana: Rideau Is Free," January 15, 2005. Available at http://www.naacpldf.org.

8. David Cole, *No Equal Justice: Race and Class in the American Criminal Justice System* (New York: The New Press, 1999), p. 103.

9. Ibid., p. 101.

10. *Duncan v. Louisiana*, 391 U.S. 145 (1968).

11. *McCleskey v. Kemp*, 481 U.S. 279 (1987) (quoting *Strauder v. West Virginia*, 100 U.S. 303 [1880]).

12. *Strauder v. West Virginia*, 100 U.S. 303 (1880).

13. Ibid., pp. 307–308.

14. Ibid., p. 309.

15. *Neal v. Delaware*, 103 U.S. 370, 394 (1881), at 393–394 (1881).

16. Ibid.

17. Ibid., p. 397.

18. Gunnar Myrdal, *An American Dilemma: The Negro Problem and Modern Democracy* (New York: Harper, 1944), p. 549.

19. Ibid., p. 549.

20. Ibid., p. 549.

21. Seymour Wishman, *Anatomy of a Jury: The System on Trial* (New York: Times Books, 1986), p. 54.

22. *Avery v. Georgia*, 345 U.S. 559 (1953).

23. *Whitus v. Georgia*, 385 U.S. 545 (1967).

24. *Avery v. Georgia*, 345 U.S. [559 (1953)] at 562.

25. Randall Kennedy, *Race, Crime, and the Law* (New York: Vintage, 1997), p. 179.

26. Ibid.

27. *Amadeo v. Zant*, 486 U.S. 214 (1988).

28. Cole, *No Equal Justice*, pp. 104–105.

29. Michael Higgins, "Few Are Chosen," *ABA Journal* February (1999): 50–51.

30. Kennedy, *Race, Crime, and the Law*, p. 239.

31. Albert W. Alschuler, "Racial Quotas and the Jury," *Duke Law Journal 44* (1995): 44.

32. Denise Lavoie, "Judge Rules on Racial Makeup of Juries," *Newsday.Com*, October 2, 2005. Available at http://www.newsday.com/news/nationwide.

33. Ibid.

34. Kennedy, *Race, Crime, and the Law*, p. 253.

35. Ibid., p. 255.

36. *U.S. v. Ovalle*, 136 F.3d 1092 (1998).

37. Alschuler, "Racial Quotas and the Jury," p. 704.

38. Cole, *No Equal Justice*, p. 126.

39. *Strauder v. West Virginia*, 100 U.S. 303 (1880) at 305; *Batson v. Kentucky*, 476 U.S. 79 (1986) at 85.

40. *Swain v. Alabama*, 380 U.S. 202, 212 (1965).

41. Kennedy, *Race, Crime, and the Law*, p. 214.

42. "Former Prosecutor Accused of Bias in Election Year," *New York Times* (March 31, 1997).

43. Ibid.

44. *Swain v. Alabama*, 380 U.S. 202 (1965).

45. Ibid., at 222.

46. Wishman, *Anatomy of a Jury*, p. 115.

47. Justice Brennan dissenting from denial of certiorari in *Thompson v. United States*, 105 S.Ct. at 445.

48. See Comment, "*Swain v. Alabama*, A Constitutional Blueprint for the Perpetuation of the All–White Jury," *Virginia Law Review 52* (1966): 1157; Note, "Rethinking Limitations on the Peremptory Challenge," *Columbia Law Review 85* (1983): 1357.

49. Brian J. Serr and Mark Maney, "Racism, Peremptory Challenges, and the Democratic Jury: The Jurisprudence of a Delicate Balance," *Journal of Criminal Law and Criminology 79* (1988): 13.

50. Batson v. Kentucky, 476 U.S. 79 (1986), at 93-94.

51. Ibid., at 96.

52. *United States v. Montgomery*, 819 F.2d at 851. The Eleventh Circuit, however, rejected this line of reasoning in *Fleming v. Kemp* [794 F.2d 1478 (11th Cir. 1986)] and *United States v. David* [803 F.2d 1567 (11th Cir. 1986)].

53. *United States v. Vaccaro*, 816 F.2d 443, 457 (9th Cir. 1987); *Fields v. People*, 732 P.2d 1145, 1158 n.20 (Colo. 1987).

54. Serr and Maney, "Racism, Peremptory Challenges, and the Democratic Jury," pp. 43–47.

55. Kennedy, *Race, Crime, and the Law*, p. 211.

56. Ibid., p. 213.

57. Serr and Maney, "Racism, Peremptory Challenges, and the Democratic Jury," p. 63.

58. 115 S.Ct. 1769 (1995). Available at http://www.lexis-nexis.com/universe.

59. Ibid.

60. Ibid. (Stevens, J., dissenting).

61. Cole, *Unequal Justice*, p. 124.

62. Robert Tharp, "Miller-El Case To Be Retried," *The Dallas Morning News*, July 8, 2005. Available at http://www.quickdfw.com.

63. Myrdal, *An American Dilemma*, pp. 547–548.

64. A study of peremptory challenges issued from 1976 to 1981 in Calcasieu Parish, Louisiana, for example, found that prosecutors excused African American jurors at a disproportionately high rate. See Billy M. Turner, Rickie D. Lovell, John C. Young, and William F. Denny, "Race and Peremptory Challenges During Voir Dire: Do Prosecution and Defense Agree?" *Journal of Criminal Justice 14* (1986): 61–69.

65. Samuel R. Gross, Kristen Jacoby, Daniel J. Matheson, Nicholas Montgomery, and Sujata Patil, "Exonerations in the United States 1989 Through 2003," *Journal of Criminal Law & Criminology 95* (2005): 523–553.

66. Ibid., p. 529.

67. Ibid.

68. Ibid., p. 547.

69. Ibid.

70. Ibid., p. 548.

71. Ibid.

72. See, for example, Christian A. Meissner and John C. Brigham, "Thirty Years of Investigating the Own-Race Bias in Memory for Faces: A Meta-Analytic Review," *Psychology, Public Policy, and Law 7* (2001): 3–35; John R. Rutledge, "They All Look Alike: The Inaccuracy of Cross-Racial Identifications," *American Journal of Criminal Law 28* (2001): 207–228.

73. "Shapiro Lashes out at Cochran over 'Race Card,'" *USA Today*, October 4, 1995.

74. Kennedy, *Race, Crime, and the Law*, pp. 286–290.

75. *Moulton v. State*, 199 Ala. 411 (1917).

76. *Miller v. North Carolina*, 583 F.2d 701 (CA 4 1978).

77. *State v. Washington*, 67 So. 930 (La. Sup. Ct., 1915).

78. *Withers v. United States*, 602 F.2d 124 (CA 6 1976).

79. *Blair v. Armontrout*, 916 F.2d 1310 (CA 8 1990).

80. *Miller v. North Carolina*, 583 F.2d 701 (CA 4 1978), 708.

81. *Blair v. Armontrout*, 916 F.2d 1310 (CA 8 1990), 1351.

82. Kennedy, *Race, Crime, and the Law*, pp. 256–257.

83. For a excellent and detailed account of this case, see Mark Curriden and Leroy Phillips, Jr., *Contempt of Court: The Turn-of-the-Century Lynching that Launched a Hundred Years of Federalism* (New York: Faber and Faber, 1999).

84. "Black Man Lynched By Mob After Getting Stay Of Execution In Rape Case 94 Years Ago Is Cleared," *Jet Magazine*, March 20, 2000. Available at http://www.jetmag.com.

85. Paul Butler, "Racially Based Jury Nullification: Black Power in the Criminal Justice System," *Yale Law Journal 105* (1995): 677–725.

86. Ibid., p. 679.

87. See, for example, *United States v. Dougherty*, 473 F.2d 1113 (D.C.Cir., 1972).

88. Butler, "Racially Based Jury Nullification," p. 679.

89. Ibid., p. 715.

90. Ibid., p. 714.

91. Ibid., p. 694.

92. Ibid., p. 719.

93. Ibid., p. 716.

94. Ibid., p. 719.

95. Ibid., p. 719.

96. Kennedy, *Race, Crime, and the Law*, pp. 295–310.

97. Ibid., p. 299.

98. Ibid., p. 299.

99. Ibid., p. 301.

100. Ibid., p. 305.

101. Ibid., pp. 305–306.

102. Ibid., p. 301.

103. Ibid., p. 310.

104. Ibid., p. 310.

7

✙

Race and Sentencing

In Search of Fairness and Justice

We must confront another reality. Nationwide, more than 40 percent
of the prison population consists of African American inmates. About
10 percent of African American men in their mid-to-late 20s are
behind bars. In some cities, more than 50 percent of young African
American men are under the supervision of the criminal justice
system . . . Our resources are misspent, our punishments too severe,
our sentences too long.
—JUSTICE ANTHONY KENNEDY, SPEAKING AT THE AMERICAN BAR
ASSOCIATION, AUGUST 2003

In 2004, the United States celebrated the 50th anniversary of *Brown v. Board of Education*, the landmark Supreme Court case that ordered desegregation of public schools. Also in 2004 the Sentencing Project issued a report entitled "Schools and Prisons: Fifty Years after *Brown v. Board of Education*."[1] The report noted that, whereas many institutions in society had become more diverse and more responsive to the needs of people of color in the wake of the *Brown* decision, the American criminal justice system had taken "a giant step backward."[2] To illustrate this, the report pointed out that in 2004 there were *nine times* as many African Americans in prison or jail as on the day the *Brown* decision was handed down—the number increased from 98,000 to 884,500. The report also noted that one of every three African American males and one of every 18 African American females born today could expect to be imprisoned at some point in his or her lifetime.[3] The authors of the report concluded that "such an outcome should be shocking to all Americans."[4]

Other statistics confirm that racial minorities—and especially young African American and Hispanic men—are substantially more likely than whites to be serving time in jail or prison. In 2004, for example, 12.6 percent of African

American males, 3.6 percent of Hispanic males, and 1.7 percent of white males in their late 20s were in jail or prison.[5] There were similar racial disparities among females. Across all age groups the incarceration rate for African American females was two and a half times greater than the rate for Hispanic females and four and a half times greater than the rate for white females.[6]

Explanations for the disproportionate number of African American and Hispanic males under the control of the criminal justice system are complex. As discussed in more detail in Chapter 9, a number of studies have concluded that most—but not all—of the racial disparity in incarceration rates can be attributed to racial differences in offending patterns and prior criminal records. Young African American and Hispanic males, in other words, face greater odds of incarceration than young white males primarily because they commit more serious crimes and have more serious prior criminal records. As the National Research Council's Panel on Sentencing Research concluded in 1983, "Factors other than racial discrimination in the sentencing process account for most of the disproportionate representation of black males in U.S. prisons."[7]

Not all of the racial disparity, however, can be explained away in this fashion. Critics contend that at least some of the overincarceration of racial minorities is the result of racially discriminatory sentencing policies and practices. As one commentator noted, "A conclusion that black overrepresentation among prisoners is not primarily the result of racial bias does not mean that there is no racism in the system."[8] The National Academy of Sciences Panel similarly concluded that evidence of racial discrimination in sentencing may be found in some jurisdictions or for certain types of crimes.

Underlying this controversy are questions concerning discretion in sentencing. To be fair, a sentencing scheme must allow the judge or jury discretion to shape sentences to fit individuals and their crimes. The judge or jury must be free to consider all *relevant* aggravating and mitigating circumstances. To be consistent, on the other hand, a sentencing scheme requires the even-handed application of objective standards. The judge or jury must take only relevant considerations into account and must be precluded from determining sentence severity based on prejudice or whim.

Critics of the sentencing process argue that judges, juries, and other members of the courtroom workgroup sometimes exercise their discretion inappropriately. Although they acknowledge that some degree of sentence disparity is to be expected in a system that attempts to individualize punishment, these critics suggest that there is *unwarranted* disparity in the sentences imposed on similarly situated offenders convicted of similar crimes. More to the point, they assert that judges impose harsher sentences on African American, Hispanic, and Native American offenders than on white offenders.

Other scholars contend that judges' sentencing decisions are not racially biased. They argue that disparity in sentencing is the result of legitimate differences among individual cases and that racial disparities disappear once these differences are taken into consideration. These scholars argue, in other words, that judges' sentencing decisions are both fair and consistent.

GOALS OF THE CHAPTER

In this chapter, we address the issue of racial disparity in sentencing. Our purpose is not simply to add another voice to the debate over the *existence* of racial discrimination in the sentencing process. Although we do attempt to determine whether racial minorities are sentenced more harshly than whites, we believe that this is a theoretically unsophisticated and incomplete approach to a complex phenomenon. It is overly simplistic to assume that racial minorities will receive harsher sentences than whites regardless of the nature of the crime, the seriousness of the offense, the culpability of the offender, or the characteristics of the victim. The more interesting question is "When does race matter?" It is this question that we attempt to answer.

RACIAL DISPARITY IN SENTENCING

There is clear and convincing evidence of two types of racial *disparity* in sentencing. The first type is derived from national statistics on prison admissions and prison populations. These statistics, which we discuss in detail in Chapter 9, reveal that the incarceration rates for African Americans and Hispanics are much higher than the rate for whites. In June 2004, for example, 4,919 of every 100,000 African American men, 1,717 of every 100,000 Hispanic men, and 717 of every 100,000 white men were incarcerated in a state or federal prison or local jail. The incarceration rates for women, although much lower than the rates for men, revealed a similar pattern: 359 of 100,000 for African Americans, 143 of 100,000 for Hispanics, and 81 of 100,000 for whites. Among males between the ages of 25 and 29 the disparities were even larger: 12,603 of every 100,000 African Americans, 3,606 of every 100,000 Hispanics, and 1,666 of every 100,000 whites were incarcerated.[9]

The second type of evidence comes from studies of judges' sentencing decisions. These studies, which are the focus of this chapter, reveal that African American and Hispanic defendants are more likely than whites to be sentenced to prison; those who are sentenced to prison receive longer terms than whites. Consider the following statistics:

- Black and Hispanic offenders sentenced under the federal sentencing guidelines in three U.S. District Courts in 1999, 2000, and 2001 received harsher sentences than white offenders. The incarceration rate was 98 percent for Hispanics, 94 percent for African Americans, and 85 percent for whites. Among those sentenced to prison, the average sentence was 102 months for African Americans, 74 months for Hispanics, and 59 months for whites.[10]

- Among offenders convicted of drug offenses in federal district courts in 1997 and 1998, the mean sentence length was 82 months for African Americans and 52 months for whites. For offenses with mandatory minimum sentences, the mean sentences were 136 months (African Americans) and 82 months (whites).[11]

- Fifty-eight percent of the African American offenders convicted of violent crimes in state courts in 2002 were sentenced to prison, compared with 47 percent of the white offenders. The figures for offenders convicted of drug offenses were 41 percent for African Americans and 32 percent for whites.[12]

- African American and Hispanic offenders convicted of felonies in Chicago, Miami, and Kansas City faced greater odds of incarceration than whites. In Chicago, 66 percent of the African Americans, 59 percent of the Hispanics, and 51 percent of the whites were incarcerated. In Miami, 51 percent of the African Americans, 40 percent of the Hispanics, and 35 percent of the whites were incarcerated. In Kansas City the incarceration rates were 46 percent (African Americans), 40 percent (Hispanics), and 36 percent (whites).[13]

Four Explanations for Racial Disparities in Sentencing

These statistics provide compelling evidence of racial disparity in sentencing. They indicate that the sentences imposed on African American and Hispanic offenders are different than—that is, harsher than—the sentences imposed on white offenders. These statistics, however, do not tell us *why* this occurs. They do not tell us whether the racial disparities in sentencing reflect racial discrimination and, if so, whether that discrimination is institutional or contextual. We suggest that there are at least four possible explanations for racial disparity in sentencing, only three of which reflect racial discrimination. Box 7.1 summarizes these explanations.

First, the differences in sentence severity could result from the fact that African Americans and Hispanics commit more serious crimes and have more serious prior criminal records than whites. Studies of sentencing decisions consistently have demonstrated the importance of these two "legally relevant" factors (see Box 7.2 for an alternative interpretation). Offenders who are convicted of more serious offenses, who use a weapon to commit the crime, or who seriously injure the victim receive harsher sentences, as do offenders who have prior felony convictions. The more severe sentences imposed on African Americans and Hispanics, then, might reflect the influence of these legally prescribed factors, rather than the effect of racial prejudice or unconscious bias on the part of judges.

Second, the differences could result from economic discrimination. As explained in Chapter 5, poor defendants are not as likely as middle- or upper-class defendants to have a private attorney or be released prior to trial. They also are more likely to be unemployed. All of these factors may be related to sentence severity. Defendants represented by private attorneys or released prior to trial may receive more lenient sentences than those represented by public defenders or held in custody prior to trial. Defendants who are unemployed may be sentenced more harshly than those who are employed. Because African American and Hispanic defendants are more likely than white defendants to be poor, economic discrimination amounts to *indirect* racial discrimination.

Third, the differences could result from overt or *direct* racial discrimination on the part of judges. Judges might take the race or ethnicity of the offender into

---

B O X   7.1   Four Explanations for Racial Disparities in Sentencing

---

African Americans and Hispanics are sentenced more harshly than whites for the
following reasons:

1.   They commit more serious crimes and have more serious prior criminal records
     than whites.
     Conclusion: Racial disparity but not racial discrimination

2.   They are more likely than whites to be poor; being poor is associated with a
     greater likelihood of pretrial detention and unemployment, both of which may
     lead to harsher sentences.
     Conclusion: Indirect (i.e., economic) discrimination

3.   Judges are biased or have prejudices against racial minorities.
     Conclusion: Direct racial discrimination

4.   The disparities occur in some contexts but not in others.
     Conclusion: Subtle (i.e., contextual) racial discrimination

---

account in determining the appropriate sentence, and prosecutors might consider
the offender's race or ethnicity in deciding whether to plea bargain and in making
sentence recommendations to the judge. If so, this implies that judges and
prosecutors who are confronted with similarly situated African American, Hispanic, and white offenders treat racial minorities more harshly than whites. It also
implies that these criminal justice officials, the majority of whom are white,
stereotype African American and Hispanic offenders as more violent, more
dangerous, and less amenable to rehabilitation than white offenders.

Fourth, the sentencing disparities could reflect both equal treatment and
discrimination, depending on the nature of the crime, the racial composition of
the victim–offender dyad, the type of jurisdiction, the age and gender of the
offender, and so on. It is possible, in other words, that racial minorities who
commit certain types of crimes (such as forgery) are treated no differently than
whites who commit these crimes, whereas those who commit other types of
crimes (such as sexual assault) are sentenced more harshly than their white
counterparts. Similarly, it is possible that racial discrimination in sentencing of
offenders convicted of sexual assault is confined to the South or to cases involving
black offenders and white victims. It is possible, in other words, that the type of
discrimination found in the sentencing process is contextual discrimination.

EMPIRICAL RESEARCH ON RACE
AND SENTENCING

Researchers have conducted dozens of studies to determine which of the four
explanations for racial disparity in sentencing is more correct and to untangle the
complex relationship between race and sentence severity. In fact, as Zatz has

---

B O X 7.2 Are Crime Seriousness and Prior Criminal Record "Legally Relevant" Variables?

Most policymakers and researchers assume that the seriousness of the conviction charge and the offender's prior criminal record are legally relevant to the sentencing decision. They assume that judges who base sentence severity primarily on crime seriousness and prior record are making legitimate, and racially neutral, sentencing decisions. But are they?

Some scholars argue that crime seriousness and prior criminal record are "race-linked" variables. If, for example, sentencing schemes consistently mandate the harshest punishments for the offenses for which racial minorities are most likely to be arrested (such as robbery and drug offenses involving crack cocaine), the imposition of punishment is not necessarily racially neutral.

Similarly, if prosecutors routinely file more serious charges against racial minorities than against whites who engage in the same type of criminal conduct, or offer less attractive plea bargains to racial minorities than to whites, the more serious conviction charges for racial minorities will reflect these racially biased charging and plea bargaining decisions. An African American defendant who is convicted of a more serious crime than a white defendant, in other words, may not necessarily have engaged in more serious criminal conduct than his white counterpart.

Prior criminal record also may be race-linked. If police target certain types of crimes (for example, selling illegal drugs) or patrol certain types of neighborhoods (for example, inner-city neighborhoods with large African American or Hispanic populations) more aggressively, racial minorities will be more likely than whites to "accumulate" a criminal history that then can be used to increase the punishment for the current offense. Racially biased charging and convicting decisions would have a similar effect.

If crime seriousness and prior criminal record are, in fact, race-linked in the ways outlined here, it is misleading to conclude that sentences based on these two variables are racially neutral.

---

noted, this issue "may well have been the major research inquiry for studies of sentencing in the 1970s and early 1980s."[14] The studies that have been conducted vary enormously in theoretical and methodological sophistication. They range from simple bivariate comparisons of incarceration rates for whites and racial minorities, to methodologically more rigorous multivariate analyses designed to identify direct race effects, to more sophisticated designs incorporating tests for indirect race effects and for interaction between race and other predictors of sentence severity. The findings generated by these studies and the conclusions drawn by their authors also vary.

Reviews of Recent Research

Studies conducted from the 1930s through the 1960s generally concluded that racial disparities in sentencing reflected overt racial discrimination. For example, the author of one of the earliest sentencing studies, which was published in 1935, claimed that "equality before the law is a social fiction."[15] Reviews of these early studies,[16] however, found that most of them were methodologically flawed. They usually used simple bivariate statistical techniques and they failed to control adequately for crime seriousness and prior criminal record.

The conclusions of these early reviews, coupled with the findings of its own review of sentencing research,[17] led the National Research Council's Panel on Sentencing Research to state in 1983 that the sentencing process was not characterized by "a widespread systematic pattern of discrimination." Rather, "some pockets of discrimination are found for particular judges, particular crime types, and in particular settings."[18] Marjorie Zatz, who reviewed the results of four waves of race and sentencing research conducted from the 1930s through the early 1980s, reached a somewhat different conclusion.[19] Although she acknowledged that "it would be misleading to suggest that race/ethnicity is *the* major determinant of sanctioning," Zatz nonetheless asserted that "race/ethnicity is *a* determinant of sanctioning, and a potent one at that."[20]

The two most recent reviews of research on race and sentencing confirm Zatz's assertion. Chiricos and Crawford reviewed 38 studies published between 1979 and 1991 that included a test for the direct effect of race on sentencing decisions in noncapital cases.[21] Unlike previous reviews, they distinguished results involving the decision to incarcerate or not from those involving the length of sentence decision. Chiricos and Crawford also considered whether the effect of race varied depending on structural or contextual conditions. They asked whether the impact of race would be stronger "in southern jurisdictions, in places where there is a higher percentage of Blacks in the population or a higher concentration of Blacks in urban areas, and in places with a higher rate of unemployment."[22] Noting that two-thirds of the studies that they examined had been published subsequent to the earlier reviews (which generally concluded that race did not play a prominent role in sentencing decisions), Chiricos and Crawford stated that their assessment "provides a fresh look at an issue that some may have considered all but closed."[23]

The authors' assessment of the findings of these 38 studies revealed "significant evidence of a *direct* impact of race on imprisonment."[24] This effect, which persisted even after the effects of crime seriousness and prior criminal record were controlled, was found only for the decision to incarcerate or not; it was not found for the decision on length of sentence. The authors also identified a number of structural contexts that conditioned the race/imprisonment relationship. African American offenders faced significantly greater odds of incarceration than white offenders in the South, in places where African Americans comprised a larger percentage of the population, and in places where the unemployment rate was high.

Spohn's[25] review of noncapital sentencing research that used data from the 1980s and 1990s also highlighted the importance of attempting to identify "the structural and contextual conditions that are most likely to result in racial discrimination."[26] Spohn reviewed 40 studies examining the relationship between race, ethnicity, and sentencing. This included 32 studies of sentencing decisions at the state level and 8 studies at the federal level. Consistent with the conclusions of Chiricos and Crawford, Spohn reported that many of these studies found a *direct race effect*. At both the state and federal levels, there was evidence

---

B O X 7.3   Race, Ethnicity, and Sentencing Decisions: Contextual Effects

Spohn's review of recent studies analyzing the effect of race and ethnicity on state and federal sentencing decisions identified four themes or patterns of contextual effects. These studies revealed the following:

1. Racial minorities are sentenced more harshly than whites if they

    are young and male,

    are unemployed,

    are male and unemployed,

    are young, male, and unemployed,

    have lower incomes, or

    have less education.

2. Racial minorities are sentenced more harshly than whites if they

    are detained in jail prior to trial,

    are represented by a public defender rather than a private attorney,

    are convicted at trial rather than by plea,

    have more serious prior criminal records.

3. Racial minorities who victimize whites are sentenced more harshly than other race-of-offender/race-of-victim combinations.

4. Racial minorities are sentenced more harshly than whites if they are

    convicted of less serious crimes or

    convicted of drug offenses or more serious drug offenses.

SOURCE: Cassia Spohn, "Thirty Years of Sentencing Reform: The Quest for a Racially Neutral Sentencing Process," in *Criminal Justice 2000: Policies, Process, and Decisions of the Criminal Justice System* (Washington, DC: U.S. Department of Justice, 2000).

---

that African Americans and Hispanics were more likely than whites to be sentenced to prison; at the federal level, there was also evidence that African Americans received longer sentences than whites.[27]

Noting that "[e]vidence concerning direct racial effects . . . provides few clues to the circumstances under which race matters,"[28] Spohn also evaluated the 40 studies included in her review for evidence of indirect or contextual discrimination. Although she acknowledged that some of the evidence was contradictory—for example, some studies revealed that racial disparities were confined to offenders with less serious prior criminal records, whereas others reported such disparities only among offenders with more serious criminal histories—Spohn nonetheless concluded that the studies revealed four "themes" or "patterns" of contextual effects. Box 7.3 summarizes these themes.

The first theme or pattern revealed was that the combination of race/ethnicity and other legally irrelevant offender characteristics produces greater sentence disparity than race/ethnicity alone. That is, the studies demonstrated that certain types of racial minorities—males, the young, the unemployed, the less educated—are singled out for harsher treatment. Some studies found that each of these offender characteristics, including race/ethnicity, had a direct effect on sentence outcomes but that the combination of race/ethnicity and one or more of the other characteristics was a more powerful predictor of sentence severity than any characteristic individually. Other studies found that race/ethnicity had an effect only if the offender was male, young, and/or unemployed.[29]

The second pattern of indirect/interaction effects was that a number of process-related factors conditioned the effect of race/ethnicity on sentence severity.[30] Some of the studies revealed, for example, that pleading guilty, hiring a private attorney, or providing evidence or testimony in other cases resulted in greater sentence discounts for white offenders than for African American or Hispanic offenders. Other studies showed that racial minorities paid a higher penalty—in terms of harsher sentences—for being detained prior to trial or for having a serious prior criminal record. As Spohn noted, these results demonstrate that race and ethnicity influence sentence outcomes through their relationships with earlier decisions and suggest that these process-related determinants of sentence outcomes do not operate in the same way for racial minorities and whites.

The third theme or pattern concerned an interaction between the race of the offender and the race of the victim. Consistent with research on the death penalty (which is discussed in Chapter 8), two studies found that African Americans who sexually assaulted whites were sentenced more harshly than either African Americans who sexually assaulted other African Americans or whites who sexually assaulted whites. Thus, "punishment is contingent on the race of the victim as well as the race of the offender."[31]

The final pattern of indirect/interaction effects, which Spohn admitted was "less obvious" than the other three,[32] was that the effect of race/ethnicity was conditioned by the nature of the crime. Some studies found that racial discrimination was confined to less serious—and thus more discretionary—crimes. Other studies revealed that racial discrimination was most pronounced for drug offenses or, alternatively, that harsher sentencing of racial minorities was found only for the most serious drug offenses.[33]

The fact that a majority of the studies reviewed by Chiricos and Crawford and by Spohn found that African Americans (and Hispanics) were more likely than whites to be sentenced to prison, even after taking crime seriousness and prior criminal record into account, suggests that racial discrimination in sentencing is not a thing of the past. Although the contemporary sentencing process may not be characterized by "a widespread systematic pattern of discrimination,"[34] it is not racially neutral.

Race/Ethnicity, Sentence Outcomes, and Conflict Theory   Spohn's conclusion that race/ethnicity interacts with or is conditioned by other predictors of sentence severity is consistent with the arguments put forth by Peterson and Hagan.[35] They asserted that the contradictory findings of early research exploring the effect of race on sentencing resulted in part from an oversimplification of conflict theory, the principal theoretical model used in studies of race and criminal punishment (see Chapter 3 for a detailed discussion of conflict theory).

Most researchers simply test the hypothesis that racial minorities will be sentenced more harshly than whites, assuming, either explicitly or implicitly, that racial minorities will receive more severe sentences than whites regardless of the characteristics of the offender, the nature of the crime, the race of the victim, or the relationship between the victim and the offender.

As Hawkins notes, however, conflict theory "does not support a simplistic expectation of greater punishment for blacks than whites under all circumstances."[36] Rather, conflict theorists argue that "the probability that criminal sanctions will be applied varies according to the extent to which the behaviors of the powerless conflict with the interests of the power segments."[37]

Crimes that threaten the power of the dominant class will therefore produce harsher penalties for African Americans who commit those crimes. Crimes that pose relatively little threat to the system of white authority, however, will not necessarily result in harsher sanctions for African Americans.[38] According to this view, African Americans who murder, rape, or rob whites will receive harsher sentences, whereas African Americans who victimize members of their own race will be treated more leniently. As Peterson and Hagan note,

> When black offenders assault or kill black victims, the devalued status of the black victims and the paternalistic attitudes of white authorities can justify lenient treatment... When blacks violate white victims, the high sexual property value attached to the white victims and the racial fears of authorities can justify severe treatment.[39]

Criminal justice scholars have proposed revising the conflict perspective on race and sentencing to account for the possibility of interaction between defendant race and other predictors of sentence severity. Hawkins, for example, argues for the development of a more comprehensive conflict theory that embodies race-of-victim and type-of-crime effects.[40] Similarly, Peterson and Hagan argue for research "that takes context-specific conceptions of race into account."[41]

As Spohn's review of recent research demonstrates, researchers examining the linkages between race and sentence severity have begun to heed these suggestions. They have begun to conduct research designed to identify the circumstances under which African Americans will be sentenced more harshly than whites. They have begun to design studies that attempt to determine "when race matters."

WHEN DOES RACE/ETHNICITY MATTER?

Research conducted during the past two decades clearly demonstrates that race/ethnicity interacts with or is conditioned by (1) other legally irrelevant offender characteristics, (2) process-related factors, (3) the race of the victim, and (4) the nature and seriousness of the crime. A comprehensive review of these studies is beyond the scope of this book. Instead, we summarize the findings of a few key studies. We begin by summarizing the results of two studies that found both direct and indirect racial/ethnic effects. We then review the findings of a series of

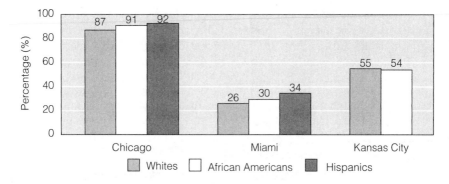

FIGURE 7.1 Estimated Probabilities of Incarceration for Offenders Convicted of Burglary

studies that explore the intersections among race, ethnicity, gender, age, employment status, and sentence severity. We also review studies that examine differential treatment of interracial and intraracial crime. We then discuss the findings of studies examining the effect of race on sentencing for different types of offenses and the findings of a number of studies that focus explicitly on the relationship between race and sentence severity for drug offenders. Our purpose is to illustrate the subtle and complex ways in which race influences the sentencing process.

Race/Ethnicity and Sentencing: Direct and Indirect Effects

A number of methodologically sound studies have concluded that African American and Hispanic offenders are sentenced more harshly than whites. Spohn and DeLone, for example, compared the sentences imposed on African American, Hispanic, and white offenders convicted of felonies in Chicago, Kansas City, and Miami in 1993 and 1994.[42] They controlled for the legal and extralegal variables that affect judges' sentencing decisions: the offender's age, gender, and prior criminal record; whether the offender was on probation at the time of the current offense; the seriousness of the conviction charge; the number of conviction charges; the type of attorney representing the offender; whether the offender was detained or released prior to trial; and whether the offender pled guilty or went to trial.

Spohn and DeLone found evidence of racial discrimination in the decision to incarcerate or not in two of the three jurisdictions. Although race had no effect on the likelihood of incarceration in Kansas City, both African Americans and Hispanics were more likely than whites to be sentenced to prison in Chicago, and Hispanics (but not African Americans) were more likely than whites to be incarcerated in Miami. The data presented in Figure 7.1 illustrate these results more clearly. The authors used the results of their multivariate analyses to calculate the estimated probability of imprisonment for a "typical" white, African American, and Hispanic offender who was convicted of burglary in each of the three cities.[43]

These estimated probabilities confirm that offender race had no effect on the likelihood of incarceration in Kansas City; 55 percent of the whites and 54 percent of the African Americans convicted of burglary were sentenced to prison. In Chicago, however, there was about a 4 percentage-point difference between white offenders and African American offenders and between white offenders and Hispanic offenders. In Miami, the difference between white offenders and Hispanic offenders was somewhat larger; even after the other legal and extralegal variables were taken into consideration, 34 percent of the Hispanics, but only 26 percent of the whites, received a prison sentence.

Spohn and DeLone also compared the sentences imposed on offenders who were incarcerated. They found that race/ethnicity had no effect on the length of the prison sentence in Chicago or Miami. In Kansas City, however, African Americans convicted of drug offenses received 14 months longer than whites convicted of drug offenses; African Americans convicted of property crimes received sentences that were nearly 7 months longer than those imposed on whites convicted of these crimes.

Consistent with the explanations presented in Box 7.1, Spohn and DeLone also found evidence of economic discrimination. When they analyzed the likelihood of pretrial detention, controlling for crime seriousness, the offender's prior criminal record, and other factors associated with the type and amount of bail required by the judge, they found that African Americans and Hispanics faced significantly higher odds of pretrial detention than whites in Chicago and Miami, and that African Americans were more likely than whites to be detained in Kansas City. They also found that pretrial detention was a strong predictor of the likelihood of incarceration following conviction. Thus, African American and Hispanic defendants were more likely than whites to be detained prior to trial, and those who were detained were substantially more likely than those who were released to be incarcerated.

The authors of this study were careful to point out that the race effects they uncovered, although statistically significant, were "rather modest"[44] and that the seriousness of the offense and the offender's prior criminal record were the primary determinants of sentence outcomes. They noted, however, that the fact that offender race/ethnicity had both direct and indirect effects, coupled with the fact that female offenders and those who were released prior to trial received substantially more lenient sentences than male offenders and those who were detained before trial, suggests that "judges' sentencing decisions are not guided *exclusively* by factors of explicit legal relevance."[45] They concluded that judges' sentencing decisions reflect "stereotypes of dangerousness and culpability that rest, either explicitly or implicitly, on considerations of race, gender, pretrial status, and willingness to plead guilty."[46] (See Box 7.4 for a discussion of sentencing outcomes for Native Americans.)

Are Hispanics Sentenced More Harshly than Whites *and* African Americans?   A study of sentencing decisions in the state of Pennsylvania, where judges use sentencing guidelines, compared the relative harshness of sentences imposed on Hispanic and African American offenders. Arguing that "Hispanic defendants may seem even more

B O X 7.4 Native Americans and Sentencing Disparity

Most studies investigating the effect of race on sentence outcomes focus exclusively on African Americans and whites. There are relatively few studies that include Hispanics and even fewer that include other racial minorities, such as Native Americans.

Young[56] asserted that the failure of criminal justice researchers to address issues relating to Native Americans "means that Native Americans are viewed in terms of narrow ethnocentric stereotypes (e.g., drunken savage)." Lujan[57] similarly contended that the stereotype of the "drunken Indian" makes Native Americans more vulnerable to arrest for alcohol-related offenses and that stereotypical perceptions of reservation life as unstable and conducive to crime may lead to longer sentences for Native Americans.

The few studies that do examine sentence outcomes for Native Americans have produced mixed results. Some studies found that Native Americans and whites are sentenced similarly once crime seriousness, prior record, and other legally relevant variables are taken into account.[58] Other studies concluded that Native Americans adjudicated in federal[59] and state[60] courts are sentenced more harshly than similarly situated whites or that Native Americans serve significantly more of their prison sentence before parole or release than whites do.[61]

One study used data on offenders incarcerated in Arizona state correctional facilities in 1990 to compare sentence lengths for Native Americans and whites.[62] Alvarez and Bachman found that whites received longer sentences than Native Americans for homicide, but Native Americans received longer sentences than whites for burglary and robbery.

Alvarez and Bachman speculated that these findings may reflect the fact that homicide tends to be intraracial, whereas burglary and robbery are more likely to be interracial. Whites may have received longer sentences for homicide, in other words, because their victims were also likely to be white, whereas the victims of Native Americans usually were other Native Americans. As the authors note, "Because the lives of American Indian victims may not be especially valued by U.S. society and the justice system, these American Indian defendants may receive more lenient sentences for their crime." Similarly, Native Americans convicted of burglary or robbery may have received harsher sentences than whites convicted of these crimes because their victims were more likely to be "higher-status Caucasians."[63]

Alvarez and Bachman concluded that their study demonstrates "the need for more crime-specific analyses to investigate discriminatory practices in processing and sentencing minority group members, especially American Indians."[64]

culturally dissimilar and be even more disadvantaged" than African Americans, Steffensmeier and Demuth hypothesized that Hispanic offenders would be sentenced more harshly than either white offenders or African Americans offenders.[47] They based this hypothesis on a number of factors, including the perceived threat posed by growing numbers of Hispanic immigrants; stereotypes that link Hispanics with drug trafficking and that characterize them as 'lazy, irresponsible, low in intelligence, and dangerously criminal"; and the relative powerlessness of Hispanic Americans in the political arena.[48] As the authors noted, "We expect that the specific social and historical context involving Hispanic Americans exacerbates perceptions of their cultural dissimilarity and the 'threat' they pose in ways that will contribute to their harsher treatment in criminal courts."[49]

When they looked at the raw data, Steffensmeier and Demuth found that Hispanics were sentenced to prison more often than either African Americans or whites. The incarceration rates for nondrug offenses were 46.2 percent (whites), 62.9 percent (African Americans), and 66.8 percent (Hispanics). The differences were even larger for drug offenses: 52.3 percent (whites), 69.9 percent (African Americans), and 87.4 percent (Hispanics).[50] These differences diminished, but did not disappear, when the authors controlled for the seriousness of the offense, the offender's criminal history, the mode of conviction, and the offender's age. In nondrug cases, African Americans were 6 percent more likely and Hispanics were 18 percent more likely than whites to be incarcerated. In drug cases, there was a 7 percentage-point difference in the probabilities of incarceration for African Americans and whites and a 26 percentage-point difference in the probabilities for Hispanics and whites.[51] For both types of crimes, then, African Americans faced higher odds of incarceration than whites, and Hispanics faced higher odds of incarceration than both whites and African Americans.

Steffensmeier and Demuth stated that their findings were consistent with hypotheses "drawn from the writings on prejudice and intergroup hostility suggesting that the specific social and historical context facing Hispanic Americans will exacerbate perceptions of their cultural dissimilarity and the 'threat' they pose."[52] They illustrated this with comments made by a judge in a county with a rapidly growing Hispanic population:

> We shouldn't kid ourselves. I have always prided myself for not being prejudiced but it is hard not to be affected by what is taking place. The whole area has changed with the influx of Hispanics and especially Puerto Ricans. You'd hardly recognize the downtown from what it was a few years ago. There's more dope, more crime, more people on welfare, more problems in school.[53]

This judge's comments suggest that "unconscious racism"[54] may infect the sentencing process. Concerns about the changes in the racial/ethnic makeup of a community, coupled with stereotypes linking race and ethnicity to drug use and drug-related crime and violence, may interact to produce harsher treatment of racial minorities by criminal justice officials who have always "prided themselves for not being prejudiced." As Greenberg notes, individuals who have ambivalent attitudes about race "may engage in automatic invidious stereotyping and may act on the basis of these stereotypes."[55]

Race/Ethnicity, Gender, Age, and Employment: A Volatile Combination?

In an article exploring the "convergence of race, ethnicity, gender, and class on court decisionmaking," Zatz urged researchers to consider the ways in which offender (and victim) characteristics jointly affect case outcomes.[65] As she noted, "Race, gender, and class are the central axes undergirding our social structure. They intersect in dynamic, fluid, and multifaceted ways."[66]

The findings of a series of studies conducted by Darrell Steffensmeier and his colleagues at Pennsylvania State University illustrate these "intersections." Research published by this team of researchers during the early 1990s concluded that race,[67] gender,[68] and age[69] each played a role in the sentencing process in Pennsylvania. However, it is interesting to note, especially in light of its later research findings,[70] that the team's initial study of the effect of race on sentencing concluded that race contributed "very little" to our understanding of judges' sentencing decisions.[71] Although the incarceration (jail or prison) rate for African Americans was 8 percentage points higher than the rate for whites, there was only a 2 percentage-point difference in the rates at which African Americans and whites were sentenced to prison. Race also played "a very small role in decisions about sentence length."[72] The average sentence for African American defendants was only 21 days longer than the average sentence for white defendants. These findings led Kramer and Steffensmeier (1993: 373) to conclude that "if defendants' race affects judges' decisions in sentencing ... it does so very weakly or intermittently, if at all."[73]

This conclusion is called into question by Steffensmeier, Ulmer, and Kramer's more recent research,[74] which explores the ways in which race, gender, and age interact to influence sentence severity. They found that each of the three legally irrelevant offender characteristics had a significant direct effect on both the likelihood of incarceration and the length of the sentence: African Americans were sentenced more harshly than whites, younger offenders were sentenced more harshly than older offenders, and males were sentenced more harshly than females. More important, they found that the three factors interacted to produce substantially harsher sentences for one particular category of offenders—young, African American males—than for any other age–race–gender combination. According to the authors, their results illustrate the "high cost of being black, young, and male."[75]

Although the research conducted by Steffensmeier and his colleagues provides important insights into the judicial decisionmaking process, their findings also suggest the possibility that factors other than race, gender, and age may interact to affect sentence severity. If, as the authors suggest, judges impose harsher sentences on offenders perceived to be more deviant, more dangerous, and more likely to recidivate, and if these perceptions rest, either explicitly or implicitly, on "stereotypes associated with membership in various social categories,"[76] then offenders with constellations of characteristics other than "young, black, and male" may also be singled out for harsher treatment.

The validity of this assertion is confirmed by the results of a recent replication and extension of the Pennsylvania study. Spohn and Holleran examined the sentences imposed on offenders convicted of felonies in Chicago, Miami, and Kansas City.[77] Their study included Hispanics and African Americans and tested for interactions between race, ethnicity, gender, age, and employment status. They found that none of the four offender characteristics had a significant effect on the length of the sentence in any of the three jurisdictions but that each of the characteristics had a significant effect on the decision to incarcerate or not in at least one of the jurisdictions. As shown in Part A of Table 7.1, in Chicago, African

TABLE 7.1   Do Young, Unemployed African American and Hispanic Males
Pay a Punishment Penalty?

Differences in the Probabilities of Incarceration:
The Effect of Race, Ethnicity, Gender, Age, and Employment Status

A. Probability Differences	Chicago	Miami	Kansas City
African Americans versus whites	+12.1%	not significant	not significant
Hispanics versus whites	+15.3%	+10.3%	(not applicable)
Males versus females	+22.8%	not significant	+21.1%
Unemployed versus employed	not significant	(not applicable)	+9.3%
Age 21–29 versus age 17–20	+10.0%	+9.5%	+10.8%

Differences in the Probabilities of Incarceration: Male Offenders only

B. Probability Differences between Whites aged 30–39 and	Chicago	Miami	Kansas City
African Americans, 17–29	+18.4%	+14.7%	+12.7%
Hispanics, 17–29	+25.1%	+18.2%	(not applicable)
Whites, 17–29	not significant	not significant	+14.4%
African Americans, 30–39	+23.3%	not significant	not significant
Hispanics, 30–39	not significant	+18.5%	(not applicable)

C. Probability Differences between Employed Whites and			
Unemployed African Americans	+16.9%	(not applicable)	+13.0%
Unemployed Hispanics	+23.5%	(not applicable)	(not applicable)
Unemployed Whites	not significant	(not applicable)	not significant
Employed African Americans	not significant	(not applicable)	not significant
Employed Hispanics	not significant	(not applicable)	(not applicable)

SOURCE: Cassia Spohn and David Holleran, "The Imprisonment Penalty Paid by Young, Unemployed Black and Hispanic Male Offenders," *Criminology* 38 (2000): Tables 3, 5, 6.

American offenders were 12.1 percent more likely than white offenders to be sentenced to prison; Hispanics were 15.3 percent more likely than whites to be incarcerated. In Miami, the difference in the probabilities of incarceration for Hispanic offenders and white offenders was 10.3 percent. Male offenders were more than 20 percent more likely than female offenders to be sentenced to prison in Chicago and Kansas City, and unemployed offenders faced significantly higher odds of incarceration than employed offenders (+9.3 percent) in Kansas City. In all three jurisdictions, offenders aged 21–29 were about 10 percent more likely than offenders aged 17–20 to be sentenced to prison.[78] Race, ethnicity, gender, age, and employment status, then, each had a direct effect on the decision to incarcerate or not.

Like Steffensmeier and his colleagues, Spohn and Holleran found that various combinations of race/ethnicity, gender, age, and employment status were better predictors of incarceration than any variable alone. As shown in Part B of Table 7.1, young African American and Hispanic males were consistently more likely than middle-aged white males to be sentenced to prison. These offenders, however, were not the only ones singled out for harsher treatment. In Chicago, young African American and Hispanic males and middle-aged African American males faced higher odds of incarceration than middle-aged white males. In Miami, young African American and Hispanic males and older Hispanic males were incarcerated more often than middle-aged white males. In Kansas City, both young African American males and young white males faced higher odds of incarceration than middle-aged whites. These results led Spohn and Holleran to conclude that "in Chicago and Miami the combination of race/ethnicity and age is a more powerful predictor of sentence severity than either variable individually, while in Kansas City age matters more than race."[79]

The findings of the studies conducted by Steffensmeier and his colleagues and by Spohn and Holleran confirm Richard Quinney's assertion, which he made 35 years ago, that "judicial decisions are not made uniformly. Decisions are made according to a host of extra-legal factors, including the age of the offender, his race, and social class."[80] Their findings confirm that dangerous or problematic populations are defined "by a mix of economic *and* racial ... references."[81] African American and Hispanic offenders who are also male, young, and unemployed may pay a higher punishment penalty than white offenders or other types of African American and Hispanic offenders.

Why Do Young, Unemployed Racial Minorities Pay a Punishment Penalty?

The question, of course, is *why* young, unemployed racial minorities are punished more severely than other types of offenders—why "today's prevailing criminal predator has become a euphemism for young, black males."[82]

A number of scholars suggest that certain categories of offenders are regarded as more dangerous and more problematic than others and thus more in need of formal social control. Spitzer, for example, used the term "social dynamite"[83] to characterize that segment of the deviant population that is viewed as particularly threatening and dangerous; he asserted that social dynamite "tends to be more youthful, alienated and politically volatile" and contended that those who fall into this category are more likely than other offenders to be formally processed through the criminal justice system.[84] Building on this point, Box and Hale argued that unemployed offenders who are also young, male, and members of a racial minority will be perceived as particularly threatening to the social order and thus will be singled out for harsher treatment.[85] Judges, in other words, regard these types of "threatening" offenders as likely candidates for imprisonment "in the belief that such a response will deter and incapacitate and thus defuse this threat."[86]

Steffensmeier and his colleagues advanced a similar explanation for their finding "that young black men (as opposed to black men as a whole) are the defendant subgroup most at risk to receive the harshest penalty."[87] They interpreted their results using the "focal concerns" theory of sentencing. According to this perspective, judges' sentencing decisions reflect their assessment of the blameworthiness or culpability of the offender; their desire to protect the community by incapacitating dangerous offenders or deterring potential offenders; and their concerns about the practical consequences, or social costs, of sentencing decisions. Because judges rarely have enough information to accurately determine an offender's culpability or dangerousness, they develop a "perceptual shorthand" based on stereotypes and attributions that are themselves linked to offender characteristics such as race, gender, and age. Thus, according to these researchers,

> Younger offenders and male defendants appear to be seen as more of a threat to the community or not as reformable, and so also are black offenders, particularly those who also are young and male. Likewise, concerns such as "ability to do time" and the costs of incarceration appear linked to race-, gender-, and age-based perceptions and stereotypes.[88]

The conclusions proffered by Spohn and Holleran, who noted that their results are consistent with the focal concerns theory of sentencing, are very similar. They suggested that judges, who generally have limited time in which to make decisions and have incomplete information about offenders, "may resort to stereotypes of deviance and dangerousness that rest on considerations of race, ethnicity, gender, age, and unemployment."[89] Young, unemployed African American and Hispanic males, in other words, are viewed as more dangerous, more threatening, and less amenable to rehabilitation; as a result, they are sentenced more harshly.

Differential Treatment of Interracial and Intraracial Sexual Assault

There is compelling historical evidence that interracial and intraracial crimes were treated differently. Gunnar Myrdal's examination of the Southern court system in the 1930s, for example, revealed that African Americans who victimized whites received the harshest punishment, whereas African Americans who victimized other African Americans were often "acquitted or given a ridiculously mild sentence. . . ."[90] Myrdal also noted that "it is quite common for a white criminal to be set free if his crime was against a Negro."[91]

These patterns are particularly pronounced for the crime of sexual assault. As Brownmiller has noted, "No single event ticks off America's political schizophrenia with greater certainty than the case of a black man accused of raping a white woman."[92] Evidence of this can be found in pre-Civil War statutes that prescribed different penalties for African American and white men convicted of sexual assault. As illustrated in Box 7.5, these early laws also differentiated between the rape of a white woman and the rape of an African American woman.

B O X 7.5   **Pre-Civil War Statutes on Sexual Assault: Explicit Discrimination Against African American Men Convicted of Raping White Women**

Virginia Code of 1819
The penalty for the rape or attempted rape of a white woman by a slave, African American, or mulatto was death; if the offender was white, the penalty was 10–21 years.

Georgia Penal Code of 1816
Death penalty for rape or attempted rape of a white woman by slaves or free persons of color. Term of not more than 20 years for rape of a white woman by a white man. White man convicted of raping an African American woman could be fined or imprisoned at the court's discretion.

Pennsylvania Code of 1700
The penalty for the rape of a white woman by an African American man was death; penalty for attempted rape was castration. The penalty for a white man was 1–7 years in prison.

Kansas Compilation of 1855
An African American man convicted of raping a white woman was to be castrated at his own expense. Maximum penalty for a white man convicted of raping a white woman was 5 years in prison.[93]

Differential treatment of interracial and intraracial sexual assaults continued even after passage of the Fourteenth Amendment, which outlawed explicit statutory racial discrimination. In the first half of the 20th century, African American men accused of, or even suspected of, sexually assaulting white women often faced white lynch mobs bent on vengeance. As Wriggens noted, "The thought of this particular crime aroused in many white people an extremely high level of mania and panic."[94] In a 1907 Louisiana case, the defense attorney stated:

> Gentlemen of the jury, this man, a nigger, is charged with breaking into the house of a white man in the nighttime and assaulting his wife, with the intent to rape her. Now, don't you know that, if this nigger had committed such a crime, he never would have been brought here and tried; that he would have been lynched, and if I were there I would help pull on the rope.[95]

African American men who escaped the mob's wrath were almost certain to be convicted. Those who were convicted were guaranteed a harsh sentence. Many, in fact, were sentenced to death; 405 of the 453 men executed for rape in the United States from 1930 to 1972 were African Americans.[96] According to Brownmiller, "Heavier sentences imposed on blacks for raping white women is an incontestable historic fact."[97] As we show, it is not simply a historic fact. Research conducted during the past 2 decades illustrates that African American

T A B L E 7.2 **Incarceration of Offenders Convicted of Sexual Assault:
A Hypothetical Example of the Effect of Offender–Victim Race**

Example: 2,000 men convicted of sexual assault. Analysis reveals that incarceration rate for African Americans is very similar to the rate for whites.

1,000 convicted African American offenders	460 incarcerated = 46% incarceration rate
1,000 convicted white offenders	440 incarcerated = 44% incarceration rate

Problem: Similarities are masking differences based on the race of the victim.

1,000 African American Offenders	460 incarcerated (46%)
800 cases with African American victims	320 incarcerated (40%)
200 cases with white victims	140 incarcerated (70%)
1,000 White Offenders	440 incarcerated (44%)
300 cases with African American victims	90 incarcerated (30%)
700 cases with white victims	350 incarcerated (50%)

Thus, the incarceration rate varies from 30% (for whites who assaulted African Americans) to 70% (for African Americans who assaulted whites).

men convicted of raping white women continue to be singled out for harsher treatment.

Offender–Victim Race and Sentences for Sexual Assault   Researchers analyzing the impact of race on sentencing for sexual assault have argued that focusing only on the race of the defendant and ignoring the race of the victim will produce misleading conclusions about the overall effect of race on sentencing. They contend that researchers may incorrectly conclude that race does not affect sentence severity if only the race of the defendant is taken into consideration. Table 7.2 presents a hypothetical example to illustrate how this might occur. Assume that 460 of 1,000 African American men (46 percent) and 440 of 1,000 white men (44 percent) convicted of sexual assault in a particular jurisdiction were sentenced to prison. A researcher who focused only on the race of the offender would therefore conclude that the incarceration rates for the two groups were nearly identical.

Assume now that the 1,000 cases involving African American men included 800 cases with African American victims and 200 cases with white victims and that 320 of the 800 cases with African American victims and 140 of the 200 cases with white victims resulted in a prison sentence. As shown in Table 7.2, although the overall incarceration rate for African American offenders is 46 percent, the rate for crimes involving African American men and white women is 70 percent, whereas the rate for crimes involving African American men and African American women is only 40 percent. A similar pattern—an incarceration rate of 50 percent for cases with white victims but only 30 percent for cases with African American victims—is found for sexual assaults involving white offenders. The similar incarceration rates for African American and white offenders mask large differences based on the race of the victim.

The findings of empirical research suggest that this scenario is not simply hypothetical. LaFree, for example, examined the impact of offender–victim race on the disposition of sexual assault cases in Indianapolis.[98] He found that African American men who assaulted white women were more likely than other offenders to be sentenced to prison. They also received longer prison sentences than any other offenders.

LaFree concluded that his results highlighted the importance of examining the racial composition of the offender–victim pair. Because the law was applied *most* harshly to African Americans charged with raping white women but *least* harshly to African Americans charged with raping African American women, simply examining the overall disposition of cases with African American defendants would have produced misleading results.

Walsh[99] reached a similar conclusion. When he examined the sentences imposed on offenders convicted of sexual assault in a metropolitan Ohio county, he found that neither the offender's race nor the victim's race influenced the length of the sentence. In addition, the incarceration rate for white defendants was *higher* than the rate for African American defendants.

Further analysis, however, revealed that African Americans convicted of assaulting whites received more severe sentences than those convicted of assaulting members of their own race. This was true for those who assaulted acquaintances and for those who assaulted strangers. As Walsh noted, "The leniency extended to blacks who sexually assault blacks provides a rather strong indication of disregard for minority victims of sexual assault."[100]

Somewhat different results were reported by Spohn and Spears,[101] who analyzed a sample of sexual assaults bound over for trial from 1970 through 1984 in Detroit Recorder's Court. Unlike previous research, which controlled only for offender–victim race and other offender and case characteristics, the authors of this study also controlled for a number of victim characteristics. They controlled for the age of the victim, the relationship between the victim and the offender, evidence of risk-taking behavior on the part of the victim, and the victim's behavior at the time of the incident. They compared the incarceration rates and the maximum sentences imposed on three combinations of offender–victim race: African American–African American, African American–white, and white–white.

In contrast to the results reported by LaFree and Walsh, Spohn and Spears found that the race of the offender–victim pair did not affect the likelihood of incarceration. The sentences imposed on African Americans who assaulted whites, however, were significantly longer than the sentences imposed on whites who assaulted whites or African Americans who assaulted African Americans. The average sentence for African American-on-white crimes was more than 4 years longer than the average sentence for white-on-white crimes and more than 3 years longer than the average sentence for African American-on-African American crimes. These results, according to the authors, reflected discrimination based on the offender's race and the victim's race.[102]

To explain the fact that offender–victim race affected the length of sentence but had no effect on the decision of whether to incarcerate, the authors suggested that judges confronted with offenders convicted of sexual assault may have

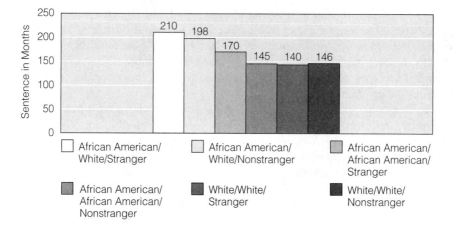

FIGURE 7.2 Offender's Race, Victim's Race, Relationship, and Length of Sentence

SOURCE: Cassia Spohn and Jeffrey Spears, "The Effect of Offender and Victim Characteristics on Sexual Assault Case Processing Decisions," *Justice Quarterly 3* (1996): 649–679.

relatively little discretion in deciding whether to incarcerate. As they noted, "Because sexual assault is a serious crime … the 'normal penalty' may be incarceration. Judges may have more latitude, and thus more opportunities to consider extralegal factors such as offender/victim race, in deciding on the length of the sentence."[103]

Spohn and Spears also tested a number of hypotheses about the interrelationships among offender race, victim race, and the relationship between the victim and the offender. Noting that previous research has suggested that crimes between intimates are perceived as less serious than crimes between strangers, they hypothesized that sexual assaults involving strangers would be treated more harshly than assaults involving intimates or acquaintances regardless of the offender's race or the victim's race. Contrary to their hypothesis, they found that the offender–victim relationship came into play only when both the offender and the victim were African American. African Americans convicted of assaulting African American strangers received harsher sentences than African Americans convicted of assaulting African American intimates or acquaintances; they were more likely to be incarcerated, and those who were incarcerated received longer sentences.[104]

The data presented in Figure 7.2 illustrate these differences. The authors used the results of their multivariate analysis of sentence length to calculate adjusted sentence means for each of the six combinations of offender race, victim race, and the relationship between the victim and the offender. These adjusted rates take all of the other independent variables into account. They show that three types of offenders received substantially longer sentences than the other three types. The harshest sentences were imposed on African Americans who victimized whites (strangers or nonstrangers) and on African Americans who victimized African American strangers. More lenient sentences were imposed on African Americans who assaulted African American nonstrangers and on whites who assaulted whites (strangers or nonstrangers).

As the authors noted, these results suggest that judges consider the offender's race, but not the relationship between the victim and offender, in determining the appropriate sentence for offenders convicted of assaulting whites. Regardless of the relationship between the victim and the offender, African Americans who victimized whites received longer sentences than whites who victimized whites. However, judges do consider the relationship between the victim and offender in determining the appropriate sentence for African Americans convicted of sexually assaulting other African Americans. Judges apparently believe that African Americans who sexually assault African Americans who are strangers to them deserve harsher punishment than those who sexually assault African American friends, relatives, or acquaintances.

Considered together, the results of these studies demonstrate that criminal punishment is contingent on the race of the victim as well as the race of the offender. They demonstrate that *"the meaning of race varies, and that, despite simplistic interpretations of conflict theory, both differential severity and leniency are possible."*[105] The harshest penalties will be imposed on African Americans who victimize whites, and the most lenient penalties will be imposed on African Americans who victimize other African Americans. (See Box 7.6 for information on groups' perceptions of the severity of sanctions.)

The Effect of Race on Sentencing for Various Types of Crimes

The studies summarized thus far highlight the importance of testing for interaction between offender race/ethnicity and other factors, such as the age, gender, and employment status of the offender and the race of the victim. The importance of "rethinking the conflict perspective on race and criminal punishment"[110] is also demonstrated by the results of studies examining the effect of race on sentence severity for various types of crimes. Some researchers, building on Kalven and Zeisel's "liberation hypothesis,"[111] assert that African Americans will be sentenced more harshly than whites only in less serious cases.

The liberation hypothesis suggests that jurors deviate from their fact-finding mission in cases in which the evidence against the defendant is weak or contradictory. Jurors' doubts about the evidence, in other words, liberate them from the constraints imposed by the law and free them to consider their own sentiments or values. When Kalven and Zeisel examined jurors' verdicts in rape cases, they found that jurors' beliefs about the victim's behavior at the time of the attack (for example, whether the victim was intoxicated or under the influence of drugs, whether the victim was walking alone late at night or in a bar by herself) were much more likely to influence their verdicts if the victim was raped by an unarmed acquaintance than if the victim was raped by a stranger armed with a gun or a knife.

The liberation hypothesis suggests that in more serious cases the appropriate sentence is strongly determined by the seriousness of the crime and by the defendant's prior criminal record. In these types of cases, judges have relatively little discretion and thus few opportunities to consider legally irrelevant factors such as race. In less serious cases, on the other hand, the appropriate sentence is

---

B O X 7.6   Perceptions of the Severity of Sanctions: Do African Americans Evaluate Prison Differently than Whites?

Studies of sentencing decisions assume that prison is a harsher punishment than probation, a county jail sentence, or other alternatives to incarceration. But is this necessarily this case? Is it possible that some people would rather serve time in prison than be subjected to electronic monitoring, ordered to perform community service, or placed on intensive supervision probation? More to the point, is it possible that African Americans would evaluate the severity of these sanctions differently than whites?

   To answer these questions, Peter Wood and David May asked 113 probationers to rate the severity of prison and a number of alternatives to incarceration.[106] Respondents were given descriptions of 10 alternative sanctions and then were asked to indicate how many months of the alternative they would be willing to do to avoid serving a sentence of 4, 8, or 12 months of imprisonment in a medium-security facility. The authors used these responses to calculate the percentage of respondents who would choose each prison term rather than *any* duration of the alternative sanction. They found that African Americans were much more likely than whites to choose prison rather than an alternative; this was true for each of the alternative sentences. For example,

- 22.2 percent of African Americans, but only 13.2 percent of whites, said that they would rather serve 4 months in prison than any time on electronic monitoring; 17 percent of African Americans, but only 11.5 percent of whites, said that they would rather serve a year in prison than any time on electronic monitoring.

- Six times as many African Americans as whites said that they would rather spend time in prison than be placed on intensive supervision probation (ISP). For example, 26.8 percent of African Americans said that they would rather serve a year in prison than any time on ISP; for whites, the figure was only 3.8 percent.

- The percentage of African Americans who said they would rather spend 8 months in prison than any time in county jail was 24.1 percent, compared to 13.5 percent of whites.[107]

   Wood and May also asked the respondents about their reasons for wanting to avoid alternative sanctions. Like their evaluations of the sanctions themselves, these varied depending on the race of the respondent. Twice as many African Americans as whites reported that a "very important reason" for avoiding alternative sanctions was that the officials in charge of these programs were too hard on participants—they wanted to catch them and send them back to prison. Similarly, 38.9 percent of African Americans, but only 18.9 percent of whites, said that abuse by officials overseeing the programs was a very important reason for avoiding them. African Americans also were more likely than whites to believe that serving time in prison is less of a hassle and that the program rules for alternative sanctions were too hard to follow. Because African Americans believe that the risk of revocation is high, they are "less willing to gamble on alternatives and more likely to choose prison instead."[108]

   According to the authors of this study, their findings raise questions about the deterrent value of imprisonment for African Americans. Although they admitted that they did not know whether African Americans' preference for prison over alternative sanctions was due to a belief that doing time in prison was easier or that the risk of revocation made alternatives too risky, the authors did conclude that "a brief prison term may be more of a deterrent for whites than for blacks."[109]

not clearly indicated by the features of the crime or the defendant's criminal record, which may leave judges more disposed to bring extralegal factors to bear on the sentencing decision.

Consider, for example, a case of sexual assault in which the offender, who has a prior conviction for armed robbery, raped a stranger at gunpoint. This case clearly calls for a severe sentence; all defendants who fall into this category, regardless of their race or their victim's race, will be sentenced to prison for close to the maximum term.

The appropriate sentence for a first-time offender who assaults an acquaintance with a weapon other than a gun, however, is not necessarily obvious. Some defendants who fall into this category will be incarcerated, but others will not. This opens the door for judges to consider the race of the defendant or the race of the victim in determining the appropriate sentence.

The Liberation Hypothesis and Offenders Convicted of Violent Felonies

Spohn and Cederblom used data on defendants convicted of violent felonies in Detroit to test the hypothesis that racial discrimination in sentencing is confined to less serious criminal cases.[112] Although they acknowledged that all of the cases included in their data file are by definition "serious cases," they argued that some are more serious than others: Murder, rape, and robbery are more serious than assault; crimes in which the defendant used a gun are more serious than those in which the defendant did not use a gun; and crimes in which the defendant had a prior felony conviction are more serious than those in which the defendant did not have prior convictions.

As shown in Table 7.3, which summarizes the results of their analysis of the likelihood of incarceration (controlling for other variables linked to sentence severity), the authors found convincing support for their hypothesis. With only one exception, race had a significant effect on the decision of whether to incarcerate only in less serious cases. African Americans convicted of assault were incarcerated at a higher rate than whites convicted of assault; there were no racial differences for the three more serious offenses. Similarly, race affected the likelihood of incarceration for defendants with no violent felony convictions, but not for those with a prior conviction; for defendants who victimized acquaintances, but not for those who victimized strangers; and for defendants who did not use a gun to commit the crime, but not for those who did use a gun.

Spohn and Cederblom concluded that their results provided support for Kalven and Zeisel's liberation hypothesis, at least with respect to the decision to incarcerate. They also concluded that their findings offered important insights into judges' sentencing decisions. According to the authors,

> When the crime is serious and the evidence strong, judges' sentencing decisions are determined primarily by factors of explicit legal relevance— the seriousness of the conviction charge, the number of conviction charges, the nature of the defendant's prior criminal record, and so on. Sentencing decisions in less serious cases, however, reflect the influence of extralegal as well as legal factors.[113]

T A B L E 7.3   The Effect of Race on the Likelihood of Incarceration
for Various Types of Cases in Detroit

	Effect of Race on Incarceration: Statistically Significant?
Most serious conviction charge	
Murder	No
Robbery	No
Rape	No
Other sex offenses	No
Assault	Yes
Prior criminal record	
Violent felony conviction	No
No violent felony conviction	Yes
Relationship between offender and victim	
Strangers	No
Acquaintances	Yes
Use of a weapon	
Offender used a gun	No
Offender did not use a gun	Yes
Injury to victim	
Offender injured victim	Yes
Offender did not injure victim	Yes

SOURCE: Adapted from Cassia Spohn and Jerry Cederblom, "Race and Disparities in Sentencing: A Test of the Liberation Hypothesis," *Justice Quarterly* 8 (1991): 305–327.

Racial Discrimination in the Sentencing of Misdemeanor Offenders?   Most of the research on sentencing examines the sentences imposed on offenders convicted of felonies. There is relatively little research testing for racial discrimination in the sentencing of individuals convicted of misdemeanor offenses. Because the lower courts where misdemeanor cases are handled usually have huge caseloads and informal, nonadversarial procedures for delivering what is often referred to as "assembly-line justice," one might predict that the likelihood of racially disparate decisions would be even greater in these courts than in the more formal felony courts.

Research by Leiber and Blowers addressed this issue.[114] They used data from an urban jurisdiction in a southeastern state to test for racial differences in a series of outcomes in misdemeanor cases. One of the dependent variables they examined was whether the case was assigned "priority status." This case-screening decision, which was made based on the defendant's prior criminal record or the facts in the case, identified cases that warranted priority prosecution. Two other dependent variables were whether the defendant was convicted and whether the defendant was sentenced to jail or prison.

When they examined the case prioritization variable, they found that cases involving assaults, cases in which the victim was a stranger to the offender, and cases involving offenders with prior criminal histories were more likely to be prioritized. They also found that cases involving African Americans were significantly more likely than those involving whites to be prioritized. Regarding the conviction and incarceration variables, they found that more serious cases had greater odds of conviction and incarceration and that the race of the offender did not affect either of these decisions. However, both decisions were affected by the status of the case; cases labeled as priority status cases were more likely to result in convictions and sentences to jail or prison.[115] The effect of race on these decisions, in other words, was indirect rather than direct. Cases involving African Americans were more likely to be prioritized and, as a result, were more likely than cases involving whites to result in conviction and incarceration. In these misdemeanor cases, then, African Americans were treated more harshly than whites when the case was characterized as serious rather than nonserious.

The results of these studies demonstrate that the criteria used by judges to determine the appropriate sentence will vary depending on the nature of the crime and the defendant's prior criminal record. More to the point, they demonstrate that *the effect of race on sentence severity will vary.* Judges impose harsher sentences on African Americans than on whites under some circumstances and for some types of crime; they impose similar sentences under other circumstances and for other types of crime. The fact that race does not affect sentence severity for *all* cases, in other words, does not mean that judges do not discriminate in *any* cases. (For a discussion of differences in the sentences imposed by judges of different races/ethnicities see "Focus on an Issue: Does It Make a Difference? A Comparison of the Sentencing Decisions of African American, Hispanic, and White Judges.")

Sentencing and the War on Drugs

The task of assessing the effect of race on sentencing is complicated by the War on Drugs, which critics contend has been fought primarily in minority communities. Tonry, for example, argued that "urban black Americans have borne the brunt of the War on Drugs."[116] More specifically, he charged that "the recent blackening of America's prison population is the product of malign neglect of the war's effects on black Americans."[117] Miller similarly asserted, "The racial discrimination endemic to the drug war wound its way through every stage of the processing—arrest, jailing, conviction, and sentencing."[118] Mauer's criticism is even more pointed. He asserted that " ... the drug war has exacerbated racial disparities in incarceration while failing to have any sustained impact on the drug problem."[119]

Comments such as these suggest that racial minorities will receive more punitive sentences than whites for drug offenses. This expectation is based in part on theoretical discussion of the "moral panic" surrounding drug use and the War on Drugs.[120] Moral panic theorists argue that society is characterized by a variety of common-sense perceptions about crime and drugs that result in community intolerance for such behaviors and increased pressure for punitive

(*continued on p. 262*)

Focus on an Issue

Does It Make a Difference? A Comparison of the Sentencing Decisions of African American, Hispanic, and White Judges

Historically, most state and federal judges have been white males. Although the nation's first African American judge was appointed in 1852, by the mid-1950s there were only a handful of African Americans presiding over state or federal courts. During the 1960s and 1970s, civil rights leaders lobbied for increased representation of African Americans at all levels of government, including the courts. By 1989 there were nearly 500 African American judges on the bench nationwide.

Those who champion the appointment of racial minorities argue that African American and Hispanic judges could make a difference. They contend that increasing the number of racial minorities on state and federal courts will alter the character of justice and the outcomes of the criminal justice system. Because the life histories and experiences of African Americans and Hispanics differ dramatically from those of whites, the beliefs and attitudes they bring to the bench also will differ. Justice A. Leon Higginbotham Jr., an African American who retired from the U.S. Court of Appeals for the Third Circuit in 1993, wrote, "The advantage of pluralism is that it brings a multitude of different experiences to the judicial process."[158] More to the point, he stated that "someone who has been a victim of racial injustice has greater sensitivity of the court's making sure that racism is not perpetrated, even inadvertently."[159] Judge George Crockett's assessment of the role of the black judge was even more pointed: "I think a black judge . . . has got to be a reformist—he cannot be a member of the club. The whole purpose of selecting him is that the people are dissatisfied with the status quo and they want him to shake it up, and his role is to shake it up."[160]

Assuming that African American judges agree with Judge Crockett's asser-

tion that their role is to "shake it up," how would this affect their behavior on the bench? One possibility is that African American (and Hispanic) judges might attempt to stop—or at least slow—the flow of young African American (and Hispanic) men into state and federal prisons. If African American judges view the disproportionately high number of young African American males incarcerated in state and federal prisons as a symptom of racial discrimination, they might be more willing than white judges to experiment with alternatives to incarceration for offenders convicted of nonviolent drug and property crimes. Welch and her colleagues make an analogous argument. Noting that African American judges tend to view themselves as liberal rather than conservative, they speculate that African American judges might be "more sympathetic to criminal defendants than whites judges are, since liberal views are associated with support for the underdog and the poor, which defendants disproportionately are."[161] Other scholars similarly suggest that increasing the number of African American judges would reduce racism in the criminal justice system and produce more equitable treatment of African American and white defendants.[162]

Statements made by African American judges suggest that they might bring a unique perspective to the courts. Smith's[163] survey of African American judges throughout the United States revealed that these judges believed that their presence on the bench reduced racial discrimination and promoted equality of justice. A Philadelphia judge, for instance, stated that the mere presence of African American judges "has done more than anything I know to reduce police brutality and to reduce illegal arrests and things of that sort."[164] Moreover, nearly half of the respondents stated that African American judges should exercise their powers to protect the rights of African American defendants. One Michigan judge remarked that African American judges should state that "everybody's going to get equal justice," by saying that, "you're going to give blacks something that they haven't been getting in the past."[165]

DECISIONMAKING BY AFRICAN AMERICANS AND WHITE FEDERAL JUDGES

As more African Americans have been appointed or elected to state and federal trial courts, it has become possible to compare their decisions with those of white judges. Two studies examined the consequences of the affirmative action policies of President Carter, who appointed a record number of African Americans to the federal courts. (Carter appointed 258 judges to the federal district courts and courts of appeals; 37, or 14 percent, of those appointed were African Americans. In contrast, only 7 of the 379 (1.8 percent) persons appointed to the federal bench by President Reagan were African American.)

Walker and Barrow[166] compared decisions handed down by the African American and white district court judges appointed by President Carter. The question they asked was, "Did it make a difference that President Carter appointed unprecedented numbers of women and minorities to the bench as opposed to filling vacancies with traditional white, male candidates?"[167] The authors found no differences in criminal cases or in four other types of cases. In criminal cases African American judges ruled in favor of the defense 50 percent of the time; white judges ruled in favor of the defense 48 percent of the time. These

similarities led the authors to conclude that black judges do not view themselves as advocates for the disadvantaged or see themselves as especially sympathetic to the policy goals of minorities.

Gottschall[168] examined decisions in the U.S. Courts of Appeals in 1979 and 1981. He compared the decisions of African American and white judges in terms of "attitudinal liberalism," which he defined as "a relative tendency to vote in favor of the legal claims of the criminally accused and prisoners in criminal and prisoner's rights cases and in favor of the legal claims of women and racial minorities in sex and race discrimination cases."[169]

In contrast to Walker and Barrow, Gottschall found that the judge's race had a "dramatic impact" on voting in cases involving the rights of criminal defendants and prisoners. African American male judges voted to support the legal claims of defendants and prisoners 79 percent of the time, as compared to only 53 percent for white male judges. African American judges, however, did not vote more liberally than white judges in race or sex discrimination cases. Gottschall concluded, "Affirmative action for blacks *does* appear to influence voting on the courts of appeals in cases involving the rights of the accused and prisoners, where black voting is markedly more liberal than is that of whites."[170]

DECISIONMAKING BY AFRICAN AMERICAN AND WHITE STATE JUDGES

Research comparing the sentencing decisions of African American and white state court judges also has yielded mixed results. Most researchers have found few differences and have concluded that the race of the judge is not a strong predictor of sentence severity.[171] Two early studies, for example, found few differences in the

(continued)

(*continued*)

sentencing behavior of African American and white judges. Engle[172] analyzed Philadelphia judges' sentencing decisions. He found that although the judge's race had a statistically significant effect, nine other variables were stronger predictors of sentence outcomes. He concluded that the race of the judge exerted "a very minor influence" overall.[173] Uhlman's[174] study of convicting and sentencing decisions in "Metro City" reached a similar conclusion. African American judges imposed somewhat harsher sentences than white judges, but the differences were relatively small. And both African American and white judges imposed harsher sentences on African American defendants than on white defendants. Moreover, there was more "behavioral diversity" among the African American judges than between African American and white judges. Some of the African American judges imposed substantially harsher sentences than the average sentence imposed by all judges, whereas other African American judges imposed significantly more lenient sentences. These findings led Uhlman to conclude that "Black and white judges differ little in determining both guilt and the punishment a defendant 'deserves' for committing a crime in Metro City."[175]

A later study of sentencing decisions in "Metro City" reached a different conclusion. Welch, Combs, and Gruhl[176] found that African American judges were more likely than white judges to send white defendants to prison. Further analysis led them to conclude that this difference reflected African American judges' tendency to incarcerate African American and white defendants at about the same rate and white judges' tendency to incarcerate African American defendants more often than white defendants. They also found, however, that African American judges, but not whites judges, favored defendants of their own race when determining the length of the prison sentence.

These results led them to conclude that "black judges provide more than symbolic representation."[177] According to these authors, "To the extent that they equalize the criminal justice system's treatment of black and white defendants, as they seem to for the crucial decision to incarcerate or not, [black judges] thwart discrimination against black defendants. In fact, the quality of justice received by both black and white defendants may be improved."[178]

A study of sentencing decisions by African American and white judges on the Cook County (Chicago) Circuit Court reached a similar conclusion.[179] Spears found that African American judges sentenced white, African American, and Hispanic offenders to prison at about the same rate, whereas white judges sentenced both African American and Hispanic offenders to prison at a significantly higher rate than white offenders. In fact, compared to white offenders sentenced by white judges, African American offenders sentenced by white judges had a 13 percent greater probability of imprisonment; for Hispanic offenders sentenced by white judges, the difference was 15 percent. Like the Metro City study, then, this study found that white judges sentenced racial minorities more harshly than whites and concluded that having African American judges on the bench "does provide more equitable justice."[180]

Spohn's[181] analysis of the sentences imposed on offenders convicted of violent felonies in Detroit Recorder's Court produced strikingly different results and led to very different conclusions. Like Engle and Uhlman, Spohn uncovered few meaningful differences between African American and white judges. She found that African American judges were somewhat more likely than white judges to sentence offenders to prison, but that judicial race had no effect on the length of sentence. Like Engle, she concluded that "the effect of judicial race, even where significant, was clearly overshadowed by the effect of the other independent variables."[182] Spohn also tested for interaction between the race of the judge, the race of the offender, and the race of the victim—that is, she attempted to determine, first, if African American and white judges treated African American and white offenders differently and, second, if African American and white judges imposed different sentences on African American offenders who victimized other African Americans, African American offenders who victimized whites, white offenders who victimized other whites, and white offenders who victimized African Americans.

Spohn's research highlighted the similarities in the sentences imposed by African American and by white judges. African American judges sentenced 72.9 percent of African American offenders to prison, whereas white judges incarcerated 74.2 percent, a difference of less than 2 percentage points. The adjusted figures for white offenders were 65.3 percent (African American judges) and 66.5 percent (white judges), again a difference of less than 2 percentage points. More important, these data reveal that both African American and white judges sentenced African American defendants more harshly than white defendants. For both African American and white judges, the adjusted incarceration rates for African American offenders were 7 percentage points higher than for white offenders. Moreover, African American judges sentenced offenders to prison at about the same rate as white judges, regardless of the racial makeup of the offender–victim pair.

These findings led Spohn to conclude that there was "remarkable similarity"[183] in the sentencing decisions of African American and white judges. They also led her to question the assumption that discrimination against African American defendants reflects prejudicial or racist attitudes on the part of white criminal justice officials. As

she noted, "Contrary to expectations, both black and white judges in Detroit imposed harsher sentences on black offenders. Harsher sentencing of black offenders, in other words, cannot be attributed sole to discrimination by white judges."[184] Spohn suggested that her findings contradicted the widely held assumption that African Americans do not discriminate against other African Americans and conventional wisdom about the role of African American judges. She concluded "that we should be considerably less sanguine in predicting that discrimination against black defendants will decline as the proportion of black judges increases."[185]

To explain her unexpected finding that both African American and white judges sentenced African American defendants more harshly than white judges, Spohn suggested that African American and white judges might perceive African American offenders as more threatening and more dangerous than white offenders. Alternatively, she speculated that at least some of the discriminatory treatment of African American offenders might be the result of concern for the welfare of African American victims. African American judges, in other words, "might see themselves not as representatives of black defendants but as advocates for black victims. This, coupled with the fact that black judges might see themselves as potential victims of black-on-black crime, could help explain the harsher sentences imposed on black offenders by black judges."[186]

Spohn acknowledged that because we do not know with any degree of certainty what goes through a judge's mind during the sentence process, these explanations were highly speculative. As she put it, "We cannot know precisely how the race of the offender is factored into the sentencing equation. Although the data reveal that both black and white judges sentence black offenders more

(continued)

(*continued*)
harshly than white offenders, the data do not tell us *why* this occurs."[187]

DECISIONMAKING BY HISPANIC AND WHITE JUDGES

Although most research examining the effect of judicial characteristics on sentencing has focused on the race of the sentencing judge, there is one study that compares the sentencing decisions of Anglo and Hispanic judges in two southwestern jurisdictions.[188] Holmes and his colleagues found that Hispanic judges sentenced Anglo and Hispanic offenders similarly, whereas Anglo judges sentenced Hispanics more harshly than Anglos. In fact, the sentences imposed on Hispanic offenders by Hispanic and Anglo judges were very similar to the sentences imposed by Hispanic judges on Anglo offenders. What was different, according to these researchers, was that Anglo judges sentenced Anglo offenders more leniently. Thus, "Anglo judges are not so much discriminating against Hispanic defendants as they are favoring members of their ethnic groups."[189]

REASONS FOR SIMILARITIES IN DECISIONMAKING

Although there is some evidence that African American and Hispanic judges sentence racial minorities and whites similarly, and that white judges give preferential treatment to white offenders, the bulk of the evidence suggests that judicial race/ethnicity makes very little difference.

The fact that African American, Hispanic, and white judges decide cases similarly is not particularly surprising. Although this conclusion challenges widely held presumptions about the role of African American and Hispanic criminal justice officials, it is not at odds with the results of other studies comparing African American and white decisionmakers. As noted in Chapter 4, studies have documented similarities in the behavior of African American and white police officers.

Similarities in judicial decisionmaking can be attributed in part to the judicial recruitment process, which produces a more or less homogeneous judiciary. Most judges recruited to state courts are middle or upper class and were born and attended law school in the state in which they serve. Even African American and white judges apparently share similar background characteristics. Studies indicate that "both the black and white benches appear to have been carefully chosen from the establishment center of the legal profession."[190] The judicial recruitment process may screen out candidates with unconventional views.

These similarities are reinforced by the judicial socialization process, which produces a subculture of justice and encourages judges to adhere to prevailing norms, practices, and precedents. They also are reinforced by the courtroom work group—judges, prosecutors, and defense attorneys who work together day after day to process cases as efficiently as possible. Even unconventional or maverick judges may be forced to conform. As one African American jurist noted, "No matter how 'liberal' black judges may believe themselves to be, the law remains essentially a conservative doctrine, and those who practice it conform."[191]

---

action.[121] Many theorists argue that this moral panic can become ingrained in the judicial ideology of sentencing judges, resulting in more severe sentences for those—that is, African Americans and Hispanics—believed to be responsible for drug use, drug distribution, and drug-related crime.[122]

B O X 7.7 Drug-Free School Zones: A Racially Neutral Policy?

Dematric Young was 20 years old when he was convicted of selling a small amount of cocaine to an undercover narcotics agent in North Lubbock, Texas. Young sold the drugs from his room in the Sunset Motel, a rundown place in a largely Hispanic neighborhood that, unknown to him, was located within 1,000 feet of Cavazos Junior High School. The normal sentence for Young's crime under Texas law would have been about 10 years. Because Young sold the drugs in a "drug-free school zone," he was sentenced to serve 38 years in prison.[124]

The Texas law under which Young was sentenced was modeled after the Federal Drug-Free School Zones Act (21 U.S.C. § 860 [1984]), which was enacted "to reduce the presence of drugs in the schools by threatening those who distributed drugs near schools with heavy penalties." The law, which doubles the maximum sentences for drug offenses that occur within the protected zones, is applicable to offenders who are convicted of distributing, possessing with intent to distribute, or manufacturing a controlled substance in or on, or within 1,000 feet of, the real property comprising a public or private elementary, vocational, or secondary school; a public or private college, junior college, or university; a playground; or housing facility owned by a public housing authority or within 100 feet of a public or private youth center, swimming pool, or video arcade facility.

Laws similar to this have been enacted in most states. Although they are designed to prevent the sale of drugs to children by moving drug dealing away from schools, critics contend that the statutes are irrational in that they assume that all drug sales near a school involve children or are more dangerous to children than drug sales that occur farther away from schools. Critics also argue that the laws transform entire urban areas—indeed, entire cities—into school zones and that this is most likely to occur in the inner-city neighborhoods populated by poor African Americans and Hispanics. A study of New Bedford, Massachusetts, for example, found that "most of the urban core falls within the enhanced-penalty area" and that more than three-fourths of all drug-dealing cases within the city limits occurred within school zones. This study also found that the drug dealers who were arrested within the school zones were not selling drugs to children and that most of them were arrested when school was not in session.[125]

A report by the Justice Policy Institute reached similar conclusions about the impact of the drug-free school zone law in New Jersey.[126] Noting that the New Jersey law used a broad definition of "schools" that included day-care centers and vocational training centers, the report concluded that "in New Jersey's poorest urban centers, minority offenders find themselves blanketed in drug free school zones." The report also noted that "a more suburban county, with fewer African American and Hispanic residents and a less dense distribution of 'schools' might experience less enforcement of school-zone laws, placing fewer Whites at risk of arrest and imprisonment."

As these reports suggest, drug-free school zone statutes, which are racially neutral on their face, may have racially discriminatory effects.

Racial Disparities in Sentences Imposed for Drug Offenses   As demonstrated in earlier chapters and summarized in what follows, there is ample evidence that the War on Drugs has been fought primarily in minority communities (see also Box 7.7, Drug-Free School Zones). In 2000, Human Rights Watch, a New York–based watchdog organization, issued a report titled *Punishment and Prejudice.*[123] The report analyzed nationwide prison admission statistics and presented the results of the first state-by-state analysis of the impact of drug offenses on prison admissions for African Americans and whites. The authors of the report alleged that the War on Drugs, which is "ostensibly color blind," has been waged "disproportionately against black Americans." As they noted, "The statistics we have compiled present a unique—and devastating—picture of the price black Americans have paid in each state for the national effort to curtail the use and sale of illicit drugs." In support of this conclusion, the report noted that:

- African Americans constituted 62.6 percent of all drug offenders admitted to state prisons in 1996; in certain states, the disparity was much worse—in Maryland and Illinois, for example, African Americans comprised 90 percent of all persons admitted to state prisons for drug offenses.

- Nationwide, the rate of drug admissions to state prison for African American men was 13 times greater than the rate for white men; in 10 states, the rates for African American men were 26 to 57 times greater than those for white men.

- Drug offenders accounted for 38 percent of all African American prison admissions, but only 24 percent of all white prison admissions; in New Hampshire, drug offenders accounted for 61 percent of all African American prison admissions.

- The disproportionate rates at which African Americans are sentenced to prison for drug offenses "originate in racially disproportionate rates of arrest." From 1979 to 1998, the percentage of drug users who were African American did not vary appreciably; however, among those arrested for drug offenses, the percentage of African Americans increased significantly. In 1979 African Americans comprised 10.8 percent of all drug users and 21.8 percent of all drug arrests; in 1998, African Americans comprised 16.9 percent of all drug users and 37.3 percent of all drug arrests.

The authors of the report stated that their purpose was "to bring renewed attention to extreme racial disparities in one area of the criminal justice system— the incarceration of drug law offenders." They also asserted that, although the high rates of incarceration for all drug offenders are a cause for concern, "the grossly disparate rates at which blacks and whites are sent to prison for drug offenses raise a clear warning flag concerning the fairness and equity of drug law enforcement across the country, and underscore the need for reforms that would minimize these disparities without sacrificing legitimate drug control objectives."

Critics of the report's conclusions, which they branded "inflammatory," argued that the statistics presented did not constitute evidence of racial discrimination. "There will be inevitably, inherently, disparities of all sorts in the enforcement of any kind of law," said Todd Graziano, a senior fellow in legal studies at the Heritage Foundation. Critics noted that because the illegal drug trade flourishes in inner-city, minority neighborhoods, the statistics presented in the report could simply indicate that African Americans commit more drug crimes than whites.

There are now a number of studies that focus on racial disparities in sentences imposed on drug offenders. Moreover, the results of these studies are somewhat inconsistent. Some researchers find that African American and Hispanic drug offenders are sentenced more harshly than white drug offenders;[127] other researchers conclude either that there are few if any racial differences[128] or that racial minorities convicted of certain types of drug offenses are sentenced more leniently than their white counterparts.[129]

We summarize the results of three studies comparing the sentences imposed on African American, Hispanic, and white drug offenders. All of these studies used data on offenders sentenced since the initiation of the War on Drugs. The first two studies[130] used data on offenders sentenced in state courts; the third[131] analyzed data on offenders sentenced under the Federal Sentencing Guidelines.

Sentencing of Drug Offenders in Three State Courts   Spohn and Spears used data on offenders convicted of felony drug offenses in Chicago, Kansas City, and Miami in 1993 and 1994 to test the hypothesis that African Americans and Hispanics would be sentenced more harshly than whites. They found that Hispanics, but not African Americans, faced greater odds of incarceration than whites in Miami, but that racial minorities and whites were sentenced to prison at about the same rate in Chicago and Kansas City. Similarly, they found that African Americans received longer sentences than whites in Kansas City but that the sentences imposed on racial minorities and whites were very similar in Chicago and Miami.

These similarities and differences are illustrated by the estimated probabilities of incarceration and the adjusted mean sentences for each racial group in each jurisdiction (Table 7.4). The estimated probabilities of incarceration are calculated for a "typical" offender (e.g., male, 30 years old, convicted of one count of an offense involving cocaine, one prior felony conviction) and take all of the other independent variables included in the analysis into account. They reveal substantial interjurisdictional variation in the likelihood of a prison sentence. They also confirm that race/ethnicity affected the probability of a prison sentence only in Miami.

The data presented in Table 7.4 reveal that the typical drug offender faced much higher odds of imprisonment in Chicago than in Kansas City or Miami. Three of every four offenders, regardless of race, were sentenced to prison in Chicago, compared with only one of every three, again regardless of race, in Kansas City. In Miami, in contrast, the odds of a prison sentence were much lower, particularly for white drug offenders. In this jurisdiction, the typical Hispanic drug offender was twice as likely as the typical white offender to be sentenced to prison.

The authors explained that the low rate of imprisonment in Miami reflects the fact that those convicted of less serious drug offenses normally were sentenced to the Dade County Jail rather than to state prison. As shown in Table 7.4, in Miami the odds of incarceration (in either jail or prison) were very similar to the odds of imprisonment in Chicago. When the authors used overall incarceration, rather than imprisonment, they found that the predicted probabilities for African American, Hispanic, and white drug offenders were very similar. As they noted, "In Miami, then, judges appear to take the offender's ethnicity into account in deciding between prison and either jail or probation, but not in deciding between some form of incarceration and probation."[132]

TABLE 7.4 **Predicted Probabilities of Incarceration and Adjusted Sentences for African American, Hispanic, and White Drug Offenders in Three Cities**

	Chicago	Miami	Kansas City
Probability of prison sentence			
African American	.796	.177	.370
Hispanic	.789	.227	NA
White	.765	.111	.341
Probability of a jail or prison sentence: Miami			
African American		.812	
Hispanic		.804	
White		.774	
Adjusted prison sentence (in months)			
African American	38.61	46.73	73.11
Hispanic	47.03	58.49	NA
White	41.35	56.51	58.12

SOURCE: Adapted from Cassia Spohn and Jeffrey Spears, "Sentencing of Drug Offenders in Three Cities: Does Race/Ethnicity Make a Difference?" in *Crime Control and Criminal Justice: The Delicate Balance*, Darnell F. Hawkins, Samuel L. Meyers Jr. , and Randolph N. Stone, eds. (Westport, CT: Greenwood , 2002).

The data presented in Table 7.4 also illustrate the authors' finding that judges in Kansas City imposed much longer sentences on African American than on white drug offenders. The mean sentence for African Americans was 73.11 months, compared with only 58.12 months for white offenders. In Chicago and Miami, however, the mean sentences imposed on whites were very similar to those imposed on African Americans and Hispanics. There were, however, more substantial differences in the sentences imposed on African American and Hispanic offenders. Hispanics received almost 15 months longer than African Americans in Miami and more than 8 months longer than African Americans in Chicago. In all three jurisdictions, then, one group of offenders received significantly longer sentences— African Americans in Kansas City and Hispanics in Miami and Chicago.

The authors of this study admitted that they were "somewhat puzzled"[133] by their finding that Hispanics were sentenced more harshly than African Americans in Miami and Chicago. They explained that they expected the "moral panic" surrounding drug use, drug distribution, and drug-related crime[134] to produce harsher sentences for both African Americans and Hispanics, who make up the majority of drug offenders in each jurisdiction. According to Spohn and Spears,

> The fact that harsher treatment was reserved for Hispanics in Miami, while unexpected, is not particularly surprising; arguably, the most enduring perception about drug importation and distribution in Miami is that these activities are dominated by Hispanics of various nationalities. This explanation, however, is less convincing with regard to our finding that Hispanics received longer sentences than blacks in Chicago.[135]

Further analysis of the sentences imposed in Chicago revealed that only certain types of Hispanic offenders—those convicted of the most serious drug offenses, those with a prior felony conviction, and those who were unemployed at the time of arrest—received longer sentences than African American offenders. The authors stated that this pattern of results suggests that judges in Chicago "may be imposing more severe sentences on offenders characterized as particularly problematic."[136] It suggests that Chicago judges use ethnicity, offense seriousness, prior record, and employment status to define what might be called a "dangerous class"[137] of drug offenders. The Hispanic drug offender who manufactures or sells large quantities of drugs, who is a repeat offender, or who has no legitimate means of financial support may be perceived as particularly dangerous and particularly likely to recidivate.

Sentencing of Drug Offenders in Washington State   Research conducted in Washington State also examined the effect of race on sentencing decisions in drug cases. Steen, Engen, and Gainey interviewed criminal justice officials about their perceptions of typical drug cases and drug offenders and the factors they used to differentiate among drug cases.[138] They found that decisionmakers used three offender characteristics—gender, prior record, and whether the offender was using or dealing drugs—to construct a stereotype of a dangerous drug offender. Males with prior felony convictions who were convicted of drug-delivery offenses involving cocaine, heroin, or methamphetamine were perceived as more dangerous and threatening than other types of drug offenders.

As shown in Table 7.5, Steen and her colleagues also found that African Americans were more likely than whites to have the characteristics stereotypical of a dangerous drug offender. African Americans were more likely than whites to be male, to be drug dealers rather than drug users, and to have prior felony convictions. African Americans also were more likely than whites to have all of the characteristics of a dangerous drug offender; 16 percent of the African Americans, but only 6 percent of the whites, were male offenders with prior felony convictions who were convicted of drug dealing. According to the authors, "this disproportionality, along with cultural stereotypes, makes decision makers more inclined to expect this 'worst case' behavior from black offenders (especially black males) than from white offenders."[139] As a result, whites who match the stereotype of a dangerous drug offender will be seen as atypical, and their behavior will be subjected to more judicial scrutiny; African Americans who match the stereotype, however, will be perceived as typical and their cases will be handled in a routine fashion.

The results of the authors' analysis of the decision whether to incarcerate revealed that African Americans were substantially more likely than whites to be incarcerated and that offenders whose characteristics matched those of the dangerous drug offenders had higher odds of incarceration than offenders whose characteristics were at odds with the stereotype. Males were 56 percent more likely than females to be incarcerated, and the odds of incarceration were 23 times greater for dealers than for nondealers and 8 times greater for offenders with prior felony convictions than for those without prior felonies. When the authors partitioned the data by the race of the offender, they found that, although being a drug

T A B L E 7.5 Race and the Stereotype of a Dangerous Drug Offender: Percentage of Whites and African Americans Having Characteristics Stereotypical of a Dangerous Drug Offender

	Whites (%)	African Americans (%)
Offender is male	74	82
Offender is a drug dealer	14	27
Offender has at least one prior felony conviction	48	68
Offender Groups		
Offender is a male dealer with prior felony convictions	6	16
Offender is a male dealer without prior felony convictions	5	6
Offender is a male nondealer with prior felony convictions	32	41
Offender is a male nondealer with no prior felony convictions	31	18
Offender is a female dealer	3	4
Offender is a female nondealer with prior felony convictions	9	8
Offender is a female nondealer without prior felony convictions	14	6

dealer had a significant effect on the likelihood of incarceration for both white offenders and African American offenders, it had a significantly larger effect for whites than for blacks. Being a dealer increased the odds of incarceration 27 times for white offenders, compared to 9 times for African American offenders.[140] Further analysis revealed that fitting the stereotype of a dangerous drug offender (i.e., a male dealer with prior felony convictions) also affected the likelihood of incarceration for white offenders more than for African American offenders.[141]

The authors interpreted their finding that matching the stereotype of a dangerous drug offender had a more pronounced effect on the severity of the sentence for whites than for African Americans as reflecting "greater leniency in the sentencing of less-threatening white offenders, compared to blacks, as opposed to greater punitiveness in the sentencing of the most threatening white offenders."[142] All offenders—whites as well as African Americans—who matched the stereotype of a dangerous offender were sentenced to jail or prison. Probation was not an option for these dangerous offenders. Among less serious offenders, however, judges sent whites to jail or prison less often than African Americans. The authors concluded that their results suggested that "decision makers are more likely to define low-level black offenders as a threat to public safety, and therefore deserving of incarceration, than similarly situated white offenders."[143] (For additional discussion of dangerous drugs and dangerous drug offenders, see "Focus on an Issue: Penalties for Crack and Powder Cocaine.")

The findings of these two state-level studies provide clues regarding the contexts in which race and ethnicity matter in sentencing drug offenders. They suggest that decision makers' beliefs about the dangerousness of and degree of threat posed by white, Hispanic, and African American offenders are intertwined

Focus on an Issue
Penalties for Crack and Powder Cocaine

Federal sentencing guidelines for drug offenses differentiate between crack and powder cocaine. In fact, the guidelines treat crack cocaine as being 100 times worse than powder cocaine. Possession of 500 grams of powder cocaine, but only 5 grams of crack, triggers a mandatory minimum sentence of 5 years. Critics charge that this policy, although racially neutral on its face, discriminates against African American drug users and sellers, who prefer crack cocaine to powder cocaine. More than 90 percent of the offenders sentenced for crack offenses in federal courts are African American. Those who defend the policy, however, suggest that it is not racially motivated; rather, as Randall Kennedy, an African American professor at Harvard Law School, contends, the policy is a sensible response "to the desires of law-abiding people—including the great mass of black communities—for protection against criminals preying on them."[145]

In 1993 Judge Lyle Strom, the chief judge of the United States District Court in Nebraska, sentenced four African American crack dealers to significantly shorter prison terms than called for under the guidelines. In explanation, Strom wrote, "Members of the African American race are being treated unfairly in receiving substantially longer sentences than Caucasian males who traditionally deal in powder cocaine."[146]

Strom's decision was overturned by the Eighth Circuit Court of Appeals in 1994. The three-judge panel ruled that even if the guidelines are unfair to African Americans, that is not enough to justify a more lenient sentence than called for under the guidelines. Other federal appellate courts have upheld the 100-to-1 rule, holding that the rule does not violate the equal protection clause of the Fourteenth Amendment (see, for example, *U.S. v. Thomas*, 900 F.2d 37 [4th Cir. 1990]; *U.S. v. Frazier*, 981 F.2d 92 [3rd Cir. 1992]; and *U.S. v. Latimore*, 974 F2d 971 [8th Cir. 1992].

In 1996 the U.S. Supreme Court ruled 8-1 that African Americans who allege that they have been singled out for prosecution under the crack cocaine rule must first show that whites in similar circumstances were not prosecuted.[147] The case was brought by five African American defendants from Los Angeles, who claimed that prosecutors were systematically steering crack cocaine cases involving African Americans to federal court, where the 100-to-1 rule applied, but steering cases involving whites to state court, where lesser penalties applied. The Court stated that a defendant who claimed he or she was a victim of selective prosecution "must demonstrate that the federal prose-cutorial policy had a discriminatory effect and that it was motivated by a discriminatory purpose."

The United States Sentencing Commission has recommended that the penalties for crack and powder cocaine offenses be equalized. In 1995 the Commission recommended that the 100-to-1 ratio be changed to a 1-to-1 ratio. Both Congress and former President Clinton rejected this amendment. In May 2002 the Commission "unanimously and firmly" reiterated its earlier position that "the various congressional objectives can be achieved more effectively by decreasing substantially the 100-to-1 drug quantity ratio."[148] The Commission rec-ommended increasing the quantity levels that trigger the mandatory minimum penalties for crack cocaine. They recom-mended that the 5-year mandatory min-imum threshold be increased to at least 25 grams and that the 10-year mandatory

(continued)

(*continued*)
minimum threshold be increased to at least 250 grams. The Commission also recommended that Congress repeal the mandatory minimum sentence for simple possession of crack cocaine.

The Commission's 2002 report also noted that the majority (85 percent in 2000) of offenders subject to the harsh penalties for drug offenses involving crack cocaine were African American. Although the Commissioners acknowledged that this did not necessarily prove that "the current penalty structure promotes unwarranted disparity based on race," they cautioned that "even the perception of racial disparity [is] problematic because it fosters disrespect for and lack of confidence in the criminal justice system."[149]

---

with their assumptions about crime and criminality. As Steen and her colleagues noted, "stereotypes about both crimes and criminals affect the way cases are perceived and decisions are made."[144]

Sentencing of Drug Offenders in the Federal Courts   Albonetti[150] examined sentences imposed on drug offenders under the federal sentencing guidelines for evidence of bias against racial minorities. Although the federal guidelines were designed to reduce judicial discretion in sentencing and, as a result, to eliminate "unwarranted sentencing disparity among defendants with similar records who had been found guilty of similar criminal conduct,"[151] both judges and prosecutors retain some discretion. Albonetti was particularly interested in determining the degree to which prosecutorial charging and plea bargaining decisions work to the disadvantage of racial minorities. As she noted, "Under the federal guidelines, a prosecuting attorney can circumvent the guideline-defined sentence through charging, guilty plea negotiations, and motions for a sentence that is a departure from the guideline sentence."[152]

Albonetti used 1991–1992 data on drug offenders sentenced in federal district courts to test a number of hypotheses concerning the relationship between the offender's race/ethnicity, the prosecutor's "process-related decisions,"[153] and sentence severity. She hypothesized, first, that African American and Hispanic offenders will be sentenced more harshly than similarly situated white offenders. She also hypothesized that African American and Hispanic offenders "will receive less benefit"[154] from pleading guilty and from guideline departures[155] than will white offenders. White offenders, in other words, will receive greater sentence reductions than either African American or Hispanic offenders if they plead guilty or if the judge accepts the prosecutor's motion for a departure from the guidelines.

In support of her first hypothesis, Albonetti found that both African American and Hispanic drug offenders received more severe sentences than white drug offenders. These results were obtained after all of the legally relevant variables (i.e., offense severity, criminal history, type of drug offense, and number of counts) and process-related factors (i.e., whether the defendant pled guilty and whether the defendant's sentence was a departure from the guidelines) were taken into consideration.

Regarding her second research question, Albonetti found that pleading guilty produced a similar reduction in sentence severity for all three groups of offenders.

The effect of a guideline departure, however, varied among the three groups, with whites receiving a significantly greater benefit than either African Americans or Hispanics. Among white defendants, a guideline departure produced a 23 percent reduction in the probability of incarceration; the comparable figures for African Americans and Hispanics were 13 percent and 14 percent, respectively. According to the author, "These findings strongly suggest that the mechanism by which the federal guidelines permit the exercise of discretion operates to the disadvantage of minority defendants."[156]

Albonetti also found that white offenders received a larger sentence reduction than African American or Hispanic offenders as a result of being convicted for possession of drugs rather than drug trafficking and that whites benefitted more from educational achievements than did racial minorities. She concluded that the pattern of results found in her study suggests that "the federal sentencing guidelines have not eliminated sentence disparity linked to defendant characteristics for defendants convicted of drug offenses in 1991-92."[157] (As detailed in the "Focus on an Issue: Penalties for Crack and Powder Cocaine" there is considerable controversy regarding the sentences mandated for offenses involving crack and powder cocaine.)

SENTENCING REFORM: THE QUEST FOR A "JUST" PUNISHMENT SYSTEM

Concerns about disparity, discrimination, and unfairness in sentencing led to a "remarkable burst of reform"[192] that began in the mid-1970s and continues today. The initial focus of reform efforts was the indeterminate sentence, in which the judge imposed a minimum and maximum sentence and the parole board determined the date of release. The parole board's determination of when the offender should be released rested on its judgment of whether the offender had been rehabilitated or had served enough time for the particular crime. Under indeterminate sentencing, sentences were tailored to the individual offender and discretion was distributed to the criminal justice officials who determined the sentence and to corrections officials and the parole board. The result of this process was "a system of sentencing in which there was little understanding or predictability as to who would be imprisoned and for how long."[193]

Challenges to the Indeterminate Sentence

Both liberal and conservative reformers challenged the principles underlying the indeterminate sentence and called for changes designed to curb discretion, reduce disparity and discrimination, and achieve proportionality and parsimony in sentencing. Liberals and civil rights activists argued that indeterminate sentencing was arbitrary and capricious and therefore violated defendants' rights to equal protection and due process of law.[194] They charged that indeterminate sentences were used to incapacitate those who could not be rehabilitated and that offenders' uncertainty about their date of release contributed to prison unrest. Liberal critics also were apprehensive about the potential for racial bias under indeterminate sentencing schemes. They asserted that "racial discrimination in the criminal justice system was epidemic, that judges, parole boards, and corrections officials could not be trusted, and that tight controls on officials' discretion offered the only way to limit racial disparities."[195]

Political conservatives, however, argued that the emphasis on rehabilitation too often resulted in excessively lenient treatment of offenders who had committed serious crimes or had serious criminal histories.[196] They also charged that sentences that were not linked to crime seriousness and offender culpability were unjust.[197] These conservative critics championed sentencing reforms designed to establish and enforce more punitive sentencing standards. Their arguments were bolstered by the findings of research demonstrating that most correctional programs designed to rehabilitate offenders and reduce recidivism were ineffective.[198]

After a few initial "missteps," in which jurisdictions attempted to *eliminate* discretion altogether through flat-time sentencing,[199] states and the federal government adopted structured sentencing proposals designed to *control* the discretion of sentencing judges. A number of states adopted determinate sentencing policies that offered judges a limited number of sentencing options and included enhancements for use of a weapon, presence of a prior criminal record, or infliction of serious injury. Other states and the federal government adopted sentence guidelines that incorporated crime seriousness and prior criminal record into a sentencing "grid" that judges were to use in determining the appropriate sentence. Other reforms enacted at both the federal and state level included mandatory minimum penalties for certain types of offenses (especially drug and weapons offenses), "three-strikes-and-you're-out " laws that mandated long prison sentences for repeat offenders, and truth-in-sentencing statutes that required offenders to serve a larger portion of the sentence before being released.

This process of experimentation and reform revolutionized sentencing in the United States. Thirty years ago every state and the federal government had an indeterminate sentencing system and "the word 'sentencing' generally signified a slightly mysterious process which ... involved individualized decisions that judges were uniquely qualified to make."[200] The situation today is much more complex. Sentencing policies and practices vary enormously on a number of dimensions, and there is no longer anything that can be described as the American approach.

The reforms enacted during the past 30 years clearly were *designed* to ameliorate discrimination in sentencing. Sentencing guidelines explicitly prohibit consideration of the offender's race, ethnicity, gender, or social class; they shift the focus of sentencing away from the personal characteristics of the offender to the nature and seriousness of the offense and the culpability of the offender. Mandatory minimum sentence statutes and three-strikes laws are applicable to *all* offenders—regardless of race, ethnicity, gender, or social class—whose offense, conduct, and prior record qualify them for these sentence enhancements. If these laws are applied as intended, legally irrelevant offender characteristics should not affect sentencing decisions in jurisdictions with sentencing guidelines; likewise, offender characteristics should not affect the application of mandatory minimum penalties or three-strikes-and-you're-out provisions.

Race/Ethnicity and the Federal Sentencing Guidelines

'The findings of a comprehensive review of recent federal and state sentencing research suggests that the sentencing reforms have not achieved their goal of eliminating unwarranted racial disparity.[201] Spohn reviewed eight methodologically sophisticated studies of sentences imposed under the federal sentencing guidelines.[202] She found that each of these studies revealed that racial minorities were sentenced more harshly than whites, either for all offenses or for some types of offenses. Moreover, racial disparities were not confined to the decision to incarcerate or not and the length of the prison sentence. Compared to whites, African Americans and Hispanics were less likely to be offered a sentence reduction for acceptance of responsibility[203] or for providing substantial assistance in the prosecution of another offender.[204] Among those who did receive a departure for substantial assistance, the sentence discount that African Americans and Hispanics received was less than the discount that whites received.[205] And African Americans and Hispanics were more likely than whites to be sentenced at or above the minimum sentence indicated by applicable mandatory minimum sentencing provisions.[206]

The fact that significant racial differences were found for each of the various alternative measures of sentence severity is interesting. Although the federal sentencing guidelines severely constrain judges' discretion in deciding between prison and probation and in determining the length of the sentence, they place only minimal restrictions on the ability of judges (and prosecutors) to reduce sentences for substantial assistance or acceptance of responsibility. Mandatory minimum sentences also can be avoided through charge manipulation. As Albonetti notes, "[T]hese process-related decisions offer potential avenues through which prosecutors [and judges] can circumvent guideline-defined sentence outcomes."[207] The validity of this assertion is confirmed by the fact that each of the six federal-level studies that examined an alternative measure of sentence severity found evidence of direct discrimination against both African American and Hispanic offenders.

These findings are confirmed by a study of federal sentencing decisions.[208] Using data on male offenders convicted of drug and nondrug offenses from 1993 to 1996, Steffensmeier and Demuth compared sentence outcomes for four groups of offenders: whites, African Americans, white Hispanics, and African American Hispanics. As shown in Part A of Table 7.6, which presents descriptive data on sentence outcomes, the likelihood of incarceration was substantially longer and the mean prison sentence was significantly shorter for white offenders than for racial minorities. Whites also were more likely than racial minorities to receive a downward departure and a departure for providing substantial assistance.

These differences did not disappear when the authors controlled for offense seriousness, prior criminal record, and other relevant predictors of sentence severity. As shown in Part B of Table 7.6, which presents the differences in the

T A B L E 7.6 **Race/Ethnicity and Sentence Outcomes: Male Offenders in U.S. District Courts, 1993–1996**

A. Descriptive Data

	NONDRUG OFFENSES		HISPANIC		DRUG OFFENSES		HISPANIC	
	White	African American	White	African American	White	African American	White	African American
Percentage imprisoned	67.1	78.1	73.2	75.2	88.1	96.7	95.7	97.2
Mean sentence (months)	44.0	70.6	53.4	77.2	70.5	122.6	78.2	95.3
Downward departure (%)	9.0	5.4	7.7	4.0	5.4	4.8	6.8	6.0
Substantial assistance departure (%)	114.1	10.4	12.8	6.7	38.0	31.2	28.0	26.1

B. Differences in the Probability of Incarceration and Mean Prison Sentence

	NONDRUG OFFENSES		HISPANIC		DRUG OFFENSES		HISPANIC	
	White	African American	White	African American	White	African American	White	African American
Probability of incarceration		+5%	+7%	+6%		+11%	+16%	+20%
Mean prison sentence (difference in months)		+1	+4	+16		+16	+19	+23

SOURCE: Darrell Steffensmeier and Stephen Demuth, "Ethnicity and Sentencing Outcomes in U.S. Federal Courts: Who Is Punished More Harshly?" *American Sociological Review 65* (2000).

likelihood of incarceration and the mean prison sentence for racial minorities compared to whites, racial minorities were sentenced more harshly than whites. The differences were particularly pronounced for drug offenses. African American Hispanics were 20 percent more likely than whites to be sentenced to prison, and their sentences averaged 23 months longer than those imposed on whites. Similarly, white Hispanics faced a 16 percent greater likelihood of incarceration and 19 months longer in prison than whites. African Americans were 11 percent more likely than whites to be sentenced to prison; those who were incarcerated received sentences that averaged 16 months longer than those imposed on whites.[209]

Further analysis revealed that a considerable amount of the differential treatment of Hispanics was due to the fact that they were less likely than whites to receive either downward departures or substantial assistance departures. These findings led Steffensmeier and Demuth to conclude that "the ethnic disparities found in our analysis are real and meaningful—they support our theoretical hypotheses and they also raise some concerns about the equal application of the law and the wherewithal of the sentencing guidelines in reducing sentencing disparities of any kind."[210]

A second study of sentences imposed under the federal sentencing guidelines compared sentence severity for whites, African Americans, Hispanics, Native Americans, and Asian Americans.[211] This study focused on whether the offender received a sentence at the top or the bottom of the guideline range. Under the federal sentencing guidelines, the appropriate sentence is determined by the offender's criminal history category and offense seriousness score; the cell where these two factors intersect reflects the appropriate sentence range. For each cell on the sentencing grid, the maximum of the range cannot exceed the minimum of the range by more than 25 percent or 6 months (whichever is greater). The range of punishment for an offender with an offense seriousness score of 20 and a criminal history score of 4, for example, is 51 to 63 months; if the offense score is 30 and the criminal history score is 6, the range is 168 to 210 months. In imposing sentence, then, the judge could, without departing either upward or downward, sentence the offender to any term between 168 and 210 months.

Everett and Wojtkiewicz divided each sentencing range into fourths and then determined whether the sentence fell into the first, second, third, or fourth quarter of the range. When they looked at the raw data, they found that African Americans, Hispanics, and Native Americans were all more likely than whites to be sentenced at the top of the range; Asians were less likely than whites to be sentenced at the top of the range. The figures were 24.3 percent for African Americans, 22.6 percent for Hispanics, 22.3 percent for Native Americans, 17.3 percent for whites, and 15.0 percent for Asian Americans. The pattern was reversed for sentencing at the bottom of the range: 59.2 percent of African Americans, 59.9 percent of Native Americans, and 60.8 percent of Hispanics were sentenced at the bottom of the range, compared to 68.5 percent of whites and 72.9 percent of Asian Americans.[212]

The authors then controlled for other offender characteristics (gender, age, education, and citizenship status) and for the variables measuring the seriousness of the offense, the offender's criminal history, the type of disposition in the case, and the region of the country in which the case was adjudicated. They found that African Americans, Hispanics, and Native Americans still received longer sentences than whites.[213] They also found that, whereas African Americans received longer sentences than whites for all types of offenses (drug, economic, violent, immigration, and firearms offenses), Hispanics received longer sentences than whites only for economic, drug, and violent crimes, Native Americans received longer sentences than whites only for violent crimes, and Asian Americans received longer sentences than whites only for immigration offenses. These results led the authors to conclude that racial/ethnic bias had not been eliminated by the implementation of the federal sentencing guidelines. Rather, "offenders are sanctioned partially for what they have done (offense characteristics, criminal history), for who they are (race/ethnicity, age, gender) and also for what they may fail to do during the punishment process (plead guilty or express remorse)."[214]

Race/Ethnicity and State Sentencing Reforms

Evidence concerning the impact of state sentencing reforms is inconsistent. Petersilia's[215] analysis of California's determinate sentencing system found that African Americans and Hispanics were more likely than whites to be sentenced to prison; racial minorities who were incarcerated also received longer sentences and served a longer time in prison. An examination of sentences imposed by judges in Minnesota before and after the implementation of guidelines showed that the impact of race and socioeconomic status declined but did not disappear.[216] The authors also found that race affected sentencing indirectly through its effect on prior criminal record and use of a weapon. They concluded that disparities under the guidelines "are slightly more subtle, but no less real."[217] Dixon's[218] study of sentencing under the Minnesota guidelines, however, found that offender race was unrelated to sentence severity.

A series of studies examining sentencing under Pennsylvania's guidelines demonstrates the subtle ways in which race/ethnicity can affect sentence outcomes.[219] As noted earlier, the sentencing guidelines found in Pennsylvania are "looser" than those found in Minnesota or in the federal system; judges in Pennsylvania have considerably more discretion, and thus more opportunities to consider extralegal factors, than do judges in other jurisdictions.

One study used Pennsylvania data to explore the effect of race/ethnicity on the likelihood that the judge would depart from the guidelines.[220] Kramer and Ulmer examined both dispositional departures, in which the guidelines call for incarceration but the judge chooses an alternative to incarceration, and durational departures, in which the judge imposes a jail or prison term that is longer or shorter than the term specified by the guidelines. They found that African American offenders were less likely than white offenders to receive a dispositional departure; the downward durational departures given to African Americans also were smaller than those given to whites. The authors found similar results when they compared the sentences imposed on Hispanic and white offenders.

When Kramer and Ulmer examined the reasons given by judges for departures, they found evidence suggesting that race-linked stereotypes affected these decisions. The most common reasons given for departures were as follows: the

In the Courts: The Constitutionality of Hate-Crime Sentencing Enhancements—*Wisconsin v. Mitchell* (508 U.S. 47 [1993])

In 1989 Todd Mitchell, a 19-year-old African American, and a group of his friends accosted Gregory Reddick, a 14-year-old white boy, beat him severely, and stole his tennis shoes. Mitchell and his friends had just watched the movie, "Mississippi Burning," which depicts Ku Klux Klan terrorism against African Americans in the South during the 1960s. They were standing outside an apartment complex in Kenosha, Wisconsin, discussing the movie, when Reddick walked by. Mitchell asked his friends, "Do you feel hyped up to move on some white people?" He then pointed to Reddick and said, "There goes a white boy....Go get him!" The beating put Reddick in a coma for 4 days and he suffered permanent brain damage.

Mitchell was convicted of aggravated battery, an offense that ordinarily carries a maximum sentence of 2 years in prison. The jury, however, found that Mitchell had intentionally selected his victim because of the boy's race, in violation of Wisconsin's hate-crime statute. That law, which increased the maximum sentence for Mitchell's crime to 7 years, enhances the maximum penalty for an offense whenever the defendant "intentionally selected the person against whom the crime . . . is committed . . . because of the race, religion, color, disability, sexual orientation, national origin, or ancestry of that person" (Wis. Stat. §939.6435[1][b]). The judge sentenced Mitchell to 4 years in prison for the aggravated battery.

Mitchell challenged his conviction and sentence, arguing that the hate-crime statute infringed on his First Amendment right to freedom of speech. The Wisconsin Supreme Court agreed, holding that the statute "violates the First Amendment directly by punishing what the legislature has deemed to be offensive thought." The Court rejected the state's claim that the statute punished only conduct (that is, the intentional selection of a victim on the basis of race) and stated that "the Wisconsin legislature cannot criminalize bigoted thought with which it disagrees."

In 1993 the United States Supreme Court upheld the hate-crime statute and ruled that Mitchell's First Amendment rights were not violated by the application of the sentencing enhancement provision. Writing for a unanimous court, Chief Justice Rehnquist stated that the primary responsibility for determining penalties for criminal behavior rests with the legislature, which can differentiate among crimes based on their seriousness and the degree of harm they inflict on victims and on society. Justice Rehnquist noted that this was the case with the hate-crime statute: The Wisconsin legislature had decided that bias-inspired conduct was more harmful and thus had enhanced the penalties for these types of crimes. Although he acknowledged that "a defendant's abstract beliefs, however obnoxious to most people, may not be taken into consideration by a sentencing judge," Rehnquist stated that trial judges are not barred from considering the defendant's racial animus toward his victim. (The decision in this case is available online at http://straylight.law.cornell.edu/. Search for *Wisconsin v. Mitchell*.)

defendant expressed remorse or appears to be a good candidate for rehabilitation; the defendant pled guilty; the defendant is caring for dependents; the defendant is employed; and the defendant's prior record is less serious than his or her criminal history score suggests. As the authors note, "When these reasons are given by judges, they are given more often for women, whites, and (obviously) those who pleaded guilty."[221] For a discussion of another type of race-linked sentencing statute, see "In the Courts: The Constitutionality of Hate-Crime Sentencing Enhancements—*Wisconsin v. Mitchell* (508 U.S. 47 [1993])."

In discussing the ways in which these reasons reflected race-linked stereotypes, the authors state:

> Although these judges do not explicitly mention factors such as race or gender, it is plausible that the process of 'sizing up' a defendant's 'character and attitude' in terms of whether he or she is a candidate for a departure below guidelines may involve the use of race and gender stereotypes and the behavioral expectations they mobilize ..."[222]

Kramer and Ulmer conclude that "... departures below guidelines are an important locus of race and gender differences in sentencing."[223]

Have Sentencing Guidelines Increased the Likelihood of Racial Discrimination?

Michael Tonry has suggested that sentence guidelines actually may have exacerbated the problem of racial disparity in sentencing. His critique of sentence guidelines focuses on the prohibition against consideration of offenders' "special circumstances."[224] Under sentence guidelines, the harshness of the sentence depends on the severity of the offense and the offender's prior criminal record; judges are not supposed to consider factors such as the offender's employment status, marital status, family situation, or education.

Although Tonry acknowledged that these restrictions were designed to prevent unduly lenient sentences for affluent offenders and unduly harsh sentences for poor offenders, he argued that in reality they have harmed "disadvantaged and minority offenders, especially those who have to some degree overcome dismal life chances." Tonry characterized these restrictions as "mistakes":

> They may have been necessary mistakes that showed us how to protect against aberrantly severe penalties and exposed the injustices that result when sentencing shifts its focus from the offender to the offense. Mistakes they were, however, and we now know how to do better.[225]

"Doing better," according to Tonry, means allowing judges to consider factors other than the offender's crime and prior criminal record. Tonry argued that "neither offenders nor punishments come in standard cases"[226] and stated that a just punishment system would require judges to consider the offender's personal circumstances and the effects of punishment on the offender and the offender's family (Box 7.8). He asserted that a just system would allow judges to mitigate sentences for disadvantaged inner-city youth, who face greater temptations to commit crimes than do affluent suburban youth. It also would allow judges to mitigate sentences for "offenders from deprived backgrounds who have achieved some personal successes."[227] The problem is that current federal and state sentence guidelines usually do not allow judges to make these distinctions.

It thus appears that reformers' hopes for determinate sentencing and sentence guidelines have not been fully realized. Although overt discrimination against African Americans is less likely, discrimination in sentencing has not disappeared.

B O X 7.8 **The Illusion of Like-Situated Offenders**

Michael Tonry suggested that those who call for proportionality in punishment mistakenly assume that it is possible to place individuals into a manageable number of categories composed of "like-situated offenders." He suggested that this is an "illusion" because "neither offenders nor punishments come in standard cases."

> Consider a minority offender charged with theft who grew up in a single-parent, welfare-supported household, who has several siblings in prison, and who was formerly drug dependent, but who has been living in a common-law marriage for 5 years, has two children whom he supports, and who has worked steadily for 3 years at a service station—first as an attendant, then an assistant mechanic, and now a mechanic. None of these personal characteristics was supposed to influence the sentencing decision, and certainly not to justify imposing a noncustodial sentence on a presumed prison-bound offender.

Tonry also objected to the fact that sentence guidelines do not take account of the "collateral effects" of punishment.

> Incarceration for a drug crime for a woman raising children by herself may result in the breakup of her family and the placement of her children in foster homes or institutions or in homes of relatives who will not be responsible care providers. Incarceration of an employed father and husband may mean loss of the family's income and car, perhaps the breakup of a marriage . . .

According to Tonry, "To ignore that collateral effects of punishments vary widely among seemingly like-situated offenders is to ignore things that most people find important."

SOURCE: Michael Tonry, *Malign Neglect* (New York: Oxford University Press, 1995), pp. 155–157.

As Zatz has concluded, the sentencing procedures currently being used "are less blatantly biased than were their predecessors, and are cloaked with the legitimacy accruing from formalized rules ... Differential processing and treatment is now veiled by legitimacy, but it is a legitimacy in which certain biases have become rationalized and institutionalized."[228]

CONCLUSION

Despite dozens of studies investigating the relationship between defendant race and sentence severity, a definitive answer to the question, "Are racial minorities sentenced more harshly than whites?" remains elusive. Although a number of studies have uncovered evidence of racial discrimination in sentencing, others have found that there are no significant racial differences.

The failure of research to produce uniform findings of racial discrimination in sentencing has led to conflicting conclusions. Some researchers assert that racial discrimination in sentencing has declined over time and contend that the predictive power of race, once relevant legal factors are taken into account, is quite low. Other researchers claim that discrimination has not declined or disappeared but simply has become more subtle and difficult to detect. These researchers argue that discrimination against racial minorities is not universal but is confined to certain types of cases, certain types of settings, and certain types of defendants.

We assert that the latter explanation is more convincing. We suggest that, although the sentencing process in most jurisdictions today is not characterized by overt or systematic racism, racial discrimination in sentencing has not been eliminated. We argue that sentencing decisions in the 1990s reflect *contextual discrimination.* Judges in some jurisdictions continue to impose harsher sentences on racial minorities who murder or rape whites and more lenient sentences on racial minorities who victimize members of their own racial/ethnic group. Judges in some jurisdictions continue to impose racially biased sentences in less serious cases; in these "borderline cases" racial minorities get prison, whereas whites get probation. In jurisdictions with sentencing guidelines, judges depart from the presumptive sentence less often when the offender is African American or Hispanic than if the offender is white. Judges, in other words, continue to take race into account, either explicitly or implicitly, when determining the appropriate sentence.

It thus appears that although flagrant racism in sentencing has been eliminated, equality under the law has not been achieved. Today, whites who commit crimes against racial minorities are not beyond the reach of the criminal justice system, African Americans suspected of crimes against whites do not receive "justice" at the hands of white lynching mobs, and racial minorities who victimize other racial minorities are not immune from punishment. Despite these significant changes, inequities persist. Racial minorities who find themselves in the arms of the law continue to suffer discrimination in sentencing.

DISCUSSION QUESTIONS

1. Why is evidence of racial disparity in sentencing not necessarily evidence of racial discrimination in sentencing? What are the alternative explanations?

2. Some researchers argue that racial stereotypes affect the ways in which decisionmakers, including criminal justice officials, evaluate the behavior of racial minorities. What are the stereotypes associated with African Americans? Hispanics? Native Americans? Asian Americans? How might these stereotypes affect judges' sentencing decisions?

3. Do you agree or disagree with the argument (see Box 7.2) that crime seriousness and prior criminal record are not legally relevant variables?

4. Based on Spohn's (2000) review of research on race and sentencing, how would you answer the question, "When does race matter?"

5. Research reveals that young, unemployed African American and Hispanic males pay a higher punishment penalty than other types of offenders. What accounts for this?

6. Spohn and Spears's study of sentencing decisions in sexual assault cases revealed that judges imposed the harshest sentences on African Americans who sexually assaulted whites (strangers or nonstrangers) and on African Americans who sexually assaulted African American strangers. They imposed much more lenient sentences on African Americans who sexually assaulted African American friends, relatives, and acquaintances and on whites who victimized other others (strangers or nonstrangers). How would you explain this pattern of results?

7. As discussed in Box 7.6, African Americans are more likely than whites to be willing to serve time in prison rather than be sentenced to some alternative to incarceration such as electronic monitoring or intensive supervision probation. What accounts for these racial differences in perceptions of the severity of sanctions?

8. The federal sentencing guidelines currently mandate a 5-year minimum prison sentence for possession of 5 grams of crack cocaine or 500 grams of powder cocaine. Is this policy racially biased? Should the 100-to-1 ratio be reduced? Should it be eliminated?

9. Those who champion the appointment/election of racial minorities to the bench argue that African American and Hispanic judges could make a difference. Why? Does research comparing the sentencing decisions of white judges to those of African American or Hispanic judges confirm or refute this assumption?

10. The sentencing reforms adopted during the past three decades were designed to structure discretion and eliminate unwarranted disparity in sentence outcomes. Has this goal been achieved?

11. Do you agree with the Supreme Court's decision (*Wisconsin v. Mitchell*) upholding sentencing enhancements for hate crimes? Why or why not?

NOTES

1. The Sentencing Project, "Schools and Prisons: Fifty Years after *Brown v. Board of Education*." Available at http://www.sentencingproject.org/pdfs/brownvboard.pdf.

2. Ibid., p. 5.

3. Ibid.

4. Ibid., p. 5.

5. Bureau of Justice Statistics, *Prison and Jail Inmates at Midyear 2004* (Washington, DC: U.S. Department of Justice, 2005), p. 1.

6. Ibid., p. 11.

7. Alfred Blumstein, Jacqueline Cohen, Susan E. Martin, and Michael Tonry, *Research on Sentencing: The Search for Reform*, Volume I (Washington, DC: National Academy Press, 1983).

8. Michael Tonry, *Malign Neglect: Race, Crime, and Punishment in America* (New York: Oxford University Press, 1995), p. 49.

9. Bureau of Justice Statistics, *Prison and Jail Inmates at Midyear 2004* (Washington, DC: U.S. Department of Justice, 2005), Table 14.

10. Cassia Spohn, *Charging and Sentencing Decisions in Three U.S. District Courts: A Test of the Assumption of Uniformity in the Federal Sentencing Process*. Final Report to the National Science Foundation, 2004.

11. Paula Kautt and Cassia Spohn, "*Crack*-ing Down on Black Drug Offenders? Testing for Interactions Among Offenders' Race, Drug Type, and Sentencing Strategy in Federal Drug Sentences," *Justice Quarterly* 19 (2000): 2–35.

12. Bureau of Justice Statistics, *State Court Sentencing of Convicted Felons, 2002* (Washington, DC: U.S. Department of Justice, 2004), p. 24.

13. Cassia Spohn and Miriam DeLone, "When Does Race Matter? An Analysis of the Conditions Under Which Race Affects Sentence Severity," *Sociology of Crime, Law, and Deviance* 2 (2000): 3–37.

14. Marjorie Zatz, "The Changing Forms of Racial/Ethnic Biases in Sentencing," *Journal of Research in Crime and Delinquency* 25 (1987): 69–92, p. 69.

15. Thorsten Sellin, "Race Prejudice in the Administration of Justice," *American Journal of Sociology* 41 (1935): 212–217, p. 217.

16. John Hagan, "Extra-legal Attributes and Criminal Sentencing: An Assessment of a Sociological Viewpoint," *Law & Society Review* 8 (1974): 357–383; Gary Kleck, "Racial Discrimination in Sentencing: A Critical Evaluation of the Evidence with Additional Evidence on the Death Penalty," *American Sociology Review* 43 (1981): 783–805.

17. John Hagan and Kristin Bumiller, "Making Sense of Sentencing: A Review and Critique of Sentencing Research," in *Research on Sentencing: The Search for Reform*, Alfred Blumstein, Jacqueline Cohen, Susan Martin, and Michael Tonry, eds. (Washington, DC: National Academy Press, 1983).

18. Blumstein, Cohen, Martin, and Tonry, *Research on Sentencing: The Search for Reform*, p. 93.

19. Zatz, "The Changing Forms of Racial/Ethnic Biases in Sentencing."

20. Ibid., p. 87.

21. Theodore G. Chiricos and Charles Crawford, "Race and Imprisonment: A Contextual Assessment of the Evidence," in *Ethnicity, Race, and Crime: Perspectives Across Time and Place*, Darnell F. Hawkins, ed. (Albany: State University of New York Press, 1995).

22. Ibid., p. 282.

23. Ibid., p. 300.

24. Ibid., p. 300.

25. Spohn, "Thirty Years of Sentencing Reform: A Quest for a Racially Neutral Sentencing Process," in *Policies, Processes, and Decisions of the Criminal Justice System*, vol. 3, *Criminal Justice 2000* (Washington, DC: U.S. Department of Justice, 2000).

26. Hagan and Bumiller, "Making Sense of Sentencing," p. 21.

27. Spohn, "Thirty Years of Sentencing Reform," pp. 455–456.

28. Ibid., p. 458.

29. Ibid., pp. 460–461.

30. Ibid., pp. 466–467.

31. Ibid., p. 469.

32. Ibid., p. 461.

33. Ibid., pp. 469–473.

34. Blumstein, et al., *Research on Sentencing*, vol. 1, p. 93.

35. Darnell F. Hawkins, "Beyond Anomalies: Rethinking the Conflict Perspective on Race and Criminal Punishment," *Social Forces* 65 (1987): 719–745.

36. Ibid., p. 724.

37. Richard Quinney, *The Social Reality of Crime* (Boston: Little, Brown, 1970), p. 18.

38. Hawkins, "Beyond Anomalies," p. 736.

39. Ruth Peterson and John Hagan, "Changing Conceptions of Race: Toward an Account of Anomalous Findings in Sentencing Research," *American Sociological Review* 49 (1984): 56–70.

40. Hawkins, "Beyond Anomalies."

41. Peterson and Hagan, "Changing Conceptions of Race," p. 69.

42. Cassia Spohn and Miriam DeLone, "When Does Race Matter? An Analysis of the Conditions Under Which Race Affects Sentence Severity," *Sociology of Crime, Law and Deviance 2* (2000): 3–37.

43. These estimated probabilities are adjusted for the effects of the other legal and extralegal variables included in the multivariate analysis. See Spohn and DeLone, "When Does Race Matter?" for a description of the procedures used to calculate the probabilities.

44. Spohn and DeLone, "When Does Race Matter?" p. 29.

45. Ibid.

46. Ibid., p. 30.

47. Darrell Steffensmeier and Stephen Demuth, "Ethnicity and Judges' Sentencing Decisions: Hispanic–Black–White Comparison," *Criminology 39*: 145–178.

48. Ibid.

49. Ibid., p. 153.

50. Ibid., Table 2.

51. Ibid., Table 3.

52. Ibid., p. 170.

53. Ibid., p. 168.

54. David F. Greenberg, "'Justice' and Criminal Justice," in *Crime Control and Criminal Justice: The Delicate Balance*, Darnell F. Hawkins, Samuel L. Meyers Jr., and Randolph N. Stone (Westport, CT: Greenwood, 2002), p. 330.

55. Ibid., p. 331.

56. Iris Marion Young, *Justice and the Politics of Difference* (Princeton, NJ: Princeton University Press, 1990), p. 59.

57. Carol Chiago Lujan, "Stereotyping by Politicians: Or 'The Only Real Indian Is the Stereotypical Indian," in *Images of Color, Images of Crime*, Coramae Richey Mann and Marjorie Zatz (Los Angeles: Roxbury, 1998).

58. Steve Feimer, Frank Pommersheim, and Steve Wise, "Marking Time: Does Race Make a Difference? A Study of Disparate Sentencing in South Dakota," *Journal of Crime and Justice 13* (1990): 86–102; Frank Pommersheim and Steve Wise, "Going to the Penitentiary: A Study of Disparate Sentencing in South Dakota," *Criminal Justice and Behavior 16* (1989): 155–165.

59. B. Swift and G. Bickel, *Comparative Parole Treatment of American Indians and Non-Indians at United States Federal Prisons.* (Washington, DC: Bureau of Social Science Research, 1974.)

60. Alexander Alvarez and Ronet D. Bachman, "American Indians and Sentencing Disparity: An Arizona Test," *Journal of Criminal Justice 24* (1996): 549–561; Edwin L. Hall and Albert A. Simkins, "Inequality in the Types of Sentences Received by Native Americans and Whites," *Criminology 13*: 199–222.

61. Ronet D. Bachman, Alexander Alvarez, and C. Perkins, "The Discriminatory Imposition of the Law: Does It Affect Sentence Outcomes for American Indians?" in *Native Americans, Crime and Justice*, Marianne O. Nielsen and Robert A. Silverman, eds. (Boulder, CO: Westview Press, 1996); Timothy S. Bynum and Raymond Paternoster, "Discrimination Revisited: An Exploration of Frontstage and Backstage Criminal Justice Decision Making," *Sociology and Social Research 69* (1984): 90–108.

62. Alvarez and Bachman, "American Indians and Sentencing Disparity."

63. Ibid., p. 558.

64. Ibid.

65. Zatz, "The Convergence of Race, Ethnicity, Gender, and Class on Court Decisionmaking: Looking Toward the 21st Century," in *Policies, Processes, and Decisions of the Criminal Justice System*, vol. 3, *Criminal Justice 2000* (Washington, DC: U.S. Department of Justice, 2000).

66. Ibid., p. 540.

67. John H. Kramer and Darrell Steffensmeier, "Race and Imprisonment Decisions," *The Sociological Quarterly 34* (1993): 357–376.

68. Darrell Steffensmeier, John Kramer, and Cathy Streifel, "Gender and Imprisonment Decisions," *Criminology 31* (1993): 411–446.

69. Darrell Steffensmeier, John Kramer, and Jeffery Ulmer, "Age Differences in Criminal Sentencing," *Justice Quarterly 12* (1995): 701–719.

70. Darrell Steffensmeier, Jeffery Ulmer, and John Kramer, "The Interaction of Race, Gender, and Age in Criminal Sentencing: The Punishment Cost of Being Young, Black, and Male," *Criminology 36* (1998): 363–397.

71. Kramer and Steffensmeier, "Race and Imprisonment Decisions," p. 370.

72. Ibid., p. 368.

73. Ibid., p. 373.

74. Ibid.

75. Ibid., p. 789.

76. Ibid., p. 768.

77. Cassia Spohn and David Holleran, "The Imprisonment Penalty Paid by Young Unemployed Black and Hispanic Male Offenders," *Criminology 38* (2000): 281–306.

78. Ibid., pp. 291–293.

79. Ibid., p. 301.

80. Quinney, *The Social Reality of Crime*, p. 142.

81. Dario Melossi, "An Introduction: Fifty Years Later, Punishment and Social Structure in Contemporary Analysis," *Contemporary Crises 13* (1989): 311–326.

82. Gregg Barak, "Between the Waves: Mass-Mediated Themes of Crime and Justice," *Social Justice 21* (1994): 133–147.

83. Spitzer, "Toward a Marxian Theory of Deviance," *Social Problems 22* (1975): 638–651, p. 645.

84. Ibid., p. 646.

85. Steven Box and Chris Hale, "Unemployment, Imprisonment, and Prison Overcrowding," *Contemporary Crises 9* (1985): 209–228.

86. Ibid., p. 217.

87. Steffensmeier, Ulmer, and Kramer, "The Interaction of Race, Gender and Age in Criminal Sentencing," p. 789.

88. Ibid., p. 787.

89. Spohn and Holleran, "The Imprisonment Penalty Paid by Young, Unemployed Black and Hispanic Male Offenders," p. 301.

90. Gunnar Myrdal, *An American Dilemma: The Negro Problem and Modern Democracy* (New York: Harper and Brothers, 1944), p. 551.

91. Ibid., p. 553.

92. Susan Brownmiller, *Against Our Will: Men, Women and Rape* (New York: Bantam Books, 1975).

93. Jennifer Wriggins, "Rape, Racism, and the Law," *Harvard Women's Law Journal 6* (1983): 103–41.

94. Wriggins, "Rape, Racism, and the Law."

95. Ibid., p. 109.

96. Marvin E. Wolfgang and Marc Reidel, "Race, Judicial Discretion and the Death Penalty," *Annals of the American Academy 407* (1973): 119–133; Marvin E. Wolfgang and Marc Reidel, "Rape, Race and the Death Penalty in Georgia," *American Journal of Orthopsychiatry 45* (1975): 658–668.

97. Brownmiller, *Against Our Will*, p. 237.

98. Gary D. LaFree, *Rape and Criminal Justice: The Social Construction of Sexual Assault* (Belmont, CA: Wadsworth, 1989).

99. Anthony Walsh "The Sexual Stratification Hypothesis and Sexual Assault in Light of the Changing Conceptions of Race," *Criminology 25* (1987): 153–173.

100. Ibid., p. 167.

101. Cassia Spohn and Jeffrey Spears, "The Effect of Offender and Victim Characteristics on Sexual Assault Case Processing Decisions," *Justice Quarterly 13* (1996): 649–679.

102. Ibid., p. 663.

103. Ibid., p. 675.

104. Ibid., p. 665.

105. Peterson and Hagan, "Changing Conceptions of Race," p. 67.

106. Peter B. Wood and David C. May, "Racial Differences in Perceptions of the Severity of Sanctions: A Comparison of Prison with Alternatives," *Justice Quarterly 20* (2003): 605–631.

107. Ibid., p. 618.

108. Ibid., pp. 623–624.

109. Ibid., p. 628.

110. Hawkins, "Beyond Anomalies," p. 719.

111. Harry Kalven Jr. and Hans Zeisel, *The American Jury* (Boston: Little, Brown: 1966).

112. Cassia Spohn and Jerry Cederblom, "Racial Disparities in Sentencing: A Test of the Liberation Hypothesis," *Justice Quarterly 8* (1991): 305–327.

113. Ibid., p. 323.

114. Michael J. Leiber and Anita N. Blowers, "Race and Misdemeanor Sentencing," *Criminal Justice Policy Review 14* (2003): 464–485.

115. Ibid., pp. 475–477.

116. Michael Tonry, *Malign Neglect: Race, Crime, and Punishment in America* (New York: Oxford University Press, 1995), p. 105.

117. Ibid., p. 115.

118. Jerome G. Miller, *Search and Destroy: African-American Males in the Criminal Justice System* (Cambridge, England: Cambridge University Press, 1996), p. 83.

119. Marc Mauer, *Race to Incarcerate*, (New York: The New Press, 1999), p. 143.

120. William J. Chambliss, "Crime Control and Ethnic Minorities: Legitimizing Racial Oppression by Creating Moral Panics" in *Ethnicity, Race, and Crime: Perspectives Across Time and Place*, Darnell F. Hawkins, ed. (Albany, NY: State University of New York Press, 1995); Tonry, *Malign Neglect.*

121. Phillip Jenkins, "'The Ice Age:' The Social Construction of a Drug Panic," *Justice Quarterly 11* (1994): 7–31.

122. For a review of this research, see Theordore G. Chiricos and Miriam DeLone, "Labor Surplus and Punishment: A Review and Assessment of Theory and Evidence," *Social Problems 39* (1992): 421–446.

123. Human Rights Watch. *Punishment and Prejudice: Racial Disparities in the War on Drugs*, vol. 12, no. 2 (G), May 2000. Available at http://www.hrw.org/reports/2000/usa/.

124. John Gould, "Zone defense: drug–free school zones were supposed to keep dealers away from kids. But what happens when the zones engulf whole cities," *Washington Monthly*, June 11, 2002.

125. William Brownsberger and Susan Aromaa, "An Empirical Study of the School Zone Law in Three Cities in Massachusetts. Available online at http://www.jointogether.org/sa/files/pdf/schoolzone.pdf.

126. Vincent Schiraldi and Jason Ziedenberg, *Costs and Benefits? The Impact of Drug Imprisonment in New Jersey* (Washington, DC: Justice Policy Institute, 2003).

127. Theordore G. Chiricos and William D. Bales, "Unemployment and Punishment: An Empirical Assessment," *Criminology 29* (1991): 701–724; John H. Kramer and Darrell Steffensmeier, "Race and Imprisonment Decisions"; Martha Myers, "Symbolic Policy and the Sentencing of Drug Offenders," *Law & Society Review 23* (1989): 295–315; Sara Steen, Rodney L. Engen, and Randy R. Gainey,

"Images of Danger and Culpability: Racial Stereotyping, Case Processing, and Criminal Sentencing," *Criminology 45* (2005): 435–468; James D. Unnever, "Direct and Organizational Discrimination in the Sentencing of Drug Offenders," *Social Problems 30* (1982): 212–225 [note: Unnever found significant differences between African Americans and whites but not between Hispanics and whites].

128. Cassia Spohn and Jeffrey Spears, "Sentencing of Drug Offenders in Three Cities: Does Race/Ethnicity Make a Difference?" in *Crime Control and Criminal Justice: The Delicate Balance*, Darnell F. Hawkins, Samuel L. Meyers, Jr. and Randolph N. Stone, eds. (Westport, CT: Greenwood, 2002); Unnever "Direct and Organizational Discrimination in the Sentencing of Drug Offenders."

129. See the earlier discussion of Peterson and Hagan, "Changing Conceptions of Race."

130. Spohn and Spears, "Sentencing of Drug Offenders in Three Cities;" Steen, et al., "Images of Danger and Culpability."

131. Celesta A. Albonetti, "Sentencing Under the Federal Sentencing Guidelines: Effects of Defendant Characteristics, Guilty Pleas, and Departures on Sentence Outcomes for Drug Offenses, 1991–1992," *Law & Society Review 31* (1997): 789–822.

132. Spohn and Spears, "Sentencing of Drug Offenders in Three Cities," p. 29.

133. Ibid.

134. See William J. Chambliss, "Crime Control and Ethnic Minorities" and Tonry, *Malign Neglect*.

135. Spohn and Spears, "Sentencing of Drug Offenders in Three Cities," p. 29.

136. Ibid. pp. 29–30.

137. Jeffrey S. Adler, "The Dynamite, Wreckage, and Scum in our Cities: The Social Construction of Deviance in Industrial America," *Justice Quarterly 11* (1994): 33–49.

138. Steen, Engen, and Gainey, pp. 441–444.

139. Ibid., p. 444.

140. Ibid., Table 2.

141. Ibid., p. 454.

142. Ibid., p. 460.

143. Ibid., p. 461.

144. Ibid., p. 464.

145. Randall Kennedy, "Changing Images of the State: Criminal Law and Racial Discrimination: A Comment," *Harvard Law Review* 107(1994): 1255, 1278. See also Randall Kennedy, *Race, Crime, and the Law* (New York: Vintage Books, 1997).

146. *Omaha World Herald*, April 17, 1993, p. 1.

147. *U.S. v. Armstrong*, 116 S.Ct. 1480, 1996.

148. United States Sentencing Commission, *Report to the Congress: Cocaine and Federal Sentencing Policy* (Washington, DC: U.S. Sentencing Commission, 2002), p. viii.

149. Ibid.

150. Albonetti, "Sentencing Under the Federal Sentencing Guidelines."

151. 28 U.S.C, 991(b)(1)(B)(Supp. 1993).

152. Albonetti, "Sentencing Under the Federal Sentencing Guidelines," p. 790.

153. Ibid.

154. Ibid., p. 780.

155. Albonetti notes (p. 817) that most of the departures in these cases were "judicial decisions to comply with prosecutorial motions based on the defendant having provided substantial assistance to the government in the prosecution of others."

156. Ibid., p. 818.

157. Ibid., pp. 818–819.

158. Linn Washington, *Black Judges on Justice: Perspectives from the Bench*, (New York: The New Press, 1994), p. 11.

159. Ibid., pp. 11–12.

160. George Crockett, "The Role of the Black Judge," in *The Criminal Justice System and Blacks*, D. Georges-Abeyie, ed. (New York: Clark Boardman, 1984), p. 393.

161. Susan Welch, Michael Combs, and John Gruhl, "Do Black Judges Make a Difference?" *American Journal of Political Science 32* (1988): 126–136.

162. Crockett, "The Role of the Black Judge"; Welch, Combs, and Gruhl, "Do Black Judges Make a Difference?"

163. Michael David Smith, *Race Versus Robe: The Dilemma of Black Judges* (Port Washington, NY: Associated Faculty Press, 1983).

164. Cited in Smith, *Race Versus Robe*, p. 80.

165. Cited in Smith, *Race Versus Robe*, p. 81.

166. Thomas G. Walker and Deborah J. Barrow, "The Diversification of the Federal Bench: Policy and Process Ramifications," *Journal of Politics 47* (1985): 596–617.

167. Ibid., pp. 613–614.

168. Jon Gottschall, "Carter's Judicial Appointments: The Influence of Affirmative Action and Merit Selection on Voting on the U.S. Courts of Appeals," *Judicature 67* (1983): 165–173.

169. Ibid., p. 168.

170. Ibid., p. 173.

171. Charles Donald Engle, *Criminal Justice in the City: A Study of Sentence Severity and Variation in the Philadelphia Court System.* (Ph.D. dissertation, Temple University, 1971); Cassia Spohn, "Decision Making in Sexual Assault Cases: Do Black and Female Judges Make a Difference?" *Women & Criminal Justice 2* (1990): 83–105; Thomas M. Uhlman, "Black Elite Decision Making: The Case of Trial Judges," *American Journal of Political Science 22* (1978): 884–895.

172. Engle, *Criminal Justice in the City.*

173. Ibid., pp. 226–227.

174. Thomas M. Uhlman, *Racial Justice: Black Judges and Defendants in an Urban Trial Court* (Lexington, MA: Lexington Books, 1979).

175. Ibid., p. 71.

176. Welch, Combs, and Gruhl, "Do Black Judges Make a Difference?"

177. Ibid., p. 134.

178. Ibid.

179. Jeffrey W. Spears, *Diversity in the Courtroom: A Comparison of the Sentencing Decisions of Black and White Judges and Male and Female Judges in Cook County Circuit Court.* (PhD dissertation, University of Nebraska at Omaha, 1999).

180. Ibid., p. 135.

181. Cassia Spohn, "The Sentencing Decisions of Black and White Judges: Expected and Unexpected Similarities," *Law & Society Review 24* (1990): 1197–1216.

182. Ibid., p. 1206.

183. Ibid., p. 1211.

184. Ibid., p. 1212–1213.

185. Ibid., p. 1213.

186. Ibid., p. 1214.

187. Ibid.

188. Malcolm D. Holmes, Harmon M. Hosch, Howard C. Daudistel, Dolores A. Perez, and Joseph B. Graves, "Judges' Ethnicity and Minority Sentencing: Evidence Concerning Hispanics," *Social Science Quarterly 74* (1993): 496–506.

189. Ibid., p. 502.

190. Uhlman, "Black Elite Decision Making," p. 893.

191. Bruce McM. Wright, "A Black Broods on Black Judges," *57 Judicature* (1973): pp. 22–23.

192. Samuel Walker, *Taming the System: The Control of Discretion in Criminal Justice, 1950–1990* (New York: Oxford University Press, 1993), p. 112.

193. U.S. Department of Justice, Bureau of Justice Assistance, *National Assessment of*

Structured Sentencing, (Washington, DC: Government Printing Office, 1996), p. 6.

194. American Friends Service Committee, *Struggle for Justice: A Report on Crime and Punishment in America* (Boston: Little, Brown, 2971); Kenneth C. Davis, *Discretionary Justice: A Preliminary Inquiry* (Baton Rouge: Louisiana State University Press, 1969); Marvin Frankel, *Criminal Sentences: Law Without Order* (New York: Hill and Wang, 1972).

195. Tonry, *Malign Neglect,* p. 164.

196. See, for example, Ernest van den Haag, *Punishing Criminals: Confronting a Very Old and Painful Question* (New York: Basic Books, 1975); James Q. Wilson, *Thinking about Crime* (New York: Basic Books, 1975).

197. Andrew von Hirsch, *Doing Justice: The Choice of Punishments* (New York: Hill and Wang, 1976).

198. Robert Martinson, "What Works? Questions and Answers about Prison Reform," *Public Interest 24* (1974): 22–54.

199. Walker, *Taming the System,* p. 123.

200. Michael Tonry, *Sentencing Matters,* (New York: Oxford University Press, 1996), p. 3.

201. Spohn, "Thirty Years of Sentencing Reform."

202. The eight studies of federal sentencing decisions included in the review were the following: Albonetti, "Sentencing Under the Federal Sentencing Guidelines;" Ronald S. Everett and Barbara C. Nienstedt, "Race, Remorse, and Sentence Reduction: Is Saying You're Sorry Enough?" *Justice Quarterly 16* (1999): 99–122; Patrick Langan, "Sentence Reductions for Drug Traffickers for Assisting Federal Prosecutors" (unpublished manuscript); Linda D. Maxfield and John H. Kramer, *Substantial Assistance: An Empirical Yardstick Gauging Equity in Current Federal Policy and Practice* (Washington, DC: U.S. Sentencing Commission, 1998); Douglas C. McDonald and Kenneth E. Carlson,

Sentencing in Federal Courts: When Does Race Matter? (Washington, DC: U.S. Department of Justice, 1993); Brent L. Smith and Kelly R. Damphouse, "Punishing Political Offenders: The Effect of Political Motive on Federal Sentencing Decisions," *Criminology 34* (1996): 289–321; U.S. Sentencing Commission, *Special Report to the Congress: Mandatory Minimum Penalties in the Federal Criminal Justice System* (Washington, DC: U.S. Sentencing Commission, 1991); U.S. Sentencing Commission, *Substantial Assistance Departures in the United States Courts* (Washington, DC: U.S. Sentencing Commission, 1995).

203. Everett and Nienstedt, "Race, Remorse, and Sentence Reduction: Is Saying You're Sorry Enough?"

204. Langan, "Sentence Reductions for Drug Traffickers for Assisting Federal Prosecutors" Maxfield and Kramer, *Substantial Assistance: An Empirical Yardstick Gauging Equity in Current Federal Policy and Practice*; U.S. Sentencing Commission, *Substantial Assistance Departures in the United States Courts.*

205. Maxfield and Kramer, *Substantial Assistance: An Empirical Yardstick Gauging Equity in Current Federal Policy and Practice.*

206. U.S. Sentencing Commission, *Special Report to the Congress: Mandatory Minimum Penalties in the Federal Criminal Justice System.*

207. Albonetti, "Sentencing Under the Federal Sentencing Guidelines," p. 790.

208. Darrell Steffensmeier and Stephen Demuth, "Ethnicity and Sentencing Outcomes in U.S. Federal Courts: Who Is Punished More Harshly?" *American Sociological Review 65* (2000): 705–729.

209. Ibid., p. 718.

210. Ibid., p. 725.

211. Ronald S. Everett and Roger A. Wojtkiewicz, "Difference, Disparity, and Race/Ethnic Bias in Federal Sentencing," *Journal of Quantitative Criminology 18* (2002): 189–211.

212. Ibid., Table I.

213. Ibid., Table III.

214. Ibid., p. 208.

215. Joan Petersilia, *Racial Disparities in the Criminal Justice System* (Santa Monica, CA: RAND, 1983).

216. Terance D. Miethe and Charles A. Moore, "Socioeconomic Disparities Under Determinate Sentencing Systems: A Comparison of Preguideline and Postguideline Practices in Minnesota," *Criminology 23* (1985): 337–363.

217. Ibid., p. 358.

218. Jo Dixon, "The Organizational Context of Criminal Sentencing," *American Journal of Sociology 100* (1995): 1157–1198.

219. Kramer and Steffensmeier, "Race and Imprisonment Decisions"; John H. Kramer and Jeffery T. Ulmer, "Sentencing Disparity and Departures from Guidelines," *Justice Quarterly 13* (1996): 81–106; Jeffery T. Ulmer and John H. Kramer, "Court Communities Under Sentencing Guidelines: Dilemmas of Formal Rationality and Sentencing Disparity," *Criminology 34* (1996): 383–408.

220. Kramer and Ulmer, "Sentencing Disparity and Departures from Guidelines."

221. Ibid., p. 99.

222. Ibid.

223. Ibid., p. 101.

224. Tonry, *Malign Neglect*, pp. 170–172.

225. Tonry, *Malign Neglect*, p. 190.

226. Tonry, *Malign Neglect*, p. 155.

227. Tonry, *Malign Neglect*, p. 160.

228. Zatz, "The Changing Forms of Racial/Ethnic Biases in Sentencing," p. 87.

8

⚵

The Color of Death
Race and the Death Penalty

> We may not be capable of devising procedural or substantive rules
> to prevent the more subtle and often unconscious forms of racism from
> creeping into the system . . . discrimination and arbitrariness could not be
> purged from the administration of capital punishment without sacrificing
> the equally essential component of fairness—individualized sentencing.
> —SUPREME COURT JUSTICE HARRY BLACKMUN[1]

In January 2003, Illinois Governor George Ryan ignited national debate by announcing that he had commuted the sentences of all of the state's 167 death row inmates to life in prison.[2] He justified his unprecedented and highly controversial decision, which came 3 years after he announced a moratorium on executions, by stating that "our capital system is haunted by the demon of error: error in determining guilt and error in determining who among the guilty deserves to die." Governor Ryan, who left office 2 days after making the announcement, also stated that he was concerned about the effects of race and poverty on death penalty decisions. He acknowledged that his decision would be unpopular but stated that he felt he had no choice but to strike a blow in "what is shaping up to be one of the great civil rights struggles of our time."

Similar views were expressed by Supreme Court Justice Harry A. Blackmun, who announced in February 1994 that he would "no longer tinker with the machinery of death."[3] In an opinion dissenting from the Court's order denying review in a Texas death penalty case, Blackmun charged the Court with coming "perilously close to murder" and announced that he would vote to oppose all future death sentences. He also stated that the death penalty was applied in an arbitrary and racially discriminatory manner. "Rather than continue to coddle the Court's delusion that the desired level of fairness has been

290

achieved and the need for regulation eviscerated," Blackmun wrote, "I feel morally and intellectually obligated simply to concede that the death penalty experiment has failed."[4]

Governor Ryan and Justice Blackmun are not alone in their assessment of the system of capital punishment in the United States. Legal scholars, civil libertarians, and state and federal policymakers also have questioned the fairness of the process by which a small proportion of convicted murderers is sentenced to death and an even smaller proportion is eventually executed.[5] As a lawyer who defends defendants charged with capital crimes put it, "You are dealing with a group of people who are in this situation not so much because of what they did, but because of who they are. And who they are has a lot to do with the color of their skin and their socio-economic status."[6] Echoing Justice Blackmun, these critics contend that "the most profound expression of racial discrimination in sentencing occurs in the use of capital punishment."[7]

As these comments demonstrate, controversy continues to swirl around the use of the death penalty in the United States. Although issues other than race and class animate this controversy, these issues clearly are central. The questions asked and the positions taken by those on each side of the controversy mimic to some extent the issues that dominate discussions of the noncapital sentencing process. Supporters of capital punishment contend that the death penalty is administered in an even-handed manner on those who commit the most heinous murders; they also argue that the restrictions contained in death penalty statutes and the procedural safeguards inherent in the process preclude arbitrary and discriminatory decisionmaking. Opponents contend that the capital sentencing process, which involves a series of highly discretionary charging, convicting, and sentencing decisions, is fraught with race- and class-based discrimination; moreover, they argue that the appellate process is unlikely to uncover, much less remedy, these abuses.

GOALS OF THE CHAPTER

In this chapter, we address the issue of racial discrimination in the application of the death penalty. We begin with a discussion of Supreme Court decisions concerning the constitutionality of the death penalty. We follow this with a discussion of racial differences in attitudes toward capital punishment. We then present statistics on death sentences and executions and summarize the results of empirical studies examining the effect of race on the application of the death penalty. The next section discusses *McCleskey v. Kemp*,[8] the Supreme Court case that directly addressed the question of racial discrimination in the imposition of the death penalty. We conclude with a discussion of recent calls for a moratorium on the death penalty and legislation intended to reform the capital sentencing process.

THE CONSTITUTIONALITY
OF THE DEATH PENALTY

The Eighth Amendment to the United States Constitution prohibits "cruel and unusual punishments." The determination of which punishments are cruel and unusual, and thus unconstitutional, has been left to the courts. According to the Supreme Court,

> Punishments are cruel when they involve torture or lingering death; but the punishment of death is not cruel, within the meaning of that word as used in the Constitution. It implies there is something inhuman and barbarous, something more than the mere extinguishment of life.[9]

Whatever the arguments may be against capital punishment, both on moral grounds and in terms of accomplishing the purposes of punishment—and they are forceful—the death penalty has been employed throughout our history, and, in a day when it is still widely accepted, it cannot be said to violate the constitutional concept of cruelty.[10]

Although the Supreme Court consistently has stated that punishments of torture violate the Eighth Amendment, the Court has never ruled that the death penalty itself is a cruel and unusual punishment.

Furman v. Georgia

In 1972 the Supreme Court ruled in *Furman v. Georgia* that the death penalty, as it was being administered under then-existing statutes, was unconstitutional.[11] The 5-4 decision, in which nine separate opinions were written, did not hold that the death penalty *per se* violated the Constitution's ban on cruel and unusual punishment. Rather, the majority opinions focused on the procedures by which convicted defendants were selected for the death penalty. The justices ruled that because the statutes being challenged offered no guidance to juries charged with deciding whether to sentence convicted murderers or rapists to death, there was a substantial risk that the death penalty would be imposed in an arbitrary and discriminatory manner.

Although all of the majority justices were concerned about the arbitrary and capricious application of the death penalty, the nature of their concerns varied. Justices Brennan and Marshall wrote that the death penalty was inherently cruel and unusual punishment. Justice Brennan argued that the death penalty violated the concept of human dignity, whereas Justice Marshall asserted that the death penalty served no legitimate penal purpose. These justices concluded that the death penalty would violate the Constitution under any circumstances.

The other three justices in the majority concluded that capital punishment as it was then being administered in the United States was unconstitutional. These justices asserted that the death penalty violated both the Eighth Amendment's ban on cruel and unusual punishment and the Fourteenth Amendment's requirement of equal protection under the law. Justice Douglas stated that the procedures used in administering the death penalty were "pregnant with discrimination." Justice Stewart focused on the fact that the death penalty was "so wantonly and so freakishly imposed." Justice White found "no meaningful basis for distinguishing the few cases in which [the death penalty] is imposed from the many cases in which it is not."[12]

The central issue in the *Furman* case was the meaning of the Eighth Amendment's prohibition of cruel and unusual punishment, but the issue of racial discrimination in the administration of the death penalty was raised by three of the five justices in the majority. Justices Douglas and Marshall cited evidence of discrimination against defendants who were poor, powerless, or African American. Marshall, for example, noted that giving juries "untrammeled discretion" to impose a sentence of death was "an open invitation to discrimination."[13] Justice Stewart, although asserting that "racial discrimination has not been proved," stated that Douglas and Marshall "have demonstrated that, if any basis can be discerned for the selection of these few to be sentenced to die, it is the constitutionally impermissible basis of race."[14]

The Impact of *Furman*   The impact of the *Furman* decision was dramatic. The Court's ruling "emptied death rows across the country" and "brought the process that fed them to a stop."[15] Many commentators argued that *Furman* reflected the Supreme Court's deep-seated concerns about the fairness of the death penalty process; they predicted that the Court's next step would be the abolition of capital punishment. The Court defied these predictions, deciding to regulate capital punishment rather than abolish it.

Also as a result of the *Furman* decision, the death penalty statutes in 39 states were invalidated. Most of these states responded to *Furman* by adopting new statutes designed to narrow discretion and thus to avoid the problems of arbitrariness and discrimination identified by the justices in the majority. These statutes were of two types. Some required the judge or jury to impose the death penalty if a defendant was convicted of first-degree murder. Others permitted the judge or jury to impose the death penalty on defendants convicted of certain crimes, depending on the presence or absence of aggravating and mitigating circumstances. These "guided-discretion" statutes usually required a bifurcated trial in which the jury first decided guilt or innocence and then decided whether to impose the death penalty. They also provided for automatic appellate review of all death sentences.

Post-*Furman* Decisions

The Supreme Court ruled on the constitutionality of the new death penalty statutes in 1976. The Court held that the mandatory death penalty statutes enacted by North Carolina and Louisiana were unconstitutional,[16] both because they provided no opportunity for consideration of mitigating circumstances and because the jury's power to determine the degree of the crime (conviction for first-degree murder or for a lesser included offense) opened the door to the type

---

B O X 8.1   Georgia's Guided Discretion Death Penalty Statute

Under Georgia law, if the jury finds at least one of the following aggravating circumstances it may, but need not, recommend death:[181]

1. The offense was committed by a person with a prior record of conviction for a capital felony or by a person who has a substantial history of serious assaultive criminal convictions.

2. The offense was committed while the offender was engaged in the commission of another capital felony, or aggravated battery, or burglary or arson in the first degree.

3. The offender knowingly created a great risk of death to more than one person in a public place by means of a weapon or device that would normally be hazardous to the lives of more than one person.

4. The offender committed the offense of murder for himself or another, for the purpose of receiving money or any other thing of monetary value.

5. The murder of a judicial officer, former judicial officer, district attorney or solicitor, or former district attorney or solicitor during or because of the exercise of his official duty.

6. The offender caused or directed another to commit murder or committed murder as an agent or employee of another person.

7. The offense was outrageously or wantonly vile, horrible, or inhuman in that it involved torture, depravity of mind, or an aggravated battery to the victim.

8. The offense was committed against any peace officer, corrections employee, or fireman while engaged in the performance of his or her official duties.

9. The offense was committed by a person in, or who has escaped from, the lawful custody of a peace officer or place of lawful confinement.

10. The murder was committed for the purpose of avoiding, interfering with, or preventing a lawful arrest or custody in a place of lawful confinement, of himself (or herself) or another.

---

of "arbitrary and wanton jury discretion"[17] condemned in *Furman*. The Justices stated that the central problem of the mandatory statutes was their treatment of all defendants "as members of a faceless, undifferentiated mass to be subjected to the blind infliction of the penalty of death."[18]

In contrast, the Supreme Court ruled that the guided discretion death penalty statutes adopted by Georgia, Florida, and Texas did not violate the Eighth Amendment's prohibition of cruel and unusual punishment.[19] In *Gregg v. Georgia* the Court held that Georgia's statute—which required the jury to consider and weigh 10 specified aggravating circumstances (see Box 8.1), allowed the jury to consider mitigating circumstances, and provided for automatic appellate review—channeled the jury's discretion and thereby reduced the likelihood that the jury would impose arbitrary or discriminatory sentences.[20] According to the Court,

No longer can a jury wantonly and freakishly impose the death sentence; it is always circumscribed by the legislative guidelines. In addition, the review function of the Supreme Court of Georgia affords additional assurance that the concerns that prompted our decision in *Furman* are not present to any significant degree in the Georgia procedure applied here.[21]

Since 1976 the Supreme Court has handed down additional decisions on the constitutionality of the death penalty. With the exception of *McCleskey v. Kemp*, which we address later, these decisions do not focus on the question of racial discrimination in the application of the death penalty. The Court has ruled that the death penalty cannot be imposed on a defendant convicted of the crime of rape[22] and that the death penalty can be imposed on an offender convicted of felony murder if the offender played a major role in the crime and displayed "reckless indifference to the value of human life."[23] In 2002 the Court ruled that the execution of someone who is mentally handicapped is cruel and unusual punishment in violation of the Eighth Amendment,[24] and in 2005, the Court ruled 5-4 that the Eighth and Fourteenth Amendments forbid the imposition of the death penalty on offenders who were younger than age 18 when their crimes were committed.[25]

ATTITUDES TOWARD CAPITAL PUNISHMENT

In *Gregg v. Georgia*, the seven justices in the majority noted that both the public and state legislatures had endorsed the death penalty for murder. The Court stated that "it is now evident that a large proportion of American society continues to regard it as an appropriate and necessary criminal sanction." Public opinion data indicate that the Court was correct in its assessment of the level of support for the death penalty. In 1976, the year that *Gregg* was decided, 66 percent of the respondents to a nationwide poll said that they favored the death penalty for persons convicted of murder.[26] By 1997 three-fourth of those polled voiced support for the death penalty. Although the exoneration of death row inmates and subsequent decisions to impose a moratorium on executions (discussed later) led to a decline in support, in October 2003, 64 percent of Americans still reported that they favored the death penalty for people convicted of murder.[27]

The reliability of these figures has not gone unchallenged. In fact, Supreme Court Justices themselves have raised questions about the reliability and meaning of public opinion data derived from standard "do you favor or oppose?" polling questions. Justice Marshall observed in his concurring opinion in *Furman* that Americans were not fully informed about the ways in which the death penalty was used or about its potential for abuse. According to Marshall, the public did not realize that the death penalty was imposed in an arbitrary manner or that "the burden of capital punishment falls upon the poor, the ignorant, and the underprivileged members of society."[28] Marshall suggested that public opinion data demonstrating widespread support for the death penalty should therefore be given little weight in determining whether capital punishment is consistent with "evolving standards of decency." In what has become known as the "Marshall Hypothesis,"[29] he stated that "the average citizen" who knew "all the facts presently available regarding capital punishment would . . . find it shocking to his conscience and sense of justice."[30]

Researchers also have raised questions about the poll results,[31] suggesting that support for the death penalty is not absolute but depends on such things as the circumstances of the case, the character of the defendant, or the alternative punishments that are available. Bowers, for example, challenged the conclusion that "Americans solidly support the death penalty" and suggested that the poll results have been misinterpreted.[32] He argued that instead of reflecting a "deep-seated or strongly held commitment to capital punishment," expressed public support for the death penalty "is actually a reflection of the public's desire for a genuinely harsh but meaningful punishment for convicted murderers."[33]

In support of this proposition, Bowers presented evidence from surveys of citizens in a number of states and from interviews with capital jurors in three states. He found that support for the death penalty plummeted when respondents were given an alternative of life in prison without parole plus restitution to the victim's family; moreover, a majority of the respondents in every state preferred this alternative to the death penalty. Bowers also found that about three-fourths of the respondents, and 80 percent of jurors in capital cases, agreed that "the death penalty is too arbitrary because some people are executed and others are sent to prison for the very same crimes." Bowers concluded that the results of his study "could have the critical effect of changing the perspectives of legislators, judges, the media, and the public on how people think about capital punishment."[34]

Consistent with Bowers' results, recent public opinion polls reveal that most Americans believe that innocent people are sometimes convicted of murder. These polls also suggest that respondents' beliefs about the likelihood of wrongful convictions affect their views of the death penalty. A Harris poll conducted in July 2001 found that 94 percent of those polled believed that innocent people are "sometimes" convicted of murder; only 3 percent stated that this "never happens."[35] When respondents were asked, "If you believed that quite a substantial number of innocent people are convicted of murder, would you then believe in or oppose the death penalty for murder," 53 percent said that they would oppose the death penalty, compared to 36 percent who stated that they would continue to support it.

It is also clear that there are significant racial differences in support for the death penalty. The 2001 Harris poll, for example, found that 73 percent of whites and 63 percent of Hispanics expressed support for the death penalty, compared to only 46 percent of African Americans.[36] In fact, as shown in Figure 8.1, since 1976 the percentage of respondents who report that they support the death penalty has been consistently higher among whites than among African Americans. Beliefs about the fairness of the death penalty and estimates of the number of innocent people convicted of murder also vary by race and ethnicity. Fifty-nine percent of whites, but only 32 percent of African Americans, stated that they believed the death penalty was applied fairly.[37] African American respondents estimated that 22 of every 100 people convicted of murder were innocent. In contrast, the estimate was 15 of every 100 for Hispanic respondents and 10 of every 100 for white respondents.[38]

Researchers have advanced a number of explanations to account for these consistent racial differences. Some attribute African American opposition to

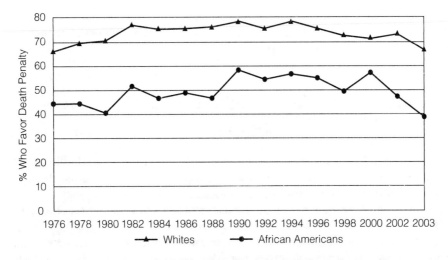

FIGURE 8.1 African American and White Attitudes Toward Capital Punishment for People Convicted of Murder, 1976–2003

SOURCE: Data from Bureau of Justice Statistics, *Sourcebook of Criminal Justice Statistics 2003* (Washington, DC: U.S. Government Printing Office, 2003).

perceptions of racial bias in the application of the death penalty.[39] Others contend that white support is associated with racial prejudice.[40] One study, for example, found that antipathy to African Americans (which was measured by two items asking respondents to indicate their attitudes toward living in a majority-black neighborhood or having a family member marry an African American) and belief in racial stereotypes (believing that African Americans are lazy, unintelligent, violent, and poor) predicted white respondents' support for the death penalty.[41] As the authors noted, "Simply put, many White people are both prejudiced against Blacks and are more likely to favor capital punishment."[42] The authors concluded that their finding of an association between racial prejudice and support for the death penalty suggests "that public sentiment may be an unacceptable indicator of contemporary standards of appropriate punishment for persons convicted of homicide."[43]

There also is evidence of geographic variation in support for the death penalty and that these variations can be explained by features of the social context, such as the homicide rate, the political climate, and the size of the minority population.[44] Eric Baumer and his colleagues found that support for the death penalty in 268 jurisdictions ranged from less than 50 percent to more than 90 percent. As they noted, this finding of geographic variation in support for the death penalty "challenges conventional wisdom and popular portrayals that support for capital punishment in the United States is universally high."[45] They also found that support for the death penalty was higher among respondents who lived in areas with high homicide rates, among people who lived in politically conservative jurisdictions, and among respondents who lived in areas with higher percentages of African Americans in the population. Community contextual characteristics, in other words, shaped citizens' attitudes toward the death penalty. This suggests that attitudes toward capital punishment are determined not only by individual characteristics, including race/ethnicity, but also by the characteristics of the communities in which people live.

RACE AND THE DEATH PENALTY: THE EMPIRICAL EVIDENCE

The Supreme Court's decisions regarding the constitutionality of the death penalty have been guided by a number of assumptions. In the *Furman* decision, the five justices in the majority assumed that the absence of guidelines and procedural rules in then-existing death penalty statutes opened the door to arbitrary, capricious, and discriminatory decisionmaking. In *Gregg*, the Court affirmed the guided discretion statutes on their face and assumed that the statutes would eliminate the problems condemned in *Furman*. The Court assumed that racial discrimination was a potential problem under the statutes struck down in *Furman* but would not be a problem under the statutes approved in *Gregg* and the companion cases.

In this section we address the validity of these assumptions. We begin by presenting statistics on the application of the death penalty. We then discuss the results of pre-*Furman* and post-*Furman* studies investigating the relationship between race and the death penalty. We also examine recent research on the federal capital sentencing process.

Statistical Evidence of Racial Disparity

There is clear evidence of racial disparity in the application of the death penalty. Despite the fact that African Americans make up only 13 percent of the United States population, they have been a much larger proportion of offenders sentenced to death and executed, both historically and during the post-*Gregg* era. There also is compelling evidence that those who murder whites, and particularly African Americans who murder whites, are sentenced to death and executed at disproportionately high rates. For example, the state of Georgia, which generated both *Furman* and *Gregg*, carried out 18 executions between 1976 and 1994. Twelve of those executed were African Americans; 6 of the 12 were sentenced to death by all-white juries. Sixteen of the 18 people executed had killed whites.[46]

The pattern found in Georgia casts doubt on the Supreme Court's assertion in *Gregg* that the disparities that prompted their decision in *Furman* will not be present "to any significant degree"[47] under the guided discretion procedures. Other evidence also calls this into question. Consider the following statistics:

- Of the 3,415 people under sentence of death in the United States in July 2005, 1,432 (42 percent) were African Americans; 350 (10 percent) were Hispanic, and 1,533 (46 percent) were white.[48]

- Of the 47 females on death row in 2003, 15 (31.9 percent) were African American.[49]

- African Americans make up approximately half of the death row populations in Washington, Georgia, North Carolina, South Carolina, Ohio, Delaware, and Mississippi; they constitute nearly two-thirds of those on death row in Arkansas, Pennsylvania, Maryland, Idaho, and Louisiana.[50]

- Twenty-three of the 36 offenders sentenced to death by the federal courts from 1993 through 2005 were African American, 12 were white, and 1 was Native American.[51]

- Of the 985 prisoners executed from 1976 through 2005, 571 (58 percent) were white, 331 (34 percent) were African American, 62 (6 percent) were Hispanic, and 21 (2 percent) were Native American or Asian.[52]

- Of the 1,449 victims of those executed from 1977 through 2005, 1,165 (80.4 percent) were white, 198 (13.7 percent) were African Americans, 58 (4 percent) were Hispanics, and 28 (2 percent) were Native Americans or Asians. During this period, approximately 50 percent of all murder victims were African Americans.[53]

- From 1977 through 2005, 55 percent of the prisoners executed were whites convicted of killing other whites, 21 percent were African Americans convicted of killing whites, 11 percent were African Americans convicted of killing other African Americans, and only 1.2 percent were whites convicted of killing African Americans.[54]

- Among those executed from 1930 through 1972 for the crime of rape, 89 percent (405 of the 455) were African Americans.[55] During this period, Louisiana, Mississippi, Oklahoma, Virginia, West Virginia, and the District of Columbia executed 66 African American men, but not a single white man, for the crime of rape.[56]

- Among those sentenced to death for rape in North Carolina from 1909 to 1954, 56 percent of the African Americans, but only 43 percent of the whites, were eventually executed.[57]

- Twenty percent of the whites, but only 11 percent of the African Americans, sentenced to death for first-degree murder in Pennsylvania between 1914 and 1958 had their sentences commuted to life in prison.[58]

These statistics clearly indicate that African Americans have been sentenced to death and executed "in numbers far out of proportion to their numbers in the population."[59] They document racial disparity in the application of the death penalty, both prior to *Furman* and following *Gregg*.[60] As we have noted frequently throughout this book, however, disparities in the treatment of racial minorities and whites do not necessarily constitute evidence of racial discrimination.

Racial minorities may be sentenced to death at a disproportionately high rate, not because of discrimination in the application of the death penalty, but because they are more likely than whites to commit homicide—the crime most frequently punished by death. As illustrated by the hypothetical examples presented in Box 8.2, the appropriate comparison is not the number of African Americans and whites sentenced to death during a given year or over time. Rather, the appropriate comparison is the percentage of death-eligible

---

B O X 8.2   Discrimination in the Application of the Death Penalty: Hypothetical Examples

---

Example 1
- 210 death-eligible homicides with African American offenders: 70 offenders (30 percent) receive the death penalty.
- 150 death-eligible homicides with white offenders: 50 offenders (30 percent) receive the death penalty.
- Conclusion: No evidence of discrimination, despite the fact that a disproportionate number of African Americans are sentenced to death.

Example 2
- 210 death-eligible homicides with African American offenders: 90 offenders (43 percent) receive the death penalty.
- 150 death-eligible homicides with white offenders: 30 offenders (20 percent) receive the death penalty
- Conclusion: Possibility of discrimination because African Americans are more than twice as likely to be sentenced to death.

---

homicides involving African Americans and whites that result in a death sentence.

The problem with the hypothetical examples presented in Box 8.2 is that there are no national data on the number of death-eligible homicides or on the race of those who commit or who are arrested for such crimes. Kleck, noting that most homicides are intraracial, used the number of African American and white homicide *victims* as a surrogate measure.[61] He created an indicator of "execution risk" by dividing the number of executions (for murder) of persons of a given race in a given year by the number of homicide victims of that race who died in the previous year.[62] Using data from 1930 through 1967, Kleck found that the risk of execution was somewhat greater for whites (10.43 executions per 1,000 homicides) than for African Americans (9.72 executions per 1,000 homicides) for the United States as a whole but that African Americans faced a greater likelihood of execution than whites in the South (10.47 for African Americans versus 8.39 for whites).[63] He concluded that the death penalty "has not generally been imposed for murder in a fashion discriminatory toward blacks, except in the South."[64]

None of the statistics cited here, including the execution rates calculated by Kleck, prove that the death penalty has been imposed in a racially discriminatory manner, in the South or elsewhere, either before the *Furman* decision or after the *Gregg* decision. As we pointed out earlier, conclusions of racial discrimination in sentencing rest on evidence indicating that African Americans are sentenced more harshly than whites after other legally relevant predictors of sentence severity are taken into account.

Even if it can be shown that African Americans face a greater risk of execution than whites, we cannot necessarily conclude that this reflects racial prejudice or

T A B L E 8.1 **Criminal History Profile of Prisoners under Sentence of Death in the United States, 2003**

	Race of Prisoner		
	African American **(n = 1,404)**	**Hispanic** **(n = 369)**	**White** **(n = 1,541)**
Prior felony conviction	69.8% (899)	58.7% (200)	61.8% (879)
Prior homicide conviction	8.5 (117)	6.9 (25)	8.3 (125)
On parole at time of capital offense	17.7 (222)	21.6 (72)	14.4 (199)

SOURCE: Department of Justice, Bureau of Justice Statistics, *Capital Punishment 2003* (Washington, DC: U.S. Government Printing Office, 2004), Table 8.

racial discrimination. The difference might be the result of legitimate legal factors—the heinousness of the crime or the prior criminal record of the offender, for example—that juries and judges consider in determining whether to sentence the offender to death. If African Americans are sentenced to death at a higher rate than whites because they commit more heinous murders than whites or because they are more likely than whites to have a prior conviction for murder, then we cannot conclude that criminal justice officials or juries are making racially discriminatory death penalty decisions.

The data presented in Table 8.1 provide some evidence in support of this possibility. Among prisoners under sentence of death in 2003, African Americans were more likely than either Hispanics or whites to have a prior felony conviction. African Americans and Hispanics also were more likely than whites to have been on parole when they were arrested for the capital offense. There were, however, very few differences in the proportions of whites and racial minorities who had a prior homicide conviction.

Just as the presence of racial disparity does not necessarily signal the existence of racial discrimination, the absence of disparity does not necessarily indicate the absence of discrimination. Even if it can be shown that African Americans generally face the same risk of execution as whites, we cannot conclude that the capital sentencing process operates in a racially neutral manner. Assume, for example, that the crimes for which African Americans are sentenced to death are less serious than those for which whites are sentenced to death. If this is the case, apparent equality of treatment may be masking race-linked assessments of crime seriousness. Moreover, as we noted in our discussion of the noncapital sentencing process, it is important to consider not only the race of the offender but the race of the victim as well. If African Americans who murder whites are sentenced to death at a disproportionately high rate, and African Americans who murder other African Americans are sentenced to death at a disproportionately low rate, the overall finding of "no difference" in the death sentence rates for African American and white offenders may be masking significant differences based on the race of the victim. As Johnson wrote in 1941,

---

B O X 8.3   **Executions of Whites for Crimes Against African Americans: Exceptions to the Rule?**

Since 1608 there have been about 16,000 executions in the United States (Radelet, 1989, p. 531). Of these, only 30, or about two-tenths of 1 percent, were executions of whites for crimes against African Americans. Historically, in other words, there has been one execution of a white for a crime against an African American for every 533 recorded executions.

Michael Radelet (1989) believes that these white offender–black victim cases, which would appear to be "theoretically anomalous" based on the proposition that race is an important determinant of sentencing, are not really "exceptions to the rule" (p. 533). Although he acknowledges that each case is in fact anomalous if *race alone* is used to predict the likelihood of a death sentence, Radelet suggests that these cases are consistent with a more general theoretical model that uses the *relative social status* of defendants and victims to explain case outcomes. These cases are consistent with "the general rule that executions almost always involve lower status defendants who stand convicted for crimes against victims of higher status" (p. 536).

Radelet's examination of the facts in each case revealed that 10 of the 30 cases involved white men who murdered slaves, and 8 of these 10 involved men convicted of murdering a slave who belonged to someone else. The scenario of one case, for example, read as follows:

> June 2, 1854. Texas. James Wilson (a.k.a. Rhode Wilson). Wilson had been on bad terms with a powerful white farmer, and had threatened to kill him on several occasions. One day Wilson arrived at the farm with the intention of carrying out the threats. The farmer was not home, so Wilson instead murdered the farmer's favorite slave (male) (p. 538).

According to Radelet, cases such as this are really "economic crimes" in which the true victim is not the slave himself but the slave's owner. As he notes, "Slaves are property, the

---

If caste values and attitudes mean anything at all, they mean that offenses by or against Negroes will be defined not so much in terms of their intrinsic seriousness as in terms of their importance in the eyes of the dominant group. Obviously, the murder of a white person by a Negro and the murder of a Negro by a Negro are not at all the same kind of murder from the standpoint of the upper caste's scale of values ... instead of two categories of offenders, Negro and white, we really need four offender–victim categories, and they would probably rank in ser-iousness from high to low as follows: (1) Negro versus white, (2) white versus white, (3) Negro versus Negro, and (4) white versus Negro.[65]

Evidence in support of Johnson's rankings is presented in Box 8.3, which focuses on the "anomalous" cases in which whites have been executed for crimes against African Americans. According to Radelet, "the scandalous paucity of these cases, representing less than two-tenths of 1 percent of known executions, lends further support to the evidence that the death penalty in this country has been discriminatorily applied."[66]

There is now a substantial body of research investigating the relationship between race and the death penalty. Most, but not all, of the research tests for

wealth of someone else, and their rank should be measured accordingly." James Wilson was sentenced to death not because he killed a slave, but because he destroyed the property of someone of higher status than himself. Similarly, the death sentences imposed on the two men who killed their own slaves were meant to discourage such brutality, which might threaten the legitimacy of the institution of slavery.

The 20 remaining cases of whites who were executed for crimes against African Americans involved one of the following:

- An African American victim of higher social status than his white murderer (five cases)
- A defendant who was a marginal member of the white community—a tramp, a recent immigrant, a hard drinker (four cases)
- A defendant with a long record of serious criminality (seven cases)
- Murders that were so heinous that they resulted in "an unqualified disgust and contempt for the offender unmitigated by the fact of his or the victim's race" (pp. 534–535).

Based on his analysis of these 30 cases, Radelet concluded that "it was not primarily outrage over the violated rights of the black victim or the inherent value of the victim's life that led to the condemnation" (p. 536). Rather, the 30 white men executed for crimes against African Americans were sentenced to death because their crimes threatened the institution of slavery, involved a victim of higher social status than the defendant, or involved a defendant who was a very marginal member of the community. As Radelet noted, "The data show that the criminal justice system deems the executioner's services warranted not simply for those who *do something* but who also *are someone*" (p. 536 [emphasis in original]).

both race-of-defendant and race-of-victim effects. Some of these studies are methodologically sophisticated, both in terms of the type of statistical analysis used and in terms of the number of variables that are taken into consideration in the analysis. Other studies use less sophisticated statistical techniques and include fewer control variables.

We summarize the results of these studies—presenting the results of the pre-*Furman* studies first and then the results of the post-*Gregg* studies. Our purpose is to assess the validity of the Supreme Court's assumptions that race played a role in death penalty decisions prior to *Furman* but that the guided discretion statutes enacted since 1976 have removed arbitrariness and discrimination from the capital sentencing process.

Pre-*Furman* Studies

We noted in our discussion of the Supreme Court's decision in *Furman v. Georgia* that three of the five justices in the majority mentioned the problem of racial discrimination in the application of the death penalty. Even two of the dissenting justices—Chief Justice Burger and Justice Powell—acknowledged the existence of historical evidence of discrimination against African Americans. Justice Powell also stated, "If a Negro defendant, for instance, could demonstrate that members of his race were being singled out for more severe punishment than others charged with the same offense, a constitutional violation might be established."[67]

Several studies suggest that African Americans, and particularly African Americans who murdered or raped whites, were "singled out for more severe punishment" in the pre-*Furman* era.[68] Most of these studies were conducted in the South. Researchers found, for example, that African Americans indicted for murdering whites in North Carolina from 1930 to 1940 faced a disproportionately high risk of a death sentence,[69] that whites sentenced to death in nine Southern and border states during the 1920s and 1930s were less likely than African Americans to be executed,[70] and that African Americans sentenced to death in Pennsylvania were less likely than whites to have their sentences commuted to life in prison and more likely than whites to be executed.[71]

Garfinkel's[72] study of the capital sentencing process in North Carolina during the 1930s revealed the importance of taking both the race of the offender and the race of the victim into account. Garfinkel examined three separate decisions: the grand jury's decision to indict for first-degree murder; the prosecutor's decision to go to trial on a first-degree murder charge (in those cases in which the grand jury returned an indictment for first-degree murder); and the judge or jury's decision to convict for first-degree murder (and thus to impose the mandatory death sentence).

As shown in Figure 8.2, which summarizes the movement of death-eligible cases from one stage to the next, there were few differences based on the race of the offender. In fact, among defendants charged with first-degree murder, white offenders were *more* likely than African American offenders to be convicted of first-degree murder, and thus to be sentenced to death; 14 percent of the whites, but only 9 percent of the African Americans, received a death sentence.

In contrast, there were substantial differences based on the race of the victim, particularly in the decision to convict the defendant for first-degree murder. Only 5 percent of the defendants who killed African Americans were convicted of first-degree murder and sentenced to death, compared to 24 percent of the defendants who killed whites.

The importance of considering both the race of the offender and the race of the victim is further illustrated by the data presented in Figure 8.3. Garfinkel's analysis revealed that African Americans who killed whites were more likely than any of the other race-of-offender/race-of-victim groups to be indicted for, charged with, or convicted of first-degree murder. Again, the differences were particularly pronounced at the trial stage of the process. Among offenders charged with first-degree murder, the rate of conviction for first-degree murder ranged from 43 percent for African Americans who killed whites, to 15 percent for whites who killed whites, to 5 percent for African Americans who killed African Americans, to 0 percent for whites who killed African Americans. The overall probability of a death sentence (that is, the probability that an indictment for

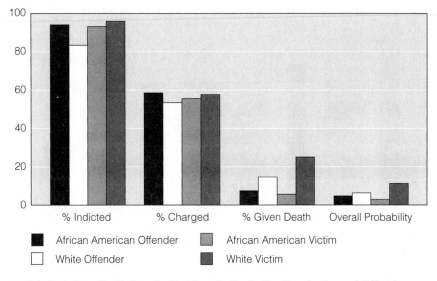

F I G U R E 8.2 Death Penalty Decisions in North Carolina, by Race of Offender and Victim, 1930–1940

SOURCE: Date obtained from Harold Garfinkel, "Research Note on Inter- and Intra-Racial Homicides," *Social Forces* 27 (1949), Tables 2 and 3.

homicide would result in a death sentence) revealed similar disparities. African Americans who killed whites had a substantially higher overall probability of a death sentence than any of the other three groups.

The results of Garfinkel's study suggest that there were pervasive racial differences in the administration of capital punishment in North Carolina during the 1930s. Although Garfinkel did not control for the possibility that the crimes committed by African Americans and the crimes committed against whites were more serious, and thus more likely to deserve the death penalty, the magnitude of the differences "cast[s] doubt on the possibility that legally relevant factors are responsible for these differences."[73]

Studies of the use of capital punishment for the crime of rape also reveal overt and pervasive discrimination against African Americans in the pre-*Furman* era. These studies reveal that "the death penalty for rape was largely used for punishing blacks who had raped whites."[74] One analysis of sentences for rape in Florida from 1940 through 1964, for example, revealed that 54 percent of the African Americans convicted of raping whites received the death penalty, compared to only 5 percent of the whites convicted of raping whites. Moreover, none of the eight whites convicted of raping African Americans were sentenced to death.[75]

Wolfgang and Reidel's[76] study of the imposition of the death penalty for rape in 12 southern states from 1945 through 1965 uncovered a similar pattern. As shown in Table 8.2, they found that 13 percent of the African Americans, but only 2 percent of the whites, were sentenced to death. Further analysis revealed that cases in which

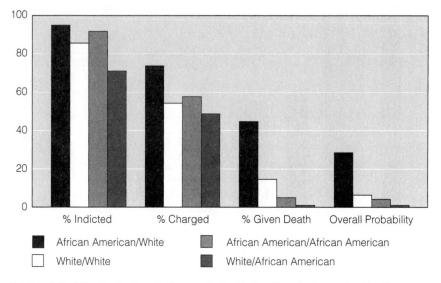

F I G U R E 8.3 Death Penalty Process in North Carolina, by Race of Offender and Victim

SOURCE: Date obtained from Harold Garfinkel, "Research Note on Inter- and Intra-Racial Homicides," *Social Forces* 27 (1949), Tables 2 and 3.

T A B L E 8.2 **Race and the Death Penalty for Rape in the South, 1945–1965**

	Sentenced to Death		Not Sentenced to Death	
	n	%	n	%
Race of offender				
African American	110	13	713	87
White	9	2	433	98
Race of offender/victim				
African American /white	113	36	204	64
All other combinations	19	2	902	98

SOURCE: Marvin E. Wolfgang and Marc Reidel, "Race, Judicial Discretion, and the Death Penalty," *Annals of the American Academy* 407 (1973): 129, Tables 1 and 2.

African Americans were convicted of raping whites were 18 times more likely to receive a death penalty than were cases with any other racial combinations.

These differences did not disappear when Wolfgang and Reidel controlled for commission of a contemporaneous felony or for other factors associated with the imposition of the death penalty. According to the authors, "All the nonracial factors in each of the states analyzed 'wash out,' that is, they have no bearing on the imposition of the death penalty in disproportionate numbers upon blacks. The only variable of statistical significance that remains is race."[77]

Critics of the pre-*Furman* research note that most researchers did not control for the defendant's prior criminal record, for the heinousness of the crime, or for other predictors of sentence severity. Kleck, for example, although admitting that additional controls probably would not eliminate "the huge racial differentials in use of the death penalty" for rape, asserted that the more modest differences found for homicide might disappear if these legal factors were taken into consideration.[78]

A handful of more methodologically sophisticated studies of capital sentencing in the pre-*Furman* era control for these legally relevant factors. An analysis of death penalty decisions in Georgia, for example, found that African American defendants and defendants who murdered whites received the death penalty more often than other equally culpable defendants.[79] These results were limited, however, to borderline cases in which the appropriate sentence (life in prison or death) was not obvious.

An examination of the capital sentencing process in pre-*Furman* Texas also found significant racial effects.[80] Ralph and her colleagues controlled for legal and extralegal factors associated with sentence severity. They found that offenders who killed during a felony had a higher probability of receiving the death penalty, as did nonwhite offenders and offenders who killed whites. In fact, their analysis revealed that the race of the victim was the most important extralegal variable; those who killed whites were 25.2 percent more likely to be sentenced to death than those who killed nonwhites. The authors concluded, "Overall we found a significant race-linked bias in the death sentencing of non–Anglo-American murderers; the victim's race, along with legal factors taken together, emerged as the pivotal element in sentencing."[81]

The results of these studies, then, reveal that the Supreme Court was correct in its assumption of the potential for racial discrimination in the application of the death penalty in the pre-*Furman* era. The death penalty for rape was primarily reserved for African Americans who victimized whites. The evidence with respect to homicide, although less consistent, also suggests that African Americans, and particularly African Americans who murdered whites, were sentenced to death at a disproportionately high rate. We now turn to an examination of the capital sentencing process in the post-*Gregg* period.

Post-*Gregg* Studies

In *Gregg v. Georgia* the Supreme Court upheld Georgia's guided discretion death penalty statute and stated that "the concerns that prompted our decision in *Furman* are not present to any significant degree in the Georgia procedure applied here."[82] The Court, in essence, predicted that race would not affect the capital sentencing process in Georgia or in other states with similar statutes. Critics of the Court's ruling were less optimistic. Wolfgang and Reidel, for example, noted that the post-*Furman* statutes narrowed, but did not eliminate, discretion. They suggested that "it is unlikely that the death penalty will be applied with greater equity when substantial discretion remains in these post-*Furman* statutes."[83]

B O X 8.4   Discrimination in the Georgia Courts: The Case of Wilburn Dobbs

Statistical evidence of racial disparities in the use of the death penalty, although important, cannot illustrate the myriad ways in which racial sentiments influence the capital sentencing process.

Consider the case of Wilburn Dobbs, an African American on death row since 1974 in Georgia for the murder of a white man (case described in Bright, 1995, pp. 912–915). The judge trying his case referred to him in court as "colored" and "colored boy," and two of the jurors who sentenced him to death admitted after trial that they used the racial epithet "nigger." Moreover, the court-appointed lawyer assigned to his case, who also referred to Dobbs as "colored," stated on the morning of trial that he was "not prepared to go to trial" and that he was "in a better position to prosecute the case than defend it." He also testified before the federal court hearing Dobbs's appeal that he believed that African Americans were uneducated and less intelligent than whites and admitted that he used the word "nigger" jokingly (pp. 912–913).

The federal courts that heard Dobbs's appeals ruled that neither the racial attitudes of the trial judge or the defense attorney nor the racial prejudice of the jurors required that Dobbs's death sentence be set aside. The Court of Appeals, for instance, noted that although several of the jurors made statements reflecting racial prejudice, none of them "viewed blacks as more prone to violence than whites or as morally inferior to whites" (*Dobbs v. Zant*, 963 F.2d 1403, 1407 [11th Cir. 1991], cited in Bright, 1995, n. 7).

The Court's reasoning in this case led Stephen Bright to conclude that "racial discrimination which would not be acceptable in any other area of American life today is tolerated in criminal courts" (p. 914).

Other commentators predicted that the guided discretion statutes would simply shift discretion, and thus the potential for discrimination, to earlier stages in the capital sentencing process. They suggested that discretion would be transferred to charging decisions made by the grand jury and the prosecutor. Thus, according to Bowers and Pierce, "under post-*Furman* capital statutes, the extent of arbitrariness and discrimination, if not their distribution over stages of the criminal justice process, might be expected to remain essentially unchanged." Compelling evidence supports this hypothesis. (See also Box 8.4.) Studies conducted during the past 3 decades document substantial discrimination in the application of the death penalty under post-*Furman* statutes. In fact, a 1990 report by the United States General Accounting Office (GAO) concluded that there was "a pattern of evidence indicating racial disparities in the charging, sentencing, and imposition of the death penalty after the *Furman* decision."[84]

The GAO evaluated the results of 28 post-*Gregg* empirical studies of the capital sentencing process. They found that the race of the victim had a statistically significant effect in 23 of the 28 studies; those who murdered whites were more likely to be charged with capital murder and to be sentenced to death than those who murdered African Americans. The authors of the report noted that the race of the victim affected decisions made at all stages of the criminal justice process. They concluded that these differences could not be explained by the defendant's prior criminal record, by the heinousness of the crime, or by other legally relevant variables.

T A B L E 8.3 **Death Penalty Decisions in Post-*Furman* Georgia**

Offender and Victim Race	Overall Death-Sentencing Rate	Prosecutor's Decision to Seek Death Penalty	Jury's Decision to Impose Death Penalty
African American/White	.35 (45/130)	.58 (72/125)	.58 (45/77)
White/White	.22 (51/230)	.38 (85/224)	.56 (51/91)
African American/African American	.06 (17/232)	.15 (34/231)	.40 (14/35)
White/African American	.14 (2/14)	.21 (3/14)	.67 (2/3)

SOURCE: David C. Baldus, George G. Woodworth, and Charles A. Pulaski Jr., *Equal Justice and the Death Penalty* (Boston: Northeastern University Press, 1990), Tables 30 and 34.

With respect to the effect of the race of the defendant, the GAO report concluded that the evidence was "equivocal."[85] The report noted that about half of the studies found that the race of the defendant affected the likelihood of being charged with a capital crime or receiving the death penalty; most, but not all, of these studies found that African Americans were more likely than whites to be sentenced to death. The authors of the report also stated that, although some studies found that African Americans who murdered whites faced the highest odds of receiving the death penalty, "the extent to which the finding was influenced by race of victim rather than race of defendant was unclear."[86]

A comprehensive review of the post-*Gregg* research is beyond the scope of this book.[87] Instead, we summarize the results of three studies. The first, a study of the capital sentencing process in Georgia,[88] is one of the most sophisticated studies conducted to date. It also figured prominently in the Supreme Court's decision in *McCleskey v. Kemp*. The second is a study of capital sentencing patterns in eight states,[89] and the third is a study of death sentencing for California homicides during the 1990s.[90] We then discuss recent research on the federal capital sentencing process.

Race and the Death Penalty in Georgia David Baldus and his colleagues analyzed the effect of race on the outcomes of more than 600 homicide cases in Georgia from 1973 through 1979.[91] Their examination of the raw data revealed that the likelihood of receiving a death sentence varied by both the race of the offender and the race of the victim. The first column of Table 8.3 shows that 35 percent of the African Americans charged with killing whites were sentenced to death, compared to only 22 percent of the whites who killed whites, 14 percent of the whites who killed African Americans, and 6 percent of the African Americans who killed other African Americans.

Baldus and his co-authors also discovered that the race of the victim played an important role in both the prosecutor's decision to seek the death penalty and the jury's decision to impose the death penalty (see columns 2 and 3, Table 8.3). The victim's race was a particularly strong predictor of the prosecutor's decision to seek or waive the death penalty. In fact, Georgia prosecutors were nearly four times more likely to request the death penalty for African American offenders convicted of killing whites than for African American offenders convicted of killing African Americans. The effect of the race of the victim was less pronounced when the offender was white; prosecutors sought the death penalty in 38 percent of the cases with white offenders and white victims but only 21 percent of the cases with white offenders and African American victims.

The authors of this study then controlled for more than 200 variables that might explain these disparities; they included detailed information on the defendant's background and prior criminal record, information concerning the circumstances and the heinousness of the crime, and measures of the strength of evidence against the defendant. They found that inclusion of these controls did not eliminate the racial differences. Although the race of the offender was only a weak predictor of death penalty decisions once these legal factors were taken into consideration, the race of the victim continued to exert a strong effect on both the prosecutor's decision to seek the death penalty and the jury's decision to impose the death penalty. In fact, those who killed whites were more than four times as likely to be sentenced to death as those who killed African Americans.

Further analysis revealed that the effects of race were not uniform across the range of homicide cases included in the analysis. It was not surprising that race had little effect on decisionmaking in the least aggravated cases, in which virtually no one received the death penalty, or in the most heinous cases, in which a high percentage of murderers, regardless of their race or the race of their victims, were sentenced to death. Rather, race played a role primarily in the mid-range of cases where decisionmakers could decide either to sentence the offender to life in prison or impose the death penalty. In these types of cases, the death-sentencing rate for those who killed whites was 34 percent, compared to only 14 percent for those who killed African Americans.

These findings led Baldus and his colleagues to conclude that the race of the victim was "a potent influence in the system"[92] and that the state of Georgia was operating a "dual system" for processing homicide cases. According to the authors, "Georgia juries appear to tolerate greater levels of aggravation without imposing the death penalty in black victim cases; and, as compared to white victim cases, the level of aggravation in black victim cases must be substantially greater before the prosecutor will even seek a death sentence."[93]

Anthony Amsterdam's[94] analysis was even more blunt. Noting that 9 of the 11 murderers executed by Georgia between 1973 and 1988 were African American and that 10 of the 11 had white victims, Amsterdam asked, "Can there be the slightest doubt that this revolting record is the product of some sort of racial bias rather than a pure fluke?"[95]

Some commentators would be inclined to answer this question in the affirmative. They would argue that the statistics included in the Baldus study are not representative of death penalty decisions in the United States as a whole; rather, they are peculiar to Southern states such as Georgia, Texas, Florida, and Mississippi. A study by Gross and Mauro addressed this possibility.

Death Penalty Decisions in Eight States   Gross and Mauro examined death penalty decisions in the post-*Gregg* era (1976 to 1980) in eight states—Arkansas, Florida, Georgia, Illinois, Mississippi, North Carolina, Oklahoma, and Virginia.[96]

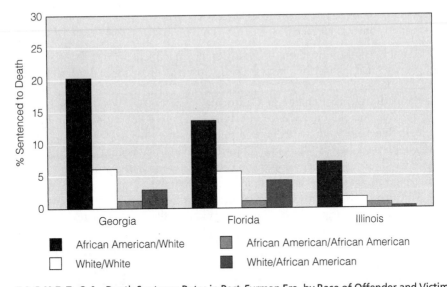

FIGURE 8.4 Death Sentence Rates in Post-*Furman* Era, by Race of Offender and Victim

SOURCE: Data obtained from Samuel R. Gross and Robert Mauro, *"Death and Discrimination: Racial Disparities in Capital Sentencing* (Boston: Northeastern University Press, 1989.

They found that the risk of a death sentence was much lower for defendants charged with killing African Americans than for defendants charged with killing whites in each of the eight states included in their study. In Georgia and Mississippi, for example, those who killed whites were nearly 10 times as likely to be sentenced to death as those who killed African Americans. The ratios for the other states included in the study were 8:1 (Florida), 7:1 (Arkansas), 6:1 (Illinois, Oklahoma, and North Carolina), and 5:1 (Virginia).

The authors also discovered that African Americans who killed whites faced the greatest odds of a death sentence. Figure 8.4 presents the percentages of death sentences by race of suspect and race of victim for the three states with the largest number of death-eligible cases. In Georgia, 20.1 percent of the African Americans who killed whites were sentenced to death, compared to only 5.7 percent of the whites who killed whites, 2.9 percent of the whites who killed African Americans, and less than 1 percent (0.8 percent) of the African Americans who killed African Americans. There were similar disparities in Florida and Illinois. In fact, in these three states only 32 of the 4,731 cases with African American defendants and African American victims resulted in a death sentence, compared to 82 of the 621 cases involving African American defendants and white victims.

These racial disparities did not disappear when Gross and Mauro controlled for other legally relevant predictors of sentence severity. According to the authors,

> The major factual finding of this study is simple: there has been racial discrimination in the imposition of the death penalty under post-*Furman* statutes in the eight states that we examined. The discrimination is based on the race of the victim, and it is a remarkably stable and consistent

phenomenon... The data show "a clear pattern, unexplainable on grounds other than race."[97]

Like the Baldus study, then, this study of the capital sentencing process in eight states showed that the race of the victim was a powerful predictor of death sentences.

Race and the Death Penalty in California   The two studies described previously provide compelling evidence of victim-based racial discrimination in the use of the death penalty in the years immediately following the *Gregg* decision. Recent research in states such as Maryland,[98] North Carolina,[99] Virginia,[100] Ohio,[101] and California[102] provides equally compelling evidence of racial disparities in the capital sentencing process during the 1990s and early 2000s.

Research conducted in California illustrates this more recent trend. In 2005 California had the largest death row population in the United States, with 648 inmates under sentence of death.[103] Of those on death row, 39 percent were white, 36 percent were African American, 20 percent were Hispanic, 3 percent were Asian, and 2 percent were Native American.

To determine whether these figures reflected racial/ethnic bias in the imposition of the death penalty in California, Pierce and Radelet examined the characteristics of all people sentenced to death in the state from 1990 through 2003 (for homicides committed from 1990 to 1999). They found that offenders who killed whites were 3.7 times more likely to be sentenced to death than offenders who killed African Americans; those who killed whites were 4.7 times more likely to be sentenced to death than those who killed Hispanics.[104] To address the possibility that these differences were because the murders of whites were more aggravated or more heinous than the murders of nonwhites, the authors divided the homicides in their sample into three categories: those with no aggravating circumstances, those with one aggravating circumstance, and those with two aggravating circumstances. As the authors noted, "If homicides that victimize whites are indeed more aggravated than other homicides, death sentencing rates will be similar across each category of victim's race/ethnicity for each level of aggression."[105]

The results presented in Table 8.4 do not support the hypothesis that those who kill whites are sentenced to death more often because their crimes are more heinous. Although the death sentencing rate increased for each of the three groups as the number of aggravating circumstances increased, for each level of aggravation, those who killed whites were substantially more likely than those who killed African Americans or Hispanics to be sentenced to death. These findings were confirmed by the results of a multivariate analysis, which simultaneously controlled for the number of aggravating circumstances, the race/ethnicity of the victim, and the population density and racial makeup of the county in which the crime occurred. The authors found that those who killed African Americans or Hispanics were significantly less likely than those who killed whites to be sentenced to death. They concluded that "the data clearly show that the race and ethnicity of homicide victims is associated with the imposition of the death penalty."[106]

TABLE 8.4 Race and the Death Penalty in California, Controlling for Aggravating Circumstances

	Death Sentence Rate per 100 Offenders	Ratio of White Victim Rate/ Other Victim Rate
No Aggravating Circumstances		
White Victim	0.775	—
African American Victim	0.102	7.60
Hispanic Victim	0.070	11.07
One Aggravating Circumstance		
White Victim	4.560	—
African American Victim	1.999	2.28
Hispanic Victim	1.583	2.88
Two Aggravating Circumstances		
White Victim	24.286	—
African American Victim	12.162	2.00
Hispanic Victim	14.773	1.64

SOURCE: Glenn L. Pierce and Michael L. Radelet, "The Impact of Legally Inappropriate Factors on Death Sentencing for California Homicides, 1990–1999," *Santa Clara Law Review 46* (2005), Table 6. Reprinted by permission.

Race and the Death Penalty in the Post-*Gregg* Era   The results of the death penalty studies conducted in the post-*Gregg* era provide compelling evidence that the issues raised by the Supreme Court in *Furman* have not been resolved. The Supreme Court's assurances in *Gregg* notwithstanding, racial discrimination in the capital sentencing process did not disappear as a result of the guided-discretion statutes enacted in the wake of the *Furman* decision. Methodologically sophisticated studies conducted in Southern and non-Southern jurisdictions and in the 1990s as well as the 1970s and 1980s consistently conclude that the race of the victim affects death sentencing decisions. Many of these studies also conclude that the race of the defendant, or the racial makeup of the offender–victim pair, influences the capital sentencing process.

According to Austin Sarat, professor of jurisprudence and political science at Amherst College, "the post-*Furman* effort to rationalize death sentences has utterly failed; it has been replaced by a policy that favors execution while trimming away procedural protection for capital defendants. This situation only exacerbates the incompatibility of capital punishment and legality."[107] Scott W. Howe, a professor of criminal law at Chapman University School for Law, similarly contends that widespread evidence of racial disparity in capital sentencing undermines "confidence in the neutrality of capital selection nationwide . . . The studies, considered as a group, imply racial discrimination."[108] (See Box 8.5 for a discussion of the effect of the race and gender of the victim on the capital sentencing process.)

B O X 8.5   The Death Penalty and the Race and Gender of the Victim: Are Those Who Kill White Women Singled Out for Harsher Treatment?

Research on the application of the death penalty reveals that those who kill whites are more likely than those who kill African Americans to be sentenced to death. There also is evidence that those who kill females are more likely than those who kill males to receive the death penalty. This raises the question, "Are those who kill white women sentenced to death at a disproportionately high rate?"

To answer this question, Williams and Holcomb analyzed data on homicides in Ohio for the years 1981 to 1994.[182] When they looked at the raw data, they found that white females made up only 15 percent of all homicide victims but 35 percent of all death sentences. Cases in which the offender was a white male and the victim was a white female made up 12 percent of all homicides but 28 percent of all death sentences; cases in which the offender was an African American male and the victim was a white female made up 2 percent of homicide cases but 8 percent of death sentences.[183]

Multivariate analysis confirmed these findings. The authors controlled for the race, gender, and age of the victim and the offender; whether a gun was used; whether the victim and offender were strangers; whether the homicide involved another felony or multiple victims; and the location of the crime. They found that homicides with female victims were more than twice as likely as those with male victims to result in a death sentence and that homicides with white victims were about one and a half times more likely as those with African American victims to result in death sentence. Further analysis revealed that offenders who victimized white females had significantly higher odds of being sentenced to death than offenders who victimized African American females, African American males, or white males.[184]

Williams and Holcomb concluded that the results of their study, which they acknowledged provided only a preliminary test of their hypothesis, suggested "that the central factor in understanding existing racial disparity in death sentences may be the severity with which those who kill White females are treated relative to other gender–race victim combinations."[185] This suggests that criminal justice officials and jurors who make death penalty decisions believe that homicides involving white women are especially heinous and that those who kill white women are therefore more deserving of death sentences than those who kill men or women of color.

Race and the Federal Capital Sentencing Process

As noted earlier, state legislatures moved quickly to revise their death penalty statutes in the wake of the 1972 *Furman* decision. The federal government, however, did not do so until 1988, when passage of the Anti-Drug Abuse Act made the death penalty available for certain serious drug-related offenses. The number of federal offenses for which the death penalty is an option increased substantially as a result of legislation passed during the mid-1990s. The Federal Death Penalty Act of 1994 added more than 40 federal offenses to the list of capital crimes, and the Antiterrorism and Effective Death Penalty Act of 1996 added an additional four offenses.[109]

The Department of Justice has adopted a set of standards and procedures—commonly known as the "death penalty protocol"—to govern death penalty decisions in federal cases. According to this protocol, a United States Attorney cannot seek the death penalty without prior written authorization from the Attorney General. The steps in the capital case review process are as follows:[110]

- U.S. Attorneys are required to submit all cases involving a charge for which the death penalty is a legally authorized sanction—regardless of whether the attorney recommends seeking the death penalty—to the Capital Case Unit of the Criminal Division for review;

- The Capital Case Unit reviews the case and prepares an initial analysis and recommendation regarding the death penalty;

- The case is forwarded to the Attorney General's Capital Case Review Committee, which is composed of senior Justice Department lawyers—the members of the committee meet with the U.S. Attorney and defense counsel responsible for the case, review documents submitted by all parties, and make a recommendation to the Attorney General.

- The Attorney General makes the final decision regarding whether to seek the death penalty.

According to the Department of Justice, these procedures are designed to ensure that the federal capital sentencing process is fair and equitable: "Both the legal rules and the administrative procedures that currently govern federal capital cases incorporate extensive safeguards against any influence of racial or ethnic bias or prejudice."[111]

The Department of Justice has conducted two studies of the federal capital sentencing process. The first study, which was released in 2000, revealed that from 1995 to 2000, U.S. Attorneys forwarded for review 682 death-eligible cases. Of the defendants in these cases, 81 percent were racial minorities: 324 (48 percent) were African American; 195 (29 percent) were Hispanic, and 29 (4 percent) were Native American, Asian, and other races.[112] This study also revealed, however, that participants in the review process were less likely to recommend (or to seek) the death penalty if the defendant was a racial minority. As shown in Table 8.5, U.S. Attorneys recommended the death penalty in 36 percent of the cases involving white defendants, compared with 25 percent of those involving African American defendants and 20 percent of those involving Hispanic defendants. There was a similar pattern of results for the Capital Case Unit's recommendation (to the Attorney General) to request the death penalty, the Attorney General's decision to authorize the U.S. Attorney to file a notice of intent to seek the death penalty; and the Department of Justice's final decision to seek the death penalty.

The data presented in Table 8.5 demonstrate that, although the Justice Department's study did not find racial bias in the decisions that followed the U.S. Attorney's initial decision to submit the case for review, it did find that a significant majority of the cases that were submitted for review involved African American and Hispanic defendants. Then-Attorney General Janet Reno stated that

T A B L E 8.5 Race/Ethnicity and the Federal Death Penalty: 1995–2000

		Race of the Defendant			
	Total	White	African American	Hispanic	Other
Number (% of total) of cases submitted for review	682	134 (20%)	324 (47%)	195 (29%)	29 (4%)
Rate at which U.S. Attorneys recommended seeking the death penalty	.27	.36	.25	.20	.52
Rate at which the Review Committee recommended seeking the death penalty	.30	.40	.27	.25	.50
Rate at which the attorney general approved filing of notice of intent to seek the death penalty	.27	.38	.25	.20	.46
Rate at which the Department of Justice sought the death penalty	.23	.33	.22	.16	.41

SOURCE: U.S. Department of Justice, *The Federal Death Penalty System: A Statistical Survey (1998–2000)* (Washington, DC: Author), pp. 10–11.

she was "sorely troubled" by these findings, adding that "we must do all we can in the federal government to root out bias at every step." Reno's concerns were echoed by then-U.S. Deputy Attorney General Eric Holder, an African American prosecutor who oversaw the study. He said that he was "both personally and professionally disturbed by the numbers."[113] Publication of the report also led President Clinton to grant a 6-month reprieve to Juan Raul Garza, a Mexican American from Texas who was scheduled to be executed in January 2001. In granting the reprieve, Clinton stated, "The examination of possible racial and regional bias should be completed before the United States goes forward with an execution in a case that may implicate the very questions raised by the Justice Department's continuing study."[114]

Attorney General Reno ordered the Department of Justice to gather additional data about the federal capital sentencing process. The results of this study, which was overseen by Janet Reno's successor, John Ashcroft, were released in 2001.[115] Unlike the first study, which examined only those cases that were charged as capital crimes and submitted for review, this study included an analysis of cases in which the facts would have supported a capital charge but the defendants were not charged with a capital crime (and thus the case was not submitted for review). The results of the second study were generally similar to those of the first. Within the larger pool of cases examined in the follow-up study, which included 973 defendants, 17 percent (166) were white, 42 percent (408) were African American, and 36 percent (350) were Hispanic. Consistent with the results of the 2000 study, "potential capital cases involving Black or Hispanic defendants were less likely to result in capital charges and submission of the case to the review procedure . . . likewise [these cases] were less likely to result in decisions to seek the death penalty."[116]

The 2001 report, which noted that the proportion of racial minorities in federal capital cases was substantially greater than the proportion of racial minorities in the general population, concluded that "the cause of this disproportion is not racial or ethnic bias, but the representation of minorities in the pool of potential federal capital cases."[117] The report attributed the overrepresentation of African Americans and Hispanics in the federal capital case pool to a number of factors, including the fact that federal law enforcement officers focused their attention on drug trafficking and related criminal violence. According to the report,

> In areas where large-scale, organized drug trafficking is largely carried out by gangs whose memberships is drawn from minority groups, the active federal role in investigating and prosecuting these crimes results in a high proportion of minority defendants in federal cases, including a high proportion of minority defendants in potential capital cases arising from the lethal violence associated with the drug trade. This is not the result of any form of bias, but reflects the normal factors that affect the division of federal and state prosecutorial responsibility.[118]

Opponents of the death penalty criticized the 2001 report, and the Justice Department's interpretation of the data, on a number of grounds. The American Civil Liberties Union (ACLU), for example, asserted that there were a number of problems with the study, which it characterized as "fatally flawed."[119] The ACLU noted that the report did not address questions regarding the prosecution of cases in the federal system rather than the state system or examine whether race/ethnicity played a role in these decisions or in U.S. Attorneys' decisions to enter into plea bargains. The ACLU asserted that Attorney General Ashcroft reached a "premature" conclusion that "racial bias has not played a role in who is on federal death row in America," adding, "This remarkable conclusion is not only inaccurate, but also dangerous, because it seeks to give Americans the impression that our justice system is fair when in fact there is substantial evidence that it is not."[120]

On June 11, 2001, Timothy McVeigh, who was convicted of a number of counts stemming from the 1995 Oklahoma City bombing, became the first federal offender since 1963 to be put to death. The execution of Juan Raul Garza, a Texas marijuana distributor who was sentenced to death in 1993 for the murder of three other drug traffickers, followed 8 days later. By July 2005, there were 36 offenders on federal death row: 23 were African American, 12 were white, and 1 was Native American.[121]

Explanations for Disparate Treatment

Researchers have advanced two interrelated explanations for the higher death penalty rates for homicides involving African American offenders and white victims and the lower rates for homicides involving African American offenders and African American victims.

The first explanation builds on conflict theory's premise that the law is applied to maintain the power of the dominant group and to control the behavior of individuals who threaten that power.[122] It suggests that crimes involving African American offenders and white victims are punished most harshly because they pose the greatest threat to "the system of racially stratified state authority."[123] Some commentators further suggest that in the South the death penalty may be imposed more often on African Americans who kill whites "because of a continuing adherence to traditional southern norms of racial etiquette."[124]

The second explanation for the harsher penalties imposed on those who victimize whites emphasizes the race of the victim rather than the racial composition of the victim–offender dyad. This explanation suggests that crimes involving African American victims are not taken seriously, that crimes involving white victims are taken very seriously, or both. It also suggests that the lives of African American victims are devalued relative to the lives of white victims. Thus, crimes against whites will be punished more severely than crimes against African Americans regardless of the offender's race. Some commentators suggest that these beliefs are encouraged by the media, which plays up the murders of wealthy whites but ignores those involving poor African Americans and Hispanics. The publicity accorded crimes involving middle-class and wealthy white victims also influences prosecutors to seek the death penalty more often in these types of cases than in cases involving poor racial minorities. According to David Baldus, "If the victim is black, particularly if he's an unsavory character, a drug dealer, for example, prosecutors are likely to say, 'No jury would return a death verdict.'"[125]

Most researchers have failed to explain adequately *why* those who victimize whites are treated more harshly than those who victimize African Americans. Gross and Mauro[126] suggest that the explanation, at least in capital cases, may hinge on the degree to which jurors are able to identify with the victim. The authors argue that jurors take the life-or-death decision in a capital case very seriously. To condemn a murderer to death thus requires something more than sympathy for the victim. Jurors will not sentence the defendant to death unless they are particularly horrified by the crime, and they will not be particularly horrified by the crime unless they can identify or empathize with the victim. According to Gross and Mauro:

> In a society that remains segregated socially if not legally, and in which the great majority of jurors are white, jurors are not likely to identify with black victims or to see them as family or friends. Thus jurors are more likely to be horrified by the killing of a white than of a black, and more likely to act against the killer of a white than the killer of a black.[127]

Bright[128] offers a somewhat different explanation. He contends that the unconscious racism and racial stereotypes of prosecutors, judges, and jurors, the majority of whom are white, "may well be 'stirred up'" in cases involving an African American offender and a white victim.[129] In these types of cases, in other words, officials' and jurors' beliefs that African Americans are violent or morally inferior, coupled with their fear of African Americans, might incline them to seek or to impose the death penalty. Bright also asserts that black-on-white murders generate more publicity and evoke greater horror than other types of crimes. As he notes, "Community outrage, ... the social and political clout of the family in the community, and the amount of publicity regarding the crime are often far more important in determining whether death is sought than the facts of the crime or the defendant's record and background."[130]

McCLESKEY V. KEMP: THE SUPREME COURT AND RACIAL DISCRIMINATION IN THE APPLICATION OF THE DEATH PENALTY

Empirical evidence of racial discrimination in the capital sentencing process has been used to mount constitutional challenges to the imposition of the death penalty. African American defendants convicted of raping or murdering whites have claimed that the death penalty is applied in a racially discriminatory manner in violation of both the equal protection clause of the Fourteenth Amendment and the cruel and unusual punishment clause of the Eighth Amendment.

These claims have been consistently rejected by state and federal appellate courts. The case of the Martinsville Seven, a group of African American men who were sentenced to death for the gang-rape of a white woman, was the first case in which defendants explicitly argued that the death penalty was administered in a racially discriminatory manner.[131] It also was the first case in which lawyers presented statistical evidence to prove systematic racial discrimination in capital cases. As explained in more detail in "In the Courts: The Case of the Martinsville Seven," the defendants' contention that the Virginia rape statute had "been applied and administered with an evil eye and an unequal hand"[132] was repeatedly denied by Virginia appellate courts.

The question of racial discrimination in the application of the death penalty also has been addressed in federal court. In a series of decisions, the Courts of Appeals ruled, first, that the empirical studies used to document systematic racial discrimination did not take every variable related to capital sentencing into account and, second, that the evidence presented did not demonstrate that the appellant's *own* sentence was the product of discrimination.[144]

The Supreme Court directly addressed the issue of victim-based racial discrimination in the application of the death penalty in the case of *McCleskey v. Kemp*.[145] Warren McCleskey, an African American, was convicted and sentenced to death in Georgia for killing a white police officer during the course of an armed robbery. McCleskey claimed that the Georgia capital sentencing process was administered in a racially discriminatory manner. In support of his claim, he offered the results of the study conducted by Baldus and his colleagues.[146] As noted earlier, this study found that African Americans convicted of murdering whites had the greatest likelihood of receiving the death penalty.

The Supreme Court rejected McCleskey's Fourteenth and Eighth Amendment claims. Although the majority accepted the validity of the Baldus study, they

In the Courts: The Case of the Martinsville Seven

Just after dark on January 8, 1949, Ruby Floyd, a 32-year-old white woman, was assaulted and repeatedly raped by several men as she walked in a predominately black neighborhood in Martinsville, Virginia.[133] Within a day and a half, seven African American men had been arrested; when confronted with incriminating statements made by their co-defendants, all of them confessed. Two months later, a grand jury composed of four white men and three African American men indicted each defendant on one count of rape and six counts of aiding and abetting a rape by the other defendants.

The defendants were tried in the Seventh Judicial Circuit Court, located in Martinsville. Before the legal proceedings began, Judge Kennon Caithness Whittle, who presided over all of the trials, called the prosecutors and defense attorneys into his chambers to remind them of their duty to protect the defendants' right to a fair trial and to plead with them to "downplay the racial overtones" of the case. He emphasized that the case "must be tried as though both parties were members of the same race."[134]

Although prosecutors took Judge Whittle's admonitions to heart and emphasized the seriousness of the crime and the defendants' evident guilt rather than the fact that the crime involved the rape of a white woman by African American men, the "racial overtones" of the case inevitably surfaced. Defense attorneys, for example, moved for a change of venue, arguing that inflammatory publicity about the case, coupled with widespread community sentiment that the defendants were guilty and "ought to get the works,"[135] meant that the defendants could not get a fair trial in Martinsville. Judge Whittle, who admitted that it might be difficult to find impartial jurors and acknowledged that some jurors might be biased against the defendants because of their race, denied the motion, asserting that "no mass feeling about these defendants"[136] had surfaced. Later, prosecutors used their peremptory challenges to exclude the few African Americans who remained in the jury pool after those who opposed the death penalty had been excused for cause. As a result, each case was decided by an all-white jury. The result of each day-long trial was the same—all seven defendants were found guilty of rape and sentenced to death. On May 3, 1949, less than 4 months after the assault on Ruby Floyd, Judge Whittle officially pronounced sentence and announced that four of the defendants were to be executed on July 15, and the remaining three were to be executed on July 22. Noting that this gave the defendants more than 60 days to appeal, he stated, "If errors have been made I pray God they may be corrected."[137]

The next 19 months witnessed several rounds of appeals challenging the convictions and death sentences of the Martinsville Seven. The initial petition submitted by attorneys for the NAACP Legal Defense Fund, which represented the defendants on appeal, charged the trial court with four violations of due process. Although none of the charges focused directly on racially discriminatory practices, allegations of racial prejudice were interwoven with a number of the arguments. Appellants noted, for example, that prior to 1866 Virginia law specified that the death penalty for rape

---

nonetheless refused to accept McCleskey's argument that the disparities documented by Baldus signaled the presence of unconstitutional racial discrimination. Justice Powell, writing for the majority, argued that the disparities were "unexplained" and stated, "At most, the Baldus study indicates a discrepancy that appears to correlate with race."[147] The Court stated that the Baldus study was "clearly insufficient to

could be imposed only on African American men convicted of raping white women and that even after the law was repealed virtually all of those sentenced to death for rape had been African American. They also stated that the trial judge's questioning of prospective jurors about capital punishment and subsequent exclusion of those who were opposed to the imposition of the death penalty sent the unmistakable message that "only one penalty would be appropriate for the offenders."[138]

These appeals failed at both the state and federal level. The Virginia Supreme Court of Appeals voted unanimously to affirm the convictions. Chief Justice Edward W. Hudgins, who wrote the opinion, vehemently denied appellants' assertions that the death penalty was reserved for blacks, noting that there was not "a scintilla of evidence" to support it.[139] Hudgins also chastised the defendants' attorneys for even raising the issue, contending that it was nothing more than "an abortive attempt to inject into the proceedings racial prejudice."[140]

The defendants appealed the decision to the U.S. Supreme Court, but the Court declined to review the case. This prompted the NAACP attorneys to adopt a radically different strategy for the next round of appeals. Rather than challenging the defendants' convictions and death sentences on traditional due process grounds, the attorneys mounted a direct attack on the discriminatory application of the death penalty in Virginia. Martin Martin and Samuel Tucker, the NAACP attorneys who argued in support of the defendants' *habeas corpus* petition, presented statistical evidence documenting a double standard of justice in Virginia rape cases. Noting that 45 African Americans, but not a single white, had been executed for rape since 1908, Tucker stated that African Americans were entitled to the same protection of the law as whites and concluded "if you can't equalize upward [by executing more whites], we must equalize downward."[141]

In an opinion that foreshadowed the Supreme Court's decision in *McCleskey v. Kemp* a quarter of a century later, Judge Doubles, who was presiding over the Hustings Court of the City of Richmond, denied the petition. Judge Doubles stated, first, that there was no evidence of racial discrimination in the actions of the six juries that sentenced the Martinsville Seven to death or in the performance of other juries in similar cases. He then concluded that even if one assumed that those juries had been motivated by racial prejudice, "the petitioners could not demonstrate that an official policy of discrimination, rather than the independent actions of separate juries, resulted in the death verdicts."[142] As a result, there was no Constitutional violation.

The case then was appealed to the Virginia Supreme Court and, when that appeal failed, to the U.S. Supreme Court. In January 1951, the Supreme Court again declined to review the case. Last-minute efforts to save the Martinsville Seven failed. Four of the men were executed on February 2 and the remaining three on February 5. "After two years, six trials, five stays of execution, ten opportunities for judicial review, and two denials of executive clemency, the legal odyssey of the Martinsville Seven had ended."[143]

support an inference that any of the decisionmakers in McCleskey's case acted with discriminatory purpose."[148]

The Court also expressed its concern that accepting McCleskey's claim would open a Pandora's Box of litigation. "McCleskey's claim, taken to its logical conclusion," Powell wrote, "throws into serious question the principles that underlie our entire criminal justice system ... if we accepted McCleskey's claim that racial bias impermissibly tainted the capital sentencing decision, we would soon be faced with similar claims as to other types of penalty."[149] A ruling in McCleskey's favor, in other words, would open the door to constitutional challenges to the legitimacy, not only of the capital sentencing process, but of sentencing in general.

The four dissenting justices were outraged. Justice Brennan, who was joined in dissent by Justices Blackmun, Marshall, and Stevens, wrote, "The Court today holds that Warren McCleskey's sentence was constitutionally imposed. It finds no fault with a system in which lawyers must tell their clients that race casts a large shadow on the capital sentencing process." Brennan also characterized the majority's concern that upholding McCleskey's claim would encourage other groups—"even women"[150]—to challenge the criminal sentencing process "as a fear of too much justice" and "a complete abdication of our judicial role."[151]

Legal scholars were similarly outraged. Anthony Amsterdam, who was the lead attorney in a 1968 U.S. Court of Appeals case in which an African American man challenged his death sentence for the rape of a white woman,[152] wrote,

> I suggest that any self-respecting criminal justice professional is obliged to speak out against this Supreme Court's conception of the criminal justice system. We must reaffirm that there can be no justice in a system which treats people of color differently from white people, or treats crimes against people of color differently from crimes against white people.[153]

Randall Kennedy's analysis was similarly harsh. He challenged Justice Powell's assertion that the Baldus study indicated nothing more "than a discrepancy that appears to correlate with race," which he characterized as "a statement as vacuous as one declaring, say, that 'at most' studies on lung cancer indicate a discrepancy that appears to correlate with smoking."[154] Bright characterized the decision as "a badge of shame upon America's system of justice,"[155] and Gross and Mauro concluded that, "The central message of the *McCleskey* case is all too plain; de facto racial discrimination in capital sentencing is legal in the United States."[156] (See Box 8.6 for a discussion of the possible remedies for racial discrimination in the application of the death penalty.)

The Execution of Warren McCleskey   The Court's decision in *McCleskey v. Kemp* did not mark the end of Warren McCleskey's odyssey through the appellate courts. He filed another appeal in 1987, alleging that the testimony of a jailhouse informant, which was used to rebut his alibi defense, was obtained illegally. Offie Evans testified at McCleskey's trial in 1978 that McCleskey admitted to and boasted about killing the police officer. McCleskey argued that the state placed Evans in the jail cell next to his and instructed Evans to try to get him to talk about the crime. He contended that because he did not have the assistance of counsel at the time he made the incriminating statements, they could not be used against him.

In 1991 the Supreme Court denied McCleskey's claim, asserting that the issue should have been raised in his first appeal.[157] The Court stated that

McCleskey would have been allowed to raise a new issue if he had been able to demonstrate that the alleged violation resulted in the conviction of an innocent person. However, according to the Court, "the violation, if it be one, resulted in the admission at trial of truthful inculpatory evidence which did not affect the reliability of the guilt determination. The very statement that McCleskey now embraces confirms his guilt."[158]

After a series of last-minute appeals, requests for clemency, and requests for commutation were denied, Warren McCleskey was strapped into the electric chair at the state prison in Jacksonville, Georgia. He was pronounced dead at 3:13 A.M., September 26, 1991.

Justice Thurgood Marshall, one of three dissenters from the Supreme Court's decision not to grant a stay of execution, wrote, "In refusing to grant a stay to review fully McCleskey's claims, the court values expediency over human life. Repeatedly denying Warren McCleskey his constitutional rights is unacceptable. Executing him is inexcusable."[159]

The Aftermath of *McCleskey*: Calls for Reform or Abolition of the Death Penalty

Opponents of the death penalty viewed the issues raised in *McCleskey v. Kemp* as the only remaining challenge to the constitutionality of the death penalty. They predicted that the Court's decision, which effectively closed the door to similar appeals, would speed up the pace of executions. Data on the number of persons executed since 1987 provide support for this. Although only 25 people were executed in 1987, 11 in 1988, 16 in 1989, 23 in 1990, and 14 in 1991, the numbers began to increase in 1992. As shown in Figure 8.5, 31 people were put to death in 1992, 33 in 1993, 31 in 1994, 35 in 1995, 45 in 1996, 74 in 1997, 68 in 1998, 98 in 1999, 85 in 2000, 66 in 2001, 71 in 2002, 65 in 2003, and 59 in 2004.[160]

The increase in executions since 1991 no doubt reflects the impact of two recent Supreme Court decisions sharply limiting death row appeals. As noted previously, in 1991 the Court ruled that, with few exceptions, death row inmates and other state prisoners must raise constitutional claims on their first appeals.[161] This ruling, coupled with a 1993 decision stating that "late claims of innocence" raised by death row inmates who have exhausted other federal appeals do not automatically qualify for a hearing in federal court,[162] severely curtailed the ability of death row inmates to pursue multiple federal court appeals.

The U.S. House of Representatives responded to the Supreme Court's ruling in *McCleskey v. Kemp* by adding the Racial Justice Act to the Omnibus Crime Bill of 1994. A slim majority of the House voted for the provision, which would have allowed condemned defendants to challenge their death sentences by showing a *pattern* of racial discrimination in the capital sentencing process in their jurisdictions. Under this provision, the defendant would not have to show that criminal justice officials acted with discriminatory purpose in his or her case; rather, the defendant could use statistical evidence indicating that a disproportionate number of those sentenced to death in the jurisdiction were African Americans or had killed whites.

B O X 8.6 Racial Discrimination in Capital Sentencing: The Problem of Remedy

---

A number of commentators have suggested that the Court's reluctance to accept McCleskey's claim reflected its anxiety about the practical consequences of ruling that race impermissibly affected the capital sentencing process.[186] The Court's decision, in other words, reflected its concern about the appropriate remedy if it found a constitutional violation.

The remedies that have been suggested include the following:

1. Abolish the death penalty and vacate all existing death sentences nationwide.
   - The problem with this remedy, of course, is that it is impractical, given the level of public support for the death penalty and the current emphasis on crime control. As Gross and Mauro note, "Although abolition is a perfectly practical solution to the problems of capital punishment . . . it is not a serious option in America now."[187]

2. Vacate all death sentences in each state where there is compelling evidence of racial disparities in the application of the death penalty.
   - Although this state-by-state approach would not completely satisfy the abolitionists, according to Kennedy, it would place "a large question mark over the legitimacy of any death penalty system generating unexplained racial disparities of the sort at issue in *McCleskey*."[188]

3. Limit the class of persons eligible for the death penalty to those who commit the most heinous, the most aggravated homicides. As Justice Stevens suggested in his dissent in *McCleskey*, the Court could narrow the class of death-eligible defendants to those "categories of extremely serious crimes for which prosecutors consistently seek, and juries consistently impose, the death penalty without regard to the race of the victim or the race of the offender."[189]
   - Although not an "ideal" solution for a number of reasons, this would, as Baldus and his colleagues contend, impart "a greater degree of rationality and consistency into state death-sentencing systems than any of the other procedural safeguards that the Supreme Court has heretofore endorsed."[190]

4. Reinstate mandatory death sentences for certain crimes.
   - This remedy would, of course, require the Supreme Court to retract its invalidation of mandatory death penalty statutes. Kennedy contends that this would not solve the problem because prosecutors could refuse to charge the killers of African Americans with a capital crime and juries could decline to convict those who killed African Americans of crimes that triggered the mandatory death sentence.[191]

5. Opt for the "level-up solution,"[192] which would require courts to purposely impose more death sentences on those who murdered African Americans.
   - According to Kennedy, states in which there are documented racial disparities in the use of the death penalty could be given a choice: either condemn those who kill African Americans to death at the same rate at those who kill whites or "relinquish the power to put anyone to death."[193]

Once this pattern of racial discrimination had been established, the state would be required to prove that its death penalty decisions were racially neutral. The state might rebut an apparent pattern of racial discrimination in a case involving an

FIGURE 8.5 Executions in the United States, 1987–2004

SOURCE: NAACP Legal Defense and Educational Fund, Inc. *Death Row USA: Summer 2005.* Available at http://www.deathpenaltyinfo.org/DEATHROWUSArecent.pdf.

African American convicted of killing a white police officer, for example, by showing a consistent pattern of seeking the death penalty for defendants, regardless of race, who were accused of killing police officers.

Opponents of the Racial Justice Act argued that it would effectively abolish the death penalty in the United States. As Senator Orrin Hatch remarked, "The so-called Racial Justice Act has nothing to do with racial justice and everything to do with abolishing the death penalty."[163] The provision was a source of heated debate before it was eventually eliminated from the 1994 Omnibus Crime Bill.

THE DEATH PENALTY IN THE 21ST CENTURY

Opponents of the death penalty assumed that the Supreme Court's decision in *McCleskey v. Kemp*, coupled with the defeat of the Racial Justice Act, sounded a death knell for attempts to abolish the death penalty. They predicted that these decisions would quiet—if not extinguish—the controversy surrounding the death penalty. Contrary to their predictions, however, the controversy did not die down. In fact, a series of events at the turn of the century pushed the issue back on the public agenda:

- In February 1997, the American Bar Association (ABA) went on record as being formally opposed to the current capital sentencing system and called for an immediate moratorium on executions in the United States. The ABA report cited the following concerns: lack of adequate counsel in death penalty cases; restrictions on access to appellate courts; and racial disparities in the administration of capital punishment.[164]

- In January 2000, George Ryan, the governor of Illinois, issued a moratorium on the use of the death penalty in that state. His decision was motivated by the fact that since the death penalty was reinstated in Illinois, 12 people were

---

B O X 8.7   Death and Discrimination in Texas

On June 5, 2000 the U.S. Supreme Court set aside Victor Saldano's death sentence after lawyers for the state of Texas admitted that the decision had been based in part on the fact that he is Hispanic.[194] Saldano kidnapped Paul Green at gunpoint from a grocery store parking lot, took him to an isolated area, shot him five times, and stole his watch and wallet. At his sentencing hearing, a psychologist testified about Saldano's "future dangerousness." He noted that blacks and Hispanics were overrepresented in prison and stated that the fact that Saldano was Hispanic was an indicator of his future dangerousness. The Texas Court of Criminal Appeals upheld Saldano's death sentence, stating that allowing his ethnicity to be used as an indicator of dangerousness was not a "fundamental error."

In his appeal to the U.S. Supreme Court, Saldano disagreed with that conclusion. He stated that it is "fundamentally unfair for the prosecution to use racial and ethnic stereotypes in order to obtain a death penalty." The Texas Attorney General conceded Saldano's point. He admitted that the state had erred and joined Saldano in asking the Supreme Court to order a new sentencing hearing. After the Court's decision was announced, a spokesperson for the Texas Attorney General's Office stated that an audit had uncovered eight additional cases that might raise similar issues regarding testimony linking race and ethnicity to assessments of future dangerousness.

Questions about the fairness of the Texas death penalty process have been raised in other forums. During the summer of 2000, for example, the *Chicago Tribune* published a two-part series that focused on the 131 executions that were carried out during Texas Governor George W. Bush's tenure.[195] (Since 1977, Texas has executed 218 people, which is more than three times the number executed by any other state.[196]) The report noted that in 40 of the 131 cases the defense attorney either presented no mitigating evidence at all or called only one witness during the sentencing hearing. In 43 of the cases, the defendant was represented by an attorney who had been (or was subsequent to the trial) publicly sanctioned for misconduct by the State Bar of Texas. One attorney, for example, who had been practicing for only 17 months, was appointed to represent Davis Losada, who was accused of rape and murder. Losada was found guilty and sentenced to death after the attorney delivered a "disjointed and brief argument" in which he told the jury: "The System.

---

executed but 13 were exonerated. Governor Ryan, who called for a "public dialogue" on "the question of the fairness of the application of the death penalty in Illinois," stated that he favored a moratorium because of his "grave concerns about our state's shameful record of convicting innocent people and putting them on death row."[165] Three years later, Governor Ryan commuted the sentences of all of the state's 167 death row inmates to life in prison.

■ In May 2000, the New Hampshire legislature voted to repeal the death penalty. One legislator—a Republican and a longtime supporter of the death penalty—justified his vote for repeal by saying, "There are no millionaires on death row. Can you honestly say that you're going to get equal justice under the law when, if you've got the money, you are going to get away with it?"[166] Although the legislation was subsequently vetoed by the governor, it was the first time in more than 2 decades that a state legislature had voted to repeal the death penalty.

Justice. I don't know. But that's what y'all are going to do." He later admitted that he had a conflict of interest in the case (he previously had represented the key witness against his client) and in 1994 he was disbarred for stealing money from his clients.

Other problems cited in the *Tribune* report included the use of unreliable evidence, such as testimony by jail-house informants; the use of questionable testimony from a psychiatrist, nicknamed "Dr. Death," regarding the potential dangerousness of capital offenders; and the refusal of the Texas Court of Criminal Appeals to order new trials or sentencing hearings despite allegations of fundamental violations of defendants' rights. The report noted that since then-Governor Bush took office in 1995, the Court of Criminal Appeals affirmed 270 capital convictions, granted new trials eight times, and ordered new sentencing hearings only six times.

In September 2000, the Texas Civil Rights Project issued a comprehensive report on "The Death Penalty in Texas" that identified many of the same problems.[197] The authors of the report stated that there were "six areas where the probability of error and the probability of wrongful execution grow dramatically": appointment of counsel to represent indigent defendants; the prosecutor's decision to seek the death penalty; the jury selection process; the sentencing process; the appellate process; and the review of cases by the Board of Pardons and Parole. The report emphasized that the issue was not "a possible break at one juncture, but a probable break at two or more critical junctures."

To remedy these deficiencies, the Texas Civil Rights Project recommended that Governor Bush call for a moratorium on the death penalty in Texas. They also recommended that Governor Bush appoint a commission to review the convictions of those currently on death row; the commission would be charged with determining whether the defendant's rights to due process had been violated and whether race, social class, or both affected the death penalty process.[198] According to the report, "[i]f the State of Texas is going to continue to take the lives of people, then it needs to repair the system ..." The report concluded, "The frightening truth of the matter is that Texas is at greater risk than at anytime since it resumed executions in 1982 of killing innocent people."[199]

- In October 2000, the Texas Civil Rights Project (TCRP) released a report on the death penalty in Texas (see Box 8.7). The report identified six critical issues, including the competency of attorneys appointed to represent defendants charged with capital murder, that "decrease due process for low-income death penalty defendants and increase the probability of wrongful convictions." The report called on then–Governor George Bush to institute a moratorium on the death penalty pending the results of two studies, one of which would determine whether race and social class influenced the use of the death penalty in Texas.[167]

- During 2001 two Supreme Court Justices—Sandra Day O'Connor and Ruth Bader Ginsburg—gave speeches in which they criticized the handling of death penalty cases. O'Connor stated that "some innocent defendants have been convicted and sentenced to death" and Ginsburg noted that she "had yet to see a death case ... in which the defendant was well represented at trial."[168]

- Since 2000, bills calling for a moratorium on the death penalty have been introduced in Congress and in the state legislatures of 32 of the 38 states with the death penalty.

As these examples illustrate, concerns about the fairness and accuracy of the capital sentencing process led many to conclude that it was time to rethink the death penalty. This period of "rethinking" spawned two distinct movements: one for reform of the capital sentencing process and one for abolishing the death penalty.

The Movement to Reform the Death Penalty

Advocates of reform contend that the capital sentencing process can be "fixed." Although acknowledging that the system is not infallible, they argue that the enactment of reforms designed to ensure that innocent persons are not convicted and sentenced to death will remedy the situation. The reforms that have been proposed include increasing access to postconviction DNA testing and providing funding to pay for DNA tests requested by indigent inmates; banning the execution of the mentally handicapped; and establishing standards on qualifications and experience for defense counsel in death penalty cases.

Typical of this approach is the Innocence Protection Act of 2004 (HR 5107), a package of criminal justice reforms that President George W. Bush signed into law on October 30, 2004. The Act was part of the larger Justice for All Act, which had broad bipartisan support in the U.S. Senate and House of Representatives; this bill enhanced protection for victims of federal crimes, increased federal resources available to state and local governments to combat crimes with DNA technology, and provided safeguards designed to prevent wrongful convictions and executions. The Innocence Protection Act (Title VI of the Justice for All Act) has three important provisions. The first provision allows a person convicted of a federal crime to obtain DNA testing to support a claim of innocence, prohibits the destruction of DNA evidence in federal criminal cases while a defendant remains incarcerated, and provides funding to states to help defray the costs of postconviction DNA testing. The second provision authorizes a grant program to improve the quality of legal representation provided to indigent defendants in state capital cases. The third provision increases the maximum amount of damages that can be awarded in cases of unjust imprisonment to $100,000 per year in capital cases.[169]

One of the act's main supporters in the Senate, Patrick Leahy (Democrat from Vermont), characterized the Innocence Protection Act as "the most significant step we have taken in many years to improve the quality of justice in this country." Leahy added that DNA testing, which he called the "miracle forensic tool of our lifetimes," had revealed flaws in the death penalty process. He also stated that the bill's provisions regarding provision of counsel represent "a modest step toward addressing one of the most frequent causes of wrongful convictions in capital cases, the lack of adequate legal counsel."[170]

A similar approach was taken by the bipartisan commission appointed by Illinois Governor George Ryan after he halted executions in January 2000. The commission's report, which was issued in April 2002, recommended 85 changes in the capital sentencing process in Illinois. Included were proposals to prohibit the imposition of the death penalty based solely on the testimony of a single eyewitness, a jail-house informant, or an accomplice; videotape interrogations of suspects; establish an independent forensics laboratory; and establish a state panel to review prosecutors' decisions to seek the death penalty. The report also proposed eliminating several categories of capital crimes, including murder committed in the course of a felony. The co-chairman of the commission, Thomas P. Sullivan, a former federal prosecutor, stated that the options were to "repair or repeal" the death penalty. "Fix the capital punishment system or abolish it," he said. "There is no other principled recourse."[171]

The Movement to Abolish the Death Penalty

In contrast to those who advocate reform of the capital sentencing system, proponents of abolishing the death penalty contend that the system is fatally flawed. To support their position, these "new abolitionists"[172] cite mounting evidence of wrongful conviction of those on death row (see Box 8.8) and evidence that the death penalty is administered in an arbitrary and discriminatory manner. Like former Supreme Court Justice Harry Blackmun, they argue that it is futile to continue to "tinker with the machinery of death."

Whereas traditional abolitionists base their opposition to the death penalty on the immorality of state killing, the sanctity of human life, or the inherent cruelty of death as a punishment, the new abolitionists claim that the death penalty "has not been, and cannot be, administered in a manner that is compatible with our legal system's fundamental commitments to fair and equal treatment."[173] They contend that the implementation of procedural rules, such as those proposed by the advocates of reform, has not solved—indeed, cannot solve—the problems inherent in the capital sentencing process; the post-*Furman* reforms notwithstanding, "the death penalty remains fraught with arbitrariness, discrimination, caprice, and mistake."[174] Like Justice Blackmun, the advocates of abolition insist that "no combination of procedural rules or substantive regulations ever can save the death penalty from its inherent constitutional deficiencies."[175]

Concerns about fairness and discrimination in the capital sentencing process prompted death penalty opponents to call not for procedural reforms but for a moratorium on executions in the United States. Although these resolutions usually call for a cessation of executions until reforms designed to ensure due process and equal protection have been implemented, Sarat maintains that they "amount to a call for the abolition, not merely the cessation, of capital punishment."[176]

Sarat contends that the reforms needed to "fix" the capital sentencing process—provision of competent counsel for all capital defendants, expansion of death row inmates' rights to appeal, guaranteed access to DNA testing, and review of prosecutors' decisions to seek the death penalty—although feasible, are "hardly a likely or near-term possibility."[177] He notes, for example, that one of the reasons cited by the American Bar Association in its call for a moratorium on the death penalty is the "longstanding patterns of racial discrimination ... in courts around the country." To address this problem, the ABA calls for the

---

B O X 8.8   The Death Penalty and Wrongful Convictions

Opponents of the death penalty consistently note the possibility that an individual will be sentenced to death for a crime that he or she did not commit. Bedau and Radelet[200] have identified 350 cases in which defendants were wrongfully convicted of a homicide for which they could have received the death penalty or of a rape in which the death penalty was imposed. Of these individuals, 139 were sentenced to die; 23 eventually were executed. Another 22 people came within 72 hours of being executed.

These wrongful convictions include a number of people sentenced to death in the post-*Furman* era. In 1987, for example, Walter McMillian, an African American man who was dating a white woman, was charged with the death of an 18-year-old white female store clerk in Alabama. In spite of testimony from a dozen witnesses, who swore he was at home on the day of the murder, and despite the lack of any physical evidence, McMillian was convicted after a one-and-a-half-day trial. His conviction hinged on the testimony of Ralph Myers, a 30-year-old with a long criminal record. The jury recommended life in prison without parole, but the judge hearing the case, citing the "vicious and brutal killing of a young lady in the full flower of adulthood,"[201] sentenced McMillian to death.

Six years later, Myers recanted his testimony. He said he had been pressured by law enforcement officials to accuse McMillian and to testify against him in court. McMillian was freed in March 1993, after prosecutors conceded that his conviction was based on perjured testimony and that evidence had been withheld from his lawyers. He had spent 6 years on death row for a crime he did not commit.

A similar fate awaited Rolando Cruz, a Hispanic American who, along with co-defendant Alejandro Hernandez, was convicted in DuPage County (Illinois) Circuit Court of the 1983 kidnapping, rape, and murder of 10-year-old Jeanine Nicarico. Cruz was twice convicted and condemned to death for the crime, but both verdicts were overturned by appellate courts because of procedural errors at trial. He spent nearly 10 years on death row before he was acquitted at a third trial in November 1995. Hernandez also was convicted twice and sentenced to death once before his case was dropped following the acquittal of Cruz.[202]

This case attracted national attention for what many believed was the "railroading" of Cruz and Hernandez. Prosecutors presented no physical evidence or

---

development of "effective mechanisms" to eliminate racial discrimination in capital cases. Similarly, the National Death Penalty Moratorium Act, which was introduced in both houses of Congress in 2001 but which did not pass, would have set up a National Commission on the Death Penalty; the commission would have been charged with "establishing guidelines and procedures which … ensure that the death penalty is not administered in a racially discriminatory manner."[178] The problem, according to Sarat, is that it is not clear that any such "mechanisms," "guidelines," or "procedures" exist. As he contends,

> The pernicious effects of race in capital sentencing are a function of the persistence of racial prejudice throughout society combined with the wide degree of discretion necessary to afford individualized justice in

eyewitness testimony linking the two to the crime but relied almost exclusively on the testimony of jailhouse informants, who stated that the defendants had admitted the crime, and on questionable testimony regarding a dream about the crime that Cruz allegedly described to sheriff's deputies. They also ignored compelling evidence that another man, Brian Dugan, had committed the crime. According to one commentator, "The crime had been 'solved' by cobbling together a shabby case against Rolando Cruz and Alex Hernandez of Aurora and presenting it to a jury that convicted them and sent them to Death Row."[203]

On November 3, 1995, Judge Ronald Mehling, who was presiding at Cruz's third trial, acquitted Cruz of the charges. In a strongly worded address from the bench, Mehling stated that the murder investigation was "sloppy" and that the government's case against Cruz was "riddled with lies and mistakes." He also sharply criticized prosecutors for their handling of the "vision statement" and suggested that investigators had lied about the statement and about other evidence. "What troubles me in this case," Mehling said, "is what the evidence does not show."[204] Cruz was set free that day; Hernandez was released several weeks later.

One year later, a grand jury handed down a 47-count indictment against three of the prosecutors and four of the sheriff's deputies involved in the case. The indictment charged the deputies with repeated acts of perjury and alleged that prosecutors knowingly presented perjured testimony and buried the notes of an interview with Dugan that could have exonerated Cruz.[205] The defendants, dubbed the "DuPage Seven," were acquitted of all charges in 1999. Lawyers for Rolando Cruz, Alejandro Hernandez, and Stephen Buckley (a third defendant who had been charged in the crime) then filed a federal civil rights suit. In October 2000, the DuPage County State's Attorney agreed to pay the defendants an out-of-court settlement of $3.5 million.

These two cases are not isolated incidents. In April 2002, Ray Krone, who was convicted and sentenced to death for the murder of a cocktail waitress in 1991, became the 100th former death row prisoner to be exonerated since 1973. Krone was freed after DNA tests revealed that he was not the killer. In 2005, Derrick Jamison became the 121st death row inmate to be exonerated. He was freed and all charges were dismissed after it came to light that prosecutors in the case had withheld critical eyewitness statements and other evidence from his attorneys.

capital prosecutions and capital trials. Prosecutors with limited resources may be inclined to allocate resources to cases that attract the greatest public attention, which often will mean cases where the victim was white and his or her assailant black. Participants in the legal system—whether white or black—demonize young black males, seeing them as more deserving of death as a punishment because of their perceived danger. These cultural effects are not remediable in the near term . . .[179]

Because it may be impossible to ensure that the capital sentencing process is operated in a racially neutral manner, Sarat and others who embrace the new abolitionism maintain that the only solution is to abolish the death penalty.

CONCLUSION

The findings of research examining the effect of race on the capital sentencing process are consistent. Study after study has demonstrated that those who murder whites are much more likely to be sentenced to death than those who murder African Americans. Many of these studies also have shown that African Americans convicted of murdering whites receive the death penalty more often than whites who murder other whites. These results come from studies conducted before *Furman*, in the decade following the *Gregg* decision, and in the 1990s and beyond. They come from studies conducted in both Southern and non-Southern jurisdictions and from studies examining prosecutors' charging decisions and jurors' sentencing decisions.

These results suggest that racial disparities in the application of the death penalty reflect racial discrimination. Some might argue that these results signal contextual, rather than systematic, racial discrimination. As noted earlier, although research consistently has revealed that those who murder whites are sentenced to death at a disproportionately high rate, not all studies have found that African American offenders are more likely than white offenders to be sentenced to death.

We contend that the type of discrimination found in the capital sentencing process falls closer to the systematic end of the discrimination continuum presented in Chapter 1. Racial discrimination in the capital sentencing process is not limited to the South, where historical evidence of racial bias would lead one to expect differential treatment; it is applicable to other regions of the country as well. It is not confined to one stage of the decisionmaking process; it affects decisions made by prosecutors and juries. It also is not confined to the pre-*Furman* period, when statutes offered little or no guidance to judges and juries charged with deciding whether to impose the death penalty; it is found, too, under the more restrictive guided discretion statutes enacted since *Furman*. Moreover, this effect does not disappear when legally relevant predictors of sentence severity are taken into consideration.

With respect to the capital sentencing process, then, empirical studies suggest that the Supreme Court was overly optimistic in predicting that the statutory reforms adopted since *Furman* would eliminate racial discrimination. To the contrary, these studies document "a clear pattern unexplainable on grounds other than race."[180]

DISCUSSION QUESTIONS

1. Do you agree or disagree with the so-called "Marshall Hypothesis"—that is, that the average citizen who knew "all the facts presently available regarding capital punishment would ... find it shocking to his conscience and sense of justice"?

2. In *Gregg v. Georgia*, the Supreme Court assumed that racial discrimination would not be a problem under the guided-discretion statutes enacted in the wake of the *Furman* decision. Does the empirical evidence support or refute this assumption?

3. Explain why Michael Radelet believes that the handful of executions of whites for crimes against African Americans are not really "exceptions to the rule."

4. The procedures adopted by the Department of Justice to govern death penalty decisions in federal cases (the so-called "death penalty protocol") are designed to ensure that the federal capital sentencing process is fair and equitable. But studies conducted by the Department of Justice revealed that racial minorities were overrepresented in federal capital criminal cases and among those sentenced to death in U.S. District Courts. How did the Justice Department interpret these findings? Why did the American Civil Liberties Union conclude that the 2001 study was "fatally flawed?"

5. In the case of the Martinsville Seven a series of state and federal court rulings rejected the defendants' allegations regarding racial discrimination in the application of the death penalty; Judge Doubles, for instance, ruled that there was no evidence of racial discrimination in the actions of the six juries that sentenced the seven men to death. In *McCleskey v. Kemp*, the U.S. Supreme Court similarly ruled that there was insufficient evidence "to support an inference that any of the decisionmakers in McCleskey's case acted with discriminatory purpose." Assume that you are the lawyer representing an African American offender who has been sentenced to death. What types of evidence would you need to convince the appellate courts that decision-makers in your client's case had "acted with discriminatory purpose"? Is it realistic to assume that any offender can meet this burden of proof?

6. Consider the five remedies for racial discrimination in capital sentencing (see Box 8.5). Which do you believe is the appropriate remedy? Why?

7. In 1994 Supreme Court Justice Harry Blackmun stated that it was futile to continue to "tinker with the machinery of death." Although those who advocate abolishing the death penalty agree with this assessment, advocates of reform contend that the death penalty can be "fixed." Summarize their arguments.

8. Do you agree or disagree with our conclusion that "the type of discrimination found in the capital sentencing process falls closer to the systematic end of the discrimination continuum presented in Chapter 1"? Why?

NOTES

1. *Callins v. Collins*, 510 U.S. 1141 (1994), 1154–1155.

2. Jeff Flock, "'Blanket commutation' empties Illinois death row," CNN, January 13, 2003. Available at http://www.cnn.com/2003/LAW/01/11/illinois.death.row/html.

3. *Callins v. Collins*, 510 U.S. 1141 (1994), 1145.

4. Ibid.

5. For a discussion of the "new abolitionist policies," see Austin Sarat, "Recapturing the Spirit of *Furman*: The American Bar Association and the New

Abolitionist Politics," *Law and Contemporary Problems 61* (1998): 5–28 and Austin Sarat, *When the State Kills: Capital Punishment and the American Condition* (Princeton: Princeton University Press, 2001), chapter 9.

6. Cited in Sarat, "Recapturing the Spirit of *Furman*: The American Bar Association and the New Abolitionist Politics," p. 14.

7. Clyde E. Murphy, "Racial Discrimination in the Criminal Justice System," *North Carolina Central Law Journal 17* (1988): 171–190.

8. *McCleskey v. Kemp*, 481 U.S. 279 (1987).

9. In re Kemmler, 136 U.S. 436, 447 (1890).

10. *Trop v. Dulles*, 356 U.S. 86, 99 (1958).

11. *Furman V. Georgia*, 408 U.S. 238 (1972).

12. Ibid., at 257 (Douglas, J., concurring); at 310 (Stewart, J., concurring); at 313 (White, J., concurring).

13. Ibid., at 257 (Marshall, J., concurring).

14. Ibid., at 310 (Stewart, J., concurring).

15. Samuel R. Gross and Robert Mauro, *Death & Discrimination: Racial Disparities in Capital Sentencing* (Boston: Northeastern University Press, 1989), p. 215.

16. *Woodson v. North Carolina*, 428 U.S. 280 (1976); *Roberts v. Louisiana*, 428 U.S. 325 (1976).

17. *Woodson v. North Carolina*, 428 U.S. 280 (1976), 303.

18. Ibid., at 305.

19. *Gregg v. Georgia*, 428 U.S. 153 (1976); *Proffitt v. Florida*, 428 U.S. 242 (1976); *Jurek v. Texas*, 428 U.S. 262 (1976).

20. *Gregg v. Georgia*, 428 U.S. 153 (1976).

21. Ibid., at 206–207.

22. *Coker v. Georgia*, 433 U.S. 584, 592 (1977).

23. *Tison v. Arizona*, 107 S.Ct. 1676 (1987).

24. *Atkins v. Virginia*, 536 U.S. 304 (2002).

25. *Roper v. Simmons*, 543 U.S. 551 (2005).

26. National Opinion Research Center, *General Social Surveys, 1972–94, General Social Surveys, 1996* (Storrs, CT: The Roper Center for Public Opinion Research, University of Connecticut, 1997).

27. Bureau of Justice Statistics, *Sourcebook of Criminal Justice Statistics 2003*, Table 2.49.

28. *Furman v. Georgia*, 408 U.S. 238, at 365–66 (1972) (Marshall, J., concurring).

29. Raymond Paternoster, *Capital Punishment in America* (New York: Lexington Books, 1991), p. 72.

30. *Furman v. Georgia*, 408 U.S. 238, at 369, 1972 (Marshall, J., concurring).

31. See, for example, Robert M. Bohm, "American Death Penalty Opinion, 1936–1986: A Critical Examination of the Gallup Polls," in *The Death Penalty in America: Current Research*, Robert M. Bohm, ed. (Cincinnati: Anderson, 1991); William Bowers, "Capital Punishment and Contemporary Values: People's Misgivings and the Court's Misperceptions," *Law & Society Review 27* (1993): 157–175; James Alan Fox, Michael L. Radelet, and Julie L. Bonsteel, "Death Penalty Opinion in the Post-*Furman* Years," *New York University Review of Law and Social Change 18* (1990-91); Philip W. Harris, "Over-Simplification and Error in Public Opinion Surveys on Capital Punishment, *Justice Quarterly 3* (1986): 429–455; Austin Sarat and Neil Vidmar, "Public Opinion, the Death Penalty, and the Eighth Amendment: Testing the Marshall Hypothesis," in *Capital Punishment in the United States*, Hugo A. Bedau and Chester M. Pierce, eds. (New York: AMS Publications, 1976).

32. Bowers, "Capital Punishment and Contemporary Values," p. 162.

33. Ibid.

34. Ibid., p. 172.

35. Taylor, Humphrey, "Support for Death Penalty Still Very Strong In Spite of Widespread Belief That Some Innocent People Are Convicted of Murder," Harris Interactive. Available at www.harrisinteractive.com/harris_poll/index.asp?PID=252, Table 6.

36. Ibid.

37. Bureau of Justice Statistics, *Sourcebook of Criminal Justice Statistics 2003*, Table 2.54.

38. Taylor, "Support for Death Penalty Still Very Strong," Table 6.

39. Tom W. Smith, "A Trend Analysis of Attitudes Toward Capital Punishment, 1936–1974," in *Studies of Social Change Since 1948*, vol. 2, James E. Davis, ed. (Chicago: National Opinion Research Center, 1975), pp. 257–318.

40. Steven E. Barkan and Steven F. Cohn, "Racial Prejudice and Support for the Death Penalty by Whites," *Journal of Research in Crime and Delinquency 31* (1994): 202–209; Robert L. Young, "Race, Conceptions of Crime and Justice, and Support for the Death Penalty," *Social Psychological Quarterly 54* (1991): 67–75.

41. Barkan and Cohn, "Racial Prejudice and Support for the Death Penalty by Whites."

42. Ibid., p. 206.

43. Ibid., p. 207.

44. Eric P. Baumer, Steven F. Messner, and Richard Rosenfeld, "Explaining Structural Variation in Support for Capital Punishment: A Multilevel Analysis," *American Journal of Sociology 108* (2003): 844–875.

45. Ibid., p. 856.

46. Stephen B. Bright, "Discrimination, Death and Denial: The Tolerance of Racial Discrimination in Infliction of the Death Penalty," *Santa Clara Law Review 35* (1995): 901–950.

47. *Gregg V. Georgia*, 428 U.S. 153 (1976), at 207.

48. NAACP Legal Defense Fund, *Death Row USA* (New York: NAACP LDF, 2005).

49. U.S. Department of Justice, Bureau of Justice Statistics, *Capital Punishment, 2003* (Washington, DC: U.S. Government Printing Office, 2004), pp. 6–7.

50. Ibid., p. 5.

51. NAACP Legal Defense and Educational Fund. *Death Row USA, Summer 2005*. Available at http://www.deathpenaltyinfo.org.

52. Ibid.

53. Ibid.

54. Ibid.

55. U.S. Department of Justice, Bureau of Justice Statistics, *Capital Punishment 1991* (Washington, DC: U.S. Government Printing Office), p. 8.

56. Marvin E. Wolfgang and Marc Riedel, "Race, Judicial Discretion, and the Death Penalty," *The Annals of the American Academy of Political and Social Science 407* (1973): 119–133.

57. Elmer H. Johnson, "Selective Factors in Capital Punishment," *Social Forces 36* (1957): 165.

58. Marvin E. Wolfgang, Arlene Kelly, and Hans C. Nolde, "Comparisons of the Executed and the Commuted Among Admissions to Death Row," *Journal of Criminal Law, Criminology, and Police Science 53* (1962): 301.

59. Gary Kleck, "Racial Discrimination in Criminal Sentencing: A Critical Evaluation of the Evidence With Additional Evidence on the Death Penalty," *American Sociological Review 46* (1981): 793.

60. For example, according to Raymond Fosdick, who studied U.S. police departments shortly before the country's entry into World War I, Southern police departments had three classes of homicide. One official told Fosdick, "If a nigger kills a white man, that's murder. If a white man kills a nigger, that's justifiable homicide. If a nigger kills another nigger, that's one less

nigger." See Raymond Fosdick, *American Police Systems* (Montclair, NJ: Patterson Smith Reprint Series, 1972), p. 45 (Originally published in 1920).

61. Gary Kleck, "Racial Discrimination in Criminal Sentencing," p. 793.

62. Ibid.

63. Ibid., p. 796.

64. Ibid., p. 798.

65. Guy Johnson, "The Negro and Crime," *Annals of the American Academy* 217 (1941): 98.

66. Michael L. Radelet, "Executions of Whites for Crimes Against Blacks: Exceptions to the Rule?" *The Sociological Quarterly* 30 (1989): 535.

67. *Furman v. Georgia*, 408 U.S. 238 (1972) at 449 (Powell, J., dissenting).

68. Harold Garfinkel, "Research Note on Inter- and Intra-Racial Homicides," *Social Forces* 217 (1949): 369–381; Guy Johnson, "The Negro and Crime;" Charles S. Mangum, Jr. *The Legal Status of the Negro* (Chapel Hill, NC: North Carolina Press, 1940); Paige H. Ralph, Jonathan R. Sorensen, and James W. Marquart, "A Comparison of Death-Sentenced and Incarcerated Murderers in Pre-*Furman* Texas," *Justice Quarterly* 9 (1992): 185–209; Wolfgang, Kelly, and Nolde, "Comparison of the Executed and Commuted Among Admissions to Death Row"; Marvin E. Wolfgang and Marc Reidel, "Race, Judicial Discretion, and the Death Penalty," *Annals of the American Academy* 407 (1973): 119–133; Marvin E. Wolfgang and Marc Reidel, "Rape, Race, and the Death Penalty in Georgia," *Amer. J. Orthopsychiat* 45 (1975): 658–668.

69. Guy Johnson, "The Negro and Crime."

70. Mangum, *The Legal Status of the Negro.*

71. Wolfgang, Kelly and Nolde, "Comparisons of the Executed and Commuted Among Admissions to Death Row."

72. Garfinkel, "Research Note on Inter- and Intra-Racial Homicides."

73. William Bowers and Glenn L. Pierce, "Arbitrariness and Discrimination Under Post-*Furman* Capital Statutes," *Crime and Delinquency* 74 (1980): 1067–1100.

74. Kleck, "Racial Discrimination in Criminal Sentencing," p. 788.

75. Florida Civil Liberties Union, *Rape: Selective Electrocution Based on Race* (Miami: Florida Civil Liberties Union, 1964).

76. Wolfgang and Reidel, "Race, Judicial Discretion, and the Death Penalty."

77. Ibid., p. 133.

78. Kleck, "Racial Discrimination in Criminal Sentencing," p. 788.

79. David C. Baldus, George Woodworth, and Charles A. Pulaski, *Equal Justice and the Death Penalty: A Legal and Empirical Analysis* (Boston: Northeastern University Press, 1990).

80. Ralph, Sorensen, and Marquart, "A Comparison of Death-Sentenced and Incarcerated Murderers in Pre-*Furman* Texas."

81. Ibid., p. 207.

82. Ibid., pp. 206–207.

83. Wolfgang and Reidel, "Rape, Race and the Death Penalty in Georgia," p. 667.

84. U.S. General Accounting Office, *Death Penalty Sentencing: Research Indicates Pattern of Racial Disparities* (Washington, DC: General Accounting Office, 1990), p. 5.

85. Ibid., p. 6.

86. Ibid.

87. Studies that find either a race-of-victim or race-of-defendant effect include (but are not limited to): Stephen Arkin, "Discrimination and Arbitrariness in Capital Punishment: An Analysis of Post-*Furman* Murder Cases in Dade County, Florida, 1973–1976," *Stanford Law Review* 33 (1980): 75–101; William Bowers, "The Pervasiveness of Arbitrariness and Discrimination Under Post-*Furman* Capital Statutes," *Journal of*

Criminal Law & Criminology 74 (1983): 1067–1100; Bowers and Pierce, "Arbitrariness and Discrimination Under Post-*Furman* Capital Statutes;" Sheldon Ekland-Olson, "Structured Discretion, Racial Bias, and the Death Penalty: The First Decade After *Furman* in Texas," *Social Science Quarterly 69* (1988): 853–873; Thomas Keil and Gennaro Vito, "Race and the Death Penalty in Kentucky Murder Trials: An Analysis of Post-*Gregg* Outcomes," *Justice Quarterly* (1990): 189–207; Raymond Paternoster, "Prosecutorial Discretion in Requesting the Death Penalty: A Case of Victim-Based Racial Discrimination," *Law & Society Review 18* (1984): 437–478; Michael L. Radelet, "Racial Characteristics and the Imposition of the Death Penalty," *American Sociological Review 46* (1981): 918–927; Michael L. Radelet and Glenn L. Pierce, "Race and Prosecutorial Discretion in Homicide Cases," *Law & Society Review 19* (1985): 587–621; and Dwayne M. Smith, "Patterns of Discrimination in Assessments of the Death Penalty: The Case of Louisiana," *Journal of Criminal Justice 15* (1987): 279–286.

88. Baldus, Woodworth, and Pulaski, *Equal Justice and the Death Penalty.*

89. Gross and Mauro, *Death & Discrimination.*

90. Glenn L. Pierce and Michael L. Radelet, "The Impact of Legally Inappropriate Factors on Death Sentencing for California Homicides, 1990–99," *Santa Clara Law Review 46* (2005).

91. Baldus, Woodworth and Pulaski, *Equal Justice and the Death Penalty.*

92. Ibid., p. 185.

93. David Baldus, Charles Pulaski, and George Woodworth, "Comparative Review of Death Sentences: An Empirical Study of the Georgia Experience," *The Journal of Criminal Law & Criminology 74* (1983): 709–710.

94. Anthony Amsterdam, "Race and the Death Penalty," *Criminal Justice Ethics 7* (1988): 2, 84–86.

95. Ibid., p. 85.

96. Gross and Mauro, *Death & Discrimination,* chapters 4 and 5.

97. Gross and Mauro, *Death & Discrimination,* pp. 109–110.

98. Raymond Paternoster and Robert Brame, "An Empirical Analysis of Maryland's Death Sentencing System with Respect to the Influence of Race and Legal Jurisdiction." Available at http://ncic.org/library/018518.

99. Isaac Unah and Jack Boger, "Race and the Death Penalty in North Carolina: An Empirical Analysis: 1993–1997." Available at http://www.deathpenalty info.org.

100. "Broken Justice: The Death Penalty in Virginia." Available at http://www.aclu.org/DeathPenalty/DeathPenalty.cfm?ID=14388&c=17.

101. Andrew Welsh-Huggins, "Death Penalty Unequal," Associated Press, May 7, 2005.

102. Pierce and Radelet, "The Impact of Legally Inappropriate Factors on Death Sentencing for California Homicides, 1990–1999."

103. NAACP Legal Defense and Educational Fund, Inc., *Death Row USA, Summer 2005.*

104. Pierce and Radelet, "The Impact of Legally Inappropriate Factors on Death Sentencing for California Homicides, 1990–1999," Table 4.

105. Ibid.

106. Ibid.

107. Sarat, "Recapturing the Spirit of *Furman,*" p. 27.

108. Scott W. Howe, "The Futile Quest for Racial Neutrality in Capital Selection and the Eighth Amendment Argument for Abolition Based on Unconscious Racial Discrimination," *William & Mary Law Review 45* (2004): 2083–2166.

109. U. S. Department of Justice, *The Federal Death Penalty System: A Statistical*

Survey (1988–2000). (Washington, DC: U.S. Department of Justice, 2000), p. 4.

110. U.S. Department of Justice, *The Federal Death Penalty System: Supplementary Data, Analysis and Revised Protocols for Capital Case Review* (Washington, DC: U.S. Department of Justice, 2001), pp. 6–7.

111. Ibid., p. 5.

112. U.S. Department of Justice, *The Federal Death Penalty System: A Statistical Survey (1988–2000)*, p. 9.

113. Marc Lacey and Raymond Bonner, "Reno Troubled by DP Stats," *New York Times* (September 12, 2000), A17.

114. American Civil Liberties Union, *Federal Death Row: Is It Really Color-Blind? Analysis of June 6 Department of Justice Report on the Death Penalty*. Available at http://www.aclu.org/Congress/10614la.htm.

115. U. S. Department of Justice, *The Federal Death Penalty System: Supplementary Data, Analysis and Revised Protocols for Capital Case Review*.

116. Ibid., p. 9.

117. Ibid., p. 3.

118. Ibid.

119. American Civil Liberties Union, *Federal Death Row*.

120. Ibid.

121. Legal Defense and Educational Fund. *Death Row USA: Summer 2005*, p. 30.

122. Richard Quinney, *The Social Reality of Crime* (Boston: Little, Brown, 1970); Austin Turk, *Criminality and Legal Order* (New York: Rand McNally, 1969).

123. Darnell F. Hawkins, "Beyond Anomalies: Rethinking the Conflict Perspective on Race and Criminal Punishment," *Social Forces* 65 (1987): 726.

124. Keil and Vito, "Race and the Death Penalty in Kentucky Murder Trial," p. 204.

125. Quoted in Wissink, Stephen, "Race and the Big Needle," *Spectator Online*.

Available at http://www.spectatoronline.com/2001-03-07/news_cover.html.

126. Gross and Mauro, *Death & Discrimination*.

127. Ibid., p. 113.

128. Bright, "Discrimination, Death and Denial," pp. 903–905.

129. Ibid., pp. 904–905.

130. Ibid., p. 921.

131. For an excellent and detailed discussion of this case, see Eric W. Rise, *The Martinsville Seven: Race, Rape, and Capital Punishment* (Charlottesville: University Press of Virginia, 1995).

132. Ibid., p. 122.

133. Ibid.

134. Ibid., p. 30.

135. Ibid., p. 32.

136. Ibid., p. 35.

137. Ibid., p. 48.

138. Ibid., p. 85.

139. *Hampton v. Commonwealth*, 58 S.E.2d 288, 298 (Va. Sup. Ct., 1950).

140. Ibid.

141. Rise, *The Martinsville Seven*, p. 121.

142. Ibid., p. 124.

143. Ibid., p. 148.

144. See, e.g., *Maxwell v. Bishop*, F.2d 138 (8th Cir. 1968) *Spinkellink v. Wainwright*, 578 F.2d 582 (5th Cir. 1978); *Shaw v. Martin*, 733 F.2d 304 (4th Cir. 1984); and *Prejean v. Blackburn*, 743 F.2d 1091 (5th Cir. 1984).

145. *McCleskey v. Kemp*, 481 U.S. 279, 107 S.Ct. 1756 (1987).

146. David C. Baldus, George W. Woodworth, Charles A. Pulaski, "Monitoring and Evaluating Contemporary Death Penalty Systems: Lessons From Georgia," *University of California at Davis Law Review 18* (1985): 1375–1407.

147. *McCleskey v. Kemp*, 107 S.Ct 1756 (1987) at 1777.

148. Ibid., at p. 1769.

149. *McCleskey v. Kemp*, 481 U.S. 279 (1987), at 315 (Brennan, J., dissenting).

150. Ibid., at pp. 316–317.

151. Ibid.

152. *Maxwell v. Bishop*, 398 F.2d 138 (CA 8 1968).

153. Amsterdam, "Race and the Death Penalty," p. 86.

154. Randall Kennedy, *Race, Crime, and the Law* (New York: Vintage Books, 1998).

155. Bright, "Discrimination, Death and Denial," p. 947.

156. Gross and Mauro, *Death & Discrimination*, p. 212.

157. *McCleskey v. Zant*, 111 S.Ct. 1454 (1991).

158. Ibid.

159. *New York Times*, September 26, 1991, p. A10.

160. NAACP Legal Defense and Educational Fund, Inc. *Death Row USA: Summer 2005*, p. 9.

161. *McCleskey v. Zant*, 111 S.Ct 1454 (1991).

162. *Herrera v. Collins*, 113 S.Ct. 853 (1993).

163. Congressional Record, S4602 (April 21, 1994).

164. American Bar Association, "Whatever You Think About the Death Penalty, A System That Will Take Life Must First Give Justice: A Report from the IR&R Death Penalty Committee," 24 *W.T.R. Hum. Rts.* 22.

165. Press Release, January 31, 2000. Available at http://www.state.il.us/gov/press/00/Jan/morat.htm.

166. John Kifner, "A State Votes to End Its Death Penalty," *New York Times*, May 19, 2000, A8.

167. Press Release, Sept. 20, 2000. Available at http://www.igc.org/tcrp/press/HRR/death_penalty.htm.

168. Cited in Kenneth Jost, "Rethinking the Death Penalty," *CQ Researcher, 11* (November 16, 2001): p. 962.

169. Public Law No. 108–405.

170. Comments taken from U.S. Senator Patrick Leahy's website, http://leahy.senate.gov/press/200410/103004A.html.

171. Jodi Wilgoren, "Few Death Sentences or None Under Overhaul Proposed by Illinois Panel," *The New York Times on the Web*, April 16, 2002.

172. Austin Sarat, *When the State Kills*, pp. 246–260.

173. Ibid., p. 251.

174. *Callins v. Collins*, 510 U.S. 1141 (1994) at 1144 (Blackmun, J., dissenting).

175. Ibid., at p. 1145.

176. Sarat, *When the State Kills*, p. 255.

177. Ibid., p. 256.

178. National Death Penalty Moratorium Act of 2001, S. 223, H.R. 1038.

179. Sarat, *When the State Kills*, p. 257.

180. Gross and Mauro, *Death & Discrimination*, pp. 109–110.

181. Georgia Code Ann., §27-2534.1 (Supp. 1975).

182. Marian R. Williams and Jefferson E. Holcomb, "The Interactive Effects of Victim Race and Gender on Death Sentence Disparity Findings," *Homicide Studies* 8 (2004): 350–376.

183. Ibid., Table 2 and p. 366.

184. Ibid., Tables 3 and 4.

185. Ibid., p. 370.

186. Baldus, Woodworth, and Pulaski., *Equal Justice and the Death Penalty*, pp. 384–387; Gross and Mauro, *Death & Discrimination*, Chapter 11; Kennedy, *Race, Crime, and the Law*, pp. 340–345.

187. Gross and Mauro, *Death & Discrimination*, p. 216.

188. Kennedy, *Race, Crime, and the Law*, p. 341.

189. *McCleskey v. Kemp*, 107 S.Ct., 1756 (1987) at 1806 (Stevens, J., dissenting).

190. Baldus, Woodworth, and Pulaski, *Equal Justice and the Death Penalty*, p. 385.

191. Kennedy, *Race, Crime and the Law*, p. 343.

192. Ibid., p. 344.

193. Ibid.

194. *Saldano v. Texas*, 99-8119.

195. *Chicago Tribune*, "Flawed Trials Lead to Death Chamber," June 11, 2000; "Gatekeeper Court Keeps Gates Shut," June 12, 2000.

196. U. S. Department of Justice, Bureau of Justice Statistics, *Sourcebook of Criminal Justice Statistics, 1999* (Washington, DC: Government Printing Office, 2000).

197. Texas Civil Rights Project, *The Death Penalty in Texas: Due Process and Equal Justice . . . or Rush to Execution?* (Austin, TX: Texas Civil Rights Project, 2000).

198. Ibid., p. iv.

199. Ibid., p. ii.

200. Hugo A. Bedau and Michael L. Radelt, "Miscarriages of Justice in Potentially Capital Cases," *Stanford Law Review 40* (1987): 21–179.

201. Omaha World Herald, March 3, 1993.

202. Information about this case was obtained from articles appearing in the *Chicago Tribune* from 1995 to 1998.

203. Eric Zorn, "Dark Truths Buried in Nicarico Case May Yet See Light," *Chicago Tribune*, October 18, 1995, Section 2, p. 1.

204. *Chicago Tribune*, November 4, 1995, Section 1, pp. 1–2.

205. *Chicago Tribune*, April 9, 1998, DuPage section, p. 1.

9

⚐

Corrections in America:
A Colorful Portrait

Corrections vs. College:
Minorities in Society

The number of people under correctional supervision in the United States has increased considerably in the last 30 years, substantially outpacing population growth. During the same period, the population of people seeking higher education by attending college grew as well. In 2003 we had nearly 7 million people under some form of correctional supervision (prison, jail, probation, parole)[1] and more than 16 million people pursuing some form of higher education.[2] The United States currently has the highest incarceration rates per population than any other country in the world[3] and one of the highest higher education rates.[4]

In short, although 3 percent of the adult U.S. population is under correctional supervision, roughly twice that proportion of the adult U.S. population is attending college.[5] This profile of incarceration versus education differs drastically when assessing specific racial groups. Four times as many whites attend college than are under correctional supervision.[6] However, more African Americans and Hispanics are under some form of correctional supervision compared to attending college. The differences are particularly stark when focusing on males—nearly 20 percent of African American males and 8 percent of Hispanic males are under correctional supervision, whereas less than 3 percent of white males are under correctional supervision.[7] College attendance estimates, however, indicate that fewer than half this number of African American and Hispanic males were attending college in 2003, whereas twice as many white males were attending college than under correctional supervision.[8]

GOALS OF THE CHAPTER

This chapter describes various disparities in the ethnic and racial makeup of American correctional populations. It examines which groups are overrepresented in situations of incarceration and supervision in the community. The extent of minority overrepresentation also is explored in relation to gender distinctions, federal versus state populations, and recidivism, with an emphasis on historical fluctuations. The juxtaposition of Native American philosophies and methods of correction with the mainstream American criminal justice system is also explored.

This descriptive information is supplemented by a discussion of current research on discrimination in the correctional setting. Finally, the inmate social system, which reflects key aspects of prison life, is discussed. This section will focus on the influence of minority group status on prison subcultures and religion.

THE INCARCERATED: PRISON AND JAIL POPULATIONS

Describing incarcerated populations in the United States is a complicated task. The answer to the question, "Who is locked up?" depends on what penal institution and which inmates we are discussing. Prison population figures are descriptive counts taken on one day, often midyear. These figures are used for the purpose of describing disparity and are not standardized rates (see discussion later in this chapter). There are a number of important distinctions between prisons and jails, male and female inmates, and state and federal populations. In addition, important changes occur over time.

Prisons are distinct from jails because they serve different functions in the criminal justice system.[9] These differences may result in different levels of minority overrepresentation, so jails and prisons are discussed separately. Gender differences are also important when discussing incarceration; therefore, we also explore the issues of the racial and ethnic composition of male and female prisoner populations. State and federal prison populations must be examined separately because of the differences in state and federal crime.[10]

Minority Overrepresentation

In 2004 nearly 1.5 million people were incarcerated in federal and state prison.[15] Looking at this population through the lens of race and ethnicity of prison inmates, our primary observation about the prison population in the United States (Table 9.1, column 1) is that African Americans are strikingly overrepresented compared to their presence in the general population. Hispanics also are overrepresented but not as markedly. African Americans comprise less than 15 percent of the U.S. population but nearly 50 percent of all incarcerated offenders.

Focus on an Issue
Indigenous Justice Paradigm

In "Crime and Punishment: Traditional and Contemporary Tribal Justice," Melton observes that in many contemporary tribal communities "a dual justice system exists, one based on an American paradigm of justice and the other based on an indigenous paradigm."[11] The American justice paradigm is characterized by an adversarial system and stands apart from most religious tenants. Crimes are viewed as actions against the state, with little attention to the needs of the victim or community. The focus is on the defendant's individual rights during adjudication. Punishing the offender is generally governed by a retributive philosophy and removal from society.

In contrast, tribal justice is based on a holistic philosophy and is not easily divorced from the religious and spiritual realms of everyday life. Melton[12] attempts to distill the characteristic elements of a number of diverse American tribal justice ideologies into an indigenous justice paradigm. The holistic philosophy is the key element of this paradigm and supports a "circle of justice" where "the center of the circle represents the underlying problems and issues that need to be resolved to attain peace and harmony for the individuals and the community."[13] The corresponding values of restorative and reparative justice prescribe the actions the offender must perform to be forgiven. These values reflect the importance of the victim and the community in restoring harmony.

The influence of the American paradigm of justice on Native American communities has a long and persistent history.[14] However, the values of restorative and reparative justice are emerging in a number of programs off the reservation. In particular, the restorative justice practices of the Navajo Nation have influenced a number of new-offender rehabilitation programs, including many supported by the Presbyterian Church.

Hispanics are roughly 12 percent of the U.S. population; however, they represent nearly 20 percent of the prison population.[16] Conversely, whites (non-Hispanic) are underrepresented compared to their presence in the population—they are more than 70 percent of the general population but just more than one-third (33.5 percent) of the prison population.[17]

In recent years Hispanics have represented the fastest-growing minority group being imprisoned. They were 10.5 percent of the prison population in 1985, 15.5 percent in 1995, 16.4 percent in 2000, and 19.2 percent in 2004.[18] These increases reflect a rate twice as high as the increase for African American and white inmates.[19] Little information is available about the number of Asian, Pacific Islander, Alaska Native, and Native American prisoners because they are generally represented in a category collapsed into "Other." The representation of Asians and Pacific Islanders does not appear substantially greater than their representation in the general population. However, Native American and Alaska Natives are overrepresented compared to their representation in the U.S. populations.

Given the changes in racial categories in the U.S. census forms in 2000, prison statistics are starting to reflect the percentage of prisoners who identify

T A B L E   9.1   Racial and Ethnic Profile of State and Federal Prison Populations, by Gender at Midyear, 2004

	Combined	Female	Male
White (non-Hispanic)	33.5	44.2	33.6
African American (non-Hispanic)	45.7	33.4	41.2
Hispanic	17.6	15.6	19.5
Other (Native American, Alaskan Native, Asian, and Pacific Islander)	2.9	6.8	5.7 (combined)
Two or more races	2.9	—	—

SOURCE: Paige M. Harrison and Allen J. Beck, *Prisoners in 2004* (Washington, DC: Department of Justice, 2005). Available at www.ojp.usdoj.gov/bjs/.

themselves as being of two or more races. Although the number seems small at this point, future researchers should note that increased attention to this group is warranted.

Racial and Ethnic Female Prisoners   The picture of the racial and ethnic composition of prison populations changes slightly when focusing on gender (Table 9.1; columns 2 and 3). Because women make up less than 7 percent of federal and state prisoners, up from 5.7 percent in 1990,[20] we should not generalize patterns from predominantly male populations to females. For example, although prison populations have increased markedly in the last several years, the increase for female inmates is more rapid than for male inmates from 1995 to 2004. Over this nearly 10-year period, female prison populations have increased by 53 percent, whereas male populations increased by only 32 percent.[21]

Among female prisoners, similarities and differences exist when comparing their racial and ethnic makeup to the overall (predominately male) prison population. Although people of color represent more than half of the women incarcerated in federal and state prisons, white, non–Hispanic women make up the largest group of female prisoners (44.2 percent). This is the reverse of the male population, in which the largest racial group is African American males (42.1 percent). The percentage of female inmates who identify themselves as African American indicates an overrepresentation of African American females in prison compared to the general population, but the proportion of this overrepresentation is different than the number for the African American male population (33.4 percent compared to 41.2 percent). Notably, the percentage of female prisoners who are Hispanic is lower than the percentage of male prisoners who are Hispanic (15.6 percent compared to 19.5 percent).

Federal Racial and Ethnic Prisoners   Although state prison populations account for the majority (nearly 90 percent) of incarcerated offenders, a look at the racial and ethnic percentages of federal populations alone is warranted. Just as

TABLE 9.2 Racial and Ethnic Profile of Federal Prison Population, 2003

	Percent
Race	
White	56.4
African American	40.4
Other	3.2
Ethnicity (of any race)	
Hispanic	32.0
Non-Hispanic	68.0

SOURCE: *Sourcebook of Criminal Justice Statistics, 2003* (Washington, DC: U.S. Department of Justice, 2004). Available at www.albany.edu/sourcebook/.

state and federal laws differ, so will their prison populations because they present different offenses and unique sentencing practices (see Chapter 7). An important implication for federal prisoners is that they can expect to serve more of their original sentence than do state inmates (up to 50 percent more).[22] Also, federal prison populations are increasing at rates higher than state populations, with higher rates of change in court commitments to federal prison than to state prisons.

Comparisons between state and federal prison populations with regard to racial composition are a challenge. The U.S. Bureau of Justice Statistics (BJS) sources used to estimate the racial and ethnic composition of federal and state prison populations (Table 9.1) reflect the convention of using racial and ethnic status combined (white, non-Hispanic; African American, non-Hispanic; Hispanic, other); however, the Federal Bureau of Prisons uses the convention of measuring race and ethnicity as separate concepts (more like the U.S. Census).

The descriptive profile of the federal inmate population presented in Table 9.2 suggests an important correction in the magnitude of racial and ethnic differences in state versus federal prison populations.[23] African Americans do not appear as severely overrepresented in the federal prison population as they do in the profile of state and federal prison populations combined. In short, in the federal population alone, African Americans represent 40 percent of the population, whereas state and federal populations combined reveal roughly 46 percent are African American.

Perhaps the most startling contrast appears with the Hispanic population. When Hispanics are identified as being of any race, they represent nearly one-third (32 percent) of the federal prison population, compared to less than 20 percent of the combined prison population.

These data suggest that the overrepresentation of Hispanics in federal prison populations is hidden in the description of the racial and ethnic composition. Also the underrepresentation of whites in prison is inflated by the extraction of

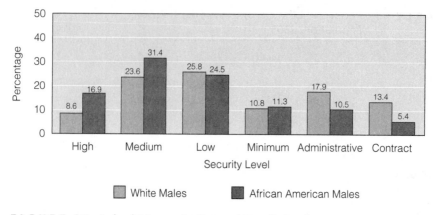

F I G U R E   9.1   Federal Prisoners by Race and Security Level

SOURCE: Bureau of Justice Statistics, *Sourcebook of Criminal Justice Statistics* (Washington, DC: Government Printing Office, 2003). Available at www.albany.edu/sourcebook/.

Hispanics (who are predominantly white) from the calculation of demographic percentages.

These differences in disparity among racial and ethnic groups are explained in large part by different patterns of offending. Whites are relatively more likely to commit and be convicted of federal offenses. African Americans, conversely, are relatively more likely to be arrested and convicted for index crimes, which are generally state offenses. Hispanics are consistently overrepresented among convicted drug offenders at the federal level and among immigration law offenders.[24]

Security Level of Facilities   When convicted offenders are committed to federal prison, they undergo a classification process that determines, among other things, what type of institution (or security level) they should be assigned to as inmates. Federal Bureau of Prison statistics offer a picture of male inmates of color by security level of the prison they are assigned to, presented in the figure above (Figure 9.1).[25] Roughly the same percentage of inmates, regardless of race, are found in the low- and minimum-security settings (about 25 percent and 10 percent, respectively). However, a larger percentage of African American inmates are in the highest two security levels compared to the white inmates. Thus, although the typical federal prison inmate is white, the typical inmate in the high-security facilities is African American.

Conclusion   Differences in the magnitude of racial disparity among the various racial and ethnic groups in prison offer more support that the impact of race/ethnicity is not a constant—that is, the impact of overrepresentation in incarceration settings varies in magnitude and quality. The racial and ethnic profile of prison inmates is to some extent conditioned by how the concepts of race and ethnicity are measured. One of the important implications of the more extreme overrepresentation of Hispanic offenders in federal prison is that offenders sentenced to federal prison serve longer sentences with more time served than those

Focus on an Issue

Correctional Personnel: Similarities and Differences on the Basis of Race

Currently, federal and state prisons have fairly equitable representation of African American citizens among correctional officers and supervisors, compared to the general population.[27] Hispanic representation among correctional personnel is still lacking.[28] Important goals include ensuring fair employment practices in government hiring and ensuring there are minority decisionmakers to cause a beneficial (and perhaps less discriminatory) impact on the treatment of minority populations.

The author's[29] review of the research in the area of attitudes and beliefs of correctional officers toward inmates and punishment ideologies suggests that respondents' views do appear to differ in many ways on the basis of race. In particular, he notes that African American officers appear to have more positive attitudes toward inmates than do white officers; however, others have found that black officers expressed a preference for greater distance between officers and inmates than did white officers.

Additionally, neither white nor African American correction officers reflect an ability to correctly identify the self-reported needs of prison inmates.

In relation to ideological issues, African American officers were more often supportive of rehabilitation than their white counterparts. African American officers also appear to be more ambivalent about the current punitive nature of the criminal justice system, indicating that the court system is often too harsh.

In short, current research does not offer a definitive answer to the question of whether minority correctional officers make different decisions. Assuming that differential decisionmaking by correction officers could be both a positive and negative exercise of discretion, at what point are differential decisions beneficial to inmates versus unprofessional or unjust? What research could be done to resolve the issue of the presence or absence of differential decisionmaking by correctional officers on the basis of race?

---

offenders sentenced to state prisons, given that federal prisoners can expect to serve 50 percent more of their original sentence than do state inmates.[26] In short, this detrimental impact of conditions of imprisonment on Hispanics would not have been known if we only examined the demographic profile offered in Table 9.1.

Race, Ethnicity, and Recidivism

The concept of recidivism can take on different meanings in different settings. Generally, the term is used to refer to offenders who return to offending after experiencing a criminal conviction and the corresponding punishment. Four key distinctions in the research on offender recidivism center on the point in the system we measure as the return to criminal behavior: (1) rearrest for a new crime (either felony or misdemeanor), (2) reconviction (in state or federal court), (3) resentence to prison, and (4) revocation of parole (technical or new offense violation). In a study of recidivism among prisoners released from 15 states, racial differences did emerge in the findings. A group of 272,111 offenders released in 1994 were followed for 3 years after their release.[30] Findings indicate that, compared to white ex-offenders, African Americans were more likely to be rearrested (72.9 percent compared to 62.7 percent), reconvicted (51.1 percent compared to 43.3 percent), resentenced (28.5 percent compared to 22.6 percent), and revoked (54.2 percent compared to 51.9 percent).[31] Conversely, non–Hispanics were more likely than Hispanics to be rearrested (71.4 percent compared to 64.6 percent), reconvicted (50.7 percent compared to 43.9 percent), and revoked (57.3 percent compared to 51.9 percent).[32] No significant differences were evident between Hispanics and non–Hispanics in terms of the likelihood of being resentenced (24.7 percent compared to 26.8 percent).[33]

Historical Trends

The overrepresentation of Americans in state and federal prisons is not a new phenomenon. Figure 9.2 provides a graphic illustration of the changing demographic composition of the prison population from 1926 to 2004. Reviewing this figure we can document a disproportionate number of African Americans in the prison population since 1926 (the beginning of national-level data collection on prison populations). The racial disparity has increased in recent years, however. In 1926 African Americans represented 9 percent of the population and 21 percent of the prison population.[34] Over time, the proportion of the prison population of African Americans increased steadily, reaching 30 percent in the 1940s, 35 percent in 1960, 44 percent in 1980, peaking at slightly more than 50 percent in the mid-1990s, and leveling off at about 45 percent in the late 1990s to the present. The representation of African Americans in the general population has never exceeded 15 percent. The African American prisoner population ratio to white prisoner population ratio was 2.5:1 in 1926, but it has reached the current ratio of 4:1.

Impact of the War on Drugs

Dramatic increases in the overrepresentation of African Americans in the prison population have occurred in a context of generally increasing prison population totals and rising incarceration rates since the early 1970s. The incarceration binge seems to be slowing in the first years of the 21st century, but it remains at a level of approximately 2 million people incarcerated in state and federal jails and prisons. Although the incarceration binge surely has multiple sources, it may reflect an impact of the war on drugs. Tonry,[35] for example, argues that the war on drugs has had a particularly detrimental effect on African American males. Evidence of this impact, he argues, can be seen by focusing on the key years affected by the war on drugs: 1980 to 1992. During this period, the number of white males incarcerated in state and federal prison increased by 143 percent; for African American males the number increased by 186 percent.[36]

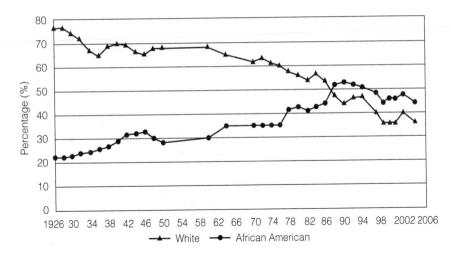

FIGURE 9.2 Admissions to State and Federal Prison, by Race, 1926–2004

SOURCE: Bureau of Justice Statistics, *Race of Prisoners Admitted to State and Federal Institutions, 1926–86* (Washington, DC: Government Printing Office , 1991); Bureau of Justice Statistics, *Correctional Populations in the United States, 1996* (Washington, DC: Government Printing Office , 1997); Bureau of Justice Statistics, *Correctional Populations in the United States, 1996* (Washington, DC: Government Printing Office, 1998); Allen J. Beck, *Prison and Jail Inmates, 1999*; Allen J. Beck and Jennifer C. Karberg, *Prison and Jail Inmates at Midyear 2000*; Allen J. Beck, Jennifer C. Karberg, Paige M. Harrison, *Prison and Jail Inmates at Midyear 2001*; Paige M. Harrison and Allen J. Beck, *Prison and Jail Inmates at Midyear 2004*. Available at www.ojp.usdoj/bjs/.

Statisticians for the BJS argue that the sources of growth for prison populations differ for white and African American inmates. Specifically, drug offenses and violent offenses account for the largest source of growth among state prison inmates. During the 10-year period from 1985 to 1995, "the increasing number of drug offenders accounted for 42 percent of the total growth of black inmates and 26 percent of the growth among white inmates."[37] Similarly, the number of African American inmates serving time for violent offenses increased by 37 percent, whereas growth among white inmates was at a higher 47 percent.[38]

As we discussed in Chapters 3 and 4, the differential impact of the war on drugs may result more from the enforcement strategies of law enforcement than from higher patterns of minority drug use. Critics argue that although the police are *reactive* in responding to robbery, burglary, and other index offenses, they are *proactive* in dealing with drug offenses. There is evidence to suggest that they target minority communities—where drug dealing is more visible and where it is thus easier to make arrests—and tend to give less attention to drug activities in other neighborhoods.

Incarceration Rates

Another way to describe the makeup of U.S. prisons is to examine incarceration *rates*. The information offered by incarceration rates expands the picture of the prison inmate offered in population totals and percentages (as outlined

TABLE 9.3 Incarceration Rates by Race/Ethnicity and Gender

	Male			Female		
	White	African American	Hispanic	White	African American	Hispanic
1990	339	2,376	817	19	125	43
1995	461	3,250	1,174	27	176	57
2001	705	4,848	1,668	67	380	119
2004	717	4,919	1,717	81	359	143

SOURCES: Paige Harrison and Allen J. Beck, *Prison and Jail Inmates at Midyear 2004* (Washington, DC: U.S. Department of Justice, 2005); Allen J. Beck, Jennifer C. Karberg, and Paige Harrison, *Prison and Jail Inmates at Midyear 2001* (Washington, DC: U.S. Department of Justice, 2002); Christopher J. Mumola and Allen J. Beck, *Prisoners, 1996* (Washington, DC: U.S. Department of Justice, 1997).

previously). Incarceration rates offer the most vivid picture of the overrepresentation of African Americans and Hispanics in prison populations. Rates allow for the standardization of population figures that can be calculated over a particular target population. For example, the general incarceration rate in 2004 was 726 per 100,000 population.[39] This number can be further explored by calculating rates that reflect the number of one race group in the prison population relative to the number of that population in the overall U.S. population.

As shown in Table 9.3, over the last decade African Americans and Hispanics have been substantially more likely than whites to be incarcerated in state and federal prisons. Although rates for all groups are increasing over time, the current rate for African American males remained the highest, at more than seven times higher than the rate for white males. Hispanic male rates were more than twice as high as the rate for white males but lower than the rate for African American males. Note that female rates of incarceration are substantially lower than male rates, but they are increasing at faster rates over time. In the current year, African American female rates of incarceration were roughly six times higher than the rate for white females. The rate for Hispanic females was twice the rate for white females; it was lower than for African American females.

These total incarceration rates fail to reveal the stark differences that occur among racial and gender groups by age. Young African American males (ages 20 to 40) have incarceration rates 2.5 times higher than the rates reported earlier in this chapter.[40] Notably, in 2004 nearly 13 percent of all young black males, ages 25 to 29, were in prison or jail.[41] The incarceration rates for Hispanic and whites males also increase for the younger age groups but in less drastic proportions compared to African Americans.[42] Moreover, less than 4 percent of young Hispanic males (ages 25 to 29) and less than 2 percent of young white males (ages 25 to 29) are incarcerated in prisons and jails.[43](See Box 9.1 for information on incarceration rates in other parts of the world.)

B O X 9.1 International Comparisons

In the international arena, the United States consistently has the highest incarceration rate in the world. According to the International Centre for Prison Studies,[44] according to a review of 211 countries in 2003, the United States has 714 people incarcerated in jails and prisons for every 100,000 people in the general population, second only to Russia, Belarus, and Bermuda (all 532 people per 100,000 population). America's neighbors have markedly lower rates, with Canada and Mexico at 116 and 182 people per 100,000 population incarcerated, respectively. Notably, more than half of the world's countries (58 percent) have incarceration rates of less than 150 per 100,000 population. European countries have among the lowest rates: England/Wales at 142, Germany at 96, Turkey at 92, France at 91, and Sweden at 75 per 100,000 population.

In 2001 The Sentencing Project also calculated that the incarceration rate for African American males in the United States was more than four times the rate of South Africa in the last years of apartheid—that is, in 1993 the incarceration rate for African American males was 3,822 per 100,000 compared to the rate of 815 per 100,000 for South African males.[45] In 2001 the incarceration rate for African American males in the U.S. soared to 4,848 per 100,000.

The racial disparity in the nation's prison populations is revealed even more dramatically by The Sentencing Project, which estimates that at some point in their lives, African American males have a 29 percent chance of serving time in prison or jail.[46] Hispanic males have a lower lifetime risk at 16 percent, whereas white males have a 4 percent chance of being incarcerated at some time during their lives.[47]

JAILS AND MINORITIES

The Role of Jail

Jail populations are significantly different than prison populations. Because jails serve a different function in the criminal justice system, they are subject to different dynamics in terms of admissions and releases. The Annual Survey of Jails[48] reveals that just more than half are being detained while awaiting trial, whereas just less than half of the daily population of all jail inmates are convicted offenders. Those awaiting trial are in jail because they were denied bail or were unable to raise bail. The other inmates are convicted offenders who have been sentenced to serve time in jail. Although the vast majority of these inmates have been convicted of misdemeanors, some convicted felons are given a "split sentence" involving jail followed by probation. Also, a small number of inmates have been sentenced and are in jail awaiting transfer to state or federal prison facilities.

Because of the jail's role as a pretrial detention center, there is a high rate of turnover among the jail population. The data used in Table 9.4 represent a static 1-day count, as opposed to an annual total of all people who pass through the jail system. Thus, *daily* population of jails is lower than prisons, but the *annual* total of people incarcerated is higher.

TABLE 9.4 Percentage of Jail Inmates by Race and Ethnicity, One-Day Count, 2004

Race/Ethnicity	Percentage
White (non-Hispanic)	44.4
African American (non-Hispanic)	38.6
Hispanic	15.2
Other (Native Americans, Alaska Natives, Asians, Pacific Islanders)	1.8

SOURCE: Paige M. Harrison and Allen J. Beck. *Prison and Jail Inmates at Midyear 2004* (Washington, DC: U.S. Department of Justice, 2005).

Minority Overrepresentation

Racial and ethnic minorities are consistently overrepresented in the nation's local jail populations; at midyear 2004, nearly 6 of 10 people in local jails were racial and ethnic minorities.[49] As Table 9.4 indicates, whereas whites make up the largest proportion of inmates in jails around the country (roughly 45 percent), African Americans are notably overrepresented compared to their representation in the general population. Hispanics represent a slightly higher percentage of the jail population than the general population. These numbers change slightly from year to year; sometimes African Americans make up the largest proportion of jail inmates, so that over time there are roughly the same number of African Americans and whites in jail. The overrepresentation of Hispanics has been higher in some years than 2004 (see 1996), indicating a more serious disparity than reflected in Table 9.4. Overall, the picture of disparity depicted by these jail numbers is essentially similar to the reflection of race and ethnicity in prison populations. (See "Focus on an Issue" for specific information about tribal jails.)

Because of the jail's function as a pretrial detention center, jail population is heavily influenced by bail decisions. If more people were released on nonfinancial considerations, the number of people in jail would be lower. This raises the questions of racial discrimination in bail setting, which we discussed in Chapter 5. As noted in that chapter, there is evidence that judges impose higher bail—or are more likely to deny bail altogether—if the defendant is a racial minority.

COMMUNITY CORRECTIONS

Nearly 7 million people were under correctional supervision in the United States in 2004 (3,175 per 100,000 population). Nearly 5 million of these offenders were supervised in the community on the status of parole or probation. Does the pattern of racial and ethnic disparity present in incarceration facilities remain in community corrections?

Focus on an Issue
Jails on Tribal Lands[50]

In 2003 more than 53,000 Native Americans were under correctional supervision (prison, jail, probation, parole) in the United States (federal, state, local, and tribal authorities combined). Most were under community supervision (29,705). The U.S. population is approximately 1 percent Native American; however, the incarceration rate for Native Americans in prison and jail facilities was 19 percent higher than the incarceration rate for all races combined (848 per 100,000 Native Americans compared to 715 per 100,000 U.S. residents).

The picture of jails on tribal lands is presented by the Bureau of Justice Statistics' "2003 Survey of Jails in Indian Country" (SJIC). The statutory meaning of "Indian country" (18 U. S. C. 1151) is all lands within an Indian reservation, dependent Indian Communities, and Indian Trust allotments. Currently, nearly 300 Native American land areas/reservations exist across 33 states. Federal regulations limit the jurisdiction and incarceration powers of tribal governments by identity of the victim and offender,

the severity of the crime, and location of the crime. Tribal sentencing authority is limited to 1 year and a $5,000 fine per offense, or both (25 U.S.C. 1153). The SJIC reveals that more than 12,000 people were admitted to jails in the first 6 months of 2003, with a total of 1,908 people on the U.S. Census date, June 30th. This population is smaller than the number of Native Americans held in locally operated city/county jails, which was estimated at 7,200 for the year 2003.

These offenders were incarcerated in 70 tribal confinement facilities; however, 43 percent of the tribal inmate population is held in 10 jails. The largest Native American tribal jail populations are found in Arizona, with additional large institutions in Oregon and North Dakota. The majority of jail facilities hold fewer than 25 inmates.

In 2003 the SJIC indicated that 56 percent of inmates being held were convicted offenders, predominantly for misdemeanor offenses. Overall, 35 percent of offenders were held for a violent offense, with 17 percent charged with domestic violence offenses.[51]

Parole: Early Release from Prison

Parole is a form of early release from prison under supervision in the community. Prison inmates are released to one of two forms of parole: discretionary parole or mandatory parole. The U.S. Department of Justice defines discretionary parole as a decision made by a parole board to "conditionally release prisoners based on a statutory or administrative determination of eligibility," whereas mandatory parole "occurs in jurisdictions using determinate sentencing statutes. Inmates are conditionally released from prison after serving a portion of their original sentence minus any good time earned."[53] It is not surprising, therefore, that parole populations are similar in racial and ethnic distribution to federal and state prison populations. In 2004 (Figure 9.3) a nearly equal percentage of white or African American people were released on parole

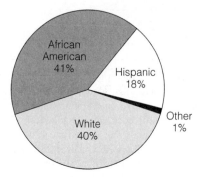

F I G U R E 9.3 State Parole Populations, by Race and Ethnicity, 2004

SOURCE: Bureau of Justice Statistics. *Probation and Parole Statistics, Summary Findings 2004.* Available at www.ojp.usdoj/bjs/.

(40 percent compared to 41 percent). Hispanics make up the other roughly 20 percent of parolees. Although African Americans and Hispanics are still over-represented in parole populations compared to their presentation in the population, the positive side of this picture of parole is that African Americans and Hispanics are making the transition to parole (arguably a positive move) in proportions similar to prison population figures. However, parole revocation figures require a closer look.

Success and Failure on Parole

A parolee "succeeds" on parole if he or she completes the terms of supervision without violations. A parolee can "fail" in one of two ways: by being arrested for another crime or by violating one of the conditions of parole release (using drugs, possessing a weapon, violating curfew, etc.). In either case, parole authorities can revoke parole and send the person back to prison.

Parole revocation, therefore, is nearly equivalent to the judge's power to sentence an offender in the first place because it can mean that offender will return to prison. The decision to revoke parole is discretionary; parole authorities may choose to overlook a violation and not send the person back to prison. This use of discretion opens the door for possible discrimination.

Most of parolees are released from state prisons. Currently, nearly 80 percent of inmates will be released to parole supervision rather than simply being released at the expiration of their sentence. Recent data indicate that 42 percent of all parolees at the state level successfully completed parole.[54] The success rate varied somewhat by racial/ethnic groups: 40.0 percent of whites, 39.0 percent of African Americans, 50.6 percent of Hispanics, and 42.2 percent of other races.[55] The percentage of parole violators by race within the year 1999 indicates that the majority of those violating parole were African American (51.8 percent), with whites representing less than one-third of violators (27.5 percent) and Hispanics representing approximately one-fifth of violators (18.3 percent).[56]

A small number of federal inmates are still eligible for parole consideration. Recent data on federal parole reveal that approximately 78 percent of

B O X 9.2   Supervision in the Community: An Uneven Playing Field?

Both parole and probation involve supervision in the community under a set of specific provisions for client behavior. One of the most common provisions is the requirement of employment. Not being able to attain or retain employment may lead to a violation of supervision conditions and unsuccessful discharge of an individual from probation or parole. Essentially, a person could be sent to prison for being unemployed. It is possible that the employment provision creates uneven hardships for minorities. In 2003 the unemployment rate for U.S. citizens, regardless of race, was 6.0 percent. This rate, of course, varies by race and ethnicity: whites 5.2 percent, African Americans 10.8 percent, and Hispanics 7.7 percent.[60] Unemployment rates also vary by age; youth between the ages of 16 and 24 have higher unemployment rates than the general population. Young people have unemployment rates two to three times higher, with the highest unemployment rates found for young (16 to 19) African Americans at 33 percent and young Hispanics at 20 percent; the lowest was for young white males, at 15.2 percent.[61] In short, ethnic- and race-specific unemployment rates vary substantially, showing the disadvantaged status of minorities in the labor market. Does this aspect of the general economy adversely affect minorities on probation and parole? If yes, could this be seen as a form of institutional discrimination?

federal parole discharges were from successful completion of parole conditions.[57] Once again, these rates vary by minority group status. Whites and other races had the highest successful completion rate of 76 percent, followed by Hispanics at 68 percent and African Americans with the lowest at 53 percent.[58] Similarly, African Americans had the highest return-to-prison rates (36 percent), with all other groups exhibiting a return rate of lower than 20 percent.[59] (See Box 9.2 for a discussion of supervision of people on parole in the community.)

Probation: A Case of Sentencing Discrimination?

Probation is an alternative to incarceration, a sentence to supervision in the community. The majority of all the people under correctional supervision are on probation, totaling more than 4 million people.[62]

The racial demographics in Figure 9.4 offer a picture of the probation population with race and ethnicity presented separately. These figures indicate that African Americans are overrepresented (30 percent) in the probation population relative to their presence in the general population.[63] Correspondingly, whites are underrepresented at 56 percent of all probationers and Hispanics are represented at roughly the same as their representation in the population.[64]

It is immediately apparent that the racial disparity for probation is not as great as it is for the prison population, however. Given that probation is a less severe sentence than prison, this difference may indicate that the advantage of receiving the less severe sentence of probation is more likely to be reserved for

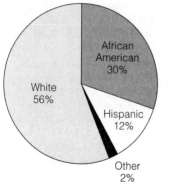

FIGURE 9.4 Probation Populations, by Race, 2004

SOURCE: Lauren E. Glaze and Seri Palla, *Probation and Parole in the United States, 2004,* Bureau of Justice Statistics (Washington, DC: U.S. Department of Justice, 2005).

whites. In a study of sentencing in California, Petersilia found that 71 percent of whites convicted of a felony were granted probation, compared with 67 percent of African Americans and 65 percent of Hispanics.[65] Similarly, Spohn and other colleagues found that in "borderline cases" in which judges could impose either a long probation sentence or a short prison sentence, whites were more likely to get probation and African Americans were more likely to get prison. (See the discussion of discrimination in sentencing in Chapter 7 and Figure 9.4.)

Community Corrections: A Native American Example

The phenomenon of drug courts in American criminal justice emerged in the late 1980s. Primarily, these specialized courts emerged in response to the growing concern over drug-related cases that were clogging the courts and filling up our jails and prisons and the perception that traditional "War on Drugs" strategies of attacking supply and incarcerating users to control demand was not producing the desired results.

The Drug Courts Program Office of the U.S. Department of Justice defines the drug court approach as departing "from the standard court approach by systematically bringing drug treatment to the criminal justice population entering the court system...In the drug court,...treatment is anchored in the authority of the judge who holds the defendant or offender personally and publicly accountable for treatment progress."[66] Essentially, local teams of judges, law enforcement officials, prosecuting attorneys, defense attorneys, probation officers, and treatment providers are using "the coercive powers of the court to force abstinence and alter behavior with a combination of intensive judicial super-vision, escalating sanctions, mandatory drug testing and strong aftercare programs."[67]

Starting in 1997, attempts have been made to adapt the drug court curric-ulum to tribal court settings. Currently, more than 40 programs exist in more than 13 states. A number of adaptations need to be made to incorporate the drug court model to the tribal court setting, but the basic philosophy of therapeutic jurisprudence is a strong compliment to many elements of indigenous justice philosophy. First, the naming of drug courts has undergone a transition to the title of "Tribal Healing to Wellness Courts." This renaming and the subsequent adaptation of procedures are designed to meet the cultural needs of individual Native communities and their long-established traditional Native concepts of justice.

The Tribal Law and Policy Institute notes that the "Tribal Healing to Wellness Courts return to a more traditional method of Justice for Indian people by 1) creating an environment that focuses on the problems underlying the criminal act rather than the acts itself and 2) stressing family, extended family and community involvement in the healing process."[68] In short, advocates argue that the Tribal Healing to Wellness Courts are "a modern revitalization of Native principles of Justice—truth, honor, respect, harmony, balance, healing, wellness, apology or contrition, restitution, rehabilitation and an holistic approach."[69] The hope is that the court will function to "restore harmony and balance to individuals, the families and the communities which have been devastated by alcohol and drug use."[70]

Tribal Healing to Wellness Courts involve a number of tribal members in the court process, including tribal elders and medicine men, to accomplish the goals of treatment and community service. Usually, part of the treatment component is the mandatory attendance at community activities reflecting traditional, cultural heritage values. Such activities include "traditional healing ceremonies, talking circles, peacemaking, sweats, sweat lodge, visits with medicine men, sun dance and vision quest," depending on the practices of the individual Native community.[71] Beyond the typical community service requirement of drug courts are the requirements of spending time with elders, tribal storytellers, or both.

All of the methods and procedures adopted by Tribal Healing to Wellness Courts are firmly grounded in traditional dispute resolution mechanisms and traditional spiritual components to promote healing to wellness. The most common issue dealt with in the Tribal Courts is the problem of alcohol abuse. Records indicate that more than 90 percent of the criminal cases that come before tribal courts have an alcohol or substance abuse component.[72] The substance abuse issues are present not just for some adults; they also are problems for some children, so some tribes have adopted courts for both groups. Juveniles also have the problem of inhalant use.[73]

The development of the Tribal Healing to Wellness Courts is often limited by the sentencing authority granted to the tribal courts. These courts have limited jurisdiction to nonmajor crimes on tribal lands and limited influence in off-reservation crimes. The Tribal Law and Policy Institute notes, however, that some Tribal Healing to Wellness Courts have agreements with state court systems to transfer jurisdiction to them when tribal members are involved in substance abuse–related offenses.[74]

Focus on an Issue
Civil Rights of Convicted Felons

Individuals convicted of felonies in the United States may experience a range of sentences from incarceration to probation. Such sentences in effect limit the civil rights of the convicted. No longer do we live in a society that views the convicted felon from the legal status of civil death, literally a slave of the state, but some civil rights restrictions endure after the convicted offender serves a judicially imposed sentence. *Collateral consequences* is a term used to refer to the statutory restrictions imposed by a legislative body on a convicted felon's rights. Such restrictions vary by state but include restrictions on employment, on carrying firearms, on holding public office, and on voting.

Forty-nine states and the District of Columbia restrict the rights of imprisoned people to vote, whereas 28 states restrict the right to vote for offenders on probation, and 32 states limit this right while on parole.[75] In most states the right to vote can be restored (automatically or by petition) after completion of the sentence (or within a fixed number of years). However, in eight states the legal prohibition on voting is permanent.[76] The Sentencing Project reports that, although some states allow for the restoration of voting rights to felony offenders who have served out their sentences, the process is not always easy.[77] In the state of Nebraska,[78] the ex-offender has their voting rights restored automatically after 2 years, but in some states the ex-offender has to apply to the Pardons Board for reinstatement.[79]

In the state of Alabama ex-offenders are required to provide a DNA sample to the Alabama Department of Forensic Sciences as part of the process of regaining the right to vote.[80] Additional restrictions on convicted felons were created with the passage of the U.S. Patriot Act. Under these provisions, ex-offenders are unable to attain certain commercial driver's licenses and are banned from transporting materials designated as hazardous waste.

Given the current increases in incarceration rates across the country, the additional penalty of disenfranchisement for convicted felons becomes an increasing concern. In short, the permanence of this measure may have unanticipated consequences. Because there is an over-representation of African American males in U.S. prisons, "significant proportions of the black population in some states have been locked out of the voting booth."[81] For example, in the state of Florida, which denies voting rights permanently to convicted felons, nearly one-third of the African American male population is not eligible to vote.[82] It has been argued that laws such as these, that have the effect of barring a substantial portion of the minority population from voting, fails to promote a racially diverse society. Should convicted offenders be allowed to earn back their right to vote as recognition of their efforts at rehabilitation? Should we change laws that have a racial impact, even if the intent is not racially motivated?

THEORETICAL PERSPECTIVES ON THE RACIAL DISTRIBUTION OF CORRECTIONAL POPULATIONS

Several theoretical arguments are advanced to explain the overwhelming overrepresentation of African Americans in the correctional system. The most fundamental question is whether prison populations reflect discrimination in the criminal justice system or other factors. One view is that the overrepresentation reflects widespread discrimination; the alternative view is that the overrepresentation results from a disproportionate involvement in criminal activity on the part of minorities. Mann[83] argues that there is systematic discrimination based on color, whereas Wilbanks[84] contends that the idea of systematic discrimination is a "myth."

The work of Alfred Blumstein offers a benchmark to explore the results of such research. Focusing on 1979 prison population data, Blumstein sought to isolate the impact of discrimination from other possible factors. The key element of his research is the following formula[85]:

X = ratio of expected black-to-white incarceration rates based only on arrest
    disproportionality/ratio of black-to-white incarceration rates actually
    observed.

Essentially, this formula compares the expected black–white disparity (X) in state prison populations based on recorded black–white disparity in arrest rates (numerator) over the observed black–white disparity in incarceration rates (denominator). Thus, accepting the argument that arrest rates are not a reflection of discrimination, Blumstein's formula calculates the portion of the prison population left unexplained by the disproportionate representation of African Americans at the arrest stage. In short, this figure is the amount of actual racial disproportionality in incarceration rates that is open to an explanation or charge of discrimination.

Overall, Blumstein found that 20 percent of the racial disparity in incarceration rates is left unexplained by the overrepresentation of African Americans at the arrest stage. Crime-specific rates indicate that results vary by crime type:[86]

All offenses	20.0 percent
Homicide	2.8 percent
Aggravated assault	5.2 percent
Robbery	15.6 percent
Rape	26.3 percent
Burglary	33.1 percent
Larceny/auto theft	45.6 percent
Drugs	48.9 percent

Arguably, the main implication of this list is that the level of unexplained disproportionality is "directly related to the discretion permitted or used in handling each of the offenses, which tends to be related to offense seriousness—the less serious the offenses (and the greater discretion), the greater the amount of the disproportionality in prison that must be accounted for on grounds other than differences in arrest."[87]

This observation is particularly salient in the context of drug offenses. Recall the arguments from Chapter 4 that contend that drug arrest decisions are subject to more proactive enforcement than most offenses. Combine this observation with the fact that during the surge of incarceration rates from 1980 to1996, the offense with the greatest impact on new commitments to prison was drug offenses. In short, the offense category indicated to suffer from the broad use of discrimination and the most opportunity for discrimination is the fastest-growing portion of new commitments to prison. Thus, Blumstein's findings, although generally not an indictment of the criminal justice system, suggest an ominous warning for the presence of discrimination during the era of the war on drugs.

Langan[88] reexamined Blumstein's argument, contending that he relied on an inappropriate dataset. Langan argued that prison admissions offered a more appropriate comparison to arrest differentials than prison populations. Langan also incorporated victim identification data as a substitute for arrest data to circumvent the biases associated with arrest. In addition to altering Blumstein's formula, he looked at 3 years of data (1973, 1979, 1982) across five offense types (robbery, aggravated assault, simple assault, burglary, and larceny). Even after making these modifications, Langan confirmed Blumstein's findings; about 20 percent of the racial overrepresentation in prison admissions was left unexplained.

In an updated analysis with 1990 prison population data, Blumstein found that the amount of unexplained variation in racially disproportionate prison populations on the basis of arrest data increased from 20 percent to 24 percent. In addition, the differentials discussed earlier on the basis of discretion and seriousness increased for drug crimes and less serious crimes, becoming smaller for homicide and robbery only.[89] This seems to confirm the argument that the war on drugs has increased the racial disparities in prison populations.

Tonry challenges Blumstein's work on several grounds.[90] He argues, first, that it is a mistake to assume that official Uniform Crime Report arrest statistics accurately reflect offending rates. As discussed in Chapter 4, there is evidence of race discrimination in arrests. This is particularly true with respect to drug arrests, which account for much of the dramatic increase in the prison populations in recent years. Second, Tonry points out that Blumstein's analysis used national-level data. Aggregating in this fashion can easily mask evidence of discrimination in certain areas of the country.

Tonry's third criticism is that Blumstein's approach could easily hide "off-setting forms of discrimination that are equally objectionable but not observable in the aggregate."[91] One example would be sentencing African American offenders with white victims more harshly, while at the same time punishing African American offenders with African American victims less harshly (see Chapter 7 for a more detailed discussion). The former represents a bias against African American offenders, and the latter is a bias against African American victims. If we aggregate the data, as Blumstein did, neither pattern is evident.

Hawkins and Hardy speak to the possibility of regional differences by looking at state-specific imprisonment rates.[92] These authors find a wide variation across the 50 states in the extent of the differential in African American imprisonment rates left unexplained by disproportionate African American arrest rates. The "worst state" was New Mexico, with only 2 percent of the difference explained by the expected impact of arrest. At the other end of the continuum, Missouri was the "best state," with 96 percent of the incarceration rates of African Americans explained by differential arrest rates. Hawkins and Hardy conclude that "Blumstein's figure of 80 percent would not seem to be a good approximation for all states."[93]

In an attempt to look past systematic racial discrimination in the criminal justice system, researchers have begun to explore the intricacies of contextual discrimination. A review by Chiricos and Crawford[94] reveals that researchers have started to study the social context's impact on the racial composition of imprisonment rates by investigating such issues as the population's racial composition, the percentage of unemployed African Americans, and the region.

The first two issues reflect the theoretical argument that communities and thus decisionmakers will be apprehensive under certain conditions and become more punitive. Specific conditions of apprehension (or threat) are related to racial mass. For example, large concentrations of African Americans will be associated with a higher fear of crime and a need to be more punitive. Michalowski and Pearson[95] found that racial composition of African Americans in a state was positively associated with general incarceration rates. However, the impact of racial composition on race-specific incarceration rates is less clear. Hawkins and Hardy[96] discovered that states with smaller percentages of African Americans were associated with more racial disparity in incarceration rates that could be accounted for by arrest rates. In contrast, Bridges and Crutchfield[97] found that states with higher percentages of African Americans in the general population were associated with lower levels of racial disparity in incarceration rates. DeLone and Chiricos[98] argue that this inconsistency is the result of an improper level of analysis. They argue that looking at state-level imprisonment and racial composition rates can be deceiving. The proper level of analysis is the level of the sentencing court. In their study of county-level incarceration rates, they found that higher levels of African Americans led to higher levels of general incarceration and African American incarceration rates.

Race-specific unemployment rates reflect the idea that idle (or surplus) populations are crime prone and in need of deterrence. This line of reasoning requires more punitive response, with higher incarceration rates when the perceived crime-prone population is idle.[99] Generally, this "threat" is measured by the unemployment rate of the perceived crime-prone population—young, African American males. DeLone and Chiricos have found that at the county level, high young African American male unemployment rates are not associated with higher general incarceration rates but are predictive of higher young African American male incarceration rates.[100] (Box 9.3 details other explanations for the racial distribution of the prison population.)

Adjustment to Prison

Research on the adjustment of men to life in prison has been available for many years, beginning with Clemmer's *The Prison Community*[105] and including Sykes' *The Society of Captives*[106] and Irwin and Cressey's "Thieves, Convicts and Inmate Culture."[107] Jacobs[108] argues that without exception these studies disregarded the issue of race, although the prison populations in the institutions under study were racially diverse.[109] Consequently, according to Jacobs, the prevailing concept of the "prison subculture" needs to be revised. Jacobs argues that race is the defining factor of the prison experience. Racial and ethnic identity defines the social groupings in prisons, the operation of informal economic systems, the organization of religious activities, and the reasons for inmate misconduct. In other words, white inmates tend to associate with white inmates, African American inmates associate with African Americans, and so on. In this respect, the racial and ethnic segregation in prison mimics society on the outside.

B O X 9.3   Additional Explanations for the Racial Distribution
of U.S. Prison Populations

Historically, some have argued that prison replaced the social control of slavery in the
South after the end of the Civil War. Given the criminalization of vagrancy and the
operation of the convict lease system, a *de facto* slavery system was invoked on those
African Americas who did not leave the South and who refused to offer their labor to
former plantation owners who needed it.[101]

Others have argued that prison has always been used to supplement the
needs of capitalism as a mechanism to control surplus populations in times of high
unemployment.[102] Specifically, African American males, who have the highest
unemployment rates, have been viewed as socially dangerous surplus populations.[103]

In the context of the war on drugs, some have argued that the increasing
African American male prison populations are a response to a moral panic about
drugs that stems from the association of crime and drug use with this population
almost exclusively.[104]

Goodstein and MacKenzie support Jacob's observations and argue that their
own "exploratory study of race and inmate adjustment to prison demonstrates
that the experience of imprisonment differs for African Americans and
whites."[110] They report that although African Americans may develop more
antiauthoritarian attitudes, and are more likely to challenge prison officials, they
appear to have fewer conflicts with fellow inmates.

Wright[111] explored the relationship between "race and economic marginality" to explain adjustment to prison. He explores the apparently common-sense
assumption that African Americans, because of their experience in the "modern
urban ghetto" (see information on the underclass in Chapter 3), will be more
"resilient" to the pains of imprisonment. In short, "ghetto life supposedly social-
izes the individual to engage in self-protection against the hostile social environment of the slum and the cold and unpredictable prison setting."[112] Using
multiple indicators of adaptation to the prison environment, Wright found that,
although economic marginality does appear to influence the ease of adjustment to
prison, this appears to be the case regardless of race.

Other research on male prison populations also indicates that race may not
always explain institutional behavior. Research on the effects of race on levels of
institutional misconduct reveals an inconsistent picture. Although some researchers find nonwhites overrepresented in inmate misconduct, Petersilia and
Honig's[113] study of three state prison systems found three different patterns in
relationships between race and rule infractions. In Michigan there was no
relationship between race and rule infractions; in California whites had significantly higher rule infractions; and in Texas, African Americans had significantly
higher rule infractions.

Flanagan[114] finds similarly inconsistent results. He argues that inmates' age at
commitment, history of drug use, and current incarceration offense are most
predictive of general misconduct rates. He does, however, find that race is an

Focus on an Issue
Mortality in Prisons and Jails[52]

Inmate mortality rates are available for state prison and local jail populations. For all causes, regardless of race, 148 per 100,000 inmates die in jails per year and 244 per 100,000 inmates die in prison per year. The 2002 figures indicate that there are significant racial/ethnic differences for all causes combined, as well as for suicide rates, with few differences for homicide rates. Both suicide and homicide rates have declined steadily since the 1980s. Currently, the rates for suicide are 47 and 14 per 100,000 inmates (jail and prison, respectively), with the rates for homicide at 3 and 4 per 100,000 inmates (jail and prison, respectively).

Suicide rates are substantially higher for whites in jail and prison than for African Americans inmates (96 per 100,000 jail inmates and 22 per 100,000 prison inmates, respectively, compared to 16 per 100,000 jail inmates and 8 per 100,000 state inmates, respectively). Hispanic inmates have a somewhat lower rate than whites (30 per 100,000 jail inmates and 18 per 100,000 prison inmates) but higher than for African American inmates.

Homicide rates in local jails for 2002 were reported at 3 per 100,000 population and do not vary across racial/ethnic groups. However, the homicide rates for state prison inmates are higher than the overall rate for Hispanics (7 per 100,000 inmates) and whites (5 per 100,000 inmates) and less than the overall rate for African American inmates (2 per 100,000 inmates).

---

important predictor for older inmates with no drug history and sentenced for an offense other than homicide. Flanagan recommends that race (among other predictors) is a variable that is inappropriate to use in assisting with the security classification of inmates as a result of its low predictive power in relation to institutional misconduct.

Research of federal prison inmates by Harer and Steffensmeier[115] offers support for the importation model of prison violence, indicating that African American inmates are significantly more likely to receive disorderly conduct reports for violence than white inmates are, but they are more likely to have lower levels of alcohol and drug misconduct reports than whites.[116] This picture reflects the differential levels of violence and drug behavior between African Americans and whites conveyed in arrest figures and assumed to characterize the general behavior patterns of these groups in American society (see Chapter 2).

Many correctional observers say that even with the numerical dominance of African Americans in correctional facilities, they are still at a disadvantage in terms of the allocation of resources. For example, Thomas argues that race operates in prison culture to guide behavior, allocate resources, and elevate white groups to a privileged status even when they are not numerically dominant.[117]

In addition to the adjustment issues related to prison life, the previous "Focus on an Issue" section raises the issue of racial differences in prison mortality rates. Are the contributing factors to this controversial situation most likely to be found in pre-prison lifestyles or to be connected to disparities in prison health care?

Race and Religion Religion often emerges as a source of solidarity among prison inmates and as a mechanism for inmates to adjust to the frustrations of the prison environment. Although religion may be seen as a benign, or even a rehabilitative influence, some religious activities in prison have been met with criticism by correctional officials and have been accepted only with federal court intervention. Concern arises when religious tenants seem to espouse the supremacy of one racial group over another.

Jacobs argues that the Black Muslim movement in U.S. prisons was a response to active external proselytizing by the church.[118] The most influential Muslim movement was the Nation of Islam, founded by Elijah Muhammad. Conley and Debro point out that, although the Nation of Islam was not particularly competitive with Christianity in the nonprison population, "it had special appeal to incarcerated Black males. In contrast to the various religious denominations, which preached religious repentance and submission and obedience to the U. S. justice system ... the Nation of Islam preached Black pride and resistance to white oppression."[119] Prison administrators overtly resisted the movement for several years. The American Correctional Association issued a policy statement in 1960 refusing to recognize the legitimacy of the Muslim religion, based on arguments that it was a "cult" that disrupted prison operations. Jacobs notes that "prison officials saw in the Muslims not only a threat to prison authority, but also a broader revolutionary challenge to American society"[120] that led to challenges of the white correctional authority.

Consequently, prison officials tried to suppress Muslim religious activities by such actions as banning the Koran. This led to lawsuits asserting the Muslim's right to the free exercise of religion. In 1962, however, the U.S. Supreme Court (*Fulwood v. Clemmer*) ordered the District of Columbia Department of Corrections to "stop treating the Muslims differently from other religious groups."[121] This decision paved the way for the Black Muslim movement to be seen as a legitimate religion and to be taken seriously as a vehicle of prison change through such avenues as litigation.

One example of the rise and subsequent influence of Native American religious groups can be found in Nebraska. The Native American Cultural and Spiritual Awareness group is composed of Native American inmates who seek to build solidarity and appreciation of Native American values.[122] This group also pursues change in the prison environment through litigation. The element of inmate-on-inmate violence and guard assaults characteristic of other groups are not apparent here.

As the direct result of litigation, Native American inmates won the right to have a sweat lodge on prison grounds and to have medicine men and women visit to perform religious ceremonies. The significance of this concession is that it happened 4 years before federal legislation dictated the recognition and acceptance of Native American religions.

Other religious movements have come to concern prison officials and social commentators because of their apparent assertions of racial supremacy. The impact of such values in a closed environment like a prison is obvious, but concerns have surfaced that the impact of these subcultures may reach outside prison walls. Are groups emerging, under the guise of religions, that promote tenants of racial hatred?

The Five Percent and Asatru movements are two groups that have prison officials concerned. The former group is made up of African Americans, and the latter is made up of whites, each emphasizing tenants of racial purity. Currently, six states censor the teachings of the Five Percenters, whereas other states label all followers as gang members.[123] The movement began in Harlem in 1964 and has spread across the country, claiming thousands of followers. Teachings include the rejection of "history, authority and organized religion" while calling themselves a nation of Gods (men) and Earths (women).[124] Although the group advocates peace and rejects drinking alcohol and using drugs, correctional officials have linked Five Percenters to violence in some state institutions. Similar to the Nation of Islam, their beliefs stress that "blacks were the original beings and must separate from white society."[125]

The Asatru followers practice a form of pagan religion based on principles of pre-Christian Nordic traditions. This religion was officially recognized in Iceland in 1972 and professes nine noble virtues, including courage, honor, and perseverance. However, prison officials claim that as this group has grown in popularity in American prisons, so has racial violence. Some critics charge that "while Asatru is a genuine religion to some followers, these modern pagan groups have been a breeding ground for right-wing extremists"[126] and attract white supremacists. Some state prison systems have taken steps to ban Asatru groups, stating security concerns. Some Asatru followers have surfaced in connection with acts of racial violence. Most notably, perhaps, is the recent case of John William King, a white male convicted of the dragging death of an African American man in Jasper, Texas. While serving a prison sentence prior to this crime, King is said to have joined an Odinist group, an Asatru variant. From this affiliation he has tattoos depicting an African American man lynched on a cross and the words "Aryan Pride."[127]

Prison Gangs

Prison gangs are an integral part of understanding the prison environment and the inmate social system. Little systematic information on prison gangs (or security threat groups) is available. However, from the states that do document such subcultures we know that they cover the racial and ethnic spectrum. Some of these gangs have networks established between prisons; across states; and most recently, with street gangs.

The Florida and Texas prison systems offer examples of the variety of prison gangs present in prisons today. The Florida Department of Corrections documented six major prison gangs; one was white, two were African American, and three were Hispanic.[128] The Texas prison system documented eight well-established prison gangs; two were white, two were African American, and four were Hispanic.[129] Following are some representative examples.

Aryan Brotherhood[130]   The Aryan Brotherhood is one of the largest prison gangs and is made up of white males. This group originated in 1967 in the San Quentin State Prison in California. They are present in numerous federal and state facilities. Their membership is dominated by inmates with white supremacist and neo-Nazi ideologies. The group is implicated in criminal enterprises in prison (both violence and contraband) and in illegal activities on the outside.[131] This group is thought to be involved in a number of inmate and staff homicides. Although the group maintains economic arrangements with the Mexican Mafia, they are long-time enemies with such groups as the La Nuestra Familia and African American prison gangs such as the Black Guerilla Family.

Black Guerilla Family[132]   The Black Guerilla Family is made up of African American males. It was founded in the San Quentin Prison in California in 1966 by a former Black Panther. This group is distinguished by a predominant political ideology: Marxist/Maoist/Lenonist communism. Its goals are to struggle to maintain dignity in prison, eradicate racism, and overthrow the U.S. government. Rival gangs are the Aryan Brotherhood, Texas Syndicate, and the Mexican Mafia. However, the group does form alliances with such groups as the Black Liberation Army and black street gangs.

Mandingo Warriors[133]   The Mandingo Warriors are made up of African American males. It came into existence after most of the Hispanic and white groups formed. These members are involved in prison violence and the *sub rosa* economic system but appear to be less organized than the other race/ethnic groups.

Mexican Mafia[134]   The Mexican Mafia was formed in the late 1950s in the youth offenders' facilities of California by former Los Angeles street gang members. The members are male and Mexican American. This group is often identified as the most active gang in the federal prison system. They are described as having a philosophy of ethnic pride and act to control the drug trafficking in the institutions. They have active relationships with the Aryan Brotherhood and urban Latino street gangs. They have intense rivalries with the Black Guerilla Family and black street gangs.

Texas Syndicate[135]   The Texas Syndicate has its origins in the California Department of Corrections. Once released, these individuals returned to Texas and entered the Texas Department of Corrections as the result of continuing criminal activity. The membership is predominately Hispanic, with the occasional acceptance of white inmates. This group is structured along paramilitary lines, has a documented history of prison violence, and will enforce rule breaking with death. A spinoff associated with this group is the predominantly white gang Dirty White Boys.

One of the management issues associated with dealing with gangs in prison is the tension created by integrating prison populations that prefer to be racially segregated. While self-sought racial segregation is a dominant feature of most residential areas in the U.S., there are legal issues that structure such segregation decisions in the prison and jail environment. See "In the Courts: Racial and Ethnic Segregation in Prison: By Law or by Choice?" for additional insight into this issue.

In the Courts: Racial and Ethnic Segregation in Prison: By Law or by Choice?

A series of court decisions have declared *de jure* racial segregation in prisons to be unconstitutional. As late as the 1970s, prisons in the South and even some in states such as Nebraska segregated prisoners according to race as a matter of official policy. Although such policies have been outlawed, inmates often self-segregate along racial and ethnic lines as a matter of choice. Most recently, the racial segregation policies of the California Department of Corrections (DOC) have been under judicial review.

In 2005 the U.S. Supreme Court, in its opinion in *Johnson v. California*, overturned a lower court ruling indicating the California DOC could *not* use racial classifications in prison to assign mandatory segregated housing based on race. The California DOC was using a race/ethnic–based classification that required mandatory residential segregation for an inmate's stay in the reception center and for the initial pairing (60 days) of the two-inmate room assignment. The DOC argues that this policy prevents violence within facilities because of the extensive nature of race-based security threat groups (gangs such as the Aryan Brotherhood, Mexican Mafia, and Black Guerilla Family). In short, correctional administrators were arguing that "separate, but equal" treatment of inmates was justified to prevent violence among inmates. Administrators note that all racial/ethnic groups are segregated at the initial phases of admission; "the DOC policy further subdivided ethnic groups so that Chinese Americans were separated from Japanese Americans and Northern California Hispanics from Southern California Hispanics."[136] Administrators also noted that no other areas in the facilities were segregated, such as the dining hall and the recreation yards.[137]

The U.S. Supreme Court's opinion striking down this policy was written by Justice Sandra Day O'Connor, where she states for the majority that in the implementation of policies such as these "there is simply no way of determining ... what classifications are in fact motivated by illegitimate notions of racial inferiority or simple racial politics. We therefore apply strict scrutiny to all racial classifications to 'smoke out' illegitimate uses of race by assuring that [government] is pursuing a goal important enough to warrant use of a highly suspect tool."[138]

Justice O'Connor also stated in her opinion that "when government officials are permitted to use race as a proxy for gang membership and violence without demonstrating compelling government interest ... society as a whole suffers."[139] She further contends that the Federal Bureau of Prisons supports the assertion that "racial integration leads to less violence in institutions and better prepares inmates for reentry into society."[140] The courts' recommendation is that "race-neutral" remedies be pursued to handle the problems associated with inmate violence. Correctional administrators should strive to avoid policies that may breed racial intolerance.

Given the clear judicial message that correctional administrators cannot pursue "separate, but equal" policies of race/ethnic–based segregation to reduce prison violence, the issue remains—to what extent should integration be *required* work, housing, recreation, and education assignments? Should administrators allow inmates to make decisions on the basis of personal preference, even if these decisions result in self-segregation? Racial tensions are a serious problem in most prisons; forcing white and African American inmates to share cells, when they are actively hostile to each other, could bring these tensions to a boil. In one instance, a white inmate felt so threatened by the politicized racial atmosphere in his prison that he filed suit asking a federal court to reverse the integration requirement and return to segregation.[141]

However, if correctional administrators bowed to the wishes of inmates on this matter they would create two problems. First, they would be actively promoting racial segregation, which is illegal. Second, they would undermine their own authority by acknowledging that inmates could veto policy they did not like.

What is the best strategy for administrators in this difficult situation? You decide.

Women in Prison

Studies addressing the imprisonment of women are less numerous than those for men, but they are increasing in number. Within this growing body of research, the issue of race is not routinely addressed either. When race is assessed the comparisons are generally limited to African Americans and whites. The evidence is mixed on the issue of whether race effects the adjustment of women to prison life.

MacKenzie[142] explains the behaviors (conflicts and misconduct reports) of women in prison on the basis of age and attitudes (anxiety, fear of victimization). She comments that the four prisons she examined are similar in racial composition, but she does not comment on whether she explored differences by race in relation to attitudes and aggressive behavior. Such research ignores the possibility that race may influence one's perception of prison life, tendencies toward aggression, age of inmate, or length of time in prison.

MacKenzie and others[143] do, in later works, address race in the demographic description of the incarcerated women. In a study of one women's prison in Louisiana, for example, they found that nonwhite women were severely overrepresented among all prisoners and even more likely to be serving long sentences. Their findings indicate unique adjustment problems for long-term inmates, but they fail to incorporate race into their explanatory observations about institutional misconduct. This omission seems contrary to the observation that nonwhite women are more likely to have longer sentences.

Race has specifically been recognized as a factor in research addressing the issue of sexual deprivation among incarcerated women. Leger[144] identifies racial dimensions to several key explanatory factors in the participation of female prisoners in lesbianism. First, the demographic information reveals that most lesbian relationships are intraracial and that no distinctions emerged by race in participation in the gay or straight groups. Second, once dividing the group by the characteristics of previous confinements (yes or no) and age at first lesbian experience, the pattern of even representation of whites and African Americans changed. African American females were overrepresented in the group indicating previous confinement, and the information about age at first arrest indicates that African American females are more likely to have engaged in their first lesbian act prior to their first arrest.

CONCLUSION

The picture of the American correctional system is most vivid in black and white, but it also has prominent images of brown. Such basic questions as "Who is in prison?" and "How do individuals survive in prison?" cannot be divorced from the issues of race and ethnicity. The most salient observation about minorities and corrections is the striking overrepresentation of African Americans in prison populations. In addition, this overrepresentation is gradually increasing in new court commitments and population figures. Explanations for this increasing overrepresentation are complex.

The most obvious possibility is that African American criminality is increasing. This explanation has been soundly challenged by Tonry's work, which compares the stability of African American arrest rates since the mid 1970s to the explosive African American incarceration rates of the same period.[145] He argues that a better explanation may be the racial impact of the war on drugs.

Blumstein's analysis offers another clue to the continuing increase in the African American portion of the prison population, which links discretion and the war on drugs. His work suggests that the racial disparities in incarceration rates for drug offenses are not well explained by racial disparities in drug arrest rates. Thus, the war on drugs and its impact on imprisonment may be fostering the "malign neglect" Tonry charges.

DISCUSSION QUESTIONS

1. What must a researcher do to advance a description of disparity to an argument of discrimination? In the case of prison populations, how do you advance from the demographic description of the overrepresentation of African Americans in prison to a causal analysis of discrimination by the criminal justice system?

2. In what ways is the indigenous justice paradigm in conflict with the principles of the traditional, adversarial American criminal justice system? In what ways do the principles of Native American justice complement more mainstream correctional initiatives?

3. In what way are Blumstein and colleagues' findings about the wide variation of unexplained racial disparity in prison populations according to type of offense similar to the liberation hypothesis discussed in the chapter on sentencing (Chapter 7)?

4. What correctional policies can be created from the principles of restorative justice (based indigenous justice principles)? Are these values more compatible with some offenses than others? More appropriate for some types of offenders than others?

5. Do you think prison gang formation is influenced most by external forces and the gang affiliations offenders bring to prison from the street or by the internal forces of the prison environment, such as racial composition? What arguments can you offer to support your position?

NOTES

1. U.S. Department of Justice, News Release: *National Correctional Population Reaches New High* (August 26, 2001). Available at www.ojp.usdoj/bjs/abstract/oous000.htm.

2. U.S. Census Bureau, *United States Statistical Abstract, 2000.* Available at www.census.gov/population/socdemo/school/ppl-148/tab01.text.

3. Marc Maur, *Americans Behind Bars: A Comparison of International Rates of Incarceration* (Washington, DC: The Sentencing Project, 1991).

4. http://nces.ed.gov/pubs2001/digest/.

5. U.S. Census Bureau, *United States Statistical Abstract, 2004–5*. Available at www.census.gov/.

6. Ibid.

7. Estimates calculated from U.S. Department of Justice, News Release: *National Correctional Population Reaches New High* (August 26, 2001). Available at www.ojp.usdoj/bjs/abstract/oous000.htm; Allen J. Beck and Paige M. Harrison, *Prisoners in 2000* (Washington, DC: U.S. Department of Justice, 2001). Available at www.ojp.usdoj.gov/bjs/.

8. U.S. Census Bureau, *United States Statistical Abstract, 2000* (Washington, DC: U.S. Government Printing Office). Available at www.census.gov/population/socdemo/school/ppl-148/tab01.text.

9. Harry E. Allen and Clifford E. Simonson, *Corrections in America: An Introduction*, 7th ed. (Englewood Cliffs, NJ: Prentice-Hall, 1995).

10. Ibid.

11. Ada Pecos Melton, "Crime and Punishment: Traditional and Contemporary Tribal Justice" in *Images of Color, Images of Crime*. Coramae Richey Mann and Marjorie S. Zatz, eds. (Los Angeles: Roxbury Publishing Company, 1998).

12. Ibid.

13. Ibid., p. 66.

14. See Marjorie S. Zatz, Carol Chiago Lujan, and Zoann K. Snyder-Joy, "American Indians and Criminal Justice: Some Conceptual and Methodological Considerations," in *Race and Criminal Justice* for a review of these issues.

15. Paige M. Harrison and Allen J. Beck. *Prisoners in 2004*. Bureau of Justice Statistics, 2005.

16. Ibid.

17. Ibid.

18. Beck and Harrison, *Prisoners in 2000* and Harrison and Beck, *Prisoners in 2004*.

19. Harrison and Beck, *Prisoners in 2004*.

20. Ibid.

21. Ibid.

22. Bureau of Justice Statistics, *Comparing State and Federal Inmates, 1991* (Washington, DC: Government Printing Office, 1993).

23. Bureau of Justice Statistics, *Sourcebook of Criminal Justice Statistics, 2003*, page 517. Available at www.albany.edu/sourcebook/.

24. BJS, *Comparing State and Federal Inmates, 1991*.

25. BJS, *Sourcebook, 2003*, pg 518. Note that the administrative classification is made up of special populations needing medical treatment or in pretrial detention.

26. Christopher J. Mumalo and Allen J. Beck, *Prisoners, 1996* (Washington, DC: U. S. Department of Justice, 1997).

27. *1993 Directory of Juvenile and Adult Correctional Departments, Institutions, Agencies and Paroling Authorities* (Laurel, MD: American Correctional Association, 1993).

28. Ibid.

29. John A. Arthur, "Correctional Ideology of Black Correctional Officers," *Federal Probation 58* (1994): 57–65.

30. Patrick A. Langan and David J. Levin. "Recidivism of Prisoners Released in 1994," *Bureau of Justice Statistics Report, 2002*.

31. Ibid.

32. Ibid.

33. Ibid.

34. Margaret Werner Cahalan, *Historical Corrections Statistics in the United States, 1850–1984* (Washington, DC: Government Printing Office, 1986), pp. 65–66.

35. Michael Tonry, *Malign Neglect* (New York: Oxford University Press, 1995).

36. Ibid.

37. Ibid., p. 21.

38. Ibid.

39. Harrison and Beck, *Prison and Jail Inmates at Midyear, 2004.*

40. Ibid., p. 11.

41. Ibid.

42. Ibid.

43. Ibid.

44. Roy Walmsley, *World Prison Population List*, 6th ed. International Centre for Prison Studies. Available at www.prisonstudies.org.

45. Marc Maur, *Americans Behind Bars*, 1991.

46. The Sentencing Project. "Facts about Prison and Prisoners." Available at www.sentencingproject.org.

47. Ibid.

48. *Prison and Jail Inmates*, 2004.

49. Ibid., p. 8.

50. Todd D. Minton, *Jails in Indian Country, 2003* (Washington, DC: U.S. Department of Justice, 2005). Available at www.ojp.usdoj.gov/bjs/.

51. Ibid., p. 1.

52. Christopher J. Mumola, *Suicide and Homicide in State Prisons and Local Jails* (Washington, DC: U.S. Department of Justice, 2005).

53. Timothy A. Hughes, Doris James Wilson, and Allen J. Beck, *Trends in State Parole, 1990–2000* (Washington, DC: U.S. Department of Justice, 2001), p. 2. Available at www.ojp.usdoj.gov/bjs/.

54. Ibid.

55. Ibid.

56. Ibid.

57. The Sentencing Project: Facts about Prison and Prisoners (2001). Available at www.sentencingproject.org.

58. Ibid.

59. Ibid.

60. U.S. Census Bureau, *Statistical Abstract of the United States, 2004–5.* Available at www.census.gov/.

61. Ibid.

62. Lauren E. Glaze and Seri Palla. *Probation and Parole in the United States, 2004* (Bureau of Justice Statistics, 2005).

63. Ibid.

64. Ibid.

65. Joan Petersilia, *Racial Disparities in the Criminal Justice System* (Santa Monica, CA: Rand, 1983), p. 28.

66. Tribal Law and Policy Institute. *Healing to Wellness Courts: A Preliminary Overview of Tribal Drug Courts* (Office of Justice Programs, 1999).

67. Ibid., p. 1.

68. Ibid., p. 1.

69. Ibid., p. 9.

70. Ibid., p. 9.

71. Ibid., pp. 9–10.

72. Ibid., p. 14.

73. Ibid.

74. Ibid.

75. The Sentencing Project, "Felony Disenfranchisement Laws in the United States." Available at www.sentenging project.org.

76. Ibid.

77. Ibid.

78. *Nebraska Lawmakers Restore Felons' Voting Rights* (March 11, 2005). Available at www.cnsnews.com.

79. *Omaha World Herald*, March 3, 1999, p. 22.

80. The Sentencing Project, Felony Disenfranchisement Laws.

81. *Omaha World Herald*, March 3, 1999, p. 22.

82. Ibid.

83. Coramae Richey Mann, *Unequal Justice: A Question of Color* (Bloomington, IN: Indiana University Press, 1993).

84. William Wilbanks, *The Myth of the Racist Criminal Justice System* (Monterey, CA: Brooks/Cole, 1987).

85. Alfred Blumstein, "On the Disproportionality of United States' Prison

Populations," *The Journal of Criminal Law and Criminology 73* (1982): 1259–1281.

86. Ibid., p. 1274.

87. Ibid., p. 1274.

88. Patrick Langan, "Racism on Trial: New Evidence to Explain the Racial Composition of Prisons in the United States," *Journal of Criminal Law and Criminology 76* (1985): 666–683.

89. Alfred Blumstein, "Racial Dispro-portionality in U.S. Prisons Revisited," *University of Colorado Law Review 64* (1993): 743–760.

90. Michael Tonry, *Malign Neglect* (New York: Oxford University Press, 1995), p. 67–68.

91. Ibid.

92. Darnell F. Hawkins and Kenneth A. Hardy, "Black–White Imprisonment Rates: A State-by-State Analysis," *Social Justice 16* (1989): 75–94.

93. Ibid., p. 79.

94. Theodore G. Chiricos and Charles Crawford, "Race and Imprisonment: A Contextual Assessment of the Evidence," in *Ethnicity, Race and Crime*, Darnell F. Hawkins, ed. (Albany: State University of New York Press, 1995).

95. Raymond J. Michalowski and Michael A. Pearson, "Punishment and Social Structure at the State Level: A Cross-Sectional Comparison of 1970 and 1980," *Journal of Research in Crime and Delinquency 27* (1990): 52–78.

96. Hawkins and Hardy, "Black and White Imprisonment Rates."

97. George S. Bridges and Robert D. Crutchfield, "Law, Social Standings and Racial Disparities in Imprisonment," *Social Forces 66* (1988): 699–724.

98. Miriam A. DeLone and Theodore G. Chiricos, "Young Black Males and Incarceration: A Contextual Analysis of Racial Composition," paper presented at the Annual Meetings of the American Society of Criminology, 1994.

99. Dario Melossi, "An Introduction: Fifty Years Later, Punishment and Social Structure in Comparative Analysis," *Contemporary Crises 13* (1989): 311–326.

100. DeLone and Chiricos, "Young Black Males and Incarceration."

101. W.E.B. Du Bois, "The Spawn of Slaver: The Convict-Lease System in the South," *The Missionary Review of the World 14* (1901): 737–745; Martha A. Myers, *Race, Labor and Punishment in the South* (Columbus, OH: Ohio State University Press, 1999).

102. Raymond J. Michalowski and Susan J. Carlson, "Unemployment, Imprisonment and Social Structures of Accumulation: Historical Contingency in the Rushe-Kirchheimer Hypothesis," *Criminology 37* (1999): 217–250.

103. For a review of this literature see Theodore G. Chiricos and Miriam A. DeLone, "Labor Surplus and Punish-ment: A Review and Assessment of Theory and Evidence," *Social Problems 39* (1992): 421–446.

104. Theodore G. Chiricos, "The Moral Panic of the Drug War, in Race and Criminal Justice," Michael J. Lynch and E. Britt Patterson, eds. (New York: Harrow and Heston, 1995).

105. Donald Clemmer, *The Prison Com-munity* (New York: Holt, Reinhart and Winston, 1940).

106. Gresham M. Sykes, *The Society of Captives* (Princeton: Princeton University Press, 1958).

107. John Irwin and Donald Cressey, "Thieves, Convicts and Inmate Culture," *Social Problems 10* (1962): 142–155.

108. James Jacobs, *New Perspectives on Prison and Imprisonment* (Ithaca, NY: Cornell University Press, 1983).

109. Ibid.

110. Lynne Goldstein and Doris Layton MacKenzie, "Racial Differences in

Adjustment Patterns of Prison Inmates—Prisonization, Conflict, Stress and Control," in *The Criminal Justice System and Blacks*, Daniel Georges-Abeyie, ed. (New York: Clark Boardman Company, Ltd, 1984).

111. Kevin N. Wright, "Race and Economic Marginality," *Journal of Research in Crime and Delinquency 26* (1989): 67–89.

112. Ibid., p. 67.

113. Joan Petersilia, Paul Honig, and Charles Hubay, *The Prison Experiences of Career Criminals* (Santa Monica, CA: Rand Corporation, 1980).

114. Timothy Flanagan, "Correlates of Institutional Misconduct Among Prisoners," *Criminology 21* (1983): 29–39.

115. Miles D. Harer and Darrell J. Steffensmeier, "Race and Prison Violence" *Criminology 34* (1996): 323–355.

116. Ibid.

117. Jim Thomas, "Racial Codes in Prison Culture: Snapshots in Black and White," in *Race and Criminal Justice*, Michael Lynch and Britt Patterson, eds. (New York: Harrow and Heston, 1991).

118. Jacobs, *New Perspective on Imprisonment*.

119. Darlene Conley and Julius Debro, "Black Muslims in California Prisons: The Beginning of a Social Movement for Black Prisoners in the United States," in *Race, Class, Gender and Justice in the Unites States*, Charles E. Reasons, Darlene J. Conley, and Julius Debro, eds. (Boston: Allyn and Bacon, 2002), p. 279.

120. Jacobs, *New Perspective on Imprisonment*, p. 65.

121. Ibid.

122. Elizabeth S. Grobsmith, *Indians in Prison* (Lincoln, NE: University of Nebraska Press, 1994).

123. *Omaha World Herald*, Sunday, December 6, 1998; 19-A.

124. Ibid.

125. Ibid.

126. *Omaha World Herald*, Sunday February 28, 1999; p. 1.

127. Ibid.

128. Florida Department of Corrections, "Gang and Security Groups Awareness, 2005." Available at www.dc.state.fl.us/pub/gangs.

129. Robert Fong, Ronald Vogel, and Salvador Buentello, "Prison Gang Dynamics: A Look Inside the Texas Department of Corrections," in *Corrections: Dilemmas and Directions*, Peter J. Benekos and Alida V. Merlo, eds. (Anderson Publishing Co. and Academy of Criminal Justice Sciences, 1992).

130. Florida Department of Corrections, "Gang and Security Groups Awareness, 2005." Available at www.dc.state.fl.us/pub/gangs.

131. Ibid.

132. Ibid.

133. Robert Fong, Ronald Vogel, and Salvador Buentello, "Prison Gang Dynamics: A Look Inside the Texas Department of Corrections," in *Corrections: Dilemmas and Directions*, Peter J. Benekos and Alida V. Merlo, eds. (Anderson Publishing Co. and Academy of Criminal Justice Sciences, 1992).

134. Florida Department of Corrections, "Gang and Security Groups Awareness, 2005."

135. Ibid.

136. Joseph Summerill. "Supreme Court Rules that Racially Segregating Inmates is Unconstitutional." *Corrections Today 67* (Jun 2005), p. 24–25.

137. Ibid.

138. Justice Sandra Day O'Connor cited in Summerill, *Corrections Today*, 2005.

139. Ibid.

140. Ibid.

141. Ibid.

142. Doris L. MacKenzie, "Age and Adjustment to Prison: Interactions with Attitudes and Anxiety," *Criminal Justice and Behavior* 14 (1987): 427–447.

143. Doris L. MacKenzie, James Robinson, and Carol Campbell, "Long-Term Incarceration of Female Offenders: Prison Adjustment and Coping," *Criminal Justice and Behavior* 16 (1989): 223–238.

144. Leger Robert G, "Lesbianism Among Women Prisoners: Participants and Nonparticipants," *Criminal Justice and Behavior* 14 (1987): 448–467.

145. Tonry, *Malign Neglect*.

10

✼

Minority Youth and Crime
Minority Youth in Court

> Youth in general, and young minority males in particular, often are
> demonized by legislators, the media, scholars, and the public
> at large. These attacks reinforce stereotypes and place a particularly
> heavy burden on young Black and Latino males.
> —LINDA S. BERES AND THOMAS D. GRIFFITH, "DEMONIZING YOUTH"[1]

In June 2001, Lionel Tate, an African American boy who was 12 years old when he killed a 6-year-old family friend while demonstrating a wrestling move he had seen on television, was sentenced to life in prison without the possibility of parole. Tate, who claimed that the death was an accident, was tried as an adult in Broward County, Florida; he was convicted of first-degree murder. One month later, Nathaniel Brazill, a 14-year-old African American, was sentenced by a Florida judge to 28 years in prison without the possibility of parole. Brazill was 13 years old when he shot and killed Barry Grunow, a popular 30-year-old seventh grade teacher at a middle school in Lake Worth, Florida. Although Brazill did not deny that he fired the shot that killed his teacher, he claimed that he had only meant to scare Grunow and that the shooting was an accident. Like Tate, Brazill was tried as an adult; he was convicted of second-degree murder.

These two cases raised a storm of controversy regarding the prosecution of children as adults. Those on one side argue that children who commit adult crimes, such as murder, should be treated as adults; they should be prosecuted as adults and sentenced to adult correctional institutions. As Marc Shiner, the prosecutor in Brazill's case, put it, "This was a heinous crime committed by a young man with a difficult personality who should be behind bars. Let us not forget a man's life has been taken away.[2] Those on the other side contend that prosecuting children as adults is "unwarranted and misguided." They assert that

375

children who commit crimes of violence usually suffer from severe mental and emotional problems and that locking kids up in adult jails does not deter crime or rehabilitate juvenile offenders. Although they acknowledge that juvenile offenders should be punished for their actions, they claim that incarcerating them in adult prisons for the rest of their lives "is an outrage."[3] According to Vincent Schiraldi, president of the Justice Policy Institute, "In adult prisons, Brazill will never receive the treatment he needs to reform himself. Instead, he will spend his time trying to avoid being beaten, assaulted, or raped in a world where adults prey on, rather than protect, the young."[4]

Nanthaniel Brazill is still incarcerated in the Brevard Correctional Institution. Assuming that none of his pending appeals are successful, he will not be released until 2028, when he will be 41 years old.[5] Lionel Tate's conviction, however, was overturned by a Florida appellate court in 2003. The court ruled that Tate should be retried because his competency to stand trial was not evaluated before he went to trial. The state decided not to retry Tate and instead offered him a plea agreement— Tate pled guilty to second-degree murder in exchange for a sentence to time served (which was about 3 years), plus 1 year of house arrest and 10 hours of probation.[6]

He was released from prison in January 2004. In May 2005 he was back in jail in Fort Lauderdale, Florida, after he allegedly robbed a pizza delivery man at gunpoint. Because he was on probation at the time of the crime, Tate faces a potential life sentence on the robbery charge.[7]

GOALS OF THE CHAPTER

The prosecution of children as adults, and the potential for racial bias in the decision to "waive" youth to adult court, is one of the issues we address in this chapter. We also discuss racial/ethnic patterns in victimization of juveniles and in offending by juveniles, the treatment of juveniles by the police, and police use of gang databases. We end the chapter with a discussion of the treatment of minority youth by the juvenile justice system. Consistent with the approach taken in previous chapters, our goals are to (1) explore the myths and realities about victimization of and crime by minority youth; (2) examine the relationship between the police and racial and ethnic minority youth; and (3) review recent research on racial disparities in the juvenile justice system.

YOUNG RACIAL MINORITIES AS VICTIMS AND OFFENDERS

Juveniles as Victims of Crime

In Chapter 2 we showed that, regardless of age, African Americans have higher personal theft and violent victimization rates than other racial/ethnic groups and that Hispanics generally have higher victimization rates than non-Hispanics.

TABLE 10.1 Juvenile and Adult Property Victimization Rates by Race and Ethnicity, 1996 and 1997 Combined

	Property Crime Rate (per 1,000 Population)		Property Crime Ratio (Juvenile/ Adults)
	Juvenile	Adult	
Victim race			
White	162	114	1:4[a]
African American	194	151	1:3
Other	155	108	1:4
Victim ethnicity			
Hispanic	143	133	1:1
Non-Hispanic	170	117	1:5

[a]Juvenile rate versus adult rate; significant difference at the .05 level or below.

SOURCE: Office of Juvenile Justice and Delinquency Prevention, "Juvenile Victims of Property Crimes" (Washington, DC: U.S. Department of Justice, 2000). Available at www.ncjrs.org/html/ojjdp.

However, information concerning the racial and ethnic trends in victimization for juveniles is scarce. In this section, we examine National Crime Victimization (NCVS) data, supplemented by National Incident-Based Reporting System (NIBRS) data and Supplemental Homicide Reports (SHR) from the FBI. We first discuss property victimization, followed by violent victimization and homicide victimization.

Property Crime Victimization Using information from the 1996 and 1997 National Crime Victimization Survey (NCVS), the Office of Juvenile Justice and Delinquency Prevention released a brief on "Juvenile Victims of Property Crime."[8] Their findings indicated that one of every six juveniles (defined as youth aged 12 to 17) had been the victim of property crime.[9] This rate was 40 percent higher than the property crime victimization rate for adults.[10]

Table 10.1 offers a comparison of juvenile and adult property crime victimization rates by race and ethnicity. A ratio of juvenile to adult rates higher than 1:1 indicates that the juvenile victimization rate is higher than the adult rate. The ratio of 1:4 for whites, for example, indicates that the property crime victimization rate for white juveniles is higher than the property crime victimization rate for white adults; moreover, the differences are statistically significant. This pattern is found for all three racial categories. Hispanic property crime victimization rates, however, do not vary significantly between juveniles and adults, but non-Hispanic rates do vary.

Looking at the victimization rates for juveniles only in Table 10.1, we see that African American youth have the highest property crime victimization rate, followed by white youth and "other race" (American Indian/Alaska Native and Asian/Pacific Islander) youth. With regard to ethnicity, non-Hispanic juveniles report a higher rate of property crime victimization than Hispanic juveniles. The racial pattern of property crime victimization among juveniles mirrors the overall pattern for all ages combined (see Chapter 2); both comparisons show the highest rates for African Americans. The victimization rates of Hispanic and non-Hispanic juveniles (higher rates for non-Hispanics), however, differ from the rates for all age groups combined (higher rates for Hispanics).[11]

The FBI also collects information about crime victims through the NIBRS. These data do not represent the entire U.S. population, but they do provide substantial information on the victims of crime in the jurisdictions covered. Using this information, researchers estimate that juveniles with the following characteristics have a relatively high risk for property crime victimization: "African American juveniles, juveniles in urban areas, and juveniles in the West."[12] In short, these victimization patterns closely mirror "the higher risk for adults in these categories."[13]

Violent Crime   In general, violent victimization rates are higher for younger age groups than for older age groups. For example, in 2003 the violent victimization rate for youth from 12 to 15 years old was 51.6 victimizations for every 1,000 people in that age group and the rate for youth 16 to 19 years old was 53 victimizations for every 1,000 people in that age group. In contrast, the rate for individuals who were 20 to 24 years old was 43.3 per 1,000, and the rate for those who were 25 to 34 years old was 26.4 per 1,000.[14]

Among youth ages 12 to 15, African Americans had a higher rate of victimization than whites. For all crimes of violence, the rates were 68.6 for African Americans and 48.2 for whites. For robbery, the rates were 14.0 for African Americans and 3.0 for whites, and for assault the rates were 54.6 (African Americans) and 43.9 (whites).[15]

Data on violent victimization rates broken down by age, gender, and race reveal that *young African American males* are particularly at risk.[16] These data, which are shown in Figure 10.1, reveal that in 2003 the violent victimization rate for youth between the ages of 12 and 15 was 112.3 for African American males, 60.9 for white males, 34.9 for white females, and 21.1 for African American females. The robbery victimization rate for African American males (20.8) was nearly seven times the rate for white males (3.0) or females (3.0) and was three times the rate for African American females (6.6).

African American and Hispanic youth also were more likely than white youth to be victims of crimes committed with weapons.[17] This was true for crimes committed with any weapon and for crimes committed with a firearm, and it was true for youth between the ages of 12 and 14 and youth between the ages of 15 and 17. Among the 15–17 year olds, for example, the rate of violent victimizations with a firearm for white youth was only half the rate for Hispanic youth; the rate for African American youth was even higher than the rate for Hispanic youth.

The question, of course, is why African American and Hispanic youth are more likely than whites to be the victims of violent crime. To answer this question, Lauritsen used 1995 data from the National Crime Victimization

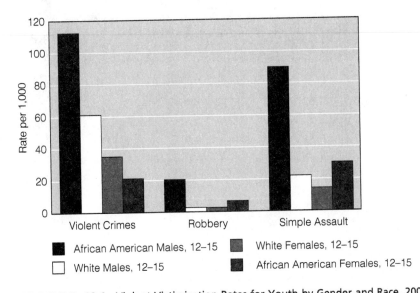

FIGURE 10.1 Violent Victimization Rates for Youth by Gender and Race, 2003

SOURCE: Bureau of Justice Statistics, Criminal Victimization in the United States, 2003—Statistical Tables (Washington, DC: U.S. Department of Justice, 2004): Table 10. Available at http://www.ojp.usdoj.edu/bjs/abstract/cvusst.htm.

Survey to explore the effects of individual, family, and community characteristics on the risk for nonlethal violence among youth.[18] She disaggregated violent incidents into incidents perpetrated by strangers and those perpetrated by nonstrangers, and she distinguished incidents that occurred in the youth's own neighborhood from those that occurred elsewhere. She found that youth living in single-parent families had higher risks for violence than those living in two-parent families and that the risk for violence was much higher for youth living in the most disadvantaged communities.[19]

According to the author of this study, "because family and community characteristics vary among racial and ethnic groups in the United States, it is important to consider differences in victimization risk across racial and ethnic groups."[20] As shown in Table 10.2, when she examined the risk for violence by race and gender, she found that young males faced a substantially higher risk of violence than young females; this was true for both stranger and nonstranger violence, for all violence, and violence that took place in the youth's own neighborhood. She also found that,

- White, African American, and Hispanic males had roughly equal risks of nonstranger violence, but young white males had a lower risk of victimization for stranger violence in their own neighborhoods than African American and Hispanic young males.

- African American girls faced much higher risks of nonstranger violence than either Hispanic or white girls, and both African American girls and Hispanic girls were more likely than white girls to be victimized by a stranger in their neighborhoods.

TABLE 10.2 Risk for Stranger and Nonstranger Violence for African American, Hispanic, and White Youth

	Stranger Violence		Nonstranger Violence	
	All Violence	Neighborhood Violence	All Violence	Neighborhood Violence
Males	34.9	20.2	25.0	14.4
African American	35.8	27.1	25.5	17.1
Hispanic	43.4	31.2	24.4	13.1
White	33.2	16.6	25.0	14.0
Females	19.8	10.1	23.1	12.8
African American	24.3	14.2	30.1	22.7
Hispanic	22.7	14.1	16.3	10.3
White	18.2	8.5	22.7	11.0

SOURCE: Janet L. Lauritsen, "How Families and Communities Influence Youth Victimization" (Washington, DC: U.S Department of Justice, 2003), Adapted from Table 5.

To determine whether these patterns could be explained by other factors, Lauritsen used analytical techniques that simultaneously controlled for individual, family, and community characteristics. She found that the amount of time the youth spent at home and the length of time the youth had lived in his or her current home had a negative effect on risk of violent victimization and that youths who lived in single-parent families faced a greater risk than those who lived in a two-parent families. She also found that youth who lived in communities with higher percentages of female-headed families and higher percentages of residents younger than age 18 had higher likelihoods of violent victimization.[21]

The most interesting finding from this analysis was that the racial and ethnic differences in risk for violent victimization disappeared when the characteristics of the youth's family and community were taken into account. The racial and ethnic differences discussed earlier "are primarily a reflection of community and family differences rather than the result of being part of a particular racial or ethnic group."[22] Thus, African American and Hispanic youth have greater risks for violent victimization than white youth because they are more likely than white youth to spend time away from home, to live in single-parent families, to have less stable living arrangements, and to live in disadvantaged communities. As Lauritsen noted, "the sources of risk are similar for all adolescents, regardless of their race or ethnicity."[23]

Homicide Victimization In 2002, 1 in every 10 murder victims was younger than age 18; 5.3 percent of the victims were younger than age 14, and 4.6 percent were between ages 14 and 17.[24] Although homicide events are fairly rare (15,870 in 2002), racial patterns and trends by age are available. The Supplemental

T A B L E 10.3 Juvenile Homicide Victimization Rates (per 100,000 population, ages 14–17) by Race and Gender

	1990	1995	2000	2002
White male	7.5	8.6	4.1	3.6
White female	2.5	2.7	1.4	1.5
African American male	59.0	63.2	25.8	22.6
African American female	10.3	11.9	4.5	6.1

SOURCE: James Allen Fox and Marianne W. Zawitz, "Homicide Trends in the United States" (Washington, DC: U.S. Department of Justice, 2004). Available at www.ojp.usdoj.gov/bjs.

Homicide Reports (SHR) collected by the FBI indicate there are important racial patterns to be found in homicide trends. As discussed in Chapter 2, African Americans generally are overrepresented both as homicide victims and offenders. Although the highest homicide rates, regardless of race and age, are found among 18 to 24 year olds, youth between the ages of 14 and 17 have rates that are similar to those for the 25 and older age group.[25]

The homicide victimization rates for 14 to 17 year olds, which are presented in Table 10.3, indicate that homicide rates declined dramatically from 1990 to 2002. For each of the four groups—white males, white females, African American males, and African American females—the rates peaked in 1995; declined substantially by 2000; and, at least for males, declined again from 2000 to 2002. Aside from the changes over time, the most startling finding revealed by the data presented in Table 10.3 concerns the differences in homicide victimization rates by race. Regardless of gender, African American juveniles have substantially higher victimization rates than white juveniles throughout the time period, the rate for African American females was approximately four times greater than the rate for white females and the rate for African American males was six to seven times greater than the rate for white males. In fact, the homicide victimization rates for African American females were higher than the rates for white males.

It thus seems clear that African American youth are overrepresented as crime victims in the United States. African American juveniles have the highest property crime victimization rates of any group, and both African Americans and Hispanics are substantially more likely than whites to be victims of violent crime, especially violent crime at the hands of a stranger. As the study conducted by Lauritsen revealed, these racial and ethnic differences can be attributed primarily to race/ethnicity-linked differences in the characteristics of youth's families and the communities in which they live.

Juveniles as Offenders

Creating a profile of the juvenile offender is not an easy task. Much of the available data rely on arrest statistics or the perceptions of crime victims. Some critics argue that the portrait of the offender based on these data is biased (because of racial differences in reporting and racial bias in decisions to arrest) and suggest that the picture of the typical offender should be taken from a population of adjudicated offenders. We discuss this alternative picture of the juvenile offender in the section on juveniles in the correctional system, which appears later in this chapter.

Juvenile Arrests   Table 10.4 presents Uniform Crime Reporting arrest data for people younger than age 18. The racial differences in these arrest statistics are similar to those for offenders in all age groups. The overrepresentation of African American youth for violent crimes is notable. In 2004 African Americans made up 46 percent of all arrests for violent Index Crimes. Among young offenders arrested for homicide and robbery, African Americans constituted 49.7 percent and 63.5 percent, respectively, of all arrestees. African American juveniles also were overrepresented among arrests for serious property (Part 1/Index) crimes, but the proportions are smaller than for violent crime (28.4 percent for serious property crime versus 46.0 percent for violent crime).

Native American youth make up less than 1 percent of the juvenile population; they were slightly overrepresented in juvenile arrest figures for Index offenses (1.2 percent of all arrestees), especially property offenses (1.4 percent of all arrestees). Asian/Pacific Islander youth, who make up less than 3 percent of the U.S. population, were not overrepresented for any Part 1/Index offenses.

The data presented in Table 10.4 reveal more variability in the race of juveniles arrested for the less serious Part 2 offenses. White juveniles were overrepresented for driving under the influence, liquor law violations, and drunkenness; they represented about 90 percent of arrestees in each category. African Americans made up fewer than 8 percent of juveniles arrested for these offenses. A similar pattern is found for vandalism, where the racial makeup of arrestees is consistent with the racial makeup of the general population. African American juveniles were overrepresented among arrestees for a number of these less serious offenses, including gambling (86.5 percent), prostitution (52.7 percent), offenses involving stolen property (42.4 percent), disorderly conduct (37.9 percent), other assaults (37.4 percent), weapons offenses (33.2 percent), fraud (28.9 percent), embezzlement (27.4 percent), and drug abuse violations (27.2 percent).

Native American/American Indian youth were overrepresented for two of the liquor-related Part 2 offenses: driving under the influence (DUI) and liquor law violations. They made up 2.6 percent of all arrests for liquor law violations and 1.7 percent of all arrests for driving under the influence. Asian/Pacific Islander youth were overrepresented only for the status offense of running away and were significantly underrepresented for offenses such as liquor violations and drug abuse violations.

Self-Reported Violent Behavior   Data on juvenile offending also come from surveys in which youth are asked to self-report delinquent acts. The National Longitudinal Survey of Adolescent Health, for example, gathered data from students attending 132 schools throughout the United States.[26] Youth between the ages of 11 and 20 were asked to indicate the number of times in the past 12 months they engaged in four types of serious violent behavior: getting into a

TABLE 10.4 Percent Distribution of Arrests by Race, Younger than 18 Years of Age, 2004

	White	African American	Native American	Asian American
Total	69.3%	25.1%	1.2%	1.7%
Part I/Index Crimes				
Murder and nonnegligent manslaughter	42.3	49.7	2.4	5.6
Forcible rape	63.1	34.7	1.4	0.8
Robbery	34.7	63.5	0.4	1.4
Aggravated assault	58.5	39.2	1.1	1.2
Burglary	70.2	27.5	1.2	1.2
Larceny-theft	69.2	27.4	1.4	2.0
Motor vehicle theft	56.8	40.2	1.3	1.7
Arson	78.5	19.1	1.1	1.4
Violent crime	51.8	46.0	0.9	1.3
Property crime	68.5	28.4	1.4	1.8
Part II Crimes				
Other assaults	60.4	37.4	1.0	1.2
Forgery and counterfeiting	77.6	19.9	1.0	1.5
Fraud	68.7	28.9	1.0	1.5
Embezzlement	68.9	27.4	1.4	2.3
Stolen property: buying, receiving, possessing	55.3	42.4	0.9	1.4
Vandalism	79.6	18.0	1.2	1.1
Weapons: carrying, possessing, etc.	64.6	33.2	0.8	1.4
Prostitution and commercialized vice	44.7	52.7	0.9	1.7
Sex offenses (except forcible rape and prostitution)	71.5	26.6	0.7	1.3
Drug abuse violations	71.1	27.2	0.9	0.8
Gambling	12.5	86.5	0.0	1.1
Offenses against family and children	78.2	20.3	0.9	0.6
Driving under the influence (DUI)	93.5	3.7	1.7	1.2
Liquor law violations	91.6	4.6	2.6	1.1
Drunkenness	89.4	7.8	2.0	0.8
Disorderly conduct	60.1	37.9	1.1	0.8
Vagrancy	76.9	22.0	0.3	0.9
All other offenses (except traffic)	73.0	24.2	1.3	1.5
Suspicion	81.5	17.8	0.7	0.0
Curfew and loitering law violations	65.8	32.3	0.6	1.3
Runaways	73.5	21.3	1.6	3.7

SOURCE: *Crime in the United States, 2004* (Washington, DC: U.S. Department of Justice, 2005).

T A B L E 10.5 Self-Reported Violent Behavior, by Race and Ethnicity: Mean Percentage Who Reported Engaging in Each Type of Violence

	Serious Fighting	Caused Injury	Pulled Knife or Gun	Shot or Stabbed	Serious Violence Scale
Asian American	.115*	.032*	.014*	.013	.17*
African American	.210*	.102*	.086*	.031*	.43*
Hispanic	.236*	.119*	.066*	.030*	.45*
Native American	.402*	.166*	.079	.009	.66*
White	.179	.074	.032	.012	.30

*Group mean is significantly different from mean for white adolescents (P $\leq$0.05).

SOURCE: Thomas L. McNulty and Paul E. Bellair, "Explaining Racial and Ethnic Differences in Serious Adolescent Violent Behavior," *Criminology 41* (2003): 709–748, Appendix 1 and Table 1.

serious fight, hurting someone badly enough to need bandages or care from a doctor or nurse, pulling a knife or gun on someone, and shooting or stabbing someone.

McNulty and Bellair used these data to examine racial and ethnic differences in violent behavior. As shown in Table 10.5, there were significant differences between white adolescents and each of the four other groups on the first two items. Asians were less likely than whites to have been in a serious fight or to have injured someone else; African Americans, Hispanics, and Native Americans, however, were more likely than whites to have engaged in these types of violent behavior. Asians also were less likely than whites to have pulled a knife or gun on someone else, but African Americans and Hispanics were more likely than whites to have pulled a gun or knife on someone or to have shot or stabbed another person.[27] McNulty and Bellair used these data to create a serious violence scale, which focused on the breadth of violent activity (that is, whether the respondent engaged in the activity or not). The scale ranged from zero (respondent had not engaged in any of the types of violent behavior) to four (respondent had engaged in all four types of violence).[28] They found that Native American adolescents were the most likely to have engaged in violent behavior (mean = .66), followed by Hispanics (.45), African Americans (.43), whites (.30), and Asians (.17). Overall, then, there were large and statistically significant differences between white youth and youth in each of the other four groups. Asians were less likely than whites to have engaged in violent behavior; Native Americans, Hispanics, and African Americans were more likely than whites to have participated in violence.

Homicide Offenders   Data on homicide offenders reveal that offending peaks at around age 18, that males are overrepresented as offenders, that roughly 50 percent of all homicides are committed by offenders known to the victim (non-strangers), and that the victim and the offender come from the same age group

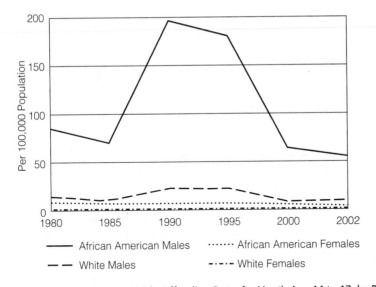

FIGURE 10.2 Homicide Offending Rates for Youth Age 14 to 17, by Race and Gender

SOURCE: James Allen Fox and Marianne W. Zawitz, "Homicide Trends in the United States," (Washington, DC: U.S. Department of Justice, 2004). Available at http://www.ojp.usdoj.edu/bjs.

and racial category. The Supplemental Homicide Reports (SHR) collected by the FBI can be used to calculate approximate rates of homicide offending by age, race, and gender. We consider these approximate rates because the data come from reports filled out by police agencies investigating homicides rather than from convicted offenders. As a consequence, these data may reflect a number of biases and should be viewed with caution.

The SHR data indicate that offending rates vary by age group and that the pattern is similar to that found for victimization rates: the 18- to 24-year-old group has the highest offending rate, followed by the 14- to 17-year-old group, with those 25 and older having the lowest offending rates.[29] Figure 10.2 displays homicide offending rates from 1980 to 2002 for white males, white females, African American males, and African American females aged 14 to 17.[30] Two trends are apparent. First, over time, the homicide offending rate for African American males has been substantially higher than the rates for the other three groups. In 2002, for example, the rate for young African American males (54.5) was six times the rate for young white males (9.2), 15 times the rate for young African American females (3.7), and more than 60 times the rate for young white females. The second trend revealed by the data is that the homicide offending rates for each group peaked in either 1990 or 1995 and declined dramatically after 1995. The rate for African American males, for example, was 194.0 in 1990, 178.6 in 1995, 63.2 in 2000, and 54.5 in 2002. For white males the rates fell from 22.0 (1990 and 1995) to 8.0 (2000).

The intraracial pattern identified in Chapter 2 for all homicides—that is, most homicides involve victims and offenders of the same race—is found for juvenile homicides as well. However, interracial homicides are more common among young perpetrators.[31]

Explaining Racial and Ethnic Differences in Violent Behavior   The data discussed thus far reveal that there are racial and ethnic differences in violent behavior among juveniles. Data on homicide indicate that African American males have the highest offending rate, and self-report data on other types of violence reveal that Asians and whites have lower rates of offending than Native Americans, Hispanics, and African Americans.

Researchers have advanced a number of explanations for these racial and ethnic differences. Although a detailed discussion of these explanations is beyond the scope of this book, they generally focus on the effects of community social disorganization,[32] individual and family-level risk factors,[33] weakened family attachments and weak bonds to school and work,[34] and involvement with delinquent peers and gangs.[35] Most studies focus on *either* individual/family influences or community-level risk factors such as social disorganization. There are very few studies that examine the causes of violent crime across these level of analysis.

An exception to this is the study by McNulty and Bellair (which we discussed earlier); this study found that Asians were significantly less likely than whites to engage in serious violent behavior and that Native Americans, Hispanics, and African Americans were more likely than whites to report they had committed violent acts.[36] To explain these differences, McNulty and Bellair controlled for individual factors (e.g., gender, age, use of alcohol/drugs, easy access to a gun, and prior violent behavior), family characteristics (e.g., type of family structure, parents' education and income), social bonds indicators (e.g., family attachment, school bonding, grades in school), involvement in gangs, exposure to violence, and community characteristics (i.e., social disorganization and residential stability). They found that the racial/ethnic differences in violent behavior disappeared when they included these explanatory factors in a single model. As they noted, "statistical differences between whites and minority groups are explained by variation in community disadvantage (for blacks), involvement in gangs (for Hispanics), social bonds (for Native Americans), and situational variables (for Asians)."[37]

The authors of this study concluded that their results had important implications for implementing policies designed to reduce youth violence. They noted, however, that "the implementation of social programs is unlikely to alter contemporary patterns of racial and ethnic group involvement in violent behavior without amelioration of the fundamental social and economic inequalities faced by minority group members."[38] (See Box 10.1 for a discussion of media's presentation on crime.)

JUVENILES OF COLOR AND THE POLICE

The racial/ethnic patterns found in data on arrests of juveniles raise questions about the general pattern of relations between the police and juveniles. We have discussed this subject in Chapter 4. It is useful to review the major points here.

B O X 10.1 Race, Crime, and the Media

In a review of more than 70 studies focusing on crime in the news, Lori Dorfman and Vincent Schiraldi, of the Berkeley Media Studies Group, asked the following questions: Does news coverage reflect actual crime trends? How does news coverage depict minority crime? Does news coverage disproportionately depict youth of color as perpetrators of crime?[140]

The authors of the report concluded that "the studies taken together indicate that depictions of crime in the news are not reflective of the rate of crime generally, the proportion of crime that is violent, the proportion of crime committed by people of color, or the proportion of crime that is committed by youth. The problem is not the inaccuracy of individual stories, but the cumulative choices of what is included in the news—or not included—presents the public with a false picture of higher frequency and severity of crime than is actually the case."[141]

Dorfman and Schiraldi noted that, although crime decreased 20 percent from 1990 to 1998, crime news coverage increased by more than 80 percent.[142] Moreover, 75 percent of the studies found that minorities were overrepresented as perpetrators;[143] more than 80 percent of the studies found that more attention was paid to white victims than to minority victims.[144] The authors concluded that the studies revealed that a "misinformation synergy" occurs in the way crime news is presented in the media.[145] The result is a message that crime is constantly on the increase; the offenders are young, minority males; and their victims are white.

First, juveniles have a high level of contact with the police, and juveniles of color have particularly high rates of contact. Several factors explain this pattern. Most important, young people tend to be out on the street more than adults. This is simply a matter of lifestyle related to the life cycle. Low-income juveniles are even more likely to be out in public than middle-class youth. Middle-class and wealthy people have more opportunities for indoor recreation: family rooms, large back yards, and so on. A study of juvenile gangs in the 1960s found that gang members regarded the street corner as, in effect, their private space.[39] At the same time, juveniles are more likely to be criminal offenders than middle-age people. Criminal activity peaks between ages 14 and 24. For this reason, the police are likely to pay closer attention to juveniles—and to stop and question them on the street—than to older people (for further discussion of this, see "Focus on an Issue: The Use of Gang Databases").

Second, in large part because of the higher levels of contact, juveniles consistently have less favorable attitudes toward the police. Age and race, in fact, are the two most important determinants of public attitudes, with both young people and African Americans having the most negative view of the police. As Chapter 4 explains, the attitudes of Latinos are less favorable than non-Latino whites but not as negative as those of African Americans. When age and race are combined, the result is that young African Americans have the most negative attitudes toward the police.[40]

Attitudes—and behavior that reflects negative attitudes—can have a significant impact on arrest rates. In his pioneering study of arrest patterns, Donald

(continued on p. 390)

Focus on an Issue
The Use of Gang Databases

In the late 1980s, California became the first state to create a computerized database of suspected gang members. Originally known as GREAT (Gang Reporting, Evaluation, And Trafficking system), by 2000 CalGang contained the names of more than 300,000 suspected gang members. In fact, the CalGang database included more names than there were students in the University of California system.[44]

As concerns about youth violence mounted during the early 1990s, other jurisdictions followed California's example. Laws authorizing law enforcement agencies to compile databases of gang members were enacted in Colorado, Florida, Illinois, Georgia, Tennessee, Texas, Minnesota, Ohio, and Virginia. The FBI also maintains a database, the Violent Gang and Terrorist Organization File, which became operational in 1995.[45]

The criteria for inclusion in a gang database—which usually includes information about the individual (name, address, physical description and/or photograph, tattoos, gang moniker), the gang (type and racial makeup), and a record of all police encounters with the individual—are vague. The Texas statute, for example, states that an individual can be included in the gang database if two or more of the following conditions are met: (1) self-admission by the individual of criminal street gang membership; (2) an identification of the individual as a criminal street gang member by an informant or other individual of unknown reliability; (3) a corroborated identification of the individual by an informant or other individual of unknown reliability; (4) evidence that the individual frequents a documented area of a criminal street gang, associates with known criminal street gang members, and uses criminal

street gang dress, hand signals, tattoos, or symbols; or (5) evidence that the individual has been arrested or taken into custody with known criminal street gang members for an offense or conduct consistent with criminal street gang activity.[46] Critics of the use of gang databases point to the third criterion—which allows entry of "associates" of gang members without evidence of actual gang membership—as especially problematic. According to a former California Attorney General, the CalGang database mixes "verified criminal history and gang affiliations with unverified intelligence and hearsay evidence, including reports on persons who have committed no crime."[47]

Other critics suggest that the gang databases, which are racially neutral on their face, are racially biased. One observer, for example, stated that "it's not a crackdown on gangs; it's a crackdown on blacks."[48] Statistics on the composition of gang databases confirm this. In 1997 in Orange County, California, for example, Latinos, who made up only 27 percent of the county population, made up 74 percent of the youth in the database; in fact, 93 percent of those included in the database were people of color. In 1993, African Americans made up 5 percent of Denver's population but 47 percent of those in the gang database; Latinos made up 12 percent of the population but 33 percent of the gang database.[49] In Schaumburg, Illinois (a suburb of Chicago), African Americans made up 3.7 percent of the village's population but 22 percent of gang members in the database.[50]

Gang database supporters counter that these statistics simply reflect the composition of criminal street gangs. The fact that most of the individuals whose names appear in gang databases are African American, Hispanic, and Asian, is not the result of racially discriminatory policing but because most of those who belong to street gangs are racial minorities. Critics, however, maintain that the vagueness of the criteria for inclusion in the database, coupled with accounts by youth of color of repeated stops and frequent questions about gang membership and the extremely high percentages of African Americans and Hispanics in gang databases in cities like Los Angeles and Denver, "support claims that the number of racial minorities who are not gang members but are included in the database is disproportionate."[51]

THE USE OF GANG DATABASES: POLICE HARASSMENT AND SENTENCE ENHANCEMENTS

Critics' concerns about racial and ethnic disparities in gang databases focus on the potential for police harassment and on the fact that in many states inclusion in a gang database may result in harsher sentences. Two incidents in California illustrate the potential for police harassment. The first took place in Garden Grove. In 1993, three Asian teens were stopped by Garden Grove police officers at a strip mall that the officers claimed was frequented by gang members. The officers questioned the youth, took down information on them that was later entered into the gang database, and took photographs of them without their permission.[52] The second incident took place in Union City. In 2002 Union City police officers called a "gang intervention meeting" at a local high school. They rounded up 60 students, most of whom were Latino and Asian, and sent them to separate classrooms based on their race/ethnicity. The students were then searched, interrogated, and photographed; the information collected and the photographs of the

students were entered into the gang database.[53] Both of these cases resulted in suits filed by the ACLU of Northern California. In the first case, a settlement was reached, in which the police department agreed to take photographs only if they had reasonable suspicion of criminal activity and written consent. The settlement in the second case is similar; it required police to destroy the photographs and other material collected during the sweep and prohibits further photographing of students for the gang database.

There also is evidence that inclusion in a gang database may lead to harsher treatment for youth convicted of crimes. In Arizona, for example, the prosecutor may increase the charges from a misdemeanor to a felony if the offense was committed for the benefit of a gang; if the youth is adjudicated delinquent, the prosecutor may request a sentence enhancement for gang-related activity.[54] In 2000, 60 percent of California voters approved Proposition 21, The Gang Violence and Juvenile Crime Prevention Act, which increased the sentence enhancements for gang-related crimes. If the crime is serious, 5 years are added to the sentence; if the crime is violent, 10 years are added. Proposition 21 also makes it easier to prosecute juveniles who are alleged gang members as adults, allows the police to use wiretaps against known or suspected gang members, and adds gang-related murder to the list of special circumstances that make offenders eligible for the death penalty."[55]

If, as critics contend, inclusion in a gang database is more likely for youth of color, these gang-related sentence enhancements, which are racially neutral on their face, may have racially discriminatory effects. As Zatz and Krecker noted, "if ascriptions of gang membership did not carry penalties, defining gang membership in racialized ways might be innocuous. . . . But allegations of gang

(continued)

(continued)
members do carry added penalties, as least in Arizona." Noting that Latino boys and girls were more likely than whites to be identified as gang members, and thus

were more likely to be subject to the penalty enhancements, they asked, how does this differ "in effect even if not in intent, from saying that the severity of sanctions is increased for Latinos?"[56]

Black found that the demeanor of the suspect was one of the important determinants of officers' decisions to make an arrest. With other factors held constant, individuals who are less respectful or more hostile are more likely to be arrested. Black then found that African Americans were more likely to be less respectful of the police and consequently were more likely to be arrested. Thus, the general state of poor relations leads to hostility in individual encounters with the police, which in turn results in higher arrest rates.[41]

A more recent study used data from the NIBRS to assess whether the likelihood of arrest varied by the race of the juvenile in incidents involving murder, a violent sex offense, robbery, aggravated assault, simple assault, or intimidation.[42] (These incidents were selected because they were the ones in which there was interaction between the offender and the victim, and victims were asked to describe the characteristics of the offender.) Pope and Snyder found that white juveniles were significantly more likely than African American juveniles to be arrested: Whites made up 69.2 percent of all juvenile offenders (based on victims' perceptions) but 72.7 percent of all juvenile offenders who were arrested. The results of a multivariate analysis that controlled for other incident characteristics (for example, the number of victims; the age, sex, and race of the victim; the relationship between the victim and the offender; and the offender's sex) revealed that the likelihood of arrest did not vary for white and nonwhite juveniles. This was true for each state and for each of the types of offenses examined. According to Pope and Snyder, "Overall, the NIBRS data offer no evidence to support the hypothesis that police are more likely to arrest nonwhite juvenile offenders than white juvenile offenders, once other incident attributes are taken into consideration."[43]

RACE/ETHNICITY AND THE JUVENILE JUSTICE SYSTEM

One particularly troubling aspect of juvenile justice as it has been constructed throughout the 20th Century is its disproportionate involvement, in an aggregate social sense, with youths from the lowest socioeconomic strata, who at least in the latter half of the 20th Century overwhelmingly have been children of color.[57]

Although most research on the effect of race on the processing of criminal defendants has focused on adults, researchers have also examined the juvenile justice system for evidence of racial discrimination. Noting that the juvenile

Focus on an Issue
The Past, Present, and Future of the Juvenile Court

The traditional view of the emergence of the juvenile court in America pictures the "child savers" as a liberal movement of the late 19th century made up of benevolent, civic-minded, middle-class Americans who worked to help delinquent, abused, and neglected children who were suffering as a result of the negative impact of the rapid growth of industrialization. Although the emergence of the juvenile court is most often described as the creation of a welfare agency for the humane treatment of children, Platt (1977) highlighted the movement's social control agenda as well. According to Platt, the "child saving movement" did little to humanize the justice system for children; instead it "helped create a system that subjected more and more juveniles to arbitrary and degrading punishments" (p. xvii).

Platt contended that the attention of the juvenile court was originally focused on a select group of at-risk youth: court personnel originally focused on the children of urban, foreign-born, poor families for their moral reclamation projects (p. xvii). Feld (1999) argued that in modern times the juvenile court continues to intervene disproportionately in the lives of minority youth. He asserted that the persistent overrepresentation of minority youth at all stages of the system is largely the consequence of the juvenile court's unstable foundation of trying to reconcile social welfare and social control agendas. This conceptual contradiction allows "public officials to couch their get-tough policy changes in terms of 'public safety' rather than racial oppression" (p. 6).

Feld argued that the social welfare and social control aims of the juvenile court are irreconcilable and that attempts to pursue and reconcile these two competing agendas have left the contemporary juvenile court in crisis. He called it "a conceptually and administratively bankrupt institution with neither a rationale nor a justification" (pp. 3–4). He also contended that the juvenile court today offers a "second-class criminal court for young people" and does not function as a welfare agency (p. 4). Feld suggested that the distinction between adult and juvenile courts should be eliminated and that social welfare agencies should be used to address the needs of youth. His suggestion would make age a mitigating factor in our traditional, adjudicatory (adult) court system.

Would this policy suggestion ease the oppressive element of the juvenile court's intervention in the lives of racial and ethnic minorities? Why or why not?

system, with its philosophy of *parens patriae*,[58] is more discretionary and less formal than the adult system, researchers suggest that there is greater potential for racial discrimination in the processing of juveniles than in the processing of adults. In cases involving juveniles, criminal justice officials are more concerned about rehabilitation than retribution, and they have discretion to decide whether to handle the case formally or informally. As a result, they have more opportunities than those who handle cases involving adults to take extralegal factors such as race/ethnicity and gender into consideration during the decisionmaking process. (See "Focus on an Issue: The Past, Present, and Future of the Juvenile Court" for a look at the development of the juvenile court.)

T A B L E 10.6   Juvenile Court Case Outcomes, 2000

	Whites (%)	African Americans (%)
Delinquent Cases		
Detained prior to juvenile court disposition	17.5	23.8
Petitioned to juvenile court	55.1	64.5
Petitioned Cases		
Adjudicated delinquent	67.2	64.2
Waived to adult court	0.5	0.8
Adjudicated Cases		
Placed out of home	22.8	26.9
Placed on probation	63.6	61.9
Dismissed	2.2	3.4

SOURCE: U.S. Department of Justice, Bureau of Justice Statistics, *Sourcebook of Criminal Justice Statistics 2003* (Washington, DC: U.S. Government Printing Office, 2004), Table 5.63. Available at http://www.albany.edu/sourcebook.

There is compelling evidence that racial minorities are overrepresented in the juvenile justice system. In 2000, for example, African Americans made up 15 percent of the U.S. population aged 10 to 17 but 28 percent of all youth in cases disposed by juvenile courts. Whites constituted approximately 80 percent of the youth population but only 69 percent of all offenders in juvenile court. African American juveniles were involved in 35 percent of person-offense cases (murder, rape, robbery, and assault), 26 percent of property-offense cases, 22 percent of drug-offense cases, and 27 percent of public-order offenses. [59] Stated another way, the total delinquency case rate for African American juveniles in 2000 (95.6) was more than twice the rate for white juveniles (46.3). [60]

There also is evidence of racial disparity in the treatment of juvenile offenders. As shown in Table 10.6, which presents nationwide data on juvenile court outcomes in 2000, African Americans were treated more harshly than whites at several stages in the juvenile justice process. African Americans were more likely than whites to be detained prior to juvenile court disposition, to be petitioned to juvenile court for further processing, and to be waived to adult court. Among those adjudicated delinquent, African Americans were more likely than whites to be placed in a juvenile facility but somewhat less likely than whites to be placed on probation. White youth, however, were more likely than African American youth to be adjudicated delinquent, and the dismissal rate was slightly higher for African Americans than for whites.

Much of the criticism of the treatment of racial minorities by the juvenile justice system focuses on the fact that racial minorities are more likely than whites to be detained in secure facilities prior to adjudication and sentenced to secure confinement following adjudication. Since 1988 the Juvenile Justice and Delinquency Prevention Act has required states to determine whether the proportion of minorities in confinement exceeds their proportion of the population. If there is disproportionate minority confinement, the state must develop and implement policies to reduce it. In the United States as a whole, African American youth made up 28 percent of the population of cases referred to juvenile court in 2000; they accounted for 35 percent of all juveniles detained pending adjudication. As shown in Table 10.6, 27 percent of African American youth who were adjudicated delinquent received an out-of-home placement disposition; for white youth, the figure was 23 percent. Among youth adjudicated delinquent for drug offenses, 31 percent of African American youth, but only 16 percent of white youth, received an out-of-home placement.[61]

Although most of the statistics on disproportionate minority confinement compare African American and white youth, there is some state-level evidence that Hispanic and Native American youth are overrepresented. In Santa Cruz County, California, for example, Hispanics comprised 33 percent of the population ages 10 through 17 but made up 64 percent of the youths incarcerated in the Juvenile Hall on any given day in 1997 and 1998.[62] A study in Colorado revealed that Hispanic youths were overrepresented at all stages in the juvenile justice system, and a study in North Dakota found that Native American youth made up 8 percent of the juvenile population but 21 percent of secure detention placements and 33 percent of secure correctional placements.[63]

A report by the Building Blocks for Youth initiative, a national project to address unfairness in the juvenile justice system and to promote nondiscriminatory and effective policies, also addressed this issue.[64] The authors of the report, *And Justice for Some*, concluded that minority youth—and especially African American youth—receive harsher treatment than white youth throughout the juvenile justice system. The differences were particularly pronounced at the beginning stages of involvement with the juvenile justice system (that is, in terms of decisions regarding intake and detention) and at the end of the process (that is, in terms of decisions regarding out-of-home placement in a secure facility). With respect to detention prior to adjudication, the report found that minority youth were overrepresented, especially for drug offenses. White youth made up 66 percent of all youth referred to juvenile courts for drug offenses but only 44 percent of those detained. African American youth made up 32 percent of the drug offenders referred to juvenile court but 55 percent of those detained.[65] There was a similar pattern for out-of-home placement: In every offense category, and especially for drug offenses, minority youth were more likely than white youth to be committed to a locked institution.[66] Mark Soler, head of the Building Blocks for Youth initiative, stated that the report painted "a devastating picture of a system that has totally failed to uphold the American promise of 'equal justice for all.'"

The figures presented in Table 10.6 and the statistics on disproportionate minority confinement do not take racial differences in crime seriousness, prior juvenile record, or other legally relevant criteria into consideration. If racial minorities are referred to juvenile court for more serious offenses or have more serious criminal histories than whites, the observed racial disparities in case processing might diminish or disappear once these factors were taken into consideration. Like research on sentencing in adult court, studies of juvenile court outcomes consistently reveal that judges base their decisions primarily on the seriousness of the offense and the offender's prior record.[67] Thus, "real differences in rates of criminal behavior by black youths account for part of the disparities in justice administration."[68]

Research conducted during the past 20 years reveals that racial differences in past and current involvement in crime do not account for all of the differential treatment of racial minorities in juvenile court. Pope and Feyerherm, for example, reviewed 46 studies published in the 1970s and 1980s.[69] They found that two-thirds of the studies they examined found evidence that racial minorities were treated more harshly, even after offense seriousness, prior record, and other legally relevant factors were taken into account. A recent review of 34 studies published from 1989 to 2001 found a similar pattern of results.[70] Eight of the 34 studies found that race, ethnicity, or both had direct effects on juvenile court outcomes; 17 reported that the effects of race/ethnicity were contextual (that is, present at only some decision points or for some types of offenders); only one study reported no race effects.[71] An analysis that focused explicitly on disproportionate minority confinement reached the same conclusion. According to Huizinga and Elliot, "Even if the slightly higher rates for more serious offenses among minorities were given more importance than is statistically indicated, the relative proportions of whites and minorities involved in delinquent behavior could not account for the observed differences in incarceration rates."[72]

The studies conducted to date also find evidence of what is referred to as "cumulative disadvantage"[73] or "compound risk"[74]—that is, they reveal that small racial differences in outcomes at the initial stages of the process "accumulate and become more pronounced as minority youths are processed further into the juvenile justice system."[75] The Panel on Juvenile Crime, for example, calculated the likelihood that a youth at one stage in the juvenile justice process would reach the next stage (the transitional probability) and the proportion of the total population younger than age 18 that reached each stage in the juvenile justice process (the compound probability).[76] The Panel did this separately for African American and white youth and then used these probabilities to calculate the African American-to-white relative risk and the African American-to-white compound risk. As shown in Table 10.7, 7.2 percent of the African American population younger than age 18, but only 3.6 percent of the white population younger than age 18, was arrested. African Americans, in other words, were twice as likely as whites to be arrested. Of those arrested, 69 percent of the African Americans and 58 percent of the whites were referred to juvenile court. Taking these differences into account resulted in a compound probability—that is, the proportion of the total youth population referred to juvenile court—of 5.0 percent for African American youth and 2.1 percent for white youth. Thus, African Americans were 2.38 times more likely than whites to be referred to juvenile court. These differences in outcomes,

T A B L E 10.7 Juvenile Justice Outcomes for African Americans and Whites: Compound Risk

Outcome	Transitional Probability[a]		Compound Probability[b]		African American-to-White Risk	
	African Americans	Whites	African Americans	Whites	Relative Risk[c]	Compound Risk[d]
Arrested	.072	.036	.072	.036	2.00:1.00	2.00:1.00
Referred to juvenile court	.690	.580	.050	.021	1.19:1.00	2.38:1.00
Case handled formally	.620	.540	.031	.011	1.15:1.00	2.82:1.00
Adjudicated delinquent/ found guilty	.550	.590	.0168	.0067	0.93:1.00	2.51:1.00
Placed in residential facility	.320	.260	.0053	.0017	1.23:1.00	3.12:1.00

[a]The transitional probability = the proportion of youth at one stage who proceed to the next stage.
[b]The compound probability = the proportion of the population under age 18 that reaches each stage in the process.
[c]The relative risk = the ratio of the African American transitional probability to the white transitional probability.
[d]The compound risk = the ratio of the African American compound probability to the white compound probability.
SOURCE: Adapted from The Panel on Juvenile Justice, *Juvenile Crime Juvenile Justice* (Washington, DC: National Academy Press, 2001), Fig. 6.3 and Table 6.5.

as Table 10.7 shows, meant that at the end of the process African Americans were more than three times as likely as whites to be adjudicated delinquent and confined in a residential facility. As the Panel pointed out, "At almost every stage in the juvenile justice process the racial disparity is clear, but not extreme. However, because the system operates cumulatively the risk is compounded and the end result is that black juveniles are three times as likely as white juveniles to end up in residential placement."[77]

In the sections that follow, we summarize the findings of five methodologically sophisticated studies. The first is a comparison of outcomes for African Americans and whites in Florida. The second is an analysis of outcomes for African American, Hispanic, and white youth in Pennsylvania. The third, which also examines the treatment of juveniles in Pennsylvania, is an exploration of the degree to which outcomes are affected by the urbanization of the jurisdiction and the youth's family situation. The fourth study is an examination of outcomes for white and African American youth in Georgia, which analyzes the degree to which admitting guilt affects adjudication and disposition. The fifth study uses data from Nebraska to explore the extent to which black males who are ages 16 and 17 are treated differently than other youth. We also discuss evidence concerning racial disparities in waivers to adult criminal court.

T A B L E 10.8   Race and Juvenile Justice Processing in Florida, 1979–1981

	Recommended for Formal Processing	Detained	Petitioned to Juvenile Court	Adjudicated Delinquent	Incarcerated/ Transferred
African Americans	59.1%	11.0%	47.3%	82.5%	29.6%
Whites	45.6	10.2	37.8	80.0	19.5
Proportion African American	34.0	30.0	32.4	33.3	43.1

SOURCE: Adapted from Donna M. Bishop and Charles E. Frazier, "The Influence of Race in Juvenile Justice Processing," *Journal of Research in Crime and Delinquency 25* (1988): 250.

Race/Ethnicity and Juvenile Court Outcomes in Five Jurisdictions

Processing Juveniles in Florida   Bishop and Frazier examined the processing of African American and white juveniles in Florida.[78] In contrast to previous researchers, most of whom focused on a single stage of the juvenile justice process, these researchers followed a cohort of 54,266 youth through the system from intake through disposition. They examined the effect of race on five stages in the process: (1) the decision to refer the case to juvenile court for formal processing (rather than close the case without further action or handle the case informally); (2) the decision to place the youth in detention prior to disposition; (3) the decision to petition the youth to juvenile court; (4) the decision to adjudicate the youth delinquent (or hold a waiver hearing in anticipation of transferring the case to criminal court); and (5) the decision to commit the youth to a residential facility or transfer the case to criminal court.

Table 10.8 displays the outcomes for African American and white youth, as well as the proportion of African Americans in the cohort at each stage in the process. These data indicate that African Americans were substantially more likely than whites to be recommended for formal processing (59.1 percent versus 45.6 percent), petitioned to juvenile court (47.3 percent versus 37.8 percent), and either incarcerated in a residential facility or transferred to criminal court (29.6 percent versus 19.5 percent). As the cohort of offenders proceeded through the juvenile justice system, the proportion that was African American increased from 34.0 percent (among those recommended for formal processing) to 43.1 percent (among those committed to a residential facility or transferred to criminal court). As Bishop and Frazier pointed out, however, these differences could reflect the fact that the African American youths in their sample were arrested for more serious crimes and had more serious prior criminal records than white youths. If this were the case, the differences would reflect racial disparity but not racial discrimination.

When the authors controlled for crime seriousness, prior record, and other predictors of juvenile justice outcomes, they found that the racial differences did

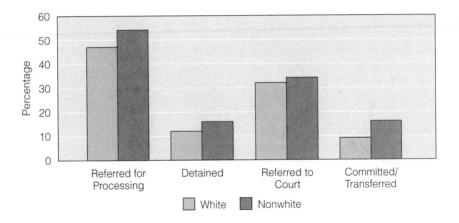

FIGURE 10.3 Juvenile Court Outcomes for "Typical" Florida Youth, 1985–1987

SOURCE: Adapted from Charles E. Frazier and Donna M. Bishop, "Reflections on Race Effects in Juvenile Justice," in *Minorities in Juvenile Justice*, Kimberly Kempf Leonard, Carl E. Pope, and William H. Feyerherm, eds. (Thousand Oaks, CA: Sage, 1995).

not disappear. Rather, African Americans were more likely than whites to be recommended for formal processing, referred to juvenile court, and adjudicated delinquent. They also received harsher sentences than whites. These findings led Bishop and Frazier to conclude that " ... race is a far more pervasive influence in processing than much previous research has indicated."[79]

A follow-up study using more recent (1985–1987) Florida data produced similar results.[80] As shown in Figure 10.3, Frazier and Bishop found that outcomes for "typical" white and nonwhite youth varied significantly. They defined a typical youth as "a 15-year-old male arrested for a misdemeanor against person (e.g., simple battery), with a prior record score consistent with having one prior referral for a misdemeanor against property (e.g., criminal mischief)."[81] Compared to his white counterpart, the typical nonwhite youth was substantially more likely to be recommended for formal processing, held in secure detention prior to disposition, and committed to a residential facility or transferred to criminal court. They also found that being detained had a significant effect on subsequent outcomes; youth who were detained were significantly more likely than those who were released to be referred to juvenile court and, if adjudicated delinquent, to be committed to a residential facility or transferred to criminal court. Thus, nonwhite youth, who were more likely than white youth to be detained, were sentenced more harshly both because of their race (a direct effect) and because of their custody status (an indirect effect).

Frazier and Bishop also conducted interviews with criminal justice officials. During the interview, the respondent was asked whether the findings of harsher treatment of nonwhites "were consistent with their experiences in Florida's juvenile justice system between 1985 and 1987."[82] Most of the intake supervisors and public defenders stated that they believed juvenile justice dispositions were influenced by the race of the youth. In contrast, only 25 percent of the prosecutors and 33 percent of the judges believed that nonwhites were treated more harshly than similarly situated whites.

Although some of the racial differentials in treatment were attributed to racial bias—that is, to prejudiced individuals or a biased system of juvenile justice—a number of respondents suggested that the race effects actually reflected differences in economic circumstances or family situations. As one prosecutor observed, "The biggest problem is the lack of money and resources. Blacks don't have the resources. Whites are more likely to have insurance to pay for treatment. The poor I saw were always poor, but the black poor were poorer yet." Other respondents cited the fact that white parents were more likely than African American parents to be able to hire a private attorney and, as a result, got more favorable plea bargains. Other officials mentioned the role played by family considerations, noting that youth from single-parent families or families perceived to be incapable of providing adequate supervision were treated more harshly than those from intact families. Although they acknowledged that this practice had a disparate effect on minority youth, most officials defended it as "fair and appropriate." As one judge stated, "Inadequate family and bad neighborhood correlate with race and ethnicity. It makes sense to put kids from these circumstances in residential facilities."[83]

Frazier and Bishop concluded that the results of their study "leave little doubt that juvenile justice officials believe race is a factor in juvenile justice processing."[84] They noted that the fact that some officials believed that race directly affected juvenile justice outcomes, whereas others thought that the effect of race was subtle and indirect, meant that "policies aimed at eradicating discrimination must focus both on individual racism and on racism in its most subtle institutional forms."[85] They offered the following recommendations:[86]

- States should establish procedures for all the agencies comprising the juvenile justice system to require reporting, investigating, and responding to professionals whose decisions appear to have been influenced by racial or ethnic bias.

- State legislatures should mandate the development of a race, ethnic, and cultural diversity curriculum that personnel at every level of the juvenile justice system should be required to complete.

- Intake policies and practices should be altered so that youths referred for screening are not rendered ineligible for diversion and other front-end programs if their parents or guardians (a) cannot be contacted, (b) are contacted but are unable to be present for an intake interview, or (c) are unable to participate in family-centered programs.

- In any situation in which persons with economic resources (e.g., income or insurance benefits) are allowed to arrange for private care as a means of diversion from the juvenile justice system or less harsh formal dispositions, precisely the same treatment services should be made available at state expense to serve the poor—whether minority or majority race youths.

Frazier and Bishop acknowledged that these "fairly modest proposals" were unlikely to eliminate racial discrimination that had "survived for generations in a legal environment that expressly forbids it." Nonetheless, they were "cautiously optimistic" that their recommendations would have some effect. As they stated, "if implemented with a genuine interest in their success, such policies will both help reduce discriminatory actions and promote equal justice."[87]

Processing Juveniles in Pennsylvania   Leonard and Sontheimer[88] explored the effect of race and ethnicity on juvenile justice case outcomes in Pennsylvania. Although African Americans and Hispanics accounted for only 19 percent and 4 percent, respectively, of the general youth population in the 14 counties included in the study, they comprised 46 percent (African Americans) and 7 percent (Hispanics) of all referrals to juvenile court.[89]

Like the two studies discussed earlier, this study used a multivariate model to examine the effect of race/ethnicity on a series of juvenile justice outcomes. Leonard and Sontheimer found that both African American and Hispanic youth "were more likely than whites with similar offenses, prior records, and school problems to have their cases formally processed, especially in nonrural court settings."[90] They also found that minority youth were significantly more likely than whites to be detained prior to adjudication and that detention was a strong predictor of subsequent outcomes. African American and Hispanic youth, in other words, were detained more frequently than whites and, as a result, were more likely than whites to be adjudicated delinquent and to be placed in a residential facility following adjudication.

Leonard and Sontheimer suggest that their findings have important policy implications. In particular, they recommend that

> [The] criteria used by individual intake officers should be evaluated to determine whether factors that may more often negatively affect minorities are accorded importance. Racially neutral criteria in detention decisions should be established . . . Cultural bias, including value judgments not based on fact (such as notions that minority parents may not provide adequate supervision for their children or that certain neighborhoods are not conducive to growing up well) must not influence detention.[91]

Intake and Disposition Decisions in Pennsylvania   A second study of juvenile justice decisionmaking in Pennsylvania focused on two stages in the process: the decision to formally refer a youth to the juvenile court rather than handle the case informally and the decision to place the youth in a secure detention facility following adjudication.[92] As shown in Table 10.9, which displays the bivariate relationships between the two outcomes and the legal and extralegal variables that may affect those outcomes, DeJong and Jackson found that African American and Hispanic youth were more likely than white youth to be referred to juvenile court; they also were more likely to be committed to a detention facility. The likelihood of a formal referral also was greater for youth with the following characteristics: male, age 15 and older, living in a single-parent (mother only) family, not in school, charged with a drug offense, charged with a felony, and with two or more prior arrests. A similar pattern of results was found for the decision to place the youth in a secure facility.

T A B L E 10.9 **The Characteristics of Youth Formally Referred to Juvenile Court and Placed in Secure Confinement Following Disposition in Pennsylvania**

	Formally Referred (%)	Placed in Secure Facility (%)
Race/Ethnicity		
White	49.5	14.9
African American	61.4	17.8
Hispanic	59.4	22.9
Gender		
Male	57.5	17.1
Female	38.4	12.9
Age		
12 and below	43.7	11.8
13	50.0	14.3
14	51.9	17.5
15	56.9	12.7
16	58.6	21.0
17 and above	54.7	17.1
Living with mother only	65.9	17.8
Living with both parents	55.1	10.7
In school	61.0	15.8
Not in school	68.2	22.6
Charge type		
Property	66.2	16.1
Violent	61.2	15.9
Drug	71.6	23.7
Other	29.6	15.6
Charge seriousness		
Felony	78.5	19.5
Misdemeanor	35.8	12.5
Number of prior arrests		
None	48.7	10.5
One	64.7	22.9
Two	70.1	32.2
Three or more	76.4	35.8

SOURCE: Adapted from Christina DeJong and Kenneth C. Jackson, "Putting Race into Context: Race, Juvenile Justice Processing, and Urbanization," *Justice Quarterly 15* (1998): 487–504, Table 2.

Further analysis of the data using multivariate techniques led DeJong and Jackson to conclude that race/ethnicity did not have a significant effect on either outcome once the other variables were taken into consideration. Although Hispanics were significantly more likely than whites and African Americans to be formally referred to juvenile court, the referral rates for African American and white youth did not differ. And neither Hispanics nor African Americans faced greater odds than whites of commitment to a secure facility. The race of the youth, however, did affect these outcomes indirectly. In particular, white youth who lived with both parents were less likely than those who lived in single-parent families to be formally referred to juvenile court or placed in secure confinement following disposition. Among African American youth, however, living with both parents rather than in a single-parent household did not have these positive effects. As DeJong and Jackson pointed out, "Black youths are treated the same whether they are living with parents or with their mothers only; for these youths, family status does not protect against [formal referral or] incarceration."[93] In addition, African American youth, but not white youth, were treated more harshly in rural counties than in urban or suburban counties.

DeJong and Jackson speculated that the fact that family status did not affect outcomes for African American youth might be the result of juvenile justice officials' stereotyped beliefs about African American families—that is, officials "may view all black fathers as absentee" or "may view the black family structure as weak."[94] If this is the case, African American youth who live in two-parent families would not be regarded as better candidates for diversion or for treatment within the community than those who live in single-parent families. This type of subtle discrimination may be more common than the overt discrimination that characterized the system in earlier eras.[95]

Adjudication and Disposition Decisions in Georgia   A study of juvenile court outcomes in Georgia focused on the interaction between the race of the juvenile and admitting or denying the crime.[96] Ruback and Vardaman posited two opposing effects for admitting/denying guilt—one based on the youth's potential for rehabilitation and the other based on due process considerations. They asserted that if the primary goal of the juvenile justice system was rehabilitation, then indicators of amenability to rehabilitation should be important predictors of case disposition. Because admitting guilt signals that the youth accepts responsibility for his actions and feels remorse and also indicates that the youth may be a good candidate for treatment rather than punishment, an admission of guilt should—again, if rehabilitation is the goal—lead to more lenient treatment. However, if the goal of the court is to punish the guilty, *denial* of guilt might lead to more lenient treatment. This might be particularly true, according to Ruback and Vardaman, in large urban jurisdictions with heavy caseloads. If the youth denies that he is guilty, the court must hold an evidentiary hearing and prove the charges. Prosecutors might prefer to dismiss the case rather than use their limited resources to secure a conviction.

Ruback and Vardaman found that, whereas African Americans were over-represented in juvenile court populations, in the 16 Georgia counties they examined, white youth were treated more harshly than African American youth.[97] White juveniles (43 percent) were more likely than African American juveniles (39 percent) to be adjudicated delinquent, and African American juveniles (29 percent) were more likely than white juveniles (23 percent) to have their cases dismissed. The authors also found that white youth were substantially more likely to admit the crimes they were accused of committing: 66 percent of the whites, compared to only 51 percent of the African Americans, admitted their guilt.

When Ruback and Vardaman compared adjudication outcomes for African American and white youth, controlling for crime seriousness, prior record, whether the case was heard in an urban or rural county, whether the youth admitted guilt, and the youth's age and gender, they found that race had no effect. Admitting guilt, however, had a strong effect on the likelihood of being adjudicated delinquent. Youth who admitted their guilt were more likely to be adjudicated delinquent. The odds of being adjudicated delinquent also were higher in rural than in urban counties.

The authors of the study concluded that the harsher treatment of white youth could be attributed to two factors. First, whites were more likely than African Americans to admit guilt and admitting guilt led to a higher likelihood of being adjudicated delinquent. Second, cases involving whites were more likely than those involving African Americans to be processed in rural courts, where the odds of being adjudicated delinquent were higher.[98] They also suggested that their results might reflect judges' beliefs that whites youths would be more likely to benefit from the interventions and services available to the court. Thus,

> an intervention by the court may be deemed more likely to affect the future behavior of white juveniles (who generally have shorter legal histories), while the same intervention with Black juveniles (who generally have longer legal histories) may be perceived as wasted effort. It may be . . . that only white juveniles are believed to be worth investing resources in so as to reduce the chances of their committing future crimes.[99]

Ruback and Vardaman maintained that this also might explain why white youth admitted their guilt at a higher rate than African American youth. Juvenile justice officials might have urged whites to admit the crime so that they could receive an informal adjustment and court intervention.

Race/Ethnicity, Gender, and Age: Juvenile Justice in Nebraska   The studies discussed thus far all tested for the direct effects of race/ethnicity—that is, these studies examined whether African American and Hispanic youth were treated more harshly than white youth. Kwak used Nebraska data to examine the interactions among age, gender, race/ethnicity, and four juvenile court outcomes: detention, petition, adjudication, and disposition.[100] He controlled for the seriousness of the offense, the youth's prior delinquency referrals, whether the case was handled by a separate juvenile court or a regular county court, and the year of the referral. He found that each of the offender characteristics affected some or all of the outcomes: youth of color generally were treated more harshly than white youth, younger offenders were treated more leniently than offenders who were between the ages of 13 and 17, and males were more likely than females to be petitioned and transferred to legal custody.[101]

Kwak then compared outcomes for African American males who were 16 or 17 years old with outcomes for other categories of offenders. Although he found differences for each of the four outcomes, the most consistent outcomes were found for the disposition decision, which was measured by a dichotomous variable that differentiated between decisions that transferred the legal custody of the youth (that is, transferred the youth to a secure facility or into the custody of a public agency) and those that did not (that is, probation, dismissal of charges with a warning from the judge, or a fine). As shown in Table 10.10, African American males, aged 16 and 17, received substantially harsher dispositions than all of the other groups, except for Hispanic females aged 10 through 12; black males aged 13 through 15; Hispanic males aged 13 through 15; and Native American males aged 16 and 17. Of particular interest is the fact that white males, regardless of age, were substantially less likely than 16- and 17-year-old African American males to have their legal custody transferred to a secure facility or a state agency. The probability differences were 21.0 percent for white males, aged 10 through 12; 13.9 percent for white males, aged 13 through 15; and 17.7 percent for white males, aged 16 and 17. Overall, then, male teenagers of color, and especially African American male teenagers, were treated more harshly than other offenders.

In summary, the results of the studies reviewed here suggest that the effect of race/ethnicity on juvenile court outcomes is complex. Some researchers conclude that race and ethnicity have direct or overt effects on case outcomes. Research conducted in Florida and Pennsylvania, for example, found that racial minorities were treated more harshly than whites at several stages in the juvenile justice process, including detention, and that detention had significant "spillover effects" on subsequent adjudication and disposition decisions. Other researchers conclude that the effect of race/ethnicity is indirect rather than direct. Research conducted in Pennsylvania, for instance, found that living in a two-parent family benefited whites but not African Americans, whereas research in Georgia found that the *harsher* treatment of white youth reflected their higher rates of admitting guilt and a greater likelihood of being prosecuted in rural rather than urban jurisdictions. A study conducted in Nebraska revealed that teenage boys were singled out for harsher treatment if they were racial minorities, and especially if they were African Americans.

These studies also suggest that the effect of race on juvenile justice outcomes may vary from one jurisdiction to another and highlight the importance of conceptualizing decisionmaking in the juvenile justice system as a process. According to Secret and Johnson,[102] "in examining for racial bias in juvenile justice system decisions, we must scrutinize each step of the process to see whether previous decisions create a racial effect by changing the pool of offenders at subsequent steps." The importance of differentiating among racial and ethnic groups is also clear. As one author noted, "Circumstances surrounding the case processing of minority youths not only may be different from those for whites, but also may vary among minority groups."[103]

T A B L E 10.10 Differences in the Probabilities of Placement in a Secure Facility or Transfer to a State Agency

Probability Differences Between African American Males, Ages 16 and 17, and . . .

White Female	
Age 10–12	-18.7%
Age 13–15	-17.2%
Age 16–17	-18.8%
African American Female	
Age 10–12	-26.1%
Age 13–15	-6.8%
Age 16–17	-19.6%
Hispanic Female	
Age 10–12	Not significant
Age 13–15	-12.2%
Age 16–17	-22.6%
Native American Female	
Age 10–12	-28.0%
Age 13–15	-12.0%
Age 16–17	-16.8%
White Male	
Age 10–12	-21.0%
Age 13–15	-13.9%
Age 16–17	-17.7%
African American Male	
Age 10–12	-12.8%
Age 13–15	Not significant
Age 16–17*	Reference Category
Hispanic Male	
Age 10–12	-26.3%
Age 13–15	Not significant
Age 16–17*	Not significant
Native American Male	
Age 10–12	-24.0%
Age 13–15	-6.6%
Age 16–17	Not significant

*Figures are the differences in the probabilities of placement in a secure facility or transfer to a state agency for youth in each group and African American males, ages 16 and 17. For example, the probability was 18.7 percent less for white females between the ages of 10 and 12 and African American males who were 16 or 17.

SOURCE: Dae-Hoon Kwak, "The Interaction of Age, Gender, and Race/Ethnicity on Juvenile Justice Decision Making in Nebraska." Unpublished master's thesis, University of Nebraska at Omaha, 2004.

Transfer of Juveniles to Criminal Court

In 2003 juveniles accounted for 9 percent of all arrests for murder/manslaughter, 16 percent of all arrests for forcible rape, 24 percent of all arrests for robbery, and 14 percent of all arrests for aggravated assault.[104] The number of juveniles arrested increased 100 percent between 1985 and 1994[105] but declined by 18 percent from 1994 to 2003.[106] Juvenile arrests for *violent* crimes increased from 66,976 in 1985 to 117,200 in 1994 (an increase of 75 percent) but declined to 92,300 (a decrease of 32 percent) in 2003.

The increase in juvenile crime during the 1980s and early 1990s, coupled with highly publicized cases of very young children accused of murder and other violent crimes, prompted a number of states to alter procedures for handling certain types of juvenile offenders. In 1995, for example, Illinois lowered the age of admission to prison from 13 to 10. This change was enacted after two boys, ages 10 and 11, dropped a 5-year-old boy out of a 14th-floor window of a Chicago public housing development. In 1996 a juvenile court judge ordered that both boys, who were then 12 and 13, be sent to a high-security juvenile penitentiary; her decision made the 12-year-old the nation's youngest inmate in a high-security prison.[107]

Other states responded to the increase in serious juvenile crime by lowering the age when children can be transferred from juvenile court to criminal court, expanding the list of offenses for which juveniles can be waived to criminal court, or both. A report by the United States General Accounting Office indicated that between 1978 and 1995, 44 states passed new laws regarding the waiver of juveniles to criminal court; in 24 of these states the new laws increased the population of juveniles that potentially could be sent to criminal court.[108] California, for example, changed the age at which juveniles could be waived to criminal court from 16 to 14 years (for specified offenses); Missouri reduced the age at which children could be certified to stand trial as adults from 14 to 12 years.

By 2004 there were 15 states with mandatory waiver in cases that met certain age, offense, or other criteria and 15 states with a rebutable presumption in favor of waiver in certain kinds of cases. Currently, all but four states give juvenile court judges the power to waive jurisdiction over juvenile cases that meet certain criteria—generally, a minimum age, a specified type or level of offense, and/or a sufficiently serious record of prior delinquency.[109] And 15 states have direct file waiver provisions, which allow the prosecutor to file certain types of juvenile cases directly in criminal court. (See Box 10.2 for the criteria that courts can use in making the waiver decision.)

A report by the National Center for Juvenile Justice noted that the number of delinquency cases waived to criminal court increased by 70 percent from 1985 to 1994 but declined by 54 percent between 1994 and 2000.[110] (The report attributed the decline in the number of cases waived to criminal court in part to statutory changes that excluded certain cases from juvenile court or allowed prosecutors to file serious cases directly in criminal court.). During most of this time period, the waiver rate was highest for person offenses; from 1989 to 1992, the rate was higher for drug offenses than for person offenses. It is not surprising that cases involving older youth were more likely than those involving youths 15

B O X 10.2 *Kent v. United States* [383 U.S. 541 (1966)]: Criteria
Concerning Waiver of Jurisdiction from Juvenile
Court to Adult Court

In 1996 the United States Supreme Court ruled in *Kent v. United States* that waiver hearings must measure up to "the essentials of due process and fair treatment." The court held that juveniles facing waiver are entitled to representation by counsel, access to social services records, and a written statement of the reasons for the waiver. In an appendix to its opinion, the court also laid out the "criteria and principles concerning waiver of jurisdiction." The criteria that courts are to use in making the decision are as follows:

- The seriousness of the alleged offense and whether protection of the community requires waiver.

- Whether the alleged offense was committed in an aggressive, violent, premeditated, or willful manner.

- Whether the alleged offense was against persons or against property.

- Whether there is evidence on which a Grand Jury may be expected to return an indictment.

- The desirability of trial and disposition of the entire offense in one court when the juvenile's associates are adults who will be charged with a crime in criminal court.

- The sophistication and maturity of the juvenile as determined by consideration of his home, environmental situation, emotional attitude, and pattern of living.

- The record and previous history of the juvenile.

- The prospects for adequate protection of the public and the likelihood of reasonable rehabilitation of the juvenile by the use of procedures, services, and facilities currently available to the Juvenile Court.

---

and younger to be waived and that cases involving males were substantially more likely than those involving females to be waived.[111]

There also is evidence that cases involving racial minorities are more likely than those involving whites to be transferred to criminal court. For example:

- In 2000 the percentage of delinquency cases waived to criminal court nationwide was 0.5 percent for white youth and 0.8 percent for African American youth. Among offenders charged with drug offenses, the rate was 0.4 for white youth and 1.5 percent for African American youth.[112]

- In 1996 youth of color accounted for 75 percent of Los Angeles County's population between the ages of 10 and 17 but accounted for 95 percent of the youths whose cases were waived to adult court; Asian Americans were 3 times more likely than white youth, Hispanics were 6 times more likely than white youth, and African Americans were 12 times more likely than white youth to be waived to adult court.[113]

- African American youth comprised 60 percent and Hispanics made of 10 percent of juveniles waived to adult court in Pennsylvania in 1994; white youth made up only 28 percent of these cases.[114]

- African Americans made up 80 percent of all waiver request cases in South Carolina from 1985 through 1994. Of the cases involving African American youth, 81 percent were approved for waiver to adult court, compared to only 74 percent of the cases involving white youth.[115]

Decisions to transfer juveniles to adult criminal courts are important because of the sentencing consequences of being convicted in criminal, rather than juvenile court. Although there is some evidence that transferred youth are treated more leniently in criminal court than they would have been in juvenile court[116]—in large part because they appear in criminal court at a younger age and with shorter criminal histories than other offenders—most studies reveal just the opposite. Fagan, for example, compared juvenile and criminal court outcomes for 15- and 16-year-old felony offenders in New York (where they were excluded from juvenile court) and New Jersey (where they were not).[117] He found that youth processed in criminal courts were twice as likely as those processed in juvenile courts to be incarcerated.

A more recent study compared sentencing outcomes of juveniles (those younger than age 18) and young adults (those ages 18 to 24) processed in Pennsylvania's adult criminal courts from 1997 to 1999.[118] When they examined the raw data, Kurlycheck and Johnson found that the mean sentence imposed on juvenile offenders was 18 months, compared to only 6 months for young-adult offenders. These differences did not disappear when the authors controlled for the seriousness of the offense, the offender's criminal history, the offense type, whether the case was settled by plea or trial, and the offender's gender. Once these factors were taken into consideration, juveniles still received sentences that were 83 percent harsher than those imposed on young adults.[119] Further analysis revealed that "'being juvenile' resulted in a 10-percent greater likelihood of incarceration and a 29-percent increase in sentence length."[120]

These findings led Kurlychek and Johnson to suggest that "the transfer decision itself is used as an indicator of incorrigibility, threat to the community, and/or lack of potential for rehabilitation, resulting in a considerable 'juvenile penalty.'"[121] Evidence that African American and Hispanic youth face higher odds of being transferred to adult court than do white youth suggests that this "juvenile penalty" is not applied in a racially neutral manner.

Explaining Disparate Treatment of Juvenile Offenders

The studies discussed previously provide compelling evidence that African American and Hispanic juveniles are treated more harshly than similarly situated white juveniles. The question, of course, is why this occurs. Secret and Johnson[122] suggest that juvenile court judges may attribute positive or negative characteristics to offenders based on their race/ethnicity. Judges may use extralegal characteristics such as race to create "a mental map of the accused person's underlying character" and to predict his or her future behavior.[123] As Mann notes, officials' attitudes "mirror the stereotype of minorities as typically violent, dangerous, or threatening."[124] Alternatively, according to Secret and Johnson, the harsher treatment of African American and Hispanic juveniles might reflect both class and race biases on the part of juvenile court judges. As conflict theory posits, "the individual's economic and social class and the color of his skin ... determine his relationship to the legal system."[125]

These speculations regarding court officials' perceptions of minority and white youth have not been systematically tested. Researchers assume that findings of differential treatment of racial minorities signal the presence of race-linked stereotypes or racially prejudiced attitudes, but there have been few attempts to empirically verify either the existence of differing perceptions of white and minority youth or the degree to which these perceptions can account for racial disparities in the juvenile justice system.

A study by Bridges and Steen[126] addressed this issue by examining 233 narrative reports written by juvenile probation officers in three counties in the state of Washington during 1990 and 1991. The narratives, which were used by the court in determining the appropriate disposition of the case, were based on interviews with the youth and his or her family and on written documents such as school records and juvenile court files. Each narrative included the probation officer's description of the youth's crime and assessment of the factors that motivated the crime, an evaluation of the youth's background, and an assessment of his or her likelihood of recidivism. The information gleaned from these narratives was used "to explore the relationship between race; officials' characterizations of youths, their crimes, and the causes of their crimes; officials' assessments of the threat of future crime by youths; and officials' sentence recommendations."[127]

Bridges and Steen's review of the narratives revealed that probation officers described African American and white youth and their crimes differently. They tended to attribute crimes committed by whites to negative environmental factors (poor school performance, delinquent peers, dysfunctional family, use of drugs or alcohol) but to attribute crimes committed by African Americans to negative personality traits and "bad attitudes" (refusal to admit guilt, lack of remorse, failure to take offense seriously, lack of cooperation with court officials). They also found that probation officers judged African American youth to have a significantly higher risk of reoffending than white youth.

Further analysis, which controlled for the juvenile's age, gender, and prior criminal history and for the seriousness of the current offense, confirmed these findings. As the authors note, "Being black significantly reduces the likelihood of negative *external* attributions by probation officers and significantly increases the likelihood of negative *internal* attributions, even after adjusting for severity of the presenting offense and the youth's prior involvement in criminal behavior."[128] To illustrate these differences, the authors discuss the narratives written for two very similar cases of armed robbery, one involving a black youth and one involving a white youth. The black youth's crime was described as "very dangerous" and as "premeditated and willful," and his criminal behavior was attributed to an amoral character, lack of remorse, and no desire to change. In contrast, the white youth was portrayed as an "emaciated little boy" whose crime was attributed to a broken home, association with delinquent peers, and substance abuse.

Bridges and Steen's examination of the factors related to probation officers' assessments of the risk of reoffending revealed that youth who committed more serious crimes or had more serious criminal histories were judged to be at higher risk of future offending. Although none of the offender's demographic characteristics, including race, was significantly related to assessments of risk, probation officers' attributions of delinquency did affect these predictions. Youth whose delinquency was attributed to negative internal causes were judged to be at higher risk of future delinquency than youth whose crimes were attributed to negative external factors. According to Bridges and Steen, "This suggests that youths whose crimes are attributed to internal causes are more likely to be viewed as 'responsible' for their crimes, engulfed in a delinquent personality and lifestyle, and prone to committing crimes in the future."[129]

The authors of this study concluded that race influenced juvenile court outcomes indirectly. Probation officers were substantially more likely to attribute negative internal characteristics and attitudes to African American youth than to white youth; these attributions, in turn, shaped their assessments of dangerousness and their predictions of future offending. As Bridges and Steen state, "Insofar as officials judge black youths to be more dangerous than white youths, they do so because they attribute crime by blacks to negative personalities or their attitudinal traits and because black offenders are more likely than white offenders to have committed serious offenses and have histories of prior involvement in crime."[130]

The results of this study illustrate the "mechanisms by which officials' perceptions of the offender as threatening develop or influence the process of legal decision-making."[131] They suggest that perceptions of threat and, consequently, predictions about future delinquency are influenced by criminal justice officials' assessments of the causes of criminal behavior. Thus, "officials may perceive blacks as more culpable and dangerous than whites in part because they believe the etiology of their crimes is linked to personal traits" that are "not as amenable to the correctional treatments the courts typically administer."[132]

JUVENILES UNDER CORRECTIONAL SUPERVISION

As the previous section illustrates, the racial makeup of juveniles at key stages of the juvenile justice system varies by decision type. Generally, nonwhite youth (the majority of whom are African American) are overrepresented at every stage of decisionmaking. Nonwhite youth also are at greater risk of receiving harsher sanctions than white youth. For example, nonwhite youth are detained in secure custody prior to their juvenile court hearing at rates that exceed those for white youth, regardless of the seriousness of the delinquency offense. There has been a decline in the proportion of white youth detained but an increase in the proportion of African American youth in custody.[133]

Table 10.11 presents data on the racial and ethnic makeup of juvenile offenders who were placed in a secure residential facility in 1999 after being adjudicated delinquent.[134] White and Asian American youth are underrepresented

TABLE 10.11 Racial and Ethnic Profile of Juvenile Offenders in Residential Placement, 1999

Most Serious Offense	Percentage of Youth in Residential Placement in Each Racial/Ethnic Group				
	White	African American	Hispanic	Native American	Asian American
Total	38	38	18	2	2
Delinquency Cases	37	40	19	2	2
Criminal homicide	23	44	24	3	6
Sexual Assault	52	31	13	2	1
Robbery	19	55	22	1	3
Aggravated Assault	29	40	25	2	3
Simple Assault	43	37	15	2	1
Burglary	43	34	18	2	2
Theft	43	38	15	2	1
Auto theft	36	38	21	2	3
Drug trafficking	16	65	18	0	1
Weapons	39	39	18	2	2
Status Offenses	54	31	10	2	1

SOURCE: Office of Juvenile Justice and Delinquency Prevention, *Juveniles in Corrections* (Washington, DC: Office of Juvenile Justice and Delinquency Prevention, 2004), p. 9.

among youth in residential placement, whereas African American, Hispanic, and Native American/Alaskan Native youth generally are overrepresented. For all of the criminal offenses except for sexual assault, youth of color made up at least half of all youth in secure residential facilities. African American and Hispanic youth made up 68 percent of the youth in residential placement for criminal homicide, 77 percent of the youth in a secure facility for robbery, and 83 percent of the youth in a secure facility for drug trafficking. For status offenses (i.e., running away from home and truancy), however, whites comprised the largest proportion of offenders placed in secure confinement. Racial minorities were overrepresented in residential placement in every state in the United States, and in some states there were more than twice as many racial minorities in secure facilities as there were in the juvenile population. For instance, racial minorities made up 37 percent of the juvenile population, but 84 percent of those in residential placement, in New Jersey. The figures were 15 percent (population) and 59 percent (residential placement) for Wisconsin, 18 percent (population) and 55 percent (residential placement) for Rhode Island, and 25 percent (population) and 77 percent (residential placement) for Connecticut.[135]

Another way to gauge the extent of overrepresentation of racial and ethnic groups placed in residential facilities by the juvenile court is to examine custody

T A B L E 10.12 Juvenile Custody Rates (per 100,000) by Racial and Ethnic Categories, 1999

White (non-Hispanic)	212
African American (non-Hispanic)	1,004
Hispanic	485
Native American/Alaskan Native	632
Asian American/Pacific Islander	182

SOURCE: Office of Juvenile Justice and Delinquency Prevention, *Juveniles in Corrections* (Washington, DC: Office of Juvenile Justice and Delinquency Prevention, 2004), p. 11.

rates calculated for each racial and ethnic group (Table 10.12). Consistent with the results discussed previously, important differences exist across race and ethnicity. For every 100,000 African American juveniles living in the United States, 1,004 were in a residential placement facility in 1999; in contrast, the rate was 632 for American Indians, 485 for Hispanics, and 212 for whites. Moreover, in half of the states, the minority custody rate exceeded the white rate by more than 3 to 1. In four states (Connecticut, New Jersey, Pennsylvania, and Wisconsin), the ratio of minority to nonminority rates was more than 8 to 1.[136]

There also is evidence that African American males are incarcerated in state prisons at disproportionality high rates. In 1999 people younger than age 18 accounted for only 2 percent of all new court commitments to adult prisons; in the 37 states that provided data to the National Corrections Reporting Program, there were 5,600 new court commitments involving youth younger than 18 at the time of admission.[137] Almost all of these youth (96 percent) were male and more than half of them (57 percent) were African American males. African American males made up 57 percent of new admissions for homicide, 75 percent of new admissions for robbery, and 84 percent of new admissions for drug offenses.[138]

CONCLUSION

The victimization and offending patterns for juveniles mirror those for adults. Juveniles of color, and particularly African American males, face a higher risk of victimization than white juveniles. This pattern is found for property crime, violent crime, and homicide. In fact, the homicide victimization rate for young African American females is higher than the rate for young white males.

Although the common perception of the juvenile offender is that he or she is a person of color,[139] the data discussed in this chapter indicate that whites constitute the majority of juvenile offenders for most crimes. The notable exceptions (among the more serious index offenses) are robbery, where more than half of those arrested are African American, and murder and nonnegligent manslaughter, where African American youth comprise nearly half of all arrestees. The overrepresentation of African American juveniles in arrest statistics is not a constant, however. The most pronounced disparities are found for violent crimes, where from one-third to one-half of all arrestees are African American. There is less racial disparity for property offenses; for these crimes, between one-fourth and one-third of those arrested are African American. Further, whites are overrepresented among arrestees for many of the drug and alcohol offenses.

Methodologically sophisticated research reveals that racial and ethnic differences in juvenile victimization and offending rates can be attributed in large part to family and community characteristics. African American and Hispanic youth are more likely than white youth to be the victims of violent crime because they spend more time away from home, and are more likely to live in single-parent households and disadvantaged communities. Similarly, the higher rates of violent offending found among minority youth than white youth reflect the fact that minority youth are more likely to live in disadvantaged neighborhoods, to be members of gangs, and to have weak bonds to social institutions such as schools. The sources of risk of victimization and offending are similar for all teenagers, but the likelihood of experiencing these risk factors is higher for youth of color than for white youth.

The results of studies examining the effect of race/ethnicity on juvenile justice processing decisions suggest that the juvenile justice system, like the criminal justice system for adults, is not free of racial bias. There is compelling evidence that racial minorities are treated more harshly than whites at various points in the juvenile justice process. Most importantly, minority youth are substantially more likely than white youth to be detained pending disposition, adjudicated delinquent, and waived to adult court. They also are sentenced more harshly than their white counterparts, at least in part because of the tendency of criminal justice officials to attribute their crimes to internal (personality) rather than external (environmental) causes.

DISCUSSION QUESTIONS

1. Describe the characteristics of juvenile victims of crime. Are they similar to or different than the characteristics of adult victims of crime?

2. There is a common perception that the typical juvenile offender is a person of color. Is this an accurate perception?

3. Why is there greater potential for racial discrimination in the juvenile justice system than in the adult justice system?

4. What are the dangers inherent in allowing police to use gang databases in investigating crimes?

5. Studies of the juvenile justice system reveal that racial minorities are subject to "cumulative disadvantage" or "compound risk." Explain what this means and why it is a cause for concern.

6. We suggest that preliminary evidence indicating that African American juveniles are more likely than white juveniles to be waived to adult court

should be confirmed by additional research that incorporates legally relevant criteria other than the seriousness of the offense. What other variables should be taken into consideration?

7. Although studies reveal that African American, Hispanic, and Native American youth are treated more harshly than white youth at several stages of the juvenile justice process (even after the seriousness of the offense and the offender's prior juvenile record are taken into consideration), they do not tell us why these disparities occur. How would *you* explain these differences? How do Bridges and Steen account for them?

NOTES

1. Linda S. Beres and Thomas D. Griffith, "Demonizing Youth," *Loyola of Los Angeles Law Review 34* (2001): 747–767.

2. Kate Randall, "Another Florida Teenager Receives Harsh Adult Prison Sentence." Available at http://www.wsws.org/articles/2001/aug2001.

3. "Juvenile Justice Experts Decry Severity of Life in Adult Prison for Nathaniel Brazill." Available at http://www.cjcj.org.

4. Ibid.

5. Susan Spencer-Wendel, "Nathaniel Brazill Would Have Graduated From High School This Week," *Palm Beach Post*, May 22, 2005.

6. "Lionel Tate Released," CNN.com, January 27, 2004. Available at http://www.cnn.com/2004/LAW/01/26/wrestling.death/.

7. Andrew Ryan, "Lionel Tate Accused of Firing Mother's Handgun Randomly on Street," Sun-Sentinel.com. Available at http://www.sun-sentinel.com/news/local/broward.

8. Office of Juvenile Justice and Delinquency Prevention, "Juvenile Victims of Property Crimes" (Washington, DC: U.S. Department of Justice, 2000).

9. Ibid.

10. Office of Juvenile Justice and Delinquency Prevention, "Juvenile Victims of Property Crimes."

11. Ibid., p. 5.

12. Ibid.

13. Ibid.

14. Bureau of Justice Statistics, *Criminal Victimization in the United States, 2003: Statistical Tables*. Table 3. Available at http://www.ojp.usdoj.gov/bjs/abstract/cvusst.htm.

15. Ibid., Table 9.

16. Ibid., Table 10.

17. Bureau of Justice Statistics, *Weapon Use and Violent Crime* (Washington, DC: U.S. Department of Justice, 2003): Figures 1 and 2.

18. Janet L. Lauritsen, "How Families and Communities Influence Youth Victimization," *OJJDP Juvenile Justice Bulletin* (Washington, DC: U.S. Department of Justice, 2003).

19. Ibid., pp. 5–6.

20. Ibid., p. 7.

21. Ibid., pp. 8–9.

22. Ibid., p. 9.

23. Ibid.

24. James Allen Fox and Marianne W. Zawitz, "Homicide Trends in the United States" (Washington, DC: U.S. Department of Justice, 2004). Available at www.ojp.usdoj.gov/bjs.

25. Ibid.

26. Thomas McNulty and Paul E. Bellair, "Explaining Racial and Ethnic Differences

in Serious Adolescent Violent Behavior," *Criminology 41* (2003): 709–748.

27. Ibid., Appendix 1.

28. Ibid., p. 719.

29. Ibid.

30. Ibid.

31. Ibid.

32. See, for example, Robert J. Sampson and William Julius Wilson, "Toward a Theory of Race, Crime, and Urban Inequality," in *Crime and Inequality*, John Hagan and Ruth D. Peterson, eds. (Stanford, CA: Stanford University Press, 1995); and Clifford R. Shaw and Henry D. McKay, *Juvenile Delinquency and Urban Areas* (Chicago: University of Chicago Press, 1942).

33. Michael R. Gottfredson and Travis Hirschi, *A General Theory of Crime* (Stanford, CA: Stanford University Press, 1985); Douglas S. Massey and Nancy A. Denton, *American Apartheid: Segregation and the Making of the Underclass* (Cambridge, MA: Harvard University Press, 1993); and William Julius Wilson, *When Work Disappears: The World of the New Urban Poor* (New York: Knopf, 1996).

34. Stephen A. Cernkovich and Peggy C. Giordano, "School Bonding, Race, and Delinquency," *Criminology 30* (1992): 261–291; Travis Hirschi, *Causes of Delinquency* (Berkeley, CA: University of California Press, 1969).

35. Ronald L. Akers, *Social Learning and Social Structure: A General Theory of Crime and Deviance* (Boston: Northeastern University Press, 1994); Malcom Klein, *The American Street Gang* (New York: Oxford University Press, 1995).

36. McNulty and Bellair, "Explaining Racial and Ethnic Differences in Serious Adolescent Violent Behavior."

37. Ibid., p. 709.

38. Ibid., p. 736.

39. Carl Werthman and Irving Piliavin, "Gang Members and the Police," in *The Police: Six Sociological Essays*, David J. Bordua, ed. (New York: Wiley, 1967), p. 58.

40. Gallup Poll data, reported in Bureau of Justice Statistics, *Sourcebook of Criminal Justice Statistics 2000*, online edition, www.albany.edu/sourcebook, Table 2.16.

41. Donald Black, "The Social Organization of Arrest," in Donald Black, *The Manners and Customs of the Police* (New York: Academic Press, 1980).

42. Carl E. Pope and Howard N. Snyder, *Race as a Factor in Juvenile Arrests* (Washington, DC: Office of Juvenile Justice and Delinquency Prevention, 2003.)

43. Ibid., p. 6.

44. Ryan Pintado-Vertner, "How is Juvenile Justice Served? Racially Biased System Just Sweeps Troubled Youths Under the Rug," *San Francisco Chronicle*, February 27, 2000.

45. Stacey Leyton, "The New Blacklists: The Threat to Civil Liberties Posed by Gang Databases," in *Crime Control and Social Justice: The Delicate Balance*, Darnell F. Hawkins, Samuel L. Meyers Jr., and Randolph N. Stone, eds. (Westport, CT: Greenwood, 2003).

46. Texas Art. 61-02. Available at http://www.iir.com/nygc/gang-legis/gang_databases.htm.

47. Leyton, "The New Blacklists," p. 115.

48. Rev. Oscar Tillman, senior official of the Denver NAACP, quoted in Dirk Johnson, "2 Out of 3 Young Black Men in Denver Are on Gang Suspect List," *N.Y. Times*, December 11, 1993, at A8.

49. Leyton, "The New Blacklists," p. 120 and Note 114.

50. John Moreno Gonzales, "Response to Violence; Anti-Gang Bill Revived," *Newsday*, November 12, 2004, at A18.

51. Leyton, "The New Blacklists," p. 121.

52. Daniel C. Tsang, "Garden Grove's Asian Mug File Settlement." Available at

http://sun3.lib.uci.edu/~dtsang/ggamfs.htm.

53. Stella Richardson, "ACLU Wins Major Settlement for Union City Students," *ACLU News*, Summer 2005. Available at http://www.alcunc.org/aclunews/news0508/unioncity.html.

54. Marjorie S. Zatz and Richard P. Krecker Jr., "Anti-gang Initiatives as Racialized Policy," in *Crime Control and Social Justice: The Delicate Balance*, Darnell F. Hawkins, Samuel L. Meyers Jr., and Randolph N. Stone, eds. (Westport, CT: Greenwood, 2003).

55. Nicholas Espiritu, "(E)racing Youth: The Racialized Construction of California's Proposition 21 and the Development of Alternate Contestations," *Cleveland State Law Review 52* (2005): 189–217.

56. Zatz and Krecker, "Anti-Gang Initiatives as Racialized Policy," p. 192.

57. Philip W. Harris, Wayne N. Welsh, and Frank Butler, "A Century of Juvenile Justice," in Volume 1, *Criminal Justice 2000, The Nature of Crime: Continuity and Change* (Washington, DC: National Institute of Justice, 2000), p. 360.

58. Literally translated as "father of the country," this phrase refers to the government's right and obligation to act on behalf of a child (or a person who is mentally ill).

59. National Center for Juvenile Justice, *Juvenile Court Statistics 2000* (Washington, DC: Office of Juvenile Justice and Delinquency Prevention, 2004), p. 19.

60. Ibid., p. 20.

61. Ibid., p. 47.

62. Judith A. Cox, "Addressing Disproportionate Minority Representation Within the Juvenile Justice System." Available at the website for Building Blocks for Youth (http://www.buildingblocksforyouth.org). The author of this report noted that steps taken by the Santa Cruz County Probation Office led to a decrease in the percentage of those held who were Hispanic; it declined from 64 percent in 1997/1998 to 46 percent in 2000.

63. Office of Juvenile Justice and Delinquency Prevention, *Disproportionate Minority Confinement 2002 Update* (Washington, DC: U.S. Department of Justice, 2004), p. 3.

64. Building Blocks for Youth, *And Justice for Some* (Washington, DC: Building Blocks for Youth, 2000).

65. Ibid., p. 9.

66. Ibid., p. 15.

67. See, for example, Donna M. Bishop and Charles S. Frazier, "Race Effects in Juvenile Justice Decision-Making: Findings of a Statewide Analysis," *Journal of Criminal Law and Criminology 86* (1996): 392–413.

68. Barry C. Feld, *Bad Kids: Race and the Transformation of the Juvenile Court* (London and New York: Oxford University Press, 1999), p. 266.

69. Carl E. Pope and William H. Feyerherm, "Minority Status and Juvenile Justice Processing: An Assessment of the Research Literature (Part I)," *Criminal Justice Abstracts 22* (1990): 327–335.

70. Carl E. Pope, Rich Lovell, and Heidi M. Hsia, *Disproportionate Minority Confinement: A Review of the Research Literature from 1989 Through 2001*, (Washington, DC: U.S. Department of Justice, 2004).

71. Ibid., p. 6.

72. David Huizinga and Delbert S. Elliot, "Juvenile Offenders: Prevalence, Offender Incidence, and Arrest Rates by Race," *Crime and Delinquency 33* (1987): 206–223.

73. Donna M. Bishop and Charles E. Frazier, "The Influence of Race in Juvenile Justice Processing," *Journal of Research in Crime and Delinquency 25* (1988): 242–263.

74. Panel on Juvenile Crime, *Juvenile Crime Juvenile Justice*, p. 254.

75. Pope and Feyerherm, "Minority Status and Juvenile Justice Processing," p. 334.

76. Ibid., pp. 254–258.

77. Ibid., p. 257.

78. Bishop and Frazier, "The Influence of Race in Juvenile Justice Processing."

79. Ibid., p. 258.

80. Charles E. Frazier and Donna M. Bishop, "Reflections on Race Effects in Juvenile Justice," in *Minorities in Juvenile Justice*, Kimberly Kempf Leonard, Carl E. Pope, and William H. Feyerherm, eds. (Thousand Oaks, CA: Sage, 1995).

81. Ibid., p. 25.

82. Ibid., p. 28.

83. Ibid., p. 35.

84. Ibid., p. 40.

85. Ibid., p. 41.

86. Ibid., pp. 41–45.

87. Ibid., p. 45.

88. Kimberly Kempf Leonard and Henry Sontheimer, "The Role of Race in Juvenile Justice in Pennsylvania," in *Minorities in Juvenile Justice*, Kimberly Kempf Leonard, Carl E. Pope, and William H. Feyerherm, eds. (Thousand Oaks, CA: Sage, 1995).

89. Ibid., p. 108.

90. Ibid., p. 119.

91. Ibid., pp. 122–123.

92. Christina DeJong and Kenneth C. Jackson, "Putting Race Into Context: Race, Juvenile Justice Processing, and Urbanization," *Justice Quarterly 15* (1998): 487–504.

93. Ibid., p. 501.

94. Ibid., p. 502.

95. A study of juvenile justice outcomes in Ohio also found evidence of indirect discrimination. This study revealed that African American youth whose families were receiving welfare benefits were more likely than African American youth whose families were not on welfare to be placed in secure confinement following adjudication. The same pattern was not observed for whites. According to the authors, this suggests that "only minority families on welfare are regarded as unsuitable for supervising their delinquent children." Bohsiu Wu and Angel Ilarraza Fuentes, "The Entangled Effects of Race and Urban Poverty," *Juvenile and Family Court Journal 49* (1998): 41–53.

96. R. Barry Ruback and Paula J. Vardaman, "Decision Making in Delinquency Cases: The Role of Race and Juveniles' Admission/Denial of the Crime, *Law and Human Behavior 21* (1997): 47–69.

97. Ibid., p. 52.

98. Ibid., p. 59.

99. Ibid., p. 67.

100. Dae-Hoon Kwak, "The Interaction of Age, Gender, and Race/Ethnicity on Juvenile Justice Decision Making in Nebraska." Unpublished master's thesis, University of Nebraska at Omaha, 2004.

101. Ibid., Table 5.

102. Philip E. Secret and James B. Johnson, "The Effect of Race on Juvenile Justice Decision Making in Nebraska: Detention, Adjudication, and Disposition, 1988–1993," *Justice Quarterly 14* (1997): 445–478.

103. Ibid., p. 274.

104. Office of Juvenile Justice and Delinquency Prevention, *Juvenile Arrests 2003*, p. 4.

105. U.S. Department of Justice, Federal Bureau of Investigation, *Crime in the United States 1994* (Washington, DC: U.S. Government Printing Office, 1995), pp. 227–228.

106. Office of Juvenile Justice and Delinquency Prevention, *Juvenile Arrests 2003*, p. 3.

107. "Chicago Boy, 12, Will Be Youngest in U.S. Prison," *Omaha World Herald*, January 31, 1996.

108. United States General Accounting Office, *Juvenile Justice: Juveniles Processed in*

Criminal Court and Case Dispositions (Washington, DC: GAO, 1995), p. 2.

109. National Center for Juvenile Justice, *Which States Waive Juveniles to Criminal Court?* (Pittsburgh, PA: National Center for Juvenile Justice, 2004).

110. National Center for Juvenile Justice, *Juvenile Court Statistics 2000*, p. 34.

111. Ibid., p. 36.

112. Ibid., p. 37.

113. Mike Males and Dan Macallair, *The Color of Justice: An Analysis of Juvenile Justice Adult Court Transfers in California* (Washington, DC: Justice Policy Institute, 2000).

114. Office of Juvenile Justice and Delinquency Prevention, *Juvenile Transfers to Criminal Court in the 1990s: Lessons Learned from Four Studies* (Washington, DC: Office of Juvenile Justice and Delinquency Prevention, 2000).

115. Ibid., p. 13.

116. See, for example, Office of Juvenile Justice and Delinquency Prevention, *Major Issues in Juvenile Justice Information and Training Youth in Adult Courts–Between Two Worlds* (Washington, DC: Office of Juvenile Justice and Delinquency Prevention, 1982).

117. Fagan, Jeffrey. *The Comparative Impacts of Juvenile and Criminal Court Sanctions on Adolescent Offenders* (Washington, DC: Office of Justice Programs, National Institute of Justice, 1991).

118. Megan C. Kurlychek and Brian D. Johnson, "The Juvenile Penalty: A Comparison of Juvenile and Young Adult Sentencing Outcomes in Criminal Court," *Criminology 42* (2004): 485–515.

119. Ibid., p. 500.

120. Ibid., p. 502.

121. Ibid., p. 505.

122. Secret and Johnson, "The Effect of Race on Juvenile Justice Decision Making in Nebraska."

123. Ibid., p. 450.

124. Coramae Richey Mann, *Unequal Justice: A Question of Color* (Bloomington, IN: Indiana University Press, 1993), p. 255.

125. R. Lefcourt, "The Administration of Criminal Law," in *Criminal Justice in America*, Richard Quinney, ed. (Boston: Little Brown, 1974).

126. George S. Bridges and Sara Steen, "Racial Disparities in Official Assessments of Juvenile Offenders: Attributional Stereotypes as Mediating Mechanisms," *American Sociological Review 63*: 554–570.

127. Ibid., p. 558.

128. Ibid., pp. 563–564.

129. Ibid., p. 564.

130. Ibid., p. 567.

131. Ibid., p. 567.

132. Ibid., p. 567.

133. Office of Juvenile Justice and Delinquency Preventions, *Juvenile Court Statistics 2000*.

134. Office of Juvenile Justice and Delinquency Prevention, *Juveniles in Corrections* (Washington, DC: Office of Juvenile Justice and Delinquency Prevention, 2004).

135. Ibid., p. 10.

136. Ibid., p. 11.

137. Ibid., p. 19.

138. Ibid., p. 21.

139. Jeffrey Reiman, *The Rich Get Richer and the Poor Get Prison.*

140. Lori Dorfman and Vincent Schiraldi, "Off Balance: Youth, Race and Crime in the News," Executive Summary. Berkeley Media Studies Group, 2001. Available at www.buildingblocksforyouth.org/media/.

141. Ibid. p. 3

142. Ibid. p. 4.

143. Ibid.

144. Ibid.

145. Ibid. p. 8.

11

The Color of Justice

Race, ethnicity, and crime are bound together in American society. It is impossible to discuss policing, sentencing, the death penalty, or employment in the criminal justice system without confronting issues of race and ethnicity. Moreover, most Americans believe there is a close link. Perceptions of crime and justice involve issues of race and ethnicity. Many of those perceptions reflect distortions rooted in stereotypes and prejudice.

Other Americans take a different but equally extreme position. They believe that it is inaccurate and misleading to suggest that crime is synonymous with African American crime and argue that our current crime control policies—which emphasize more police, higher bail, harsher sentences—have a disparate effect on African Americans and Hispanics. These critics also believe that those who argue that the solution to the crime problem is to "lock 'em up and throw away the key" usually visualize the faces behind the bars as black, brown, or red. They suggest that racism permeates the criminal justice system and insist that racially biased decisions are the norm, not the exception to the general rule, of impartiality.

This book has attempted to sort out the facts and the myths and to reach an understanding of the racial and ethnic aspects of criminal justice based on a clear-eyed look at the evidence. The basic controversy is whether there is discrimination in the system, and if there is, how much. Some people believe there are no serious patterns of discrimination, apart from occasional lapses by bad officials. Others argue that discrimination against African Americans and other people of color is pervasive and systematic, that it occurs in all parts of the justice system and in all regions of the country.

We argue that the truth lies somewhere between these two extremes. To say that there is no discrimination ignores many of the complexities of crime in the United States and presents an overly optimistic view of the treatment of people of color by the system. Arguing that discrimination is pervasive and systematic, however, ignores some important data about how the system works.

We believe that a fair assessment of the evidence indicates that the criminal justice system is characterized by obvious disparities based on race and ethnicity.

It is impossible to ignore the disproportionate number of minorities arrested, imprisoned, and on death row. Some of the decisions that produce these results involve discrimination. It is impossible to ignore the recent cases of innocent people who have been exonerated by DNA evidence. Most of these people are people of color. It is also impossible to ignore the underemployment of African Americans and Hispanics in the justice system. The question we have wrestled with in this book, however, is whether there is *systematic* racial and ethnic discrimination. After considering all of the evidence, we conclude that the U.S. criminal justice system is characterized by *contextual* discrimination—that is, discrimination occurs in certain parts of the justice system but not necessarily all parts all the time. Understanding this point is often difficult, but it is also what makes the study of race, crime, and justice so fascinating. There are no simple answers, and the pursuit of evidence-based answers is the challenge and the reward of studying criminal justice.

RACE, CRIME, AND JUSTICE

The overriding goal of this book is to separate fact from fiction and myth from reality. We have shown that it is inaccurate and misleading to equate crime with African American crime and to characterize the typical victim as white, the typical offender as African American, and the typical crime as an interracial act of violence. Victimization data consistently reveal that African Americans and Hispanics are more likely than whites to fall victim to household and personal crime. The racial differences are particularly pronounced for crimes of violence, especially murder and robbery. Crime statistics also reveal that *intra*racial crimes occur more often than *inter*racial crimes.

As a result of this, African Americans have been the primary beneficiaries of the great crime drop in the United States since the early 1990s. The dramatic decline in homicides, particularly gun crimes among young men, has primarily meant fewer deaths among young African American men.

It is less clear that the picture of the typical offender as African American is inaccurate. Certainly more whites than racial minorities are arrested each year, but this is a consequence of the fact that whites comprise 80 percent of the U.S. population and people of color make up only 20 percent, rather than a reflection of a more pronounced propensity toward crime among whites. If we examine arrest *rates*, the picture changes: African Americans are arrested at a disproportionately high rate.

Although criminal justice scholars and policymakers continue to debate the meaning of the disproportionately high African American arrest rate—with some arguing that it reflects a higher offending rate and others that it signals selective enforcement of the law—there is no denying the fact that African Americans are arrested more often than one would expect, particularly for crimes of violence such as murder, rape, and robbery. The explanation for this overrepresentation is complex, incorporating social, economic, and political factors.

| Systematic Discrimination | Institutionalized Discrimination | Contextual Discrimination | Individual Acts of Discrimination | Pure Justice |

FIGURE 11.1 Discrimination Continuum

It thus seems clear that one cannot paint an accurate picture of crime in the United States without relying to some extent on race and ethnicity. Race and crime *are* linked, although not necessarily in the ways that most Americans assume.

We also have shown that the criminal justice system is neither completely free of racial bias nor systematically racially biased. In Chapter 1 we suggested that there are different types and degrees of racial discrimination (Figure 11.1). At one end of the "discrimination continuum" is pure justice, which means that there is no discrimination at any time, place, or point in the criminal justice system. At the other end is systematic discrimination, which means that discrimination prevails at all stages of the criminal justice system, in all places, and at all times.

We suggest that the U.S. criminal justice system falls between the two ends of the continuum. More specifically, we suggest that the system is characterized by *contextual discrimination*. Racial minorities are treated more harshly than whites at some stages of the criminal justice process (e.g., the decision to seek or impose the death penalty) but no differently than whites at other stages of the process (e.g., the selection of the jury pool). The treatment accorded racial minorities is more punitive than that accorded whites in some regions or jurisdictions, but it is no different than that accorded whites in other regions or jurisdictions. For example, some police departments tolerate excessive force directed at racial minorities or the use of racial profiling, whereas others do not. Racial minorities who commit certain types of crimes (e.g., drug offenses or violent crimes against whites) or who have certain types of characteristics (e.g., they are young, male, and unemployed) are treated more harshly than whites who commit these crimes or have these characteristics.

We are not arguing that the U.S. criminal justice system *never* has been characterized by systematic racial discrimination. In fact, the evidence discussed in earlier chapters suggests just the opposite. The years preceding the civil rights movement (pre-1960s) were characterized by blatant discrimination directed against African Americans and other racial minorities at all stages of the criminal justice process. This pattern of widespread discrimination was not limited to the South; it was found throughout the United States.

Until fairly recently, crimes against African Americans and calls for help from minority communities often were ignored by the police. Racial minorities suspected of crimes, and particularly those suspected of crimes against whites, were more likely than whites to be harassed by the police or subject to racial profiling. They also were more likely than whites to be arrested, subjected to excessive force, and the victims of deadly force.

Also until rather recently, racial minorities who were arrested were routinely denied bail, tried by all-white juries without attorneys to assist them in their defense, and prosecuted and convicted on less-than-convincing evidence. Racial minorities convicted of crimes were sentenced more harshly than whites. They were more likely than whites to be incarcerated and more likely than whites to be sentenced to death and executed.

Our analysis of current research on race and the criminal justice system leads us to conclude that the situation today is somewhat different. Although the contemporary criminal justice system is not characterized by pure justice, many of the grossest racial inequities have been reduced, if not eliminated. Reforms mandated by the U.S. Supreme Court or adopted voluntarily by the states have tempered the blatant racism directed against racial minorities by criminal justice officials.

The Supreme Court consistently has affirmed the importance of protecting criminal suspects' rights. The Court has ruled, for example, that searches without warrants generally are unconstitutional, that confessions cannot be coerced, that suspects must be advised of their rights and provided with attorneys to assist them in their defense, that jurors must be chosen from a representative cross-section of the population, and that the death penalty cannot be administered in an arbitrary and capricious manner.

Most of these decisions reflect the Court's concern with general procedural issues rather than racial discrimination. The Court, in other words, was attempting to safeguard the rights of *all* criminal defendants. Nevertheless, some observers argue that the Supreme Court's consideration of these procedural issues often was "influenced by the realization that in another case they might affect the posture of a Negro in a hostile southern court."[1]

Even when the Court did not explicitly address the question of racial discrimination in the criminal justice system, its rulings on general procedural issues did lead to improvements in the treatment of racial minorities. By insisting that the states protect the rights of all defendants—racial minorities as well as whites—the Supreme Court rulings discussed earlier led indirectly to the elimination of racially biased criminal justice practices and policies. Coupled with reforms adopted voluntarily by the states, these decisions made systematic racial discrimination unlikely.

We want to reiterate that we are not suggesting that racial discrimination has been completely eliminated from the American criminal justice system. It is certainly true that in the early 21st century, whites who commit crimes against African Americans are not beyond the reach of the criminal justice system, African Americans suspected of crimes against whites do not receive "justice" at the hand of white lynch mobs, and African Americans who victimize other African Americans are not immune from punishment. Despite these significant changes, racial inequities persist. As we have shown in the preceding chapters, African Americans and other racial minorities continue to suffer both overt and subtle discrimination within the criminal justice system. Persuasive evidence indicates that racial minorities suffer discrimination at the hands of the police. They are subject to racial profiling and they are more likely than whites to be shot and killed, arrested, and victimized by excessive physical force. In addition, there is evidence of police misconduct directed at racial minorities and evidence that police departments fail to discipline officers found guilty of misconduct.

Compelling evidence also points to discrimination within the court system. Supreme Court decisions and statutory reforms have not eliminated racial bias in decisions regarding bail, charging, plea bargaining, jury selection, and juvenile justice processing. Discrimination in sentencing also persists. Judges in some jurisdictions continue to impose harsher sentences on African American offenders who murder or rape whites and more lenient sentences on African Americans who victimize other African Americans. Judges also impose racially biased sentences in less serious cases; in these "borderline cases," people of color are more likely to get a prison term, whereas whites are more likely to get probation. Partly as a consequence of these discriminatory sentencing practices, the number of African Americans incarcerated in U.S. jails and prisons has swelled; African Americans now comprise a majority of those incarcerated.

We are particularly troubled by the persistence of racial discrimination at two of the most critical stages in the criminal justice process—police use of deadly force and the application of the death penalty. The effect of racial bias in these irrevocable life-or-death decisions is profound. The fact that it persists is deeply disturbing.

Court rulings and policy changes designed to regulate deadly force and death penalty decisions have made racial discrimination less likely. Studies reveal that the ratio of African Americans to whites killed by the police has dropped from approximately 8:1 to 4:1. Studies also reveal that the gross racial disproportions that characterized death penalty decisions earlier in this century, and particularly those that characterized decisions to impose the death penalty for the crime of rape, no longer exist.

Some other important reforms have occurred in recent years. The development of DNA technology has resulted in the exoneration of people wrongfully convicted of serious crimes. Some of these people were facing death sentences. The majority have been African Americans. Some reformers such as the Innocence Project have argued that the use of DNA technology and other reforms will prevent miscarriages of justice from occurring in the first place. This is a promising development, and we will have to see if these reforms are in fact implemented and if they make a difference. There has also been a major effort to eliminate discrimination in traffic enforcement. Reform efforts include data collection, policies to guide officers in making stops, and better training and supervision. We will also have to monitor the future to see if these efforts produce positive results.

This clearly is progress. However, we cannot ignore the fact that discrimination remains in these two critical decisions—both of which involve the ultimate decision to take the life of another person. Moreover, the fact that discrimination persists in the face of legal efforts to eradicate it suggests that decision making in these two areas reflects racial stereotypes and deeply buried racial prejudices. It suggests that police officers' definitions of dangerousness, and thus their willingness to use deadly force, depend to some degree on the race of the suspect. It suggests that judges' and jurors' assessments of the heinousness of a crime, and thus their willingness to impose the death penalty, are influenced by the race of the offender and the race of the victim.

Our analysis of race and crime in the United States suggests that those who conclude that "the criminal justice system is not racist"[2] are misinformed. Although reforms have made systematic racial discrimination—discrimination in all stages, in all places, and at all times—unlikely, the U.S. criminal justice system has never been, and is not now, color blind.

NOTES

1. Archibald Cox, *The Warren Court* (Cambridge: Harvard University Press, 1968), p. 6.

2. William Wilbanks, *The Myth of a Racist Criminal Justice System* (Belmont, CA: Wadsworth, 1987), p. 10.

Selected Bibliography

Adler, Jeffery S. "The Dynamite, Wreckage, and Scum in our Cities: The Social Construction of Deviance in Industrial America." *Justice Quarterly 11* (1994): 33–49.

Akers, Ronald L. *Social Learning and Social Structure: A General Theory of Crime and Deviance.* Boston: Northeastern University Press, 1994.

Albonetti, Celesta A. "An Integration of Theories to Explain Judicial Discretion." *Social Problems 38* (1991): 247–266.

Albonetti, Celesta A. "Criminality, Prosecutorial Screening, and Uncertainty: Toward a Theory of Discretionary Decision Making in Felony Case Processing." *Criminology 24* (1986): 623–644.

Albonetti, Celesta A. "Sentencing Under the Federal Sentencing Guidelines: Effects of Defendant Characteristics, Guilty Pleas, and Departures on Sentencing Outcomes for Drug Offenses, 1991–1992." *Law & Society Review 31* (1997): 789–822.

Albonetti, Celesta A., Robert M. Hauser, John Hagan, and Ilene H. Nagel. "Criminal Justice Decision Making as a Stratification Process: The Role of Race and Stratification Resources in Pretrial Release." *Journal of Quantitative Criminology 5* (1989): 57–82.

Allen, James Paul, and Eugene James Turner. *We The People: An Atlas of America's Ethnic Diversity.* New York: Macmillan, 1988.

Alschuler, Albert W. "Racial Quotas and the Jury." *Duke Law Journal 44* (1995): 44.

Alvarez, Alexander, and Ronet D. Bachman. "American Indians and Sentencing Disparity: An Arizona Test," *Journal of Criminal Justice 24* (1996): 549–561.

American Bar Association. *Race and the Law: Special Report.* Chicago: American Bar Association, February 1999.

American Bar Association. "Whatever You Think About the Death Penalty, A System That Will Take Life Must First Give Justice: A Report from the IR&R Death Penalty Committee." 24 W.T.R. *Hum. Rts.* 22 (1997).

American Bar Association Commission on Racial and Ethnic Diversity in the Profession. *Miles to Go 2000: Progress of Minorities in the Legal Profession.* Chicago: American Bar Association, 2000.

American Civil Liberties Union, *Driving While Black*. New York: ACLU, 1999.

American Civil Liberties Union, *Federal Death Row: Is It Really Color-Blind? Analysis of June 6 Department of Justice Report on the Death Penalty*. Available at http://www.aclu.org/Congress/10614la.htm.

American Correctional Association. *1993 Directory of Juvenile and Adult Correctional Departments, Institutions, Agencies and Paroling Authorities*. Laurel, MD: American Correctional Associations, 1993.

American Friends Service Committee. *Struggle for Justice: A Report on Crime and Punishment in America*. Boston: Little, Brown, 1971.

Amsterdam, Anthony. "Race and the Death Penalty." *Criminal Justice Ethics* 7 (1988): 84–86.

Anderson, Philip S. "Striving for a Just Society." *ABA Journal*. February (1999): 66.

Arthur, John A. "Correctional Ideology of Black Correctional Officers." *Federal Probation* 58 (1994): 57–65.

Austin, J., Krisberg, B., and Litsky, P. "The Effectiveness of Supervised Pretrial Release." *Crime and Delinquency 31* (1985): 519–537.

Bachman, Ronet D., Alexander Alvarez, and C. Perkins. "The Discriminatory Imposition of the Law: Does It Affect Sentence Outcomes for American Indians?" In *Native Americans, Crime and Justice*, Marianne O. Nielsen and Robert A. Silverman, eds., Boulder, CO: Westview Press, 1996.

Baldus, David C., Charles Pulaski, and George Woodworth. "Comparative Review of Death Sentences: An Empirical Study of the Georgia Experience." *The Journal of Criminal Law & Criminology 74* (1983): 661–673.

Baldus, David C., George Woodworth, and Charles A. Pulaski. *Equal Justice and the Death Penalty: A Legal and Empirical Analysis*. Boston: Northeastern University Press, 1990.

Baldus, David C., George Woodworth, and Charles A. Pulaski. "Monitoring and Evaluating Contemporary Death Penalty Systems: Lessons from Georgia." *University of California at Davis Law Review 18* (1985): 1375–1407.

Barak, Gregg. "Between the Waves: Mass-Mediated Themes of Crime and Justice." *Social Justice 21* (1994).

Barak, Gregg, Jeanne M. Flavin, and Paul S. Leighton. *Class, Race, Gender, and Crime: Social Realities of Justice in America*. Los Angeles: Roxbury, 2001.

Barkan, Steven E. and Steven F. Cohn. "Racial Prejudice and Support for the Death Penalty by Whites." *Journal of Research in Crime and Delinquency 31* (1994): 202–209.

Baumer, Eric P., Steven F. Messner, and Richard Rosenfeld. "Explaining Structural Variation in Support for Capital Punishment: A Multilevel Analysis." *American Journal of Sociology 108* (2003).

Bayley, David H. and Harold Mendelsohn. *Minorities and the Police: Confrontation in America*. New York: The Free Press, 1969.

Bedau, Hugo A., and Michael L. Radelet. "Miscarriages of Justice in Potentially Capital Cases." *Stanford Law Review 40* (1987): 21–179.

Beres, Linda S. and Thomas D. Griffith. "Demonizing Youth." *Loyola of Los Angeles Law Review 34* (2001): 747–768.

Berk, Richard and Alec Campbell. "Preliminary Data on Race and Crack Charging Practices in Los Angeles." *Federal Sentencing Reporter 6* (1993).

Bernstein Nagel, Ilene, William R. Kelly, and Patricia A. Doyle. "Societal Reaction to Deviants: The Case of Criminal Defendants." *American Sociological Review 42* (1977): 743–755.

Bernstein Nagel, Ilene, Edward Kick, Jan T. Leung, and Barbara Schultz. "Charge Reduction: An Intermediary State in the Process of Labeling Criminal Defendants." *Social Forces 56* (1977).

Bing, Robert. "Politicizing Black-on-Black Crime: A Critique of Terminological Preference." In *Black-on-Black Crime*, P. Ray Kedia, ed., Bristol, IN: Wyndham Hall Press, 1994.

Bishop, Donna M. and Charles E. Frazier. "The Influence of Race in Juvenile Justice Processing." *Journal of Research in Crime and Delinquency 25* (1988): 242–263.

Bishop, Donna M. and Charles E. Frazier. "Race Effects in Juvenile Justice Decision-Making: Findings of a Statewide Analysis." *Journal of Criminal Law and Criminology 86* (1996): 392–414.

Black, Donald. *The Manners and Customs of the Police*. New York: Academic Press, 1980.

Black, Donald. "The Social Organization of Arrest." In *The Manners and Customs of the Police*, Donald Black, ed. (New York: Academic Press, 1980).

Blumberg, Abraham S. "The Practice of Law as a Confidence Game: Organizational Cooptation of a Profession." *Law & Society Review 1* (1967): 15–39.

Blumstein, Alfred. "On the disproportionality of United States' Prison Populations." *The Journal of Criminal Law and Criminology 73* (1982): 1259–1281.

Blumstein, Alfred, Jacqueline Cohen, Susan E. Martin, and Michael Tonry. *Research on Sentencing: The Search for Reform*, Vol. I. Washington, DC: National Academy Press, 1983.

Bohm, Robert M. "American Death Penalty Opinion, 1936–1986: A Critical Examination of the Gallup Polls." In *The Death Penalty in America: Current Research*. Robert M. Bohm, ed. Cincinnati: Anderson, 1991.

Boland, Barbara (INSLAW Inc.). *The Prosecution of Felony Arrests*. Washington DC: Bureau of Justice Statistics (1983).

Bowers, William. "Capital Punishment and Contemporary Values: People's Misgivings and the Court's Misperceptions." *Law & Society Review 27* (1993): 157–176.

Bowers, William. "The Pervasiveness of Arbitrariness and Discrimination Under Post-Furman Capital Statutes." *The Journal of Criminal Law & Criminology 74* (1983): 1067–1100.

Bowers, William and Glenn L. Pierce. "Arbitrariness and Discrimination Under Post-*Furman* Capital Statutes." *Crime and Delinquency 74* (1980): 1067–1100.

Box, Steven and Chris Hale. "Unemployment, Imprisonment, and Prison Overcrowding." *Contemporary Crises 9* (1985): 209–228.

Bridges, George S. *A Study on Racial and Ethnic Disparities in Superior Court Bail and Pre-Trial Detention Practices in Washington*. Olympia, WA: Washington State Minority and Justice Commission, 1997.

Bridges, George S., and Robert D. Crutchfield. "Law, Social Standing and Racial Disparities in Imprisonment." *Social Forces 66* (1988): 699–724.

Bridges, George S. and Sara Steen. "Racial Disparities in Official Assessments of Juvenile Offending: Attributional Stereotypes as Mediating Mechanisms." *American Sociological Review 65* (1998): 554–570.

Bright, Stephen B. "Discrimination, Death and Denial: The Tolerance of Racial Discrimination in the Infliction of the Death Penalty." *Santa Clara Law Review 35* (1995): 901–950.

Bright, Stephen B. and Patrick J. Keenan. "Judges and the Politics of Death: Deciding Between the Bill of Rights and the Next Election in Capital Cases," *Boston University Law Review 75* (1995): 759–835.

Brosi, Kathleen B. *A Cross-City Comparison of Felony Case Procession.* Washington DC: Institute for Law and Social Research, 1979.

Browning, Sandra Lee, Francis T. Cullen, Liqun Cao, Renee Kopache, and Thomas J. Stevenson. "Race and Getting Hassled by the Police: A Research Note." *Police Studies 17* (No. 1 1994): 1–11.

Brownmiller, Susan. *Against Our Will: Men, Women and Rape*, New York: Bantam Books, 1975.

Building Blocks for Youth. *And Justice For Some.* Washington, DC: Building Blocks for Youth, 2000.

Bureau of Justice Statistics. *Black Victims.* Washington, DC: Government Printing Office, 1990.

Bureau of Justice Statistics. *Capital Punishment 1991.* Washington, DC: U.S. Department of Justice, 1992.

Bureau of Justice Statistics. *Contacts between Police and the Public: Findings from the 1999 National Survey*, NCJ 184057. Washington, DC: U.S. Government Printing Office, 2001. Available at www.ncjrs.org.

Bureau of Justice Statistics. *Criminal Victimization in the United States, 2003: Statistical Tables.* Available at http://www.ojp.usdoj.gov/bjs/abstract/cvusst.htm.

Bureau of Justice Statistics. *Felony Defendants in Large Urban Counties, 2000.* Washington DC: U.S. Department of Justice, 2003.

Bureau of Justice Statistics. *Hispanic Victims.* Washington, DC: Government Printing Office, 1990.

Bureau of Justice Statistics. *Policing and Homicide, 1976–98: Justifiable Homicide by Police, Police Officers Murdered by Felons.* Washington, DC: U.S. Government Printing Office, 2001.

Bureau of Justice Statistics. *Pretrial Release of Felony Defendancy, 1992.* Washington, DC: U.S. Department of Justice (1994): 13–14.

Bureau of Justice Statistics. *Prison and Jail Inmates at Midyear 2001.* Washington, DC: U.S. Department of Justice, 2002.

Bureau of Justice Statistics. *Prison and Jail Inmates at Midyear 2004.* Washington, DC: U.S. Department of Justice, 2005.

Bureau of Justice Statistics. *Police Use of Force: Collection of National Data.* Washington, DC: Government Printing Office, 1997.

Bureau of Justice Statistics. *Weapon Use and Violent Crime.* Washington, DC: U.S. Department of Justice, 2003.

Burns, Haywood. "Black People and the Tyranny of American Law." *The Annals of the American Academy of Political and Social Sciences 407* (1973): 156–166.

Butler, Paul. "Racially Based Jury Nullification: Black Power in the Criminal Justice System." *Yale Law Journal 105* (1995): 677–725.

Bynum, Timothy S. and Raymond Paternoster. "Discrimination Revisited: An Exploration of Frontstage and Backstage Criminal Justice Decision Making." *Sociology and Social Research 69* (1984): 90–108.

Cahalan, Margaret Werner. *Historical Corrections Statistics in the United States, 1850–1984.* Washington, DC: Government Printing Office, 1986.

Campbell, Anne. *Girls in the Gang: A Report from New York City.* Oxford: Basil Blackwell, 1984.

Campbell, Anne. *The Girls in the Gang.* 2nd ed. Cambridge, MA: Basil Blackwell, 1991.

Carter, Dan T. *Scottsboro: A Tragedy of the American South.* Baton Rouge: Louisiana State University Press, 1969.

Carter, David L. "Hispanic Interaction with the Criminal Justice System in Texas: Experiences, Attitudes, and Perceptions." *Journal of Criminal Justice 11* (1983): 213–227.

Carter, Terry. "Divided Justice." *ABA Journal* February (1999): 42–45.

Casper, Jonathan D. *Criminal Courts: The Defendant's Perspective.* Englewood Cliffs, NJ: Prentice Hall, 1978.

Casper, Jonathan D. "'Did You Have a Lawyer When You Went to Court?' No, I Had a Public Defender." *Yale Review of Law & Social Action 1* (1971): 4–9.

Cernkovich, Stephen A. and Peggy C. Giordano. "School Bonding, Race, and Delinquency." *Criminology 30* (1992).

Chambers, David L., Timothy T. Clydesdale, William C. Kidder, and Richard O. Lempert. "The Real Impact of Eliminating Affirmative Action in American Law Schools: An Empirical Critique of Richard Sander's Study." *Stanford Law Review 57* (2005): 1855–1898.

Chambliss, William J. "Crime Control and Ethnic Minorities: Legitimizing Racial Oppression by Creating Moral Panics." In *Ethnicity, Race, and Crime: Perspectives Across Time and Place*, Darnell F. Hawkins, ed. Albany, NY: State University of New York Press, 1995.

Chin, Ko-Lin, Jeffrey Fagan, and Robert J. Kelly. "Patterns of Chinese Gang Extortion" *Justice Quarterly 9* (1992): 625–646.

Chiricos, Theodore G. "The Moral Panic of the Drug War." In *Race and Criminal Justice*, Michael J. Lynch and E. Britt Patterson, eds. New York: Harrow & Heston, 1995.

Chiricos, Theodore G. and William D. Bales. "Unemployment and Punishment: An Empirical Assessment." *Criminology 29* (1991): 701–724.

Chiricos, Theodore G. and Charles Crawford. "Race and Imprisonment: A Contextual Assessment of the Evidence." In *Ethnicity, Race and Crime*, Darnell F. Hawkins ed., Albany: State University of New York Press, 1995.

Chiricos, Theodore G. and Miriam A. DeLone. "Labor Surplus and Punishment: A Review and Assessment of Theory and Evidence." *Social Problems 39* (1992): 421–446.

Clarke, S. H. and G. G. Koch. "The Influence of Income and Other Factors on Whether Criminal Defendants Go To Prison." *Law & Society Review 11* (1976): 57–92.

Cole, David. *No Equal Justice: Race and Class in the American Criminal Justice System.* New York: New Press, 1999.

Covey, Herbert C., Scott Menard, and Robert J. Franzese. *Juvenile Gangs.* Springfield, IL: Charles C. Thomas, 1992.

Cox, Judith A. "Addressing Disproportionate Minority Representation Within the Juvenile Justice System." Available at http://www.buildingblocksforyouth.org.

Crockett, George. "The Role of the Black Judge." In *The Criminal Justice System and Blacks*, D. Georges-Abeyie, ed. New York: Clark Boardman, 1984.

Crutchfield, Robert D., Joseph G. Weis, Rodney L. Engen, and Randy R. Gainey. *Racial and Ethnic Disparities in the Prosecution of Felony Cases in King County*. Olympia Washington: Washington State Minority and Justice Commission, 1995.

Curriden, Mark and Leroy Phillips Jr. *Contempt of Court: The Turn-of-the-Century Lynching that Launched a Hundred Years of Federalism*. New York: Faber and Faber, 1999.

D'Alessio, Stewart J. and Lisa Stolzenberg. "Race and the Probability of Arrest" *Social Forces 81* (2003): 1381–1397.

Davis, Kenneth Culp. *Discretionary Justice: A Preliminary Inquiry*. Baton Rouge: Louisiana State University Press, 1969.

Death Penalty Information Center. *The Death Penalty in 2001: Year-End Report*. Washington, DC: Death Penalty Information Center, 2001.

Decker, David L., David Shichor, and Robert M. O'Brien. *Urban Structure and Victimization*. Lexington, MA: D.C. Heath, 1982.

Decker, Scott H. "Citizen Attitudes Toward the Police: A Review of Past Findings and Suggestions for Future Policy." *Journal of Police Science and Administration 9* (1981): 80–87.

DeJong, Christina and Kenneth C. Jackson. "Putting Race Into Context: Race, Juvenile Justice Processing, and Urbanization." *Justice Quarterly 15* (1998): 487–504.

Demuth, Stephen and Darrell Steffensmeier. "The Impact of Gender and Race-Ethnicity in the Pretrial Release Process." *Social Problems 51* (2004): 222–242.

Dixon, Jo. "The Organizational Context of Criminal Sentencing." *American Journal of Sociology 100* (1995): 1157–1198.

Dorfman, Lori and Vincent Schiraldi, "Off Balance: Youth, Race and Crime in the News" Executive Summary. Berkeley Media Studies Group, 2001. Available at www.buildingblocksforyouth.org/media/.

Du Bois, W.E.B. "The Spawn of Slavery: The Convict-Lease System in the South." *The Missionary Review of the World 14* (1901): 373–745.

Dulaney, W. Marvin. *Black Police in America*. Bloomington: Indiana University Press, 1996.

Elliot, Delbert, David Huizinga, Brian Knowles, and Rachel Canter. *The Prevalence and Incidence of Delinquent Behavior: 1976–1980: National Estimates of Delinquent Behavior by Sex, Race, Social Class and Other Selected Variables*. Boulder, CO: Behavioral Research Institute, 1983.

Engel, Jeremy. "Federal Judge Approves $4.5 Million Settlement in Pratt Case." *Metropolitan News-Enterprise, Capitol News Service*. May 1, 2000.

Engle, Charles Donald. *Criminal Justice in the City: A Study of Sentence Severity and Variation in the Philadelphia Court System*. Ph.D. dissertation, Temple University, 1971.

Esbensen, Finn-Aage and David Huizinga. "Gangs, Drugs and Delinquency." *Criminology 31* (1993): 565–590.

Espiritu, Nicholas. "(E)racing Youth: The Racialized Construction of California's Proposition 21 and the Development of Alternate Contestations." *Cleveland State Law Review 52* (2005).

Everett, Ronald S. and Barbara C. Nienstedt. "Race, Remorse, and Sentence Reduction: Is Saying You're Sorry Enough?" *Justice Quarterly 16* (1999): 99–122.

Everett, Ronald S. and Roger A. Wojtkiewicz. "Difference, Disparity, and Race/Ethnic Bias in Federal Sentencing." *Journal of Quantitative Criminology 18* (2002).

Fagan, Jeffrey. *The Comparative Impacts of Juvenile and Criminal Court Sanctions on Adolescent Offenders*. Washington, DC: Office of Justice Programs, National Institute of Justice, 1991.

Fagan, Jeffrey. "The Social Organization of Drug Use and Drug Dealing Among Urban Gangs." *Criminology 27* (1989): 633–666.

Farnworth, Margaret and Patrick Horan. "Separate Justice: An Analysis of Race Differences in Court Processes." *Social Science Research 9* (1980): 381–399.

Farrell, Ronald A. and Victoria L. Swigert. "Prior Offense Record as a Self-Fulfilling Prophecy." *Law & Society Review 12* (1978): 437–453.

Feeley, Malcolm M. *The Process Is the Punishment: Handling Cases in a Lower Criminal Court*. New York: Russell Sage Foundation, 1979.

Feimer, Steve, Frank Pommersheim, and Steve Wise. "Marking Time: Does Race Make a Difference? A Study of Disparate Sentencing in South Dakota." *Journal of Crime and Justice 13* (1990): 86–102.

Feld, Barry C. *Bad Kids: Race and the Transformation of the Juvenile Court*. New York: Oxford University Press, 1999.

Flowers, Ronald Barri. *Minorities and Criminality*. Westport: Greenwood Press, 1988.

Fong, Robert, Ronald Vogel, and Salvador Buentello. "Prison Gang Dynamics: A Look Inside the Texas Department of Corrections." In *Corrections: Dilemmas and Directions*, Peter J. Benekos and Alida V. Merlo, eds. Highland Heights, KY: Anderson Publishing Co. and Academy of Criminal Justice Sciences, 1992.

Foote, Caleb. "Compelling Appearance in Court: Administration of Bail in Philadelphia." *University of Pennsylvania Law Review 102* (1954): 1031–1079.

Fosdisk, Raymond. *American Police Systems*. Montclair, NJ: Patterson Smith Reprint Series, 1972.

Fox, James Allen, Michael L. Radelet, and Julie L. Bonsteel. "Death Penalty Opinion in the Post-*Furman* Years." *New York University Review of Law and Social Change 18* (1990–91): 499–528.

Fox, James Allen and Marianne W. Zawitz. *Homicide Trends in the United States*. Washington DC: U.S. Department of Justice, 2004. Available at www.ojp.usdoj. gov/bjs.

Frankel, Marvin. *Criminal Sentences: Law Without Order*. New York: Hill and Wang, 1972.

Frazier, Charles E. and Donna M. Bishop. "Reflections on Race Effects in Juvenile Justice." In *Minorities in Juvenile Justice*, Kimberly Kempf Leonard, Carl E. Pope, and William H. Feyerherm, eds. Thousand Oaks, CA: Sage, 1995.

Fyfe, James J. "Who Shoots? A Look at Officer Race and Police Shooting." *Journal of Police Science and Administration 9* (1981): 367–382.

Fyfe, James J. "Blind Justice: Police Shootings in Memphis." *Journal of Criminal Law and Criminology 73* (1982): 707–722.

Garfinkel, Harold. "Research Notes on Inter- and Intra-Racial Homicides." *Social Forces 27* (1949): 369–381.

Geller, William A. and Hans Toch, eds. *And Justice For All*. Washington, DC: Police Executive Research Forum, 1995.

Geller, William A. and Michael S. Scott. *Deadly Force: What We Know*. Washington, DC: Police Executive Research Forum, 1992.

Gilliard, Darrell K. and Allen Beck. *Prisoners, 1993*. Washington, DC: U.S. Department of Justice, 1994.

Goldcamp, John S. "Danger and Detention: A Second Generation of Bail Reform." *The Journal of Criminal Law and Criminology 76* (1985): 1–74.

Goodstein, Lynne and Doris Layton MacKenzie. "Racial Differences in Adjustment Patterns of Prison Inmates—Prisonization, Conflict, Stress and Control." *The Criminal Justice System and Blacks*, Daniel Georges-Abeyie, ed. New York: Clark Boardman Company, Ltd., 1984.

Gottfredson, Michael R. and Travis Hirschi. *A General Theory of Crime*. Stanford, CA: Stanford University Press, 1985.

Gottschall, Jon. "Carter's Judicial Appointments: The Influence of Affirmative Action and Merit Selection on Voting on the U.S. Courts of Appeals." *Judicature 67* (1983): 167–173.

Greenberg, David F. "'Justice' and Criminal Justice." *Crime Control and Criminal Justice: The Delicate Balance*, Darnell F. Hawkins, Samuel L. Meyers Jr., and Randolph N. Stone, eds. Westport, CT: Greenwood, 2002.

Greenfeld, Lawrence and Steven K. Smith. *American Indians and Crime*. Washington, DC: Bureau of Justice Statistics, 1999.

Grobsmith, Elizabeth S. *Indians in Prison*. Lincoln: University of Nebraska Press, 1994.

Gross, Samuel R., Kristen Jacoby, Daniel J. Matheson, Nicholas Montgomery, and Sujata Patil. "Exonerations in the United States 1989 through 2003." *Journal of Criminal Law & Criminology 95* (2005).

Gross, Samuel R. and Robert Mauro. *Death & Discrimination: Racial Disparities in Capital Sentencing*. Boston: Northeastern University Press, 1989.

Hacker, Andrew. *Two Nations: Black and White, Separate, Hostile, Unequal*. New York: Scribners, 1992.

Hagan, John. "Extra-Legal Attributes and Criminal Sentencing: An Assessment of a Sociological Viewpoint." *Law & Society Review 8* (1974): 357–383.

Hagan, John. "Parameters of Criminal Prosecution: An Application of Path Analysis to a Problem of Criminal Justice." *Journal of Criminal Law and Criminology 65* (1975).

Hagan, John and Kristin Bumiller. "Making Sense of Sentencing: A Review and Critique of Sentencing Research." *Research on Sentencing: The Search for Reform*. Alfred Blumstein, Jacqueline Cohen, Susan Martin, and Michael Tonry, eds. Washington, DC: National Academy Press, 1983.

Hagedorn, John M. *People and Folks*. Chicago: Lake View Press, 1989.

Hall, Edwin L. and Albert A. Simkins. "Inequality in the Types of Sentences Received by Native Americans and Whites." *Criminology 13* (1975): 199–222.

Hamm, Mark S. *American Skinheads*. Westport, CT: Praeger, 1994.

Hanson, Roger A. and Brian J. Ostrom. "Indigent Defenders Get the Job Done and Done Well." *Criminal Justice: Law and Politics*, 6th edition, George Cole, ed. Belmont, CA: Wadsworth, 1993.

Harlow, Caroline Wolf. *Hate Crime Reported by Victims and Police*. Washington, DC: U.S. Department of Justice, 2005.

Harris, David. *Profiles in Injustice: Why Racial Profiling Doesn't Work.* New York: New Press, 2002.

Harris, Mary G. *Cholas: Latino Girls in Gangs.* New York: AMS Press, 1988.

Harris, Philip W. "Over-Simplification and Error in Public Opinion Surveys on Capital Punishment." *Justice Quarterly 3* (1986): 429–455.

Harris, Philip W., Wayne N. Welsh, and Frank Butler. "A Century of Juvenile Justice." *Criminal Justice 2000, The Nature of Crime: Continuity and Change,* Vol. I. Washington, DC: National Institute of Justice, 2000.

Hawkins, Darnell F. "Beyond Anomalies: Rethinking the Conflict Perspective on Race and Criminal Justice." *Social Forces 65* (1987): 719–745.

Hawkins, Darnell F. "Ethnicity: The Forgotten Dimension of American Social Control." In Inequality, Crime, and Social Control, George S. Bridges and Martha A. Myers, eds. Boulder, CO: Westview Press, 1994.

Hawkins, Darnell F., ed. *Ethnicity, Race, and Crime.* Albany, NY: State University of New York Press, 1995.

Hawkins, Darnell F. and Kenneth A. Hardy. "Black-White Imprisonment Rates: A State-by-State Analysis." *Social Justice 16* (1989): 75–94.

Hayden, George, Joseph Senna, and Larry Siegel. "Prosecutorial Discretion in Peremptory Challenges: An Empirical Investigation of Information Use in the Massachusetts Jury Selection Process," *New England Law Review 13* (1978): 768–790.

Herbst, Leigh, and Samuel Walker. "Language Barriers in the Delivery of Police Services: A Study of Police and Hispanic Interactions in a Midwestern City." *Journal of Criminal Justice 29,* no. 4 (2001): 329–340.

Higgins, Michael. "Few Are Chosen." *ABA Journal.* February (1999): 253.

Hindelang, Michael J. "Race and Involvement in Common Law Personal Crimes." *American Sociological Review 43* (1978): 93–109.

Hirschi, Travis. *Causes of Delinquency.* Berkeley, CA: University of California Press, 1969.

Hoffman, Morris B. "Peremptory Challenges: Lawyers Are From Mars, Judges Are From Venus," 3 Green Bag 2d 135 (Winter 2000). Available at http://www.lexis-nexis.com/universe.

Holmes, Malcolm D., Howard C. Daudistel, and Ronald A. Farrell. "Determinants of Charge Reductions and Final Dispositions in Cases of Burglary and Robbery." *Journal of Research in Crime and Delinquency 24* (1987).

Holmes, Malcolm D., Harmon M. Hosch, Howard C. Daudistel, Dolores A. Perez, and Joseph B. Graves, "Judges' Ethnicity and Minority Sentencing: Evidence Concerning Hispanics." *Social Science Quarterly 74* (1993): 496–506.

Holmes, Malcolm D., Harmon M. Hosch, Howard C. Daudistel, Dolores A. Perez, and Joseph B. Graves, "Ethnicity, Legal Resources, and Felony Dispositions in Two Southwestern Jurisdictions," *Justice Quarterly 13* (1996): 11–30.

Howe, Scott W. "The Futile Quest for Racial Neutrality in Capital Selection and the Eighth Amendment Argument for Abolition Based on Unconscious Racial Discrimination." *William & Mary Law Review 45* (2004): 2083.

Huff, C. Ronald, ed., *Gangs in America.* Newbury Park, CA: Sage, 1990.

Huizinga, David, and Delbert S. Elliot. "Juvenile Offenders: Prevalence, Offender Incidence, and Arrest Rates by Race." *Crime and Delinquency 33* (1987): 206–223.

Human Rights Watch, *Shielded From Justice: Police Brutality and Accountability in the United States*. New York: Human Rights Watch, 1998.

Human Rights Watch. *Punishment and Prejudice: Racial Disparities in the War on Drugs*, Vol. 12, No. 2 (G), May 2000. Available at http://www.hrw.org/reports/2000/usa/.

Humphries, Drew, John Dawson, Valerie Cronin, Phyllis Keating, Chris Wisniewski, and Jennine Eichfeld. "Mothers and Children, Drugs and Crack: Reactions to Maternal Drug Dependency." In *The Criminal Justice System and Women*, 2nd edition, Barbara Raffel Price and Natalie J. Sokoloff, eds. New York: McGraw-Hill, 1995.

Jacobs, James. *New Perspectives on Prison and Imprisonment*. Ithaca: Cornell University Press, 1983.

Jaynes, Gerald David and Robin M. Williams, Jr., eds. *A Common Destiny: Blacks and American Society*. Washington, DC: National Academy Press, 1992.

Jenkins, Phillip. "'The Ice Age:' The Social Construction of a Drug Panic." *Justice Quarterly 11* (1994): 7–31.

Johnson, Elmer H. "Selective Factors in Capital Punishment." *Social Forces 36* (1957): 165.

Johnson, Guy. "The Negro and Crime." *Annals of the American Academy 217* (1941): 93–104.

Johnson, Sheri Lynn. "Black Innocence and the White Jury." *University of Michigan Law Review 83* (1985): 1611–1708.

Johnstone, J.W.C. "Youth Gangs and Black Suburbs." *Pacific Sociological Review 24* (1981): 355–375.

Jost, Kenneth. "Rethinking the Death Penalty." *CQ Researcher, 11*, November 16, 2001.

Kalven, Harry Jr. and Hans Zeisel. *The American Jury*. Boston: Little, Brown, 1966.

Katz, Charles M. and Cassia Spohn. "The Effect of Race and Gender on Bail Outcomes: A Test of an Interactive Model." *American Journal of Criminal Justice 19* (1995): 161–184.

Kautt, Paula and Cassia Spohn. "*Crack*-ing Down on Black Drug Offenders? Testing for Interactions Among Offenders' Race, Drug Type, and Sentencing Strategy in Federal Drug Sentences." *Justice Quarterly 19* (2002): 2–35.

Keil, Thomas and Gennaro Vito. "Race and the Death Penalty in Kentucky Murder Trials: An Analysis of Post–Gregg Outcomes." *Justice Quarterly* (1990): 189–207.

Kempf, Kimberly Leonard and Henry Sontheimer. "The Role of Race in Juvenile Justice in Pennsylvania." In *Minorities and Juvenile Justice*, Kimberly Kempf Leonard, Carl E. Pope, and William H. Feyerherm, eds. Thousand Oaks, CA: Sage, 1995.

Kennedy, Randall. "Changing Images of the State: Criminal Law and Racial Discrimination: A Comment." *Harvard Law Review 107* (1994): 1255–1278.

Kennedy, Randall. *Race, Crime, and the Law*. New York: Vintage Books, 1997.

Kerner Commission. *Report of the National Advisory Commission on Civil Disorders*. New York: Bantam Books, 1968.

Kleck, Gary. "Racial Discrimination in Criminal Sentencing: A Critical Evaluation of the Evidence with Additional Evidence on the Death Penalty." *American Sociological Review 46* (1981): 783–805.

Klein, Kitty and Blanche Creech. "Race, Rape, and Bias: Distortion of Prior Odds and Meaning Changes," *Basic and Applied Social Psychology 3* (1982): 21.

Klein, Malcolm W. *The American Street Gang*. New York: Oxford University Press, 1995.

Klein, Malcolm W., Cheryl Maxson, and Lea C. Cunningham. "'Crack,' Street Gangs and Violence." *Criminology 29* (1991): 623–650.

Klein, Stephen, Joan Petersilia, and Susan Turner. "Race and Imprisonment Decisions in California." *Science 247* (1990): 812–816.

Klinger, David. "Demeanor or Crime?: Why 'Hostile' Citizens Are More Likely to be Arrested." *Criminology 32* (1994): 475–493.

Knepper, Paul. "Race, Racism and Crime Statistics." *Southern Law Review 24* (1996): 71–112.

Kramer, John H. and Darrell Steffensmeier. "Race and Imprisonment Decisions." *Sociological Quarterly 34* (1993): 357–376.

Kramer, John H. and Jeffery T. Ulmer. "Court Communities Under Sentencing Guidelines: Dilemmas of Formal Rationality and Sentencing Disparity." *Criminology 34* (1996).

Kramer, John H. and Jeffery T. Ulmer. "Sentencing Disparity and Departures From Guidelines." *Justice Quarterly 13* (1996): 81–105.

Kurlychek, Megan C. and Brian D. Johnson. "The Juvenile Penalty: A Comparison of Juvenile Adult Sentencing Outcomes in Criminal Court." *Criminology 42* (2004).

Kwak, Dae-Hoon. "The Interaction of Age, Gender, and Race/Ethnicity on Juvenile Justice Decision Making in Nebraska." Unpublished Master's Thesis, University of Nebraska at Omaha, 2004.

LaFree, Gary D. "The Effect of Sexual Stratification by Race on Official Reactions to Rape." *American Sociological Review 45* (1980): 842–854.

LaFree, Gary D. *Rape and Criminal Justice: The Social Construction of Sexual Assault.* Belmont, CA: Wadsworth, 1989.

Langan, Patrick. "Sentence Reductions For Drug Traffickers For Assisting Federal Prosecutors." (Unpublished manuscript).

Lauritsen, Janet L. "How Families and Communities Influence Youth Victimization." (OJJDP Juvenile Justice Bulletin). Washington DC: U.S. Department of Justice, 2003.

Leadership Conference on Civil Rights. *Justice on Trial: Racial Disparities in the American Criminal Justice System.* Washington, DC: Leadership Conference on Civil Rights, 2000.

Lee, Harper. *To Kill a Mockingbird.* New York: Warner Books, 1960.

Lefcourt, R. "The Administration of Criminal Law." In *Criminal Justice in America*, Richard Quinney, ed. Boston: Little Brown, 1974.

Leiber, Michael J. "A Comparison of Juvenile Court Outcomes for Native Americans, African Americans, and Whites." *Justice Quarterly 11* (1994): 255–279.

Leiber, Michael J. and Anita N. Blowers. "Race and Misdemeanor Sentencing." *Criminal Justice Policy Review 14* (2003): 464–485.

Levin, Martin Howard. "The Jury in a Criminal Case: Obstacles to Impartiality." *Criminal Law Bulletin 24* (1988): 492–520.

Levine, James P. *Juries and Politics.* Pacific Grove, CA: Brooks Cole, 1992.

Lewis, Anthony. *Gideon's Trumpet.* New York: Vintage Books, 1964.

Leyton, Stacey. "The New Blacklists: The Threat to Civil Liberties Posed by Gang Data-bases." In *Crime Control and Social Justice: The Delicate Balance*, Darnell F. Hawkins, Samuel L. Meyers, Jr., and Randolph N. Stone, eds. Westport, CT: Greenwood, 2003.

Lujan, Carol Chiago. "Stereotyping by Politicians: Or 'The Only Real Indian Is the Stereotypical Indian.'" In *Images of Color, Images of Crime*, Coramae Richey Mann and Marjorie Zatz, eds. Los Angeles: Roxbury, 1998.

Lynch, Michael J., and E. Britt Patterson, eds. *Race and Criminal Justice*. New York: Harrow and Heston, 1991.

Males, Mike and Dan Macallair. *The Color of Justice: An Analysis of Juvenile Justice Adult Court Transfers in California*. Washington, DC: Justice Policy Institute, 2000.

Mangum Jr., Charles S. *The Legal Status of the Negro*. Chapel Hill, NC: North Carolina Press, 1940.

Mann, Coramae Richey. *Unequal Justice: A Question of Color*. Bloomington, IN: University of Indiana Press, 1993.

Martinson, Robert. "What Works? Questions and Answers about Prison Reform." *Public Interest 24* (1974): 22–54.

Mason, Alpheus Thomas and William M. Beaney. *American Constitutional Law*. Englewood Cliffs, NJ: Prentice-Hall, 1972.

Massey, Douglas S. and Nancy A. Denton. *American Apartheid: Segregation and the Making of the Underclass*. Cambridge, MA: Harvard University Press, 1993.

Mather, Lynn. *Plea Bargaining or Trial?* Lexington, MA: Heath, 1979.

Mauer, Marc. *Americans Behind Bars: A Comparison of International Rates of Incarceration*. Washington, DC: The Sentencing Project, 1990.

Mauer, Marc. *Race To Incarcerate*. New York: New Press, 1999.

Mauer, Marc. *Young Black Men and the Criminal Justice System: A Growing National Problem*. Washington, DC: The Sentencing Project, 1990.

Mauer, Marc and Tracy Huling. *Young Black Americans and the Criminal Justice System: Five Years Later*. Washington, DC: The Sentencing Project, 1995.

Maxfield, Linda Drazga and John H. Kramer. *Substantial Assistance: An Empirical Yardstick Gauging Equity in Current Federal Policy and Practices*. Washington, DC: United States Sentencing Commission, 1998.

McDonald, Douglas C. and Kenneth E. Carlson. *Sentencing in the Federal Courts: Does Race Matter?* Washington, DC: U.S. Department of Justice, 1993.

McIntyre, Lisa J. *The Public Defender: The Practice of Law in the Shadows of Repute*. Chicago: University of Chicago Press, 1987.

McNulty, Thomas and Paul E. Bellair "Explaining Racial and Ethnic Differences in Serious Adolescent Violent Behavior." *Criminology 41* (2003): 701–730.

Meissner, Christian A., and John C. Brigham. "Thirty Years of Investigating the Own-Race Bias in Memory for Faces: A Meta-Analytic Review." *Psychology, Public Policy, and Law 7* (2001): 3–35.

Melossi, Dario. "An Introduction: Fifty Years Later, Punishment and Social Structure in Comparative Analysis." *Contemporary Crises 13* (1989): 311–326.

Melton, Ada Pecos. "Crime and Punishment: Traditional and Contemporary Tribal Justice." In *Images of Color, Images of Crime*, Coramae Richey Mann and Marjorie S. Zatz, eds. Los Angeles: Roxbury, 1998.

Michalowski, Raymond J. and Susan J. Carlson. "Unemployment, Imprisonment and Social Structures of Accumulation: Historical Contingency in the Rushe-Kirchheimer Hypothesis." *Criminology 37* (1999): 217–250.

Michalowski, Raymond J., and Michael A. Pearson. "Punishment and Social Structure at the State Level: A Cross-Sectional Comparison of 1970 and 1980." *Journal of Research in Crime and Delinquency 27* (1990): 52–78.

Miethe, Terance D. and Charles A. Moore. "Socioeconomic Disparities Under Determinate Sentencing Systems: A Comparison of Preguideline and Postguideline Practices in Minnesota." *Criminology 23* (1985): 337–363.

Miller, Jerome. *Search and Destroy: African-American Males in the Criminal Justice System.* Cambridge: Cambridge University Press, 1996.

Moore, J. D. and Vigil R. Garcia. "Residence and Territoriality in Chicano Gangs." *Social Problems 31* (1983): 182–194.

Morrison, Toni. *Beloved: A Novel.* New York: Plume, 1988.

Murphy, Clyde E. "Racial Discrimination in the Criminal Justice System." *North Carolina Central Law Journal 17* (1988): 171–190.

Myers, Martha. "Symbolic Policy and the Sentencing of Drug Offenders." *Law & Society Review 23* (1989): 295–315.

Myers, Martha. *Race, Labor and Punishment in the South.* Columbus: Ohio State University Press, 1999.

Myers, Martha. *The Effects of Victim Characteristics in the Prosecution, Conviction, and Sentencing of Criminal Defendants.* Unpublished Ph.D. Dissertation, Bloomington: Indiana University (1977).

Myrdal, Gunnar. *An American Dilemma: The Negro Problem and Modern Democracy.* New York: Harper and Brothers, 1944.

NAACP Legal Defense and Educational Fund. *Death Row USA, Winter 2002.* Available at http://www.deathpenaltyinfo.org/DEATHROWUSArecent.pdf.

NAACP Legal Defense and Educational Fund. *Death Row USA, Summer 2005.* Available at http://www.deathpenaltyinfo.org/DEATHROWUSArecent.pdf.

NAACP Legal Defense and Educational Fund. "Justice Prevails in Louisiana: Rideau Is Free." January 15, 2005. Available at http://www.naacpldf.org.

National Center for Juvenile Justice. *Juvenile Court Statistics 2000.* Washington, DC: Office of Juvenile Justice and Delinquency Prevention, 2004.

National Center for Juvenile Justice. *Which States Waive Juveniles to Criminal Court?* Pittsburgh, PA: National Center for Juvenile Justice, 2004.

National Opinion Research Center. *General Social Surveys, 1972–94, General Social Surveys, 1996.* Storrs, CT: The Roper Center for Public Opinion Research, University of Connecticut, 1997.

Nardulli, Peter F., James Eisenstein, and Roy B. Flemming. *The Tenor of Justice: Criminal Courts and the Guilty Plea Process.* Chicago: University of Chicago Press, 1988.

Neubauer, David W. *America's Courts and the Criminal Justice System*, 7th edition. Belmont, CA: Wadsworth, 2002.

Nobiling, Tracy, Cassia Spohn, and Miriam DeLone. "A Tale of Two Counties: Unemployment and Sentence Severity." *Justice Quarterly 15* (1998): 459–485.

Note. *Batson v. Kentucky*: Challenging the Use of the Peremptory Challenge." *American Journal of Criminal Law 15* (1988): 298.

O'Brien, Robert M. "The Interracial Nature of Violent Crimes: A Reexamination." *American Journal of Sociology 92* (1987): 817–835.

Office of Juvenile Justice and Delinquency Prevention. *Juvenile Court Statistics 2000.*

Office of Juvenile Justice and Delinquency Prevention. *Juvenile Victims of Property Crimes.* Washington, DC: U.S. Department of Justice, 2000.

Office of Juvenile Justice and Delinquency Prevention. *Juvenile Transfers to Criminal Court in the 1990s: Lessons Learned from Four Studies.* Washington, DC: Office of Juvenile Justice and Delinquency Prevention, 2000.

Office of Juvenile Justice and Delinquency Prevention. *Juveniles in Corrections.* Washington, DC: Office of Juvenile Justice and Delinquency Prevention, 2004.

Office of Juvenile Justice and Delinquency Prevention. *Disproportionate Minority Confinement 2002 Update.* Washington, DC: U.S. Department of Justice, 2004.

Olsen, Jack. *Last Man Standing: The Tragedy and Triumph of Geronimo Pratt.* New York: Doubleday, 2000.

Panel on Juvenile Crime. *Juvenile Crime Juvenile Justice.* Washington, DC: National Academy Press, 2001.

Pate, Anthony M. and Lorie Fridell. *Police Use of Force* (2 vols.). Washington, DC: The Police Foundation, 1993.

Paternoster, Raymond. "Discrimination Revisited: An Exploration of Frontstage and Backstage Criminal Justice Decision Making." *Sociology and Social Research 69* (1984): 90–108.

Paternoster, Raymond. "Prosecutorial Discretion in Requesting the Death Penalty: A Case of Victim-Based Racial Discrimination." *Law & Society Review 18* (1984): 437–478.

Paternoster, Raymond. *Capital Punishment in America.* New York: Lexington Books, 1991.

Paternoster, Raymond and Robert Brame. "An Empirical Analysis of Maryland's Death Sentencing System with Respect to the Influence of Race and Legal Jurisdiction." Available at http://ncic.org/library/018518.

Peak, K. and J. Spencer. "Crime in Indian Country: Another Trail of Tears." *Journal of Criminal Justice 15* (1987): 485–494.

Petersilia, Joan. *Racial Disparities in the Criminal Justice System.* Santa Monica, CA: Rand, 1983.

Peterson, Ruth D. and John Hagan. "Changing Conceptions of Race: Towards an Account of Anomalous Findings of Sentencing Research." *American Sociological Review 49* (1984): 56–70.

Pierce, Glenn L. and Michael L. Radelet. "The Impact of Legally Inappropriate Factors on Death Sentencing for California Homicides, 1990–99." *Santa Clara Law Review 46* (2005).

Platt, Anthony M. *The Child Saver: The Invention of Delinquency*, 2nd ed. Chicago: University of Chicago Press, 1977.

Police Executive Research Forum. *Racially Biased Policing: A Principled Response.* Washington, DC: PERF, 2001.

PolicyLink. *Community-Centered Policing: A Force for Change.* Oakland, CA: PolicyLink, 2001.

Pommersheim, Frank and Steve Wise. "Going to the Penitentiary: A Study of Disparate Sentencing in South Dakota." *Criminal Justice and Behavior 16* (1989): 155–165.

Pope, Carl E. and William H. Feyerherm. "Minority Status and Juvenile Justice Processing: An Assessment of the Research Literature (Part I), *Criminal Justice Abstracts 22* (1990): 327–335.

Pope, Carl E., Rich Lovell, and Heidi M. Hsia. *Disproportionate Minority Confinement: A Review of the Research Literature from 1989 Through 2001.* Washington, DC: U.S. Department of Justice, 2004.

Pope, Carl E. and Howard N. Snyder. *Race as a Factor in Juvenile Arrests.* Washington, DC: Office of Juvenile Justice and Delinquency Prevention, 2003.

Quinney, Richard. *The Social Reality of Crime*. Boston: Little, Brown, 1970.

Radelet, Michael L. "Racial Characteristics and the Imposition of the Death Penalty." *American Sociological Review 46* (1981): 918–927.

Radelet, Michael L. "Executions of Whites for Crimes Against Blacks: Exceptions to the Rule?" *The Sociological Quarterly 30* (1989): 529–544.

Radelet, Michael L. and Glenn L. Pierce. "Race and Prosecutorial Discretion in Homicide Cases." *Law & Society Review 19* (1985): 587–621.

Ralph, Paige H., Jonathan R. Sorensen, and James W. Marquart. "A Comparison of Death-Sentenced and Incarcerated Murderers in Pre-Furman Texas." *Justice Quarterly 9* (1992): 185–209.

Ramirez, Deborah A. "Affirmative Jury Selection: A Proposal To Advance Both the Deliberative Ideal and Jury Diversity," *University of Chicago Legal Forum* 1998: 161.

Ramirez, Deborah A., Jack McDevitt, and Amy Farrell. *A Resource Guide on Racial Profiling Data Collection Systems: Promising Practices and Lessons Learned*. Washington DC: U.S. Department of Justice, 2000.

Randall, Kate "Another Florida Teenager Receives Harsh Adult Prison Sentence." Available at http://www.wsws.org/articles/2001/aug2001.

Reasons, Charles E., Darlene J. Conley, and Julius Debro. *Race, Class, Gender, and Justice in the United States*. Boston: Allyn and Bacon, 2002.

Reddy, Marlita A., ed. *Statistical Record of Black America*. Detroit: Gale Research, 1997.

Reddy, Marlita A., ed. *Statistical Record of Hispanic Americans*. Detroit: Gale Research, 1993.

Reiman, Jeffrey. *The Rich Get Richer and Poor Get Prison*. Boston: Allyn & Bacon, 1995.

Reiss, Albert J. *The Police and the Public*. New Haven: Yale University Press, 1971.

Rise, Eric W. *The Martinsville Seven: Race, Rape, and Capital Punishment*. Charlottesville: University Press of Virginia, 1995.

Roberts. Dorothy. "Punishing Drug Addicts Who Have Babies: Women of Color, Equality, and the Right of Privacy." *Harvard Law Review 104* (1991): 1419–1454.

Ruback, R. Barry and Paula J. Vardaman. "Decision Making in Delinquency Cases: The Role of Race and Juveniles' Admission/Denial of the Crime." *Law and Human Behavior 21* (1997): 47–69.

Rutledge, John R. "They All Look Alike: The Inaccuracy of Cross-Racial Identifications." *American Journal of Criminal Law 28* (2001).

Sampson, Robert J. and William Julius Wilson. "Toward a Theory of Race, Crime, and Urban Inequality." In *Crime and Inequality*, John Hagan and Ruth D. Peterson, eds. Stanford, CA: Stanford University Press, 1995.

Sander, Richard H. "A Systematic Analysis of Affirmative Action in American Law Schools." *Stanford Law Review 57* (2004): 367–585.

Sarat, Austin. "Recapturing the Spirit of Furman: The American Bar Association and the New Abolitionist Politics." *Law and Contemporary Problems 61* (1998): 5–28.

Sarat, Austin. *When the State Kills: Capital Punishment and the American Condition*. Princeton, NJ: Princeton University Press, 1998.

Sarat, Austin and Neil Vidmar. "Public Opinion, the Death Penalty, and the Eighth Amendment: Testing the Marshall Hypothesis." In *Capital Punishment in the United States*, Hugo A. Bedau and Chester M. Pierce, eds. New York: AMS Publications, 1976.

Schiraldi, Vincent and Jason Ziedenberg. *Costs and Benefits? The Impact of Drug Imprisonment in New Jersey.* Washington, DC: Justice Policy Institute, 2003.

Secret, Philip E. and James B. Johnson. "The Effect of Race on Juvenile Justice Decision Making in Nebraska: Detention, Adjudication, and Disposition, 1988–1993." *Justice Quarterly 14* (1997): 445–478.

Sellin, Thorsten. "Race Prejudice in the Administration of Justice." *American Journal of Sociology 41* (1935): 312–317.

Sentencing Project, The. *Facts about Prison and Prisoners.* Available at www.sentencingproject.org (April 2002).

Sentencing Project, The. *Felony Disenfranchisement Laws in the United States.* Available at www.sentencingproject.org (November 2002).

Sentencing Project, The. *Schools and Prisons: Fifty Years after Brown v. Board of Education.* Available at http://www.sentencingproject.org/pdfs/brownvboard.pdf.

Serr, Brian J. and Mark Maney. "Racism, Peremptory Challenges, and the Democratic Jury: The Jurisprudence of a Delicate Balance." *Journal of Criminal Law and Criminology 79* (1988): 1–65.

Shaw, Clifford R. and Henry D. McKay. *Juvenile Delinquency and Urban Areas.* Chicago: University of Chicago Press, 1942.

Silberman, Charles E. *Criminal Violence, Criminal Justice.* New York: Random House, 1978.

Skogan, Wesley G. and Susan M. Hartnett. *Community Policing: Chicago Style.* New York: Oxford University Press, 1997.

Skolnick, Jerome. "Social Control in the Adversary System." *Journal of Conflict Resolution 11* (1967): 67.

Smith, Brent L. and Kelly R. Damphouse. "Punishing Political Offenders: The Effect of Political Motive on Federal Sentencing Decisions." *Criminology 34* (1996): 289–321.

Smith, Douglas A., Christy Visher, and Laura A. Davidson. "Equity and Discretionary Justice: The Influence of Race on Police Arrest Decisions." *Journal of Criminal Law and Criminology 75* (1984): 234–249.

Smith, Michael David. *Race Versus Robe: The Dilemma of Black Judges.* Port Washington, NY: Associated Faculty Press, 1983.

Smith, Tom. "A Trend Analysis of Attitudes Toward Capital Punishment, 1936–1974." In *Studies of Social Change Since 1948: Vol. 2,* James E. Davis, ed. Chicago: National Opinion Research Center, 1975.

Snell, Tracy. *Correctional Populations in the United States 1992.* Washington, DC: Department of Justice, 1995.

Song, John Huey-Long. "Attitudes of Chinese Immigrants and Vietnamese Refugees Toward Law Enforcement in the United States." *Justice Quarterly 9* (1992) 703–719.

Sorensen, Jon and Donald H. Wallace. "Prosecutorial Discretion in Seeking Death: An Analysis of Racial Disparity in the Pretrial Stages of Case Processing in a Midwestern County." *Justice Quarterly 16* (1999): 559–578.

Spears, Jeffrey W. *Diversity in the Courtroom: A Comparison of the Sentencing Decisions of Black and White Judges and Male and Female Judges in Cook County Circuit Court.* PhD dissertation, University of Nebraska at Omaha, 1999.

Spitzer, Steven. "Toward a Marxian Theory of Deviance." *Social Problems 22* (1975): 638–651.

Spohn, Cassia. "Decision Making in Sexual Assault Cases: Do Black and Female Judges Make a Difference?" *Women & Criminal Justice 2* (1990).

Spohn, Cassia. "The Sentencing Decisions of Black and White Judges: Expected and Unexpected Similarities." *Law & Society Review 24* (1990): 1197–1216.

Spohn, Cassia. "Crime and the Social Control of Blacks: Offender/Victim Race and the Sentencing of Violent Offenders." In Inequality, Crime & Social Control, George S. Bridges and Martha A. Myers, eds. Boulder, CO: Westview Press, 1994.

Spohn, Cassia. "Thirty Years of Sentencing Reform: A Quest for a Racially Neutral Sentencing Process." In *Policies, Processes, and Decisions of the Criminal Justice System*, Vol. 3, *Criminal Justice 2000*. Washington, DC: U.S. Department of Justice, 2000.

Spohn, Cassia and Jerry Cederblom. "Race and Disparities in Sentencing: A Test of the Liberation Hypothesis." *Justice Quarterly 8* (1991): 305–327.

Spohn, Cassia and Miriam DeLone. "When Does Race Matter? An Analysis of the Conditions Under Which Race Affects Sentence Severity." *Sociology of Crime, Law, and Deviance 2* (2000): 3–37.

Spohn, Cassia, John Gruhl, and Susan Welch. "The Effect of Race on Sentencing: A Re–Examination on an Unsettled Question." *Law & Society Review 16* (1981–82): 71–88.

Spohn, Cassia, John Gruhl, and Susan Welch. "The Impact of the Ethnicity and Gender of Defendants on the Decision to Reject or Dismiss Felony Charges." *Criminology 25* (1987): 175–191.

Spohn, Cassia and David Holleran. "The Imprisonment Penalty Paid by Young Unemployed Black and Hispanic Male Offenders." *Criminology 38* (2000): 281–306.

Spohn, Cassia and Jeffrey Spears. "The Effect of Offender and Victim Characteristics on Sexual Assault Case Processing Decisions." *Justice Quarterly 13* (1996): 649–679.

Spohn, Cassia and Jeffrey Spears. "Sentencing of Drug Offenders in Three Cities: Does Race/Ethnicity Make a Difference?" In *Crime Control and Criminal Justice: The Delicate Balance*, Darnell F. Hawkins, Samuel L. Meyers, Jr., and Randolph N. Stone, eds. Westport, CT: Greenwood, 2002.

Steen, Sara, Rodney L. Engen, and Randy R. Gainey. "Images of Danger and Culpability: Racial Stereotyping, Case Processing, and Criminal Sentencing." *Criminology 45* (2005).

Steffensmeier, Darrell and Stephen Demuth. "Ethnicity and Sentencing Outcomes in U.S. Federal Courts: Who Is Punished More Harshly?" *American Sociological Review 65* (2000): 705–729.

Steffensmeier, Darrell and Stephen Demuth. "Ethnicity and Judges' Sentencing Decisions: Hispanic-Black-White Comparison." *Criminology 39* (2001): 145–178.

Steffensmeier, Darrell, John Kramer, and Cathy Streifel. "Gender and Imprisonment Decisions." *Criminology 31* (1993): 411–443.

Steffensmeier, Darrell, John Kramer, and Jeffery Ulmer. "Age Differences in Criminal Sentencing." *Justice Quarterly 12* (1995): 701–719.

Steffensmeier, Darrell, Jeffery Ulmer, and John Kramer. "The Interaction of Race, Gender, and Age in Criminal Sentencing: The Punishment Cost of Being Young, Black, and Male." *Criminology 36* (1998): 363–397.

Stryker, R., Ilene Nagel, and John Hagan. "Methodology Issues in Court Research: Pretrial Release Decisions for Federal Defendants." *Sociological Methods and Research 11* (1983): 460–500.

Sudnow, David. "Normal Crimes: Sociological Features of the Penal Code in the Public Defender's Office." *Social Problems 12* (1965): 255–277.

Swift, B. and G. Bickel. *Comparative Parole Treatment of American Indians and Non-Indians at United States Federal Prisons.* Washington, DC: Bureau of Social Science Research, 1974.

Texas Civil Rights Project. *The Death Penalty in Texas: Due Process and Equal Justice . . . or Rush to Execution?* Austin, TX: Texas Civil Rights Project, 2000.

Thernstrom, Stephan and Abigail Thernstrom. *America in Black and White: One Nation, Indivisible.* New York: Simon & Schuster, 1997.

Thomas, Jim. "Racial Codes in Prison Culture: Snapshots in Black and White." In *Race and Criminal Justice*, Michael Lynch and Britt Patterson, eds. New York: Harrow and Heston, 1991.

Thomas, Wayne. *Bail Reform in America.* Berkeley, CA: University of California Press, 1976.

Tonry, Michael. *Malign Neglect: Race, Crime and Punishment in America.* New York: Oxford University Press, 1995.

Tonry, Michael. *Sentencing Matters.* New York: Oxford University Press, 1996.

Toy, Calvin. "A Short History of Asian Gangs in San Francisco." *Justice Quarterly 9* (1992): 645–665.

Tuch, Steven A. and Ronald Weitzer. "Racial Differences in Attitudes toward the Police." *Public Opinion Quarterly 61* (1997): 643–663.

Turk, Austin. *Criminality and Legal Order.* New York: Rand McNally, 1969.

Turner, Billy M., Rickie D. Lovell, John C. Young, and William F. Denny. "Race and Peremptory Challenges During Voir Dire: Do Prosecution and Defense Agree?" *Journal of Criminal Justice 14* (1986): 61–69.

Uhlman, Thomas M. "Black Elite Decision Making: The Case of Trial Judges." *American Journal of Political Science 22* (1978): 884–895.

Uhlman, Thomas M. *Racial Justice: Black Judges and Defendants in an Urban Trial Court.* Lexington, MA: Lexington Books, 1979.

Ulmer, Jeffery T. and John H. Kramer. "Court Communities Under Sentencing Guidelines: Dilemmas of Formal Rationality and Sentencing Disparity." *Criminology 34* (1996): 383–407.

Unnever, James D. "Direct and Organizational Discrimination in the Sentencing of Drug Offenders." *Social Problems 30* (1982).

U.S. Department of Health and Human Services, Substance Abuse and Mental Health Services Administration. *National Household Survey on Drug Abuse: Population Estimates 1994.* Rockville, MD: U.S. Department of Health and Human Services, 1995.

U.S. Department of Justice. *The Police and Public Opinion.* Washington, DC: Government Printing Office, 1977.

U.S. Department of Justice. *The Federal Death Penalty System: A Statistical Survey (1988–2000).* Washington, DC: U.S. Department of Justice, 2000.

U.S. Department of Justice. *The Federal Death Penalty System: Supplementary Data Analysis and Revised Protocols for Capital Case Review.* Washington, DC: U.S. Department of Justice, 2001.

U.S. Department of Justice, Bureau of Justice Assistance. *National Assessment of Structured Sentencing.* Washington, DC: Government Printing Office, 1996.

U.S. Department of Justice, Bureau of Justice Statistics. *Comparing Federal and State Inmates, 1991.* Washington, DC: U.S. Government Printing Office, 1993.

U.S. Department of Justice, Bureau of Justice Statistics. *Sourcebook of Criminal Justice Statistics, 1999.* Washington, DC: U.S. Government Printing Office, 2000.

U.S. Department of Justice, Bureau of Justice Statistics. *Sourcebook of Criminal Justice Statistics, 2003* Washington, DC: U.S. Government Printing Office, 2004.

U.S. Department of Justice, Bureau of Justice Statistics. *Capital Punishment 2000.* Washington, DC: U.S. Government Printing Office, 2001.

U.S. Department of Justice, Bureau of Justice Statistics. *Capital Punishment 2003.* Washington, DC: U.S. Government Printing Office, 2004.

U.S. Department of Justice, Federal Bureau of Investigation. *Crime in the United States 1994.* Washington, DC: U.S. Government Printing Office, 1995.

U.S. General Accounting Office. *Death Penalty Sentencing: Research Indicates Pattern of Racial Disparities.* Washington, DC: General Accounting Office, 1990.

U.S. General Accounting Office. *Juvenile Justice: Juveniles Processed in Criminal Court and Case Dispositions* Washington, DC: General Accounting Office, 1995.

Unah, Isaac and Jack Boger. "Race and the Death Penalty in North Carolina: An Empirical Analysis: 1993–1997." Available at http://www.deathpenaltyinfo.org.

United States Sentencing Commission. *Sourcebook of Federal Sentencing Statistics.* Washington DC: United States Sentencing Commission, 1998.

United States Sentencing Commission. *Special Report to the Congress: Mandatory Minimum Penalties in the Federal Criminal Justice System.* Washington, DC: U.S. Sentencing Commission, 1991.

United States Sentencing Commission. *Substantial Assistance Departures in the United States Courts.* Washington, DC: U.S. Sentencing Commission, 1995.

United States Sentencing Commission. *Report to the Congress: Cocaine and Federal Sentencing Policy.* Washington, DC: U.S. Sentencing Commission, 2002.

van den Haag, Ernest. *Punishing Criminals: Confronting a Very Old and Painful Question.* New York: Basic Books, 1975.

Vera Institute of Justice. *Felony Arrests: Their Prosecution and Disposition in New York City's Courts.* New York: Longman, 1981.

Vigil, James D. *Barrio Gangs.* Austin, TX: University of Texas Press, 1988.

von Hirsch, Andrew. *Doing Justice: The Choice of Punishments.* New York: Hill & Wang, 1976.

Wakeling, Stewart, Miriam Jorgensen, Susan Michaelson, and Manley Begay. *Policing on American Indian Reservations: A Report to the National Institute of Justice.* Washington, DC: U.S. Government Printing Office, 2001.

Walker, Samuel. "Racial Minority and Female Employment in Policing: The Implications of 'Glacial' Change." *Crime and Delinquency 31* (1985): 555–572.

Walker, Samuel. *Taming the System: The Control of Discretion in Criminal Justice, 1950–1990,* New York: Oxford University Press, 1993.

Walker, Samuel. "Complaints Against the Police: A Focus Group Study of Citizen Perceptions, Goals, and Expectations." *Criminal Justice Review 22* (1997): 207–225.

Walker, Samuel. *Police Interactions with Racial and Ethnic Minorities: Assessing the Evidence and Allegations.* Washington, DC: Police Executive Research Forum, 2000.

Walker, Samuel. *Police Accountability: The Role of Citizen Oversight.* Belmont CA: Wadsworth, 2001.

Walker, Samuel. "Searching for the Denominator: Problems with Police Traffic Stop Data and an Early Warning System Solution." *Justice Research and Policy 3* (Spring 2001): 63–95.

Walker, Samuel, and Molly Brown. "A Pale Reflection of Reality: The Neglect of Racial and Ethnic Minorities in Introductory Criminal Justice Textbooks." *Journal of Criminal Justice Education 6,* no. 1 (Spring 1995): 61–83.

Walker, Samuel, and K. B. Turner. *A Decade of Modest Progress: Employment of Black and Hispanic Police Officers, 1982–1992.* Omaha: University of Nebraska Press, 1992.

Walker, Thomas G. and Deborah J. Barrow. "The Diversification of the Federal Bench: Policy and Process Ramifications." *Journal of Politics 47* (1985): 596–617.

Walsh, Anthony. "The Sexual Stratification Hypothesis in Light of Changing Conceptions of Race." *Criminology 25* (1987): 153–173.

Washington, Linn. *Black Judges on Justice: Perspectives from the Bench.* New York: The New Press, 1994.

Way, H. Frank. *Criminal Justice and the American Constitution.* North Scituate, MA: Duxbury Press, 1994.

Weisburd, David, Rosann Greenspan, Edwin E. Hamilton, Kellie Bryant, and Hubert Williams. *The Abuse of Police Authority: A National Study of Police Officers' Attitudes.* Washington DC: The Police Foundation, 2001.

Weisenburger, Steven. *Modern Medea.* New York: Hill & Wang, 1998.

Weitzer, Ronald. "Racial Discrimination in the Criminal Justice System: Findings and Problems in the Literature." *Journal of Criminal Justice 24* (1996): 313.

Weitzer, Ronald. "Racialized Policing: Residents' Perceptions in Three Neighborhoods." *Law & Society Review 34,* no. 1 (2000): 129–156.

Welch, Susan, Michael Combs, and John Gruhl. "Do Black Judges Make a Difference?" *American Journal of Political Science 32* (1988): 126–136.

Werthman, Carl and Irving Piliavin. "Gang Members and the Police." In *The Police: Six Sociological Essays,* David J. Bordua, ed. New York: Wiley, 1967.

Wheeler, Gerald R. and Carol L. Wheeler. "Reflections on Legal Representation of the Economically Disadvantaged: Beyond Assembly Line Justice." *Crime and Delinquency 26* (1980): 319–332.

Wice, Paul B. *Chaos in the Courthouse: The Inner Workings of the Urban Municipal Courts.* New York: Praeger, 1985.

Wilbanks, William. "Is Violent Crime Intraracial?" *Crime and Delinquency 31* (1985): 117–128.

Wilbanks, William. *The Myth of a Racist Criminal Justice System.* Monterey: Brooks/Cole, 1987.

Williams, Marian R. and Jefferson E. Holcomb. "The Interactive Effects of Victim Race and Gender on Death Sentence Disparity Findings." *Homicide Studies 8* (2004).

Wilson, James Q. *Thinking About Crime.* New York: Basic Books, 1975.

Wilson, William Julius. *The Truly Disadvantaged.* Chicago: University of Chicago Press, 1987.

Wilson, William Julius. *When Work Disappears: The World of the New Urban Poor.* New York: Knopf, 1996.

Wishman, Seymour. *Anatomy of a Jury: The System on Trial.* New York: Times Books, 1986.

Wolfgang, Marvin E., Arlene Kelly, and Hans C. Nolde. "Comparisons of the Executed and the Commuted Among Admissions to Death Penalty." *Journal of Criminal Law, Criminology, and Police Science 53* (1962): 301–311.

Wolfgang, Marvin E. and Marc Reidel. "Race, Judicial Discretion, and the Death Penalty." *The Annals of the American Academy of Political and Social Science 407* (1973): 119–133.

Wolfgang, Marvin E. and Marc Reidel. "Rape, Race and the Death Penalty in Georgia." *American Journal of Orthopsychiatry 45* (1975): 658–668.

Wood, Peter B. and David C. May. "Racial Differences in Perceptions of the Severity of Sanctions: A Comparison of Prison with Alternatives." *Justice Quarterly 20* (2003).

Wriggins, Jennifer. "Rape, Racism, and the Law." *Harvard Women's Law Journal 6* (1983): 103–141.

Wright, Bruce McM. "A Black Broods on Black Judges." *Judicature 57* (1973): 22–23.

Wu, Bohsiu and Angel Ilarraza Fuentes. "The Entangled Effects of Race and Urban Poverty." *Juvenile and Family Court Journal 49* (1998): 41–53.

Young, Iris Marion. *Justice and the Politics of Difference.* Princeton, NJ: Princeton University Press, 1990.

Young, Robert L. "Race, Conceptions of Crime and Justice, and Support for the Death Penalty." *Social Psychological Quarterly 54* (1991).

Zatz, Marjorie S. "Pleas, Priors and Prison: Racial/Ethnic Differences in Sentencing." *Social Science Research 14* (1985): 169–193.

Zatz, Marjorie S. "The Changing Form of Racial/Ethnic Biases in Sentencing." *Journal of Research in Crime and Delinquency 25* (1987): 69–92.

Zatz, Marjorie S. "The Convergence of Race, Ethnicity, Gender, and Class on Court Decisionmaking: Looking Toward the 21st Century." In *Policies, Processes, and Decisions of the Criminal Justice System*, Vol. 3, *Criminal Justice 2000.* Washington, DC: U.S. Department of Justice, 2000.

Zatz, Marjorie S., Carol Chiago Lujan, and Zoann K. Snyder-Joy. "American Indians and Criminal Justice: Some Conceptual and Methodological Considerations." In *Race and Criminal Justice*, Michael J. Lynch and E. Britt Patterson, eds. New York: Harrow & Heston, 1995.

Zatz, Marjorie S. and Richard P. Krecker, Jr. "Anti-Gang Initiatives as Racialized Policy." In *Crime Control and Social Justice: The Delicate Balance*, Darnel F. Hawkins, Samuel L. Meyers, Jr., and Randolph N. Stone, eds. Westport, CT: Greenwood, 2003.

Zorn, Eric. "Dark Truths Buried in Nicarico Case May Yet See Light." *Chicago Tribune* (October 19, 1995), sec. 2, p. 1.

Index